The Lord's Watchman

The Lord's Watchman

A Life of Edward Irving (1792–1834)

Tim Grass

PICKWICK *Publications* · Eugene, Oregon

THE LORD'S WATCHMAN
A Life of Edward Irving (1792–1834)

Copyright © 2012 Tim Grass. All rights reserved. Except for brief quotations in critical publications or reviews, no part of this book may be reproduced in any manner without prior written permission from the publisher. Write: Permissions, Wipf and Stock Publishers, 199 W. 8th Ave., Suite 3, Eugene, OR 97401.

Pickwick Publications
An Imprint of Wipf and Stock Publishers
199 W. 8th Ave., Suite 3
Eugene, OR 97401

www.wipfandstock.com

First published in the UK in 2011 by Paternoster, an imprint of Authentic Media, 52 Presley Way, Crownhill, Milton Keynes, MK8 0ES, UK

PAPERBACK ISBN 13: 978-1-62032-620-6

HARDCOVER ISBN 13: 978-1-4982-6567-6

Cataloging-in-Publication data:

Grass, Tim.

The Lord's watchman : a life of Edward Irving (1792–1834) / Tim Grass.

xiv + 356 p. ; 23 cm. Includes bibliographical references and index.

ISBN 13: 978-1-62032-620-6

1. Irving, Edward, 1792–1834. 2. Catholic Apostolic Church—Biography. 3. Theologians—Scotland—Biography. I. Title.

BX6593.I7 G73 2012

CONTENTS

Preface	*vii*
List of Illustrations	*xi*
List of Abbreviations	*xi*
Map: Irving's Scotland	*xv*

1. Earl Life in Annan, 1792–1805 — 1
2. Edinburgh, 1805–09 — 8
3. Haddington, 1809–12 — 12
4. Kirkcaldy, 1812–18 — 16
5. Assistant to Thomas Chalmers: Edinburgh and Glasgow, 1818–21 — 27
6. Call to London and Farewell to Glasgow, 1821–22 — 40
7. Taking London by Storm, 1822–23 — 51
8. Irving as a Preacher, 1822–25 — 61
9. Marriage and Family Life, 1823–25 — 81
10. Three Life-changing Friendships, 1823–25 — 92
11. Pastor, 1826–30 — 106
12. Scot and Churchman, 1826–30 — 132
13. Prophetic Student, 1826–30 — 148
14. Christological Heretic? — 174
15. Witness to the Truth, 1828–31 — 190
16. The Port Glasgow Manifestations, March 1830 Onwards — 204
17. The Manifestations in London, July 1830 – November 1831 — 216
18. The Presbytery Moves against Irving, December 1831 – May 1832 — 244
19. Deposed as Pastor, May 1832 – March 1833 — 264
20. Ordained as Angel, March 1833 – August 1834 — 276
21. 'If I die, I die unto the Lord', September – December 1834 — 289

22. Epilogue 300

Appendix I: Irving's Family *304*
Appendix II: A Chronology of Irving's Life *305*
Appendix III: Contents of Irving's Collected Writings *309*

Bibliography *315*

Index *349*

Preface

Although a number of biographies of Edward Irving have appeared, the first the year after he died and the most recent in 1984, one has overshadowed them all, that of Margaret Oliphant. Her *Life of Edward Irving* appeared in 1862 in a two-volume edition, of which a one-volume abridgement, somewhat amended in response to family criticisms, was rapidly produced. The work was a best-seller and has rightly won praise for the way in which it deploys his own letters to bring him to life in a manner matched by few other biographies of the period; full use has been made of it in what follows, and readers of my book will find that it does not replace hers. Yet it has also been criticized, partly because it sometimes reads more like one of the author's novels than a work of biography, partly because of its tendency to hero-worship, and partly because it is undoubtedly weaker when discussing aspects of Irving's theology, a subject on which the author confessed herself out of her depth. Catholic Apostolics have tended to feel that the book was valuable so far as it went, but vitiated by the author's inability to discern what they saw as the work of the Holy Spirit among them, thus rendering her judgements unreliable on matters such as tongues and prophecy or Irving's relationship with the apostles.

Another influential portrayal has been Thomas Carlyle's *Reminiscences*, written in 1866. A recent editor has spoken of Carlyle's 'love and admiration for Irving, combined with complete scepticism about his beliefs'.[1] He made no secret of his distaste for men such as Henry Drummond, or of his attempts to persuade Irving to drop his advocacy of the tongues and focus on more rational and this-worldly concerns. In the light of these factors, as well as his tendency to overstate a case, we should no more take the work at face value than we should another reaction against an excessively supernaturalist form of religion, Edmund Gosse's *Father and Son*. Both are about their author as much as their subject; in this case, about Carlyle's friendship with Irving and evaluation of him, rather than Irving as he was in himself, as

---

[1] *CL*, 26.205n.

Carlyle himself acknowledged.² And that means we should be cautious about accepting his judgement that Irving was brought down by tongues-speaking fanatics and power-hungry apostles. Nevertheless, on occasion he could be highly perceptive, as in his comments about the revival of interest in Irving in literary and theological circles during the 1860s:

> He was scornfully forgotten at the time of his death; having indeed sunk a good while before out of the notice of the more intelligent classes. There has since been and now is, in the new theological generation, a kind of revival of him, on rather weak and questionable terms, sentimental mainly, and grounded on no really correct knowledge or insight . . .³

One other work deserves notice here: that by Harry Whitley, then minister of St Giles, Edinburgh, whose short introduction appeared in 1955. This has the merit of including considerable excerpts from Irving's writings. Whitley had been brought up in the Catholic Apostolic Church and wrote favourably of the continuities between Irving and the body often referred to by his name, offering the judgement that 'the Catholic Apostolic Church preserves more of the real Irving than either those within or those without have allowed'.⁴ It, like Irving, was Bible-based, liturgical, sacramental and charismatic.⁵ However, oral tradition within that body is that his work was 'not approved of'.

Other works will be discussed at suitable points in the text, which may be located from the Index. Whilst several on various aspects of Irving's thought have appeared since 1970, none have attempted a comprehensive overview of his life and thought. This book tries to fill that gap. It seeks to take account of almost a century and a half of scholarly investigation of Irving's thought and to draw upon considerable quantities of letters and manuscript material to which Mrs Oliphant either did not have access or which she did not think to use. Much of this is used here for the first time.

---

[2] Thomas Carlyle, *Reminiscences*, ed. C. E. Norton (London: J. M. Dent, 1932), 307.

[3] Ibid. 170.

[4] H. C. Whitley, *Blinded Eagle: an Introduction to the Life and Teaching of Edward Irving* (London: SCM, 1955), 82.

[5] Ibid. 82–83.

A word about my structure may be helpful. Mrs Oliphant follows a fairly strict chronological order, which has the great merit of taking the reader through the events of Irving's life. However, it makes it more difficult to pick out the key themes running through the narrative. Whilst I have followed such an order for the first (1792–1822) and last (July 1830 – December 1834) parts of his life, I have divided the intervening period into two (1822–5 and January 1826 – July 1830), and within each I have adopted a thematic approach. An outline chronology of his life appears as Appendix II.

So why the unusual title? The answer to that begins, oddly enough, with the follow-up to this book: a history of the Catholic Apostolic Church, which will be entitled *The Lord's Work*. As the two books belong together, I wanted to find a similar title for this one, one which sums up how Irving saw himself: hence *The Lord's Watchman*. Without going into detail here, he believed that God had charged him as a minister with warning the church of the deadly peril which she was in, and also of warning the nation. He believed that Britain was a nation in covenant with God, and that apostasy from that covenant, as represented by such trends as political reform and Catholic emancipation, would incur divine judgement on church and nation. The image, which Irving uses as one description of the faithful minister, draws on Ezekiel 33, in which God commissions Ezekiel as a watchman and warns him that if Israel perishes as a result of his failure to warn them of the consequences of their sin, he will be held accountable for their blood.

My own interest in Irving goes back twenty-five years, beginning with his attempt to integrate aspects of Reformed theology and charismatic practice at a point where I was trying to do the same. In time, a doctoral thesis on ecclesiology followed, in which Irving played a part. At various points since then I have written and spoken on him. But a full-length biography has been on my mind to undertake ever since floating the idea fifteen years ago with the late Professor Colin Gunton, then my doctoral supervisor, who has played a key role in the resurgence of interest in Irving which has taken place over the last forty years. Gratitude is therefore due to Jeremy Mudditt, Anthony Cross and all those at Paternoster who commissioned and oversaw this project.

I would like to thank those who have so readily assisted me. In particular, descendants of Irving have readily made available material for consultation, read draft chapters, offered hospitality, and encouraged me to keep at it, particularly Miss Penny Howell, Mrs Elizabeth Martin and her family, Professor John Martin and Mrs Rosemary Owen. Several others have generously served as peer reviewers for all or part of the manuscript: Dr David Allen, Miss Rene Anderson, Peter Elliott, Dr Nick Needham and Mrs Barbara Waddington. Hospitality on a number of visits to Edinburgh has been readily provided by Katy and David Pudney. A grant from the Friends of Annandale and Eskdale Museums assisted with the costs of research and provided tangible evidence of continuing interest in Irving in his home town. Many libraries and archives have offered their assistance, especially the Albury Historical Society, the Banner of Truth Trust, the Bodleian Library, the British Library, the Dumfries & Galloway National Health Service Archives, Edinburgh University Library (Special Collections), the Evangelical Library, the London Metropolitan Archive, Lumen (formerly Regent Square) United Reformed Church, the National Archives of Scotland, the National Library of Scotland, New College Library, the University of St Andrews Library (Special Collections) and the United Reformed Church Historical Society. The Drummond Family Papers are used by kind permission of His Grace the Duke of Northumberland, and the Strutt archives by kind permission of the fifth Baron Rayleigh. Finally, I owe a great deal to Ann, my wife, who has lived with my enthusiasm for Irving for more years than she may care to remember.

Tim Grass
May 2009

For the American edition, the opportunity has been taken to correct some typographical errors. My thanks to Gordon W. Simmonds for spotting a number of these.

Tim Grass
November 2011

List of illustrations

1. The Fish Cross, Annan; Irving was born in one of the cottages in the background, in Butts Street
2. Part of Edinburgh University (now known as Old College); Irving attended lectures here as an Arts student
3. Kirkcaldy parish church; Irving's father-in-law John Martin was minister here, and in 1828 thirty-five lives were lost when part of a gallery collapsed
4. The only known photograph of the Caledonian Church in Hatton Garden, long after it had been vacated by Irving's congregation
5. Admission tickets for the Caledonian Church, issued in 1824 (on loan to the London Metropolitan Archive, ref. LMA/4358/C/002/6 & 7)
6. The Irvings lived in this house in London's Claremont Square from 1825 to 1828
7. The National Scotch Church from the north-west at the end of the nineteenth century
8. Interior of the National Scotch Church as it was in Irving's time (on loan to the London Metropolitan Archive, ref. LMA/4358/C/002)
9. Communion tokens were issued to members, entitling them to take part in the Lord's Supper; these examples were issued by the National Scotch Church in 1827
10. Detail of a portrait of Irving by Faithful Christopher Pack
11. A page from the National Scotch Church burial register, showing the entry for the burial of Irving's son Gavin in 1829
12. Annan Old Parish Church, where Irving was baptized, ordained and deposed
13. This memorial tablet to Irving was erected at Regent Square about 1870; it is not known whether it survived the old building's demolition in the 1960s
14. The statue of Irving's closest friend, Thomas Carlyle, which stands near his house in Chelsea
15. This statue of Irving in the churchyard at Annan was erected in 1892
16. This blue plaque on Irving's house in Claremont Square describes Irving as 'Founder of the Catholic Apostolic Church', an assertion which continues to engender debate

Thanks are due to the following for permission to reproduce illustrations: picture 1: Annan Museum; pictures 5, 8, 9: United Reformed Church Historical Society, Westminster College, Cambridge; pictures 10, 11: Lumen (formerly Regent Square) United Reformed Church, London; picture 13: Miss P. Howell.

List of Abbreviations

BDEB:	Donald M. Lewis, ed., *The Blackwell Dictionary of Evangelical Biography 1730–1860*, 2 vols, Oxford: Blackwell, 1995
DL:	British Library
BLO:	Bodleian Library
BT:	Banner of Truth Trust, Edinburgh
CL:	Charles Richard Sanders et al., eds, *The Collected Letters of Thomas and Jane Welsh Carlyle*, 36 vols so far, Durham, NC: Duke University Press, 1970 onwards
CO:	*Christian Observer*
CW:	Edward Irving, *Collected Writings*, ed. Gavin Carlyle, 5 vols, London: Alexander Strahan, 1864–6
DFP:	Alnwick Castle, Drummond Family Papers, held by the Duke of Northumberland; Drummond's religious letters and papers have been microfilmed and the films deposited in the Bodleian Library, Oxford
ECI:	*Edinburgh Christian Instructor*
EM:	*Evangelical Magazine*
ER:	*Eclectic Review*
EUL:	Edinburgh University Library, Special Collections
Fasti:	Hew Scott, ed., *Fasti Ecclesiae Scoticanae*, rev. ed. William S. Crockett and Francis Grant, 7 vols, Edinburgh: Oliver & Boyd, 1915–28 (first publ. 1866–71), online at http://www.dwalker.pwp.blueyonder.co.uk/Ministers%20Index.htm; both versions have been used
JEH:	*Journal of Ecclesiastical History*
JPHSE:	*Journal of the Presbyterian Historical Society of England*
LMA:	London Metropolitan Archive
MS:	manuscript
MW:	*Morning Watch*
NAS:	National Archive of Scotland
NCL:	New College Library, Edinburgh

NLS:	National Library of Scotland
n.p.:	no publisher shown
n.pl.:	no place of publication shown
ODNB:	*Oxford Dictionary of National Biography*, online version
Oliphant, *Life*:	references with volume and page number are to the first edition: Mrs [M. O. W.] Oliphant, *The Life of Edward Irving, Minister of the National Scotch Church, London*, 2 vols, London: Hurst and Blackett, 1862; references with only a page number are to the 5th edn: London: Hurst and Blackett, n.d.[c.1865]
PW:	Edward Irving, *Prophetical Works*, ed. Gavin Carlyle, 2 vols, London: Alexander Strahan, 1867/70
QJP:	*Quarterly Journal of Prophecy*
repr.:	reprinted
RS:	Lumen (formerly Regent Square) United Reformed Church archives, London
RSCHS:	*Records of the Scottish Church History Society*
URCHS:	United Reformed Church Historical Society archive, now at Westminster College, Cambridge

Quotations from the Bible are taken from the Authorized (King James) Version.

Spelling and punctuation in quotations are reproduced from the original, and hence are not always consistent; editorial additions are in square brackets.

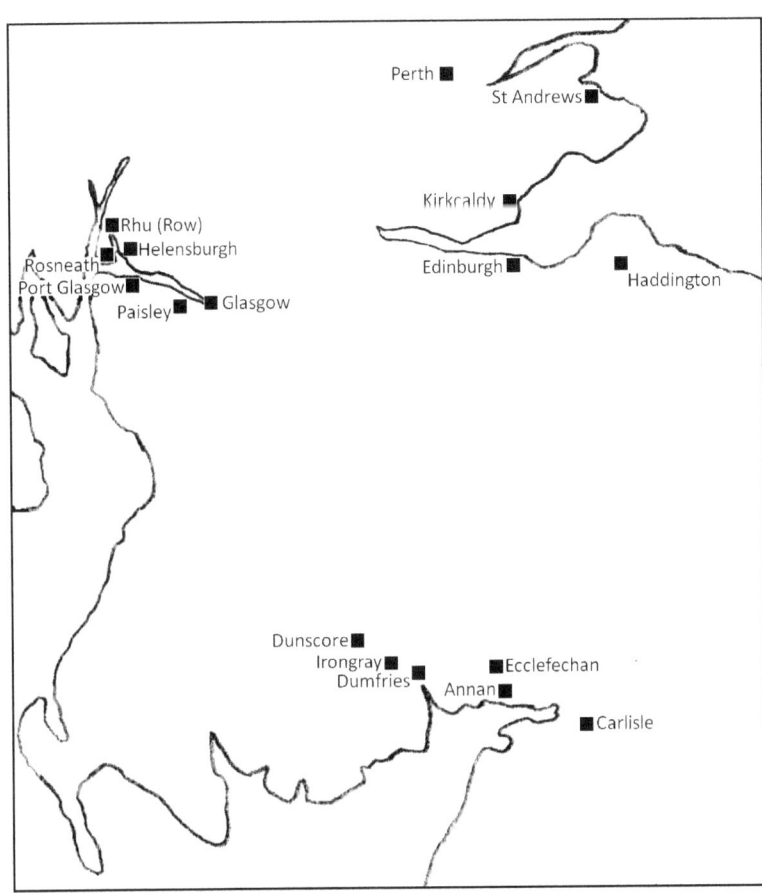

Irving's Scotland

CHAPTER 1

Early Life in Annan, 1792–1805

It was on 4 August 1792, the same day as Percy Bysshe Shelley, that Edward Irving first saw the light of day. He was born in the small Dumfriesshire town of Annan, in a small dwelling in Butts Street, near the Fish Cross.[1] The house has been demolished and is now the site of a bus stand, but a plaque which marked his birthplace may still be seen in the town's museum. A royal burgh since 1538, with a population of about a thousand, as well as three markets, Annan was an economic centre for the farming villages around. Industries included iron foundries and a cotton works. Its location near the border with England, at the lowest point of the Solway Firth where a foot crossing was possible, had ensured for it a turbulent history, but by the eighteenth century things were settling down, and it became a busy port with ships sailing to Liverpool, Whitehaven and other places around the Irish Sea.[2]

Edward was the son of Gavin and Mary Irving. Gavin (1758–1832), a tanner, was described by one later writer as 'a silent and somewhat austere man, with rigid notions of discipline'.[3] The author Thomas Carlyle (1795–1881), who grew up in the same area and whose father knew that branch of the Irvings, described Gavin as 'a tallish man, of rugged countenance, which broke out oftenest into some innocent fleer of merriment, or readiness to be merry, ... a prudent, honest-hearted, rational person, but made no pretension to superior gifts of mind'.[4] The family were 'all cheerfully quiet, rational and honest people, of a good-natured and prudent turn, – something of what might be called a kindly vanity, a very harmless self-esteem,

---

[1] Mrs Oliphant, in her influential biography of Irving, wrongly stated that the house was near the town cross: *Life*, 6; this is corrected by Andrew Landale Drummond, *Edward Irving and his Circle: Including some Consideration of the 'Tongues' Movement in the Light of Modern Psychology* (London: James Clarke, [1937]), 15, and confirmed by local information.

[2] See Anon., 'The Statistical Accounts of Scotland: Account of 1791–99 vol. 19: Annan, County of Dumfries', http://stat-acc-scot.edina.ac.uk//link/1791-99/Dumfries/Annan/, accessed 22 October 2005; Frank Miller, 'Edward Irving and Annan', *Records of the Scottish Church History Society*, repr. in idem, *Poems from the Carlyle Country: Together with Papers on Two of Carlyle's Early Friends and some Fragments in Prose* (Glasgow: Jackson Son & Co., 1937), 39–47.

[3] William W. Andrews, *Edward Irving: A Review* (2nd edn, Glasgow: David Hobbs, 1900), 16. Irving's own conception of the father-son relationship may be gathered from his series of sermons 'On Family and Social Religion': *CW*, 3.217–339.

[4] Thomas Carlyle, *Reminiscences*, ed. C. E. Norton (London: J. M. Dent, 1932), 171 (subsequent references are to this edition unless indicated otherwise).

doing pleasure to the proprietor and hurt to nobody else, was traceable in all of them'. In Carlyle's opinion, none were distinguished by their intellectual capacities, except perhaps in an undeveloped form.[5] Some of them were farmers; one became a tobacconist. Irvings had lived in the area since the eleventh century, the ancestral seat being Bonshaw, a few miles to the north-east, just off the modern A74(M), the motorway between Carlisle and Glasgow.

Gavin did comfortably well for himself and served as Baillie (local magistrate) in the town. Carlyle comments that he 'married well, perhaps rather above his rank'.[6] His wife Mary (1764–1840), *née* Lowther (most of the children carried this as their middle name), was, in Mrs. Oliphant's words, 'the handsome and high-spirited daughter of a small landed proprietor in the adjacent parish of Dornoch [Dornock]'.[7] One who remembered her described her as 'a portly, buxom dame, full of animation, very demonstrative and eloquent, who, on meeting one of her neighbours in the street, would stand and discourse most vigorously on the topics of the day'; the animation and eloquence, along with Gavin's quiet dignity, would reappear in her celebrated son.[8] Her great-grandfather, Thomas Howy, had been the parish minister from 1703 to 1753, and a persistent if undocumented tradition claimed that she was descended from Huguenot refugees.[9] Mary 'had much of fluent speech in her, and of management; thrifty, assiduous, wise, if somewhat fussy; for the rest, an excellent house-mother, I believe, full of affection and tender anxiety for her children and husband.'[10] She evidently possessed a measure of natural gentility; Edward later lamented that 'Evangelicalism ... has spoiled both the minds and the bodies of the women of Scotland – there are no women now like my mother.'[11] According to a close friend of hers, Edward was 'a spirity little man, but would do anything for his mother'.[12] Nine children were born to Gavin and Mary, not all of whom survived to adulthood.[13] Edward grew into a strong child, although he early developed a squint. A medical friend of his later suggested that it arose from one eye being obscured by the

---

[5] Ibid. 171.

[6] Ibid. 172.

[7] Oliphant, *Life*, 1.

[8] James Dodds, *Personal Reminiscences and Biographical Sketches* (Edinburgh: Macniven & Wallace, 1887), 33.

[9] Some sources refer to these ancestors as Albigenses, but as this term refers to a French branch of the medieval Cathars it is incorrect. 'Howie' (in various spellings) is a common Ayrshire surname; Irving referred to a famous branch of the family, the Howies of Lochgoin in the north-east of the county, whom he claimed as his kinsfolk: Oliphant, *Life*, 1.120. From that branch came John Howie (1735–93), author of *Scots Worthies*, which described the sufferings of the seventeenth-century Scottish Covenanters. It held a similar place of honour in Scottish homes to that held in English ones by Bunyan's *Pilgrim's Progress*.

[10] Carlyle, *Reminiscences*, 172.

[11] Oliphant, *Life*, 7.

[12] Dodds, *Personal Reminiscences*, 35.

[13] For a family tree, see Appendix I.

side of the cradle and thus unable to focus on the light coming in from the window.[14]

Education was highly esteemed throughout Scotland, and the Irving family, like many others, sought to ensure that each of their sons received a professional training. John (1790–1822) became a surgeon, Edward a minister, and George (1804–33) a doctor. Edward received his primary and secondary education in his home town, first at the hands of a Peggy Paine,[15] and then under Adam Hope (1756–1823). Hope, who had intended becoming a minister but was prevented by 'backwardness', was to leave a lasting impression on this scholar, as on others; for one thing he was ruthless in his deployment of the Socratic method to question his pupils, thereby exposing their ignorance and the logical consequences of their ill-considered answers, and for another he was a member of a dissenting denomination known as the Burgher Seceders, a point to which we shall return shortly.[16] Irving recalled how he

> received a classical education first under Mr Hope and then under Mr Dalgliesh, the first of these teachers I shall remember while I have the remembrance of any thing, if ever I rise to any eminence in the world ..., it shall, [sic] be attributed totally to Mr Hope whose instructions it may have pleased the Almighty to prosper and from whose care of my early education I have derived that activity of mind which I know how to value and which I hope will accompany me through life.[17]

One reviewer claimed that the discipline Irving experienced as a schoolboy affected his temper and conception of discipline,[18] although from Carlyle's description it does not appear that Hope was at all extreme in his approach, preferring to detain students until they had worked out the right answer to his question, rather than inflict physical punishment on them.[19]

In 1803, Hope closed his school and joined the staff of the newly opened Annan Academy under the Rev. William Dalgliesh (1771/2–1846), where he taught for the next sixteen years. Edward made the same move for the remainder of his school

---

[14] Oliphant, *Life*, 6.

[15] Some sources (e.g. Anon., 'No. XII. The Rev. Edward Irving, M.A. Late Minister of the National Scotch Church', *Annual Biography and Obituary* 20 (1836), 138–56, at 139; cf. Oliphant, *Life*, 7) claim that she was the aunt of the radical writer Tom Paine, but given that he came from Thetford in Norfolk and was born in 1737, this is scarcely plausible: Drummond, *Irving*, 16; Miller, 'Irving and Annan', 43.

[16] Carlyle, *Reminiscences*, 174–5.

[17] Edward Irving, 'Diary. Haddington 18th July 1810', fols 73–4: 4 August (in private hands). Cf. Carlyle: 'through life, you could always notice, overhung by such strange draperies, and huge superstructures so foreign to it, something of that old primeval basis of rigorous logic and clear articulation laid for him in boyhood by old Adam Hope': *Reminiscences*, 175.

[18] [John Tulloch], Review of Mrs Oliphant's *Life* and Story's *Memoir*, *Edinburgh Review* 116 (1862), 426-60, at 430.

[19] Carlyle, *Reminiscences*, 174–5.

career.[20] Although a bright student, he was better known for his athletic abilities.[21] In time, he was to be well over six feet in height, and to earn the nickname 'Longshanks'.[22] Among his near neighbours was Hugh Clapperton (1788–1827), later to achieve fame as an explorer in West Africa; when both had achieved fame, they renewed acquaintance in London, and Clapperton's last communication to England was apparently addressed to Irving.[23] One of Clapperton's colleagues was Irving's brother-in-law, Robert Dickson. It is worth pointing out here that men such as Irving, Clapperton, and Carlyle (who also attended Annan Academy[24]), were successful because of their background, and not in spite of it. It would be wrong to regard them as rising above it; indeed, Irving made it a priority to visit his family at least every year, even after he was in great demand as a famous preacher. Furthermore, he never lost the attitude of open-handed small-town hospitality with which he had grown up, an attitude which was to cost him dearly on occasion in London.

Annan's Old Parish Church was to be a significant place for Edward: here he was baptized, ordained, and deposed from the ministry. The minister from 1784 to 1825 was the Rev. William Moncrieff, whose father had been minister before him for many years. Although the early years of his ministry had seen the building of the church, to which a spire was added in 1810, he appears to have become a rather sad example of ministerial laxity: inclined to drink, the parishioners regarded him with a sort of kindly contempt. Carlyle thought that this and the impact of Hope's method of teaching meant that local people were, as a result, 'more given to sceptical free-thinking than other places'.[25] Irving would in time be accused first of scepticism and then of credulity, a duality which has resulted in varying estimates of what he would have taught had he lived longer. However, at this age it was hero-worship which played a greater part in his thinking. The south-west of Scotland had been a stronghold of the seventeenth-century Covenanters, so called because of their adherence to the covenants made by Scottish leaders of church and state to uphold Presbyterianism as the established faith and the basis of the nation's laws, and to oppose anything inconsistent with it; the best known was the Solemn League and Covenant of 1638. Belief in a nation covenanted to uphold the Reformed faith (that branch of Protestantism rooted in the teaching and practice of John Calvin and Huldreich Zwingli, among others) led them to oppose Stuart rule, under which

---

[20] Frank Miller, *A Bibliography of the Parish of Annan: With Biographical Memoranda respecting the Authors catalogued* (Dumfries: reprinted from the *Transactions of the Dumfriesshire and Galloway Natural History and Antiquarian Society*, 1925), 38–9, 42; Drummond, *Irving*, 16; Simon Heffer, *Moral Desperado: A Life of Thomas Carlyle* (London: Phoenix, 1996), 30.

[21] Oliphant, *Life*, 9.

[22] *CL*, 1.315: Carlyle to William Graham, 28 January 1821.

[23] Oliphant, *Life*, 14; Drummond, *Irving*, 18.

[24] He left his rather negative impressions on record in *Sartor Resartus*, in which the academy appeared in the disguise of 'Hinterschlag'.

[25] Carlyle, *Reminiscences*, 176.

repeated attempts were made to reintroduce episcopacy to Scotland. Thousands died in the struggle to maintain 'the crown rights of the Redeemer' over the Scottish church; stories of their heroism and readiness to die for their beliefs abounded, and the population of southern and south-western Scotland long continued to venerate their memory. We shall see that Edward was deeply affected by the covenanting tradition, as would be evident in his writings (especially those which touched on the implications of contemporary political developments for the church's standing), and in the emphasis on Britain as a nation in covenant with God which was carried over into the scheme of prophetic interpretation adopted by the Albury circle and the Catholic Apostolic Church.[26] During his boyhood, he claimed that he visited almost all of the Covenanters' graves (presumably referring to those within reach of Annan).[27]

As a lad of about ten years old, Edward used on occasion to join a group who walked to the Burgher Seceder meeting house at Ecclefechan, a town slightly larger than Annan which lay about seven miles to the north. Among the group was Adam Hope.[28] A secession from the Church of Scotland took place in 1733 over the issue of patronage (the right of appointment of a minister to a living), but the Seceders themselves divided in 1747 over the legitimacy of taking the Burgess Oath promising to uphold the true Christian religion as professed in Scotland, which was required of those holding civic office. The Burghers allowed the swearing of the oath, while the Anti-Burghers rejected it. Each party in turn divided over other matters.[29] By contrast with most English Dissent, Scottish secessions often occurred because the established church was deemed to be insufficiently committed to the form of religion enshrined in its own Confessions of Faith and Books of Discipline. As Carlyle put it, 'all Dissent in Scotland is merely stricter adherence to the National

---

[26] On the Albury circle, see ch. 13; on the movement which became the Catholic Apostolic Church, see ch. 20, and my book, *The Lord's Work: A History of the Catholic Apostolic Church* (Paternoster, forthcoming).

[27] Edward Irving, *Preliminary Discourse to the Work of Ben Ezra*, cxciii, quoted by Liam Upton, '"Our Mother and our Country": The Integration of Religious and National Identity in the Thought of Edward Irving (1792–1834)', in Robert Pope, ed., *Religion and National Identity: Wales and Scotland c. 1700–2000* (Cardiff: University of Wales Press, 2001), 242–67, at 244. Miller suggested that Irving may not have relished his connections with the Irvings of Bonshaw because one of them had taken a lead in persecuting the Covenanters: 'Irving and Annan', 40. For an earlier example of such an attitude in another branch of the family, see Dodds, *Personal Reminiscences*, 34.

[28] From 1807 there was a Burgher Seceder minister attached to the newly formed congregation at Annan, the Rev. William Glen (1778–1849); Hope served as clerk to its kirk session. Glen appears to have become a friend of Irving's, since the latter made an effort to see him to say farewell as he left his contentious congregation to take up missionary service at Astrakhan in 1817: Carlyle, *Reminiscences*, 177, 189–91; Miller, *Bibliography*, 34–5.

[29] J. H. S. Burleigh, *A Church History of Scotland* (London: Oxford University Press, 1960), endpaper chart.

Kirk in all points'.[30] Moreover, in parts of the country it was the dissenting groups which held aloft the torch of serious religion: 'A man who awoke to the belief that he actually had a soul to be saved or lost was apt to be found among the Dissenting people, and to have given up attendance on the Kirk.'[31] Carlyle was brought up in the Ecclefechan congregation, and described its minister, John Johnston, as 'the priestliest man I ever under any ecclesiastical guise was privileged to look upon'.[32] It is possible that such a man influenced Irving's own conception of the ministry, in which the priestly element played a larger role than was customary for Presbyterian ministers. His congregation was a growing one, which in 1805 planted several daughter congregations in Annan and elsewhere.[33]

Since his father was by now a magistrate, and would have attended the parish church in that capacity, Mrs Oliphant thought that Edward's visits to Ecclefechan were probably restricted to summer evenings or occasions when there was no service at his own church.[34] Doubtless one of the attractions was the presence of his uncle George (1754–1822), who belonged to the meeting.[35] However, it appears that his parents disapproved, and his older brother John refused to accompany him.[36]

Oliphant was probably right in asserting that it was 'unlikely that any premature love for sermons or discrimination of their quality was the cause' of Irving's excursions, but she also made the point that the Seceder elders 'unconsciously prepared the germs of that old-world stateliness of speech and dignity of manner which afterwards distinguished their pupil'.[37] Whilst influenced by new movements of thought, Irving hankered after aspects of a world which was fast passing away and sought to recapture them in his ministry.[38] According to Carlyle, Edward's connections with the Seceders were 'brief, but I believe ineffaceable through life';[39] he persisted 'Possibly a year or two, – or occasionally, almost till he went to College.' Yet 'Edward's religion in after years, though it ran always in the blood and life of him, was never shrieky or narrow'.[40]

---

[30] Carlyle, *Reminiscences*, 176.

[31] Ibid. 176.

[32] Ibid. 26. Cf. his father's reference to the minister as 'our priest', in James Anthony Froude, *Thomas Carlyle: A History of the First Forty Years of his Life 1795–1835* (2 vols, London: Longmans, Green, 1882), 1.45: James Carlyle to Thomas Carlyle, 12 February 1817.

[33] Ian Campbell, *Thomas Carlyle* (Edinburgh: Saltire Society, 1993; first publ. 1974), 6.

[34] Oliphant, *Life*, 14–15.

[35] Carlyle, *Reminiscences*, 170–1.

[36] Ibid. 178.

[37] Oliphant, *Life*, 12, 13.

[38] Cf. Anne M. Skabarnicki, 'Annandale Evangelist and Scotch Voltaire: Carlyle's *Reminiscences* of Edward Irving and Francis Jeffrey', *Scotia* 4 (1980), 16–30.

[39] Carlyle, *Reminiscences*, 176.

[40] Ibid. 178. This is corroborated by Irving's own later criticisms of conventicle religion, which addressed the in-group and showed no concern for those outside.

Early Life in Annan, 1792–1805

There was another minister among Irving's forebears, to whom Edward would owe a great debt. This was the Rev. Bryce Johnston (1747–1805), minister at Holywood, near Dumfries, and author of a two-volume *Commentary on the Revelation of St. John* (1794). His father John was Provost of Annan and married Thomas Howy's daughter Elizabeth. Bryce's sister was to be Edward's maternal grandmother.[41] On the occasion of his eighteenth birthday, reviewing the course of his life so far, Irving recorded his debt to Johnston as

> a man whose early death I shall ever regret as a Dispensation of Providence which deprived me of a well wisher and friend united in the person of a near relation. A person so well calculated and so much disposed to give a good advice, to correct your errors and direct your studies I never expect to meet with. I am particularly interested in his death from another circumstance: about that time it was always a part of my morning and evening prayer that my father might receive the means of compleating my education. Dr B. Johnstone died and left my mother about £500 – my Desire was granted but at a very dear rate _ Let this teach me to pray for Gods [sic] direction in those things to ask from him.[42]

It would appear, then, that the legacy from his great-uncle enabled Edward to attend university. The next chapter will explore what university life in Edinburgh was like.

---

[41] *Fasti*, 2.276; Miller, *Bibliography*, 39, 49; Miller incorrectly states that Bryce Johnston married Elizabeth Howy.

[42] Irving, 'Diary', fol. 75.

CHAPTER 2

Edinburgh, 1805–09

Edward left for university at thirteen, his father accompanying him as far as Moffat, about twenty-five miles north of Annan. Some years later, he could still recall the agony of parting and of being separated from his family and from the places which had been so familiar to him.¹ According to Mrs Oliphant, he was accompanied by his brother, John, who was to study medicine, and both were under the charge of some relatives of Hugh Clapperton; the brothers lodged together in the Old Town, then a notoriously unsavoury warren of tenements.² However, Edward's own recollection was that he left for Edinburgh on 7 November 1805 with a cousin, William Irving, with whom it was intended that he should lodge; they were committed to the charge of one John M'Whir.³

University life in Scotland differed quite considerably from that in contemporary England. Saunders provides an illuminating summary:

> There was no entrance examination; students came directly from the parish schools, sometimes only 14 or 15 years old and from the burgh schools at a slightly more advanced age. They selected their classes with or without the intention of graduating, paid the fees for each subject, and made their own arrangements for a winter's study. There was no supervision of living quarters. They could be secured at cheap rates and the country student was regularly supplied with provisions by his family. Some students helped to support themselves by tutoring or literary hack work and such opportunities were eagerly welcomed for in addition to the money earned they gave access to superior circles where raw manners were polished and important contacts made. But in the summer half of the year a country student returned to work on the farm and the earnings of the long vacation might cover the expenses of the winter.⁴

Little is known of Irving's university days, although it is possible to reconstruct the course of his studies to some extent. The curriculum for the Arts degree was remarkably wide-ranging. It fell into three parts: language and literature (including the Latin and Greek classics); philosophy and ethics (including Logic and Moral

---

¹ Edward Irving, 'Diary. Haddington 18ᵗʰ July 1810', fol. 85: 6 August (in private hands).
² Oliphant, *Life*, 15.
³ Irving, 'Diary', fol. 74–5: 4 August.
⁴ Laurance James Saunders, *Scottish Democracy 1815–1840: The Social and Intellectual Background* (Edinburgh: Oliver and Boyd, 1950), 307.

Philosophy); and mathematics and physics (then known as Natural Philosophy). By contrast with English institutions, Philosophy dominated the Scottish curriculum; even in mathematics, science, language, and literature, much attention was given to the first principles and the metaphysical grounding of each discipline.[5] The shortcoming of such a broad-brush deductive approach was that 'the immature student exposed to university discussion was accused of superficiality; he was precociously developed by a rapid change of subject, by wide views and by desultory reading'.[6] It cannot be said that Irving's preaching was entirely free from this fault.

Rebuilding of the university, to a design by Robert Adam, had begun before Irving was born, and would not be completed until the 1820s. Space was at a premium, whether for the library (which was inadequately accommodated) or for the lecturers, who often found themselves with audiences of two hundred or more.[7] As Saunders indicates, students in Scottish universities were usually left to fend for themselves, with the encouragement of an occasional food parcel from home; those from a modest background such as the Irvings' would have endured a frugal existence, although during the 1820s it was possible to find board and lodging in the city for 7s. or 7s. 6d. per week.[8] University fees were two or three guineas[9] a year, and a student could get by on no more than £20, as the session lasted only from November till May.[10] Mrs Oliphant suggests that Edward probably did the journeys to and from home by foot, stopping in wayside cottages for something to eat.[11] Doubtless this fostered his ability to relate to people from the humblest social backgrounds without being guilty of condescension. Poor as he undoubtedly was, he nevertheless took care of his appearance. Carlyle recollected Irving visiting Annan Academy in 1808: 'Irving was scrupulously dressed, black coat, ditto tight pantaloons in the fashion of the day; clerical black his prevailing hue; and looked very neat, self-possessed, and enviable: a flourishing slip of a youth; with coal-black hair, swarthy clear complexion; very straight on his feet, and, except for the glaring squint alone, decidedly handsome.'[12]

Throughout these years, he appears to have maintained a varied diet of reading, although relatively little of it was strictly theological, and almost none of it was drawn from the Reformed tradition, whether British or Continental. A significant theological discovery which he made during this period, and a surprising one for a devotee of the Covenanting tradition, was the sixteenth-century apologist for

---

[5] George Elder Davie, *The Democratic Intellect: Scotland and her Universities in the Nineteenth Century* (Edinburgh: University Press, 1961), 13–14; Saunders, *Scottish Democracy*, 353.

[6] Saunders, *Scottish Democracy*, 355.

[7] For an excellent portrayal, see Ian Campbell, *Thomas Carlyle* (Edinburgh: Saltire Society, 1993; first publ. 1974), ch. 2.

[8] Ibid. 361.

[9] A guinea was £1 1s.

[10] Cf. Campbell, *Carlyle*, 17.

[11] Oliphant, *Life*, 18.

[12] Carlyle, *Reminiscences*, 180.

Anglicanism Richard Hooker: the story goes that Irving discovered Hooker's *Laws of Ecclesiastical Polity* in an Annandale farmhouse, perhaps on his journeys between home and university. As for general literature, his reading seems to have been on the lighter side; a friend recalled how he used to read or recite passages from Macpherson's Ossian, a rather florid poet whose works he carried around in a pocket edition.[13]

The vast majority of Arts students did not graduate, particularly at Edinburgh; a full set of class tickets certifying attendance and diligence was seen as more valuable than a degree.[14] Edward, however, was awarded his degree in 1809, having attracted the attention of two of the leading teachers of the day: Professor Christison and Sir John Leslie.[15] Both took an active interest when he began his independent career,[16] recommending him to the Burgh of Haddington as a master for their new Mathematical School. Here he began in the spring of 1809 after spending one term as a student in the Divinity hall.[17]

Taking the occasion of his eighteenth birthday to look back over his life so far, he recorded that although he was determined to become a 'clergyman' of the Church of Scotland, he commenced his studies at Edinburgh 'long before I was able to judge the inclination of my own mind'.[18] It appears to have been during his time as an

---

[13] Drummond, *Irving*, 20; Oliphant, *Life*, 19. The eighteenth-century writer James Macpherson claimed to have discovered and translated an epic poem in Gaelic telling the story of a third-century Scottish king, Fingal, written by his son, Ossian. First published in 1762, Macpherson's work achieved immense popularity, even though it was generally recognized to be a fraud: Anon., 'Ossian: Fact or Fiction', http://www.bbc.co.uk/legacies/myths_legends/scotland/highland/, accessed 13 March 2009.

[14] Saunders, *Scottish Democracy*, 308. For example, during the 1820s Edinburgh's Faculty of Arts had an enrolment of over eight hundred, following a four-year course; yet an average of just ten students graduated each year: ibid. 355.

[15] Christison (1753–1820) was Professor of Humanity (i.e. Latin) from 1806; Leslie (1766–1832) was Professor of Mathematics: Thomas Carlyle, *Reminiscences*, ed. K. J. Fielding and Ian Campbell (Oxford: Oxford University Press, 1997), 449–50.

[16] Oliphant, *Life*, 18–20.

[17] Mrs Oliphant is incorrect in dating this to 1810: ibid. 20. On 16 February 1809 the Town Council wrote to Leslie seeking a teacher for the proposed school. Irving was elected, on Leslie's recommendation, on 27 March 1809, at a salary of £20, with additional fees of 15s. per quarter for teaching mathematics and 10s. for geography: James Miller, *The Lamp of Lothian or The History of Haddington* (Haddington: Sinclair, 1900), 197. This is supported by another local writer, John Martine, who stated that Irving's first recorded borrowing from the library in Haddington was on 3 July 1809, when he took out a volume of Robert Burns' poetry: *Reminiscences of the Royal Burgh of Haddington* (Edinburgh: John Menzies, 1883), 204. The library's borrowing records for this period have survived, and show that, as far as theological reading was concerned, Irving had a distinct preference for English Anglican authors: Edinburgh, NLS, MS 16481, 'Account of Books borrowed from the public Library of the Town of Haddington from 1st April 1792 and forward'.

[18] Irving, 'Diary', fol. 73: 4 August.

Arts student that he formed the intention of becoming a minister. By contrast with the Arts curriculum, the Divinity course was far more restricted in its coverage than would be expected today, comprising Systematic Theology, Hebrew, and Ecclesiastical History. Candidates had to show evidence of graduation in Arts or attendance at what amounted to a 'full course of philosophy'.[19] The course involved four years' full-time study or a year's full-time or 'regular' attendance and five years' 'irregular' attendance (in which a student would study by themselves, visiting the University twice a year to deliver set discourses or take examinations). Even full-time study was not onerous, since at Edinburgh the Divinity session lasted just four months. Graduation in divinity was honorary, no degree being awarded. During the 1820s, Edinburgh had about 150 'regular' Divinity students and 100 'irregular'.[20] We shall see in the next chapter that Edward learned more about the ministry by observation than by reading, and that what he learned did not give him too high an opinion of the profession's contemporary exponents.

---

[19] Saunders, *Scottish Democracy*, 348.

[20] Ibid. 349–50. Irving enrolled as an irregular student on 16 November 1809, his sponsoring presbytery and parish both being listed as Haddington: Edinburgh, EUL, 'The Roll-Book of Students of Divinity in the University of Edinburgh, From November 17th 1801 to April 9th 1831'.

CHAPTER 3

Haddington, 1809–12

Haddington, the county town of East Lothian (then known as Haddingtonshire), was the possible birthplace of one of Irving's heroes, the sixteenth–century Protestant reformer John Knox, who was educated there. By the early nineteenth century it had become a quiet but fairly prosperous market town, about seventeen miles east of Edinburgh on the road to London, set in the middle of good farmland, with a population at the 1811 census of 4,370, about two–thirds of which would have been in the town itself. The population, whilst educated to a basic level, were reputed to be neither great readers nor well-informed, although it was said that most families possessed a Bible, the Catechism, and a few suitable religious works.[1]

Edward's career as a schoolmaster there appears to have got off to a very promising start, according to Mrs Oliphant's account.[2] Whilst a strict disciplinarian, his firmness evidently brought encouraging results, and out of school he proved a ready companion to his pupils, who used to accompany him on astronomical and trigonometric excursions in which he had the use of some scientific instruments and from which he was capable of being distracted into more athletic pursuits. As well as teaching in the school, on Wednesday afternoons he taught at Saltoun Hall, where Lady Cathcart had engaged him to tutor her daughters Mary and Augusta. On Saturdays, he used to walk to the nearby village of Bolton, where he spent the afternoon at the manse; apart from the friendship of the minister, Andrew Stewart, it was here that he formed (or possibly renewed) the acquaintance of a fellow divinity student, Robert Story, whom we shall meet later on.[3]

One excursion which Edward and some of his students made was to walk to Edinburgh for a midweek evening service in the fashionable St George's Church, at which Dr Thomas Chalmers was due to speak.[4] They made their way to an

---

[1] Anon., *Second Statistical Account of Scotland: Haddington, County of Haddington (1834–45)*, 2.1–17, http://stat-acc-scot.edina.ac.uk/link/1834-45/Haddington/haddington/; George Barclay, *Statistical Account of Scotland 1791–99*, 6.535–42, http://stat-acc-scot.edina.ac.uk/link/1791-99/Haddington/Haddington/; both accessed 15 November 2005.

[2] Oliphant, *Life*, ch. 3.

[3] Edward Irving, 'Diary. Haddington 18th July 1810', fol. 9: 18 July (in private hands); Oliphant, *Life*, 27.

[4] Chalmers (1780–1847) experienced an evangelical conversion around 1811, when already in the parish ministry. Thereafter he quickly became one of the leading lights of Evangelicalism north of the border, and Irving would become his assistant in Glasgow

unoccupied pew, but were prevented from entering it by a man who claimed that it was taken. When Irving's remonstrance that by this point in the service it could no longer be reserved for its holder proved unavailing, he raised his arm and threatened the astonished man, 'Remove your arm, or I will shatter it in pieces!'[5] It was not the last time that he would display such an imperious attitude.[6]

Valuable light is shed on Irving's time in Haddington by the diary which he kept from 18 July to 30 August 1810.[7] Evidently a keen sermon taster, he was already becoming an acute critic of the preaching under which he sat; in his diary, he recounted some sermons in great detail, and he appears to have attended other churches as well as the Church of Scotland, such as the Tabernacle (from its name, this probably belonged to the Independents).[8] In one entry he set down his homiletic philosophy – the earliest occasion on which he did so. He disapproved of extempore preaching as likely to be poorly structured; in his view, 'A good discourse may be compared to a good machine, every wheel has a peculiar object and yet contributes in some degree to the general design of the whole'.[9] As a true Presbyterian, he asserted the priority of preaching in worship: 'Next to a correct private life due attention to pulpit discourses is the first object of a clergyman. They ought to be made level to the capacity of the weakest mind, and yet in such a manner as to be useful to all.' He believed that poor preparation risked producing infidels and careless attenders, who could not be reclaimed. Even his own minister, Dr Lorimer,[10] whom he otherwise liked a good deal, he deemed deficient in this respect.[11] As for eloquence, then so highly regarded:

(see ch. 5). He led the seceders in forming the Free Church of Scotland at the Disruption of 1843: William Hanna, *Memoirs of the Life and Writings of Thomas Chalmers D.D. LL.D.* (4 vols, Edinburgh: Sutherland and Knox, 1850).

[5] Oliphant, *Life*, 25.

[6] For another attempt to gain access to a pew, during the General Assembly of 1816, see Oliphant, *Life*, 40. This one ended with the destruction of the pew door, but he was still unable to gain a place. A third such incident occurred around 1819, when he was accompanying some young ladies to a public meeting and calmly threatened to 'annihilate' the hapless functionary who was refusing them access: Oliphant, *Life*, 1.86.

[7] Kept in detail while it lasted, it ends suddenly, and although Mrs Oliphant drew on a journal which he kept in the autumn of 1825, neither that nor any other similar document appears to have survived.

[8] Irving, 'Diary', fol. 100: 12 August. Independents in Scotland owed their origins in large measure to the labours of the Haldane brothers Robert (1764–1842) and James (1768–1851); their churches were marked by plural lay leadership, weekly observance of the Lord's Supper, and vigorous evangelism; see Alexander Haldane, *The Lives of Robert Haldane of Airthrey, and of his Brother, James Alexander Haldane* (2nd edn, London: Hamilton, Adams, 1852).

[9] Irving, 'Diary', fol. 119: 19 August.

[10] Robert Lorimer (1765–1848) was Church of Scotland minister of Haddington from 1796 until he joined the Free Church of Scotland in 1843: *Fasti*, Haddington, 370, accessed 8 November 2005.

[11] Irving, 'Diary', fol. 120: 19 August.

There appears to me to be two great distinctions in the eloquence of the pulpit. The first and real kind draws the attention from the speaker to the subject and keeps it steadily to this one object. The second sort which is of a spurious nature, tends to lead your mind from the matter of the discourse to the person who delivers it.[12]

He also confided to his diary his thoughts regarding marriage: 'I have almost formed the resolution never to marry except I can find a woman of a truly religious principle and a consistent practice as well as a sound judgement who is willing to join her fortune to mine'.[13] But that did not stop him envying a friend who had formed a romantic attachment: 'Oh that I possessed the affections & esteem of some religious, well informed, well disposed & good tempered girl. To meet with a person of such a description should be esteemed the happiest circumstance of my life.'[14] The moralizing spilled over into his family relationships: on one occasion he recorded that he was writing a letter to his sister Jenny (Jenet), who was a year or two younger than him, on such topics as 'the inutility and dangerous consequences of novels'.[15]

It was at Haddington that Edward met the young lady who was to become his first love. A local doctor, Dr Welsh, asked Professor Leslie to send a tutor for his nine-year-old daughter, 'for whose training he entertained more ambitious views than little girls are generally the subjects of'.[16] Leslie recommended Irving, who was already resident in the town. He tutored Jane from six until eight in the mornings, and again each evening.[17] The work was quite well paid: for teaching Jane Latin an hour a day, he was paid £1 11s. 6d. a month in 1812.[18] Edward was welcomed into the Welshes' civilized household (as he was into others in the locality, including that of Gilbert Burns, brother of the poet Robert Burns and treasurer of the Bolton auxiliary of the British and Foreign Bible Society[19]). He also acquired a reputation as something of a sceptic, possibly in part because he tended to superlative language in expressing his opinions; Dr Welsh expressed the opinion that 'This youth will scrape a hole in everything he is called on to believe'.[20] However, the reputation may have been due to the fact that he was keen on mathematics, and also taught Jane logic, 'to the great tribulation of the household, in which the little philosopher pushed her inquiries into the puzzling metaphysics of life'.[21] More than scepticism, speculation seems to have

---

[12] Ibid. fols 122–3: 19 August.
[13] Ibid. fol. 22: 22 July.
[14] Ibid. fol. 124: 19 August.
[15] Ibid. fol. 15: 18 July.
[16] Oliphant, *Life*, 22.
[17] Ibid. 23.
[18] Virginia Surtees, *Jane Welsh Carlyle* (Wilton, Salisbury: Michael Russell, 1986), 10.
[19] Oliphant, *Life*, 26; Peter Dobson, 'A Journey Through East Lothian Places and Personalities', http://www.grantsbraes.org.uk/pdf/a-journey-through-east-lothian.pdf, accessed 13 March 2009.
[20] Oliphant, *Life*, 24.
[21] Ibid. 23.

marked his outlook during these years, and his taste for speculative theology once brought him into disagreement with Dr Lorimer over the profitability of considering the destiny of human beings in heaven: when the minister ventured to hint that there were more important topics for him to be thinking about, Edward's response was 'Dare you or I deprive God of the glory and thanks due to his name, for this exceeding great reward?'[22]

Irving's annual salary was £35, considerably more than that of the Rector of the Grammar School (£22 5s.) or the master of the English department (£20). Nevertheless, in 1812 he wrote to the Burgh Council requesting an increase; it seems that he had already been approached to take up a position in Kirkcaldy, but wished to remain where he was because he appreciated the consideration he had been shown by the Council and others.[23] The letter was laid before the Council on 23 September, but a move to raise his salary by £15 was defeated; accordingly, the following week's meeting records the Council's acceptance of his letter of resignation.[24] He was on the move; and although his time in Kirkcaldy would prove to be a more eventful period than the years in Haddington, he was happy to return to the town on a number of occasions over the next decade to preach and to visit the Welshes.

---

[22] Ibid. 26.

[23] W. Forbes Gray and J. H. Jamieson, *A Short History of Haddington* (Stevenage: SPA Books, 1995; first publ. Edinburgh: East Lothian Antiquarian & Field Naturalists' Society, 1944), 134.

[24] Edinburgh, NAS, Haddington Burgh Registers, B30/13/21, 'Council Book 1806–1812': 23 and 30 September 1812; B30/19/4, 'Treasurer's Accounts 1803–35'.

CHAPTER 4

Kirkcaldy, 1812–18

The scene now changes to Kirkcaldy, the third small town with which Irving was to be associated. By 1843, this port and textile manufacturing town, with its neighbouring communities, numbered about 15,000 inhabitants; the population of the town itself increased from 3,747 in 1811 to about 5,400 in 1841. It sprawled along the coast of the Firth of Forth, about ten miles to the north of Edinburgh.[1]

In 1812, the professional people of the town, headed by the parish minister, the Rev. John Martin, decided to start a new school, which became known as Kirkcaldy Academy, 'of higher pretensions' than the parish school. Applying to Professor Christison for a recommendation, Irving's name was given them, and that autumn he was duly appointed. Two rooms were fitted up for him, and another as a classroom, in premises on Oswald's Wynd which were used on Sundays by the Bereans, a religious group which had commenced in 1773 and eventually merged with the Congregationalists.[2] Although located in modest premises, the new institution proved successful. Such was the devotion Irving inspired in his students that they took for themselves the nickname 'Irvingites', a title afterwards applied to members of the religious body in whose founding he played a leading role, the Catholic Apostolic Church. Irving's appearance was as striking as his pedagogical success; now somewhat over six feet in height, he often wore a tartan coat in which red predominated. With the help of an assistant, he had responsibility for the entire curriculum, everything from his beloved Mathematics, through Latin, to his equally beloved Milton, large sections of whose *Paradise Lost* he got the scholars to learn by heart. As at Haddington, Irving spent his holidays surveying or in physical activity, accompanied by a group of students.[3] Drummond thought that Irving's interest in science 'ought to have corrected his later tendency to "over-belief"', a tendency of which he began allegedly to show signs while in Kirkcaldy, but such a judgement rests upon the questionable assumption that credulity was a significant aspect of his

---

[1] John Alexander, 'Second Statistical Account of Scotland, Kirkcaldy, County of Fife', vol. 9, 740–70, http://stat-acc-scot.edina.ac.uk/link/1834-45/Fife/Kirkcaldy/, accessed 15 November 2005.

[2] John Campbell, *The Church and Parish of Kirkcaldy: From the Earliest Times till 1843* (Kirkcaldy: Alex Page, 1904), 196, 204. The location is sometimes given as Hill Place, which runs off Oswald's Wynd.

[3] Oliphant, *Life*, 29–33, 41.

later interest in charismatic phenomena.[4] More solidly based is his assessment of Irving as 'doubtless an educational pioneer in getting his pupils to observe nature for themselves and in teaching them the use of such scientific instruments as he could command'.[5]

In many respects, Irving's tenure at Kirckaldy was a success. He was not a mere time-server waiting until an opening should arise for him to enter on his true vocation; in one letter to Martin, who as minister would have played an important role in the school's management, he responded to proposals that the range of subjects taught in the school be extended by suggesting that an additional assistant be employed and twenty-five new scholars be sought. He outlined clear strategies for managing the extra work involved, and offered to forego the salary increase which such an increased workload might be seen as entailing.[6] Among his pupils appears to have been his brother George, who was a schoolboy in Kirkcaldy in the late summer of 1816, when Carlyle recalled being met by him on arriving in the town for a visit; surprisingly, from the description it does not appear that the two brothers shared the same lodgings.[7] In November 1817 Carlyle, by now installed as master in a rival institution (about which more below), wrote that he had recently attended the examination of Irving's academy, at which 'He acquitted himself dextrously, and seemed to give general satisfaction.'[8] For a short period Irving tried taking in private pupils to board, but eventually gave it up; for this purpose he lived in the

---

[4] Andrew Landale Drummond, *Edward Irving and his Circle: Including some Consideration of the 'Tongues' Movement in the Light of Modern Psychology* (London: James Clarke, [1937]), 21, 28.

[5] Ibid. 25.

[6] Irving to the members of the committee of the Kirkcaldy Subscription School, January 1814 (in private hands).

[7] Thomas Carlyle, *Reminiscences*, ed. C. E. Norton (London: J. M. Dent, 1932), 186. George appears to have caused his family, especially Edward, some concern. One of Carlyle's correspondents, Andrew Wallace, referred to a 'Memorial of Studies' prepared by Edward for George and covering a range of academic subjects. Although unable to locate it, Wallace was able to quote its conclusion: 'Finally – Gather knowledge from every source – from reading, from hearing, from observing every thing about you from interrogating modestly, yet anxiously; and let all your knowledge be accurate & minute'. Edward reminded him that unlike others in his class, he had only his industry to get him on in the world. He must not allow his classmates to distract him: they could afford to be idle, but he could not. He was to remember their parents' hopes for him, and how Edward had laboured for him. Edward urged him to read the Greek New Testament often and carefully, for it was able to make him wise to salvation. The advice was evidently needed, for, as Wallace recalled concerning George, who appears to have been a fellow student: 'we continued intemperate as long as we remained in Edinb^h [Edinburgh] together'. Nevertheless, he gave promise of eminence as a doctor, and read Greek more fluently than anyone else Wallace knew: Edinburgh, NLS, MS 1771, fols 136–7: Andrew Wallace to Carlyle, 20 October 1874.

[8] *CL*, 1.116: Carlyle to James Johnston, 20 November 1817.

schoolhouse at Abbotshall, a neighbouring community which was originally part of Kirkcaldy.[9]

On the other hand, there is evidence that Irving's firm discipline caused problems. The story is well known of the joiner who, from his premises nearby, heard the cries of pain coming from the school and appeared in the doorway, axe in hand, asking ironically whether he needed any assistance.[10] In December 1815, a complaint was made against him by a father whose son had had his ears pulled after failing to decline a Latin noun (given Irving's physical strength and willingness to use it when necessary, this must have been a painful experience). Irving defended himself vigorously to Martin; with the prospect of a general meeting (presumably of parents and those involved in the school's management) to consider his conduct as master, he saw the matter not as a personal dispute between him and the father in question, but in terms of a struggle for his authority over his pupils.[11] A few days later, he claimed that 'in the Kingdom there is not a school in which so much is done with less punishment, than has been in ours for the last year'. He therefore refused to apologize to the complainant, even though doing so would have put an end to the matter.[12] Mrs Oliphant described his character at this period as 'specially distinguished by a certain cheerful, cordial pugnacity, and readiness, when occasion called for it, to adopt a boldly offensive line of tactics in support of his own dignity and independence, or those of his class'.[13] Such dogged insistence on standing his ground was to remain a feature of his approach to ministry, and undoubtedly exacerbated the process by which the soundness of his doctrinal opinions was investigated from the late 1820s.

Dissatisfaction with Irving's disciplinary methods may perhaps have been a factor leading to Carlyle's arrival at a rival establishment in 1816. Carlyle recalled that some had become dissatisfied with Irving's severity, bought off the master of the parish school, and sought a replacement. However, as Christison (who recommended him for the post) wrote to Carlyle, the town was big enough to support two schools. Indeed, by 1843 it had no less than fifteen.[14] Again, it was Martin who approached him, on behalf of the Town Council, and he was given responsibility for teaching Latin, higher French, Geography, Arithmetic, elementary Geometry, Bookkeeping, and on occasion Greek.[15]

---

[9] Oliphant, *Life*, 40.

[10] Ibid. 30.

[11] Irving to the Rev. John Martin, 25 December 1815 (in private hands). Such an outlook would reappear in 1833, in the tensions between him and the apostles and prophets by then emerging in his church.

[12] Irving to the Rev. John Martin, 28 December 1815 (in private hands).

[13] Oliphant, *Life*, 37.

[14] Alexander, 'Kirkcaldy', 766; Carlyle, *Reminiscences*, 184; Campbell, *Kirkcaldy*, 205; Drummond, *Irving*, 25: Christison to Carlyle, 16 May 1816; Simon Heffer, *Moral Desperado: A Life of Thomas Carlyle* (London: Phoenix, 1996), 40.

[15] Virginia Surtees, *Jane Welsh Carlyle* (Wilton, Salisbury: Michael Russell, 1986), 24.

Although the two men were teaching in rival institutions, it was during these years that their friendship blossomed. Irving's first and unpropitious encounter with Carlyle had taken place in Edinburgh at Christmas 1815, in the house of a mutual acquaintance; on discovering that the younger man, like himself, came from Annandale, Irving plied him with a raft of peremptory questions concerning the health, marriages and births of local families. The topic was of no interest to Carlyle, and he resented Irving's manner, which was marked by 'something of unconscious unquestionable superiority, of careless natural *de haut en bas*'.[16] The younger man protested, which hurt his questioner a little; but from such unpromising beginnings a close friendship developed. Throughout their lives, with all the changes of opinion and circumstance which each underwent, Carlyle claimed that such unpleasantness never marked any of their later disagreements.[17]

Their next meeting was in Annan during the summer of 1816; Irving had heard that Carlyle was coming to Kirkcaldy, but offered him all assistance and hospitality. In his words, 'Two Annandale people must not be strangers in Fife!'[18] He was as good as his word: on Carlyle's first visit to him there, he offered his rival free use of his library. Among the eclectic choice of writers on offer were Gibbon (whose *Decline and Fall of the Roman Empire* made a marked impact on Carlyle) and Hume, which could not have done anything to arrest his growing inability to accept orthodox Christian belief (a problem, given his status as an 'irregular' Divinity student whose father hoped to see him enter the Church of Scotland ministry), as well as plenty of French and English literary classics.[19] We may wonder what effect some of these writers had on Irving. He did not fall prey to religious scepticism, but his sermons do indicate an awareness of some of the challenges which they presented. It seems likely, therefore, that the influence of these writers was felt in the area not of what he believed but in his approach to preaching: during the early 1820s he focused on the need to present the faith in forms appropriate to unbelievers, rather than speaking to the in-group. Certainly he appears to have been well able to extract the main points from his reading, as Carlyle explained:

> Irving himself, I found, was not, nor had been, much of a reader; but he had, with solid ingenuity and judgment, by some briefer process of his own, fished out correctly from many books the substance of what they handled, and of what conclusions they came to; this he possessed, and could produce, in an *honest* manner always, when occasion came ... he had gathered, by natural sagacity and

---

[16] Carlyle, *Reminiscences*, 183; cf. Heffer, *Moral Desperado*, 39–40. Incidentally, the idea that Irving and Carlyle were school-friends is incorrect; Carlyle did not enter Annan Academy until 1806, after Irving had left. Carlyle's family attended the Ecclefechan Burgher Seceder meeting, and his father was close friends with Irving's uncle, but the two lads did not become friends at that point.

[17] Carlyle, *Reminiscences*, 184. The course of their relationship is surveyed by Peter Elliott in his forthcoming Murdoch University thesis, 'Edward Irving: Romantic Theology in Crisis', ch. 5.

[18] Ibid. 185.

[19] Ibid. 186–7; Heffer, *Moral Desperado*, 41.

insight, from conversation and inquiry, a great deal of practical knowledge, or information on things extant round him ... . He had a most hearty, if not very refined, sense of the ludicrous ... . His wide just sympathies, his native sagacities, honest-heartedness and good-humour, made him the most delightful of companions.[20]

If Irving was no great thinker himself, it is clear that Carlyle nevertheless valued his friendship highly. Occasionally the two of them would get the boat across the Firth of Forth to Edinburgh; they would buy books and meet up with friends from student days, 'cleverish people mostly, but of no culture or information'. Irving would sometimes call on one of the city's ministers, but by all accounts did not think very highly of them,[21] a remarkable judgement given that among them was Andrew Thomson (1778–1831), the vigorous leader of the Evangelicals in the Church of Scotland and founder of the *Edinburgh Christian Instructor*, which was intended to counter the sceptical tendencies of the *Edinburgh Review*. Carlyle's assessment was not much more positive: they were by no means all stupid, but were without exception 'narrow, ignorant and barren to us two'.[22]

Yet it was to be a minister, John Martin, whose home was Irving's chief resort during his years in Kirkcaldy. Carlyle described him as 'a precise, innocent, didactic kind of man ... a clear-minded, brotherly, well-intentioned man',[23] and Mrs Oliphant called him 'an irreproachable parish priest, of respectable learning and talents and deep piety'.[24] Martin was an Evangelical, and belonged to a clerical dynasty; his son Samuel (1802–54) was also to become a minister, joining the Free Church of Scotland in 1843.[25] Whilst they would come to disagree strongly with aspects of Irving's developing theology, they nevertheless remained close friends with him, not least because one of the Martin daughters, Isabella (1797–1854), would become Edward's wife. According to Mrs Oliphant, the engagement occurred shortly after Isabella had ceased to be a student of Edward's, but no more precise dating is possible.[26]

---

[20] Carlyle, *Reminiscences*, 187. A little earlier, Carlyle wrote that Irving 'did not want some due heat of temper' but 'the basis of him at all times was fine manly sociality, and the richest truest good-nature' (ibid. 184).

[21] Ibid. 193.

[22] Ibid. 194.

[23] Ibid.

[24] Oliphant, *Life*, 34.

[25] On John Martin (1768–1837), see Anon., *Remains of the late Reverend John Martin, D.D. Minister of Kirkaldy: Consisting of Sermons, Essays, and Letters. With a Memoir* (Edinburgh: William Oliphant, 1838). On Samuel (1802–54), see John Duns, *Memoir of the late Rev. Samuel Martin, Minister of the Free Church, Bathgate* (Edinburgh: W. P. Kennedy, 1854).

[26] Oliphant, *Life*, 34. Writers give varying dates for the length of the engagement, but these appear to be surmise based on such things as the length of his stay in Kirkcaldy. The fact is that no clear indication can be found. Before any formal engagement was contracted, there may have been an informal understanding that the two would marry once

Carlyle had no great admiration for Isabella, although his judgement was affected by holding her in measure responsible for what he saw as his friend's decline into enthusiastic excess after taking up with the charismatic manifestations of tongues and prophecy from 1830. He described her as being:

> of bouncing, frank, gay manner and talk, studious to be amiable; but never quite satisfactory, on the side of *genuineness*. ... She was very ill-looking withal; a skin always under blotches and discolourment; muddy grey eyes, which for their part never laughed with the other features; pock-marked, ill-shapen, triangular kind of face, with hollow cheeks and long chin: decidedly unbeautiful as a young woman. ... Her maternal ill-qualities came out in her afterwards, as a *bride* (or engaged young lady), and still more strongly as a wife: – poor woman, it was never with her will; you could perceive she always had her father's strong and true wish to be good, had not her difficulties been quite *too* strong; – but it was and is very visible to me she (unconsciously, for much the greater part), did a good deal aggravate all that was bad in Irving's London position, and impeded his wise (instead of unwise) profiting by what was really good in it.[27]

In his opinion, Isabella's shortcomings were her mother's fault: Mrs Martin's undesirable qualities, he claimed came out in her children; the older woman was 'visibly proud as well as vain; of a snappish, rather uncomfortable manner; betokening, even in her kindness, steady egoism and various splenetic qualities'.[28]

In spite of (or perhaps because of) his low estimation of most of the ministers he encountered, Irving continued to pursue his real ambition – the ministry.[29] By 1815, he completed his six years of theological study; according to the Kirkcaldy Presbytery minutes, Martin proposed on 23 November 1814 that Irving be taken on probationary trials. The General Assemblies of 1698, 1782 and 1813 had laid down qualifications for those seeking to enter the ministry of character, piety, general education, and theological study. The last involved the candidate in preparing a homily (a discourse on a biblical text); an exegesis (a Latin discussion of a particular theological issue or 'head of divinity', to establish the extent of his linguistic proficiency and skill in argument, and to be defended before two or three ministers); an exercise (half an hour of exegesis and paraphrase of a text, and half an hour

---

Irving found a living: cf. Anon., 'No. XII. The Rev. Edward Irving, M.A. Late Minister of the National Scotch Church', *Annual Biography and Obituary* 20 (1836), 138–56, at 140.

[27] Thomas Carlyle, *Reminiscences*, eds. K. J. Fielding and Ian Campbell (Oxford: Oxford University Press, 1997), 227–8.

[28] Carlyle, *Reminiscences*, eds Fielding and Campbell, 227.

[29] It was claimed that for three months around 1811 Irving acted in a local theatre company, but that he left on conclusion of his probationary period as his acting skills were not up to the mark: Anon., 'Records of a Stage Veteran – IV', *New Monthly Magazine*, no. 43 (March 1835), 356–60, at 359; cf. *Times*, 2 March 1835. This could have occurred between his graduation and his move to Haddington in 1809, but neither I nor the archivist of Lumen (formerly Regent Square) United Reformed Church, Mrs Barbara Waddington, have uncovered any corroboratory evidence.

drawing out doctrinal and practical propositions and application from the text); a lecture (an exposition of a longer portion of the Scriptures, often a chapter); a 'popular sermon'. Beyond all these, several of which were undertaken before the congregation, the candidate was supposed to be tested on the reading and interpretation of a portion of the Greek New Testament and the reading and exposition of part of a Hebrew Psalm, his grasp of sacred chronology, church history, hard passages in the Bible, 'cases of conscience' (issues relating to personal spiritual and moral life), and church government and discipline.[30] It must have been a daunting prospect, even for one so confident of his calling as Irving was, but on 25 January 1815,

> he being strictly examined agreeably to the Act and the Presbytery satisfied with his answers to the questions put, & his translation of the passages of Greek and Latin prescribed to him directed their Clerk to transmit the circular letters intimating their resolution to recommend him to the Synod of Fife at their next meeting for leave to admit him to probationary trials.

Leave was evidently given, although not mentioned in the Synod's minutes, since on 12 April we find him being prescribed for his trial a lecture on John 15.1–6 (addressed to the clergy who could thus assess the extent of his expository gifts), a homily on 2 Timothy 3.5 (a text which would form the peg on which he hung one of his prophetic writings, *The Last Days*), a Latin exegesis, an exercise in criticism of the Greek text of Ephesians 2.16, and a popular sermon on Proverbs 13.20 (by which his homiletic ability could be tested); altogether a daunting set of discourses to prepare. Nevertheless, he acquitted himself honourably: two weeks later, he delivered his exegesis and homily, and on 21 June the rest of his discourses were examined, all being approved. Irving, having offered his subscription to the Westminster Confession, was licensed to preach.[31] This was not ordination, which followed only when a licentiate had secured a call to serve a parish, but it did enable him to exercise a preaching ministry wherever he was invited to do so, and so to seek a call.[32]

---

[30] Laurance James Saunders, *Scottish Democracy 1815-1840: The Social and Intellectual Background* (Edinburgh: Oliver and Boyd, 1950), 348; Stewart Mechie, 'Education for the Ministry in Scotland since the Reformation', *RSCHS* 14 (1983), 115-33, 161-78, at 124–5.

[31] Edinburgh, NAS, CH2/224/10, Presbytery of Kirkcaldy, minute book 1809–33, fols 137, 143, 145, 148–9; quotation at fol. 143.

[32] There was a tradition in Haddington that Irving was licensed by the Presbytery there in 1813, and that he preached his first sermon in Bolton church: John Martine, *Reminiscences and Notices of the Parishes of the County of Haddington* (repr. Haddington: East Lothian Council, 1999), 30. However, although Irving had been recommended by them to study for the ministry, I found no references to him in the Presbytery minute books, and it is inconceivable that he would have undergone the trials for licensing in a second presbytery if the first had already licensed him.

His first sermon, in his home town of Annan, was a success because he proved his ability to preach without notes (as ministers were expected to do) after dropping them part way through and then, on retrieving them, crumpling them up in front of the large congregation who had turned out to hear him.[33] However, his efforts in and around Kirkcaldy were less well received. Although the parish records make no reference to Irving's ministry, it is likely that his experiences of preaching there did much to shape his low opinion of the contemporary religious world. The church, which seated 1,500 people and had been rebuilt in 1807, would have been well filled for Martin, but Irving was considered to have too much 'grandeur' as a preacher and the congregations would be thinner when it was known that he was to preach.[34] On one occasion, while Irving was preaching a member of the congregation got up, banged open the door of his pew, and stalked down the aisle and out of the church.[35] Carlyle was in a minority when he remembered Irving's 'often, and notable, preaching, in those Kirkcaldy years', but his penetrating assessment is worth quoting at length; already, certain aspects of Irving's mature homiletic style were manifesting themselves, notably his preference for high-flown language and his unsparing denunciation of sin:

Irving's preachings as a Licentiate ... were always interesting to whoever had acquaintance with him ... . we enjoyed the broad potency of his delineations, exhortations and free flowing eloquencies, which all had a manly and original turn; and then afterwards there was sure to be, on the part of the public, a great deal of criticising pro and contra, which also had its entertainment for us. From the first, Irving read his discourses, but not in a servile manner; and of attitude, gesture, elocution, there was no neglect: – his voice was very fine; melodious depth, strength, clearness its chief characteristics; I have head more pathetic voices, going more direct to the heart, ... but recollect none that better filled the ear. He affected the Miltonic or Old-English Puritan style, and strove visibly to imitate it more and more, till almost the end of his career, when indeed it had become his own, and was the language he used in utmost heat of business, for expressing his meaning. At this time, and for years afterwards, there was something of preconceived intention visible in it, in fact of real 'affectation,' as there could not well help being ...

On the whole, poor Irving's style was sufficiently surprising to his hide-bound Presbyterian public; and this was but a slight circumstance to the novelty of the matter he set forth upon them. Actual practice: 'If this thing is true, why not do it? You had better do it; there will be nothing but misery and ruin in not doing it!' – that was the gist and continual purport of all his discoursing; – to the astonishment and deep offence of hide-bound mankind. There was doubtless something of rashness in the young Irving's way of preaching; nor perhaps quite enough of pure, complete and serious conviction (which ought to have lain *silent* a good while before it took to speaking): in general I own to have felt that there was present a certain inflation or spiritual bombast in much of this, a trifle of unconscious

---

[33] Oliphant, *Life*, 36.
[34] Alexander, 'Kirkcaldy', 761–2; Oliphant, *Life*, 36–7.
[35] Carlyle, *Reminiscences*, 196; Oliphant, *Life*, 36–7.

playactorism (highly unconscious, but not quite absent) which had been unavoidable to the brave young prophet and reformer. But brave he was; and bearing full upon the truth, if not yet quite attaining it ... In Irving's Preaching there was present or prefigured, generous opulence of ability in all kinds (except perhaps the very highest kind, not even prefigured?); but much of it was still crude ...[36]

Mrs Oliphant considered that there could have been a measure of justice in the complaints about his preaching, given how his rich style might have sounded in youth while still half-formed. During this period, however, she claimed that he gained 'deep insight into, and deeper impatience of, the common conventionalities of the pulpit', reflecting on his apparent failure, and the reasons why lesser men were more appreciated – a process of thought which, she asserted, came to fruition in his published works.[37]

In outlining the process by which Irving sought and received a call to a parish, it is germane to explain the structure of the contemporary Church of Scotland: adopting the Presbyterian polity favoured by most Reformed churches, the basic unit was the kirk session, composed of the minister and elders of the local congregation.[38] Parishes were grouped into presbyteries comprising ministers and representative lay elders; licensing and ordination were the prerogatives of the presbytery. Presbyteries were grouped into synods. The whole church gathered together in Edinburgh each May in the form of the General Assembly, composed of ministers and elders selected by presbyteries, universities, and royal burghs (Annan was to select Irving to represent it in 1829). This was the supreme court for disciplinary matters, and it formulated the church's canon law, often in response to overtures from the lower courts.[39]

At the parish level, there was a dual system of government which owed much to Reformed belief in the interdependence of church and state.

> The parish state was constituted in civil and ecclesiastical law. The governing institution in each parish was the board of heritors, composed of the landowners; as a statutory body supervised by the Court of Session in Edinburgh, the board was required to provide a church of set proportions, a manse, parish school and glebe, and was required to ensure arrangements for the payment of the minister, schoolmaster and beadle. A second body was the kirk session, composed of the minister as chair (or moderator) and lay elders (usually farmers and larger

---

[36] Carlyle, *Reminiscences*, 194–6.

[37] Oliphant, *Life*, 36–7.

[38] Elders were to share the spiritual oversight of the congregation, and the administration of church discipline, with the minister.

[39] Stewart J. Brown, *Thomas Chalmers and the Godly Commonwealth in Scotland* (Oxford: Oxford University Press, 1982), 43–4.

tradesmen), which held responsibility for imposing Church discipline on the people ...[40]

The overlap was given visible expression by the tendency for heritors to be appointed as elders. One of the heritors might be the patron of the parish, which meant that he had the responsibility of appointing a minister to the living.[41] It was the issue of patronage which caused more discontent than anything else in the Church of Scotland, and which would precipitate the Disruption in 1843. The problem lay in the way appointments were made: should the patron take account of the congregation's wishes and appoint a minister whom they considered suitable, or should he appoint one who appealed to his own tastes? Was the minister to be a man of the people or part of an enlightened oligarchy alongside the patron and other heritors? Those who stressed the importance of the patron's wishes were known as Moderates, while those who believed that the congregation's wishes should be paramount were called Populars, Highflyers, or Evangelicals. Doctrinal division in the church followed very similar lines to the division over patronage. Both parties would have subscribed to the Westminster Confession of Faith, the Church of Scotland's main doctrinal standard and that by which Scripture was to be interpreted. However, the preaching of the Moderates tended to focus more on Christian duties and frequently was indistinguishable from a religion of good works, with little comment on Calvinistic doctrine, whereas Evangelicals set forth a much fuller understanding of the way of salvation as expounded in the Confession. The eighteenth century had been marked by a long Moderate ascendancy in the church's higher courts, but this was now being challenged by a resurgence of Evangelicalism which owed much to men such as Chalmers and Thomson. By the 1830s, it would achieve dominance in the Church of Scotland.

Irving is not easy to place in this scheme. In some ways, he was more like the Moderates than like the Evangelicals, in that he always looked down on ministers who merely reflected popular views instead of challenging and stretching their congregations. Furthermore, he always felt a sense of distance between himself and the outlook of contemporary Evangelicals, which led him to stand aloof from many of their pet societies and to engage in outspoken criticism of their activism. On the other hand, he was always a doctrinal preacher, and a firm adherence to Calvinistic teaching about salvation found increasingly explicit exposition in his sermons during the mid-1820s: so we find him stressing the divine initiative in saving human beings, their inability to save themselves, and the doctrine of 'election' – that God chooses those who are to be saved through Christ. Later, as we shall see, his views would change; but throughout his life he remained a doctrinal preacher.

---

[40] Callum G. Brown, 'Rotavating the Kailyard: Re-imagining the Scottish "Meenister" in Discourse and the Parish State since 1707', in Nigel Aston and Matthew Cragoe, eds, *Anticlericalism in Britain c. 1500–1914* (Stroud: Sutton, 2001), 138–58, at 139.

[41] Saunders, *Scottish Democracy*, 18.

At this point, however, the issue which faced him was that of obtaining a call from a parish to serve as their minister; it has been asserted that the availability of openings was such that the 'stickit minister' (as a licentiate unable to secure a call was often known) was usually so because of personal incapacity,[42] but such a verdict must not be pressed too far in Irving's case, since his inability to secure a call appears to have been due in part to his reluctance to play the system. Like the Evangelicals, he had no desire to be intruded on an unwilling congregation, and thus was not prepared to take steps to curry favour with patrons of possible vacant parishes. Callum Brown has claimed that by the 1790s, probably every parish outside the Highlands had seen a disputed presentation.[43] Irving could not have been unaware of the frequency of these, and this would have reinforced his decision not to go where the congregation did not want him. But since he was dependent on receiving an approach from a congregation, what was he to do if no congregation approached him? This was his dilemma, and it seems likely that his decision to leave Kirkcaldy was motivated by the recognition that he was never going to get anywhere by remaining there. By the spring of 1818, it was becoming clear that he was ready for a move. Carlyle wrote to an Annandale friend: 'I's time here will expire in five months, and it does not seem probable that he will renew his engagements. At present he is very fond of preaching and the bible-society. He sometimes speaks of going to Edin*r* [Edinburgh] to live by private teaching – and devote his time to pulpit eloquence …'[44] That summer, Irving resigned his post and moved to Edinburgh, determined to find his way honourably into the ministry.

---

[42] Ibid. 350.
[43] Brown, 'Rotavating the Kailyard', 143.
[44] *CL*, 1.125: Carlyle to James Johnston, 30 April 1818.

CHAPTER 5

Assistant to Thomas Chalmers: Edinburgh and Glasgow, 1818–21

In the summer of 1818, Irving took rooms in Duff's Lodgings, 35 Bristo Street, Edinburgh, near the university. Back among friends from student days, he determined to put the time to good use by broadening his academic horizons. He 'used to give breakfasts to Intellectualities he fell in with',[1] and attended college classes during the following winter in Chemistry and Natural History, as well as studying French and Italian.[2]

In November, Carlyle followed him to Edinburgh.[3] The friendship evidently benefited Carlyle; on one occasion he assured a friend concerned about his happiness that he had Irving to talk with 'about chemistry or the moral sublime',[4] and referred to their both attending a natural history class.[5] Carlyle participated in a 'Philosophical Association' which Irving was instrumental in establishing, and at which six or eight ex-students read papers to each other.[6] Irving continued to encourage him to make free with his library. On the other hand, Carlyle recalled that 'A visible gloom occasionally hung over Irving, his old strong sunshine only getting out from time to time.'[7] As a licentiate without a call, he was one of many 'stickit ministers' at a time when provision outstripped demand; he was, in Mrs Oliphant's words, 'a man fully licensed and qualified to preach, whom nobody cared to hear'.[8] According to Carlyle, 'Irving's outlooks in Edinburgh were not of the best, considerably checkered with dubiety, opposition, or even flat disfavour in some quarters'.[9] Part of the problem, as we have seen, was his objection to the patronage system; but it also appears that his zeal to maintain the supreme authority of the Bible in all matters of faith led him on at least one occasion to shock his hearers by condemning ecclesiastical formulae (such as the Westminster Confession).[10] Irving

---

[1] Thomas Carlyle, *Reminiscences*, ed. C. E. Norton (London: J. M. Dent, 1932), 206.

[2] Oliphant, *Life*, 41–2.

[3] Simon Heffer, *Moral Desperado: A Life of Thomas Carlyle* (London: Phoenix, 1996), 46.

[4] *CL*, 1.149: Carlyle to Robert Mitchell, 27 November 1818.

[5] Ibid. 1.152: Carlyle to his mother, 17 December 1818.

[6] Oliphant, *Life*, 1.80–1.

[7] Carlyle, *Reminiscences*, 206–7.

[8] Oliphant, *Life*, 42.

[9] Carlyle, *Reminiscences*, 206.

[10] Oliphant, *Life*, 1.83.

was never one to temper his message out of consideration for the reaction it might receive, and hence liable to alienate congregations looking for a minister.

With time to think about how he would prosecute the work of the ministry, he burned all his old sermons and began to compose new ones along different lines. To a friend he wrote, 'Rejected by the living, I conversed with the dead',[11] which may account for some of the richness of his sermonic style. As he lacked opportunities to preach, he wrote the kind of sermons which would speak to hearers such as he himself had been while at Kirkcaldy, dissatisfied with the general run of contemporary preaching, a point to be kept in mind when examining the popularity of his preaching during his early years in London.[12] In July 1819 he wrote to Carlyle, 'I have been preaching at such a rate as to excite no small speculation in this mighty city'.[13] But still no call came his way. What was he to do with his life? He formed the idea of becoming a missionary on the apostolic model, wandering from place to place without means of material support like a Romantic hero. To that end, he persevered with his language study, and at the back of his mind was the thought of going to Persia (where John Malcolm from Eskdale (about twenty-five miles from Annan) had recently made a name for himself as the East India Company's representative to the court of the Shah[14]) after a preliminary tour through Europe. He was clearly unsettled; in March he wrote to John Martin that he proposed to go on a kind of Grand Tour to Paris via Rotterdam, then to Geneva, Florence, Rome, Naples and Sicily, and to winter at Paris or a German university, returning to Kirkcaldy the following spring. On his return he proposed 'to betake myself with heart and hand to the preaching of the Gospel, to seek for the first assistancy that is open, and to give myself to the only duty which is congenial to my mind [,] the preaching of the Gospel to a congregation of immortal beings'. Apparently this idea had been in his mind over a year earlier, before leaving Kirkcaldy, and derived strength from his confessed inability to remain inactive.[15]

His opinion of the workings of the Church of Scotland continued to grow more negative; after the General Assembly of 1819, he wrote to Carlyle that 'I could dwell upon the rich harvest of insight into character, which I gathered from the debates of the General Assembly; and of the lack of genius and honesty which took from its

---

[11] William Hanna, *Memoirs of the Life and Writings of Thomas Chalmers D.D. LL.D.* (4 vols, Edinburgh: Sutherland and Knox, 1850), 2.283; the friend was the Rev. Craig of Rothesay.

[12] Oliphant, *Life*, 43. One who knew Irving well stated that as a student he had paced the quadrangle exclaiming: 'There seems to me to be a new style of preaching possible': A. H. Charteris, 'Edward Irving', in *Teachers and Preachers of Recent Times* (Edinburgh: William P. Nimmo, 1881), 176–89, at 189.

[13] Edinburgh, NLS, MS 1764, fol. 153: Irving to Carlyle, 16 July 1819.

[14] Oliphant, *Life*, 45 (where, incorrectly, she gives Annandale).

[15] Irving to the Rev. John Martin, 31 March 1819 (in private hands).

value, and of the rankness and superfluity of vulgarity and bad temper and party zeal, which were as the thistles and ragworts and tares of the crop'.[16]

It was therefore something of a surprise when he was invited by Andrew Thomson to preach at St George's, the more so because Thomson intimated that Chalmers would be there, and that he was looking for an assistant for his Glasgow parish. Irving preached, and in a letter to John Martin on 2 August said that Thomson had described his sermon as 'the production of no ordinary mind'. Yet no inquiry ensued, and it seemed more than ever impossible that he would find an opening in the profession to which he felt called.[17] In a depressed state of mind, he packed his books and belongings and sent them home; he went to Greenock, meaning to sail round the coast and so home to bid his parents farewell before embarking on the life of a wandering missionary. Arriving at the port, he determined to take the first boat out. As luck (or Providence) would have it, he ended up sailing to Belfast. There, his lack of baggage or motive for travel excited the suspicions of the authorities, and he had to apply for assistance to a leading Presbyterian minister, the Rev. Dr Samuel Hanna, in order to obtain his release. With his spirits on the way to being restored after some time spent in Hanna's welcoming home, Irving spent a couple of weeks walking through the province.[18] According to Carlyle, Irving

> examined the peasants and the clergy of Ulster; the Giant's causeway[,] the city of Derry, and other strange objects. His stay in Colerain might have been protracted, had not a letter from Dr Chalmers recalled him to Glasgow, where he is finally engaged (if a month['s] probation should be favourable) to serve as that Rev*d* person's assistant in discharging the complicated duties of St John's parish. The Doctor's application originated from a sermon which he heard our friend deliver in Thomson's church.[19]

---

[16] James Anthony Froude, *Thomas Carlyle: A History of the First Forty Years of his Life 1795–1835* (2 vols, London: Longmans, Green, 1882), 2.70: Irving to Carlyle, 4 June 1819.

[17] Carlyle, *Reminiscences*, 208; Oliphant, *Life*, 46–8. Chalmers' silence was due to his preoccupation with a crisis which followed the conclusion of his ministry at the city's Tron church in preparation for the opening of St John's, and the continuing opposition of some to his plans for a radically different approach to poor relief (see below). This was complicated by the announcement on 10 August that Chalmers was being put forward as a candidate for the chair of Natural Philosophy at Edinburgh University; although his name was withdrawn a few days later, his elders at St John's threatened to resign *en bloc*. He remained away while things calmed down, only returning on 23 September. St John's was formally opened three days later: Stewart J. Brown, *Thomas Chalmers and the Godly Commonwealth in Scotland* (Oxford: Oxford University Press, 1982), 125–8.

[18] Oliphant, *Life*, 48–9. Hanna's son would marry Chalmers' daughter and become his father-in-law's biographer.

[19] *CL*, 1.197: Carlyle to John Fergusson, 25 September 1819.

In his absence, a letter from Chalmers had arrived at Annan. Unable to decipher the Doctor's handwriting (a problem shared by many subsequent researchers), Gavin forwarded it to his son in Coleraine with a covering note. Edward obeyed, only to find the great man out of town. On his return, he invited Irving to be his assistant; the latter was too scrupulous to allow himself to be forced on the congregation, and insisted on preaching first. He was not confident of his reception, even with Chalmers' support: 'I will preach to them if you think fit … but if they bear with my preaching, they will be the first people who have borne with it!' However, Chalmers had his way and it was only after moving to Glasgow that Irving preached at St John's.[20] The congregation liked him, although some thought him somewhat flowery, but the decisive factor ensuring their compliance was that Chalmers had chosen him.[21] Before that, Carlyle had written:

> You will rejoice with me that Irving, [sic] has in so honourable a way, obtained admittance to the career, whither his principles and feelings have long been exclusively directed. He has a fair field: and if (somewhat contrary to my hopes) his fervid genius do not prompt him into extravagancies, from which more stupid and less honest preachers are exempted, his success, I doubt not, will be brilliant. He was humble but not undesirous to prove himself, last Monday, when I accompanied him a few miles on his way. Bid good speed to poor Irving; and pray that neither the absurd nostrums, which Dr C. intends to apply forthwith, to the Glasgow weavers, nor any other obstacle may thwart his well-meant endeavours.[22]

Among Chalmers' 'absurd nostrums' was his belief that even in urban areas the needs of the poor could be met without recourse to the mechanisms adopted in England, such as handouts from charities or local officials. In his view, a traditional source, the 'plate' held by two elders at the church door on the Sabbath, could provide the necessary funds, and division of the parish into small 'localities' of sixty to a hundred families, each visited regularly by an elder (responsible for their spiritual welfare) and a deacon (who would inquire into their temporal circumstances, encourage them to adopt a thrifty and upright lifestyle, and as a last resort recommend them to the kirk session as recipients of financial assistance), would facilitate a thorough knowledge of the needs of every household in the parish. His objective was to remove, not poverty, but the dependence of the poor on handouts.

---

[20] By 25 September he was writing from his Glasgow address: cf. Edinburgh, NLS, MS 1764, fol. 163: Irving to Carlyle, 25 September 1819.

[21] Hanna, *Chalmers*, 2.284; Oliphant, *Life*, 49–51, quotation at 51. Callum Brown draws attention to the centrality of the sermon as 'the acid test of the Presbyterian minister' in such procedures as in preaching before a congregation with a view to their issuing a call: 'Rotavating the Kailyard: Re-imagining the Scottish "Meenister" in Discourse and the Parish State since 1707', in Nigel Aston and Matthew Cragoe, eds, *Anticlericalism in Britain c. 1500–1914* (Stroud: Sutton, 2001), 138–58, at 140; thus, when Irving's preaching was deemed unacceptable, the verdict amounted to questioning his call to the ministry.

[22] *CL*, 1.197: Carlyle to John Fergusson, 25 September 1819.

He persuaded the Town Council of Glasgow to create a new parish in which he could try out his social theories: carved out from existing parishes to the east of the centre, St John's contained about 11,000 people.[23]

It was a challenging time and place in which to attempt such an experiment. The city's population grew from about 110,000 in 1811 to over 147,000 ten years later. A considerable proportion of this growth was due to immigration: the Lowlands saw the enclosure of land and the consequent disappearance of farms tenanted by more than one family, while the Highlands saw the collapse of traditional sources of income such as fishing, cattle-rearing and kelp-gathering. There was also a substantial influx of people from Ireland. By 1819, the population of Chalmers' parish included 14.5% who were Irish-born, as well as 15.8% other non-Scots. At the same time as this population growth, the textile industry shared in the economic recession which affected Britain from about 1810. Handloom weaving being the main activity in St John's and surrounding parishes (occupying over 40% of the employed population), mechanization had a disproportionate effect on the locality. Many immigrants who had taken it up now found themselves reduced to penury, and lacked the family support network which would have sustained members of rural communities. To make things worse, the unsanitary conditions in which many were forced to live contributed to a rising mortality rate. It is not surprising that there should have been unrest: a one-day strike in the city in December 1819 was followed by widespread fear of a radical revolution, troops were stationed in the city for three months during 1820, and the so-called 'radical war' that April brought 60,000 workers out on strike in various towns for a week.[24]

Irving found lodgings at 34 Kent Street, between Gallowgate and London Road, east of the old city centre, in an area of unplanned development. He proved to be 'a like-minded and noble-hearted associate' to Chalmers. Each Sunday, there were three services in the church itself, and a morning service in a schoolroom at the east end of the parish. The two men alternated, one conducting morning and evening services in the church, and the other conducting the schoolroom service and the afternoon service in the church. In the mornings Irving lectured his way through Luke, and Chalmers through Romans; they repeated each lecture a few weeks later in the evening service, which had a different congregation, being intended for the parishioners and the poor rather than the middle classes who could afford the high seat-rents charged earlier in the day.[25] Each locality in the parish contained at least one Sabbath School, there being a total in 1819 of thirty-five, with a little over a thousand children on their

---

[23] On Chalmers' social thought, see Brown, *Chalmers*.

[24] J. H. S. Burleigh, *A Church History of Scotland* (London: Oxford University Press, 1960), 316; Andrew L. Drummond and James Bulloch, *The Scottish Church 1688–1843: The Age of the Moderates* (Edinburgh: Saint Andrew Press, 1973), 173–4; Andrew Gibb, *Glasgow: the Making of a City* (London: Croom Helm, 1983), 105–10; T. C. Smout, *A History of the Scottish People 1560–1830* (London: Fontana, 1985), 218, 395, 418–19.

[25] Hanna, *Chalmers*, 2.284.

registers.²⁶ The schools had to be monitored, and Chalmers and Irving also met regularly with the teachers as a group. But it was in visiting that Irving was preeminently successful. Although he arrived in Glasgow at a time of considerable social tension, he moved freely and fearlessly among the restive weavers, and made firm friends with many of them. Even Dissenters (40% of the population of the parish²⁷) and Roman Catholics appear to have accepted him. The story is told of how he won over one radical shoemaker by demonstrating his knowledge of leatherwork, derived from his father, on his visits to the home.²⁸ In a letter to his brother-in-law James Fergusson, a few months after arrival, he noted that he had visited three hundred families and found them 'in general both able and willing to entertain the religious lesson and improvement arising out of it', which Mrs Oliphant thought may have been due to his tender way of dealing with people at a personal level.²⁹ Whilst he assisted in Chalmers' schemes, he also acted on his own initiative in a way which Chalmers might not have approved, as when he disposed of a legacy he received by giving away a pound note each day.³⁰

Although Irving had a deep admiration for Chalmers (and for Mrs Chalmers, whom he described as his second mother), this was not matched by a similar admiration for the Doctor's assistants: 'Dr. Chalmers, though a most entire original by himself, is surrounded with a very prosaical sort of persons [sic], who please me something by their zeal to carry into effect his philosophical schemes, and vex me much by their idolatry of him. ... Every minister in Glasgow is an oracle to certain class of devotees.'³¹ This was an example of the tendency in towns to court popularity in order to fill the pews with high-paying renters and thus ensure the parish's financial solvency.³² It would have been such people who would turn back from going into church if they heard that Irving, rather than 'himself', 'the Doctor', was to preach. But they were not altogether to be blamed: Chalmers described Irving's preaching as being 'like Italian music, appreciated only by connoisseurs', or a spell, binding on a few but making no impact on most.³³ His homiletic style, whilst developing through practice, was as yet unripe.

In and out of the pulpit, Irving was a man with what we might call 'presence'. Mrs Oliphant recorded that he was variously taken for a highland chief, a cavalry officer or a brigand leader; Chalmers' comment was that whatever people thought he was, he always struck them as a leader.³⁴ His solemnity of appearance, manners, and

---

²⁶ James Cleland, *The Rise and Progress of the City of Glasgow, Comprising an Account of its Public Buildings, Charities, and other Concerns* (Glasgow: James Brash, 1820), chart between pages 228 and 229.
²⁷ Ibid. 288.
²⁸ Oliphant, *Life*, 57–8.
²⁹ Ibid. 54.
³⁰ Ibid. 60.
³¹ Froude, *Carlyle*, 1.83: Irving to Carlyle, 14 March 1820.
³² Brown, 'Rotavating the Kailyard', 149.
³³ Oliphant, *Life*, 60–1.
³⁴ Ibid. 51.

diction combined to give him a priestly bearing which was, to say the least, uncommon in ministers of the Church of Scotland. On entering a home, he would utter the blessing 'Peace be to this house', and was accustomed to bless the children he found.[35] Mrs Oliphant recorded an anecdote about a Glasgow dinner-party at which a young man made some uncomplimentary remarks about clergy as a class and Irving in particular, whereupon the latter called for prayer for this miscreant who had 'attacked the Lord in the person of his servant'. Whether it actually happened was unclear, but it was certainly characteristic of the man.[36] Beyond St John's, Irving served as joint-secretary of the Glasgow auxiliary of the British and Foreign Bible Society from early 1821; on one occasion, it was reported that his address at the presentation of Bibles to sixteen convicts about to be 'transported' (perhaps to Australia) bought tears to the eyes of several of them.[37]

The busy life of an urban minister did not prevent Irving from maintaining a deep devotion to his family. Indeed, his holidays with them were probably something of a safety valve; from his observations, Carlyle was convinced that Irving on his visits home was 'happier perhaps than ever elsewhere'.[38] He also made time to go home whenever necessary. In the spring of 1821, he rushed to Annan where his sister Elizabeth was seriously ill. Irving recorded that he had been used to bring her peace with God by 'making known to her the revelation of mercy'.[39] In a letter to Chalmers, he explained: 'I find her conscience in considerable disquietude and longing for the peace of the Gospel. In the present state of this parish [presumably a reference to the younger Moncrieff's ministry], it was not possible she should have been enlightened in the knowledge of Christ'. He never saw such a striking instance of the effects of evangelical truth, and drew from this the conclusion that Christ was the physician of the body as well as of the soul – a conclusion which should not be forgotten when examining his later interest in the charismatic manifestations of tongues, prophecy, and healing. Their conversations had, he believed, done her more good than all the medicines she had been prescribed.[40] On a happier note, his sister Agnes (known in the family as Nancy) married Warrand Carlile (1796–1881) on 24 September that year, and Edward was delighted to be 'Bryde-groom's man'.[41]

---

[35] Ibid. 58–9.

[36] Ibid. 63–4.

[37] *Glasgow Herald*, 23 February 1821, 12 November 1821.

[38] Carlyle, *Reminiscences*, 229.

[39] NLS, MS 1764, fol. 201: Irving to Carlyle, 26 April 1821.

[40] Edinburgh, NCL, Chalmers MSS CHA 4.18.4: Irving to Chalmers, postmarked 6 April 1821.

[41] NLS, MS 1764, fol. 189: Irving to Carlyle, 21 September 1820. In spite of the differing spelling, Carlile was distantly related to Thomas, coming from a branch of the family which had moved from Annan a century before (one member of whom was a minister – described as one of the Carlisles [sic] of Paisley – for whom Irving had officiated in Dublin): NLS, MS 1764, fol. 179: Irving to Carlyle, 10 July 1820. After Nancy died in 1829, Warrand trained for the ministry and later served as a missionary in the West Indies; their son the Rev. Gavin Carlyle (1827–1919) would edit Irving's

At the end of 1819, Carlyle commented that Irving's popularity 'is said to be great beyond example. Chalmers even is thought to look with some anxiety at the pillars of his throne'.[42] The following May, he told a friend that Irving 'succeeds wonderfully'.[43] By August 1820 he could write: 'Upon the whole, I augur great things from Irving. Circumstances have directed all the current of his powers into the channel of preaching; his views are not so likely to change now; he is fairly in the ring too; his opponents are but pigmies'. He compared him to a famous boxer of the day, Mendoza, apparently with reference to his size and build; the comparison was not entirely inappropriate, in view of Irving's pugnacity.[44]

He was in a good position to evaluate Irving's progress in this way, for the two appear to have shared their hopes and ambitions with each other as with nobody else. Although Irving and Carlyle were taking divergent paths, Irving continued to be concerned for his friend's welfare as he struggled to launch himself on a literary career. In December 1819, Irving urged him to keep writing as the only way of getting himself known.[45] The advice he gave during these months regarding writing and the likelihood of most people not receiving what Carlyle would write, seems to see him as set in a similar position to Irving himself, as one whose worth and superiority would only be recognised by a select few. We find him trying to encourage the morose and dyspeptic Carlyle: 'if I was a prophet, I know to whom I would predict many days of honour & influence & all else earthly which goes to combine a happy condition'.[46] Yet Irving himself stood in need of encouragement, too. In March 1820, he wrote that he felt he had no chance of receiving a call to another new church in Glasgow, St James's; he felt that he lacked standing and friends. Perhaps making a virtue out of necessity, he claimed that he was not ambitious of it in any case as he had his hands full assisting Chalmers; how could he manage, therefore, with a whole parish?[47]

It must have been discouraging, therefore, when at the end of a visit to Glasgow in April Carlyle confessed to his friend that he no longer believed in the same way as Irving did.[48] Once destined for the ministry, he had abandoned the idea several years earlier; now he openly admitted that he was abandoning orthodox Christian belief. Near the end of his life, he confessed that he would have done well to keep closer to Carlyle.[49] But it is hard to see how some measure of distancing could have been avoided, given that their views of the world were becoming radically different. Nevertheless, Irving continued to write to him in the same vein as before, with no

---

collected works for publication in the mid-1860s: Anon., 'Colonial CD Books: Carlile', http://www.colonialcdbooks.com/carlile.htm, accessed 15 May 2009.

[42] *CL*, 1.218: Carlyle to Robert Mitchell, 30 December 1819.
[43] Ibid. 1.250: Carlyle to James Johnston, 6 May 1820.
[44] Ibid. 1.269–70: Carlyle to John Fergusson, 5 August 1820.
[45] Edinburgh, NLS, MS 1764, fol. 167: Irving to Carlyle, 20 December 1819.
[46] Ibid. fol. 180: Irving to Carlyle, 10 July 1820.
[47] Ibid. fol. 173: Irving to Carlyle, 14 March 1820.
[48] Carlyle, *Reminiscences*, 225; Heffer, *Moral Desperado*, 52.
[49] Carlyle, *Reminiscences*, 233.

hint of embarrassment when speaking of matters of faith, perhaps in the hope of winning him back.

On a more down to earth topic, Irving informed Carlyle excitedly in July that he had just spent nearly two weeks 'with what maiden do you think one whose name will shock you as it does me, one of whom I am very proud & with whom I am well nigh in love ... Margaret Gordon'. (She and Irving had been on a walking tour with two companions.) Regaining control of his affections, he assured his friend that 'in all this there was no love, but there was most delightful sympathy in some of the sublimest scenes of nature, and also in some of the most disturbing feelings of the heart'.[50] Irving saw her off for London on 4 July, and did not see her again until he visited the city in December 1821, when he found her beginning to assume the air of the *grande dame*, and his feelings towards her cooled.[51] This doubtless reflects the growing awareness of each that their differing social backgrounds would have made marriage very difficult if not impossible.

In another letter, Irving commented that nothing, not even the company of his family, to whom he was deeply devoted, delighted him so much as the intellectual stimulation provided by Carlyle's company. Moving into a more didactic mode, he advised his friend that a sublimely virtuous life was as needful to great literary performance as were understanding and wisdom. At the end of the letter, with all the confidence of an unmarried clergyman in the making, he added, 'I mean to make a general letter to my sisters upon the bringing up of their children'.[52]

Concerned for his friend, Irving invited him to spend Christmas 1820 in Glasgow; the result was a follow-up invitation to Carlyle to spend some months with him because Irving thought he was uncomfortable in Edinburgh.[53] Given Carlyle's repeated problems in finding satisfactory lodgings, this was quite probably the case. During the General Assembly of 1821, Irving returned the favour and visited Carlyle; even then, he appeared to be doing the giving and Carlyle the receiving, Carlyle telling his brother that 'The man could not have been kinder to me, had he been a brother.'[54] Throughout, as Carlyle wrote in June 1821, 'The

---

[50] Edinburgh, NLS, MS 1764, fol. 179: Irving to Carlyle, 10 July 1820. One of Irving's former pupils, she was well-born but had been living with a widowed aunt at Kirkcaldy after the death of her parents. Carlyle was attracted to her, and claimed that Irving, 'it was sometimes thought, found her very interesting, could the Miss-Martin bonds have allowed, which they never would': Carlyle, *Reminiscences*, 256. On Margaret Gordon, see Raymond Clare Archibald, *Carlyle's First Love, Margaret Gordon, Lady Bannerman: An Account of her Life, Ancestry and Homes, her Family and Friends* (London: John Lane the Bodley Head, 1910).

[51] Archibald, *Carlyle's First Love*, 66, 68, 70–1; cf. *CL*, 1.414n: William Graham to Carlyle, 8 February 1822.

[52] NLS, MS 1764, fols 187–8: Irving to Carlyle, n.d. but marked as possibly dating from August 1820.

[53] *CL*, 1.297: Carlyle to his father, 18 December 1820; 301 (Carlyle to Alexander Carlyle, 2 January 1821 [erroneously dated 1820].

[54] Ibid. 1.363: Carlyle to Alexander Carlyle, 6 June 1821.

excellent Irving delights in making all around him happy: a miserable creature in his neighbourhood is to him like a disease of his own.'[55] Small wonder that a recent biographer of Carlyle comments that Irving 'seems at every moment in Carlyle's early development to have been there opening doors for him'.[56] It was Irving, too, who recommended Carlyle for his first London post, as tutor to the sons of an Anglo-Indian judge named Charles Buller.[57]

During his visit to Edinburgh, Irving took Carlyle to Haddington, where he had been engaged to preach, and introduced him to Jane Welsh.[58] One aspect of the Irving story which has accentuated the myth of him as a Romantic hero concerns his own relationship with Jane. Was he, as has usually been thought, in love with her but unable to marry because he was already understood to be engaged to Isabella Martin? Mrs Oliphant, as well as Carlyle's first major biographer, J. A. Froude, thought that he was, whereas Carlyle's nephew, Alexander, considered that he was no more than a friend and that the story had resulted from Jane's habitual use of exaggerated language in speaking of her male friends. The recollections of Jane's friend in later life, the garrulous Geraldine Jewsbury, were preserved by Thomas Carlyle (though he thought them overstated):

> I don't know at what period she knew Irving, but he loved her, and wrote letters and poetry (very true and touching): but there had been some vague understanding with another person, not a definite engagement, and she insisted that he must keep to it and not go back from what had once been spoken. There had been just then some trial, and a great scandal about a Scotch minister who had broken an engagement of marriage: and she could not bear that the shadow of any similar reproach should be cast on him. Whether if she had cared for him very much she could or would have insisted on such punctilious honour, she did not know herself ...[59]

Before offering a verdict, we need to establish the facts. Alexander Carlyle, as part of his running quarrel with Froude, included a lengthy note on the relationship between Irving and Jane Welsh, attempting to prove that she never was in love with him; in it he printed most of their letters and analysed the language used. In his view Irving was a friend to her, but often inconsiderate in his failure to write, and that this was sufficient to explain her annoyance.[60] In the course of his argument, Alexander Carlyle quoted the surviving part of Irving's sonnet 'To a Lock of my Lady's Hair, which reached me through hairbreadth 'scapes', which he connected with one or other of Irving's trips to Ireland (during the summers of 1819 and 1820) because of a

---

[55] Ibid. 1.365: Carlyle to William Graham, 12 June 1821.

[56] Heffer, *Moral Desperado*, 55.

[57] Ibid. 60–1.

[58] Laurence and Elisabeth Hanson, *Necessary Evil: The Life of Jane Welsh Carlyle* (London: Constable, 1952), 35.

[59] Carlyle, *Reminiscences*, 42.

[60] Alexander Carlyle, ed., *The Love Letters of Thomas Carlyle and Jane Welsh* (2 vols, London: John Lane, The Bodley Head, 1909), 2.400–26.

reference to its having crossed the sea to reach him.[61] A recent biographer of Jane who accepts the traditional version of events, Virginia Surtees, suggests that Jane sent the lock of hair as a keepsake after hearing from Edward of his time in the Highlands with Margaret Gordon,[62] which would indicate a date of the summer of 1820 for the poem.

On the back of the paper on which the sonnet was written were two incomplete lines from a letter to Jane, of which it formed a part. These read: 'I have resolved to see neither Isabella nor her father before I' and 'cannot brook the sight of either until this be explained and until'.[63] Whilst these have often been taken as implying that Irving was about to desert Isabella, Alexander Carlyle pointed out that they need not refer to anything more than a temporary estrangement. He went on to surmise that Irving, 'not the most discreet of Letter-writers at any time', had complained to Jane about the Martins.[64] As for Jane's comment that she once loved Irving passionately, his assessment was that she habitually used exaggerated language about her 'lovers', and points out that there were many of them.[65] In his opinion, Irving probably loved Margaret Gordon far more.[66] The motivation for Alexander Carlyle's lengthy exercise in revisionism was the desire to counter Froude's claim that Thomas and Jane never really loved each other.[67] However, there are problems with his account. There is no reason why Geraldine Jewsbury's recollections, whilst possibly overstated, should not have a core of truth in them. Quite what transpired between Irving and the Martins is not recorded in any primary source which I have seen, and Isabella was to die well before the story of her husband's romantic life became common currency through Mrs Oliphant's biography. Their son, Martin, had been reluctant that his father's life should be written by one who did not accept the work for which he gave up his reputation,[68] and family criticisms resulted in alterations to the second edition of her work, but there is no evidence that he ever alleged inaccuracy in her handling of this topic. Likewise, whilst he was distressed at the portrayal of the episode in Froude's edition of Carlyle's *Reminiscences*, first published in 1881, it is unclear whether this was because it was inaccurate, or simply because he thought it inappropriate to discuss the matter in public.[69] Froude, who earned criticism for his uncommon insistence on presenting a 'warts and all' picture of Carlyle, did not remove the passages dealing with it in the second edition, whereas he did remove the uncomplimentary description of Isabella quoted above. Probably, then, we should

---

[61] Ibid. 2.404. Irving would continue to use this poetic form in later life; examples appear in his *Exposition of Revelation*.

[62] Surtees, *Jane Welsh Carlyle*, 21.

[63] Carlyle, ed., *Love Letters*, 2.405.

[64] Ibid. 406.

[65] Ibid. 407.

[66] Ibid. 410.

[67] Ibid. 411.

[68] Cambridge, URCHS, letter 29: M. H. Irving to Auntie Anne [Mrs W. Hamilton], 17 May 1860.

[69] URCHS, letter 30: J. A. Froude to Martin H. Irving, n.d. (copy).

conclude that Martin Irving had not challenged the accuracy of the portrayal, and that the traditional understanding is in essentials correct: Irving had been in love with Jane (and he may have given this freer expression at a time when he had quarrelled with Isabella or her father), but that his sense of honour, of which there is plenty of evidence throughout his life, dictated that he marry Isabella.

In 1825, Jane herself was to confess to Thomas that she had once loved Irving passionately, and that she had persuaded him to keep his obligation to Isabella:

> I told you that I did not care for Edward Irving, took pains to make you believe this– It was false; I loved him – must I say it – *once* passionately loved him– Would to Heaven that this were all! It might not perhaps lower me much in your opinion for he is no unworthy man, and if I showed weakness in loving one whom I knew to be engaged to another, I made amends in persuading him to marry that other and preserve his honour from reproach: but I have concealed and disguised the truth: and for this I have no excuse ...[70]

It would seem probable that Irving had made up his mind not to marry Jane before introducing Carlyle to her in May 1821. In his subsequent contacts with Jane, he tried to play the role of friend and spiritual adviser,[71] as well as assuring her and her mother of his willingness to fill the gap left by the death of Dr Welsh in 1819.[72] Just a few days after his visit to Haddington in June 1821, he begged her not to abandon her faith,[73] and expressed his concern about her love of Romantic writers such as Rousseau and Byron, and the way Carlyle had been leading her to drink deeply of the spring of German literature.[74] Nevertheless, he was still conscious of his deep feelings for her:

> My well-beloved friend and pupil, when I think of you my mind is overspread with the most affectionate and tender regard which I neither know how to name nor to describe. One thing I know, it would long ago have taken the form of the most devoted attachment, but for one intervening circumstance, and have shewed and pleaded itself before your heart by a thousand actions from which I must now restrain myself. Heaven grant me its grace to restrain myself and, forgetting my own enjoyment, may I be enabled to combine unto your single self all that duty and plighted faith leave at my disposal.[75]

---

[70] Kenneth J. Fielding and David R. Sorensen, eds, *Jane Carlyle: Newly Selected Letters* (Aldershot: Ashgate, 2004), 16: Jane Welsh to Thomas Carlyle, 24 July 1825.

[71] Hanson and Hanson, *Necessary Evil*, 36. It is clear from later letters that Jane was less than appreciative of his efforts.

[72] Edward Irving to Jane Welsh, 5 June 1821, quoted in Carlyle, *Love Letters*, 2.413. He signs this letter 'Your affectionate friend and instructor'.

[73] Ibid. 412: Edward Irving to Jane Welsh, 5 June 1821.

[74] Ibid. 413: Edward Irving to Thomas Carlyle, 12 June 1821.

[75] Hanson and Hanson, *Necessary Evil*, 47: Edward Irving to Jane Welsh, 6 March 1822.

Irving visited Haddington again on 5 July 1822 to bid farewell before moving to London; before that, Jane had complained that she had not heard from him for six weeks, and criticized his silence as unaccountable. Surtees argues that giving up Irving was not a noble sacrifice on Jane's part: 'Hers was the bitter response of a proud woman prepared to hurt the man who had occasioned the wound. Possessive jealousy of Irving ... was tarnishing the determination ascribed to her by posterity Her bitter pronouncements were the voice of one who had sacrifice forced upon her.'[76] Certainly she displayed a penchant for 'catty' comments about him during the early years of his life in London, as we shall notice, but it is questionable whether this need imply too much more than a consciousness that their paths were headed in different directions and a rejection of the ideas which he was proclaiming to such effect.

Although he threw himself into the work in Glasgow, Irving nevertheless looked forward to the day when he would be able to take charge of his own parish. In 1821, he experienced a double disappointment in this respect. As he explained to Carlyle, 'Kinfauns [a Perthshire village] went to one better backed, and Hamilton went to one earlier promised'.[77] As at other points when his way appeared to be blocked up, he considered the possibility of going overseas. He was offered a call to Jamaica during his Glasgow years, and would probably have accepted it but for the intervention of others.[78] At the beginning of 1822 another call came from the influential Scotch Presbyterian congregation in New York, which, Carlyle reported, was offering an annual salary of £1,000: 'On the whole Irving deserves it all and more. I believe him to be about the best man in the Scottish Church, both for head and heart. I have not heard whether he means to go across the ocean: I hope & partly expect, not.'[79] He was right: but Irving must have found the offer tempting, especially when contrasted with his difficulties in securing advancement in Britain. Eventually, however, his desires were to be fulfilled, but in what looked like a most unpromising situation.

---

[76] Surtees, *Jane Welsh Carlyle*, 33–4.

[77] *CL*, 1.356n: Irving to Carlyle, 26 April 1821.

[78] William Jones, *Biographical Sketch of the Rev. Edward Irving, A.M. late Minister of the National Scotch Church, London: With Extracts from, and Remarks on his Principal Publications* (London: John Bennett, 1841), 7; cf. Oliphant, *Life*, 67 (she sees Irving's friends as responsible, whereas Jones thinks his relatives were the ones who dissuaded him).

[79] *CL*, 2.35: Carlyle to John Fergusson, 11 February 1822.

CHAPTER 6

Call to London and Farewell to Glasgow, 1821–2

The Caledonian Chapel, in London's Hatton Garden, was a small and struggling Presbyterian cause, which owed its origin to the Highland Society of London. This body had been founded late in the eighteenth century and worked for the welfare of Highlanders in the metropolis as well as in Scotland. A fund started about 1808 to provide a Gaelic-speaking ministry in the capital drew enough income to maintain a preacher and to acquire a chapel; an asylum appeal was also launched at that time, to provide a home and an education for orphaned children of Scottish soldiers and sailors, but this failed for several years to secure sufficient funds. The latter project was all but abandoned, but was rescued by an artist, Andrew Robertson, who was a leading light among the Scottish expatriate community. A former Swedenborgian chapel in Cross Street was purchased in 1812, and the Gaelic Chapel was dedicated in 1813, under the auspices of the Highland Society of London. In 1815 an Act of Parliament was passed, establishing the Caledonian Asylum, which was likewise overseen by the Highland Society; the asylum was opened in 1817, and maintained a close link with the chapel until the Disruption, the scholars attending each Sunday. Around 1818, the Gaelic Chapel became the Caledonian Chapel.

The vendor of the chapel had been happy to receive two-thirds of the purchase price and to accept a claim on the building for the balance. However, he eventually threatened legal proceedings, and so the managers made an agreement in 1816 with the asylum directors whereby the chapel's trust deeds were transferred to the asylum. The directors were happy to do so, not only because it would be a vital part of their provision for the spiritual welfare of the boys in their care, but also because a good preacher would be able to attract a congregation and so secure financial support for the asylum. Unfortunately, the first two ministers, James Boyd and Alec Macnaughton, had brief ministries: Boyd was successful but accepted a call elsewhere, while Macnaughton's ministry was not successful, and he left in December 1820. The directors kept the church going during the ministerless period, but their quest for a man to fill the pulpit was made the more difficult by a requirement built into the trust deeds that the minister should conduct regular services in Gaelic.[1]

---

[1] John Hair, *Regent Square: Eighty Years of a London Congregation* (London: James Nisbet, 1899), 5–8, 24–7; George G. Cameron, *The Scots Kirk in London* (Oxford: Becket, 1979), 104–7. The chapel was repurchased by the Swedenborgians when the congregation moved to Regent Square in 1827, and used by them until 1872, when it was taken over by a firm of manufacturing chemists. It no longer exists.

Word reached London of Chalmers' assistant, and some of the officers of the Caledonian Chapel commissioned a friend who knew the congregation to speak to Irving about it: 'Well do I remember the morning, when, as I sat in my lonely apartment, meditating the uncertainties of a preacher's calling, and revolving in my mind purposes of missionary work, this stranger stepped in upon my musing, and opened to me the commission with which he had been charged.'[2] Once again, an opportunity came to Irving at a point when he was unsettled regarding his future course. Having been dissuaded from taking charge of a Presbyterian congregation in Kingston, Jamaica, his ideas of becoming a missionary had returned.[3]

Although he knew no Gaelic, Irving was engaged to preach in London for three Sundays from 24 December 1821. With breathless enthusiasm and pardonable vanity, Irving wrote to tell Carlyle of his reception:

> I have preached, but I shall not repeat the compliments which burst upon me. It is so new a thing to me to be praised in my preaching, I know not how to look. At Glasgow ... when praised it is with reservation often with cold and unprofitable admonition. And Dr C. sometimes in his retailing of the public opinion makes me feel all black in my prospects. Here I have been hailed with the warmest reception. They anticipate great things. Talk of having the Duke of York the President of the Asylum present at a Charity sermon Sunday week and much more which it is needless to repeat. One thing would have made your heart feel; my audience was almost entirely young Scotsmen – no fathers, no mothers, no sisters – seat-fulls of youths – and how grave[,] how attentive.[4]

Writing in more measured tones to Chalmers, and with an eye on the latter's particular interests, he recorded that his preaching was 'very acceptable' and the congregation 'larger than was expected', three-quarters of it young Scotsmen (doubtless including past and present inmates of the asylum):

> ... here you will observe there is agency enough if it could be excited to godly and benevolent ends. The Scotsmen in London, having nothing else after business to engage them, and no choice of society, and being themselves detached from all family society at home, are a prey to amusement and dissipations, to which they are the more inclined that they burst upon them with the freshness of novelty, and the more incited by the vigorous health and constitution which they grow up with in the temperate region of morals from which they come.

He also refers to spending a morning with the examining committee of the London Missionary Society (evidently he had not ruled out the idea of becoming a

---

[2] Edward Irving, *The Last Days: A Discourse on the Evil Character of these our Times, proving them to be the 'Perilous Times' of the 'Last Days'* (London: J. Nisbet, 1850), xxxiv.

[3] Oliphant, *Life*, 67.

[4] Edinburgh, NLS, MS 1764, fol. 211: Irving to Carlyle, 26 December 1821. The talk came to fruition; the Duke attended Irving's preaching; and Irving was presented with the Bible which the Duke had used.

missionary, but he was not particularly impressed with this body). Irving's stay in London was extended by another Sabbath in order that the committee which had invited him could test his attractiveness by giving potential hearers from the upper ranks of society an opportunity of returning after hearing him at a charity sermon on behalf of the asylum on the third Sunday of his visit.[5] Writing to Jane Welsh on 9 February, he boasted that he had been solicited to publish the charity discourse, but that he had 'refused till my apprehensions of truth be larger, and my treatment of it more according to the models of modern and ancient times'. He described how 'My countrymen of the first celebrity, especially in art, welcomed me to their society, and the first artist in the city drew an admirable half-length miniature of me in action'.[6] Jane was none too impressed, telling a friend: 'Mr. Irving is making a *horrible* noise in London, where he has got a church – He tells me, in his last, that his head is quite turned with the admiration he has received – and really I believe him –'.[7] It may have been Jane, who elsewhere recorded her assessment in similar vein, who analysed the roots of his vanity:

> He was vain ... but it was a vanity proceeding out of what was best and most lovable in him, – his childlike simplicity and desire to be loved; his crystal transparency of character letting every little weakness show through it as frankly as his noblest qualities; and, above all, out of his loyal, his divine trust in the absolute truth and sincerity, and the generous sympathy and good-will, of all who made friendly advances towards him.[8]

Among those who heard him were two sisters, both married to retired Anglo-Indian judges, Mrs Strachey and Mrs Buller. Mrs Buller, who had not gone to hear him with any great expectations, was nonetheless greatly impressed, and sought his advice the next day regarding the education of her sons. Irving immediately suggested appointing Carlyle as their tutor.[9]

On his return to Glasgow, he reflected that:

> I have taken new wing by my visit to London. I see my way distinctly – my intellect is putting out new powers at least I fancy so – and if God endow me with his grace I foresee service to his church. My ambition (a sanctified one I trust) is taking another direction no less than an endeavour to bring the spirit and power of the ancient eloquence into the pulpit, which appears to me the only place in modern manners for its revival. ... It is for an audience chiefly I am so fond of London – perhaps as much for a school to learn in by conversation & observation, for which I

---

[5] Edinburgh, NCL, Chalmers MSS, CHA 4.18.6: Irving to Chalmers, 24 December 1821; Oliphant, *Life*, 70. He was anxious not to go into print without having something distinctive to say: London, RS, EIL 09, William Dinwiddie to Irving, [January?] 1822; EIL 10, Irving to Dinwiddie, 26 January 1822.

[6] Oliphant, *Life*, 69.

[7] *CL*, 2.44: Jane Welsh to Eliza Stoddard, 3 March [?20 February] 1822.

[8] Oliphant, *Life*, 63.

[9] *CL*, 2.4–5n.

think nature has fitted me more than by Books. I have a wonderful aptitude to sympathise with men – their manner of feeling & of thinking also is clear to me, and even when false [it is] interesting from a desire to set them right.[10]

Clearly London would provide scope for him to test out his theories, just as St John's had provided Chalmers with scope to test out his. But there were obstacles in the way. The congregation formed a committee to secure him as their minister, but they were unable to get the trustees to free them from the requirement regarding Gaelic services. Robertson claimed it would be sufficient to appoint a schoolmaster who could take these, but most of the directors believed that the minister was the one legally required to do so. Irving expressed his willingness to learn Gaelic in six months in order to fulfil the requirement, though he was forced to backtrack somewhat after consultation with experts in Edinburgh. The directors, however, obtained an Act of Parliament which absolved them from their agreement by enabling them to repay what the Gaelic Fund had supplied towards the purchase cost of the building. Pending the passage of this bill, the office-bearers (who, with the congregation, had initially invited Irving for a month at their own risk, independently of the directors) decided to act independently of the directors once again. Accordingly, on 2 April the congregation resolved to hire a chapel if necessary, in order to be free to call Irving as their minister. A meeting of his friends four days later supported this, authorizing the elders to ask the directors to rent the Caledonian Chapel to the congregation, or to find another building. On 8 April Robertson informed Irving that pending the passage of the bill through Parliament, the directors had agreed to let the church to the congregation.[11]

There was another problem. Only fifty heads of families signed the call, not enough to ensure an adequate stipend for a minister. Without the guarantee of a stipend from the congregation, the Church of Scotland would not ordain a candidate, and the Presbytery of London therefore demurred. It seems likely that the financial aspect formed part of the description of the congregation's low state given to Irving before he came to London. His correspondence with William Dinwiddie, an elder who acted as correspondent on behalf of the congregation and its office-bearers, dealt at length with financial matters. Irving wished that he could preach to them for nothing, working to support himself, but the spirit of the age required that those who preached the gospel should live by it (he had 1 Corinthians 9.14 in mind here, but seems to have overlooked the fact that this was, according to Paul, a divine ordinance and not merely a social convention). Accordingly, he informed Dinwiddie that he could not afford to come to London for less than £200 per annum. They reached an agreement that he should be guaranteed £150 plus half the proceeds, after expenses, of the seat-rents (it was expected that these would amount to £600 or £700

---

[10] NLS, MS 1764, fols 221–2: Irving to Carlyle, 9 February 1822.

[11] Oliphant, *Life*, 71–3; Hair, *Regent Square*, 31–3. Mrs Oliphant was therefore incorrect to say that the problem was a parliamentary allowance, and that the Duke of York secured the setting aside of the Gaelic stipulation for receiving it: there was no allowance, and the Duke did not act in this way.

annually). Irving also insisted that he would only come down if he was the sole candidate for the position, serving them on a trial basis.[12] Some years later, he claimed that his response to the initial approach had been to declare his readiness to preach without remuneration if necessary, a step which earned him criticism from other ministers; this may have been because he declared his willingness to seek ordination after his settlement, an action which would have been regarded as irregular. He had been, he asserted, ready to come to London 'almost on any conditions' to preach the gospel. In the end, however, the congregation's generosity made such gestures unnecessary.[13] Indeed, as Irving told Carlyle in April: 'I have received the call, most respectably signed; and, what with subscriptions and the first of the seat-rents, the security of £500 a year'.[14] Such an income was easily the largest of any Church of Scotland minister in London, although the boast was not made to impress but in order to assure Carlyle that he could now entertain him as he deserved.

A sense of unsettlement surfaced from time to time in his letters during this period, perhaps as a reaction to the uncertainty of the situation. On 21 February he reassured the office-bearers in London that God would provide for him if they were unable to proceed with the call: he had been offered (but refused) charge of a chapel of ease in Dundee, and interest in him had been shown from New York.[15] Whilst apparently somewhat depressed about his prospects, he maintained his idealistic outlook. To Dr Martin, he wrote: 'There are a few things which bind me to the world, and but a very few ... one is to make a demonstration for a higher style of Christianity, something more magnanimous, more heroical than this age affects. God knows with what success.'[16] There was also an element of foreboding. As he wrote to Carlyle on 29 April, 'There is an independence about my character, a want of resemblance with others, especially with others of my profession, that will cause me to be apprehended ill of.'[17] It was probably around this time that he confided in Robertson:

> There is a sea of troubles, ... for my notions of a clergyman's office are not common, nor likely to be in everything approved. There is a restlessness in my mind after a state of life less customary, more enterprising, more heroical, if I might apply the word to a sacred use, certainly more apostolical. My notions of pulpit eloquence differ from many of my worthy brethren. In truth I am an adventurer on ground untried, and am therefore full of anxieties. But we are not ignorant, like the world, of a sufficient strength, to which I would look. Oh! many things distress

---

[12] London, RS, including EIL 01, Irving to Dinwiddie, 6 November 1821; EIL 03, Dinwiddie to Irving, 12 November 1821 [draft].

[13] Irving, *Last Days*, xxxv–xxxvi; Oliphant, *Life*, 71–2.

[14] NLS, MS 1764, fol. 227: Irving to Carlyle, 29 April 1822.

[15] Oliphant, *Life*, 71. Irving had refused to pay a second visit to London that February in order to build on the enthusiasm created by his first, lest it appear like hunting for a pastoral settlement: Hair, *Regent Square*, 45–6.

[16] Ibid. 72–3.

[17] Ibid.

me which cannot be told, and kill all ambitions, at least denude them of their glare. These also the Lord will help me through, if I trust Him.[18]

A later biographer comments that 'This letter reveals Irving's visionary bias. It reveals undue self-consciousness. It reveals also the danger of undefined aims of heroic achievement. Even at this early stage in his career, with surprising success ahead, one can observe an erratic strain in his personality that was later to prove his ruin.'[19] In Irving's defence we may note the undoubted challenges which he and the congregation had had to face, and his experience of working in a situation where another was seeking to make their own vision a reality. The latter appears to have stimulated his own thinking about his vision for ministry, and how he might fulfil it.

Once the call had been offered and accepted, Irving returned to Annan for his ordination in June.[20] The proposal had been put to the Presbytery by Moncrieff (the minister who had baptized him), who produced the call from London, an extract of his licence to preach from Kirkcaldy, and a certificate of his moral character and ministerial usefulness from Glasgow. The Presbytery prescribed him another set of trial discourses: a lecture on Luke 6.1, a homily on John 1.5, an exegesis of a theological proposition in Latin, an exercise in Greek criticism on Ephesians 4.16, a popular sermon on John 5.39 ('Search the Scriptures', a text from which he preached at Haddington soon after,[21] thus doubtless getting good use from his material), Greek and Hebrew translations, and the first half of the sixteenth century (presumably a historical exercise).[22] Irving was examined on most of these at the next meeting, on 5 June, and preached his popular sermon at the meeting a fortnight later. Receiving unanimous approval, the moderator was enjoined to ordain him with prayer and the laying on of hands of the Presbytery. This took place immediately, after Irving had given satisfactory answers to the questions enjoined by the General Assembly to be put to probationers, the moderator delivering a suitable address to the new minister.[23] Although the congregation in Hatton Garden were impatient for Irving to make his way south and begin his ministry, he insisted upon spending two days after his

---

[18] Hair, *Regent Square*, 34.

[19] Andrew Landale Drummond, *Edward Irving and his Circle: Including some Consideration of the 'Tongues' Movement in the Light of Modern Psychology* (London: James Clarke, [1937]), 46.

[20] Irving assured his London congregation that he would use his personal influence to expedite the ordination process: RS, EIL 18, Irving to the elders and congregation of the Caledonian Chapel, 17 April 1822 [copy]; this contrasts with his declared unwillingness to do anything of the kind when seeking a call.

[21] An eye-witness recalled him preaching on this text, to a very large and attentive congregation: John Martine, *Reminiscences of the Royal Burgh of Haddington* (Edinburgh: John Menzies, 1883), 204.

[22] Edinburgh, NAS, CH2/13/5, Presbytery of Annan, minutes 1813–28, fols 260–1.

[23] Ibid. fols 262–4.

ordination in baptizing his sisters' children and attending the family gatherings customarily held on such occasions.[24]

Chalmers also wished his assistant to minister in St John's for one last time. The initial plan was for Irving to assist on the communion Sunday, 30 June, but when Chalmers became indisposed he asked Irving to conduct the actual sacrament service.[25] Irving might not have succeeded in winning over the whole congregation, but he left behind him a coterie of enthusiastic supporters, and before departing he was presented with a gold watch, chain and seals, worth £60.[26] He preached a *Farewell Discourse to the Congregation and Parish of St John's, Glasgow*, on the text 'Finally, brethren, farewell' (2 Corinthians 13.11), which became his first published work.[27] In it he showed his confidence by departing from the custom on such occasions of preaching on some useful topic with a brief and forced concluding application to the parting, in order to give a parting charge like those of Christ or Paul, in which he could express his feelings for them and his desires for their welfare.[28] It is an idealistic utterance, in the best sense, advocating a faith in God which is worked out in every aspect of Christian service as well as daily life. He applied his injunction more particularly to those who were in the same position as he had so lately been as a licentiate:

> most especially let the youth destined for the holy ministry stand aloof from the unholy influences under which the Church hath fallen; from the seats of power and patronage let them stand aloof; from the boards of ecclesiastical intrigue on both sides of the Church, let them stand aloof; from glozing the public ear, and pampering the popular taste, with unprofitable though acceptable matter, let them stand aloof; and while thus dissevered from fawning, intriguing and pandering, let them draw near to God, and drink inspiration from the milk of His word; and though poor as the first disciples of Christ, without staff, without scrip, still, like the first disciples of Christ, let them labour in the ministry of the word and in prayer with their families, their kindred, their neighbourhood, the poor who will welcome them, the sick who desire them, and the young who need them ...[29]

The apostolic ideal which he lauded here would be more fully expounded a couple of years later, in *Missionaries after the Apostolical School*.

Looking back, Irving testified that God had translated him from the sight of much in the church which grieved and which could not be amended, to be with men who were doing a great work, 'to the bosom of a city which is the Mount Zion of the

---

[24] RS, EIL 21, Irving to the elders, 14 June 1822.

[25] RS, EIL 23, Irving to the elders and congregation of the Caledonian Chapel, 20 June 1822. Irving also informed them he would need to break his journey in the east of Scotland to attend to an important matter (this would have been his leave-taking of Jane Welsh).

[26] *Glasgow Herald*, 22 July 1822.

[27] Irving, *CW*, 3.343–62; first publ. Glasgow: Chalmers and Collins, 1822.

[28] Ibid. 345.

[29] Ibid. 347–8.

Christian world, whence the law and the testimony are going forth to the ends of the earth'.[30] The parish was fortunate in possessing 'the voice of the most eloquent, and the assiduities of the most tender-hearted of Scottish pastors, who hath gathered around him a host of the most pious and devoted agents'.[31] So fulsome was Irving's eulogy of his colleague, that Grace Chalmers got hold of the printer's proofs and toned it down before it went to press, much to Irving's annoyance when he saw the finished item.[32]

This congregation, 'almost the first in which our preaching was tolerated', had been the sphere for him to gain experience. He recognized that his imperfections had alienated some, but claimed that many among 'this intelligent and independent congregation of citizens' had heard him with profit.[33] There were, he asserted, two sorts of preachers, which he compared to ships (nautical metaphors recur from time to time in his thinking about ministry): traders followed the safe routes, while adventurers took risks which enabled them to discover more. Among the latter were Paul, Luther and Calvin. Irving's own mentor, Chalmers, 'without sacrificing the gospel of Christ, hath diverged further than any of his age from the approved course of preaching, and launched a bold adventure of his own into the ocean of religious speculation'.[34] It was the adventurer whom the world needed to see more of:

> There are ministers enow [enough] to hold their flock in pasture and in safety. But where are they to make inroad upon the alien, to bring in the votaries of fashion, of literature, of sentiment, of policy, and of rank, who are content in their several idolatries to do without piety to God, and love to Him whom He hath sent? Where are they to lift up their voice against simony, and arts of policy, and servile dependence upon the great ones of this earth, and shameful seeking of ease and pleasure, and anxious amassing of money, and the whole cohort of evil customs which are overspreading the ministers of the church?[35]

That being so, preachers needed to learn how to communicate to those outside the church. He challenged the narrow tastes of most congregations and preachers, which he saw as derived from the conventicle model of preaching, addressed to insiders:

> we are pleading against those Shibboleths of a sect, those forms of words which now do not feed the soul with understanding, but are in truth as the time-worn and bare trunks of those trees from which the Church was formerly nourished, and which now have in them neither sap nor nourishment. We are pleading for a more natural

---

[30] Ibid. 348–9.

[31] Ibid. 358. This, of course, was not what he had written to Carlyle in private!

[32] William Hanna, *Memoirs of the Life and Writings of Thomas Chalmers D.D. LL.D.* (4 vols, Edinburgh: Sutherland and Knox, 1850), 2.401–2.

[33] *CW*, 3.358–9.

[34] Ibid. 350–1.

[35] Ibid. 351.

style of preaching, in which the various moral and religious wants of men shall be met, artlessly met with the simple truths of revelation ...[36]

His tribute to the congregation was fulsome: 'This place has been the cradle of my clerical character'; it had restored his self-confidence, which was failing, restored him to the church from which despair had almost weaned him, and restored his sense of vocation.[37] Even closer was his bond with the inhabitants of the parish, whose struggle to maintain their dignity amid destitution he painted in vivid terms:

> There have I sitten, with little silver or gold of my own to bestow, with little command over the charity of others, and heard the various narratives of hardship, narratives uttered for the most part with modesty and patience, oftener drawn forth with difficulty than obtruded on your ear, – their wants, their misfortunes, their ill-requited labour, their hopes vanishing, their families dispersing in search of better habitations, the Scottish economy of their homes giving way before encroaching necessity, debt rather than saving their condition, bread and water their scanty fare, hard and ungrateful labour the portion of their house, – all this have I often seen and listened to within naked walls, the witness, oft the partaker, of their miserable cheer, with little or no means to relieve.[38]

In spite of their poverty and his inability to do much to relieve it, he found them deeply responsive to his ministrations. They, not the carping critics of his preaching, were the ones whose verdict really mattered:

> God above doth know my destiny; but though it were to minister in the halls of nobles, and the courts and palaces of kings, He can never find for me more natural welcome, more kindly entertainment, and more refined enjoyment than He hath honoured me within this suburb parish of a manufacturing city. My theology was never in fault round the fires of the poor, my manner never misinterpreted, my good intentions never mistaken.[39]

'Here was the popularity worth the having', and he seized another opportunity to challenge the introversion of contemporary Christianity. Visiting among the poor was an activity which could easily be taken up, yet the churches in general appeared to neglect it:

> Would that in this age, when our clergy and our laity are ever and anon assembling in public to take measures for the moral and religious welfare of men, they were found as diligently occupying this more retired, more scriptural, and more natural region! Would they were as instant for the poor, the irreligious, the unprotected of

---

[36] Ibid. 352.
[37] Ibid. 353.
[38] Ibid. 354.
[39] Ibid. 355.

their several parishes, and several neighbourhoods, as they are for the tribes, whose dwellings are remote, and whose tongue is strange!⁴⁰

Such activity could do much to lessen the social discontent then evident: if the Church of Scotland, to which the people owed so much, would again become the people's church, then a sense of their national character would overpower disaffection and discontent.⁴¹

Irving only published the discourse after William Collins, one of the elders, encouraged him to do so.⁴² But it soon began to attract attention and excite controversy, as would be the case with all his published writings of any size. Carlyle wrote:

> I have heard a great deal about this 'farewell address' – a proof at least that it is no common performance. All people seem agreed in applauding the delineation he gives of his intercourse with the poor at St John's; almost (but not altogether) all in condemning large masses of the rest. Irving will redeem what is faulty and make good what is defective, all in due season, beyond a doubt.⁴³

Once again, Carlyle analysed Irving's sermons, comparing them with those of Chalmers, who was the foremost evangelical preacher in Scotland at the time:

> Irving's Discourses were far more opulent in ingenious thought than Chalmers's, which indeed were usually the triumphant on-rush of *one* idea with its satellites and supporters; but Irving's wanted in definite *head*, that is, steady invariably evident *aim*, what one might call definite *head* and *backbone;* so that, on arriving, you might see clearly where and how. ... He had many thoughts, pregnantly expressed, but they did not tend all one way. The reason was, there were in him infinitely more thoughts than in Chalmers; and he took far less pains in setting them forth. ... Originality and truth of purpose were undeniable in it; but there was withal, both in the matter and the manner, a something which might be suspected of affectation; a noticeable preference and search for striking quaint and ancient locutions; a style modelled on the Miltonic Old-Puritan; something too in the delivery which seemed elaborate and of forethought, or might be suspected of being so.⁴⁴

It was not only the structure and manner of Irving's preaching which gave rise to criticism, but the content. Writing to a mutual friend from Edinburgh that March, Carlyle had foreshadowed its doctrinally controversial nature:

---

⁴⁰ Ibid. 356.

⁴¹ Ibid. 357.

⁴² David Keir, *The House of Collins: The Story of a Scottish Family of Publishers from 1789 to the Present Day* (London: Collins, 1952), 69.

⁴³ *CL*, 2.192: Carlyle to William Graham, 30 October 1822.

⁴⁴ Thomas Carlyle, *Reminiscences*, ed. C. E. Norton (London: J. M. Dent, 1932), 216–17.

Irving, as you know, was here preaching lately. Nothing since the days of Knox or the Erskines has excited so much speculation in the theological world as his appearance here. They think him the cleverest and strangest person they have ever fallen in with. ... He was touching on the Catechisms: I could fancy the *Closehead* [Ecclefechan Seceders] folks, if he had read that sermon to them, all rising as one man to cast him forth of the Tabernacle, or at least withdrawing *en masse*, with the most wintry air imaginable, and leaving him to utter his 'heresies' to empty benches and bare walls. At Edinr they proceeded more moderately: some admired, several did not, most knew not what to think. I have not listened to a sermon displaying equal mind in my whole life.[45]

London, as the centre of gravity of British culture and religion, would provide Irving with unique opportunities as a preacher. Visiting his friend Robert Story before leaving Scotland, he informed the party, then rowing across Gare Loch: 'I hope yet to go deep into the ocean of truth.'[46] It would not be long, as we shall see, before he found himself in uncharted and stormy waters.

---

[45] *CL*, 2.73: Carlyle to David Hope, 23 March 1822.
[46] Oliphant, *Life*, 74.

CHAPTER 7

Taking London by Storm, 1822–5

Writing to Grace Chalmers soon after his arrival in London, Irving described his voyage south. He left Glasgow on 8 July and sailed from Leith on the steamship *James Watt* two days later, having presumably visited Haddington in the meantime. The passengers, who were delighted when he offered his services as chaplain, spent the mornings reading, and the evenings 'in talk and tales at which I was clearly dubbed the Apollo of the assembly, until they declared if I preached as I told stories I would have no equal in the South'.[1] Within a year many would come to just that conclusion; from the very beginning of his ministry in London, Irving was something of a phenomenon.

Although the office-bearers of the Caledonian Chapel had hoped to secure Chalmers' services for the induction, his indisposition and their inability to find a replacement meant that Irving introduced himself to the pulpit on 14 July 1822, preaching from Acts 10.29, 'Therefore I came unto you without gainsaying, as soon as I was sent for: I ask therefore for what intent ye have sent for me?'[2] This was to be the first of a series of sermons on Peter's discourse to Cornelius, indicating that from the start Irving adopted a systematic approach to his choice of sermon topic, a practice which was not as common then among Evangelicals as it later became. According to a report in the *Glasgow Herald*, he 'pointed out on the one hand the duties incumbent on him in the exercise of his sacred office, and on the other those obligations on the part of the flock under his charge towards himself, and his resolution to promote the cause of his Master, and act a faithful part towards those who came under his Ministry'.[3] One who went to hear him that Sunday was an import and export merchant, James Simpson (1781-1849). Hitherto inclined to wander from church to church as a sermon taster, Simpson and his wife Jane soon joined the Caledonian Chapel.[4] They would grow close to the Irvings before falling out with them in 1832 (see chapter 19).

In September, Irving left for a few weeks' break in Yorkshire and Scotland; writing to his congregation from Bolton Abbey in Yorkshire, he expressed the hope

---

[1] Edinburgh, NCL, Chalmers MSS, CHA 7.1.23: Irving to Grace Chalmers, 15 July 1822.

[2] London, RS, EIL25: Irving to Dinwiddie, 8 July 1822; Oliphant, *Life*, 76–7. Most of his sermon had to be written *en voyage*.

[3] *Glasgow Herald*, 22 July 1822.

[4] Edinburgh, NLS, Acc.12489/14, John Home Simpson, Typescript work on the Simpsons and their relationship to Irving, chs 1–2.

that by him, or by someone else more worthy, God would testify against 'the high places and strong holds of vanity and error and false philosophy in which Satan hath intrenched himself'.⁵ Here we see both his concern to engage with contemporary society (which he viewed in negative terms) and his continuing diffidence: he went on to assure the church that if they should ever choose to dispense with his services in favour of the ministry of another, he would accept their verdict and submit to the will of God – a curious comment to make when he had only just taken up the charge. On his return, the Presbytery of London inducted him as minister of the Caledonian Chapel on 16 October. (The elders, it seems, had wanted Chalmers to perform the ceremony, and Irving had brought three of them to meet him on his visit to London in August, but he now had no time to accede to their request.⁶) At the conclusion of the service, the presbytery and congregation gave Irving the right hand of fellowship, and he was 'cordially and unanimously admitted a member of Presbytery'.⁷ An induction dinner was held at the Freemasons' Tavern, Irving chairing and about two hundred gentlemen being present; a reporter noted that ministers from the Church of England and from Dissenting causes joined their Presbyterian colleagues in welcoming him.⁸

From the start, the chapel was well attended. That autumn, Irving wrote to a friend: 'The people have received me with open arms; the church is already regularly filled; my preaching, though on the average of one hour and a quarter, listened to with the most serious attention, my mind plentifully endowed with thought and feeling'.⁹ He soon found that he had his work cut out, as he explained to Carlyle:

> My business has grown upon my hands into the double of what I had calculated on. Each week I have to produce two discourses, and whether it is that my mind has taken more important views of the questions I handle, or that the young and thoughtful audience before me, makes me more careful that my argument be more complete and my whole discourse more cogent, certain it is they extend under my hands to at least an hour's length ... ... every week I have to write in the best state to which I am equal, as much as would make three or four ordinary discourses, and to refresh my mind with reading, and meet the various calls upon my time and thought, which together have occupied me to an extent I have not yet known.

---

⁵ RS, EIL26: Irving to the Caledonian Church, 28 September 1822.

⁶ William Hanna, *Memoirs of the Life and Writings of Thomas Chalmers D.D. LL.D.* (4 vols, Edinburgh: Sutherland and Knox, 1850), 2.348: Chalmers to Mrs. Chalmers, 24 September 1822. Irving himself invited Chalmers to preach for him while in London: Irving to Chalmers, 9 September 1822 (NCL, Chalmers MSS, CHA 4.21.7). Mrs Oliphant is presumably incorrect in identifying the visit she describes in August 1822 with the occasion of Irving's induction: *Life*, 77–9.

⁷ Cambridge, URCHS, 'Minutes of the Scots Presbytery of London. Vol. 1. Aug. 1772 to Mar 19. 1823', fols 361–2.

⁸ 'Caledonian Church', *Morning Chronicle*, 22 October 1822, 4 (taken from the *Representative*, 20 October 1822, 331).

⁹ John Hair, *Regent Square: Eighty Years of a London Congregation* (London: James Nisbet, 1899), 37.

Nevertheless, he complained at what he saw as the lack of high minds and profound thought in London.[10] A few months later, however, he told Carlyle that he was enjoying the greater intellectual freedom which the city provided: 'I do feel like a man floating in a sea of thought'. Such a demanding ministry required him to spend every day except Monday alone until dinner in preparation; on Mondays, he allowed himself the diversion of some time in the country or practical philanthropy in the city.[11]

Further testimony to his success came in a letter to Mrs Welsh:

> Already my Church overflows, & many are the testimonies which are brought to me of happy effects from my preaching I have dispensed the sacrament to more communicants than have ever before sat down in the place. And there are already £3000 subscribed to build a new church which will be finished in less than a year to contain 2000 people and cost towards £10,000. But that above all which gives me happiness, is the liberty I enjoy of testifying without any restraint my full conception of that blessed Gospel of which I am the unworthy minister.[12]

According to Carlyle, 'Like another Boanerges he is cleaving the hearts of the Londoners in twain, attending Bible societies, Presbyterian dinners, Religious conventions of all kinds; preaching and speculating and acting so as to gain universal notoriety and very general approbation.'[13] Chalmers thought that he was 'prospering in his new situation, and seems to feel as if in that very station of command and congeniality whereunto you have long known him to aspire. I hope that he will not hurt his usefulness by any kind of eccentricity or imprudence.'[14] This note of caution would continue to feature in Chalmers' reports on the progress of Irving's ministry. A thriving market in portraits and engravings of Irving sprang up, though he does not appear to have sat for any except that made by Andrew Robertson during his first visit to London.

What is said to have brought the crowds flocking in was a reference made by the then Foreign Secretary, George Canning, in a speech. The biographer of one of Canning's friends, the politician and philosopher Sir James Mackintosh, explains what happened:

> the first time he [Mackintosh] heard Mr. Irving preach, he was very much struck with a beautiful expression of his in a prayer for a family who had lost their parents: 'We pray for those orphans who have been deprived of their parents, and are now thrown on the fatherhood of God.' M. said he had repeated this to Canning, who

---

[10] Edinburgh, NLS, MS 1764, fol. 233: Irving to Carlyle, 23 September 1822.
[11] Ibid. fol. 243: Irving to Carlyle, 14 February 1823.
[12] Ibid. fol. 237: Irving to Mrs Welsh, 6 December 1822.
[13] *CL*, 2.237: Carlyle to Alexander Carlyle, 20 December 1822.
[14] Hanna, *Chalmers*, 2.355: Chalmers to Mrs Chalmers, 3 October 1822.

started at the expression, and expressed great admiration of it. He made M. take him to the Scotch Church the next Sunday.[15]

Thereafter, in Mrs Oliphant's words,

> A discussion took place in the House of Commons in which the revenues of the Church were referred to, and the necessary mercantile relation between high talent and good *pay* insisted upon. ... Canning told the house that, so far from universal was this rule, that he himself had lately heard a Scotch minister, trained in one of the most poorly endowed of churches, and established in one of her outlying dependencies, possessed of no endowment at all, preach the most eloquent sermon that he had ever listened to.[16]

A recent researcher has claimed that she was incorrect in stating that this took place in the House of Commons.[17] But wherever the reference was made, it evidently started something. From that point, it became the thing to do to hear Irving; on Sunday mornings a long line of carriages could be seen outside the chapel during service time, indicative of the presence of the great and the good. Among Irving's regular hearers were Brougham, Canning, the Duke of Sussex, the Earl of Aberdeen and the philosopher Sir James Graham.[18] According to one report, 'the woman who has the care of the church, and who was perfectly satisfied with her salary while she had but cobwebs to sweep from the empty seats, has struck for wages, because the preaching of Mr. Irving so crowds the church that the good lady has much extra labour'.[19]

Applications for sittings rose from fifty to 1,500. This created a problem, since the chapel could not seat more than six hundred; it seems that the increase was due in part to some judicious 'puffing' by the managers, who sent out five hundred copies of a circular letter announcing the abilities of the new occupant of their pulpit to Scots in London.[20] For those who did not hold a sitting, entrance was by ticket only. As some critics pointed out, the poor were thereby effectively excluded from Irving's pulpit ministrations. There were far more applications for sittings than the

---

[15] Robert James Mackintosh, ed., *Memoirs of the Life of the Right Honourable Sir James Mackintosh* (2 vols, London: Edward Moxon, 1835), 2.477.

[16] Oliphant, *Life*, 79–80.

[17] The researcher is Liam Upton, in some unpublished work; he points out that there is no reference to such a discussion in *Hansard*, nor in any biography of Irving preceding Mrs Oliphant. At present, his only published writing is '"Our Mother and our Country": The Integration of Religious and National Identity in the Thought of Edward Irving (1792–1834)', in Robert Pope, ed., *Religion and National Identity: Wales and Scotland c. 1700–2000* (Cardiff: University of Wales Press, 2001), 242–67.

[18] Hair, *Regent Square*, 39.

[19] 'Caledonian Church', 4.

[20] 'No. XII. The Rev. Edward Irving, M.A. Late Minister of the National Scotch Church', *Annual Biography and Obituary* 20 (1836), 138–56, at 143; cf. 'Caledonian Church', 4.

chapel could cope with, and in the spring a proposal was revived to build a new and larger sanctuary, worthy of being called 'the National Scotch Church'. Robertson (who, with William Hamilton, later to become Irving's brother-in-law, and Dinwiddie, had been a prime mover in bringing Irving to London) had mooted such a project early in 1822, before Irving had settled; whilst the need to accommodate the burgeoning congregation was one factor which led to its being taken up again, another was the concern for the spiritual welfare of Scotsmen in London, which Irving shared to the full. By December 1822, the elders were actively considering the project.[21]

At a meeting of the congregation on 19 May 1823, therefore, it was unanimously resolved to build a new church, which would be part of the Church of Scotland, and to begin receiving subscriptions towards the cost. The letter announcing this was accompanied by an 'Address' (signed by Irving and Dinwiddie as senior elder, but probably drafted by Irving) which explained the need for a building on the magnificent scale: at least 100,000 Scots and their descendants were resident in the London area, but under 5,000 of them were attached to any Scottish church. They were unlikely to join English churches due to their early religious training, so they tended to neglect religion altogether. Many who spent part of the year in London either attended no place of worship or returned north with a love for forms of religion which Scotland had never approved of. The aim was to build a church which would attract first-rank ministers, but it was also hoped that the higher ranks of society could thus be 'retained in the communion of our Church'.[22]

A piece of ground was purchased for £1,500 in Regent Square; this had been laid out early in 1820, but the first houses were not built until 1829.[23] An advertisement in *The Times* for 27 February 1824 invited designs for a church to accommodate 1,800. The winning design was set aside, however (to the architect's annoyance), because although it had been suited to the church's financial resources, the representatives of the Highland Society (which had been so closely involved with the cause's origins) wanted a grander building, which would reflect well on Scotland as a nation. They therefore chose a design by William Tite, later to achieve fame through the station buildings he designed for the London and South Western Railway. It had a frontage modelled on the west end of York Minster, with two towers rising a hundred feet; schools were to be added at a later stage.[24] This was to saddle the congregation with a financial burden which took many years to discharge and which required the publication of several appeals for funds.[25]

---

[21] Hair, *Regent Square*, 45–8.

[22] London, LMA, LMA/4358/C/002/3, Printed letter announcing the decision to build a new church, 19 May 1823, in a scrap book of items relating to the Caledonian Chapel and the National Scotch Church.

[23] H. V. Molesworth Roberts, '"Regent Square" The Cathedral of English Presbyterianism', *JPHSE* 10 (1952–5), 54–8, at 56.

[24] Anon., 'New Scotch Church for the Rev. E. Irving', *The Mirror*, no. 98 (14 August 1824).

[25] Hair, *Regent Square*, 49–50, 53.

On 1 July 1824, the foundation stone for the new building was laid by the Earl of Breadalbane, deputising for the Duke of Clarence and St Andrews, who was indisposed.[26] After prayer, Irving delivered an address. Under the stone were buried a vase, a glass plate, and a bottle. The plate was inscribed with 1 Kings 8.27[27] (in Hebrew), 1 Peter 2.6[28] (in English), and an English inscription commemorating the event. The bottle contained a list of subscribers to the building fund, and an account of the church with the names of its office-bearers. No less than 1,700 admission tickets to the ceremony were sold.[29] Carlyle went along, but 'Of the Address, which was going on when we arrived, I could hear nothing, such the confusing crowd and the unfavourable locality (a muddy chaos of rubbish and excavations, Irving and the actors shut off from us by a circle of rude bricklayers' planks): but I well remember Irving's glowing face, streaming hair, and deeply-moved tones, as he spoke'.[30]

Irving's sermon, on 'The Spiritual and national Benefits resulting from the Erection of a New Church' (1 Chronicles 29.1–19), demonstrated his deep though not uncritical attachment to the Kirk.[31] He explained that the new building would be attached to the Church of Scotland, and was to be called 'National' because it was 'for a sign to our nation, and for the gathering together of the scattered people of our nation'.[32] Foreshadowing later works which would manifest his unease with the Westminster Confession, he praised the Kirk's sixteenth-century foundation documents, the Scots Confession (1560), and the two Books of Discipline (1560, 1578):

> The Westminster Confession of Faith, and the Assembly's Catechism were approved and appointed to be used by our churches; and every candidate for the ministry is now required to subscribe the same. But we have a confession of faith a century older than that, with two books of discipline for the regulation of the church; which are much more to my taste and feeling; and which contain the exact spirit of the founders of our church, and of the Reformation.[33]

---

[26] Lord Breadalbane had invited the Irvings to dinner on their honeymoon: Thomas Carlyle, *Reminiscences*, ed. C. E. Norton (London: J. M. Dent, 1932), 240.

[27] 'But will God indeed dwell on the earth? behold, the heaven and heaven of heavens cannot contain thee; how much less this house that I have builded?'

[28] 'Wherefore also it is contained in the scripture, Behold I lay in Sion a chief corner stone, elect, precious: and he that believeth on him shall not be confounded.'

[29] Hair, *Regent Square*, 331–3, taken from a report in *The Times*.

[30] Carlyle, *Reminiscences*, 258.

[31] Edward Irving, *Thirty Sermons ... Preached during the First Three Years of his Residence in London: From the Accurate Notes of Mr. T. Oxford, Short-Hand Writer* (London: John Bennett, 1835), 117–26. According to Irving's assistant from 1830-2, David Brown, the name was chosen because Irving could not bear to be regarded as a Dissenter: David Brown, 'Personal Reminiscences of Edward Irving', *The Expositor*, 3rd series, 6 (1887), 216–28, 257–73, at 218.

[32] Irving, *Thirty Sermons*, 124.

[33] Ibid., 121.

His unease – perhaps as yet only half-conscious – is also evident from his comment that whilst his church rejected Arminianism, he refused to call its doctrine Calvinistic, because they took no man's name, because it was unlike what was being preached in England as Calvinism, and because when the Church of Scotland was founded Calvin was known as a preacher and not as a system builder. Elsewhere, however, he not only upheld Calvinistic doctrines – such as the election of individuals to salvation, the covenant of grace through which the blessings won by Christ become the enjoyment of believers, and the perseverance of true believers – but also defended the Calvinist reformers.[34]

* * *

Not everyone approved of Irving's meteoric rise to popularity. One reviewer's pen ran away with him:

> All London is at present afflicted with an epidemic frenzy, the nidus of which is the Caledonian Chapel in Hatton Garden. A Scotch Presbyterian Preacher has succeeded in propagating a mania which threatens, for a time at least, to make dreadful inroads on the sanity of the British Metropolis. ... Never, in truth, was there any madness like this. It has radiated to the whole circumference of society, and infected all classes. Lord Liverpool has become crazy, Mr Canning has been addled, Sir James Mackintosh has been astonished, and the sternness of Brougham transformed into the meekness of a new-born babe ... The eloquence of Orator Irving, like the breath of the Simoom, or the stroke of death, has levelled all distinctions. There ... may be seen, side by side, cheek for jowl, the Whig and the Tory, the High-Churchman and the Sectary, the infidel and the true believer ...[35]

More soberly, Carlyle was convinced that popularity was bad for Irving:

> On the whole our friend's mind seems to have improved but little since he left us. He [is as] full as ever of a certain hearty unrefined good-will, for which I honour him as I have always done: his faculties also have been quickened in the hot-bed of Hatton Garden, but affectation and vanity have grown up as rankly as other worthier products. It does me ill to see a strong and generous spirit distorting itself into a thousand foolish shapes; putting wilfully on the fetters of a thousand prejudices, very weak tho' very sanctified; dwindling with its own consent from a true and manly figure into some thing far too like a canting preacher of powerful sermons. He mistakes too: this popularity is different from fame.[36]

However, the fashion for hearing Irving soon passed. Thereafter, admission was still by ticket, but the upper ranks no longer came. According to Carlyle, their presence had induced him to think 'That Christian Religion was to be a truth again,

---

[34] e.g. *CW*, 3.75–8.

[35] Anon., 'Irving's Four Orations, and Argument in Nine Parts', *Edinburgh Magazine* 13 (1823), 214–18, at 214.

[36] *CL*, 2.460–1: Carlyle to Jane Welsh, 22 October 1823.

not a paltry form, and to rule the world, – he, unworthy, even he the chosen instrument!' He believed that Irving never gave up this hope, even when it had been blasted, and that this was the key to understanding his later course,[37] but in so saying he misunderstood his friend. The Sunday following the laying of the foundation stone of his new church, Irving referred to the peril ensuring from the congregation's popularity with those of rank and dignity; this they had endured for the spiritual benefit of those who seldom heard the word; but it was not good for being built together as a church.[38]

Whilst many came simply to observe the 'Irving phenomenon', and would in time desert the Caledonian Chapel for newer excitements, he continued to draw crowds wherever he was announced to preach. There were not lacking those who had been affected by his ministry: Isabella told her mother that many had testified that his preaching and his conduct of other parts of worship, had been blessed to turning them from darkness to light (a biblical metaphor drawn from Acts 26.18, and commonly used to denote an evangelical experience of conversion).[39] At each communion service (held twice a year), numbers of new communicants were received, each of whom Irving would have interviewed privately in order to ascertain their spiritual condition. It would appear that he used these communion sabbaths to preach evangelistically. For example, in an undated but early sermon on 'Christ the Propitiation' (from Romans 3.25), he explained that forgiveness meant nothing to the irreligious, or those who rest in the performance of their religious duties. It was for those who knew their sinful condition. He concluded, therefore, with an evangelistic appeal.[40]

Irving clearly had a pastoral concern to apply an evangelical understanding of the Gospel to the spiritual needs of those he met, but was determined from the start to avoid becoming a party man: 'For myself I am resolved to thrust my head into none of their cabals, but to join myself to my people, and walk straight forward in the path of honesty and truth … … … in all this city I find not one body whose maxims I could heartily go into'.[41] This was undoubtedly a factor in his relative unpopularity among Evangelicals, and it was made worse by his tendency to criticise them in his published sermons.[42] Even before his theological creativity began to blossom, he was frustrated with what he saw as a lack of content in contemporary Evangelicalism. After meeting Sir Thomas Baring and Wilberforce, he wrote them off as 'essentially stupid people, blighted with a loss of faculties, and an overgrowth of prosing'. Evangelicalism, Irving alleged, 'makes converts, but knows not what to

---

[37] Carlyle, *Reminiscences*, 254.
[38] *CW*, 3.380.
[39] Isabella Irving to Mrs Martin, 24 December 1823 (in private hands).
[40] Irving, *Thirty Sermons*, 49–57.
[41] NCL, Chalmers MSS, CHA 4.21.5: Irving to Chalmers, 20 July 1822.
[42] Another factor was doubtless his failure to use accepted terminology, and the tendency on occasion to present the gospel in a way which could be understood as laying down a new law rather than offering a way to salvation which was not based on law-keeping: cf. *CW*, 4.146–8.

make of its converts when they are made.' In a sermon preached to the Hibernian Society in May 1825, he warned:

> to the Evangelical body of the Church of England, which I did once look upon as a star in the gloom, and to the spiritual of all churches and sects ... , I have this to say, that if they will preach less a dogmatical, and more a personal Gospel; that is, present the persons of the Godhead, thus purposing, thus speaking, and thus acting, for men, rather than the abstract purpose, word, and action, if they will go about to separate a church from the worldly mass by preserving the sacraments, those bulwarks of the visible church, full of meaning, and pure in application, as far as man can preserve them, the Lord may be pleased to make them the bearers of his standard; but if not, (and faint, faint are my hopes,) if they go about to court the favour of princes and prelates, and put their trust in their growing numbers, or in their Shibboleths of shallowest doctrine, or in their favourite preachers and approved books, then let them mark that it was spoken and said unto them by one that loves them much, though him they have little loved, that they also shall die away like an untimely birth, and bring forth no fruit of reformation to the land, and shall be cast out with that general casting out of the Gentile church which is now at hand ...[43]

Not surprisingly, he felt somewhat isolated, as he had done in Scotland, although he was sustained by the love of his flock. Many saw his aloofness as evidence of conceit; even his aunt in Dumfries, Irving told Chalmers, was sending him a book on humility in an attempt to cure his alleged vainglory![44]

Yet he could be contemplated as a possible successor to the evangelical Robert Gordon, a friend who was minister of Hope Park Chapel in Newington, Edinburgh.[45] In the spring of 1825 a deputation waited on Irving to inquire whether he would be willing to accept a call. Over the next couple of months he evidently gave the matter protracted thought, and in a letter to his wife early in July he asks her advice. He feels that London can offer no home 'either to our family or my ministrations, and all the love of my people cannot make it a home'. The Scots have not returned to the church in numbers as he had hoped, and he would have liked to do battle with the anti-Christian forces which he saw as headquartered in Edinburgh, but he recognizes that leaving London would break many hearts, disperse the flock, and destroy the prospects of the proposed national church.[46] A meeting of the congregation on 14 July deputed the elders to convey to him their deep desire that he would remain, in response to which he wrote a letter two days later setting out the arguments on each side. In it he assured his congregation that he intended to stay; among the reasons he

---

[43] Edward Irving, 'The Cause and the Remedy of Ireland's Evil Condition', in *Sermons, Lectures, and Occasional Discourses* (3 vols, London: R.B. Seeley & W. Burnside, 1828), 3.1224–5.

[44] Chalmers MSS, CHA 4.26.59: Irving to Chalmers, 10 March 1823.

[45] *Fasti*, 1.61: online at http://www.dwalker.pwp.blueyonder.co.uk/Fasti%20Web%20pages/p.%2061%20St%20Giles.htm, accessed 19 May 2009.

[46] Oliphant, *Life*, 1.231, 236–8.

gave were their assurance of support for him in his labours; his belief that he had not preached the whole of his message; a sense that the members of the Kirk were in the worst spiritual condition of any group in London; and the love which the congregation had shown for him, his family and his ministry. But he maintains his independence by reserving the right to move elsewhere should God call him to do so.[47]

* * *

In spite of Irving's ministerial idiosyncracies, Carlyle began in time to think that his hope of better things for his friend was being fulfilled. As he wrote to his brother,

> I think him much more pleasant than when we last met: he has begun to see that there is nothing supernatural in his situation; he is leaner and in weaker health, so his spirits are less ebullient, and the honest practical substantial expressions of his intellect and heart have again got uppermost. His popularity without being furious as it once was is still great, long rows of coaches crowd daily to his sooty-looking meagre chapel; nor are ladies of rank wanting among the weekly applicants for tickets of admission. However he is ceasing to be a Lion – and I trust becoming something humbler and more abiding.[48]

The key, Carlyle felt, was Irving's recognition that 'he must content himself with patient well-doing and liberal tho' not immoderate success; not taking the world by one fierce onslaught, but by patient and continued sapping and mining as others do'.[49] In this, as we shall see, he misread his friend's ability to adopt a more conciliatory approach to ministry. In the next chapter, we shall see how his confrontational style affected the reception of his first published volume of sermons.

---

[47] Irving to the members and office-bearers of the Caledonian Church, 16 July 1825. My thanks to Kirkcaldy Museum and Art Galleries for supplying me with a photocopy of this letter. See also James Simpson, 'J. G. S. Journals 1806 to 1830', 14 July 1825, and Irving's reply of 16 July to the Edinburgh deputation: NLS, MS 1001, fols 119–20.
[48] *CL*, 3.90: Carlyle to John A. Carlyle, 24 June 1824.
[49] Ibid. 3.167: Carlyle to James Carlyle sr, 4 October 1824.

CHAPTER 8

Irving as a Preacher, 1822–5

In this chapter we shall take a break from tracing Irving's life history, in order to examine his preaching during the early years in London. This enables us to look at a neglected aspect of his theology – his social thought – and to explore what part was played by his preaching in making him such a phenomenon in 1823. Assessments of his preaching have varied widely, A. L. Drummond calling him 'the greatest preacher between Whitefield and Spurgeon',[1] while Jane Welsh described him as 'that stupendous ass the Orator'.[2] Various aspects of Irving have been studied in depth, but his preaching has rarely attracted the attention it deserves.[3] Yet, in Callum Brown's phrase, the sermon was 'the acid test of the Presbyterian minister',[4] and the vocation to preach shaped Irving's theology. On trial for heresy in 1833, he asserted 'I speak for the sanctification of my flock'. What he believed and taught was shaped by what he believed God had called him to do – to preach, and in so doing to break fresh ground.

Irving's ministry has been divided into four phases: moral, doctrinal, millenarian, and charismatic.[5] These overlap to a considerable extent, but the scheme is still helpful in charting the changing emphases of his preaching. The period covered by this chapter falls under the first heading. The main source for Irving's sermons during this period is his *Collected Writings*, edited by his nephew, Gavin Carlyle. Comparison of some of them with the original published versions leads me to believe that Carlyle was in fact a very faithful editor.[6] Apart from Irving's own

---

[1] Andrew L. Drummond, 'Edward Irving: Rise and Fall of a Prophet', *The Times*, 7 December 1934.

[2] *CL*, 3.69: Jane Welsh to Carlyle, 20 May 1824.

[3] Perhaps the best exception is Andrew Landale Drummond, *Edward Irving and his Circle: Including some Consideration of the 'Tongues' Movement in the Light of Modern Psychology* (London: James Clarke, [1937]), ch. 4.

[4] Callum G. Brown, 'Rotavating the Kailyard: Re-imagining the Scottish "Meenister" in Discourse and the Parish State since 1707', in Nigel Aston and Matthew Cragoe, eds, *Anticlericalism in Britain c. 1500–1914* (Stroud: Sutton, 2001), 138–58, at 140.

[5] R. Herbert Story, 'Edward Irving' in Anon., ed., *Scottish Divines 1505–1872* (Edinburgh: Macniven and Wallace, 1883), 225–72, at 239.

[6] This is corroborated by family correspondence from the period when Gavin Carlyle was working on his uncle's writings; he was assisted by Irving's daughter Isabella (1834–78) and her husband, the historian S. R. Gardiner (1829–1902). They supplied him with the original manuscripts left in their charge by Irving's son Martin (1831–1912) when he emigrated to Australia in 1856: S. R. Gardiner to Martin Irving, 25

writings, there are two other important sources. A volume of *Thirty Sermons* appeared just after his death; these had been taken down in shorthand, and many appear in other locations. Whilst they usually give a good indication of the content, they are perhaps rather more polished than the original discourses. In spite of the claim that all were preached during his first three years in London, a number can be assigned to later years. Reports of a number of Irving's sermons also appeared in a weekly publication designed for sermon-tasters, *The Pulpit*. Again, we cannot treat these reports as completely accurate, but they do give a fair idea of the content of the sermons.

With the aid of these sources, and of references in his correspondence and in Mrs Oliphant's *Life*, it is possible to reconstruct Irving's preaching programme to a fair degree, and so to gain an idea of his primary concerns; this may help those who wish to trace his theological development in more detail than a biography can do. Between 1822 and 1825, it appears that he preached the following series:

1822–3	Morning series of sermons on Peter's discourse to Cornelius (Acts 10), lasting over a year[7]
1822–4	Evening series of lectures on the opening chapters of Luke, which apparently reached the beginning of Luke 5 by Spring 1824; it was continued (with breaks) until at least 1829, by which time he appears to have completed Luke 8[8]
1823 Spring	Evening series of sermons on judgement to come, later published[9]
1823 Spring	(Evening?) series of sermons on the Christian life[10]
1823 Summer	'On John the Baptist' (fifteen lectures)[11]

September 1863 (in private hands). Gardiner had the right of veto on all items for inclusion as well as that of seeing and approving the proof pages: S. R. Gardiner to Martin Irving, 19 January 1864 (in private hands).

The sermons which comprise Volume 2 were first issued as *Sermons and Lectures* (London: Alexander Strahan, 1864).

[7] *CW*, 3.504.

[8] He referred to this series in a letter to Mrs Welsh of 6 December 1822: *CL*, 2.416–17n. Some were published in his *Thirty Sermons*, others in *The Pulpit* and *The Preacher*.

[9] *For the Oracles of God, Four Orations: For Judgment to Come, an Argument, in Nine Parts* (London: T. Hamilton, 1823). One preached on 6 April 1823 (on Matt. 25.46) was reported in *The Pulpit*, no. 1 (23 April 1823), 3–5, and described by the reporter as 'one of a series of sermons of uncommon excellence, which Mr. Irving has delivered on the Last Judgment' (ibid. 4).

[10] The first, on James 1.18, was preached on 11 May 1823: *The Pulpit*, no. 6 (28 May 1823), 88–9.

1822–3?	'On Intellectual Life' (two sermons) and 'On Moral Life' (four sermons)[12]
1823?	'The Temptation' (five lectures)[13]
1823–4	'On Prayer' (fourteen discourses)[14]
1823–4	'On Praise' (four discourses)[15]
1823–4?	'On Family and Social Religion' (nine sermons)[16]
1825 Summer	'Homilies on Baptism'[17]
1825 November	Preaching on Wednesdays from John 14, and expounding Hebrews on Sunday mornings
1825 Nov.–Dec.	'Idolatry' (seven sermons)[18]
1825 Nov. onwards	Sermons on the Incarnation[19]

Preaching on the Sunday following the laying of the foundation stone of his new church, Irving admitted that before he knew what the congregation could bear, he had kept to the offer of salvation; 'We argued the insufficiency of an intellectual and moral, the degradation of a sensual, and the necessity of a spiritual life.' Although apprehensive about moving on to the privileges of God's people, his reception was such that he now felt full liberty to declare God's mind. 'It is the most glorious privilege of an intellectual and spiritual man to have an audience before whom he may display all his convictions of truth.'[20] A measure of this development can be discerned in the above table.

Irving's choice of topics seems unusually well-balanced and wide-ranging expository fare for an evangelical preacher of this period, but what arrested people was his pulpit manner, his preaching style, and the pointed nature of his application. He was noteworthy for his straight talking about the Last Judgement, which, according to one reporter, had rarely been treated in 'such an awakening yet rational

---

[11] *CW*, 2.1–187. The fifth lecture was delivered in July 1823 (cf. *Thirty Sermons*, 9–18). This series and that on 'The Temptation' may have formed part of the series on Luke.

[12] *CW*, 4.100–77; I date these sermons to this period because of their approach, style, intended audience, and relative lack of theological content.

[13] Ibid. 2.189–243.

[14] Ibid. 3.1–162.

[15] A series on 'Social Worship' (probably the same one) was noted as ongoing in *The Pulpit*, no. 46 (4 March 1824), 241.

[16] *CW*, 3.215–339.

[17] Published in 1827; cf. *CW*, 2.247–434.

[18] Ibid. 4.3–99; cf. Oliphant, *Life*, 122.

[19] Later published as *Sermons, Lectures, and Occasional Discourses*, Vol. I: *The Doctrine of the Incarnation Opened, in Six Sermons* (London: R. B. Seeley & W. Burnside, 1828); cf. *CW*, 5.1–446, 563–7. For the dating, cf. Oliphant, *Life*, 219–20.

[20] *CW*, 3.378.

way'.²¹ Furthermore, he was not afraid to refer to contemporary figures by name in criticizing their views, a practice which led many to attend to see who would be the next to feel the weight of his wrath. But when he was not trying to tailor his presentation to the opinion-formers, and was speaking more as a pastor to his flock, he was capable of sustained exposition. This is seen to its best in his series of lectures on John the Baptist, which were also marked by repeated and frank evangelistic appeals. Their interest lies partly in the way that he expounded John's character and ministry as a paradigm for modern ministers, 'the type of every herald of salvation'.²² Indeed, he saw himself as a John the Baptist figure:²³

> The Baptist's office is gone much into disuse – so much so, that had I not a flock to feed and edify in holiness, as well as an audience to convert, I would willingly forego the preaching of mercy, address myself to topics of warning, expostulation, and denouncement, and leave the people to their chance of peace and comfort, which, it seemeth to me, they could not miss, go whither their feet might carry them to the house of God.²⁴

Because of its directness and its grounding in experience of ministry among the poor in Glasgow and London, Irving's preaching also introduced a note of social critique which was none too common in contemporary evangelical pulpits. One of his earliest biographers wrote: 'that generally forgotten function of the Christian ministry, social censorship, goes far to account for his unparalleled power of attraction and influence; for ailing men, though but vaguely conscious of their maladies, and not in earnest about their cure, will delight in having them described'.²⁵

Whilst Irving always got on well with the poor on a personal level, he did not often aim his sermons at their needs. His motivation was to reach those who were not being touched by existing preaching.²⁶ For example, it may have been during 1822-3 that he preached six sermons 'On Intellectual Life' and 'On Moral Life'. These were addressed to men of understanding, attempting to persuade them that Christianity was not anti-intellectual but rather set the intellect free to realize its true potential. To reach such an audience, it was 'necessary that the preachers of religion should be strong in intellect as well as spirit, that they may constrain the wisdom

---

²¹ *The Pulpit*, no. 1 (23 April 1823), 4.

²² *CW*, 2.24, cf. 181.

²³ When a stained glass window commemorating Irving was installed in St Mungo's Cathedral, Glasgow, in 1861, he was represented as John the Baptist; and the Catholic Apostolic Church has seen him as fulfilling such a ministry in relation to its own appearance.

²⁴ *CW*, 2.163.

²⁵ Washington Wilks, *Edward Irving: An Ecclesiastical and Literary Biography* (London: William Freeman, 1854), 43.

²⁶ As he wrote to Jane Welsh, 'I meditate a work upon the alienation of clever men from their Maker': Drummond, *Irving*, 79: Irving to Jane Welsh, 9 September 1822.

and understanding and knowledge of the times to their proper occupation of glorifying the living God'.[27]

One occasion when he did speak directly to the poor, however, was on 24 March 1824, when he preached at the opening of a new Church of Scotland in Birmingham, choosing for his text Genesis 3.17-19.[28] Taking as his title, 'The Curse as it hath degraded Man through excess of Bodily Labour, and the Deliverance from the same', he presented the Gospel as the true way of ameliorating the condition of the working poor. Human beings, he explained, were distinguished from animals by possessing understanding, reason, and conscience. Each of these faculties found employment in Paradise, but since the Fall work saw them subjected to the animal nature, and in time annihilated. Irving showed the change which the Fall brought about in the condition of Adam and Eve; the effects of excessive bodily labour; and the remedy for these evils. Excessive labour

> First, ... ground them down with toils, than which nothing tends more to the humiliation of the mind. Secondly, it directed the powers of the understanding to objects terminating in sensual enjoyment. Thirdly, it directed to things seen and temporal the noble feelings of the mind, hope, desire, ambition, and built upon them pride, vanity, envy, and every evil passion; by which means the whole soul became worldly and carnal, as we find it, and the higher faculties in which man had his delight were altogether dead ...[29]

To rekindle the spiritual life of the poor, it was necessary to go a long way in simplifying things (e.g. by using concrete rather than abstract terms), because their only concern was with physical things; in spirit, such materialism was also found among the better classes.

As for work itself, 'it is not in the fact of labouring, but in that for which we labour, that the evil consists'.[30] Workers needed a higher objective, which could ennoble their labour (he cited Scotland as an example, because its labouring classes sought to provide for their children's education and their family's independence). Merely to lessen the amount of labour would not ultimately improve their condition:

> ... simply to call upon the people to relax in their industry, and to lay down their laborious work of cherishing this niggard earth, and its raw productions, and thereby think that he improveth their condition, is truly, first, to diminish the

---

[27] *CW*, 4.113. As with many of his early sermons, these portray the truths of religion and divine revelation not as mysterious but as easy to grasp; the ethos is reminiscent of the seventeenth-century English Latitudinarians or the eighteenth-century Scottish Moderates.

[28] Edward Irving, *Sermons, Lectures and Occasional Discourses*. Vol.III: *On Subjects National and Prophetical, seven Discourses* (London: R. B. Seeley & W. Burnside), 1025-93; cf. the abbreviated report of part of the sermon in *The Pulpit*, no. 52 (15 April 1824), 337-41.

[29] *Sermons*, 3.1050-1.

[30] Ibid. 1062.

means which are possessed of health, contentment, and happiness; and, next, to injure that very condition of the people which he seeketh to amend. For industry and full occupation, are, we know, two of the best conditions for honesty and virtue. And idleness is the surest inlet to vice and profligacy; and though it be true that excessive labour brutalizes human nature, it is no less true that complete idleness brutalizes it more.[31]

Taking slavery as a case study, Irving asserted that St Paul did not do what a modern philanthropist would have done to ameliorate their condition, nor did he see the possibility of levelling consequences, such as some now feared, as an argument against preaching the Gospel to slaves. He did not attempt to civilize before Christianizing, as some were attempting to do overseas; neither did he interfere in civil questions (here Irving had in mind the advocates of the emancipation of slaves, and other social levellers). Nevertheless, social reform did follow because the Gospel transformed the attitudes of those who accepted it.

* * *

Whilst Irving's popularity as a preacher was undeniable, the reasons for it were harder to make out; as one journalist wrote, 'No one knows what to make of him.'[32] One writer has summarized them as his intellect, his oratory (this was an age which prized oratorical skill highly), his striking appearance, his pulpit bearing (Irving had what might be called a priestly conception of ministry), his well-modulated voice, and his reading of Scripture.[33] But his preaching excited strong and opposing reactions. *John Bull*, for example, described it as 'one of the most flagrant and disgusting pieces of HUMBUG which has ever been foisted upon the people of the metropolis' and expressed horror that 'those to whom we constitutionally look for the maintenance of our national institutions, flocking in crowds to listen to the ravings of presbyterian quackery', imploring them not to countenance defection from the Church of England by their presence. Condemning the fashion for preacher-hunting, the author continued:

> there is something so degrading, so theatrical, so laughable, and so contemptible, in the bustling and crowding to a Presbyterian chapel in Hatton Garden – scrambling, pushing, and squeezing for admission, with tickets, and the securing of

---

[31] Ibid. 1065–6.

[32] Anon., 'Memoir of the Rev. Edward Irving, A.M.', *European Magazine* 84 (1823), 291–3, at 292.

[33] John Hair, *Regent Square: Eighty Years of a London Congregation* (London: James Nisbet, 1899), 40. Cf. William Hazlitt's reference to the combination in Irving of superior intellect, 'uncommon height, a graceful figure and action, a clear and powerful voice, a striking, if not a fine face, a bold and fiery spirit, and a most portentous obliquity of vision': 'Rev. Mr. Irving', in idem, *The Spirit of the Age or Contemporary Portraits*, ed. E. D. Mackarness (2nd edn, Plymouth: Northcote House, 1991), 67–80, at 70.

places and ranging of carriages – for what? To hear a great, brawny Scotchman, with an accent as vulgar and abominable as HUME's, talk the most detestable nonsense that ever came from human lips.[34]

More positive was the writer Samuel Taylor Coleridge, who described him as 'the present Idol of the World of Fashion, the Revd. Mr. Irving, the super-Ciceronian, ultra-Demosthenic Pulpiteer of the Scotch Chapel'.[35] He was the greatest orator Coleridge had ever heard,[36] a verdict confirmed both by Canning and by other literary figures. Years later the essayist Thomas de Quincey recalled the 'unequalled splendour of appearance with which he convulsed all London at his first *debût*. He was, unquestionably, by many, many degrees, the greatest orator of our times.'[37] Another writer claimed that people used to ask each other 'have you heard Irving?' where they used to ask, 'were you at the opera last night?'[38] The Unitarian journalist William Hazlitt, in an article first published in 1824, commented that:

> Few circumstances show the prevailing and preposterous rage for novelty in a more striking point of view than the success of Mr. Irving's oratory. People go to hear him in crowds, and come away with a mixture of delight and astonishment. They go again to see if the effect will continue, and send others to try to find out the mystery; and in the noisy conflict between extravagant encomiums and splenetic objections, the true secret escapes observation – which is, that the whole thing is, nearly from beginning to end, a *transposition of ideas*.[39]

In other words, Irving's preaching attracted attention because in it he did things which one would not expect to be done in the pulpit, such as quoting Shakespeare, engaging with modern philosophers, and criticizing cabinet ministers.[40]

> He has, with an unlimited and daring licence, mixed the sacred and the profane together, the carnal and the spiritual man, the petulance of the bar with the dogmatism of the pulpit, the theatrical and the theological, the modern and the obsolete; – what wonder that this splendid piece of patchwork, splendid by contradiction and contrast, has delighted some and confounded others?[41]

Furthermore, 'He has found out the secret of attracting by repelling. Those whom he is likely to attack are curious to hear what he says of them: they go again, to show

---

[34] *John Bull*, no. 136 (20 July 1823), 228.

[35] S.T. Coleridge, *Collected Letters of Samuel Taylor Coleridge*, Vol. 5, ed. E. L. Griggs (Oxford: Clarendon Press, 1971), 280: Coleridge to Mrs Bent, 7 July 1823.

[36] Ibid. 286: Coleridge to Edward Coleridge, 23 July 1823.

[37] [T. de Quincey], 'Sketches of Life and Manners; from the Autobiography of an English Opium-Eater', *Tait's Edinburgh Magazine* 7 (1840), 629–37, at 631.

[38] 'Criticus', 'The Rev. Edward Irving', *European Magazine* 84 (1823), 45–8, at 47.

[39] Hazlitt, *Spirit of the Age*, 68.

[40] Ibid. 68–9.

[41] Ibid. 69.

that they do not mind it.'⁴² His appearance was no mean factor in his success: 'his imposing figure and dignified manner enable him to hazard sentiments or assertions that would be fatal to others ... Take a cubit from his stature, and his whole manner resolves itself into an impertinence.'⁴³ On the other hand, some found with his squint,⁴⁴ and he acquired the nickname 'Doctor Squintum', which had also been applied to George Whitefield – testimony, perhaps, to the more theatrical aspects of each preacher's delivery.⁴⁵

Some commented that his voice was good but not his action or style.⁴⁶ His manner also came in for scrutiny, some claiming it bordered on the theatrical:⁴⁷ according to one writer, when Irving prayed, 'his eyes were forcibly closed; his mouth was drawn into an expression so pompous as almost to be farcical; the enunciation was studied and stilted to the last degree; the gesture was ungraceful throughout, and often vehement, and the matter was a succession of scriptural phrases linked together by language, aiming not very happily at the same style'⁴⁸ – a strikingly opposed verdict to that which attracted Canning. Dorothy Wordsworth hated his rhetoric, describing the portrayal of the joys of heaven in the *Orations* as '*worse* than Methodist rant'. But she wanted to probe the secret of his popularity, so she went to see for herself.⁴⁹ Her verdict was prescient, in view of his early death:

> His person is very fine in my opinion and his action often graceful – though often far otherwise – his voice fine – reading excellent, and, while he keeps his feelings under, nothing can be finer than his manner of preaching – but it is grievous to see him wasting his powers – as he does in the latter part (especially) of his discourses – the more grievous as it is plain he must sink under such exertions while yet a young man. When I say *wasting* his powers you must understand that I mean that with less effort the effect on his hearers would be more beneficial. He wholly wants

---

⁴² Ibid. 72. For some, his boldness in this respect was to be commended: James Fleming, *The Life and Writings of the Rev. Edward Irving, M.A.* (London: Knight and Lacey, 1823), 34.

⁴³ Hazlitt, *Spirit of the Age*, 75.

⁴⁴ *John Bull*, no. 136 (20 July 1823), 228.

⁴⁵ Harry S. Stout, *The Divine Dramatist: George Whitefield and the Rise of Modern Evangelicalism* (Grand Rapids, MI: Eerdmans, 1991), 244.

A ballad under this title achieved a measure of currency: *John Bull*, no. 137 (27 July 1823), 237, repr. in Samuel Palmer, *St. Pancras; being Antiquarian, Topographical, and Biographical Memoranda, relating to the extensive Metropolitan Parish of St. Pancras, Middlesex: With some Account of the Parish from its Foundation* (London: Samuel Palmer, 1870), 179–80.

⁴⁶ 'Criticus', 'Irving', 245–6.

⁴⁷ 'The Rev. Edw. Irving, A.M.', *The Examiner*, no. 807 (14 July 1823), 453.

⁴⁸ Anon., *Trial of the Rev. Edward Irving, M.A.: A Cento of Criticism* (London: E. Brain, 1823), 26–7.

⁴⁹ Ernest De Selincourt, *Dorothy Wordsworth: A Biography* (Oxford: Clarendon, 1933), 363.

taste and judgment – but one essential I give him full credit for – *sincerity* – without which no preaching that would address the feelings can be efficacious.[50]

* * *

So what was Irving saying? To answer that, we can analyse the book which provoked so much reaction (although it has been neglected in recent writing on Irving), *For the Oracles of God, four Orations: For Judgment to Come, an Argument, in nine Parts.* The first edition appeared in July 1823.[51] In February Carlyle had written to a friend: 'Have you heard of his sermon-book? It is coming out presently. I doubt not it will cause the ear to tingle'.[52] Carlyle had good reason for his opinion.

The first part, the *Orations*, consisted of four sermons on John 5.39, 'Search the Scriptures'. The second and third may well have been preached shortly before he left Scotland.[53] The nine sermons of the second part, the *Argument*, took as their motto: 'God commandeth all men to repent: because he hath appointed a day, in the which he will judge the world in righteousness', drawn from Acts 17.30–1. These were most probably preached in London during the spring of 1823. What is interesting is that he thought of publishing them even before he had preached them; in January, he informed Chalmers that he was about to publish a book in three parts (which might in future become three books): four orations on God's oracles; an argument in five parts on judgement to come (as published, there were nine); and six or seven lectures on the Incarnation (this may have been the germ of the series which was later published as *The Doctrine of the Incarnation Opened in Six Sermons*). He intended

---

[50] Ibid. 364.

[51] The original preface is dated in the third edition, but not in the first: Irving, *For the Oracles of God* (3rd edn, London: T. Hamilton, 1824), xxii.

[52] *CL*, 2.288: Thomas Carlyle to James Johnston, [18 February 1823].

[53] In a letter to Mrs Welsh written in mid-1823, Irving requests the loan of the four sermons he left behind as a parting gift a year earlier: Virginia Surtees, *Jane Welsh Carlyle* (Wilton, Salisbury: Michael Russell, 1986), 45. According to Jane, he was already intending to get them printed when he gave them to her mother: *CL*, 2.416–17 (Jane Welsh to Carlyle, 19 August [1823]). He preached twice on this text at Haddington about 1822 (John Martine, *Reminiscences of the Royal Burgh of Haddington*, Edinburgh: John Menzies, 1883, 204), and these are probably two of the sermons in question. He had also been prescribed a 'popular sermon' on the same text as part of his trials for ordination. In his letter to Mrs Welsh of 6 December 1822, he had told her: 'Since I came to London I have preached in the Evening lectures on St. Luke, and the people are longing to have them published – and so I have devoted the profits of a first edition to the new Church, and as I intend introducing the new volume with a discourse on the preparation for reading the scriptures, and concluding it with a discourse on the advantage of obeying them, I use the liberty of requesting from you the copy I gave you of the four sermons': *CL*, 2.416–17n. In the event, he did not publish his lectures on Luke (though some appeared elsewhere), but added what became the *Argument*.

to dedicate each to an honoured friend, explaining the need for new forms of theological literature.[54]

The most controversial part of the work was the preface:

> It hath appeared to the Author of this book, from more than ten years' meditation upon the subject, that the chief obstacle to the progress of divine truth over the minds of men, is the want of its being properly presented to them. In this Christian country there are, perhaps, nine-tenths of every class who know nothing at all about the applications and advantages, of the single truths of revelation, or of revelation taken as a whole; and what they do not know, they cannot be expected to reverence or obey. This ignorance, in both the higher and the lower orders, of Religion ... , is not so much due to the want of inquisitiveness on their part, as to the want of a sedulous and skilful ministry on the part of those to whom it is entrusted.[55]

So, preachers 'must discover new vehicles for conveying the truth as it is in Jesus into the minds of the people; poetical, historical, scientific, political, and sentimental vehicles ... They prepare men for teaching gipsies, for teaching bargemen, for teaching miners; men who understand their ways of conceiving and estimating truth; why not train ourselves for teaching imaginative men and political men, and legal men and medical men?' Irving intended the book to provide examples of two such approaches; the oration, 'the best vehicle for addressing the minds of men which the world hath seen, far beyond the sermon, of which the very name hath learned to inspire drowsiness and tedium', and the argument, along the lines of ancient apologies for the Christian faith.[56]

The 'Orations' focused on the Scriptures, and how to benefit from reading them. Although neglected, the Scriptures were nothing less than the words of God himself. In contrast with contemporary neglect or formality, revelation demanded 'A DUE PREPARATION FOR RECEIVING IT. A DILIGENT ATTENTION TO IT WHILE IT IS DISCLOSING. A STRICT OBSERVANCE OF IT WHEN IT IS DELIVERED.'[57] What hindered the Bible from being efficacious in changing lives? Irving was sure that Scripture does not suffer from any shortcoming in itself.[58] The problem lay in the reader. As so often, he laid bare the evasions of his audience,

---

[54] Edinburgh, NCL, Chalmers MSS, CHA 4.21.1: Irving to Chalmers, 19 January 1822 [1823].

[55] Irving, *Orations*, v–vi.

[56] Ibid. vii–ix.

[57] Ibid. 7.

[58] In a sermon on James 1.18 delivered in May 1823, Irving criticized those who stressed the need of the Spirit's illumination in order to understand the Bible. Study of the Bible was the foundation of all spiritual knowledge. In his judgement, evangelical preachers too often portrayed it as a sealed book to all but the regenerate. So, instead of searching it, men waited for some impression from the Holy Spirit; but since the Bible was the '*legible Spirit*', if anyone wanted to understand it, they could: *The Pulpit*, no. 6 (28 May 1823), 88–9.

exploring why they were so reluctant to obey God's word. 'Obey the Scriptures or you perish' was his blunt message.[59] But he used the carrot as well as the stick; in the fourth oration, he summarized the benefits of obedience: 'the knowledge obtained; the life of heavenly enterprise begotten; and the eternal reward to be gained'.[60] In conclusion, he argued that crucial to winning back the nation was a better presentation of the Gospel;

> ... until advocates of religion do arise to make unhallowed poets, and undevout dealers in science, and intemperate advocates of policy, and all other pleaders before the public mind, give place, and know the inferiority of their various provinces to this of ours – till this most fatal error, that our subject is second-rate, be dissipated by a first-rate advocation of it – till we can shift these others into the back-ground of the great theatre of thought, by clear superiority in the treatment of our subject, we shall never see the men of understanding in this nation brought back to the fountains of living water ...[61]

The second part of the book was much longer. In the Dedication, he gave his aim as being 'to recover the great subject of Judgment to Come, from poetical visionaries on the one hand, and from religious rhapsodists on the other; and to place it upon the foundation of divine revelation, of human understanding, and the common good'.[62] In particular, he was responding to two recently published 'Visions of Judgment' by the Poet Laureate Robert Southey and by Lord Byron; the first was a sycophantic portrayal of the late king, George III, appearing before the bar of divine judgement, and the second a parody of it. In typically forthright style, Irving condemned them both as

> two most nauseous and unformed abortions, vile, unprincipled, and unmeaning – the one a brazen-faced piece of political cant, the other an abandoned parody of solemn judgment. Of which visionaries, I know not whether the self-confident tone of the one, or the ill-placed merriment of the other, displeaseth me the more. ... The men are limited in their faculties, for they, both of them, want the greatest of all faculties – to know the living God and stand in awe of his mighty power: with the one, blasphemy is virtue when it makes for loyalty; with the other, blasphemy is the food and spice of jest-making. Barren souls! – and is the land of Shakspeare and Spencer and Milton come to this! that it can procreate nothing but such profane spawn, and is content to exalt such blots and blemishes of manhood into ornaments of the age. Puny age! when religion and virtue and manly freedom have ceased from the character of those it accounteth noble. ... God send to [them] repentance, or else blast the powers they have abused so terribly; for if they repent not, they shall harp another strain at that scene they have sought to vulgarize.[63]

---

[59] Irving, *Orations*, 63.
[60] Ibid. 76.
[61] Ibid. 96.
[62] Ibid. 99.
[63] Ibid. 325–6.

Irving's work was intended as an apology (in the classical sense of a defence of Christian belief addressed to non-believers). His main contention was that:

> Man ... is made for responsibility, and for submitting himself to judgment, when all other methods fail of preserving the peace. This is the nature of man, wherever he is found and into whatever community he enters. God legislating for man hath adapted himself to this his nature, placing him under responsibility; yet taking every measure of his wisdom, and applying to every faculty of human nature by each kindly, noble method, to secure sweet harmony; putting off issues of judgment to the last, and not ringing the knell of doom until every other note and signal hath entirely failed to have effect.[64]

The work was thus 'a defence of men's responsibility to God, from the analogy of their responsibility to each other'.[65] To this end, he adopted an *ad hominem* approach, demonstrating to his hearers the mental and social benefits of adopting his views concerning divine judgement.

The directness of his approach was evident both from his portrayal of the Last Judgement and the plight of the damned (in a style whose debt to Milton is apparent to anyone who has read *Paradise Lost*), and from his defence of preaching about hell, when done in the right way:

> If ever hell were described in Scripture, as oft it is in an enthusiast's sermon, out of a fell delight in cleaving the general ear with horrid speech; if ever it was made like a torturing tool in the hands of angry priests, to torture the souls of those whose party or faction they hate, then let it be condemned and heard of no more; but if with sympathy and pity it be spoken as the sad decree gone forth against sin, and if forthwith, when it hath taken hold of the soul, recovery and restoration be preached; and a way to avoid its terrors and surmount its fears, and ascend to the bosom of God; then, I say, let it be discoursed of while there is one single creature upon earth who dotes and dreams upon its confines without any fear of its smothering and consuming effects upon the happiness and well-being of his soul.[66]

Ever his own man, he criticized the evangelical stress on the righteousness of Christ imputed to believers as their ground of acceptance before God:

> ... I am convinced, from the constant demand of the religious world for the preaching of faith and forgiveness, and their constant kicking against the preaching of Christian morals; the constant appetite for mercy, and disrelish of righteousness and judgment; or if righteousness, it be the constant demand that it should be the imputed righteousness of Christ, not our own personal righteousness; from these features of the evangelical part of men, I do greatly fear, nay, I am

---

[64] Ibid. 130.
[65] Wilks, *Irving*, 85.
[66] Irving, *Orations*, 424.

convinced that many of them are pillowing their hopes upon something else than the sanctification and changed life which the Gospel hath wrought.[67]

In fact, plenty of moderate Evangelicals would heartily have agreed with him, and the periodicals, in reviewing his book, did not disagree with this point. Another point where he considered evangelical preachers went astray was

> ... in giving too little weight to the word of God, which they hold to be a dead inefficient letter until the Spirit of God put meaning into its passages. ... Now I do not wish to go to war with the evangelical preachers, I love them so well; but I cannot help challenging them, why they preach as they wisely do, the truths of Christ crucified to the unregenerate, if so be the unregenerate can by no means lay hand upon any of these truths. ...
>
> Now, when I have often urged upon the Evangelical brethren the necessity of pressing their people to the word of God as a very mentor in all cases and conditions of life, and the folly of preaching them away from it, by casting clouds and darkness and mystery around its approach, ... they have always met me with this reply; If the book of God be intelligible to natural men, how come they to remain so ignorant of it and so disaffected to it? To this I answer, that they read it but little, many of them not at all; that when they do read it, they read it often for form's sake, ... or they read it for taste's sake ...; but if they read for edification's sake, to know God and Christ and human responsibility, then it never fareth to any reader to read in vain ...[68]

So, for Irving, 'the Word is the audible voice of the Spirit'; 'when it instructs, God instructs; when it intreats, God intreats; when it breathes tenderness, God breathes tenderness; when it offers, God offers; when it threatens, God threatens'.[69]

* * *

When Irving went into print, widely contrasting reactions were evident among reviewers. This may have been due in part to the fact that the volume was something of a curate's egg: 'We have seldom found, in a single volume, so much to praise and so much to blame as in the present.'[70] It was 'a strange mixture of beauties and faults', which would be of doubtful benefit to his reputation.[71] Many thought that he would have been better not to have published it. As one commentator put it, Irving was a speaker rather than a writer, and publication was 'one of the most injudicious and unfortunate measures he could have taken',[72] and indeed was likely to overthrow

---

[67] Ibid. 362–4.
[68] Ibid. 464–7.
[69] Ibid. 476–7.
[70] Review of *Orations*, *EM* n.s. 3 (1823), 419–21, at 419.
[71] *The Pulpit*, no. 17 (14 August 1823), 264.
[72] Fleming, *Irving*, 12; cf. Hazlitt's assertion that Irving's admirers would rather see and hear him than read him: 'the groundwork of his compositions is trashy and hackneyed, though set off by extravagant metaphors and an affected phraseology; that

the popularity which circumstances had given him.⁷³ However, the work went into its third edition before the end of the year.

One publication, *The Trial of the Rev. Edward Irving: A Cento of Criticism*, used the device of a trial, before the High Court of Common Sense, to represent the editors of a range of periodicals expressing their opinions of Irving and of one another.⁷⁴ Carlyle described it to Jane Welsh as 'something to make you and your Mother laugh till bed-time',⁷⁵ not least because of the caricatures which appeared in it. Five pulpit caricatures facing the title page were entitled: The Glance Penetrating; The Knock it into them; The Solemn Invocation; Solemn Invocation after another manner; The Crown All.⁷⁶ It ran to a fifth edition within a month,⁷⁷ and a tenth within two years, and serves as a passable compilation of published reactions to Irving's preaching, and in particular to the appearance of his *Orations*. Irving was indicted on the counts of being (i) ugly; (ii) a 'merry-andrew' (i.e. a clown or buffoon); (iii) a common quack; (iv) a common brawler; (v) a common swearer; (vi) of very common understanding; and (vii) following divisive courses, subversive of the order of his discipline and contrary to Christian fellowship and charity. He was convicted only of the last.⁷⁸

Many thought Irving able, but took objection to his antiquated style,⁷⁹ which some deemed affected and obscure.⁸⁰ The style, some thought, was linked to his belief that in the contemporary world 'whatever is, is wrong'.⁸¹ His chivalric language was deemed an inappropriate mode of addressing those who did not live in a time of turbulence like that of his heroes, the Covenanters.⁸² On the positive side, the *Sunday Times*, whilst acknowledging the defects of Irving's style and doubting whether it would be as influential as he hoped, approved of its 'vigour and manliness'.⁸³ Another paper praised his 'bold and fearless preaching, in the style and manner of the most purely intellectual age in England'.⁸⁴

---

without the turn of his head and the wave of his hand, his periods have nothing in them': *Spirit of the Age*, 77.

⁷³ Fleming, *Irving*, 37.

⁷⁴ The publication was modelled on a similar dissection of Henry Brougham in *The New Whig Guide: John Bull*, no. 144 (14 September 1823), 293.

⁷⁵ *CL*, 2.483: 29 November 1823.

⁷⁶ Anon., *Trial*, 30.

⁷⁷ Review of *Trial*, *New Evangelical Magazine* 9 (1823), 358–62, at 359. Unlike many dissenting publications, the reviewer commended it, considering its conclusions fair, and no more than Irving deserved in view of his treatment of others: ibid. 362.

⁷⁸ Anon., *Trial*, 3–4, 96.

⁷⁹ Review of *Orations*, *London Christian Instructor, or Congregational Magazine* 6 (1823), 414–19, 472–9, at 414–15.

⁸⁰ Review of *Orations*, *CO* 23 (1823), 490–502, 557–87, at 578–9.

⁸¹ [J. G. Lockhart], 'The Rev. Mr Irving's Orations', *Blackwood's Edinburgh Magazine* 14 (1823), 145–62, at 149.

⁸² *CO* 23 (1823), 563.

⁸³ 'Pulpit Oratory', *Sunday Times*, 3 August 1823, 2.

⁸⁴ 'The Rev. Edw. Irving, A.M.', 452.

Although his style was not universally approved of, several reviewers commended his energy, strength of mind, and his advocacy of the study of the Scriptures.[85] 'With all his faults ... there is an energy of mind, a vigour of intellect, a strength of reasoning, and a force of appeal, which we seldom have the privilege to witness in these later days.'[86] Whilst not 'thoroughly furnished' as a theologian, he had 'the invaluable art of setting familiar truth in a new light'.[87]

Critics were not convinced that the two types of structure in Irving's book were as novel in style as their author had claimed; the only difference between them and traditional sermons which most could see was that they were not as systematically arranged.[88] It was claimed that he refused to call them sermons because he did not want to be thought like others of his order.[89] To take this ground, he needed to know more about the state of pulpit eloquence in England. As with the social experiments of his mentor Chalmers, Irving was too quick to think his example could be followed in other circumstances. But what he did, he did well.[90] And calling them 'orations' might bring some to read them who did not read sermons.[91] Overall, the 'Argument' was seen as a better work than the 'Orations' and as more suited to his oratorical powers.[92]

Probably the most serious charge made against him was that of presumption: one writer told him that he was as yet inexperienced in the Christian life; in time, he would regret publishing such raw ideas. The surest way for Irving to progress was for him not to think too highly of his attainments and gifts at present.[93] 'Mr. Irving is but a young labourer in the Lord's vineyard, and as yet almost a stranger to this portion of it; and it ill becomes one of such few years and limited experience thus to stalk forth, dispensing his censures on all around him, and holding himself up as the only model for universal imitation.'[94] Such sweeping condemnations were regarded as evidence of conceit and of ignorance of the real world.[95] Over-familiarity in using God's name[96] was further evidence of egotism.[97] The conceit was evident in his attempt to set an example to the entire body of English clergy. A reviewer in *The*

---

[85] E.g. *EM* n.s. 3 (1823), 420.

[86] *CO* 23 (1823), 493.

[87] Review of *Orations*, *ER* n.s. 20 (1823), 193–211, at 210.

[88] *London Christian Instructor* 6 (1823), 415.

[89] *The Pulpit*, no. 12 (10 July 1823), 182.

[90] *ER* n.s. 20 (1823), 194–6.

[91] *CO* 23 (1823), 494.

[92] *EM* n.s. 3 (1823), 461; cf. *The Pulpit*, no. 16 (7 August 1823), 245.

[93] William Burns, *The Law of Christ Vindicated from Certain False Glosses of the Rev. Edward Irving, contained in his Argument on a Judgment to Come* (London: R. Hunter, 1824), 50.

[94] *The Pulpit*, no. 12 (10 July 1823), 180.

[95] Ibid. 182.

[96] John Bull, *Puritanical Treason!! The King and Honest John Bull versus Parson Irving, Doctor Collyer, and their Proselytes; or Truth Unmasking Hypocrisy, Deceit, and Bigotry! A Satirical Epistle* (London: W. Chubb, n.d.), 7.

[97] *The Pulpit*, no. 17 (14 August 1823), 263.

Pulpit commented acidly that he had thought the compliments offered in its opening number a few months earlier sufficient, but 'We find, however, that in Mr. Irving's own estimation, we had underrated him vastly.'[98]

Some resented a lately arrived Scot telling English, especially Anglican, churchmen and Christians their business.[99] It was even alleged that his main intention was to attack the Church of England.[100] On the other hand, the Scots condemned the English for their gullibility in hanging on his words![101] His Scottish background may have been a factor in his wholesale condemnation of the theatre; Carlyle likewise manifested an aversion to it.[102] Reaction to his condemnation found expression in a caricature by Cruikshank, 'The Hatton Garden Puritanical Gasometer exploded'.[103]

For some, he was too forthright in his denunciations and too blunt and detailed in his preaching about hell.[104] The radical journalist William Cobbett was quoted as calling him 'This *great brimstone merchant*'.[105] It was alleged that he worked by frightening his hearers,[106] dwelling on their fears, rather than on the pleasure and loveliness of obeying God's word.[107]

Some saw him as over-confident in the powers of the human mind to receive divine truth.[108] It was also alleged that Irving lacked a clear grasp of the Gospel,[109] a charge which has been advanced by his most recent biographer: 'Irving made no clear statement about salvation and his preaching was not accompanied by any true power from on high.'[110] Evangelicals bridled at his condemnation of their preaching and of

---

[98] *The Pulpit*, no. 12 (10 July 1823), 178; cf. Fleming, *Irving*, 22.

[99] *Country Literary Chronicle*, no. 220 (2 August 1823), 484; cf. *EM* n.s. 3 (1823), 419.

[100] [Lockhart], 'Irving's Orations', 150.

[101] 'Irving's four Orations', 215.

[102] See Ian Campbell, 'Edward Irving, Carlyle and the Stage', *Studies in Scottish Literature* 8 (1971), 166–73; Anne M. Skabarnicki, 'Annandale Evangelist and Scotch Voltaire: Carlyle's *Reminiscences* of Edward Irving and Francis Jeffrey', *Scotia* 4 (1980), 16–30.

[103] [John Bull], *Puritanical Treason*, 4–7; the caricature, the original of which is now held by the National Portrait Gallery, is reproduced as the frontispiece to 'An Actor', *Shakespeare, and Honest King George, versus Parson Irving and the Puritans; or, Taste and Common Sense, refuting Cant and Hypocrisy* (London: C. Harris, 1824).

[104] 'Irving's four Orations', 215; [Lockhart], 'Irving's Orations', 158.

[105] Anon., *Trial*, 18.

[106] Fleming, *Irving*, 20.

[107] *The Pulpit*, no. 14 (24 July 1823), 215.

[108] *London Christian Instructor* 6 (1823), 473; cf. *CO* 23 (1823), 586.

[109] *New Evangelical Magazine* 9 (1823), 362.

[110] Arnold Dallimore, *The Life of Edward Irving: Fore-runner of the Charismatic Movement* (Edinburgh: Banner of Truth, 1983), 25. In the earliest days of his London ministry this may have been true, as the following anecdote implies, although many of his published sermons do contain a clear evangelistic message:

catechisms.[111] They also wondered why he condemned English Evangelicalism so sweepingly, in effect siding with the world. They would have welcomed him as a colleague, but he placed himself as a reformer and opponent.[112]

Carlyle was, on the whole,

> sorry that Irving's preaching has taken such a turn. It had been much better, if without the gross pleasure of being a newspaper Lion and a season's wonder, he had gradually become, what he must ultimately pass for, a preacher of first rate abilities, of great eloquence and great absurdity, with a head fertile above all others in sense and nonsense, and a heart of the most honest and kindly sort.[113]

As for the book itself, 'I have read but one oration – for it is rather dull to my sense. I fear it will hardly do.'[114] Once he got further into it, he was even more critical:

> I spent the day in reading part of Irving's sermon's [sic], which I have not finished. On the whole he should not have published it – till after a considerable time. There is strong talent in it, true eloquence, and vigorous thought: but the foundation is rotten, and the building itself is a kind of monster in architecture – beautiful in parts – vast in dimensions – but on the whole decidedly a monster. ...
>
> I also told him my *true* opinion of his Book – a favourable one; but some thousand degrees below his own.[115]

And a few months later: 'I still think it was a very considerable pity that he had published them. It is not with books as with other things: *quantity* is nothing,

---

That when Irving first came to London, he was not the out-and-out minister of the Gospel of Christ which he afterwards became, is attested by many who loved him with a true love in after years, and who do not speak out of envy or misappreciation of the man. One week evening, some friends of ours went to hear Dr Waugh in London. Seated not far from them were Irving and a Congregational minister, personally unknown to each other. After service, the minister joined our friends outside, and began to talk over the discourse, which was well spoken of by all as a true exhibition of the message of the reconciliation. The minister than asked, 'Who is that singular-looking man next whom I was sitting?' 'That,' said one of our friends, 'is the new Scotch minister of the Caledonian Church.' 'Is it?' said he; 'then I have said a very awkward thing.' 'How so?' 'We spoke together of the excellence of the sermon, and of the gospel which it contained; and then I remarked that I was sorry to hear that the new Scottish minister of the Caledonian Church did not preach the gospel.' 'And what did he say in reply?' asked our friend. 'He replied, "Does he not? Then he shall do it hereafter."': [Horatius Bonar]?, 'Edward Irving', *QJP* 14 (1862), 224–47, at 229–30.

[111] *EM* n.s. 3 (1823), 420; *CO* 23 (1823), 501; *ER* n.s. 20 (1823), 205.
[112] *ER* n.s. 20 (1823), 207, 209.
[113] *CL*, 2.413–14: Carlyle to Jane Welsh, 10 August 1823.
[114] Ibid. 425: Carlyle to John Carlyle, 2 September 1823.
[115] Ibid. 440–1: Carlyle to Margaret A. Carlyle, 28 September 1823.

quality is all in all. There is stuff in that book of Irvings [sic] to have made a first-rate work of the kind out of. But it is not dressed, it is not polished.'[116]

Perhaps the most significant response, however, in the long run, came from Coleridge. When Irving sent him a copy of his *Orations*, Coleridge wrote in the front: 'Let this young man know that the world is not to be converted, but judged.' According to Irving's wife, this affected him powerfully.[117] The fruits would be seen in his later preaching, his diminished expectations, his increasingly confrontational attitude towards the authorities of church and state, and his growing interest in biblical prophecy.

* * *

Irving's response to his critics was typically robust, even belligerent. One of his sermons appears to have been preached by way of response to them, 'The Theology of the Natural Man'.[118] In it he disposed of contemporary literary and scientific portrayals of God as inadequate because they did not portray a living God who could be known personally; he explained that he was reacting to those who criticized the bad taste of Christians who spoke too freely of God and too plainly of hell. On 1 December, in the preface to the third edition of his *Orations*,[119] he asserted: 'I have been abused in every possible way, beyond the lot of ordinary men, which when I consider the quarters whence it hath come, I regard as an extraordinary honour'. He was too sure of God to be shaken by 'the opposition of wits, critics and gentlemen of taste', and too familiar with how Christ and Christians had endured to be 'tamed by paper warfare or intimidated by the terrors of a goose-quill'.[120] As for his critics, 'Their criticisms show that they are still in the gall of wickedness and the bond of iniquity'; 'for them I care not, except that they should be converted from hired scribblers into servants of truth'.[121] Replying to criticism of his style, he was not afraid

> to confess that Hooker and Taylor, and Baxter, in theology; Bacon, and Newton, and Locke, in philosophy, have been my companions, as Shakspeare and Spenser and Milton, have been in Poetry. ... They are my models of men, of Englishmen, of Authors. My conscience could find none so worthy, and the world hath acknowledged none worthier. They were the fountains of my English idiom; they taught me forms for expressing my feelings; they shewed me the construction of sentences, and the majestic flow of continuous discourse. ... They seemed to think, and feel, and imagine, and reason all at once, and the result is to take the whole man captive in the chains of sweetest persuasion.

---

[116] Ibid. 3.13: Carlyle to Alexander Carlyle, 13 January 1824.

[117] William W. Andrews, *Edward Irving: A Review* (2nd edn, Glasgow: David Hobbs, 1900), 60.

[118] *CW*, 4.504–14.

[119] Irving, *Orations* (3rd edn); the preface is dated 1 December 1823.

[120] Ibid. xi.

[121] Ibid. xii, xix–xx.

They are not always in Taste. But who is this Taste, and where are his works, that we may try what right he hath to lift his voice against such gifted men?[122]

Implicit was the idea that great ideas demand expression in a fitting style, and that poverty of style indicated poverty of thought.

* * *

Irving's appeal was partly because, as Drummond pointed out, he stood out from the run of contemporary evangelical preachers; 'he was essentially the Romantic in the pulpit at a time when Evangelicalism was losing influence because it was unimaginative and prosaic'.[123] 'Irving seems to have realised the weakness of the Presbyterian appeal to the intellect, the Methodist appeal to the emotions and the (contemporary) Anglican appeal to the moral sense'.[124] Instead, he combined them in an attempt to appeal to the whole person. He stood out partly because he had gone back to first principles and thought out his own approach to preaching. To some extent, he reinvented the wheel, as in his claim to have rehabilitated the forms of the 'oration' and the 'argument'. Yet his security in what he believed and his strong sense of a divine commission to proclaim it gave him the freedom to risk criticism by handling issues in a way which less secure preachers might not dare to do.

Often people appear to have been attracted by the oratorical form rather than the theological content of his preaching: 'He was a preacher for those who loved a good sermon rather than for those who needed a good religion. The effect of his preaching was to leave men dazzled and stupefied rather than convinced or converted; they went home wondering at the power of the orator, rather than mourning over their besetting sins and striving after amendment.'[125] A later Catholic Apostolic writer, W. W. Andrews, described Irving's preaching during this period as 'rather intellectual than doctrinal or spiritual'; in his view, Irving 'did reach their intellects and captivate their imaginations, but he did not draw them to Christ'.[126] Yet,

> defective as his preaching was during the first year or two of his ministry, great ends were doubtless answered by it. It was bold, and honest, and searching; and Christian doctrine, though not made prominent, nor set forth in theological forms, lay at the foundation. It was not heretical, nor merely moral and sentimental; but a manly and powerful exhibition of the practical side of religion; too intellectual and imaginative, no doubt, for the simplicity of the Gospel, but better fitted, perhaps, on that very account, to gain the ear of those highly-cultured and refined classes, to whom Christianity had become a worn-out thing, and who were too seldom plainly and faithfully dealt with from the pulpit. ... With all its imperfections, it was a

---

[122] Ibid. xv–xvii.

[123] Drummond, *Irving*, 53.

[124] Ibid. 60–1. Drummond was referring to the styles of preaching then current among these denominations.

[125] Ibid. 57.

[126] Andrews, *Irving*, 41, 46.

noble witness for God, and prepared the hearts of thousands for a higher message in due time.[127]

---

[127] Ibid. 48.

Chapter 9

Marriage and Family Life, 1822–5

Although Irving's marriage to Isabella was undoubtedly important for his future ministry, we cannot trace with certainty the details of the progress of his relationship with her. In September 1822, she admitted to her parents that the previous twelve months had been marked by 'somewhat singular circumstances & somewhat trying',[1] which may be a reference to the progress of the relationship. Given the understanding that marriage would follow as soon as Irving obtained a living, and Drummond's belief that the engagement had only been confirmed in 1822,[2] it is possible that the trying circumstances to which Isabella referred concerned his request to be released from his engagement in order to marry Jane Welsh, and the family's insistence that he maintain it. Irving himself referred that September to having been shaken by trial, but without compromising his integrity. Describing himself in a letter to his future mother-in-law as a 'prodigal boy', he claimed that he would several times have been shipwrecked apart from Isabella's care for him. He left Isabella to fix the precise date of the marriage, and asked her brother Samuel to act as 'bride-groom's man'.[3] As well as the vicissitudes of his relationships with Isabella, Edward's older brother John had died in India, where he was a surgeon, on 4 August 1822; Edward kept the anniversary (which was also his own birthday) thereafter as a solemn fast.[4] Informing Chalmers of John's death, Irving wrote: 'I think I could have died in his stead. He was so endeared to myself and our family – so gallant, so generous & so good.'[5] Small wonder, then, that in February 1823, according to Carlyle, Edward was still 'in a very foamy state, which he is evidently struggling to repress or conceal', and had asked him to tell Jane that he would 'never cease to love her like a brother'.[6] The marriage would not begin under auspicious circumstances,

---

[1] Isabella Martin to her parents, 9 September 1822 (in private hands).

[2] Andrew Landale Drummond, *Edward Irving and his Circle: Including some Consideration of the 'Tongues' Movement in the Light of Modern Psychology* (London: James Clarke, [1937]), 77.

[3] Irving to Mrs Martin, postmarked [22?] September 1823 (in private hands).

[4] Oliphant, *Life*, 3.

[5] Edinburgh, NCL, Chalmers MSS, CHA 4.26.59: Irving to Chalmers, 18 March 1823.

[6] *CL*, 2.292: Carlyle to Jane Welsh, 18 February 1823.

therefore: it has also been suggested that Isabella knew of his feelings for Jane and that this continued to cause tension between her and Edward.[7]

On his farewell visit to Haddington before leaving for London, Irving had told Jane that whilst he was giving Carlyle charge of her literary education, he reserved the right to oversee her religious and moral development; she asked him not to preach at her, and altogether the parting seems to have been a difficult one.[8] It is claimed that on the Sunday before his marriage (12 October), Irving preached at Haddington.[9] This seems unlikely, as he wrote to Carlyle from Kirkcaldy on the previous day,[10] but he had been due to spend a few hours in Haddington two days before that (9 October). On that occasion he left Jane a portrait of himself (presumably one of the many mass-produced that summer), and a copy of his *Orations*. He also invited her and Carlyle to spend next summer with him and Isabella in London.[11]

On 14 October 1823, Edward and Isabella were married in the manse at Kirkcaldy by her grandfather, the Rev. Samuel Martin.[12] For their honeymoon, they set out on a journey through Perthshire and central Scotland, via Glasgow to assist at Chalmers' farewell service on 9 November and speak at his farewell dinner three days later,[13] down to Annan to visit Edward's family, and across the border into England. The story goes that when they reached the border, Edward made his bride dismount and walk across into what would henceforth be her home.[14]

Irving wanted Carlyle to spend the following summer in London, so that he could see the world and also begin writing in earnest.[15] In a letter to Carlyle, Jane (perhaps

---

[7] Barbara Waddington, *The Rev. Edward Irving & the Catholic Apostolic Church in Camden and beyond*, Camden History Society Occasional Paper No. 7 (London: Camden History Society, [2007]), 59-60; cf. Oliphant, *Life*, 150.

[8] Laurence and Elisabeth Hanson, *Necessary Evil: The Life of Jane Welsh Carlyle* (London: Constable, 1952), 51.

[9] Oliphant, *Life*, 86; *CL*, 2.449n; Virginia Surtees, *Jane Welsh Carlyle* (Wilton, Salisbury: Michael Russell, 1986), 28. I have found no primary sources to confirm this.

[10] Edinburgh, NLS, MS 14836, fol. 48.

[11] *CL*, 2.445: Jane Welsh to Carlyle, [3 October 1823]; Surtees, *Jane Welsh Carlyle*, 49. Jane would not visit London until 1831: Ian Campbell, *Thomas Carlyle* (Edinburgh: Saltire Society, 1993; first publ. 1974), 71.

[12] There is some doubt about the date, which Irving had left Isabella to fix. He informed Carlyle that it would be on the 14th: NLS, MS 1764, fol. 263 (Irving to Carlyle, 8 October 1823). *The Times* also gave it as the 14th (22 October 1823, 3), but Mrs Oliphant appeared unable to make her mind up, giving it as both the 13th (*Life*, 87) and the 14th (ibid. 150). There is no entry in the relevant register for Kirkcaldy, and that in the Annan marriage register just gives the month (Irving's marriage was recorded because he was well known, not because it took place at Annan).

[13] Irving's speech at Chalmers' farewell dinner was reported in *The Pulpit*, no. 31 (20 November 1823), 9–10. For the dates, see Stewart J. Brown, *Thomas Chalmers and the Godly Commonwealth in Scotland* (Oxford: Oxford University Press, 1982), 142.

[14] Oliphant, *Life*, 88–90.

[15] *CL*, 2.456: Carlyle to John A. Carlyle, 20 October 1823.

ironically) expressed her joy at the prospect of spending a summer in London together, 'beside the One whom next to each other we love most'. She had done 'injustice to Edward Irving in supposing he had forgotten us – He loves us still – better than many hundreds of his other friends– If you can bear with "*the Lord*" and M*rs* Montague you will have great delight in his visit– Shall I like his Wife?' With a touch of sarcasm, she asked Carlyle, 'Tell me how he gets on with a wife – it must be very laughable'.[16] Perhaps it was; but the marriage proved a very happy one. However, Jane was not at all keen on visiting the Irvings; 'unless our friend doth greatly amend his ways there is little likelihood of my seeking happiness under his roof either with or without you'.[17] Not only was she wary of Isabella, but she resented Irving's failure to maintain his correspondence with her:

> Not a word from the Orator! it is unallowable! Do you know they are giving out that I am dreadfully disappointed at his marriage!!! and that he has used me very ill – *me* ill! was there ever any thing so insufferable? but it is his own blame he talked of me so absurdly– He has been telling all people that I was 'the Love of his intellect & that the woman he has married was the Love of his youth' ...[18]

In the end, Irving wrote to Carlyle to say that the delay in their moving into their new home, and the consequent need to move between various temporary abodes, made it impossible to receive a lady, though they could entertain one as simple in his habits as Carlyle.[19] It would seem that he (or Isabella) was as apprehensive of the prospect as Jane was.

Since his first visit to London, Irving's correspondence with Carlyle had become somewhat patchy. Irving does not appear to have written to him much, if at all, between February 1822 and April 1823. He was, Carlyle complained, 'one of the worst of correspondents',[20] and 'scarcely even writes to his mother'.[21] Irving's excuse, which Carlyle thought specious, was that 'he was ever ready at a moment's warning to *do* every thing in his power for his friends; but that he really had not time or topics to *write*. I scouted the idea of *time*; and told him that as to *doing*, none but prime ministers and Asiatic Monarchs could pretend to make or keep friends by that expensive method.'[22] All the same, their affection for one another remained undimmed, and Carlyle even spent a few days with the Irvings on their honeymoon. Irving was full of the possible literary openings for Carlyle in

---

[16] Ibid. 450–2: Jane Welsh to Carlyle, [14 October 1823].
[17] Ibid. 470: Jane Welsh to Carlyle, [12 November 1823].
[18] Ibid. 481: Jane Welsh to Carlyle, 26 [November 1823].
[19] Ibid. 3.67: Carlyle to Jane Welsh, 19 May 1824.
[20] Ibid. 2.342: Carlyle to William Graham, 24 April 1823.
[21] Ibid. 3.67: Carlyle to Jane Welsh, 19 May 1824. Several of Irving's postscripts to Isabella's letters to her mother (he did not often write a whole letter to her at this period) begin with a somewhat perfunctory apology that he was too busy to write properly.
[22] Ibid. 147: Carlyle to Jane Welsh, 2 September 1824.

London,[23] and 'superlatively happy', while Isabella was 'demure and quiet, though doubtless not *less* happy at heart; really comely in her behaviour ... Irving had loyally taken her as the consummate flower of all his victory in the world, – poor good *tragic* woman; better probably than the fortune she had, after all!'[24] On observing Irving in London, however, he thought him 'inwardly ... nothing like so happy as in old days, inwardly confused, anxious, dissatisfied, though, as it were, denying it to himself'.[25]

Carlyle was initially not too impressed with Isabella: she was, he told his brother, '*dead ugly*, otherwise a very decent and serviceable person'.[26] To Jane (perhaps magnifying Isabella's negative qualities) he wrote: 'His wife you will hardly like, but neither can you well dislike her. She *is* unbeautiful; has no enthusiasm, and few ideas that are not prosaic or conceited: but she possesses I believe many household virtues; she loves her husband and will love his friends.'[27] A year later he described her as 'skilful in Presbyterian philosophy and the structure of dumplings and worsted hose'.[28] However, in due course he modified his views somewhat. Visiting them on holiday at Dover in October 1824, he described her as 'a good, honest-hearted person and an excellent wife'.[29]

Mrs Oliphant expressed herself more positively:

> She stood by her husband bravely through every after vicissitude of his life; was so thorough a companion to him, that he confided to her, in detail, all the thoughts which occupied him, as will be seen in after letters; received his entire trust and confidence, piously laid him in his grave, brought up his children, and lived for half of her life a widow indeed, in the exercise of all womanly and Christian virtues. If her admiration for his genius, and the short-sightedness of love, led her rather to seek the society of those who held him in a kind of idolatry, than of friends more likely to exert upon him the beneficial influence of equals, and so contributed to the clouding of his genius, it is the only blame that has ever been attached to her. She came of a family who were all distinguished by active talent and considerable character; and with all the unnoted valour of a true woman, held on her way through the manifold agonies – in her case most sharp and often repeated – of life.[30]

Her surviving letters show her to have been a strong supporter of her husband, especially in the controversies of his later years.

---

[23] Thomas Carlyle, *Reminiscences*, ed. C. E. Norton (London: J. M. Dent, 1932), 239.

[24] Ibid. 238.

[25] Ibid. 244.

[26] Ibid. 2.456: Carlyle to John A. Carlyle, 20 October 1823.

[27] Ibid. 2.459: Carlyle to Jane Welsh, 22 October 1823.

[28] Surtees, *Jane Welsh Carlyle*, 56.

[29] *CL*, 3.167: Carlyle to James Carlyle sr, 4 October 1824; cf. his description of Isabella as 'the very model of a wife': ibid. 90: Carlyle to John A. Carlyle, 24 June 1824.

[30] Oliphant, *Life*, 87.

As he had done in Kirkcaldy, Edward continued to keep an eye on his brother George, and expressed the hope that he would turn out 'a respectable if not a distinguished man'.[31] Writing to William Hamilton in September 1823, Edward expressed a willingness to find the money George needed in order to enter one of the hospitals as a medical student.[32] Isabella did not find George too easy to deal with; expressing her exasperation at his childishness, she confessed that she could willingly box his ears.[33] Thankfully, by March she was able to inform her mother that he would be going into lodgings.[34] Soon after, the Irvings moved into their new home, 4 Myddelton Terrace, Pentonville, in an area still being developed.[35] Isabella expressed herself positively regarding the house, telling her mother that it was delightfully placed and free from the smoke of the city. Its only drawback was that it was a long way from where most of the congregation lived, and a mile from the chapel.[36] In the autumn of 1825 they moved a few hundred yards away to 4 Claremont Square; this still stands today, in a row of houses at right angles to the road leading from King's Cross to the Angel, Islington. A blue plaque on the wall testifies that Edward Irving, 'Founder of the Catholic Apostolic Church', once lived there.

* * *

Now that Irving was married, it was perhaps inevitable that he should soon feel the need to preach about domestic relationships. A series of sermons 'On Family and Social Religion', apparently preached at some point in 1823–4,[37] display a strongly theological approach; it was his declared intention to focus on the underlying principles rather than merely enforcing and illustrating a range of external duties.[38] A family, he asserted, 'is not a congregation of mortals met together for worldly ends; it is a congregation of immortals associated by the immortal bonds of affection for heavenly ends, and immortal enjoyment'.[39] Given that it 'is a little diocese of immortal souls', each father, by virtue of the promises made at baptism, 'is thus a prophet and a priest unto his child, and the law constitutes him a king. So that he mystically represents to his family the threefold relation of Christ to His people – of prophet, priest, and king.'[40] Family relationships were thus emblematic of spiritual ones.

---

[31] NLS, MS 1764, fol. 244: Irving to Carlyle, 14 February 1823.
[32] Oliphant, *Life*, 1.177.
[33] Isabella Irving to her parents, 20 January 1824 (in private hands).
[34] Isabella Irving to her mother, 26 March 1824 (in private hands).
[35] Irving's correspondence addresses indicate that he was living at no. 7 by August 1823.
[36] Isabella Irving to her mother, postmarked 24 December 1823 (in private hands).
[37] *CW*, 3.215–339.
[38] Ibid. 235.
[39] Ibid. 231.
[40] Ibid. 241.

He expanded his remit to consider the topic of friendship, something not too often preached on, which may justify the following lengthy quotation. For Irving, whose capacity for friendship was considerable, a friend could fulfil four offices:

> First, To weigh and deliberate, and give judgment upon the first fruits of our mind. Secondly, to protect us from the selfish and solitary part of our nature. Thirdly, to speak to and call out those finer and better qualities within us which the customs of this world stifle, and open up to us a career worthy of our powers. Lastly, To succour us in our straits, rally us in our defeats, and bind our spirit in its distresses. Now, as every man hath these four attributes, – infirmity of judgment, selfishness or wilfulness of disposition, inactivity and inertness of nature, and adversity of fortune, – so every man needeth the help of a friend, and should do his endeavour to obtain one. And the fourfold nature of his office requires in a good friend a fourfold qualification for discharging the several parts of it aright. For the first, sympathy with our thoughts and pursuits ...; and not only sympathy with them but understanding of them, and a solid judgment and an honest heart to give us good counsel and true upon all our plans. For the second, a generous nature which looks to the commonweal, and will not yield it to the pleasuring of a friend; also a manly and tried mind, which will not veil truth and manhood, even before a friend, so as to give in to his wilfulness, but will be an equal friend or no friend at all. For the third, a high and heroic soul, which can strike out noble duties in every path of life, and behold in all classes, ... the elements of a heaven-born nature, and the destinee of an immortal glory; and perceiving them, will stimulate us thereto, however much against the stomach of our own present inclination, or the spirit of our present life. For the fourth, a tender and a true heart, which keeps to its affections, and as it is not beguiled into friendship by outward forms or conditions, so is not alienated by the absence of them, but loves the soul, ... for its own intrinsic qualities; and while it preserves them, will love it in good report and in ill report, in prosperity and in adversity, in life and in death, and for ever. According as these qualities meet in any one, he rises in the scale of friendship; where they all combine together in one, they form a friend more precious to the soul than all which it inherits beneath the sun.[41]

* * *

Irving's theological asseverations were soon to be put to the proof. On 22 July 1824, Isabella gave birth to their first child, Edward. Father, uncle (Samuel Martin) and grandfather (John Martin) shared in conducting the baptism on 5 September. Irving told Carlyle that his new baby had been sent to soften his hard heart.[42] However, not all the visitors to the house were as besotted with the baby as its father was. Carlyle visited Irving in September 1824, but a plan that he should spend the winter there was shelved. In his view, it

---

[41] Ibid. 303–4.
[42] Carlyle, *Reminiscences*, 255.

would scarcely have been a favourable place for studying any science but the estate of religion in general and that of the Caledonian chapel in particular, as managed by various doers, delegates and other most nondescript personages; a very affected and not beautiful sister of his wife's is also to stay with them through the winter; her I might have found it a task to love. 'Pray Mr Carlyle ... are you *really* sick now, or is it only fanciful?' ... Besides Irving has a squeaking brat of a son, 'who indeed brings us many blessings, but rather interrupts our rest at nights'!⁴³

He was relieved that he was not to lodge with them; Irving, he told his mother, was 'of rough and ready habits, and his wife not by any means the pink of housekeepers'.⁴⁴ The baby, who was 'looked upon by them as if it were a cherub from on high',⁴⁵ occupied all their attention: Irving was obsessed with it, and Isabella was 'engaged in nursing it, let the house go how it will'.⁴⁶ Setting up a domestic establishment, Isabella was reliant on her family to find her suitable servants, but it would appear that those they recommended were not all that might have been desired, at least as far as the Irvings' more fastidious visitors were concerned.⁴⁷

Carlyle's first visit to London lasted from early June 1824 to the end of February 1825; in spite of his relief that he had not made his home with the Irvings, he lodged with them briefly on several occasions during the first few months.⁴⁸ After taking lodgings nearby, in Southampton Street, he often called on his friend, but Irving never or rarely called on him. In his opinion, Irving was 'a good deal unhappy', and their communication was not as free as it had been, for which Carlyle blamed Irving's pulpit popularity.⁴⁹ It was among his family, Carlyle felt, that Irving was happiest; in the autumn of 1824, he visited Irving at his parents' home in Annan, and contrasted 'the beautiful affectionate safety here, and the wild tempestuous hostilities and perils yonder'.⁵⁰ The friendship was coming under inevitable strain. When, at a missionary society meeting, Irving put down on the subscription list his dead brother John's gold watch, Carlyle regarded it as an example of the extravagant behaviour to which Irving was increasingly prone; he 'felt that for the present it was

---

⁴³ *CL*, 3.161: Carlyle to John A. Carlyle, 27 September 1824.

⁴⁴ Ibid. 195: Carlyle to Mrs. Carlyle, 12 November 1824. In any case, the Irvings had arranged to board a law student from Glasgow, James Parker, and could not take Carlyle. For this, they were to be paid £200 per annum, which Carlyle, but not the student's father, thought a very high rate: ibid.; NCL, Chalmers MSS, CHA 4.34.54 (Irving to Chalmers, 21 September 1824); CHA 4.37.40 (M. Parker to Chalmers, 29 September 1824).

⁴⁵ *CL*, 3.167: Carlyle to James Carlyle sr, 4 October 1824.

⁴⁶ Ibid. 200: Carlyle to Jane Welsh, 15 November 1824.

⁴⁷ Isabella Irving to Mrs Martin, 26 March 1824; Edward Irving to Mrs. Martin, postmarked 11 March 1824; Isabella Irving to her brother [Samuel Martin?], 8 November 1824 (all in private hands).

⁴⁸ Carlyle, *Reminiscences*, 257.

⁴⁹ Ibid. 274.

⁵⁰ Ibid. 283–4.

better to be absolved from corresponding with him'.⁵¹ Yet, even though Carlyle considered Irving 'unable to speak or act for one hour without cant, he really means to be sincere'.⁵²

Carlyle also joined Mrs Strachey, the Irvings and others on holiday at Dover in October, lodging with the Irvings. He recalled that Irving used to read to the party each evening, his choice of book being Phineas Fletcher's *Purple Island*.⁵³ The two friends regained something of their former intimacy; as Carlyle told his father, 'We talk of religion and literature and men and things, and stroll about and smoke cigars, a choice stock of which he has been presented with by some friend.'⁵⁴ Ever the workaholic, Irving informed Dinwiddie that during his three weeks there he had bathed in the sea every day, but also that he had spent three or four hours a day in study, as far as was consistent with seeking to recover his health. He may have disappointed his congregation's hopes that he would have a good break by informing them that he had no wish to join the party going to France as he had no 'spiritual kindred' there.⁵⁵ Even on holiday, his strong sense of call was never far from his thoughts; he confessed to his elders that 'There is nothing of which my spirit accuses itself more in the review which I take of my past ministry, than the want of travail of soul concerning the flock.'⁵⁶ Nevertheless, on their return to London in November Isabella expressed her belief that father and son were both better for their time by the sea.⁵⁷

At home, there was a constant stream of visitors, often responding to Irving's open invitations. 'Irving's charity was not alms, but that primitive kindness of the open house and shared meal'.⁵⁸ A close relation (probably Isabella's sister Elizabeth, who in 1828 became Mrs William Hamilton) described his daily routine to Mrs Oliphant:

---

⁵¹ Ibid. 284.

⁵² *CL*, 3.272: Carlyle to Jane Welsh, 31 January 1825.

⁵³ Carlyle, *Reminiscences*, 266–7. This was a lengthy seventeenth-century allegorical poem on the nature of man and the conflict between good and evil, edifying rather than entertaining.

⁵⁴ *CL*, 3.167: Carlyle to James Carlyle sr, 4 October 1824.

⁵⁵ London, RS, EIL30: Irving to Dinwiddie, 20 October 1824.

⁵⁶ RS, EIL30a: Irving to the Elders of the Caledonian Church, [20 October 1824].

⁵⁷ Isabella Irving to her brother [Rev. Samuel Martin?], 8 November 1824 (in private hands). Carlyle said that he joined the party early in September, but his memory was at fault here: Irving wrote to Chalmers from home on the 21ˢᵗ (NCL, Chalmers MSS, CHA 4.34.54), presumably after his return from Annan, and Carlyle himself, writing to his brother John on the 27ᵗʰ, described having found Irving at home but having been unable to stay with him because Isabella had taken the crockery, bedding and household necessities with her (*CL*, 3.159). Carlyle had arrived in Dover by 4 October, when he wrote to his father (ibid. 167), and Irving was still there on the 20ᵗʰ, when he wrote to Dinwiddie.

⁵⁸ Oliphant, *Life*, 100.

Mr Irving's rule was to see any of his friends who wished to visit him without ceremony at breakfast. Eight o'clock was the hour. Family worship first, and then breakfast. At ten he rose, bade every one good-bye, and retired to his study. He gave no audience again till after three. Two o'clock was the dinner hour; and, after that, should no one come to prevent him, he generally walked out, Mrs Irving accompanying him; and, until the baby took hooping-cough, Mr Irving almost always carried him in his arms. Some people laughed at this, but that he did not care for in the very least.

As Mrs Oliphant commented, 'To see the great preacher admired and flattered by the highest personages in the kingdom, marching along the Pentonville streets with his baby, must have been a spectacle to make ordinary men open their eyes.'[59]

Fame did not make him unapproachable; indeed, as in Glasgow, he often proved better at getting alongside the poor than did some of his lay co-workers. It is recorded that when he went visiting with some ladies in the Billingsgate district of the City, seeking to get poor families to send their children to school, he amazed them by requesting the children's attendance as a favour, rather than conveying the impression that he was the one graciously granting the favours.[60] It is another example of his willingness to challenge accepted social conventions and etiquette in order to act as he thought right and follow his Master's example.

* * *

At the end of June 1825, Isabella, who was pregnant again, took little Edward to her parents, to help him recover from whooping-cough.[61] The father was left to lodge with his friends the Montagus until he too came north on his annual holiday early in September.[62] Isabella's confinement occurred later than expected, and so her father, suspecting that Edward's sense of duty would not allow him to ask his office-bearers for a further Sabbath's leave of absence, wrote to do so.[63] On 2 October, Margaret was born, 'a fine healthy black-eyed baby who promises to be very like her Father'.[64] Irving, who had been in Edinburgh for the weekend and was unaware of his father-in-law's letter, wrote himself, asserting his desire to remain in Scotland until the baby had been baptized.[65] Later that week, he informed Dinwiddie that Edward's whooping-cough was not being helped by the east winds, and that he was going to take him to Annan the following Monday.[66] Before he could do so, Edward died at Kirkcaldy on 11 October.

---

[59] Ibid. 109.
[60] Ibid. 108–9.
[61] Ibid. 110.
[62] Ibid. 111.
[63] RS, EIL32: John Martin to William Hamilton, 1 October 1825.
[64] *CL*, 3.393n: Mrs Montagu to Jane Welsh, 18 October 1825.
[65] RS, EIL33: Irving to the Elders of the Caledonian Church, 3 October 1825. Her baptism took place on 9 October.
[66] RS, EIL34: Irving to Dinwiddie, 7 October 1825.

Given Irving's immense delight in his children, it is not surprising that he was devastated by his loss. Mrs Montagu told Jane, 'He writes to me in a state of distress that is awful, and seems quite overwhelmed by the unexpectedness of the stroke'.[67] No other event affected him as deeply, though he was to lose several more children. Visiting a deathbed a few weeks later, he noted that an attendant had closed the eyelids of the newly-deceased, 'I know not why they do so. I loved to look on Edward's.'[68]

It was not only the parents who were affected by the loss; John Martin confessed that 'the sweet boy was so singularly engaging in his dispositions & manners, that he attracted the most particular affection of us all. I hardly recollect to have been so much overcome by emotions, as I sometimes was both before & since his death.'[69] He appealed to Chalmers: 'Sympathise with your friend & brother. This day at 3 o'clock, my dear little grandson, Edward Irving, expired on his father's knees.' His illness having recurred, 'This morning, b[etw]een 4 & 5, I was summoned from my bed, to witness his dissolution, & found his father kneeling by his couch, & commending his spirit into the hands of his Redeemer.' Isabella, sadly, was not permitted to see her son for fear of infecting her daughter. Yet both parents bore their loss in a remarkable way. 'Edward has rather comforted us, than been comforted by us.' When Mrs Martin asked him how Isabella was bearing her trial, his response was: 'as well as one saint could wish another to do ... He makes his trial the motive to a resolution to set forth more & more earnestly the grace & consolations of the gospel.'[70]

The three family ministers who had baptized the child took his funeral, and Irving preached at Kirkcaldy the following Sunday afternoon from 1 Corinthians 15, 'a most powerful & impressive discourse'.[71] Irving visited some afflicted members of Martin's flock in gratitude for the consolation he and Isabella had received.[72] Soon afterwards, he left for London, Isabella staying on to regain her health. On his way through the southern uplands of Scotland, he called at each shepherd's cottage along the way, warning the occupants of their mortality.[73] Carlyle encountered him in

---

[67] *CL*, 3.393n: Mrs Montagu to Jane Welsh, 18 October 1825.

[68] Oliphant, *Life*, 165: journal for 16 November 1825.

[69] John Martin to William Hamilton, 18 October 1825 (in private hands).

[70] NCL, Chalmers MSS, CHA 4.47.4: John Martin to Chalmers, Kirkcaldy, 11 October 1825.

[71] John Martin to William Hamilton, 18 October 1825 (in private hands). On 23 October, he preached in London on 1 Cor. 15.55-7: 'O death, where is thy sting? O grave, where is thy victory? The sting of death is sin; and the strength of sin is the law. But thanks be to God, which giveth us the victory through our Lord Jesus Christ.' Perhaps this was the same sermon as he had preached the week before.

Even Carlyle was impressed by how the Irvings were sustained in their loss by their belief in the Christian gospel, though he could not understand it: Simon Heffer, *Moral Desperado: A Life of Thomas Carlyle* (London: Phoenix, 1996), 83.

[72] Oliphant, *Life*, 112, 115.

[73] Ibid. 116.

Annan, and noted that he was 'of a green hue, solemn, sad, and in bad bodily condition'; yet he bore well the death of his son, as he was full of other things.[74] His loss was made more bearable by his high view of baptism as an effectual means of saving grace for children born to believing parents. He had always believed regarding sacraments that 'when the body submitteth to the ceremony, the soul should expect and seek the grace therein contained',[75] but in the dedication of his *Homilies on Baptism* to Isabella, he stated that

> the doctrine of the holy Sacraments, which is contained in these Homilies, was made known to my mind, first of all, for the purpose of preparing us for the loss of our eldest boy; because, on that very week you went with him to Scotland, whence he never returned, my mind was directed to meditate and preach those discourses upon the standing of the baptized in the Church, which form the sixth and seventh of the Homilies on Baptism. I believe it also, because, long before our little Edward was stricken by the hand of God in Scotland, I was led to open these views to you in letters, which, by God's grace, were made efficacious to convince your mind.[76]

Back in London, Irving kept a journal over the next six weeks, posting sections periodically to his wife. He felt keenly his loneliness but, as he wrote to Isabella, 'the Lord filled me with some strong consolations when I thought that a spirit calling me father, and thee mother, might now be ministering at His throne. I do not remember ever being so uplifted in soul.'[77] It is noteworthy that his son's death did not unsettle his faith in the way that his knowledge that he could never marry Jane had done; his immediate response to Edward's death was that God was afflicting him in order to make him a more faithful minister.[78] Some years later, writing to console his sister and brother-in-law on the loss of a child, he recalled that when he lost Edward, he had learned how little he had been faithful to the covenant with God which he had made in his son's baptism, not having surrendered him completely to God, and 'to know how little of human existence is on this side the grave, and by how much the better and nobler portion of it is in eternity'.[79] In the next chapter, we shall look further into the heart and mind of this man who was always so conscious of his standing as a Christian minister.

---

[74] *CL*, 3.400: Carlyle to James Johnston, 26 October 1825.

[75] *CW*, 2.100.

[76] Ibid. 247. We shall examine Irving's thinking on the sacraments in ch. 12.

[77] Oliphant, *Life*, 119: Irving to Isabella Irving, 25 October 1825.

[78] Ibid. 113: Irving to William Hamilton, 11 October 1825.

[79] Oliphant, *Life*, 2.170: Irving to Mr and Mrs Fergusson, 17 January 1831. Irving believed that at baptism Christian parents gave up their child to God, receiving it back to care for.

CHAPTER 10

Three Life-changing Friendships, 1823–5

For all the decisiveness of his public pronouncements, and his willingness to pursue a line of thought which was often unconventional and controversial, Irving acknowledged his deep sense of indebtedness to several friends who influenced him in critical areas of his thinking. We have already seen the impact on Irving of his relationship with Chalmers; in this chapter we shall see what he gained from three friends whom he got to know during the early years of his London ministry: Coleridge, Frere, and Drummond. All were older than him, and in each case his role seems to have been that of the receiver.

Samuel Taylor Coleridge (1772–1834)

Irving's desire to present the faith in a way which caught the attention of literary men received a fulfilment in the form of the accession to his congregation of Basil Montagu and his wife, Anna. The Montagus were a couple who moved in London's literary circles, and as such just the kind of people whom Irving wished to get to know. Their home was at 25 Bedford Square, not far from the British Museum; Carlyle described it as 'a singular social and spiritual *menagerie;* which, indeed, was well known and much noted and criticised in certain Literary and other circles'.[1] It was Basil Montagu who introduced Irving to Coleridge in 1823; thereafter the two of them used to visit Coleridge at Highgate (then a village a few miles to the north of London) each Thursday evening, when he held an open house for visitors.[2]

Coleridge was a former Unitarian who had converted to Trinitarian Christianity, although he continued to seek adventurous and creative ways of expressing Christian truth in the thought-forms of contemporary philosophy. A writer whose work had a seminal influence on many thinkers, he had struggled with an addiction to opium (which had affected his output) and had been offered a home in Highgate with his friends the Gillmans. Carlyle had no great opinion of him: 'Good Irving strove always to think that he was getting priceless wisdom out of this great man; but must have had his misgivings.'[3] If he did, we have no evidence of it; indeed,

---

[1] Thomas Carlyle, *Reminiscences,* ed. C. E. Norton (London: J. M. Dent, 1932), 248.

[2] Oliphant, *Life*, 91; E. L. Griggs, ed., *Collected Letters of Samuel Taylor Coleridge*, Vol. 5 (Oxford: Clarendon, 1971), 280n, 365, 368. A survey of Coleridge's comments on Irving and the course of their relationship is offered in Peter Elliott, 'Edward Irving: Romantic Theology in Crisis', ch. 4.

[3] Carlyle, *Reminiscences,* 251–2.

Coleridge was to have a deeper intellectual influence on Irving than anybody else. The 'sage of Highgate' commended Irving for his growing mind[4] and described him as 'more earnest in his love of Truth & more fervent in his assurance that what is *truth must be* Christianity ... than almost any man, I have met with'.[5] According to Andrews:

> In the highest sense, Mr. Irving's training for the ministry began at Highgate. It was from the lips of Coleridge that he received those seeds of truth which, quickened by the Divine Spirit, brought forth the rich fruits of his teachings on the Incarnation, the Ordinances of God in society and the Church, and the future Kingdom of His Son. ... It was his communion with this remarkable man, at a time when his energetic intellect was all aglow with youthful fire, that gave the right direction to his theological studies, and lifted up the eloquent orator into the far-seeing interpreter of the ways of God to man.[6]

Irving's debt to Coleridge received controversial public acknowledgement in 1825 when he dedicated his plea *For Missionaries after the Apostolical School* to his teacher, because 'you have been more profitable to my faith in orthodox doctrine, to my spiritual understanding of the word of God, and to my right conception of the Christian Church, than any or all of the men with whom I have entertained friendship and conversation'.[7]

> I have partaken so much high intellectual enjoyment from being admitted into the close and familiar intercourse with which you have honoured me, and your many conversations concerning the revelations of the Christian faith have been so profitable to me in every sense, as a student and a preacher of the gospel, as a spiritual man and a Christian pastor, and your high intelligence and great learning have at all times so kindly stooped to my ignorance and inexperience, that not merely with the affection of friend to friend, and the honour due from youth to experienced age, but with the gratitude of a disciple to a wise and generous teacher, of an anxious inquirer to the good man who hath helped him in the way of truth, I do now presume to offer you the first-fruits of my mind since it received a new impulse towards truth, and a new insight into its depths from listening to your discourse.[8]

Such fulsome praise did nothing to endear Irving to evangelical critics. Neither did the views advanced in the work, and it is worth taking a little time to examine Irving's thinking on mission, as a case study of Coleridge's influence on him.

On several occasions during 1824–5 Irving was invited to preach anniversary or other sermons in London, in aid of missionary societies. At least four were

---

[4] Griggs, ed., *Letters of Coleridge*, 5.474: Coleridge to Daniel Stuart, 8? July 1825.

[5] Ibid. 476: Coleridge to J. Blanco White, 12 July 1825.

[6] William W. Andrews, *Edward Irving: A Review* (2nd edn, Glasgow: David Hobbs, 1900), 93.

[7] Ibid. 427. Mrs Oliphant long ago pointed out the importance of the prefaces and dedications to his works as autobiographical sources: *Life*, 91.

[8] *CW*, 1.428.

published, each of which will receive consideration at the appropriate point in the narrative:

- • to the London Missionary Society, on 13 May 1824, the first part of which was published as *For Missionaries after the Apostolical School*;[9]
- • to the Scottish Society for the Promotion of Christian Knowledge, on 17 May 1825, 'On Education';[10]
- • to the Continental Society, in May 1825, published in expanded form the following year as *Babylon and Infidelity Foredoomed of God*;[11]
- • and to the Hibernian Society, in 1825, on 'The Cause and Remedy of Ireland's Evil Condition'.[12]

The sermon to the London Missionary Society (LMS) was delivered during its three days' annual meeting. This formed part of the 'May meetings', the nearest thing Evangelicals had to a social season. Missionary societies would hold annual meetings in London during the month, and those with the time to spare could make quite a holiday of it, going from one to another and hearing the top preachers. The LMS had been founded in 1795, and became famous for its work in the South Seas. Its supporting constituency was mainly Congregational (then known as Independent), although its founding had famously been greeted as 'the funeral of bigotry'.

The venue for the sermon was Whitefield's Tabernacle in Tottenham Court Road. In spite of the heavy rain, such was the crowd that it was deemed wise for safety reasons to commence the service an hour early. Nevertheless, the congregation would get home very late that night: Irving's sermon lasted no less than three and a half hours, with two pauses for him to regain his strength while the congregation sang some verses of a hymn.[13] Even more astonishing than the length of the oration was its content, which created a furore scarcely less than that produced by his *Orations*. The accepted form was for preachers to extol the heroic work being done by the representatives of whichever society had convened the meeting, leading to an exhortation to dig deep for the collection which would follow. Irving, never one to follow convention for its own sake, struck out to do something higher, expounding

---

[9] Edward Irving, *For Missionaries after the Apostolical School, a Series of Orations: In four Parts. I. The Doctrine. II. The Experiment. III. The Argument. IV. The Duty* (London: Hamilton, Adams, 1825); cf. *CW*, 1.427–523. Only Part I was published, and in extensively revised form, but the whole sermon was reported in *The Pulpit*, nos 57 (20 May 1824), 440–6; 58 (27 May 1824), 454–62.

[10] Reported in *The Pulpit*, no. 114 (23 June 1825), 393. For a fuller version, see Irving, *Sermons, Lectures, and Occasional Discourses* (3 vols, London: R. B. Seeley & W. Burnside, 1828), 3.781–846; *CW*, 3.382–429.

[11] First publ. Glasgow: Chalmers and Collins, 1826.

[12] Irving, *Sermons*, 3.1199–1253; *CW*, 3.430–69.

[13] 'London Missionary Society', *New Evangelical Magazine* 10 (1824), 231; Oliphant, *Life*, 95–6.

what he saw as the biblical principles which should govern missionary work. This was not well received, and a report of the occasion ventured to criticize his indiscretion and tactlessness:

> Mr. Irving seems to imagine, that if the missionary cause be in danger, it is more owing to the injudicious conduct of its patrons and friends, than the open attacks of its avowed enemies. How far it was judicious to expose the errors of the missionary system (if errors exist) to upwards of three thousand persons, we do not now say.[14]

The reporter, whose opinion may have been coloured by the fact that he did not reach home until midnight, also questioned whether it was proper to speak for so long when some had already been there for four hours in a crowded building.[15]

Irving based his sermon on Jesus' commission to the twelve disciples in Matthew 10.7–42, which he took as having universal validity rather than being intended to apply to one particular situation. The main argument was that the narratives of the Twelve and the Seventy sent out by Jesus were intended to serve as models for missionaries in the same way that other passages provide exact models for pastors or for ordinary Christians. In his opinion, 'a strict adherence to these rules of our Lord would keep out improper persons from the missionary work; it would give a lie to the objectors of the world; it would stamp the highest honour on the mission itself'.[16] He acknowledged readily the usefulness of missionary societies as 'the greatest blessing God has given to men'. Their responsibilities were to select the right men, to replenish funds, and to carry Christ's commission into full effect.[17] Nevertheless, running through the whole was a vein of criticism that these societies had substituted worldly prudence for Christian faith in their policies, with deleterious consequences for the type of missionary selected and the success of the work.

It was only when he learned of the need of the widow of a missionary at Georgetown, Demerara (now Guyana), that Irving considered publishing his sermon. John Smith (1790–1824)[18] had died of tuberculosis in prison under sentence of death, and Irving, like many opponents of slavery, considered him a martyr. He intended all

---

[14] *The Pulpit*, no. 58 (27 May 1824), 461.

[15] Ibid. 461–2.

[16] Ibid. 456.

[17] Ibid. 461.

[18] Smith was a LMS missionary from 1817, whose proclamation of the Gospel was seen as subversive by local slave-owners. He soon concluded that slavery should be abolished rather than ameliorated. A minor riot in 1823 resulted in his arrest on the charges of inciting slaves to rebel (in spite of his attempts to restrain them) and not informing the authorities of his activities. A *cause célèbre*, his death was a major factor in anti-slavery agitation taking hold of Britain as a whole: *BDEB*; Ernest Marshall Howse, *Saints in Politics: The 'Clapham Sect' and the Growth of Freedom* (London: George Allen & Unwin, 1971), 158–9. Cf. Irving's comment regarding opposition to missionaries after his ideal: 'And, say the political classes, it is dangerous to the state; they cover plots under their silly pretences, and must be dealt with by the strong hand of power': *CW*, 1.452.

proceeds from the publication to go to Smith's widow. In spite of the objections which were raised, he remained convinced of his position, but concluded that it needed to be presented with a fuller examination of the Scriptures and a more reasoned argument than could be done in one discourse, and he therefore reworked and expanded it for publication. This was a lengthy process, much of it undertaken in spare moments and delayed by his poor health during the summer, only that autumn, during a few weeks' rest in Dover, was he able to see the form which the argument needed to take.[19]

Running through the book was Irving's opposition to anything which smacked of expediency. 'I remember, in this metropolis, to have heard it uttered with great applause in a public meeting, where the heads and leaders of the religious world were present, "If I were asked what was the first qualification for a missionary, I would say, Prudence; and what the second? Prudence; and what the third? still I would answer, Prudence."'[20] This he saw as the opposite of faith, defined in Hebrews 11.1 as 'the evidence of things unseen'. Such expediency had effects in other spheres, where it had resulted in the death of invisible ideals. It even led Christians to deny the possibility of conforming to the apostolic ideal.

He insisted that he was not opposed to societies in principle. As a youth he had prayed and saved for them, so 'that many years before I reached man's estate, I was chosen the manager of one of the country Bible societies, and one of the country missionary societies of Scotland'; he 'afterwards filled the office of secretary to the two chief societies in the most populous City of Scotland'. Nevertheless, he felt sure that their advocates would agree that they were not perfect.[21]

A missionary was to be 'a man of one thought, the gospel of Christ; a man of one purpose, the glory of God; a fool, and content to be reckoned a fool, for Christ; a madman, and content to be reckoned a madman, for Christ'.[22] The reverence for the ideal which he had learned from Coleridge also led him to adopt an unworldly view of such an ideal missionary. 'It was a spiritual work they had to do, therefore He disembodied (if I may so speak) and spiritualised the men who were to do it.'[23] Christ made them men of faith in order to plant faith:

> they had to deliver the nations from the idolatry of the gold and the silver, therefore He took care His messengers should have none; they had to deliver them from the idolatry of wisdom, therefore He took care they should be foolish; they had to deliver the world from the idolatry of power and might, therefore He took care they

---

[19] *CW*, 1.429–30.

[20] Ibid. 430–1.

[21] Ibid. 435–6. We noted earlier that Irving had been joint-secretary of the Bible Society's Glasgow auxiliary. He may also have been involved in an auxiliary at Bolton, near Haddington, since he knew its treasurer, Gilbert Burns: Peter Dobson, 'A Journey Through East Lothian Places and Personalities', http://www.grantsbraes.org.uk/pdf/a-journey-through-east-lothian.pdf, accessed 13 March 2009.

[22] *CW*, 1.508.

[23] Ibid. 455.

should be weak; they had to deliver the world from the idolatry of fame and reputation, therefore He took care they should be despised; they had to deliver the world from the idolatry of things that are, therefore He took care they should be as things that are not ...[24]

Therefore, missionaries must be without all the things in which men trust, in order to be wholly dependent on the Holy Spirit in the way that they sought to persuade others to be. They must have 'no purse, that is, no pecuniary emolument; no scrip, that is, no possessions; no change of raiment, that is, no pleasures or accommodations of the body; no staff, that is, no ease or pleasure of travel; no salutations by the way, that is, no ends of natural or social affection'.[25] In a perceptive anticipation of what later became widespread practice, he contended that such a missionary

> will by degrees divest himself of all those things which withdraw the people from the word of his mouth, or hinder them from apprehending the simplicity and sincerity of his spiritual purpose. He will adopt their dresses, follow their manner of life, eat with them and drink with them, and seek access to them at all their unguarded moments, that he may be always at hand to drop his words seasonably into their ear, and manifest constantly before their eye the influence of his faith over all the conditions of man, instead of merely addressing them now and then with set speeches and abstract discourses against the very time, form, and place of which, their minds are already in arms. And he will not scruple to take favours at their hand, if that will bring him into closer confidence of their souls, which it doth far more frequently than otherwise; and if not, he will work to them for his meat, teach them the arts of his country, do anything that may bring him and keep him in close and frequent contact with their personal affections: and he will learn to be of no country, that he may remove political hindrances out of the way, and he will learn to carry no temptations about with him ...[26]

Since, he argued, the conditions and challenges of missionary work have never changed, why should the characteristics which should mark the missionaries?[27] The more like the ideal, the more a missionary would be blessed; indeed, the relative lack of blessing should have made supporters of missions review their approach.[28] Following this ideal would not only lead to more blessing among the heathen, but to healing of the church's divisions, as missionaries of the apostolic stamp recognized one another.[29]

---

[24] Ibid. 455–6. Irving is echoing 1 Cor. 1.27–8.
[25] Ibid. 497–8.
[26] Ibid. 499–500.
[27] Ibid. 505–6.
[28] Ibid. 518–19.
[29] Ibid. 521.

The fullest response came, not surprisingly, from the secretary of the LMS, William Orme.³⁰ Orme argued his case robustly but graciously, winning considerable sympathy in the process from reviewers of his work, who compared its tone favourably with Irving's somewhat sweeping and allegedly ill-founded condemnations. If Irving had known those involved better, Orme thought, he might not have misunderstood or misrepresented them. As it was, Irving's ideas were confused, and he had condemned sentiments others did not hold. Moreover, the world would rejoice to see an Evangelical attacking other Evangelicals. Irving's idealism was judged to be misdirected; Orme could not see why he was so horrified at the stress on the need for prudence, since the only sort of prudence which mission societies sought was that which showed itself in the wisdom to deal with opposition and meet emergencies.³¹ The book's fundamental error was its misunderstanding of the missionary office, which confounded office and character:³² Orme asserted that all were agreed that apostles were the pattern for missionaries in terms of their character, but modern Christians did not occupy the apostolic office.³³ As for the 'Missionary Charter' in Matthew 10, everyone agreed that this was permanent too, but only for the groups which it concerned.³⁴ Some parts of it were temporary in application.³⁵ Orme did not consider that Irving's interpretation was supported by apostolic practice or by the analogy of faith, and made the telling point that the advocate of unsupported missionaries was himself in receipt of a regular salary.³⁶ He challenged Irving to suit actions to words: societies were 'ready at this moment to receive the proffer of Mr. Irving's services to any part of the world in which he may think the best opportunity is presented for acting on his own principles, and displaying the sincerity of his attachment to them'.³⁷

The *Congregational Magazine* could hardly be expected to remain unmoved, given that it was the denomination's missionary society to which Irving preached his sermon, and on which he was deemed to have cast aspersions. 'Seldom has there been presented to the world a more outrageous vituperation of all the principles on which the successful movements of christian missions have been conducted, than in the harangues of Mr. Irving.'³⁸ Like Orme, it asked why Irving should require a

---

[30] William Orme, *An Expostulatory Letter to the Rev. Edward Irving, A.M. Occasioned by his Orations for Missionaries after the Apostolical School* (London: B. J. Holdsworth, 1825).

[31] Ibid. 7, 58.

[32] Ibid. 8, 12.

[33] Ibid. 13–14.

[34] Ibid. 23, 27.

[35] Ibid. 27–9.

[36] Ibid. 38–40. Against this we may point to his willingness to come to London and preach without financial reward, his principled approach to assessing the calls to pastoral charges which had been extended to him, and the open-handed way in which he lived.

[37] Ibid. 49.

[38] Review of *Missionaries*, *Congregational Magazine* n.s. 1 (1825), 202–13, at 203.

guarantee of financial support which he condemned as illegitimate for missionaries.[39] His manner as well as his matter came in for criticism; as had happened after the appearance of *Orations*, he was attacked for presumption: 'He seems to regard himself as invested with a supernatural commission to occupy his metropolitan station, and to assume the province of a dictator on various matters, theological and ecclesiastical.'[40]

Even Coleridge, while acknowledging the work to be a 'noble specimen of manly principles and manly eloquence',[41] wondered why 'this Herculean "Oration"' had been published. Seizing on Irving's admission that 'It is not for the words, purse, scrip, raiment, staff, and friendship, that I contend', Coleridge claimed that in so saying he was conceding everything to those with whom he was taking issue, and that he had nothing else to offer.[42] Anticipating how Irving's thought would develop in later years, he accused him of failing to meet the main objection of his antagonists, which was that apostolic missionaries, unlike nineteenth-century ones, had miraculous gifts.[43] We shall see that this would be a strain in the motivation of the early seekers after miraculous gifts in the West of Scotland.[44]

One aspect of Irving's thought about mission which was not prominent in *Missionaries* but which would come to play a key role in his ecclesiology was pessimism. Initially, he had shared in the postmillennial missionary optimism which marked much early nineteenth-century Evangelicalism. In one of his sermons 'On Prayer', which may have been preached during the winter of 1823–4, he had rejoiced that:

> They who were the Church's persecutors have become her friends, and joined in society with their meanest subjects to make way for her holy laws. Nations have forborne to molest her missionary servants, who are the ambassadors of the kingdom. They have joined in a common union to send her voice through all the earth, and her words to the world's end. The heathen and barbarous powers are suing for embassies of her ministers, against whom lately their territories [sic] were barred. All Christendom is beginning to forget its partitions, and each party its long-remembered grudge. The zeal for conformity, which threatened in Protestant countries as much bloodshed as the mother of harlots drank from the cup of her abominations, is giving way to charity and forbearance. The wounds in Christ's mystical body are healing. The various members are content with their various

---

[39] Ibid. 212.

[40] Ibid. 203.

[41] Marginal note in his copy of Irving, *Missionaries*, 131 (London, BL, shelfmark C61c8).

[42] Ibid. 82.

[43] Ibid. 131.

[44] A similar view was evident among some early Brethren missionaries; one, J. V. Parnell (later Lord Congleton) would return from India in 1837, at least in part because he had not received the charismata which he believed to be essential equipment for missionary work: Tim Grass, *Gathering to His Name: The Story of Open Brethren in Britain & Ireland* (Carlisle: Paternoster, 2006), 111.

offices, and the word of the Lord is prospering apace. Heathen lands see the salvation of our God, and distant isles rejoice that the Lord God omnipotent reigneth. Oceans are crossed and continents wandered over for nations to bring unto the obedience of the truth; and God, by manifold tokens, prepares the way of His servants before them; and the hearts of the barbarous people are opened for the reception of her laws.[45]

From Coleridge, however, he was picking up a profound pessimism regarding the future of the world in which he was so successfully making his way. (We noted earlier the older man's comment that the world was not to be converted, but judged.) This may well have acted upon his existing Calvinist views, given the tendency among some Calvinists to see the elect as a minority amid an unbelieving world. He came to expect a future revolution, in which the present system would be destroyed.[46]

Coleridge also influenced Irving away from the 'evidences'-based approach to defending Christianity on the basis of the fulfilled prophecies and gospel miracles, which had marked the eighteenth century, towards an approach which stressed the capacity of Scripture to speak to the inner man. In his sermons 'On Prayer', Irving explained that: 'The Scripture is a book that is to be understood like any other book, through experience of the truth of what it contains, through the answer of head and heart, of intellect, and conscience, and feeling.'[47] The impact of Coleridge was also evident in sermons which Irving preached in 1825 at the Caledonian Chapel,[48] which were later revised and published as *The Doctrine of the Incarnation Opened in Six Sermons* (1828). About the time he received a call to Edinburgh (July 1825), he also preached two sermons on the Persons of the Trinity, which he characterized as Will, Word, and Spirit; this understanding would be foundational for his later thought, and for it he was indebted to Coleridge.[49]

James Hatley Frere (1779–1866)

James Hatley Frere was an Artillery Lieutenant who, during a lengthy period of spiritual agony and nervous breakdown, had sought to resign his commission in order to prepare for ordination. His family had resisted the idea, because of their concern at his state of health and their disapproval of his evangelical convictions. From 1805, therefore, he became a clerk at the Army Pay Office in London. Whilst he abandoned all thought of entering the ministry, he did not give up his evangelical views; indeed, within a few years he became a noted student of biblical prophecy, a

---

[45] *CW*, 3.158–9.

[46] Oliphant, *Life*, 92–3.

[47] *CW*, 3.84.

[48] O[liver]. Y[orke]., 'The Fraserians; or, the commencement of the year Thirty-Five. A Fragment', *Fraser's Magazine* 11 (1835), 1–27, at 5.

[49] Edinburgh, NLS, Acc. 12489/14, John Home Simpson, Typescript work on the Simpsons and their relationship to Irving (c. 1985), 25. For more detail, see ch. 14.

subject which at that time was still an accepted part of the wider world of intellectual discourse, and which had been given a new stimulus by the epochal events of the French Revolution and the widespread fear that something similar could happen in Britain.[50]

Carlyle wrote dismissively of Frere, whom Irving took him to meet in Frere's Whitehall office in March 1825, as 'an elderly official little gentleman ... busy in the red-tape line. This was the Honourable Something or other, great in Scripture Prophecy, in which he had started some sublime new idea, well worth prosecuting, as Irving had assured me.'[51] Coleridge was no more impressed; noting in February 1826 that Irving had lately spent a good deal of time with Frere, whom he called 'a pious and well-meaning but gloomy and enthusiastic Calvinist, and quite swallowed up in the quicksands of conjectural prophecy, – translating Ezekiel, Zachariah [sic], Daniel, and the Apocalypse into Journals and Gazettes',[52] a reference to the type of prophetic interpretation adopted by Frere. This was known as historicism, because it treated biblical prophecy as referring to specific historical events and conversely looked in the newspapers for fulfilment of specific prophecies in contemporary happenings. Perhaps the best-known features of his scheme were the identification of Napoleon Bonaparte as the Antichrist[53] and the fixing of the date of the Second Coming for 1867.

However, Irving was more impressed. As commonly portrayed, Frere was looking for somebody influential to convince of the truth of his prophetic scheme, who would then be able to advocate it with far more influence than he could himself. He found such a person in the receptive Irving,[54] who acknowledged this debt in the dedication to his first major work on Scripture prophecy, *Babylon and Infidelity Foredoomed of God*, published in 1826. Irving admitted his initial bewilderment at hearing Frere expound his interpretation of Daniel and the Apocalypse, but testified that on their second meeting, over a year later, he was so impressed with the gracious way in which Frere dealt with objectors that he found himself constrained to become Frere's pupil.[55] Writing to her mother in June 1825, Isabella included the

---

[50] On Frere, see Gabrielle Festing, *John Hookham Frere and his Friends* (London: James Nisbet, 1899); B. S. Frere, *A Record of the Frere Family of Suffolk & Norfolk* ([Stamford: the author], 1982), which quotes extensively from family correspondence.

[51] Carlyle, *Reminiscences*, 279.

[52] Quoted in Frere, *Record*, 192–3.

[53] W. H. Oliver, *Prophets and Millennialists: The Uses of Biblical Prophecy in England from the 1790s to the 1840s* ([Auckland]: Auckland University Press and Oxford University Press, 1978), 42.

[54] Oliphant, *Life*, 104.

[55] Edward Irving, *Babylon and Infidelity Foredoomed of God: A Discourse on the Prophecies of Daniel and the Apocalypse, which relate to these Latter Times, and until the Second Advent* (Glasgow: William Collins, 1828), v–vi. This may be a reference to semi-public discussions held each Wednesday afternoon during 1825: E. R. Sandeen, *The Roots of Fundamentalism: British and American Millenarianism 1800–1930* (Chicago, IL: University of Chicago Press, 1970), 16.

Freres among a list of new friends they had made. Acknowledging that Frere had 'been Edward's instructor in the Prophecies', she paid fulsome tribute to his insight into prophecy, describing him as 'the John of the present age'.[56] Indeed, it has even been claimed that Frere, whose income was not large, maintained Irving, Isabella and their child in his home for a long period.[57] Frere's sister, reading a book by Irving on biblical prophecy, commented that Irving was nothing other than a mouthpiece for her brother.[58] Irving made it clear that his part was merely to communicate to others what had been revealed, not to himself but to Frere.[59]

The ground had been prepared by Coleridge, although he came to disapprove thoroughly of Irving's preoccupation with eschatology. 'What [Frere] taught him seems to have been merely the structural and chronological features of prophecy; for insight into its spiritual power and laws he was indebted to Coleridge.'[60] From now on, prophecy was to be a central concern of Irving in his preaching and writing. By July 1825, he could inform his congregation:

> I have been occupied all the day with the finishing of a work upon those prophecies which have respect to the papacy and to infidelity, which I trust the Lord will bless to the stirring up of the church to expect speedily the coming of the Lord. My views upon this subject I have not yet fully explained to our flock but this will form, if God spare us, a part of the occupation of the next year.[61]

By the end of the year, as we shall see in a later chapter, Irving was preaching on prophetic subjects; in 1826, Frere, with Irving and Lewis Way, would found the Society for the Investigation of Prophecy. It was out of this milieu that the Albury Conferences were to be born.

Henry Drummond (1786–1860)

In social terms, Drummond and Irving were worlds apart. Whereas Irving's background had been modest and provincial, Drummond's was wealthy and urban. Educated at Harrow and Oxford (though he never took his degree), he became a partner in the family bank, the head office of which still faces Trafalgar Square (though the bank is no longer independent, having become part of the Royal Bank of Scotland in 1924). From 1810–13 he sat as a Member of Parliament for a Devon constituency, Plympton Earle, resigning for health reasons. From 1819, he lived at Albury Park in Surrey, where he acquired the reputation of being a caring if highly

---

[56] Isabella Irving to Mrs Martin, 3 June 1825 (in private hands). My guess is that Irving and Frere must have met for the first time by early 1824.

[57] Frere, *Record*, 193. I have not found any confirmatory evidence for this.

[58] Ibid. 192.

[59] Irving, *Babylon and Infidelity*, vii–viii.

[60] Andrews, *Irving*, 59.

[61] London, RS, EIL31, Irving to the Caledonian Church, 14 July 1825.

autocratic old-school Tory landlord. In 1825 he founded the chair of Political Economy at Oxford.[62]

Around 1815, Drummond had experienced an evangelical conversion. We do not know the details; it is possible that his brother Spencer (1790–1882), who was an Anglican clergyman, may have had a hand in it. He was then baptized as a believer in a chapel at Taunton belonging to a group of high Calvinist seceders from the Church of England, the 'Western Schism'.[63] He disposed of his hunting establishment, sold his house (The Grange, Northington, Hampshire), and with his wife set out for the Holy Land. Forced into port by a storm, he ended up in Geneva, where he met Robert Haldane (1764–1842), a Scottish itinerant preacher. During 1817–18, Drummond continued Haldane's efforts to foster the revival of evangelical religion in the French-speaking world which became known as the *Réveil*. Returning to England, in 1819 Drummond, with Robert Haldane and Sir Thomas Baring, founded the interdenominational Continental Society for the Diffusion of Religious Knowledge to continue the work. Rather than sending out British missionaries, it employed local agents (often theology students who had been refused ordination on account of their evangelical beliefs) to distribute Bibles and evangelical literature throughout Europe. Its activity was bankrolled to a considerable extent by Drummond, along with Haldane. In time, Drummond returned to the Church of England, as was natural in a man who was, in many ways, a pillar of the establishment.

The date of Irving's first encounter with Drummond is not possible to establish with precision, but it is likely to have been during 1824. Drummond adopted premillennial views during 1825 through hearing Irving preach, and his influence would lead to that viewpoint becoming dominant in the Continental Society.[64] His influence may also explain how Irving came to be preaching at its anniversary meetings in May 1825.[65] Irving's growing interest in biblical prophecy, and his

---

[62] On Drummond, see Hector Bolitho and Derek Peel, *The Drummonds of Charing Cross* (London: George Allen and Unwin, 1967), ch. 9; Boyd Hilton, *The Age of Atonement: The Influence of Evangelicalism on Social and Economic Thought 1785–1865* (Oxford: Oxford University Press, 1988); Timothy C. F. Stunt, *From Awakening to Secession: Radical Evangelicals in Switzerland and Britain 1815–35* (Edinburgh: T. & T. Clark, 2000); Grayson Carter, *Anglican Evangelicals: Protestant Secessions from the* Via Media, *c. 1800–1850* (Oxford: Oxford University Press, 2001).

[63] Stunt thinks that it was probably through members of the Baring family that Drummond came into contact with the 'Western Schism' and was converted: *Awakening*, 95–6. Also engaged in banking, some of them joined this movement.

[64] Another factor in Drummond's growing interest in prophecy was economic – alarm at speculation in Latin American mining shares: Henry Drummond, *Abstract Principles of Revealed Religion* (2nd edn, London: Thomas Bosworth, 1876), iii; cf. Carter, *Anglican Evangelicals*, 164.

[65] On the Continental Society, see Kenneth J. Stewart, 'A Millennial Maelstrom: Controversy in the Continental Society in the 1820s', in Crawford Gribben and Timothy C. F. Stunt, eds, *Prisoners of Hope? Aspects of Evangelical Millennialism in Britain and*

acceptance of the system of interpretation propounded by Frere, led him to conclude that, since (i) the society had been founded in order to evangelize Roman Catholic Europe, (ii) Roman Catholicism featured prominently in Frere's prophetic scheme,[66] and (iii) events appeared to be hastening rapidly towards the end, in taking a prophetic theme he could offer guidance to the society's workers in their evangelism.[67] The sermon was not summarized in its annual report, and appears to have been the cause of some controversy on account of his alleged politicization of the Christian message: both supporters and opponents of Roman Catholic emancipation understood Irving to have been expressing support for their opinions, so he decided to publish the discourse in order to clear himself of political partisanship.[68] By June it was ready, although the Preface was not written until 10 March 1826.[69] It appeared under the title *Babylon and Infidelity Foredoomed of God*.[70] The sermon was dedicated to Frere, in fulsome terms similar to those he had used of Coleridge.

If Coleridge shaped the inner dynamic of Irving's theology, and Frere its structural form, Drummond's influence was felt mainly in the way Irving related it to the contemporary church. Ultimately, the development of the Catholic Apostolic Church owed at least as much to Drummond as it did to Irving. Drummond's high Toryism gave rise to a profound social pessimism, which was reinforced both by current events and by his reading of Bible prophecy. He thus found in Irving a kindred spirit, who could provide a detailed theological undergirding for such views. In addition, Drummond shared with Irving a propensity to adopt fairly extreme views, and an aggressive outspokenness in putting them forward. Furthermore, the two shared a fairly negative opinion of the contemporary churches; this was not adopted *in spite of* their belief in establishment, but *because of* it: the church's failure to live up to its calling meant that it lay under divine judgement, and no amount of expedients in the form of missionary societies and evangelizing agencies could atone for its unfaithfulness.

In spite of their closeness in many ways, Irving continued to be wary of Drummond; in November 1825, after attending a meeting which the latter had chaired, he wrote to Isabella: 'Henry Drummond was in the chair; he is in all chairs – I fear for him. His words are more witty than spiritual; his manner is *spirituel*, not

---

Ireland, 1800–1880 (Carlisle: Paternoster, 2005), 122–49. Drummond also secured Irving a place on the society's committee in 1825: Carter, *Anglican Evangelicals*, 164.

[66] For a brief exposition of Frere's scheme, see Columba Graham Flegg, *'Gathered under Apostles': A Study of the Catholic Apostolic Church* (Oxford: Clarendon, 1992), 301–4.

[67] Cf. Oliphant, *Life*, 104–5.

[68] Ibid. 106, 108.

[69] Isabella Irving to Mrs Martin, 3 June 1825 (in private hands). It was, apparently, Isabella who conducted negotiations with potential publishers.

[70] It will be considered in ch. 13 as part of the discussion of Irving's developing eschatological views.

grave'.[71] Their relationship would be marked by occasional tension, in which their differing economic circumstances formed one factor and their clash of expectations regarding their own roles in the emerging radical movement which would become the Catholic Apostolic Church were another.

※ ※ ※

In conclusion, we may sum up what the significance of such friendships was for Irving. Like many ministers, he clearly felt a freedom to discuss intellectual concerns with his friends which could not so readily have been shared with the office-bearers and members of his congregation. It is also possible that he may half-consciously have welcomed their notice as evidence that he was becoming respectable and accepted, socially speaking, although all three were, in different ways, social misfits. Unimpressed by the contemporary world and pessimistic about its future prospects, they would greatly have reinforced the idealistic Irving's tendencies in that direction.

---

[71] Oliphant, *Life*, 176: journal for 21 November 1825. Carter considers this was when the two men first met, but offers no evidence for this: *Anglican Evangelicals*, 174.

CHAPTER 11

Pastor, 1826–30

In recent decades, the 'quest for the historical Irving' has produced a variety of pictures: we have had Irving the theologian drawing on the teaching of the early church fathers, Irving the prophetic extremist, Irving the secularizer, Irving the martyr for truth, and Irving the pioneer of charismatic renewal or (less positively) the cautionary example of what happens when a Reformed minister adopts charismatic views.[1] However, if we want to understand Irving's mind as a theologian, we should

---

[1] Examples of each are, respectively: David W. Dorries, *Edward Irving's Incarnational Christology* (Fairfax, VA: Xulon Press, 2002); Mark Rayburn Patterson, 'Designing the Last Days: Edward Irving, the Albury Circle, and the Theology of *The Morning Watch*', Ph.D. thesis, King's College, London, 2001; W. H. Oliver, *Prophets and Millennialists: The Uses of Biblical Prophecy in England from the 1790s to the 1840s* ([Auckland]: Auckland University Press and Oxford University Press, 1978); William S. Merricks, *Edward Irving: The Forgotten Giant* (East Peoria, IL: Scribe's Chamber Publications, 1983); Gordon Strachan, *The Pentecostal Theology of Edward Irving* (London: Darton Longman & Todd, 1973); Arnold Dallimore, *The Life of Edward Irving: Fore-runner of the Charismatic Movement* (Edinburgh: Banner of Truth, 1983).

It is worth commenting further at this point on recent scholarly work on Irving. Strachan's book, whilst it did not mark the beginning of the contemporary resurgence of interest in Irving, has certainly done more than any other work to foster it. Focusing on Irving's understanding of the person of Christ and (in greater detail) the work of the Holy Spirit, it was intended as both a work of serious scholarship and as an apologia for charismatic renewal, which at that stage had made little headway in the Church of Scotland of which Strachan was (and remains) a minister. Strachan was unashamed in his admiration for Irving, whom he compared successively to John the Baptist (paving the way for those who regard the gift of tongues as the initial evidence of being baptized with the Holy Spirit), Luther (standing on the Bible alone in the face of ecclesiastical opposition), and John Knox (who shot to prominence as suddenly as Irving would if the Kirk would but take Pentecostalism seriously). Irving was, Strachan argued, the first Reformed Pentecostal theologian, 'one of the few to whom it is given to uncover new systems of Scriptural truth that prove themselves subsequently to be a blessing and inspiration to millions': *Irving*, 21.

Considerably indebted to Strachan was the American Pentecostal scholar David Dorries (to date the only Pentecostal to have written a book on Irving). His work on *Edward Irving's Incarnational Christology* appeared in 2002. Its perspective may be gauged from his assertion that Irving's Christology 'merits inclusion among the most treasured deposits within the church's legacy of doctrinal truth': ibid., xiii. The author's aim was 'to vindicate the orthodoxy of Edward Irving's doctrine of the Person and work of

recognize that he saw himself as a pastor first and foremost. Similarly, if we want to understand his family relationships, we need to recognize that for him spiritual and physical fatherhood were tightly interwoven and each influenced his approach to the other; the next few chapters, dealing with the period from 1826 until mid-1830, will likewise interweave discussion of his theology, his ministry, and his family life.

* * *

In May 1827, a new and larger chapel was opened for Irving in London's Regent Square, the National Scotch Church. In some ways, the period leading up to this represents the 'high point' of his ministry. In it we see Irving the Scottish high churchman, something which in many ways he remained to the end of his life. A new building was needed to accommodate the crowds flocking to hear Irving; but we have already noted (in chapter 7) another factor at work, which predated his arrival in London. This was a desire to remedy the low esteem in which Scots in the capital held their national church, by opening a building for worship which would be worthy of the Kirk and attract those who might otherwise be lost to more inspiring Anglican places of worship.

Although the west front of the church was modelled on that of York Minster, the rest of the building was more plainly styled, and was basically a large preaching box with a gallery running round three sides of the sanctuary. The committee determined on a grand show for the opening day. Inviting Chalmers to preach, they expressed the opinion that it was deplorable that 'the Patrons of her [Scotland's] Churches should be so indifferent to her religious ordinances', and informed him that of 120,000 Scots in the London area, not 1% were in communion with any of the churches.[2] Irving followed this up with a letter on his own account. There being some uncertainty about when Chalmers could undertake the engagement, Irving explained that, according to the Building Committee, the opening could not be postponed beyond 13 May as that would occasion loss of several hundred pounds in

---

Jesus Christ': ibid. xv. He does this by means of an exhaustive survey of Irving's writings and those of his opponents. This makes the work of considerable value, although it is rather hagiographic in tone and fails to make much use of sources such as book reviews, newspaper reports and Presbytery records.

By contrast, the Canadian Baptist Arnold Dallimore wrote not to uphold Irving's charismatic views but to oppose them. His biography presents Irving's ministry as a cautionary tale about the dangers of dabbling with charismatic practices, an outlook which he shared with one of his main sources, Thomas Carlyle. The fundamental problem with Irving was, according to Dallimore, that he lacked a clear doctrinal grasp which could have preserved him from much evil. Evidence of this is sought in Irving's preaching. It is clear from the bibliography that his acquaintance with Irving's writings and published sermons was limited; had it been at all comprehensive, such a claim would not have been made.

[2] Edinburgh, NCL, Chalmers MSS, CHA 4.77.12: Irving and the elders to Chalmers, 26 February 1827.

seat rents. As for the day's proceedings, a service in the morning would be followed by a dinner for higher-class Scots in an attempt to rally them round the church. Another eminent Scot, Dr Robert Gordon of Edinburgh, was already engaged to share in the ministry on the Sabbath; Irving would 'look on in silent wonder to behold his goodness to me, and his honour to the work we are engaged in'. He was anxious for success in his request because of the efforts being made against the work and the Gospel. In inviting the two men to preach, Irving was not asking them to express agreement with his distinctive theological views, but by their presence to testify to his character, integrity, and standing in the Kirk. The letter ended positively, however, rejoicing that 'since the days of the Reformation, there never perhaps was a man more blessed in the fruitfulness of his ministry, or in the godly communion of his flock, than I have been, because I have not been ashamed of the testimony of the Lord'.[3] In agreeing to preach at the opening, Chalmers may have been killing two birds with one stone, as his main objective in visiting London was to investigate the offer of a chair at the new London University.[4]

On 29 April, Irving preached the 'Last Sermon in the Caledonian Church', on Genesis 28.10–22.[5] He took Jacob's actions in setting up an altar and making a vow as an example for the devotion of his hearers, and then reviewed the topics on which he had preached since settling with them. God allowed them to grow in peace; he had been tempted to be spoiled by admiration, but had been preserved because God allowed them to suffer opposition. Blessing had followed because they were faithful then in declaring the whole word of God. Then God began to open deeper truth to them; those who wanted to be entertained fell away, but those who wanted to learn grew closer together and the spirit of prayer grew stronger. Among the deeper truths opened to them was that of the Trinity, which, next to the Second Coming, was most fruitful in terms of souls won for Christ. From that came their knowledge of the Roman Catholic apostasy, 'which, I do well remember, we were very timorous to declare, and you were very loath to hear'.[6] God also chose them as a church among whom to plant a testimony to the Second Coming, which truth was not

---

[3] CHA 4.77.7: Irving to Chalmers, 26 March 1827.

[4] Stewart J. Brown, *Thomas Chalmers and the Godly Commonwealth in Scotland* (Oxford: Oxford University Press, 1982), 177.

[5] *CW*, 3.500–19. There was at one point a plan to retain the old building for Presbyterian worship (Chalmers MSS, CHA 4.80.45: J. Miller, Irving and W. Dinwiddie to Chalmers, [1 March 1827]). The Presbytery of London and some of the most committed in the congregation wanted to keep it for Presbytery use, and Presbytery had made available a year's rent. If a young man were willing to try and gather a flock of Scots, Irving would offer accommodation, and some of the present congregation would provide a nucleus. If blessing ensued, the freehold could be purchased, and if he were called by his congregation he could be ordained and become a pastor rather than a missionary, and help reach the 120,000 Scots. Collins had heard that the managers of the Caledonian Chapel were looking to appoint a successor there (CHA 4.70.1: William Collins to Chalmers, 10 March 1827). In the event, however, it was repurchased by the Swedenborgians that same year.

[6] *CW*, 3.507.

opened to the sixteenth-century Reformers. How should they commemorate God's goodness and his presence? By building a new house of God, and devoting their resources to him. Referring to the opening ceremonies, Irving warns his flock not to put their confidence in men because the Kirk's two most honoured ministers would be preaching, and assured them that God would not have brought them so far unless he had a message to be delivered through them.

The opening service took place at noon on Friday, 11 May. Irving was not silent but led the first part of the worship. Chalmers wrote to his wife of the 'prodigious want of tact in the length of his prayer, forty minutes, and altogether it was an hour and a half from the commencement of the service ere I began'. His judgement was that Irving 'certainly errs in the outrunning of sympathy'.[7] Much later, Chalmers referred to the service in conversation with the Quaker J. J. Gurney:

> The Congregation, in their eagerness to obtain seats, had already been assembled about three hours. Irving said, he would assist me by reading a chapter for me in the first instance. He chose the very longest chapter in the Bible, and went on with his exposition for an hour and a half. When my turn came, of what use could I be in an exhausted receiver? On another similar occasion he kindly proffered me the same aid, adding, 'I can be short.' I said, How long will it take you? He answered, 'ONLY ONE HOUR AND FORTY MINUTES.' Then, replied I, I must decline the favour.[8]

According to Jane Simpson, Irving read the story of the dedication of Solomon's Temple (1 Kings 8).[9] Charlotte Wedgwood reported to her sister Emma, later to become the wife of Charles Darwin, that Irving prayed for an hour, which she considered 'more than twice too long. Moreover his praying is so theatrical as to be disagreeable,– a much worse fault in praying than in preaching. There was an immense crowd, and quite a riot at one time made by the people outside breaking in.'[10] Chalmers, when he eventually stood up to preach, took as his text Jeremiah 6.16, 'Thus saith the Lord, Stand ye in the ways, and see, and ask for the old paths, where is the good way, and walk therein, and ye shall find rest for your souls', and it is tempting to see his title, 'On the Respect due to Antiquity',[11] as directed at Irving's predilection for what Chalmers considered dangerous novelties such as millennial speculation. In it, he called on his hearers to be willing to learn from history; for members of the Church of Scotland, that meant going back to the

---

[7] William Hanna, *Memoirs of the Life and Writings of Thomas Chalmers D.D. LL.D.* (4 vols, Edinburgh: Sutherland and Knox, 1850), 3.160.

[8] Ibid. 3.271–2; cf. Oliphant, *Life*, 208–9.

[9] Edinburgh, NLS, Acc.12489/9, Jane Simpson, Diary, 1826–8, fol. 14.

[10] Emma Darwin, *A Century of Family Letters, 1792-1896*, ed. Henrietta Litchfield, 2 vols, New York: D. Appleton, 1915, http://books.google.co.uk/books?id=vMgEA AAAIAAJ&q=%22emma+darwin%22+%22family+letters%22&dq=%22emma+darwin%22 +%22family+letters%22&pgis=1, accessed 30 April 2009.

[11] Thomas Chalmers, 'On the Respect due to Antiquity: A Sermon, Preached on Friday, May 11, 1827, at the Opening of the Scotch National Church in London', *Works*, vol. 11 (Glasgow: William Collins, n.d.), 123–59.

sixteenth-century founders and the theology and system of discipline and education which they evolved. Yet they should not follow such things slavishly, and he argued that the Reformers had been too harsh in their estimate of Roman Catholicism; indeed, he was in favour of Catholic emancipation, something which could not have pleased Irving, whose Reformed anti-Catholicism was receiving a new impetus from prophetic study.

At 5 p.m. Irving chaired a public dinner at the Freemasons' Tavern.[12] Not all approved, James Simpson recording in his diary: 'I declined being of the Dinner party, the Company being very promiscuous & after the Solemn Service of the morning I deemed [it] unsuitable'.[13] During the day, Irving presented the deacons with two silver salvers which he had been given three years earlier when opening a Church of Scotland in Liverpool. He asked for them to be engraved with the following inscription, which provides further testimony to his concern for the poor:

> These two plates I send to the National Scotch Church, London, on the 11th of May 1827, the day of its opening, that they may stand on each side of the door to receive the offerings for the poor, and all other the gifts of the congregation of the Lord in all time coming while He permits; and if at any time, which God forbid, the fountain of the people's charity should be dried up, and the poor of the Lord's house be in want of bread, of His house itself under any restraint of debt, I appoint that they shall be melted into shillings and sixpences for the relief of the same so far as they shall go.[14]

One of Irving's elders, the publisher James Nisbet, donated a pulpit Bible which Irving used and which was presented by the Kirk Session to William Hamilton, a merchant in London and one of Irving's elders as well as becoming his brother-in-law, after Irving's expulsion in 1832.[15]

In his journal for 13 May, Chalmers recorded that Peel, Coleridge, and Lords Mandeville and Farnham were present at the opening, and that Coleridge spoke with him in the vestry before and after the service.[16] Hamilton wrote to his future wife (who was one of Isabella's sisters) that the opening had been 'a gratifying success', and that Chalmers' sermon included 'an eloquent eulogium on the piety, zeal, and talents of Mr. Irving'.[17] Chalmers had agreed to publish his sermon at the opening, 'which contained a powerful defence of our excellent pastor ... not a little gratifying

---

[12] London, LMA, LMA/4358/C/002/12: lithographed letter from William Hamilton, 1 May 1827; John Hair, *Regent Square: Eighty Years of a London Congregation* (London: James Nisbet, 1899), 71.

[13] NLS, Acc. 12489/1, James Simpson, 'J. G. S. Journals 1806 to 1830', 22 May 1827.

[14] Hair, *Regent Square*, 79.

[15] Ibid. 80.

[16] Hanna, *Chalmers*, 3.160–1.

[17] Hair, *Regent Square*, 74.

to the congregation, but gall and wormwood to some of his enemies who were present'.[18]

The Building Committee were clearly strapped for cash, and on the opening day they issued a letter appealing for further donations to complete the towers.[19] A normal Sunday's collection, which was intended for the poor, averaged £4 or £5, but collections on that day amounted to £202 7s., and on the following Sunday £132 9s.[20] Shortly before the opening, the newly-elected deacons divided the church seating into four sections, each under a deacon responsible for registering names of seat-holders and collecting pew rents; 867 sittings were let straight away, with a resulting annual revenue of £1,292 7s.[21]

Irving's own first sermon in the new church, on Psalm 126.3 ('The Lord hath done great things for us; whereof we are glad'), was not preached until a fortnight later.[22] In it he calls on the congregation to render thanks to God for his goodness to them. The first blessing for which his hearers are to be thankful is that of the preaching of the word of God. Satan hates preaching; in his experience, 'the only thing against which he hath raged is the liberty which I take to myself in preaching beyond my fellows'.[23] He urges them to look at Christendom, to look at the pulpits in London, and to be thankful for this one. A second ground of thanksgiving is that through the preaching of the word, God has called out a church and ordered it apostolically. They are to bless God for the ordinances by which this has happened: a sound doctrinal confession, 'primitive' church discipline, simple forms of worship, and uncorrupted observance of the sacraments (all demonstrating Irving's deep attachment to Reformed church polity). A third ground is that these blessings are secure now; they are no longer tenants but owners of their place of worship, and a Trust deed secures it for their use. In his times of leisure, he had recently been reading Howie's *Scots Worthies*, and is thankful that they are able to gather freely – and in the sight of Episcopalians!

In his second main division, he considers why God has given the church these blessings. As their greatest blessing was that of having the word preached, God's

---

[18] Oliphant, *Life*, 207; cf. Hair, *Regent Square*, 74.

[19] LMA/4358/C/002/13.

[20] Occasionally sermons were preached in aid of particular societies; in 1828 there were sermons on behalf of the Continental Society (21 May, Andrew Thomson, £40 12s. 4d.); the Irish [Sunday] School Society (4 June, Andrew Thomson, £24 0s. 9d.); Highland Schools (8 June, Andrew Thomson – the congregation were getting good use out of him while Irving was away preaching in Scotland –, £36 15s. 10d. at two Sunday services); local schools (10 August, Irving, £40 at two Sunday services); and Spanish and Italian refugees (7 December, £192 19s. 9d. from two Sunday services): London, RS, National Scotch Church collection record book. The amount collected on the last occasion excited considerable newspaper comment, with Irving being held up as an example for others to follow.

[21] Hair, *Regent Square*, 72.

[22] *CW*, 3.520–52.

[23] Ibid. 524. We shall see below what he meant by this!

chief objective in having the new church built was that they might lead the way in testifying to sound doctrine. The Reformers had been martyred for their belief in Christ as prophet and priest; the Covenanters (uniquely among Protestants) had suffered similarly for allegiance to Christ as king. Irving saw his flock as raised up to testify to Christ's return. God also intended that they should preserve the pure discipline of the church according to the Books of Discipline, something which was especially necessary in view of the advance of radicalism and democracy among all churches. Irving testified that, in his experience, 'when the radical principle gets a footing the Holy Spirit departs'.[24] An additional objective was that of reaching out to expatriate Scots, many of whom neglected worship or were in need. In due course, we shall see that this concern, which extended to all in the neighbourhood of Regent Square, was to lead to the church calling A. J. Scott as their missionary.

* * *

The move to a larger building would test what had been achieved through Irving's ministry. He was no longer so fashionable, although it is debatable whether (as Mrs Oliphant speculates) he recognized that now he was addressing 'a congregation ... and not an age'. The office-bearers were well satisfied with the number of seat-holders and with a congregation which was usually considerably larger than that (at almost two thousand, it was probably the largest in London at the time), but his friends worried not that he would prostitute himself to popularity but that he would lose it altogether.[25] Irving's long prayers and expositions continued to present a problem. On 7 November 1825 he had written in his journal for Isabella about his kirk session meeting:

> we proceeded with good harmony and union, till they came to speak of time; and then I told them they must talk no more to me concerning the ministry of the word, for I would submit to no authority in that matter but the authority of the church, from which also I would take liberty to appeal if it gainsaid my conscience. I am resolved that two hours and a half I will have the privilege of. Write me your judgment in this matter ...[26]

Six days later, he picked up the subject again:

> I have been much exercised this last week with the possibility of some trial coming to me from the resolute stand which I have taken, and will maintain, upon the subject of the liberty of my ministry. For the spirit of authority and rule in the church begins to grow upon me, and I fear much there is not enough of the spirit of obedience in our city churches to bear it. But I am resolved, according as I am taught the duty of a minister of the Gospel, to discharge it, and consider everything that

---

[24] Ibid. 548.
[25] Oliphant, *Life*, 211–13; David Allen, 'A Belated Bouquet: A Tribute to Edward Irving (1792–1834)', *Expository Times* 103 (1991–2), 328–31, at 329.
[26] Oliphant, *Life*, 151–2.

may befall as the will of the Lord. I was telling this to Mr Dinwiddie this morning, for I find, good men, they have all their little schemes, after which they would like to see me play my part, instead of looking to me as one, under Christ's authority, to watch over the church, and to be honoured of the church.[27]

The problem appears to have been that worshippers were distracted by others who arrived late or left early. In April 1827 the session issued an appeal for punctuality on the part of seat-holders, quoting the *Directory of Public Worship* of 1645, the fullest document regulating Church of Scotland worship, to the effect that all should arrive before the service commenced and not leave until after the blessing had been pronounced. The deacons, meeting on 31 May, evidently felt that a more practical approach was needed, and asked Irving to cut the length of his services by half an hour, but he refused, brooking no interference with his prerogatives.[28]

Each year special sermons (and collections!) marked the anniversary of the church. Communion, as in most Church of Scotland congregations, was held twice a year (apparently on the first Sundays in May and November), preceded by a fast day service on the Thursday and a preparation service on the Saturday, and followed by a thanksgiving service on the Monday.[29] Following traditional practice, communion was conducted at tables placed in the central aisle, each sitting being addressed separately, with first sitting the most popular and many attenders not remaining to the end of the service.[30] At the fast day service, Irving read the Scots Confession to the congregation to remind them of the basis on which they were founded.[31]

Numbers of baptisms in the new church were at their peak substantially more than those in the old one, as the figures below indicate:[32]

1823	8 infants	0 adults
1824	16	0
1825	5	0
1826	29	4
1827	27	3
1828	35	6
1829	37	4
1830	34	0
1831	24	2

---

[27] Ibid. 159.
[28] LMA/4358/C/002/15; Hair, *Regent Square*, 76–7.
[29] Collection record book.
[30] Hair, *Regent Square*, 193.
[31] Andrew Landale Drummond, *Edward Irving and his Circle: Including some Consideration of the 'Tongues' Movement in the Light of Modern Psychology* (London: James Clarke, [1937]), 110.
[32] LMA/4358/B/006, 'Copy of Baptismal Register 1823–1855'.

The adults being baptized would probably have been converted to Christian faith under Irving's preaching, although one might have expected that at this period most such folk would have been baptized as infants. Interestingly, in January 1829 he was clearly investigating whether to baptize by immersion (something which may have arisen from his awareness of wider Christian tradition). He wrote to Chalmers on behalf of the session to ask whether the Church of Scotland permitted baptism by immersion, as was the rule in the Church of England.[33] In the name of his session he also asked the presbytery whether they might deviate from the norm of sprinkling. He was advised against innovating rashly, however, and there is no record that he adopted the practice.[34]

* * *

It would have been impossible to lead such a large flock without the assistance of dedicated church officers. A few months before the move, the congregation elected four elders and seven deacons to add to the existing three elders.[35] One new elder, Andrew Panton (like Nisbet a bookseller) became session clerk but, in spite of publishing some of Irving's works, proved a thorn in the flesh to Irving, allegedly because he adopted heterodox opinions. Isabella wrote to her sister late in 1829:

> you know or may know to what dreadful lengths the early Christians who threw off the authority of the Church & the obligation of the ordinances & means of grace & took to living in idleness having all things common were permitted to go_ Panton & his set go about making much of that text 'Give to every one that asketh' & by the sum given they measure the Christian.[36]

James Simpson, however, asserted that Panton resigned his office and left the church because he thought Irving unsound in his teaching about Christ's divine and human natures.[37] Either way, Irving was concerned to act honourably towards him. He gave William Hamilton, by now his brother-in-law and having more of a head for business than Irving ever did, power to settle his account with Panton and to terminate his business connection with him fairly and honourably.[38]

Dinwiddie, who had played such a role in Irving's coming to London and in getting the new church built to such a magnificent design, died in prison on 18

---

[33] Oliphant, *Life*, 255.

[34] Cambridge, URCHS, 'Minutes of the Scots Presbytery of London. Vol. 2. Apr. 28. 1823 to Nov. 11. 1834', fols 147–8: 20 January 1829.

[35] Hair, *Regent Square*, 71, 140. Dinwiddie had been the sole elder for some time before 1823, when Archibald Horn and David Blyth were ordained; in 1826 Hamilton, Nisbet, Duncan Mackenzie and Andrew Panton were added: ibid. 353; Isabella Irving to her parents, 29 December 1826 (in private hands).

[36] Isabella Irving to Anne Martin, 10 November 1829 (in private hands); cf. *CW*, 5.534.

[37] James Simpson, ' J. G. S. Journals 1806 to 1830', 18 September 1829.

[38] Irving to William Hamilton, London, 18 November 1829 (in private hands).

January 1830 (he had been imprisoned for debt since October 1829, his business having failed). One cannot help wondering whether Irving's course thereafter would have been quite the same if Dinwiddie had not died, given the close bond of spiritual understanding which had existed between the two men. James Simpson recorded his mystification at the session's apparent unwillingness to secure Dinwiddie's release:

> I mention what follows not as censuring Mr Irving & Kirk Session of R Church, but as a Mystery I am not now able to understand in their conduct in Mr D affairs. I have stated my great desire to get Mr D released from Prison by Court of Banc^y and having assertained [sic] that there was no Legal impediment, I went to several of Mr D's friends, not of the Session, & found them alive to my statements of the danger to Mr D's Life, or health from lying in a Prison at this season of year for 3 Months, as well as the impropriety & unchristian Spirit it would manifest on the part of the Scotch Church in London whose Interest he had been an eminent means lately of promoting, and the National Scotch Church in particular for the establishment of which he had wrought Night and Day for years. About the 1st day of Novr Mr Dinwiddie's Daughter's Funeral took Place at the Church. After it was over, I was invited into the Vestry to State my Views with regard to Mr D – present Mr <u>Irving, Horn, Hamilton, McKenzie, Blyth</u>.
>
> I did state my views as above, with arguments in favour of something being done for Mr D's release on a/c of his peculiar standing among them & towards the Church etc, and I added that I would take upon myself the providing the sum necessary for working the Commission, above the sum necessary for his relief by Insolvent Court, but to my surprise the Gentlemen present, while they seemed to feel for Mr D's circumstances, thought it better that he should remain in Prison ...[39]

Irving and the church also acquired an assistant. During a trip to Scotland in 1828 (described in chapter 15), he made the acquaintance of a minister's son from Greenock, A. J. Scott (1805–66). Sandy Scott had been preparing for the Church of Scotland ministry, having been licensed by the Presbytery of Paisley in 1827, but by the end of the year he had given this up on account of his inability to sign the Westminster Confession and had gone to Edinburgh to study medicine.[40] Irving described him as 'a precious youth, the finest and the strongest faculty for pure theology I have yet met with'.[41] He was to be the church's first missionary, working in the district around it, and Irving's assistant minister, at a salary of £150 per annum. His engagement was apparently settled at Rhu on 9 June, when Irving was preaching in the area. Initially he appears to have refused the offer of a post because he was unable to preach the required theology, but Irving told him that he was free to preach what he liked. A paper prepared by Nisbet and dated 14 August 1828 outlined his duties: to preach on Sunday afternoons and in local schools, and assist elders in

---

[39] James Simpson, 'J. G. S. Journals 1806 to 1830', 20 January 1830 [slightly altered].

[40] J. P. Newell, 'A. J. Scott and his circle' (Ph.D. thesis, New College, Edinburgh, 1981), 43.

[41] Oliphant, *Life*, 255: Irving to Chalmers, December 1828.

visiting. He helped in mission services at Swallow Street (a nearby Scottish congregation), and taught and preached among the spiritually destitute population of Westminster. Scott preached his first sermon at Regent Square on 2 November 1828.[42]

It was not long before Scott received a call, and his farewell was on 31 January 1830, although he was back at Regent Square soon after, as James Simpson recorded:

> Last Night I heard Mr Scott Preach at Regent Square on what we are to understand by the <u>Will</u> of God as expressed in first E[pistle] of John, 'If Ye Ask anything according to His <u>Will</u>', the Sermon extended to an hour, but to me it proved the least comprehensible Discourse I ever heard. Mr S is a Young Man of Talent & I believe Pious, but he seems to waste his strength by attempting to explain the subjects over which God has drawn a Veil such as the Doctrine of Election, and Christs Dying for all etc he follows Mr Irving in this Course.[43]

Irving's involvement with Scott did not end there. Called to the Church of Scotland charge at Woolwich, Scott's trials for ordination ran aground in April 1830 on the question of Christ's human nature, on which his views accorded with those of Irving. His illness led to the discussion being postponed, and in the meantime the presbytery appointed a committee to examine his doctrine; early in July they produced a formula to which Irving and Scott assented (which we shall note in chapter 17). However, Scott announced in October that, as before, he was unable to subscribe the Westminster Confession and returned the call to the presbytery. Ironically, in view of subsequent events, Irving encouraged him not to anticipate the decision of the Church of Scotland by cutting himself off from its jurisdiction. Although Irving's own views were by now under investigation, he was a member of the committee appointed to try to convince Scott that the Confession was in harmony with Scripture, but soon afterwards Irving withdrew from their jurisdiction. The church at Woolwich reissued the call early in 1831, and Scott continued to preach there, but the presbytery referred the matter to the General Assembly. The Presbytery of Paisley treated his refusal to subscribe as a resignation and deprived him of his licence on 4 May 1831. Although Scott appealed against their decision, the General Assembly confirmed it.[44]

---

[42] Collection record book; Hair, *Regent Square*, 85–7; Oliphant, *Life*, 234, 275.

[43] James Simpson, 'J. G. S. Journals 1806 to 1830', 3 March 1830. Cf. ibid. 11 June 1830: 'I said something [to Jane, his wife] regarding Mr Irving dwelling too much on controversy, and gave it as my opinion that he often attempted to explain the ways & degrees of God, which are for the present hid in a Mystery'; ibid. 12 June 1830: 'I had a good deal of conversation to day with Mr Hamilton regarding Mr Irvings dwelling so much in his Sermons on controverted points, he agreed with me that it was a pity and wish'd he would change in this respect, & again with his Discourses.'

[44] 'Presbytery of the Scots Church, London', *The Record*, no. 244 (29 April 1830), cf. no. 248 (13 May 1830); Edinburgh, NAS, CH1/2/154, 'Assembly Papers, main series' (1831); 'Minutes of Presbytery 2', fols 193, 204–7: 20 July, 21 September, 12 and 19

* * *

Before going too deeply into the controversial aspects of Irving's ministry, however, it is worth trying to sketch his approach to his calling. Irving aspired to what another great nineteenth-century preacher, the Particular Baptist C. H. Spurgeon (1834–92), would later call 'an all-round ministry'. In an essay of 1824, Irving had commended the sixteenth century reforming preacher Bernard Gilpin as an example of all-round ministerial excellence, as student, preacher, pastor, churchman and member of society.[45] He expounded these heads more fully in an *Ordination Charge* which he preached when his friend Hugh Maclean was inducted to the Scots Church at London Wall in March 1827.[46] It offered a definitive statement of his high doctrine of the ministry, but was his only writing devoted to the subject. Dallimore rightly considers it 'undoubtedly the finest production ever to come from his pen, and in its overwhelmingly challenging concept of the ministry we see Edward Irving at his best'.[47]

Irving divides the minister's responsibility into the five heads listed above. As scholar, he must keep up his studies, having in view the warfare for souls to which he is called. As preacher, he must study to conduct public worship responsibly, and that without the aid of any service book. He must know how to enable his flock to sing the psalms with understanding. Public prayer demands private reflection and meditation. Preaching has a particular end in view: 'Keep not thy people banqueting, but bring them out to do battle for the glory of God and of His Church: to which end thou shalt need to preach to them the Holy Ghost, who is the strength of battle.'[48] In celebrating the sacraments, he must not present them as 'bare and naked signs'[49] but encourage the people to approach them in faith that God uses them to convey his blessing. As pastor, he is to visit his people, yet he is always to be a man apart: in all his contacts with the flock he is never to descend to mere socializing. As churchman, he is to uphold the doctrines and discipline of the established Church of Scotland. It is not enough to care for his own congregation but he must play his part in the presbytery's efforts to reclaim Scots migrants to London. He may have fellowship with all Trinitarian believers, but should not flinch from rebuking them for their errors. Finally, as a man, he is to set a godly example in his social relationships, especially taking care to avoid the accumulation of earthly riches. No man is sufficient for these things, but through the laying on of hands Christ has endowed him with the Spirit: the gift must be stirred up that he might perform his

---

October 1830; Oliphant, *Life*, 279, 284–5; Robert Herbert Story, *Memoir of the Life of the Rev. Robert Story, Late Minister of Rosneath, Dunbartonshire* (Cambridge: Macmillan, 1862), 187; Newell, 'Scott', 87, 119 (following the *Daily News*, 26 May 1862); Dorries, *Irving's Incarnational Christology*, 40.

[45] Edward Irving, 'Introductory Essay', in William Gilpin, *The Life of Bernard Gilpin* (Glasgow: Chalmers and Collins, 1824), xii, xx–xxi.

[46] *CW*, 1.527–40.

[47] Dallimore, *Irving*, 69.

[48] *CW*, 1.531.

[49] In this he follows the Scots Confession, ch. 21.

duty faithfully. This almost sacramental understanding of ordination helps to explain why, after attending a confirmation service, Irving expressed a certain admiration for Anglican orders:

> the more I look into the Church of England, the more do I recognize the marks of a true Apostolical Church, and desire to see somewhat of the same ecclesiastical dignity transferred to the office-bearers of our Church ... [I] desire to see some more of the true primitive and Scottish character of our Church restored. I would wish every parish minister to fulfil the bishop's office, every elder the priest's, and every deacon the deacon's; and I am convinced that, till the same is attempted, through faith in the ordinances, we shall not prosper in the government and pastorship of our churches.[50]

Here we can detect the germ of his later understanding of the office of 'angel', which approximates to the second-century Ignatian understanding of the office of bishop as leader of a local worshipping community rather than a diocese; this was to become perhaps the most distinctive aspect of Catholic Apostolic orders of ministry.

His understanding of the angel's role is developed further in an exposition of the Revelation first given in Edinburgh during 1829 and extensively revised for publication in 1830–1. We shall look at their teaching on prophecy in a later chapter, but here we focus on how Irving worked out what was still very much a high Presbyterian understanding of the ministry, using this concept of the minister as angel. He asserted that 'in order to the being of a Church in any place, there must of necessity be a minister of the word to constitute it by word and sacrament.' Such a minister, addressed in Revelation 2–3 as the angel, presided over the believers in word and discipline.[51] As angel, he was Christ's messenger to the local church, and thus its head.[52] Christ looked to him as his delegate, and regarded the local church as summed up in him.[53] Churches were federated together under the headship of Christ, such confederation being needful to the recognition and ordination of ministers (who were chosen by the other angels), and thus to the existence of churches.[54] In this way, unity was maintained throughout the church; it was maintained over the course of time by the regular succession of ministers, ordination being at the hands of those already ordained.[55] As well as bearing responsibility for his flock, the angel was to contend for Christ's honour in the wider world (here Irving seems to have had in mind the Church of Scotland, which he saw as being taken over by infidelity); 'of nothing doth my conscience more loudly rebuke me, than of not having contended enough for the faith'.[56]

---

[50] Oliphant, *Life*, 247–8: Irving to Isabella Irving, 17 September 1828.
[51] *PW*, 1.172.
[52] Ibid. 1.212.
[53] Ibid. 2.291.
[54] Ibid. 1.173, 175–6.
[55] Ibid. 1.177–8.
[56] Ibid. 1.448–50.

The minister was therefore the instrument by whom Christ exercised his headship of the church for its life and nourishment. Irving recognized the awesome nature of such a conception of ministry:

> I confess for myself, that the study of this aspect of Christ as the Universal Bishop, while it hath filled me with the most exalted ideas of my calling, and delivered me, upon the one hand, from popular influence, and, on the other, from the slavish bondage of ecclesiastical polity, into the true liberty and largeness of my office; it hath, upon the other hand, impressed me with an inexpressible sense of the importance of personal completeness, blamelessness, faithfulness, watchfulness in doctrine, in discipline, in speech, in temper, in everything personal as well as official; because I see that, without such diligent perseverance, my flock must suffer loss, the Church of Christ bear scandal and my Lord himself underlie reproach in the house of His friends.[57]

Admitting that such an understanding was open to the abuse of despotism, Irving saw a counterbalance as provided by the Spirit's work in the churches. It was the harmony of the witness of the Spirit coming from the faithful with the minister's exercise of his prerogatives which enabled a congregation to maintain fidelity to the truth.[58] Christ spoke through the minister, and the Spirit answered in the churches, a conception which underlay his handling of the manifestations when they appeared.

* * *

From Irving's understanding of the ministerial office we turn to examine his approach to pastoral care. Preaching was not the only important aspect of ministry for Irving; throughout his pastoral career, he kept an open house, often at considerable cost to his health and his studies, as well as to his pocket: such was the custom among Scottish ministers. He had given his Glasgow parishioners an open invitation to visit him in London, and they took him at his word.[59] And what he was in the pulpit as the minister he also sought to be when visiting his flock, seeking to improve every occasion of spiritual conversation. Of course, this concern to be the minister at all times meant that when visiting he could be perceived as somewhat distant,[60] and this was the man who could sign a letter to his wife, 'Your most affectionate husband and pastor of your soul'.[61]

Several letters from late 1825 show this pastoral concern at work in his family relationships. He refers to writing a letter to his parents 'exhorting them against

---

[57] Ibid. 1.246–7.

[58] Ibid. 1.247.

[59] *CW*, 3.362. Perhaps this shows Irving as one of those people who needed to be loved: Drummond, *Irving*, 86.

[60] NLS, Acc. 12489/14, John Home Simpson, Typescript work on the Simpsons and their relationship to Irving, fols 10–11.

[61] Oliphant, *Life*, 119: journalfor 25 October 1825.

formality, and testifying to them the nature of a spiritual conversation'.[62] When Isabella was staying with his family, he looked to her 'to drop seasonable words into their ears, especially concerning their salvation and their little ones. For nothing is so fatal to Scotland as lethargy. I trust they are not nominal Christians; but I would fain have deeper convictions of so important a matter.'[63] But from time to time his guard slipped and he expressed concern about mundane things. On her way home Isabella was to bring him two or three pairs of good shoes from Annan; a fortnight later he reminds her, insisting that she pay for them, 'for my mother will always make herself a beggar for her children'.[64]

In the church context, he was concerned to undertake his pastoral work in a thorough and systematic manner, and doing all he could to become acquainted with his large membership. We find him meeting the Sunday School teachers each month, and preaching to the poor on the first Friday of each month.[65] As for the members in general, it appears that he wrote to each new member requesting an interview, to gain personal acquaintance.[66] The district round the church was divided into seven for visiting purposes, each part being assigned an elder and a deacon (Irving would accompany the elder on home visits).[67] Soon he began district meetings for members; there is extant a lithographed pro forma letter from Irving and one of the elders, inviting members in their district to meet at the session house at a certain time and expressing the intention of becoming acquainted with all the members for their edification and consolation.[68]

* * *

It has been claimed that Irving lost the great and the good from his congregation because he did not feed them with the truths of the Gospel, but took up with prophetic study and other distractions.[69] Such an assessment needs to be qualified in the light of an examination of his approach to preaching and the topics which he covered. As hitherto, preaching was Irving's lifeblood. Even on holiday, we find him preaching at every opportunity. He had written in the study Bible belonging to Isabella's newly-ordained brother Samuel in 1825 that 'no man is furnished for the ministry till he can unclasp his pocket-bible, and wherever it opens, discourse from it largely and spiritually unto the people'.[70]

---

[62] Ibid. 158: journal for 12 November 1825.
[63] Ibid. 192: journal for 29 November 1825.
[64] Ibid. 170, 195: journal for 18 November and 3 December 1825.
[65] Isabella Irving to her parents, 5 January 1827 (in private hands).
[66] *The Times*, 6 July 1827, 2.
[67] Collection record book; Hair, *Regent Square*, 85.
[68] LMA/4358/C/002/14.
[69] Dallimore, *Irving*, 60–1.
[70] John Duns, *Memoir of the late Rev. Samuel Martin, Minister of the Free Church, Bathgate* (Edinburgh: W. P. Kennedy, 1854), 14–15.

It was for his congregation that Irving prepared a three-volume compilation of *Sermons, Lectures and Occasional Discourses*. The first contained 'the very heart and essence of his teaching, his lofty argument and exposition of the Trinity, and its combined action in the redemption of man'; the second how to apply divine truth in preaching, and the third a range of discourses on themes to do with biblical prophecy and the spiritual state of the nation.[71] Irving explained how these three volumes hung together: 'The first part treats of the work of Christ in the flesh; the second, of the publication and propagation of the same good work amongst men; and the third, of the present aspect and condition, and the immediate prospects, of that portion of the world which hath received the preaching of the Gospel of the incarnate Word'.[72]

Although much of the work on them was undertaken at the end of 1827 and the beginning of 1828, it was not until 15 January 1829 that all three volumes appeared, according to an advertisement in that day's *Caledonian Mercury*. The delay was occasioned by a charge that Irving was guilty of heresy concerning the person of Christ. We shall examine this in chapter 14, but for now we may note that the sermons on the subject, which comprised the first volume of the three and which had been preached in 1825, were given pride of place because his office-bearers wanted them to appear first.[73] They had already been printed when Irving decided that he must add two more in order to answer the charge,[74] which he did not complete until November 1828.

The other two volumes appeared during the summer. In July he told Isabella that he had received the *Sermons*, and offered to give her all she could get for the two volumes already printed to do what she would with the proceeds.[75] A few weeks later, he informed her that he had now decided what to do about the first volume: he planned to add another discourse on the 'Method of the Incarnation' and to offer the thousand copies to any Edinburgh bookseller, as he was resolved to make known his doctrine in the heart of the Church of Scotland.[76] Isabella must have had a good head for business matters, as he then launched into detail about how the books were to be published in England. He had signed a contract with the evangelical publisher R. B. Seeley for the three volumes, in which Irving was to take the risk, pay the printers, and receive a guinea per copy, allowing the publisher five per cent; if they sold, Irving would be left with £1,000, of which about half would be profit. He planned to

---

[71] Oliphant, *Life*, 219.

[72] Irving, *Sermons, Lectures, and Occasional Discourses* (3 vols, London: R. B. Seeley & W. Burnside, 1828), 1.iii.

[73] Oliphant, *Life*, 220.

[74] This explains the pagination for the two additional sermons: inserted at pages 140 and 328, they are paginated using roman numerals following those numbers.

[75] Oliphant, *Life*, 239: Irving to Isabella Irving, 25 July 1828.

[76] Ibid. 244: Irving to Isabella Irving, 15 August 1828. Rather than burdening the church, for whose benefit he had intended to publish the *Sermons*, with the risk on them, he planned to give them *The Last Days*, an exposition of 2 Timothy 3.1–5 which Henry Drummond had either suggested or approved (and which we shall look at in ch. 13), as it would sell well and was already paid for.

have separate agents for Glasgow and Edinburgh on similar terms. A Miss M. had pressed on him £300 to pay for printing costs. 'It is a book for much good or evil, both to the Church and myself, I distinctly foresee.'[77] Clearly Irving gave as careful thought to publishing as he did to preaching, a fact not usually noticed in discussions of his influence.

We shall look now at the second volume of the Sermons, an exposition of the Parable of the Sower, which provides further insight into his approach to preaching.[78] It is dedicated to the Montagus as a couple whom God had used to guide him in the truth or to comfort him in a preacher's trials. Among other things, they had led him 'to observe more diligently the forms and aspects of human life and to comprehend more widely the ways of God's providence with men',[79] in other words to understand the nature of the human soil in which the seed of truth is sown. The preface (dated 28 September 1827) upholds the value of the Reformed custom of lecturing, which had been the regular morning practice in the Kirk. A lecture comprised two parts; the first involved exegesis (detailed explanation of the meaning of the text), and the second drew out the doctrines of the passage and applied them.

The introductory lecture was part of a course on Luke, which he had begun taking up his charge in 1822.[80] This exemplifies the Reformed practice of taking a book of the Bible and working though it verse by verse. Entitled 'How it is Possible to Teach Spiritual Things by Natural Emblems, with the Exposition of the Emblem of the Sower' and based on Luke 8.5–15, the sermon contends that God has ordained the present natural order 'for the single and express purpose of shadowing forth that future perfect condition into which it is to be brought', hence the value of a close study of this parable.[81]

Irving's pessimism comes to the surface in Lecture I, 'The Seed that Fell by the Way-side, which the Birds of the Air Snatched Away'. Here he expounds what he had learned from Coleridge – that the world was not to be converted, but judged. For all his popularity, he evidently felt it necessary to explain the relative lack of lasting response to his preaching, which he sees as symbolized by the fact that three-quarters

---

[77] Oliphant, *Life*, 245: Irving to Isabella Irving, 18 August 1828.

[78] Irving, *Sermons, Lectures, and Occasional Discourses*, vol. 2: *On the Parable of the Sower, Six Lectures*.

[79] Ibid. 331.

[80] We noted in ch. 8 that on arrival in London he had begun a series on the infancy narratives at the beginning of Luke, and a number of his surviving sermons are taken from this gospel. After preparing these discourses for the press, Irving took a break, as James Simpson records: 'Last Sabbath Mr Irving resumed his Lectures on St. Lukes Gospel which he left off about two years ago, he observed a good Providence in having arrested his progress in these Lectures, until he was more ful[l]y taught in the Subject of the Kingdom of God, and the two Natures of Christ': 'J. G. S. Journals 1806 to 1830', 18 September 1829. Before that, he had taken another break while he waited for further light on the meaning of the 'honest and good heart' in the parable, and its apparent contradiction of the scriptural teaching that the human heart is by nature wicked: Jane Simpson, Diary, 1826–8, fol. 48: 3 September 1827.

[81] Irving, *Sermons*, 2.350.

of the seed in the parable came to nothing: this, he says represents the fact that only a minority of hearers will be converted.[82] The seed falling by the wayside represents 'the blinded sensualist, who cannot believe; the self-sufficient moralist, who will not believe; the schismatic, who will believe only a favourite part; and the heretic, who preferreth to believe a falsehood'.[83] Each class presents pitfalls for the preacher; with reference to the schismatic he indicates the critical reactions which preachers then and since have encountered:

> One will not have a moral duty inculcated, another will not hear a prophecy explained; one is impatient of instruction, and will rise and go away if you do not excite his feelings, which excitement another decries as enthusiasm; another cannot receive the matter if it be read, and another dislikes that it should be spoken. You may not tell masters their duties lest ye should offend them; and if you preach of duties to rulers, you are political; and if you shew the errors of the times, you are setting yourself up for a judge of others; and if you bring forth former times in the experience of the church, you go beyond the knowledge of the people: and unless you harp upon every man's single string, you do not preach Christ. These things I do not imagine, but have sadly experienced ...[84]

Each class also provides an opportunity for him to engage in blistering condemnation of contemporary society and religion. The last (the heretic) presents a particular danger to those (especially the Evangelicals) who claim to rely on the Bible alone for their understanding of the faith. In London, where there is so much ferment and novelty, 'the true wisdom is to study the Scriptures with a careful respect and great reverence for the one faith which all sound divines and orthodox churches have maintained'.[85]

Lecture II, 'The Seed on the Rock, which was Burnt up of the Sun', argues that 'from our very childhood we are either preparing ourselves for the reception or the rejection of a preached Gospel',[86] a fact which is overlooked in the contemporary emphasis on conversion. This is relevant not only to parents and teachers, but also to hearers, whom he counsels to prepare their hearts to hear the word preached. He develops the theme further in Lecture IV, 'The Seed which Fell on the Soil of a Good and Honest Heart, and Brought Forth Abundantly'. Divine revelation involves forming the recipient as well as communicating the content, and the process of forming a soil goes on in every individual using their God-given 'faculty of self-nourishment' as they grow in knowledge of God's commands and exercise their membership of the visible church. Things are going from bad to worse, however, and the church's part can only be 'to gather together the crew, and warn them of a

---

[82] Cf. ibid. 499: 'Wherever this Gospel was to be preached, it was to be preached, as the first great lesson of it, that there were three out of four classes in the world to whom it would be preached in vain'.

[83] Ibid. 389.

[84] Ibid. 418–19.

[85] Ibid. 436.

[86] Ibid. 457.

shipwreck, to undergird the ship, and keep her afloat for a while, in hopes of reaching some shore, to betake ourselves to pieces of the wreck, and save what we can from the watery waste'.[87]

Nevertheless, even as controversy grew, Irving could on occasion express himself very positively concerning the fruitfulness of his ministry. Writing to Chalmers (probably in April 1830), he rejoiced that in the last year, almost 180 communicants had been added to his church, and testified to the fruit which his ministry was bearing among clergy in the Church of England.[88] His bullishness was borne out by James Simpson:

> Yesterday was our Sacrament Sabbath, I was much blessed of God, and Mr Irving was enabled by Gods help to do his Duty in an excelent [sic] Spirit, the Number of Communicants continue to increase on every occasion. Mr I is full of a Spirit of Love & truthfulness, & the Spirit of God gives a Power to the Word of his lips, beyond that of any Man I ever knew.[89]

Yet a few weeks later Simpson alleged that attendance was declining, which he thought was down to Irving 'dwelling so much on controversial points of Doctrine' and his preaching extempore instead of using a written manuscript, which made the sermons less interesting (even if it did conform to accepted Scottish practice).[90]

As for the topics of his sermons, I have collated all known references to his preaching, with some surprising results as far as the years from 1826 to 1830 are concerned. Firstly, as one might expect, prophecy takes a prominent place, with series on Revelation 16 in June 1827, 'The Last Days' (2 Timothy 3.1–6) from January to April 1828, and Daniel 7 on Wednesdays from March 1829, as well as two courses of lectures given in Edinburgh in 1828 and 1829 and various occasional sermons on the subject, usually based on texts from Matthew or Revelation. Prophecy also seems to have been his favourite topic when preaching away from home, doubtless because this was something which he felt had been laid on his heart to share with the wider church. But there are far fewer sermons on the person of Christ than one might have expected, given the controversial nature of his views; most are included in a short series during the summer of 1828 and another series on the Messianic psalms during the summer of 1829. Moreover, topics relating to Christian living, which had been prominent in his early ministry, continued to appear to the end of this period; evidently Irving was not the kind of preacher to allow new views of truth to cause him to overlook his congregation's need for basic instruction.

---

[87] Ibid. 662. Irving later developed this 'remnant' understanding of the church to justify the practice of separation from the Church of Scotland.

[88] Oliphant, *Life*, 281–2.

[89] James Simpson, 'J. G. S. Journals 1806 to 1830', 3 May 1830.

[90] Ibid., 27 June 1830.

* * *

What of Irving's home life? His relationship with Isabella seems initially to have been somewhat tense, although one should not make too much of what is frequently the case in a new marriage. By September 1826, however, Mrs Montagu could inform Jane Welsh that she had seen them in the country and looking happier; 'He called his wife Dear, twice in my hearing the last time I saw them together'.[91] A few months later, Mrs Montagu informed the now-married Jane that the two were living better together, and that Isabella was gaining in his affections.[92] By now, Isabella was expecting another child: Mary was born on 23 February 1827.

We find Irving concerned about his brother George, who appears to have given him some heartache while a medical student. 'I heard from George the other day by Mr R–, and I have remitted him £30 in clearing of his expenses and enabling him to return [i.e. from Paris, where he had been studying]'.[93] George would become a medical practitioner in London. Trouble of a different order came when the Irvings' house was broken into early one Sunday morning, and they were robbed of plate and clothes. According to the report, the burglars got in by boring through the kitchen door. In the parlours, they broke open desks and drawers, took books and papers and strewed them on the floor.[94] One can imagine how the family would have felt.

Healthwise, things did not look so good for the family, and we catch the first indications that all was not well with Irving himself. Yet again, it was Mrs Montagu, whose inquisitiveness appears to have been the expression of a motherly concern, who told Jane in August 1826: 'he gave me the impression that his own little girl was very unwell, and in that same terrible complaint of which the Boy died – something is wrong in the lungs of the Children, and their Father looks as if he was consumptive'.[95] On 14 December 1827, Mary died of a chest infection and croup which had come on since the Irvings returned from Norwood where they had been staying to their cold house on 8 December. It was presumably the sermons he preached the following Sunday which were published under the title 'On the Death of Children'.[96] According to Mrs Oliphant, those present said that

> he went tearless and fasting through that dark Sabbath; and coming in from his pulpit, went straight to the little coffin, and flinging himself down by it, gave way

---

[91] Edinburgh, NLS, MS 1776, fols 28–9: Mrs Montagu to [Jane] Baillie Welsh, 9 September 1826.

[92] Ibid. fol. 34: Mrs Montagu to Jane Carlyle, 8 December 1826.

[93] Oliphant, *Life*, 241: Irving to Isabella Irving, 31 July 1828.

[94] *The Examiner*, 27 January 1828.

[95] *CL*, 4.129n: Mrs Montagu to Jane Welsh, 7 August 1826.

[96] *CW*, 4.367–90. Mrs Oliphant asserts that these were preached the day after Samuel's death on 5 July 1830, stating erroneously that Samuel died on a Saturday (5 July was a Monday). Mary, however, died on a Friday, which would fit with her comment regarding these sermons that it was so late in the week that Irving had no time to find a stand-in for the Sunday: Oliphant, *Life*, 298; cf. URCHS, letter 18: John Martin to Elizabeth A. Martin, 20 December 1827.

to the agony of a strong man's grief – grief which was half or wholly prayer – an outcry to the one great Confidant of all his troubles, the faithful Lord who yet had *not* interposed to save ...[97]

His text was 2 Samuel 12.15–24, the story of the death of David's son by Bathsheba. It is worth looking at these sermons carefully because they serve as a window into his heart.

> Believing, as it is written, that no one of Christ's members ought to suffer for himself, or to rejoice for himself, but for the sake of the whole body, which is the Church, I have endeavoured, by the grace of God, to set my own sorrows to a side, and to address myself to the work of edifying God's people in that mysterious part of His providence under which so many of you are now, have been, or are yet to be fellow-sufferers with myself ...[98]

David's example in worshipping after losing his son 'doth, I feel, justify me this day in standing in my place amongst the worshippers of God and fulfilling my wonted offices as a minister of Christ'.[99] In the light of this, he highlights four truths which he believes are demonstrated by the death of infants.

1. We are shown our present condition as innately sinful and spiritually dead; God does not wait until we know good from evil before cutting us off.

> I do regard this lesson of the innate sinfulness and deadness of the creature to be so fundamental an article of faith, so needful, so indispensable to the understanding of God's glory and work in Jesus Christ, that to comprehend it, and feel it, and act under it continually, I would not grudge all the sorrow and disappointment which the loss of two unconscious infants hath caused me.[100]

2. We are shown the freeness of grace, which is no more dependent on our actions than is the death of an infant. He speaks of 'the comfort I have derived myself, and which every bereaved parent should derive from the sacrament of baptism'.[101]

3. Such cases show God's sovereignty to act as he pleases:

> there is not in the fallen world such a goodly and, delightsome object to the eye of angels or of men as an infant ere yet it hath attained to the knowledge of good and evil – its beauty, its perfectness of form, its continual appeal for help, its undoubting confidence in all, the simplicity, the guilelessness of its affections, the early notice and love of its parents, with a thousand other things which are too tender in my memory to be now exposed in a public place ...[102]

---

[97] Oliphant, *Life*, 298.
[98] *CW*, 4.367.
[99] Ibid. 369.
[100] Ibid. 369–70.
[101] Ibid. 372.
[102] Ibid. 374.

4. The Shorter Catechism described 'the chief end of man, which is to glorify God and to enjoy Him for ever'; in the light of that, Irving asserts here that this period of salvation-history is intended to demonstrate God's goodness and glory in saving those who were spiritually dead, and that applies to children too:

> Let them suffer, let them die, and let their beauty consume away in the grave, – let a father's schemes be confounded in falsehood, and a mother's hopes swallowed up in darkness, – let all this be if it is for His glory that it should be. ... Oh! it is a painful thing to a parent's heart to see his infant suffer, to see his helpless infant die; but it is a victory worthy the contendings and wrestlings of faith to submit to God, and to glorify God in the midst of it all. This, this, dear brethren, is what I have this morning endeavoured to help you to, in the way in which I have been helped to it myself.[103]

He asks their prayers that his household may exemplify these things.

That evening, he considered the question as it relates to Christian experience.

> Oh, I remember well when God gave me a son, the most hopeful of his kind, that I devoted him by a solemn covenant unto the Lord from the hour of his birth, and fondly dreamed and fondly schemed how he might be rendered most serviceable to the Church; and when the Lord cut short his life when it had little more than filled the round of one year, I was stunned and staggered for a while, until it pleased Him to reveal for my comfort what I have now taught for your edification, that the present life, compared with the life of the resurrection, is but like the life of the eaglet in the shell compared with the life of the mighty eagle who ascends into the height of the heavens, and looks into the face of the sun.[104]

He expounds the relation of parent and baptized child as one which is governed by covenant, baptism having virtually dissolved natural ties as a death and resurrection. It is the church which parents these infants, and Christ, in his officers, who finds suitable persons to exercise this guardianship – normally the parents. God, asserts Irving, is angry with his people for forgetting this duty of care. Parents and sponsors should seek to turn such an event to good use: it should quicken their love for others and awaken self-examination, since the infant is taken for their sins, not for its own. As he sums up his application, 'let every parent who hath been bereaved of his child seek to become towards God what that child of which he hath been bereaved was towards himself'.[105]

The following day, the Trustees expressed their sympathy with Irving in his loss and placed a burial vault under the church at his disposal.[106] This would have been appreciated, but what seems to have given Edward and Isabella most comfort was

---

[103] Ibid. 378.
[104] Ibid. 382.
[105] Ibid. 389–90.
[106] LMA/4358/A/006, 'Trustees Minute Book' (1825–48), fol. 12. Irving buried Mary there on 19 December: London, RS, National Scotch Church, Burial Register.

their understanding of the nature of baptism. This received expression in a series of *Homilies on Baptism* preached in the summer of 1825 and first published in 1828.[107] The chief influence on his thinking was the Scots Confession, but he found it confirmed by the Anglican Richard Hooker. Like the Genevan reformer John Calvin, the Scots Confession asserted that the sacraments were more than mere signs, and that elect infants were indeed regenerated at or after baptism, baptism was thus the means by which God's saving purpose became a reality.

Irving did not consider that the comfort which he and Isabella had received was for them alone. In the dedication ('to Isabella Irving, my wife, and the mother of my two departed children'), he writes:

> I believe in my heart, that the doctrine of the holy Sacraments, which is contained in these Homilies, was made known to my mind, first of all, for the purpose of preparing us for the loss of our eldest boy; because, on that very week you went with him to Scotland, whence he never returned, my mind was directed to meditate and preach those discourses upon the standing of the baptized in the Church, which form the sixth and seventh of the Homilies on Baptism. I believe it also, because, long before our little Edward was stricken by the hand of God in Scotland, I was led to open these views to you in letters, which, by God's grace, were made efficacious to convince your mind. I believe it, furthermore, because the thought contained in those two Homilies remained in my mind, like an unsprung seed, until it was watered by the common tears which we shed over our dying Mary. From that time forth, I felt that the truth concerning Baptism, which had been revealed for our special consolation, was not for that end given, nor for that end to be retained; and therefore I resolved, at every risk, to open to all the fathers and mothers of the Christian Church, the thoughts which had ministered to us so much consolation.

Poignantly, he closes by praying: 'May the Lord make you the mother of many children, to glorify His name for ever and ever.'[108]

In the homilies, Irving warns against two opposing errors: of disconnecting the work of the Spirit in regeneration from baptism, and of identifying it with baptism so closely that regeneration becomes something conveyed by human priestly activity rather than the gracious gift of God. Baptism, he says, is 'a birth dependent on the means of grace for its growth and perfection'.[109] It confers remission of sins and the gift of the Holy Ghost, which in Reformed terminology was denoted by regeneration, the implanting of spiritual life in the individual (he takes issue with the assumption that outward supernatural manifestations of the Spirit's power had been intended to cease after the apostolic era, arguing that these had been withdrawn as a divine judgement on the church's failure to value the gift of the Spirit). Parents are encouraged to bring their infants for baptism in faith that God bestows spiritual life through it, and if those children should fall away as they grow up, to look for their conversion as individuals already brought within God's family by baptism and

---

[107] *CW*, 2.247–432.
[108] *CW*, 2.248. One of those letters is given almost in full in Oliphant, *Life*, 239–41.
[109] *CW*, 2.262.

hence in a covenant relationship with God. Children dying in infancy are saved on account of the faith of their parents expressed in bringing them for baptism.

Whitley rightly points out that for Irving 'an understanding of baptism was fundamental to a recovery of the meaning and function of the Church'.[110] The covenant relationship into which infants are introduced by baptism brings privileges but also responsibilities; the great divide in humanity is not between those converted and those not, but between those baptized and those not; the church is composed of all the baptized, among whom are the elect who alone shall be saved (and at the end, Irving thinks, the elect will be a small minority in the church). Baptism is thus constitutive of the church as a visible body, which is a mixed body of believers and unbelievers. Those regenerated are regenerated at baptism, but not all the baptized are regenerated. This is where the mystery of God's choice of those individuals who should receive his saving grace (election) comes into play, as it is impossible in this life to make an infallible judgement concerning who in the church is elect and who is not. Whilst Mrs Oliphant confessed herself unable to see how Irving's doctrine differed from that of baptismal regeneration,[111] it is firmly within the Reformed theological tradition, and the original edition of the work included an appendix citing relevant articles from most of the major Reformed statements of faith: the Scots Confession, the Westminster Confession, the Thirty-Nine Articles (1563/71), the Second Helvetic Confession (1566), the Gallican Confession (1559), and the Belgic Confession (1561).[112]

Alongside these were a series of 'Homilies on the Lord's Supper',[113] likewise intended for publication but not actually printed until their inclusion in the *Collected Writings*. One recurrent note running through the *Homilies on Baptism* is that the baptized should not hold back from participation in the Lord's Supper, as so often happened, especially in Scottish Presbyterianism (among those of an evangelical outlook, many lifelong adherents felt spiritually unworthy to partake, often on account of a lack of assurance of their salvation). Indeed, he goes so far as to argue that refusal to ratify the faith of one's parents expressed in bringing their child for baptism amounts to spiritual suicide. In these homilies we find him arguing that a man may not normally be a Christian without an inward assurance of his spiritual standing: doubting Christians are exhorted to come to the Lord's Supper in order that their faith might be strengthened. The Lord's Table is the point where an individual 'may step out from the guardianship of others, and become responsible for himself'.[114] The rite is a commemoration of Christ's death as one who had assumed our human nature; a sacrament or oath of allegiance (here he draws on the meaning

---

[110] H. C. Whitley, *Blinded Eagle: An Introduction to the Life and Teaching of Edward Irving* (London: SCM, 1955), 66.

[111] Oliphant, *Life*, 111.

[112] Edward Irving, *Homilies on the Sacraments*. Vol. I: *On Baptism* (London: Andrew Panton, 1828), 417–32.

[113] *CW*, 2.435–642. It is impossible to determine precisely when these were originally preached.

[114] Ibid. 515.

of the Latin term *sacramentum*); a communion in which members of the church are united; and a thanksgiving (as expressed in the term 'eucharist'). Its object is to keep Christians in mind of their future destiny, that the church might not come to have a low conception of itself. Christ is present not physically but through his Spirit, who enables us to feed on Christ by faith. Partakers receive the same power of the Holy Spirit which enabled Christ to remain sinless during his life on earth. Once again, Irving's understanding of the Lord's Supper clearly belongs to the Reformed tradition, even if he expresses it in somewhat 'higher' terms than most were wont to do at this period.

In spite of the comfort which he took from such thinking, like many in such circumstances Irving struggled to reconcile his faith and his emotions; as he told Isabella in 1828: 'I often think woefully of the pair that are gone before; but I ought not.'[115] Constantly thereafter he fussed over her health. When she was visiting her family in 1828, he urged her to make a move before the onset of the cold winds which killed Edward; his concern, he explained, was because he wanted everybody back home safely.[116] Before she returned, he took up a suggestion made by Drummond and went to Harrogate to recover his health; he had, he writes, been studying too much for an outdoor constitution. But duty was calling; he tells her after just a few weeks that although the water there would do him good if he could stay, he must return to London. It is no surprise to hear him confessing how hard he found it to be apart from her and the children for six months. We know, he writes, what people will say.[117] Thankfully, his fears on that score appear to have been groundless!

One wonders whether Mary's death was a factor in the Irvings' moving from Pentonville: by 21 January 1828 they were living at 6 Euston Grove, and by 1 December 1828 had moved into a larger house at 13 Judd Place East (now demolished, but it would have been just a couple of minutes' walk from Regent Square and hence much more convenient). Death, however, continued to affect the family. The following year Mrs Montagu, seeing Isabella looking pregnant, feared that another sickly baby would be born, and went so far as to criticize Irving for what she regarded as his lack of restraint.[118] Another son, Gavin, was duly born on 28 July 1829, but it was clear that he would not survive; Irving baptized him at home, and the child lived only a few hours, being buried by his father on 4 August (his birthday and the anniversary of his brother's death).[119] Barely a month later, Isabella's grandfather died. Writing to John Martin, Irving expressed condolence on his father's death and describing the deceased as 'the last of the old and good school of Scottish Churchmen'.[120] Then in October Irving lost his sister Agnes Carlile at

---

[115] Oliphant, *Life*, 241: Irving to Isabella Irving, 31 July 1828.

[116] Ibid. 245: Irving to Isabella Irving, 18 August 1828.

[117] Ibid. 246–7: Irving to Isabella Irving, 17 September 1828.

[118] Edinburgh, NLS, MS 1776, fols 50–1: Mrs Montagu to Jane Carlyle, 3 July 1829.

[119] 'Copy of Baptismal Register 1823–1855'; Burial Register; NLS, MS 1776, fol. 52: Mrs Montagu to Jane Carlyle, 22 October 1829.

[120] Oliphant, *Life*, 2.95: Irving to John Martin, 1 September 1829.

the age of twenty-seven.[121] It is true that at this period family deaths would have been a frequent occurrence in the experience of most people, but in Irving's case they undoubtedly operated on his spirit in such a way as to strengthen his hopes for the future and hence his interest in biblical prophecy. One also wonders whether he threw himself into his work as a way of coping with loss; Mrs Oliphant notes that the family took a holiday at Brighton in September 1829, but Irving returned to preach each weekend, and in her opinion he 'seems to have at last worked himself into the condition ... of finding relaxation only in a change of work'.[122] We may ask whether this apparent inability to unwind contributed to the increasingly strident tone adopted in his writings, and perhaps to a loss of perspective on life. Some may think that the evidence in the next chapter confirms such a suggestion.

---

[121] *The Times*, 9 October 1829, 4.
[122] Oliphant, *Life*, 2.98.

Chapter 12

Scot and Churchman, 1826–30

In this chapter, we continue to evaluate Irving's approach to ministry, but this time against the broader canvas of national and religious life. Crucial to understanding this is an appreciation of the role played in Irving's approach to ministry by his Scottish patriotism and the concept of a nation in covenant with God.[1]

A sentimental example of this is 'A Tale of the Times of the Martyrs', written in August 1828 for an annual, *The Anniversary*, edited by his literary acquaintance Allan Cunningham.[2] He affirms as a Christian man and minister that he has not invented or altered anything in the story or in the manner of his receiving it. A minister belonging to a branch of his mother's family served in Nithsdale; the widow of a fellow minister moved to Glasgow with her children, and when he was about to go there as Chalmers' assistant Irving's mother's aunt charged him to visit them. On doing so, the widow told him the following story, about how a spiritually awakened young woman living in Edinburgh during the Covenanter era 'might prevent the man whom most she honoured from slaying the man whom most she loved'. Her father was Lord Provost of Edinburgh and as such was charged with hunting down the Covenanters; her love was a minister named William Guthrie, nephew of James Guthrie (the first Covenanter martyr). The girl was married to another at her father's insistence, but died of a broken heart, leaving an infant daughter to her love's charge. He cared for the child but soon she died, as did his brother or cousin who ministered at Fenwick (a famous Covenanting centre in Ayrshire), and grief made him seek to flee Scotland and abandon his ministry. Challenged when visiting Irongray (another centre of Covenanting activity, near Dumfries), he eventually agreed to become the minister there. After thirty years his grief had been assuaged to the extent that he married, and the widow told Irving that she was their daughter.

Liam Upton takes the story to be a fabrication, albeit one told in good faith by a real person, Mary Lawson, whose father James Guthrie had been minister at Irongray from 1694 to 1756. Upton argues that Irving's publication of it as oral history implies that the myth of the Covenanter struggle was more important to him than the facts. However, I doubt that the two could be so easily separated in Irving's

---

[1] On this, see Liam Upton, '"Our Mother and our Country": The Integration of Religious and National Identity in the Thought of Edward Irving (1792-1834)', in Robert Pope, ed., *Religion and National Identity: Wales and Scotland c. 1700-2000* (Cardiff: University of Wales Press, 2001), 242-67.

[2] Cf. Oliphant, *Life*, 245: Irving to Isabella Irving, 15 August 1828.

mind; rather, it would appear that his attachment to the Covenanters rendered him somewhat credulous, or that the presentation of the story as history is no more than a literary device.

More substantive, if less readable, are the sermons which Irving preached on Scottish themes, several of which were published. He was always willing to speak on behalf of Scottish societies, and in so doing to introduce some aspect of biblical teaching. A particular concern of his, however, was the expatriate Scots community. He was decidedly ambivalent regarding emigration for motives of material gain, and on one occasion advised two young men from Glasgow seeking situations that:

> this coming upon venture from a place we are occupied well, and sustained in daily food from our occupation, merely that we may rise in the world, is not a righteous thing before God, however approved by our ambitious countrymen; and though it may be successful in bringing them to what they seek, a fortune and an establishment in the world, it is generally unsuccessful in increasing them in the riches of the kingdom, in which they become impoverished every day, until they are the hardest, most secular, worldly, and self-seeking creatures which this metropolis contains. Let them come, if they have any kindred or friends to whose help they may come, or if they be in want, for then they come on an errand which the Lord may countenance; but let them come merely for desire of gain, or of getting on, and they come at Mammon's instigation, with whom our God doth not co-operate at all ...[3]

For the London Scottish Hospital, he preached a sermon in April 1826 on 'The Spiritual Economy of Scotland' which amounts to an extended appeal to London Scots not to forsake the church of their birth.[4] After a gloomy opening description of the state of his compatriots in London, he announces his theme:

> before you can understand the growth of a plant which hath been transplanted to another climate and soil, you must know the conditions from which it was taken, and the conditions into the midst of which it hath been removed. So, before we shall rightly comprehend the forms which the Scottish character assumes in this metropolis, and the diseases and derangements to which it is liable, we must study first the peculiarities of its condition in its own land, which I think are in general little understood and very imperfectly explained.[5]

In his opinion, the best Scottish preaching hardly compared with the worst of a former age; it had declined to 'an intellectual demonstration of the literal word to the natural good sense and good feeling of the people'.[6] Whilst the national character 'for understanding, morality, industry, and economy' was better than that of any other nation, the soil had become exhausted. Alleging that city congregations could not

---

[3] Ibid. 135: journal, 31 October 1825.
[4] *CW*, 3.470–99.
[5] Ibid. 471.
[6] Ibid. 472.

cope with too much matter in one sermon, he proposed to divide it into several discourses to be preached in aid of various Scottish charities. In this one, he sought to open up 'the spiritual economy of Scotland, which continued from the Reformation till the middle of the last century, when the political economy began to supplant it, and our intellectual character to be regarded as the procreative principle of the nation'.[7] Irving insisted that it was the cultivation of spiritual life which made the Scots what they were. Their character was produced by an economy which considered that the things of the soul were all, and 'the outward things – the conveniences of life, the wages of labour, the price of commodities, the political privileges, and the bodily accommodations – as mere circumstantials, which would fall into their proper place if only the spirit could be quickened to a sense of its dignity and its duties',[8] the reverse of the system of political economy which now prevailed. The preaching produced a class of peasants and farmers which could not be compared even with higher classes in other countries. Childhood memories surfaced as he recalled, in the kind of purple passage which society treasurers must have loved:

> hear them examine their households and their children, and hear them discourse by the evening fire, or in their goings forth on the Sabbath morn over hill and dale to the parish church, hear them hand down the traditions of former piety and suffering, and sharpen one another in their Christian warfare by the many examples with which every part of the country is sanctified, confirmed by the mossy graves and the gray stones and the inaccessible retreats of the martyrs, and the family legends dear to memory, – and hear them, as they come home at evening, enter at large into the discourse which they have heard, and improve its various passages, and recount a thousand recollections to which it gave rise of like discourses heard in other times and places; – oh, how dear those scenes are to my memory! When yet a child, or little more than a child, I walked many miles to hear the discoursing of a most reverend father, whose hoary image is now before me; and as we went, another and another came dropping in, till we formed a sweet society under the smiling eye of the Sabbath morn, talking words of grace and consolation and power over the soul, which God did bless with an especial blessing. And on their return, ere they parted on their several ways, and scattered over the moor to their solitary dwellings, to see them assemble in the hollow of a woody dell, and there call upon the most aged and revered of the company to conduct their worship, – the melody of their voices mingling with the tempest-like rushing of the winds in the tops of the pine-trees ...[9]

And at the heart of the whole system was the head of the household, whose leadership of family worship was, Irving claimed, monitored by the parish minister.

> I have heard my mother tell that her grandfather – who was minister of a burgh on the Border, now discriminated by Burns our poet for its intemperance – used, with

---

[7] Ibid. 474.
[8] Ibid. 475.
[9] Ibid. 478.

one of his elders, to take evening walks through the little town, in order to hear whether the voice of worship was lifted up in every dwelling; and if not, they would enter and deal with the people concerning the danger of a prayerless family. I have heard my father tell that, in the early mornings of harvest, while he and his brothers still lingered in bed, weary with the labour of reaping their father's fields, his father and mother would rise an hour before the earliest, granting mercy to their weaklier children, while, like Job, they offered the morning sacrifice for themselves and their family.[10]

The head of the household was regarded by the church as its priest, responsible for the spiritual upbringing of his children. On sabbath evenings, he would examine his children and servants on the subject of the day's preaching. Irving claimed that the church was responsible for the entire provision for youth; they were formed by the atmosphere and the whole system, not merely by the schools.

In the light of all this, he professed himself moved by how little attention was paid to the Church of Scotland by Scots in London. In an apparent reference to the loss of some to the Church of England and Nonconformity, he asked how they could cast off such a church as he had described.

* * *

This concern found fullest expression in *A Pastoral Letter ... from the Scotch Presbytery in London to the Baptized of the Scotch Church Residing in London and its Vicinity and in the Southern Parts of the Island.* Irving had begun writing this at the request of the presbytery in 1827, doubtless working on it while spending some weeks away from home during September with his family at Norwood, then a village in Surrey.[11] The letter does not appear to have made much impact, but it does express something of his heart.

The letter is provoked by a concern that multitudes of Scots are far from the ordinances of the Church of Scotland; at least a hundred thousand in the area around London have been baptized into it, but less than a thousand are communicants, and few have 'fallen away to other communions'. This lukewarmness has provoked God's displeasure. Irving goes on to list four 'Tokens of God's Wrath resting upon the Children of the Scotch Church in London': the desertion of the Kirk by Scottish nobility or Members of Parliament when in London, thus setting a bad example and hastening the separation of the Scots community from the church; the lack of concern for the church among merchants and traders which makes it necessary for ministers to spend time fund-raising; the loss of many among the 'dependent classes' to Unitarianism, heterodoxy or outright infidelity; and finally poverty: of the hundreds who had sought help from the presbytery's ministers, not one was part of a

---

[10] Ibid. 484.

[11] Cambridge, URCHS, 'Minutes of the Scots Presbytery of London. Vol. 2. Apr. 28. 1823 to Nov. 11. 1834', fols 113, 115, 118: 19 September and 21 November 1827, 16 January 1828.

congregation of any denomination. God's judgement lay upon the community as a result, in three forms: incapacity for attachment to any one congregation (here Irving condemns those who join churches which hold Socinian doctrine,[12] deny any of the Kirk's fundamental beliefs, reject presbyterian ordination, deny infant baptism, uphold Arminianism – which stressed human agency in salvation and rejected Calvinist teaching about predestination – or oppose the establishment of religion), a spirit of worldliness; and a bias to infidelity (he notes as predisposing factors the church's lack of aesthetic inducements to superstition as a counter to the working of the apostate intellect, and the infidelity of many Scottish intellectuals, especially as circulated through the *Edinburgh Review*, often a target of his criticism). The letter's pastoral instructions are weak, and one wonders whether Irving was better at diagnosis than cure. He simply urges the faithful not to become church-hoppers, to keep apart from Socinianism and popery, to avoid worldliness, to remember their baptismal privileges, and to use the means of grace fully.

On 1 January 1828 Irving preached a Fast Day sermon on Jeremiah 9.1–2 which was published at the insistence of his officers as *An Apology for the Ancient Fulness and Purity of the Doctrine of the Kirk of Scotland: A Sermon Preached on the Occasion of a Fast Appointed by the Presbytery of London, to be Held in all their Churches on the First Day of the Present Year, because of the Low Ebb of Religion among the Children of the Scottish Church Residing in these Parts*. He was convinced that only repentance and immediate reformation would avail to save the churches from the judgement which God was about to execute upon the Gentile nations. The Church of Scotland's worship, preaching, discipline and government were all rooted in its sound doctrine; but there had been a declension from the truth, beginning with the doctrine of the Trinity. The result had been a failure to understand the offices of each of the divine persons in salvation, and consequent decline in all those aspects of the church's life which marked out its boundaries as a visible body – worship, preaching, discipline and polity.

His forthright critique of the contemporary scene was bound to excite vigorous reactions. Mrs Montagu spoke of Irving as being 'again at war with the mass of Scotchmen in London from a pastoral letter, in which he holds up a glass, which does any thing but flatter them ... he speaks truth too boldly for these days'.[13] Even his wife was apprehensive about the sermon's reception, writing to her father: 'I fear you will think him very severe to the Mother Church.'[14] Neither publication was well received by reviewers, especially among the Nonconformist constituency, who often took issue with Irving's condemnation of their opposition to religious establishments. *The Baptist Magazine* regretted 'that we have not room for a full exposure of the unscriptural notions they contain, and the antichristian temper in

---

[12] Socinianism was a term used at this period to denote denial of the full divinity of Christ and the atoning character of his death; Faustus and Lelio Socinus or Sozzini were two sixteenth-century Italian reformers who opposed Calvin's teaching in this way.

[13] Edinburgh, NLS, MS 1776, fol. 43: Mrs Montagu to Jane Carlyle, 27 February 1828.

[14] Isabella Irving to John Martin, 24 January 1828 (in private hands).

which many passages are written'. The *Pastoral Letter*, it asserted, was marked by Scots nationalism, Presbyterian intolerance, and contempt of other churches. 'Unless the members of the Scottish Church have better instruction than Mr. I.'s Sermon affords, they will soon find it necessary to keep another fast.'[15] A correspondent in the *Morning Chronicle* challenged the *Pastoral Letter*'s assertion that joining another denomination amounted to apostasy while claiming to rejoice that Scots were converted in such places, and condemned the Presbytery of London as a body lacking legal standing and thus having no right to portray itself as ruling the Kirk by issuing such a publication.[16] It was self-elected, and had usurped the legal right of Scottish congregations in England to manage their own affairs.[17] A review of both works in the *Evangelical Magazine* claimed to find a discrepancy between them: the *Pastoral Letter* urged the Kirk's claims in an exclusive manner, but the *Sermon* painted such a dire picture of it as to make people think twice before joining it! The former was 'a sad compound of conceit and uncharitableness' and the latter 'a singular specimen of the pen of its very singular author', marked by the assumption of prophetic authority, a Covenanting style full of threats, and a view of the Church of Scotland as ruined and apostate. It was a gross libel to accuse its ministers of believing in Trinity out of tradition or not at all. Overall, the *Sermon* was 'a tissue of error, misrepresentation, unintelligible jargon, and almost popish assumption'.[18]

Irving's attachment to Scotland and its church was essentially a backward-looking one, contrasting a past golden age (to some extent, this was an invented tradition on his part) with present degeneracy and foretelling future ruin. Such an outlook owed something to the Romantic intellectual climate, but also to his own experiences as a youth and as a licentiate. In the rest of this chapter we shall look at how his pessimism shaped his outlook on contemporary society.

* * *

The social critique evident in Irving's earlier preaching continued to find vigorous expression, and he grounded it in a particular view of church-state relationships. This enabled him to see economic distress as a manifestation of divine judgement upon the nation. An example of this is a sermon he preached on 29 January 1826, on the occasion of a collection at the Caledonian Church for distressed manufacturers affected by a recent spate of bank failures. It was entitled 'God's Controversy with the Land' and based on the blistering condemnations of social ills in James 5.1–7.[19]

---

[15] *Baptist Magazine* 20 (1828), 309–11.
[16] *Morning Chronicle*, 6 February 1828.
[17] Ibid., 18 February 1828.
[18] *EM* n.s. 6 (1828), 147–51.
[19] Edward Irving, *Sermons, Lectures, and Occasional Discourses* (3 vols, London: R. B. Seeley & W. Burnside, 1828), 3.893–963. This was reported as 'Remarks on Commercial Distress', *The Pulpit*, no. 147 (9 February 1826), 27–8; parts also appeared in *Thirty Sermons ... Preached during the First Three Years of his Residence in London: From the Accurate Notes of Mr. T. Oxford, Short-Hand Writer* (London: John Bennett,

He describes his church as 'this place, which they would fain put to silence, that it should not presume to speak of God's national dispensations, for the sake of which it was appointed to utter truth, as well as for the private and the personal well-being of men', an indication of the breadth of his understanding of pulpit ministry.[20] Evidently he had been ferociously criticized in the public arena, 'as if I had an evil design against the country and the common weal'.[21] Yet he saw himself as responsible as a watchman (here he had Ezekiel 33 in mind, in which the prophet is given a similar commission and warned that God would require the blood of his people at Ezekiel's hand if he failed to warn them of their peril) to declare the sins of the nation. His exposition of these followed (deliberately) the approach of the Old Testament prophets, who addressed rulers, nobility and merchants.

Looking first at the sins of the rulers and nobility, he argued that they lacked a sense of responsibility towards God; it was the church's duty to expound to them their duties. The sins of the merchant classes were even worse, however, because they had resulted in the congregation of vast numbers in industrial towns, which had become centres of misery, infidelity and disaffection. Idealizing town life of a century or two earlier, in the life of which the word of God had been central, he put the change down to an increase of capital and of devotion to its accumulation. Parodying the first question of the Westminster Shorter Catechism, he asserted that 'The chief end of man is now become to glorify mammon, and to enjoy him how and while we can.' As for the people, they had lost their sense of duty to God, and obeyed the law out of fear rather than for conscience' sake, instead of reverencing those in authority as set there by God. So dark was the outlook that 'It is barely possible that the Lord may be merciful to us as a nation, and prevent the calamity of inward convulsion.'[22]

Alongside the prevailing democratic spirit, a second abomination was the brutishness and ignorance of the people, which sprang from the failure of their rulers to provide true pastors. Instead, for a long century (he had in mind the consequences of the passing of the Patronage Act in 1712[23]) there had been appointed 'drones, to waste in idleness the substance of the church; worldlings, to be a scandal to the church; formalists, to teach superstition; and Arminians, to teach false doctrine'. The worst evil of the day was the resultant spiritual darkness and consequent loss of social cohesion. Irving urged his hearers to repent and to give liberally. For the church to give and to care opened the hearts of the needy to God. And if his hearers were not convinced by spiritual or humanitarian arguments, they should consider that

---

1835) as 'The Sins of the Upper Classes', 255–69, and 'The Sins of the Common People', 270–83.

[20] Irving, *Sermons*, 3.894.

[21] Ibid.

[22] Ibid. 930.

[23] This restored the right of patrons of parish livings to appoint the minister, taking it away from the elders, heritors and congregation: Andrew L. Drummond and James Bulloch, *The Scottish Church 1688–1843: The Age of the Moderates* (Edinburgh: Saint Andrew Press, 1973), 18.

the disease which lurked in the hovels of the poor could one day claim them. So, in conclusion,

> For the sake of yourselves and families, now flourishing in health; for the sake of this land, now clear of epidemical diseases; oh! to hinder the ravages of another typhus, which rung the knell of thousands, and wrote its history in the annals of many thousand families; for the sake of human life and human happiness here at home, no less than there abroad; for the sake of the well-conditioned, as well as of the miserable; for every sake of God and man, of religion and nature, of hope and of fear, do what you can at this opportunity to succour the distressed, – and bring unto our country-men once more, the character, the enjoyment, and the condition of British subjects, and of Christian men.

Who could have kept their purses or wallets closed in the face of such an appeal?

Continuing financial crisis during the autumn of 1826 saw him preaching four sermons on 1 Timothy 6.9–10, published as 'The Deceitfulness of Riches' and 'The Love of Money'.[24] The first considered the general proposition that the love of money was the root of all evil, and the effects of it on Christians and on the populace at large. Once again, the past was held up as better than the present, and his hearers were urged to live simply and for spiritual things, and to consider the needs of the poor. The first of the four sermons on 'The Love of Money', which he saw as having possessed all classes to an unprecedented degree during recent decades, contended that the worst result of the Fall was that human beings set their love on material things rather than on God. The second sermon tackled the desire to accumulate enough to retire on and to pass on to the next generation. The aim to better one's position in the community and to rise in the world was, he asserted, sinful; among Scots it had become entwined with, and sanctified by, religion. So,

> as a minister of eternal verities, and as a pastor of the immortal soul, I do solemnly denounce, as exceeding evil in the sight of God, all desires of gain, all earnest pursuit of it, all pleasing of ourselves with the possession of it; and I do denounce, as exceeding sinful in the sight of God, the desire of wealth and worldly greatness to ourselves and to our children ...[25]

The third sermon showed the evil effects in the land of this desire: it stifled the longing to grow in faith, it had brought spiritual leanness into the church as it adopted worldly expedients to fulfil its responsibilities, and it led to the decrease of the graces of Christian character. The final sermon outlined the fatal effects of covetousness in the church; Irving applied this to the young men in his congregation in ways which demonstrated spiritual and psychological insight into the workings of temptation.

---

[24] *CW*, 4.391–401, 402–443.
[25] Ibid. 421.

*\ *\ *

A number of Irving's writings during the late 1820s deal with the relationship between church and state. This was a time when great changes were being sought and sometimes made, such as the repeal of the Test and Corporation laws in 1828, making it much easier for Dissenters to play a full part in government at all levels, and the emancipation of Roman Catholics in 1829, which cleared the way for them to sit in Parliament and hold most public offices. Electoral reform was also under review and would shortly result in far-reaching redistribution of parliamentary seats and extension of the franchise. Such changes were anathema to high Tories and especially to the Evangelicals among them, who prophesied the imminent judgement of God upon the British nation for what they regarded as apostasy from its calling. And lurking in the shadows was the ever-present fear that the turmoil and dislocation of the French Revolution could be repeated in Britain.

In Irving's thinking about church and state, we see a much greater emphasis appearing on the idea that power is from above. At the time his views were changing, he came upon and eagerly devoured the seventeenth-century Bishop Overall's *Convocation Book*. As he explained to Isabella in October 1825, it confirmed his belief

> that the maxim which since Locke's time has been the basis of all government, 'that all power is derived from the people, and held of the people for the people's good,' is in truth the basis of all revolution and radicalism, and the dissolution of all government; and that governors and judges, of whatever name, hold their place and authority of God for ends discovered in His Word, even as people yield obedience to laws and magistrates by the same highest authority. Also it pleased me to find how late sprung is the notion among our levelling dissenters, that the magistrate hath no power in the Church, and how universal was the notion among the reformers and divines that the magistrate is bound to put down idolatry and will-worship, and provide for the right religious instruction of the people.[26]

The following day he confessed himself 'a good deal shaken concerning the right of subjects to take arms against their sovereign'. The right to rebel against ungodly rulers had played an important role in Reformed political thought since the 1550s; it was argued by the seventeenth-century Scottish theologian Samuel Rutherford and was put into practice by the Covenanters. So for Irving to diverge from men who were his heroes was a radical change indeed.[27] As a later biographer put it, 'This descendant of Covenanters and Whigs announced himself a believer in the Divine Right of Kings!'[28] Milton, whose *Paradise Lost* he had praised in his *Orations*, plummeted in his estimation: he was now 'assured that Milton, in his character, was

---

[26] Oliphant, *Life*, 121–2: journal, 26 October 1825.
[27] Ibid. 123.
[28] Andrew Landale Drummond, *Edward Irving and his Circle: Including some Consideration of the 'Tongues' Movement in the Light of Modern Psychology* (London: James Clarke, [1937]), 120.

the archangel of Radicalism, of which I reckon Henry Brougham to be the archfiend'.[29] In his new outlook, as he explained to Chalmers, 'The Church is the parent of all bodies-political.'[30]

Clearly there is a greater interest in politics in his preaching and writing, but I think the change represents a development rather than a U-turn. What had been evident from the beginning was Irving's reverence for the ideal; this now included more explicit avowal of his belief that government, like the church, ruled by divine authority, that the nation was regarded by God as a Christian nation and accountable to him as such, and that purity of faith was the ultimate safeguard of healthy national life. As previously, there was in Irving no thought of practicability or compromise. He thought in terms of absolutes; if a course of action was right before God, it should be followed whatever the results. On that basis he would oppose abolition of religious tests (whether in the founding of the London University or the repeal of the Test and Corporation Acts), Roman Catholic emancipation (which imperilled Britain's Protestant allegiance), and the idea that power was derived from the people rather than bestowed from above.[31]

Along with these developments we find a more open attitude towards the Church of England. A character sketch in the *Caledonian Mercury* during his 1829 lecture series in Edinburgh claimed that

> he who formerly praised the resistance of the Cameronians to tyrannic power, has become a preacher of passive obedience; he who railed at Prelacy, has learned to call it the sister church, and has adopted into his creed doctrines of her teaching, which, if not expressly disavowed, have never been recognised by the Scottish Church; he who rested on the doctrinal part of Scripture, and waited in humble patience till the final completion should explain dark prophecies, has become an expounder of what is wrapt up in parables from men's knowledge; and all these novelties he supports with an arrogant and dogmatic tone, by dint of denunciations indicative of the most exclusive intolerance ...[32]

It is surely significant that, as the assessment just quoted implied, this development in his views coincided with his taking up the study of biblical prophecy (and, one might add, his growing friendship with the likes of Henry Drummond). One writer thought that prophetic study had 'transformed the man who had championed republican heroes and Covenanting martyrs into a wild revivalist of Church and king ecclesiasticism, a fanatical antagonist of Catholic emancipation, and a fierce detester of all that was conveyed by the mere word liberal.'[33]

---

[29] Oliphant, *Life*, 145: journal, 3 November 1825.

[30] Edinburgh, NCL, Chalmers MSS, CHA 4.77.10, Irving to Chalmers, [September, 1827].

[31] Oliphant, *Life*, 1.382–4.

[32] R., 'The Rev. Edward Irving', *Caledonian Mercury*, 21 May 1829.

[33] Unidentified newspaper cutting: Charles L. Warr, 'Edward Irving. A remarkable Scottish Minister' [1922] (in private hands).

His new thinking found controversial expression in *A Letter to the King on the Repeal of the Test and Corporation Laws, as it Affects our Christian Monarchy* (1828). In it he argued that allowing those who professed no Christian faith to hold public office amounted to signing away Britain's charter as a Christian kingdom. God would withdraw his blessing, and indeed such a concession to the democratic spirit which sought to treat all alike would incur divine judgement. The King, he argued, was responsible to Christ as having been anointed in the name of the Trinity, while the dignity of the officers of the state derived from their profession of allegiance to Christ expressed by oath and by taking the sacrament. 'It is not that the Christian Religion is patronized by the State; but that the Christian Religion is the ground and basis of the State.'[34]

Irving sent Chalmers a copy of the *Letter to the King*, which the latter thought unsatisfactory but not as bad as the sermon (presumably the *Apology*). The two men did not see eye to eye ('Irving is wild on the other side from me'[35]), and shortly after Chalmers commented that Irving's 'extravagance and obscurity have placed him far out of my sympathy and sight'.[36] The Presbytery of London, however, were somewhat more sympathetic to Irving's views, especially when it came to the question of Roman Catholic emancipation. In February 1829 they unanimously agreed to present a petition to the Lords against granting further immunities to Catholics.[37] The following month, Irving submitted some petitions for their consideration, which called for the appointment of a day of fasting and humiliation to avert God's wrath and seek forgiveness for national sins, and the appointment of a committee to examine the Church of Scotland's acts and constitutions since the sixteenth century relating to the duty of church and state towards the Roman Catholic Church and to compare these with the provisions of the bill before Parliament.[38] In April a petition 'To the King's most excellent Majesty', against Catholic emancipation, was drawn up by a committee.[39]

The church, too, appear to have supported Irving wholeheartedly, their views changing with his. On the one hand, an undated printed petition from the Caledonian Church to the House of Lords requested repeal of penal measures against Catholics; it asserted that such measures were not the way to combat error, which should be done by the preaching of the truth. To say that the Protestant Church was in danger showed a lack of faith.[40] On the other hand, a printed petition to the Lords from the minister, elders, deacons and people, dated 18 February 1829, opposed Catholic emancipation; it argued that there was nothing to prevent Catholics from

---

[34] Edward Irving, *A Letter to the King on the Repeal of the Test and Corporation Laws, as it Affects our Christian Monarchy* (London: James Nisbet, 1828), 24.

[35] William Hanna, *Memoirs of the Life and Writings of Thomas Chalmers D.D. LL.D.* (4 vols, Edinburgh: Sutherland and Knox, 1850), 3.220.

[36] Ibid. 221.

[37] 'Minutes, Vol. 2', fol. 150: 17 February 1829.

[38] Ibid. fols 158–9: 17 March 1829.

[39] Ibid. fols 160–3: 9 April 1829.

[40] London, LMA, LMA/4358/C/002/19.

worshipping as things stood, that the pope was the enemy of church and state, and that Catholics should not hold any state office. On this issue Britain, 'the great Protesting Kingdom', would stand or fall: God would judge its apostasy.[41]

Irving does seem to have become more negative in his assessment of Roman Catholicism as a result of his prophetic researches. Late in 1825, he could write to Isabella that a visitor had told him

> that in the Catholic churches of Italy he had never heard a sermon (though he had heard many) which breathed of saints' days and other mummeries, but always of solid theology, deep piety, and much unction, and that he had met with many whom he believed most spiritual. My dear, I have often more concern about the issue of the intellectual forms of our own Church, which tend to practical and theoretical infidelity, than of the sensual forms of the Romish Church, which do tend to superstition, and still preserve a faith, though it be of the sense. Anyway, I give God praise that either with us or with them He preserveth a seed.[42]

In the mid-1820s Irving argued his anti-Catholic case on different grounds from those he later adopted. For example, on 12 April 1826 he preached a sermon on behalf of the London Hibernian Society, on 'The Cause and the Remedy of Ireland's Evil Condition'.[43] The source of the evil, he contended, was not government, since English Dissenters were under the same restrictions; neither was it a matter of social class, since Northern Ireland had the same social circumstances but not the unrest. The source of the evil was rather the religious system of Roman Catholicism. Its worship was sensual rather than spiritual; it made void the Incarnation by perpetuating Christ's presence in the Sacrament; and it nullified the Spirit's work by claiming continuing miracles and by taking away his work of illuminating Scripture and his office of forgiveness of sin. The remedy was the preaching of the Word of God, its circulation, and the education of children in it (a contrast with his later concern with legislative issues).

---

[41] LMA/4358/C/002/21.

[42] Oliphant, *Life*, 160: journal, 14 November 1825.

[43] *The Pulpit*, no. 160 (11 May 1826), 225–39. The sermon also appears in Irving, *Sermons*, 3.1199–1253 (dated to May 1825) and *CW*, 3.430–69.

The *Pulpit* carried at the foot of its reproduction of his sermon, a report of a meeting of the society in which Irving made a speech. What caught the attention of the large audience was his conclusion: he said that he wished to gain his hearers' hearts and heads, and that the money would then follow. He therefore gave the society the watch which his brother John had left him, to show that he was not merely offering words, promising to redeem it as soon as he could afford to. Lord Gambier as chairman took the watch but followed Irving along the platform, urging him to take it back as they did not need such proof of his support, but he refused. He did not wish to make an ostentatious display, but sometimes it was impossible to give secretly. Irving shook Gambier's hand, 'and retired amidst the long and loud plaudits of the assembly'. The result was that liberal contributions were thrown onto the table, including purses and sums of up to £50: *The Pulpit*, no. 160 (11 May 1826), 238–9; cf. *The Times*, 9 April 1826, 4.

But as eschatology shaped his political opinions over the next few years, it served to reinforce his conviction that the Papacy was the Antichrist whose rise and fall were foretold in Scripture (a conviction which he would already have encountered in the Reformed theological tradition[44]). Quite apart from contempt for Irish Catholic fecklessness, which he manifested when working in Glasgow, he came to oppose emancipation on grounds which were ultimately theological. the King ruled by divine right and was answerable to God alone, but this was balanced by his obligation to rule according to Scripture and not according to the wishes of the people. God could and would remove a ruler who betrayed his charge.[45] By the end of 1828, he was telling Chalmers that the Albury prophetic students were 'more convinced than ever of the judgments which are about to be brought upon Christendom, and upon us most especially, if we should go into any league or confederacy with, or toleration of, the papal abomination'.[46] In the periodical set up to disseminate the views of the Albury circle, the *Morning Watch*, Irving reiterated his conviction that Rome was the apostasy, the 'mystery of iniquity', the antichristian system foretold in biblical prophecy. Only on such grounds, he claimed, could the sixteenth-century Protestant reformers be cleared of the charge of schism for separating from her.[47]

With Catholic emancipation attracting everybody's interest, from March 1829 Irving lectured to his congregation on Wednesdays on Daniel 7, drawing large audiences.[48] These lectures were published as *The Church and State Responsible to Christ, and to One Another: A Series of Discourses on Daniel's Vision of the Four Beasts*. Dedicating his work to the three generations of clergy in the Martin family, he claimed that the error of modern democratic thinkers was that

> They look upon the people as if they were not Christ's, purchased by his blood, nor cared for by his providence; and they look upon Christ as if he were not the Prince of the kings of the earth, and the Lord of all the people upon the earth: and thus they

---

[44] 'National Covenant' (1580), in Philip Schaff, ed., *The Creeds of Christendom* (3 vols; 6th edn 1931, repr. Grand Rapids, MI: Baker, 1998), 3.480–5, at 481, 484; Westminster Confession 25.6.

[45] John Hair, *Regent Square: Eighty Years of a London Congregation* (London: James Nisbet, 1899), 64.

[46] Oliphant, *Life*, 255: Irving to Chalmers, December 1828.

[47] Edward Irving, 'On the Doctrine and Manifestation and Character of the Apostasy in the Christian Church', *MW* 1 (1829), 100–15. He also argued that God had planned that the church should be a mixed company of believers and unbelievers; that the latter would be more numerous in the church than the former; that they would increase as the end approached; and that persecution would come primarily from unbelievers within the church rather than outside it.

[48] Hair, *Regent Square*, 82.

are guilty of the most deadly schism, in separating the government of nations from the government of Christ ...[49]

Rulers were responsible to obey Christ, and ministers to declare his will that it might be followed; the state was to be subject to the church in matters to do with the invisible realm, and the church to the state in matters to do with the visible realm. The two must remain separate until the return of Christ. Both held their authority from Christ, which was why they should be obeyed even if personally ungodly (here he now disagreed openly with the Reformers and Covenanters who had taught and acted otherwise). Rebellion in the state was on a level with heresy or schism in the church. Establishment of religion offered a testimony to the jurisdiction of Christ, divided in this age into state and church but in the future to be united. Therefore, Christians should remain faithful to the established churches: 'I hold it to be an act of schism to go forth and separate from any church which is not of the Apostasy.'[50] Obedience, however, did not preclude speaking plainly against error in high places of church or state. This provided the context for an examination of the teaching of the doctrinal standards of the Church of Scotland concerning Roman Catholicism, but his opposition is nuanced by the belief that 'The Papacy is the mystery of the human heart brought into manifestation. Whenever I look upon it, I tremble at the image of myself.'[51] Its great error was to attempt to unite spiritual and temporal power, thus pre-empting what Christ alone would achieve at his return; the papacy thus stood in the place which belonged to Christ alone. In view of all this, it is small wonder that he affirmed the legitimacy of seeking to establish how the future would turn out, on the basis of a study of biblical prophecy, and where the contemporary church stood in the unfolding of God's purpose. Whilst the precise day of the Second Advent was not known, he believed that it would occur within forty years.

Linked with his opposition to Catholicism was his strong disapproval of the circulation of the Apocrypha by the British and Foreign Bible Society. In 1827 controversy broke out over whether the society's agents should circulate versions of the Bible which included the Apocrypha, a practice which horrified Reformed Scots in particular. This was done in Roman Catholic areas. Irving and Drummond were among the Evangelicals who opposed the practice, as was the Continental Society.[52] Several supporters published a protest against allowing a Catholic agent in Germany, Leander van Ess, to bind his own copies of the Bible which could thus include the Apocrypha, as the society had agreed only to make grants of bound copies of the Bible as a security against circulation of the Apocrypha. Irving gave

---

[49] Edward Irving, *The Church and State Responsible to Christ, and to One Another: A Series of Discourses on Daniel's Vision of the Four Beasts* (London: J. Nisbet, 1829), vi.

[50] Ibid. 568.

[51] Ibid. 539.

[52] Alexander Haldane, *The Lives of Robert Haldane of Airthrey, and of his Brother, James Alexander Haldane* (2nd edn, London: Hamilton, Adams, 1852), 531, 538.

his signature to this protest.[53] At the society's anniversary meeting on 2 May, Irving rose to propose some anti-Apocrypha resolutions. The society should express regret for having circulated the Apocrypha; overseas it should give preference to societies circulating the pure Bible; when electing committee members, those opposed to circulating the Apocrypha should be chosen. He also called on the committee to say in public what they had said individually in private, that they were sorry for having circulated the Apocrypha with the Scriptures. Although applauded, he found no seconder.[54] However, the discontent would rumble on, reinforced by unease at co-operation with non-Trinitarians and the exclusion of prayer from the society's public meetings, until it erupted in the formation of the Trinitarian Bible Society in 1831.

* * *

Another manifestation of the decay into infidelity which Irving foresaw as preceding the Second Coming was the founding of University College London. Initially he was very much involved in discussions, until he withdrew in protest[55] at what he saw as its failure to adopt a sufficiently religious basis for its teaching or admissions policy. According to Zachary Macaulay, who was associated with the evangelical 'Clapham Sect' and thus of a more moderate stamp than Irving, 'there is a small party with our friend Irving at their head who regard us as banded to promote the reign of infidelity on the earth._ I can discover no symptoms of this evil.'[56] When Carlyle wished to apply in 1827 for a professorship of Moral Philosophy in the new institution, Irving responded coolly, commenting that his name would be of no help to his friend.[57] Nevertheless, he offered advice on how to apply,[58] and wrote him a fulsome certificate of recommendation, albeit accompanied by the warning, 'You are in bad company with Brougham.'[59] This was not a matter of anti-intellectualism, however. Irving was not opposed to academic distinctions: at the end of 1828, he requested information from Chalmers about the examination procedure for the degree of Doctor of Divinity; Sir John Sinclair had volunteered to get him one more than five years earlier, but Irving had refused as he thought that to obtain it in such a manner went against all academic discipline.[60]

---

[53] 'British and Foreign Bible Society', *Caledonian Mercury*, 10 February 1827.
[54] 'British and Foreign Bible Society', *Caledonian Mercury*, 19 May 1827; Oliphant, *Life*, 214–16.
[55] NLS, MS 665, fol. 40: Irving to Carlyle, 27 August 1827.
[56] Chalmers MSS, CHA 4.124.16: Z. Macaulay to Chalmers, 17 January 1829.
[57] NLS, MS 1765, fols 75–6: Irving to Carlyle, 21 September 1827.
[58] Ibid. fol. 77: Irving to Carlyle, 9 October 1827.
[59] Ibid. fol. 86: Irving to Carlyle, 23 January 1828.
[60] Oliphant, *Life*, 254: Irving to Chalmers, December 1828.

* * *

Despite his concern to speak to the whole range of public affairs, it is possible to see Irving as becoming progressively more withdrawn from the wider world. Inevitably, therefore, Carlyle (who had moved in the opposite direction) found it increasingly difficult to sympathize with Irving's absorption in his work. To his father he wrote in 1827. '"The Lord," he says, blesses him: his Church rejoices in "the Lord"; in fact, the Lord and he seem to be quite hand and glove. He looks unhappy, for his tone sounds hollow, like some voice from a sepulchral aisle; yet I do honestly believe there is much worth among his failings, much precious truth among all this *cant*.'[61] He continued to poke good-hearted fun at his friend, referring to him by such designations as 'the Caledonian Orator'[62] and 'his Reverence of Pentonville',[63] and to esteem him highly; but rarely did he now express any real sympathy for Irving's views. There is a sense that he felt Irving no longer inhabited the real world, surrounded as he was by supporters and busy as he was with religious matters. While both men shared a deep concern at contemporary injustice and oppression, Irving (unlike Carlyle) viewed this in the light of his God-centred view of the world and thus looked for divine intervention.[64]

Irving, for his part, continued to entertain hopes of his friend's conversion: writing to Chalmers, he described Carlyle's spiritual state, concluding with the hope that he who is not against us, is for us (cf. Luke 9.50).[65] To Carlyle himself, he wrote: 'As my faith deepens, I grow perhaps what some would think more bygotted [sic]; but assuredly not less affectionate towards those who have reverence for what I believe, for the great name and power of my God, though they have not yet attained to the same light of knowledge & conviction of faith.'[66] He put his house at Carlyle's disposal while he was away on holiday, though reading between the lines it seems that as yet it was deemed inadvisable for Isabella and Jane to meet: 'Isabella was regretting that in its present dismantled state it was not worthy to offer to your wife also if she should think of accompanying you. It is undergoing a repair in several parts to make it habitable for the winter'.[67]

Another issue which strained their friendship concerned Irving's growing preoccupation with the study of biblical prophecy and his dogmatic proclamation of the fruits of his researches. In the next chapter we shall look at how his interest in this field developed, and what his friends made of it.

---

[61] *CL*, 4.253: Carlyle to John A. Carlyle, 5 September 1827.

[62] *CL*, 4.295: Carlyle to David Hope, 12 December 1827.

[63] *CL*, 5.5: Carlyle to John A. Carlyle, 13 January 1829.

[64] Cf. Ian Campbell, *Thomas Carlyle* (Edinburgh: Saltire Society, 1993; first publ. 1974), 75.

[65] Chalmers MSS, CHA 4.77.10: Irving to Chalmers, [September, 1827].

[66] NLS, MS 3823, fol. 226: Irving to Carlyle, 31 May 1827.

[67] NLS, MS 1765, fol. 77: Irving to Carlyle, 9 October 1827.

CHAPTER 13

Prophetic Student, 1826–30

It may be surprising to many readers that during the early nineteenth century the study of biblical prophecy was an accepted mainstream intellectual pursuit. The events surrounding the French Revolution came as such a shock to the inhabitants of the eighteenth century that many in the English-speaking world were convinced that the last days spoken of in the Bible had now arrived. That being so, they set themselves to discover the 'correct' interpretation of books such as Daniel and Revelation, and to relate this to past and present events, often using the Revolution as a kind of Rosetta Stone to decode history. While some radical thinkers looked to see the existing social order overthrown by the Second Coming and associated events, many Evangelicals (including Irving and his associates) took the opposite view: strongly attached to the existing social order, they saw contemporary threats to it as manifestations of an antichristian spirit which would make increasing headway in the world order until meeting its doom at Christ's return.[1] Prophetic study assuaged their fears and perhaps also provided a basis for appeals to others to be converted.

One writer whose views influenced Irving and his circle was G. S. Faber. His thinking about prophecy focused on five key themes: recent French history, the history of the papacy, the Ottoman Empire, the future destiny of the Jewish people, and the role of England (it was hoped that England would be the maritime power spoken of in biblical prophecy as assisting the return of the Jews to their land). Irving and his friends took up the quest for prophetic evidence of England's destiny and his portrayal of a threefold enemy under the Antichrist – Turkish, infidel and papal.[2] We also saw in a previous chapter that Coleridge and Frere had given a decisive impetus to Irving's study of prophecy, and in this chapter we examine his

---

[1] On evangelical eschatological thought at this period, see D. N. Hempton, 'Evangelicalism and Eschatology', *JEH* 31 (1980), 179–94; D. W. Bebbington, *Evangelicalism in Modern Britain: A History from the 1730s to the 1980s* (London: Unwin Hyman, 1989); Crawford Gribben and Timothy C. F. Stunt, eds, *Prisoners of Hope? Aspects of Evangelical Millennialism in Britain and Ireland, 1800–1880* (Carlisle: Paternoster, 2005). On the cultural context, see Robert James Dingley, 'Some Studies in Apocalyptic Themes and Images in English Literature and Art 1790–1850' (D.Phil. thesis, University of Oxford, 1980).

[2] W. H. Oliver, *Prophets and Millennialists: The Uses of Biblical Prophecy in England from the 1790s to the 1840s* ([Auckland]: Auckland University Press and Oxford University Press, 1978), 57, 60–1, 64.

major writings on this subject between 1826 and 1830, before outlining the genesis, development and significance of the conferences for prophetic study held during the same period at Albury Park, the home of Henry Drummond. These attracted a wider group of prophetic students, of whom Irving was in many respects the leader.[3]

Irving articulated views which later found their way into much evangelical thinking, but at the same time he appears to have been the individual who did most damage to such consensus as there had been among Evangelicals. Thus Sheridan Gilley argues that Irving halted advance of moderate Evangelicalism to power by splitting it.[4] The whole of the blame for this cannot be laid at Irving's feet: Evangelicalism during this period was already fragmenting, as Grayson Carter has demonstrated.[5] Nevertheless, Irving's sermons and writings, on prophecy as on other topics, do seem to have contributed to the process by provoking equal and opposite reactions.

* * *

The earliest recorded sermon by Irving on a prophetic subject seems to have been delivered on Christmas Day 1825, when he preached on the Second Coming (which he reckoned would take place in about thirty years' time) and the impending judgement of the Gentile nations.[6] The next Sabbath, 1 January 1826, he preached again on the Second Coming. Deeper study since publishing his *Oracles of God* in 1823 had convinced him that in warning people to repent it was not enough to argue merely from uncertainty as to when they might die. The usual notions of the future state were too abstract whereas, he argued, the church had in fact held to the hope of the Second Advent since the beginning. Accordingly, he surveyed the biblical teaching regarding the expectations to be entertained by believers.[7]

---

[3] For more on Faber, Frere and Albury, see Columba Graham Flegg, *'Gathered under Apostles': A Study of the Catholic Apostolic Church* (Oxford: Clarendon, 1992), 298–304, 331–42.

[4] Sheridan Gilley, 'Edward Irving, Prophet of the Millennium', in Jane Garnett and Colin Matthew, eds, *Revival and Religion since 1700: Essays for John Walsh* (London and Rio Grande, OH: Hambledon, 1993), 95–110, at 110.

[5] Grayson Carter, *Anglican Evangelicals: Protestant Secessions from the Via Media, c. 1800–1850* (Oxford: Oxford University Press), 2001.

[6] Edinburgh, NLS, Acc. 12489/1, James Simpson, 'J. G. S. Journals, 1806 to 1830', 27 December 1825; cf. [Manuel Lacunza], *The Coming of Messiah in Glory and Majesty, Translated from the Spanish, with a Preliminary Discourse, by the Rev. Edward Irving, A.M.* (2 vols, London: L. B. Seeley, 1827; hereafter Irving, *Preliminary Discourse*), 1.iv. In the latter, Irving states that he was lecturing on 1 Thess. 5.4–7 and found that he had strayed into talking about the personal Second Advent of Christ, a topic which he had been pondering privately for several months. Thereafter he decided to proclaim the doctrine openly.

[7] Edward Irving, 'The Second Coming of Christ', in *Thirty Sermons ... Preached during the First Three Years of his Residence in London: From the Accurate Notes of Mr. T. Oxford, Short-hand Writer* (London: John Bennett, 1835), 242–54. Produced as a

Some of Irving's basic eschatological convictions are set out in one of a series of discourses, 'The Plan of the Apocalypse', which from internal evidence appears to have been delivered in 1826 and may have been part of the same series as the previous item.[8] He insists that the book is worth understanding, and that its interpretation is 'a subject by no means intricate, being accurately studied, and surely very profitable, and at present very necessary'.[9] Although it had once been mysterious to him, study had made it 'the most wonderful, spiritual, and self-demonstrating book of the whole canon; and without the right knowledge of which, no one shall apprehend the mystery of Divine Providence to the church and to the world, nor comprehend the purpose and accomplishment of the times of the Gentiles'.[10] Clearly, then, understanding the book of Revelation was not merely about things still in the future, though Irving would have plenty to say about those, but essential to a right understanding of current events. There is no need for us to get lost in the detail, but it is worth noting that Irving understood the 'earth' in biblical prophecy to denote the territory of the four empires portrayed in the book of Daniel: Babylon, Persia, Greece and Rome. These were the stage on which the divine drama of history was to be played out. In the conflict between Christ and Antichrist, the enemies of Christ were the forces of superstition, tyranny and infidelity, symbolized by the three evil spirits in Revelation 16. Since many at this time were attracted to prophetic study as a source of hope, Irving assures them that Britain would be 'sealed from the judgment [coming upon the four empires] because of our renunciation of the pope', although it would come in for its share at the final great battle of Armageddon.[11]

His belief in the special place of Britain also appeared in his speech to a meeting of the British and Foreign School Society on 21 May 1826, offering a novel argument in favour of its educational activity. Irving was not unique in noting that giving people the ability to read was essential in connection with the worldwide distribution of the Bible. But he went on to assert that this was all the more appropriate to do so now in view of the nearness of the Second Coming. We may link this with the opinion expressed elsewhere that British agencies had played the leading role in the distribution of the Scriptures which had been such a feature of the years since the French Revolution. Britain, he claimed, was 'the great garden and depositary of the great legacy of God to all mankind. To us, as to the Jews of old, God had confided his peculiar favour. In proof of this, and for this purpose, he had

---

companion volume was William Jones, *Biographical Sketch of the Rev. Edward Irving, A.M. late Minister of the National Scotch Church, London: With Extracts from, and Remarks on his Principal Publications*. These volumes were evidently compiled in order to catch the market, and were apparently part of a series: Irving, *Thirty Sermons*, 253.

[8] Irving, *Thirty Sermons*, 333–47. The date may be inferred from his reference to judgement on the papacy as beginning thirty-three years earlier, a development which he often dated elsewhere to 1793: ibid. 344.

[9] Ibid. 333.

[10] Ibid. 344.

[11] Ibid. 344–5.

preserved us from war, from inward insurrections, and had placed and continued us in unity with all nations.'[12] We shall see later, however, that Irving believed such privileges had brought with them equally weighty responsibilities, and that Britain faced divine judgement for its failure in that respect.

Further light on the principles which he adopted in interpreting biblical prophecy is shed by a sermon on Matthew 24.1–15, preached on 12 February 1826.[13] After explaining what the disciples would have expected as Jews, he draws several lessons regarding the study of prophecy. Firstly, there is a correspondence between the prophecies in the Gospels and those in the Old Testament. Secondly, exact fulfilment of prophecy in this case implies the exact fulfilment of the number of 'days' of the papal period: 1260; since, like many exegetes, Irving held that a day in prophecy was equivalent to a year in history, he saw a 1260-year period of papal domination, lasting from the Edict of Justinian in 533 (which gave universal ecclesiastical authority to the papacy) until the overthrow of the papacy in 1793.[14] He adds that Britain would, if not steadfast in the faith, experience the same troubles as the papal nations of Europe. The editor commented that Irving had made many controversial statements on such topics as the restoration of the Jews, the decline of the Gentile churches, and the prediction that the Second Advent would probably occur in 1846, followed by mass Jewish conversions and then their evangelizing the whole world.

* * *

His sermon to the Continental Society in 1825 was published in the spring of 1826 as *Babylon and Infidelity Foredoomed of God: A Discourse on the Prophecies of Daniel and the Apocalypse which relate to these Latter Times, and until the Second Advent*. In dedicating the work to Frere, he confessed that on first meeting 'you seemed to me as one who dreamed, while you opened in my ear your views of the present times, as foretold in the book of Daniel and the Apocalypse'.[15] Eventually, however, Frere answered his objections and Irving became his willing student; one of the lessons he learned was that Revelation was in fact a narrative of events in historical order. The discourse had been intended to show members of the Continental Society (which laboured in territory which had been part of the Roman Empire) what the Bible said about Roman superstition and Protestant infidelity; some who heard it considered it too political, and he published it partly in order to clear himself from this charge.

---

[12] *Morning Chronicle*, 16 May 1826.

[13] *The Pulpit*, no. 149 (23 February 1826), 49–56.

[14] This date was derived from William Cunninghame, *Dissertation on the Seals and Trumpets of the Apocalypse* (1813): Flegg, *'Gathered under Apostles'*, 329.

[15] Edward Irving, *Babylon and Infidelity Foredoomed of God: A Discourse on the Prophecies of Daniel and the Apocalypse, which relate to these Latter Times, and until the Second Advent* (Glasgow: William Collins, 1828), iii. The work was first published in a two-volume edition.

In Irving's view, prophecy was, as later exponents would have put it, more relevant than today's newspaper: 'if there be any truth in prophecy, or evidence in the fulfilment of prophecy, now is the time appointed for that second deluge of wrath, which is to sweep away the enemies of God from their place, and give the earth to Christ and his saints for a thousand years'.[16] In setting out where he thought he and his hearers stood in God's prophetic calendar, he drew on a surprising source, whose fulfilment, he claimed, had been so exact 'that I knew not how to refuse it the character of being divinely inspired' – 2 Esdras 11–12, from the Apocrypha.[17] Infidelity would overthrow superstition before being itself overthrown by God and the Gentile nations judged; the Jews would be restored to their land, converted to Christ, and evangelize the world, leading to an unparalleled harvest for the Gospel.

His conclusion offered an 'Improvement to the British Nation'. God was warning those who would hear, that they might seek refuge in him and be sealed from coming judgement. He believed that prophecy foretold the sealing of a complete nation maintaining the pure worship of Christ, and of all the nations of the former Roman Empire that could only be Great Britain. It was, he said, the firstfruits of the kingdoms of this world which were to become the kingdoms of Christ at his coming. However, that should not induce a spirit of complacency: 'when the rulers of this nation shall permit, to the worshippers of the Beast, the same honours, immunities, and trusts, which they permit to the worshippers of the true God, that day will be blackest in the history of our fate. That day our national charter is forfeited in heaven, and we are sealed no longer.'[18] From 1829, that was exactly what he thought had happened. And how did he think this would come about? 'The evils growing in the bowels of the land, which will soon strike us down, if not tim[e]ously remedied, are, the growth of infidelity in religion, and insubordination in politics.'[19] The Continental Society's agents should not try to convert Rome, but call people out of it; they should not adopt the long-term approach to mission (which was then becoming popular, and bound up with notions of the civilizing role of the missionary as an essential prerequisite for the entrance of the gospel into heathen cultures), but move from place to place, because time was short. 'The time for conversion, the time for building Churches, is gone.'[20]

It is worth remembering that many of the original readers would have been greatly interested by reports of archaeological discoveries in the Near East: apart from the fact that these were seen as confirming the divine inspiration and consequent accuracy of the Bible, they would have brought a new vividness to the prophecies concerning the 'mystical Babylon', papal Rome; it is no coincidence that the *Morning Watch* showed considerable interest in such matters. The destruction of Babylon was a popular theme in contemporary art and literature, as a neglected thesis by R. J.

---

[16] Ibid. 204.
[17] Ibid. 213.
[18] Ibid. 546.
[19] Ibid. 559.
[20] Ibid. 585.

Dingley has shown.[21] At one level, Babylon functioned as a symbol of the papacy, whose downfall was thus believed to be foretold in Revelation, with its exultant cry, 'Fallen, fallen is Babylon the Great!' (Revelation 18.2). At another, analogies could be drawn between ancient Babylon and contemporary London, reflecting pride in London's greatness but also fuelling an apprehension about the city's prospects which concentrated the more diffuse sense of imminent catastrophe felt by many members of the middle and upper classes.[22]

Such a work was bound to excite strong reactions. It was probably of this book that the Scottish lay theologian Thomas Erskine (1788–1870) wrote in 1827:

> I have been reading lately Irving's book on the Prophecies, and a very striking book it is. He writes evidently with the fullest conviction that his interpretation is right. If he is right, we are on the eve of a tremendous catastrophe, in comparison with which all the calamities of the French Revolution are as nothing. Infidelity is to destroy Popery, and to break up the very foundations of all the civil and political institutions of Europe, and then infidelity itself is to be destroyed with a fearful destruction. I have only got one volume yet, but I really think he marks the coincidence of the prophecies, and the events of the last forty years, very fairly. According to his view, our blessed Lord is Himself to appear on earth in forty years.[23]
>
> ... I am quietly looking upon the seat of the Beast, and wondering at him, at the manner of his existence, and at his duration. I have met here [Rome] with Irving's book upon the Prophecies. I don't suppose that any mere interpreter of prophecy has ever before assumed such a tone of confidence and authority. I am a little surprised that the fate of former interpreters has not warned him. He is scarcely meek enough. He seems to intend to brave and insult such of his readers as hesitate about yielding their entire consent; but it is a magnificent book, full of honest zeal.[24]

Reviewers criticized the book as largely a rehash of Frere's arguments, and seized on the granting of quasi-canonical status to a part of the Apocrypha, the more so because of Irving's prominent role in the controversy over its circulation which divided the British and Foreign Bible Society. In using 2 Esdras, he gave 'occasion to our adversaries to charge us with inconsistency in rejecting the Apocrypha, and yet making use of it when it suits our purpose'.[25] As usual, his confident and dogmatic tone invited condemnation (not least because he seemed to be claiming

---

[21] Dingley, 'Apocalyptic Themes'.

[22] Ibid. 187.

[23] W. Hanna, ed., *Letters of Thomas Erskine* (2nd edn, Edinburgh: David Douglas, 1878), 86: Erskine to Miss Christian Erskine, 12 April 1827. On Erskine, see Nicholas R. Needham, *Thomas Erskine of Linlathen: His Life and Theology, 1788–1837* (Edinburgh: Rutherford House, 1990); Don Horrocks, *Laws of the Spiritual Order: Innovation and Reconstruction in the Soteriology of Thomas Erskine of Linlathen* (Carlisle: Paternoster, 2004).

[24] Hanna, ed., *Erskine*, 87: Erskine to Chalmers, 19 April 1827.

[25] *Baptist Magazine* 18 (1826), 317–20, at 319; cf. *CO* 28 (1828), 75–6.

divine inspiration for his interpretation and placing himself between the reader and the Scriptures), as did his tendency to impute 'ignorance, stupidity, shallow-mindedness, and wickedness' to those who saw things differently.[26] As one reviewer concluded, 'we cannot conscientiously assist in the redemption of his gold watch, by recommending the perusal of these volumes to our readers.'[27]

Just before *Babylon and Infidelity* appeared, we find Coleridge arranging to meet Irving to study Revelation 'if so I might withdraw him from what I cannot regard as other than a Delusion, of a very serious nature, were it only for it's [sic] consequences on his character, and therewith on his Utility'.[28] Like the reviewers, Coleridge appears to have held Frere responsible: 'Mr Irving (as Mrs Montagu most sensibly observed) affected by Hatley Frere's solemn and intense earnestness, mistook the vividness of the impression for the force of truth – and has been preaching immeasurable lengths of Sermons, to the serious detriment of his health, and the bewilderment of his Auditors'.[29] It was, perhaps, inevitable that their friendship should cool: the essayist Henry Crabb Robinson recollected in 1828 that 'of late he has been little acquainted with Irving: he says he silenced Irving by showing how completely he had mistaken the sense of the revelations and prophecies, and then Irving kept away for more than a year'.[30]

Chalmers was likewise concerned for his friend. The day before the opening of the National Scotch Church, he went with Irving to visit Coleridge: '... Irving sits at his feet, and drinks in the inspiration of every syllable that falls from him. There is a secret, and to me, unintelligible communion of spirit between them, on the ground of a certain German mysticism, and transcendental lake poetry which I am not yet up to.' On the way home, Chalmers commented on 'the obscurity of Mr. Coleridge's utterances' and explained that 'he liked to see all sides of an idea before taking up with it'; Irving's scornful response was that 'you Scotchmen would handle an idea as a butcher handles an ox. For my part, I love to see an idea looming through the mist.'[31] The two men, in spite of their mutual regard, were finding it increasingly difficult to see each other's point of view.

On the Friday after the opening, 18 May, Irving preached on prophecy at a Hackney chapel; Robert Gordon, who was staying in London while preaching at the

---

[26] *ER* n.s. 27 (January–June 1827), 185–207, 314–36, at 203.

[27] Review of *Babylon and Infidelity*, *EM* n.s. 4 (1826), 292–4.

[28] E. L. Griggs, ed., *Collected Letters of Samuel Taylor Coleridge*, Vol. 6 (Oxford: Clarendon, 1971), 570: Coleridge to Edward Coleridge, 8 March 1826.

[29] Ibid. 557: Coleridge to Edward Coleridge, 8 February 1826.

[30] R. W. Armour and R. F. Howes. *Coleridge the Talker* (Ithaca, NH: Cornell University Press, 1940), 334. On the other hand, Peter Elliott maintains on the basis of a study of Coleridge's writings that by late 1827 he had accepted the main points of Irving's eschatology – belief in a personal Second Advent and an earthly millennium: 'Edward Irving: Romantic Theology in Crisis', ch. 4.

[31] William Hanna, *Memoirs of the Life and Writings of Thomas Chalmers D.D. LL.D.* (4 vols, Edinburgh: Sutherland and Knox, 1850), 3.160: Chalmers to Grace Chalmers, May 1827.

National Scotch Church, went to hear him, and passed on his impressions to Chalmers, who recorded that the sermon lasted two and a half hours; 'and though very powerful, yet the people were dropping away. I really fear lest his prophecies, and the excessive length and weariness of his services, may unship him altogether, and I mean to write to him seriously on the subject.'[32] The sermon was probably that on Revelation 16.13–14, 'The Three Spirits which Gather the Kings of the Earth and the whole World to the Battle of that great Day of God Almighty', which Irving preached at the Revd H. F. Burder's Independent chapel in Hackney on behalf of the Continental Society.[33] It was an elucidation of his understanding of the apocalyptic symbols of the dragon, the beast, and the false prophet, which he interpreted as:

> first, the autocratic and self-willed spirit of absolute power, which mocks the Father's sovereignty; secondly, the Papal mystery of iniquity, which assumes the threefold office of Christ, as our Prophet, Priest, and King; and, thirdly, the infidel spirit of the human intellect, levelling all distinctions, which commits the sin against the Holy Spirit, in rejecting his testimony of the Father and the Son, and thinking to constitute an enlightened, well-governed, and blessed world without them ...[34]

Irving surveyed church history to show how these Satanic spirits had been at work in it, but his anti-Catholicism was a nuanced one: Rome was a parody of Christ's kingdom, but a remarkably accurate one, from which much could be learned about the real one and in which much had been preserved, notably the Scriptures and the orthodox faith expressed in the ancient creeds. It was fitting, therefore, that Irving's next major work on prophecy should be a translation of a work by a Chilean Jesuit, Manuel Lacunza (1731–1801), *La Venida del Mesías en gloria y magestad*.

* * *

On 28 November 1825 Irving recorded in his Journal that he had begun daily Spanish lessons, partly as an act of charity towards his teacher, a needy Spanish refugee named Sottomayor; beginning with Bible, the plan was that they would also

---

[32] Oliphant, *Life*, 210. Chalmers' aversion to prophetic study should not be overstated: that October he wrote to thank one correspondent for sending him a set of lectures in manuscript form which had renewed the impulse towards prophetic study received some months earlier from reading Irving's work, confessing that he bore a share of the blame for the way in which prophetic study had been neglected in the church and avowing himself 'very much inclined' to be a millennarian: Edinburgh, NCL, Chalmers MSS, CHA 3.10.85: Chalmers to Mrs H. Paul, 20 October 1827.

[33] Edward Irving, *Sermons, Lectures, and Occasional Discourses* (3 vols, London: R. B. Seeley & W. Burnside, 1828), 3.847–92. Independents were later known as Congregationalists.

[34] Ibid. 853–4.

read *Don Quixote*.[35] Yet it was to be a very different work which would occupy Irving's attention. After he began learning Spanish he came upon Lacunza's work, which had been brought to England by an Anglican clergyman working among the Spanish people and later came into the hands of Lewis Way. It came into Irving's hands through a lady who understood Spanish and recognized the similarity of its eschatological teaching with his.[36] First published in 1812, it had been placed by the Roman Catholic authorities on the Index of Prohibited Books in 1824, and reissued in London in 1816 and 1826. The author had felt it wise to adopt the pseudonym 'Juan Josafat Ben-Ezra', perhaps in the hope of appealing to Jewish readers. Irving set about translating it, assuming that others would be as open to receive instruction from any source as he was. He had lately opposed Catholic emancipation, and now he was learning from a Catholic priest. He worked hard on it through the summer, while resting (supposedly – Irving's holidays often seem to have involved a change rather than a rest) with Isabella and the family at Beckenham and returning to London each weekend to conduct the services. He worked so closely on the book that at one point there was a risk he would lose his sight; some of his letters during this period were dictated to Isabella, and she acted as scribe for the work of translation.[37] A few friends whose spiritual and theological integrity he trusted were asked to provide comments on Irving's draft as he went along, including Chalmers, to whom he wrote in September:

> I send you herewith the first part of a work I am translating from the Spanish that it may be accessible to the Church in these lands. It was written by a learned Jesuit (by birth a Jew) named Lacunza & published in Spain about twelve years ago & is well worthy of your most careful study. I shall continue to send it to you until it is finished unless you signify to the contrary.

By that stage the printing of the work had already begun, and its cost was being covered by 'a pious lady'; after reimbursing her, profits were to go to Spanish emigrants.[38]

The Coming of Messiah in Glory and Majesty was published on 19 April 1827,[39] along with a lengthy *Preliminary Discourse* by Irving which was also published

---

[35] Oliphant, *Life*, 190. The following year, he was learning Hebrew, as James Simpson recorded: 'Mrs Simpson has attended at Revd Mr Irvings house every Tuesday for about 2 Months, to receive instruction along with Mr and Mrs Irving, Mr Reid, Mr Heith & Mr Bull, in the Hebrew Language from a Mr Newman, a Polish Jew, & lately was a Rabee [sic] among that People but who, I believe has seceded from them on acc^t of his believing the Talmud to have no Authority': 'J. G. S. Journals, 1806 to 1830', 26 December 1826.

[36] NLS, Acc.12489/9, Jane Simpson, Diary, 1826–8, fol. 6: 30 October 1826.

[37] Oliphant, *Life*, 200–2.

[38] Chalmers MSS, CHA 4.57.29: Irving to Chalmers, 12 September 1826 (in Isabella's handwriting). He also asked the Hon. J. J. Strutt, an Anglican layman and fellow prophetic student from Essex, to offer comment: Terling, Strutt letters: Irving to Strutt, 12 September 1826.

separately. He summarized the main contentions of Ben Ezra as being that the Gentile church is ripe for judgement; Christ will prepare another 'ark of testimony' (i.e. a body which both bears witness to God's truth and offers a place of shelter from his judgement) by bringing many Jews to acknowledge Christ as Messiah, who will evangelize the world; God's judgement on infidelity and anti-Christianity will conclude with the personal appearance of Christ and the resurrection and judgement of believers, inaugurating a millennium of earthly blessedness to be terminated by a final rebellion and the resurrection of all and the Last Judgement. The previous Jewish dispensation and the present Gentile one both testify to the fact that righteousness before God comes by faith rather than works; and both are to end in condemnation – in order that God may have mercy on all by bringing the Jews to acknowledge Christ and making them agents in the conversion of the world. What made the book unacceptable in Rome was Lacunza's contention that the false religion of the Antichrist would infect Christianity in general, including Catholicism, which would have sat uneasily with belief in the infallibility and indefectibility of the Roman Church. Irving accepted the main outlines of Lacunza's prophetic scheme, but disagreed with his assertion that the events of Revelation 4–22 lay entirely in the future; rather, Irving saw them as being fulfilled in the entire history of the church, and claimed that specific biblical prophecies were capable of a dual interpretation – to their own time as well as to the last times.[40] The impact of the work on Irving appears to have been significant, not so much in terms of leading to modify the scheme of prophetic interpretation which he had taken from Frere, but in terms of leading him to present the Second Advent as an object of hope for the believer and warning for the unbeliever. This emphasis was to characterize all his subsequent writing on prophecy.

After it was published, Irving sent a copy to Carlyle:

> I have translated a book out of the Spanish[.] I send it to you and to my dear friend your wife. ... The book is Theological but it is the finest specimen of Logic you ever read. And it restores that side of Christianity which has been hidden from this age, and I think by being hidden from it the age has drifted into infidelity.[41]

A postscript indicates that the work was in fact sent to Carlyle's bookseller, and a few months later Carlyle wrote to his wife: 'Edward Irvings book out of the Spanish came last night and also a copy for his father with a great bundle of preliminary discourses "to be *distributed among his kindred and addressed to them <u>with his own hand</u>"*'.[42] If the gift was intended to awaken Carlyle, it appears to have failed, as the latter saw nothing new in it:

---

[39] *Morning Chronicle*, 19 April 1827.
[40] For a useful summary of Lacunza's views and Irving's assessment of them, see Flegg, *'Gathered under Apostles'*, 304–31.
[41] NLS, MS 3823, fol. 227: Irving to Carlyle, 31 May 1827.
[42] *CL*, 4.260: Jane Welsh Carlyle to John A. Carlyle, [13 September 1827].

He does *not* seem in the least millenniary in his letters: but the same old friendly man we have long known him to be. And yet his printed works are enough to strike one blank with amazement: for if the millen[n]ium is to come upon us in twenty years and odd months, ought we not to be turning a new leaf? ... Alas! Alas! The madness of man findeth no termination, but only new shapes, the old spirit being the same. To the last, there is and will be a bee in his bonnet, which only in every new generation buzzes with a new note![43]

An unsympathetic observer might describe Irving as obsessed with prophetic study; when Robert Story was convalescing in England late in 1827 and early in 1828, Irving tried to make a match for him with a woman who, according to Irving 'knows more of the Mystery of the Papacy than any woman in England, except my wife'.[44] He continued to preach on eschatological topics 'in season and out of season'. Even at a Sunday School anniversary in Ongar, Essex, in 1827, he regaled the assembled throng (the chapel windows had been removed so that those outside could hear) with a two-hour discourse upon the battle of Armageddon; one can only wonder what the effect of his terrifying descriptions would have been on young minds present.[45] Yet underlying this was a passionate conviction concerning the truth and relevance of what he was preaching; some were put off by it, but others were riveted.

* * *

On Sunday mornings from January to May 1828, Irving preached a series of sermons from 2 Timothy 3.1–6 on 'The Last Days', indicating the characteristics which would be found in society at that period, and of course demonstrating that these characteristics marked the society of the day and therefore that the last days were imminent. The sermons were gathered together in book form as *The Last Days: A Discourse on the Evil Character of these our Times, Proving them to be the 'Perilous Times' of the 'Last Days'*.[46] His method was usually to expound the positive characteristic which was lacking in contemporary society, and then to point out the evidence of its opposite.[47] Significantly, the title page bore the text 'The vile person shall no more be called LIBERAL' (Isaiah 32.5). The work is interesting because it combines eschatological concern with the social critique which had marked

---

[43] *CL*, 4.296: Carlyle to David Hope, 12 December 1827.

[44] Robert Herbert Story, *Memoir of the Life of the Rev. Robert Story, late Minister of Rosneath, Dunbartonshire* (Cambridge: Macmillan, 1862), 125n.

[45] Josiah Gilbert, ed., *Autobiography and other Memorials of Mrs Gilbert (formerly Ann Taylor)* (2 vols, London: Henry S. King, 1874), 2.37. It was on this occasion that Isaac Taylor took the silhouette of Irving whose outline appears at the front of the first volume of Irving's *Collected Writings*: ibid. 2.93.

[46] Edward Irving, *The Last Days: A Discourse on the Evil Character of these our Times, Proving them to be the 'Perilous Times' of the 'Last Days'* (2nd edn, London: James Nisbet, 1850), 295.

[47] Ibid. 244.

his preaching ever since his arrival in London.[48] Underlying it is his intent 'to reveal an apostasy already begun in the Church, and to grow worse and worse until the end, when it should leaven the whole constitution of religious, moral, and political society, and bring in these perilous times mentioned in the text'.[49] The religious world might have a form of godliness, but it lacked its power.

The Dedication, to Dinwiddie, Hamilton, and the other members of the session and the Building Committee, offers an insight into the relationship between the topics on which his preaching focused. After his settlement, they had been

> rewarded by larger openings of Divine doctrine, and closer fellowship of the Holy Ghost, and greater increase of the flock. The doctrine especially of the blessed Trinity, and the offices sustained by the persons thereof in our salvation, I desire, for my church and for myself, to acknowledge, was then opened to us, and remained no longer, as it is to most, a believed but unknown mystery. Next the doctrine of the Gentile apostasy, as exhibited in the Papal superstition, and in Protestant liberalism, was made instrumental, under God, to deliver the church from the false hope of converting a world which standeth ripe and ready for judgment; and did set us free from the spirit of expediency, that spirit which now worketh in the religious world. To a right understanding of the present condition of the church, and its immediate judgment, we were greatly helped by attaining unto the mystery of baptism, as constituting a people in covenant, and responsible for the privileges of the covenant.[50]

Privilege brings responsibility: as a baptized nation, Britain is subject to judgment for its failure to live accordingly. He continues:

> Next in the order of God's mercies to us, we have to acknowledge his instructing of us in the true humanity of Christ – or rather, I should say, that he has enabled us to stand and suffer reproach for the most catholic and orthodox doctrine, that Christ took human nature in the fallen, and not in the unfallen state ... And now, finally, and above all, as the consummation of the whole, it pleased God to make known to us the coming of Christ in glory and in majesty, and his reign upon the earth for a thousand years, together with the resurrection of the saints, and the other mysteries of grace therewith connected.[51]

---

[48] Oliver argues that prophetic speculation is in fact a way of commenting on contemporary society: *Prophets and Millennialists*, 14–15. This is undoubtedly true, but rather than adopting a reductionist approach which sees writings on prophecy as nothing more than social comment, we should recognize that Irving and many other prophetic students (but not all) were actually looking at things the other way round, viewing contemporary society *sub specie aeternitatis*.

[49] Irving, *Last Days*, 9.

[50] Ibid. xxxviii.

[51] Ibid. xxxix.

The last days, he warns, will see not the conversion of the world but God's judgement upon its apostasy, as foreshadowed by the judgement of the Jews.[52] They 'are not yet arrived, but will begin to run from the time of God's appearing for his ancient people, and gathering them together to the work of destroying all Antichristian nations, of evangelising the world, and of governing it during the Millennium'.[53]

Giving voice to the anxieties of many of his congregation, he describes such 'perilous times' as involving 'the breaking up of the ordinances of religion and the restraints of social life'.[54] Individualism has been the order of the day, even in religion. 'This is Satan's trick with the religious world, to get them to undervalue the outward visible ordinances, offices, and canons of their several churches, under the fond conceit that they are thereby honouring the one invisible Church the more: as if one should honour the whole human race the more by trampling under foot the body of his mother'.[55] By contrast, religion should be the opposite of liberality, because it binds us to the performance of certain duties. Liberality has even affected family relationships to the point where the right of parent to direct their child's faith is denied. Parental failure results in increasing juvenile crime; 'what a burden hath the Lord laid upon his ministers, to stand amidst the wreck of a dissolving society, and, like Canute, to preach unto the surging waves!'[56]

In the church, such subjectivism and individualism springs from the evangelical awakening of the previous century, which he contrasts with traditional emphases on sound doctrine and sacramental observance:

> the Methodism of Wesley and Whitefield, ... however well meant, and over-ruled for good, yea, and productive of good, did introduce into the Church a new era of thinking and feeling with respect to the transmitted and embodied wisdom of our fathers. The obligation of the sacraments began to be forgotten in the work of conversion, and hath never since been recalled to mind. The information of doctrine and morals, and, in one word, the divine wisdom, which was wont to be embodied in preaching, passed away for quick and lively appeals to the present feelings of men,

---

[52] For the same parallel, see Irving's 'Signs of the Times, and the Characteristics of the Church', *MW* 1 (1829), 641–66; 2 (1830), 142–62. Apparently first delivered as a sermon at Regent Square, it parallels the condition of the contemporary church (especially the Evangelicals) with that of the Jews in Christ's day as delineated in Matt. 23. In the second part of the article, he argues that apart from those who will be translated to heaven before the final great time of tribulation, there will be those who are to be saved but who will have to pass through this period on earth (ibid. 161), an interpretation later designated as the 'partial rapture' theory.

[53] Irving, *Last Days*, 13–15.
[54] Ibid. 38.
[55] Ibid. 58.
[56] Ibid. 79.

addresses to their interests, presentations to their love of pleasure, food to their appetite of excitement; which continueth likewise unto this day ...[57]

Controversially, he asserts that all ministers except those who have taken up prophetic study are infected with 'liberality'.[58] He calls them to expand their horizons far beyond the mechanics of individual conversion to consider the whole purpose of God, and rejects the collapsing of every aspect of the work of redemption into the teaching that Christ paid our debt as 'Stock-Exchange divinity'.[59] He claims that if his readers' sense of holiness is offended by the idea that Christ took fallen human nature, it will be offended by having contact with sinners: they cannot go where he did not go.

A review in the *Christian Observer* described Irving as 'the Ishmael of the Christian world, his hand being against every man'.[60] *The Last Days* was too vitiated by intense feeling to be as intellectually satisfying as his earlier works, and the reviewer advised him to preach less and think more.[61] The *Evangelical Magazine* expressed the belief that if he had more to do with other denominations, he would find that many of his signs of the last days disappeared.[62] Much later, David Brown, who in 1830 succeeded Scott as Irving's assistant, considered the book 'full of exaggerated denunciations of evils seldom absent from great cities, and even at that time not peculiarly rife'. Convinced that he was living in the last days, Irving was looking for evidence to prove it to himself.[63] Nevertheless, there were those with a more positive estimate of the book. When a second edition was published in 1850, a Preface by Horatius Bonar was added, which claimed that the work 'embodies such a mass of truth, and such an amount of well-aimed admonition and warning; it forms such a minute yet such a masterly commentary upon the age and its characteristics, that it is entitled to take rank among the works specially required in our day, and robbed of which, we should suffer heavy loss'.[64]

* * *

A short work published in April 1829, *The Signs of the Times*, offers a sermonic summary of Irving's thinking about biblical prophecy which is somewhat easier to grasp, thanks to its brevity. Irving was certain that Britain and Ireland would be swiftly destroyed because they, like the Jews, had not heeded the signs of the times.

---

[57] Ibid. 306–7.
[58] Ibid. 313.
[59] Ibid. 459.
[60] *CO* 29 (1829), 503–12, 558–68, at 511; cf. Gen. 16.12.
[61] Ibid. 567.
[62] *EM* n.s. 6 (1828), 569–72, quotation at 572.
[63] David Brown, 'Personal Reminiscences of Edward Irving', *The Expositor*, 3rd ser., 6 (1887), 216–28, 257–73, at 262.
[64] Irving, *Last Days*, vii–viii. Bonar (1808–89) was a minister in the Free Church of Scotland, editor of the *Quarterly Journal of Prophecy* and a noted hymnwriter.

That catastrophe was imminent, Irving declaring himself 'solemnly and awfully convinced that we are arrived at the very upshot of the mighty purpose, the winding up of the whole matter, the opening and discovery of the deep laid and long delayed plot'.[65] Irving believed that infidelity existed in three forms: absolute power, papal superstition and infidelity. These had successively held sway over the West, but now all three were acting together.

The four kingdoms of Daniel's vision (Daniel 2), who successively tyrannized the Jews, were the Babylonians, the Medo-Persians, the Greeks and the Romans. Nineveh and Babylon were now under Turkish dominion, continuing the first; the Persians still held the territory of the Medo-Persians; the Greeks had just become independent again; and Rome was continued in the Ten Kingdoms of the West (represented by the ten toes of the image in verses 41–42). So the whole image still existed, and within the territories which it represented the Jews continued to suffer. In Daniel 7, four beasts were depicted, the fourth having ten horns. Three of these fell out to make way for a little horn which was shown speaking, to Irving symbolizing a preacher. This ecclesiastical horn took over three kingdoms first, and then the whole of the fourth beast's territory. It was slain but the others were allowed to live, though no longer to rule, representing the Roman kingdoms falling under papal rule. Britain was a Protestant nation, but Irving feared that a possible treaty with Rome was bringing it back under papal dominion. Judgement would therefore begin with the British nation, which had been specially blessed yet had despised God and come to an accommodation with the papacy. Only then would the Jews come to dominion. The worst tribulation, however, would be experienced at the hands of a Roman king, against whom stood the archangel Michael (Daniel 10–12). This was fulfilled in part in the rise of Napoleon (Daniel 11.21–40), but complete fulfilment awaited a future individual, the last king of Rome, the infidel Antichrist. A new power would put down the Antichrist; it was described as coming out of the North, which Irving took to denote Russia, allied with the remnants of the first three of the four monarchies. The Kings of the North would ally with those from the East (the ten lost tribes of Israel) to destroy the Antichrist. The ten tribes, with the two now liberated from the mystical Babylon (Rome) would settle in their land, with northern approval, but the Kings of the North would come to envy their blessing and finally oppose them, whereupon they would be destroyed.

As with all such cataclysmic predictions, readers wanted to be assured regarding their own security. Irving believed that Britain, as a Protestant nation containing a true church, had been preserved when the papal kingdoms fell in the French Revolution and the unrest which ensued. He saw no indication that God intended to destroy the true church, though it might be chastized. According to Isaiah 18, 'the land shadowing with wings' (as translated in the Authorized Version) was to be treated differently from other nations because it was to bring God's people to their

---

[65] Edward Irving, *The Signs of the Times* (London: Andrew Panton, 1829), 6.

land. Irving was convinced by the argument of Bishop Horsley[66] that it was Britain which was being referred to. It would be under the infidel Antichrist for a time but then restored. Since God was raising up men to testify to the Second Coming, he must have a future for the nation. Believers were therefore to testify against any compromise of Britain's Protestant standing. In an urgent postscript, Irving noted that the Emancipation Bill now lay before Parliament, 'this measure, the most God-forgetting, the most God-displeasing, which a nation was ever guilty of'. If church and nation would protest, then Britain might be preserved when its government was judged.[67]

* * *

We turn now to examine Irving's involvement with the Albury conferences for the study of prophecy. These were rooted in a network of like-minded leaders, often drawn into contact with Irving through his preaching. We have already encountered Frere and Drummond, but two others were Lewis Way (1772–1840) and Joseph Wolff (1795–1862).

Way was a man of considerable private means who in 1815 had provided the funds necessary to rescue the London Society for the Propagation of Christianity among the Jews (LSPCJ). Thereafter it became a missionary agency, sending Jewish Christians abroad to evangelize other Jews. Ordained in 1817, he founded a Protestant chapel in Paris in 1824. Way was also Vice-President of the Continental Society, and helped to shape its policy of seeking to call awakened individuals out of the Babylon that was apostate Christendom rather than working for the renewal of the continental churches. In 1822 he had preached a sermon along such lines on behalf of the society, entitled *The Flight out of Babylon*. From 1826 Irving was a member of the society's Business Committee.[68] Way was also active in the LSPCJ, of which Drummond was a Vice-President. In his eschatology the Jews took centre stage, something which would be reproduced in that of the Albury conferences.[69]

Wolff was a Jewish convert to Christianity who was linked with the LSPCJ and the Continental Society from 1821 until at least 1826. His travels in the East as a preacher attracted attention because of their appeal to the Romantic sensitivities of the generation. His first contact with Irving appears to have been by means of a

---

[66] Samuel Horsley (1733–1806), a high churchman and writer on biblical prophecy who before becoming Bishop of St Asaph had been Rector of Albury.

[67] Irving, *Signs*, 38–9.

[68] Kenneth J. Stewart, 'Restoring the Reformation: British Evangelicalism and the "Réveil" at Geneva 1816–1849', Ph.D. thesis, New College, Edinburgh, 1992, 327–8.

[69] On Way, see LeRoy E. Froom, *The Prophetic Faith of our Fathers* (4 vols, Washington, DC: Review & Herald, 1946), 3.418, 428, 441; *BDEB*. Many of his works appeared under the pseudonym 'Basilicus'.

letter in April 1826 recommending the bearer, an Armenian youth, to Irving for assistance in learning English in studying Christian divinity.[70]

It was in 1826 that the network began to pull together. On Easter Eve Irving, Frere, James Haldane Stewart (a clergyman whose call for prayer for the outpouring of the Holy Spirit helped to awaken expectations which for some were to be fulfilled in the restoration of the charismatic gifts in 1830) and Charles Hawtrey (secretary of the LSPCJ) met at Way's home.[71] Frere recalled in 1846 how he had been minded to form a society for prophetic study, but had concluded on the basis of Revelation 14.8 that such a society would in time arise in any case, and that if he took any steps towards doing so, it might be charged that knowledge of that prophecy had brought about an effort to fulfil it. He explained his conviction to Irving and some months later they went together to meet Way, who had just arrived in London from Paris. Way told them that he had come to England 'to impress upon the Church the duty of studying the Prophetic Scriptures with reference to the Second Coming of our Lord'. He took lodgings near Frere at Hampstead in order to study Revelation with him, and issued an invitation to a meeting on 1 June 1826 at which was formed the Society for the Investigation of Prophecy.[72] As these men began to meet regularly for the discussion of prophetic passages in the Bible, the logical next step was felt to be that of convening a residential conference. According to Drummond, this was because it was found that non-residential meetings in London did not work because participants had so many other calls on their time: they needed to get away in order to have time to study.[73]

Each Advent from 1826 to 1829, with a final conference in July 1830, several dozen prophetic students from the main British Protestant denominations, clergy and laity, were invited to spend a week at Drummond's residence at Albury Park.[74] Albury Park was (and is) an unusually idyllic and peaceful setting, with grounds first laid out by John Evelyn – one cannot help feeling a certain sense of irony that in such a setting the conference was discussing cataclysmic events associated with the overthrow of the existing world order. Drummond had bought the property on his return from Switzerland in 1819, and as befitted one of the richest men in Britain he

---

[70] J. Wolff to Irving, 28 April 1826 (in private hands). On Wolff, see *BDEB* and the works there cited.

[71] David Dale Stewart, *Memoir of the Life of the Rev. James Haldane Stewart, M.A.* (London: Thomas Hatchard, 1856), 146.

[72] J. H. Frere, *The Great Continental Revolution marking the Expiration of the Times of the Gentiles, A.D. 1847–8* (London: J. Hatchard, 1848), 85–7: excerpt reproduced from the *Prophetic Herald*, January 1846. Froom claims that the conference was Way's suggestion: *Prophetic Faith*, 3.449.

[73] [Henry Drummond], ed., *Dialogues on Prophecy* (3 vols, London: James Nisbet, 1828–9), 1.i–ii.

[74] For details of the participants, see Flegg, *'Gathered under Apostles'*, 36–8, and the sources there cited.

was 'both a generous and improving landlord'.[75] Not only so, but he was a munificent host, as Irving recorded in a vivid picture of proceedings at the first conference, provided as a postscript to his *Preliminary Discourse to Ben Ezra*.[76] Participants met at the commencement of Advent, from 30 November until 8 December, under the moderation of the Rector of Albury, Hugh M'Neile.[77] They considered:

> First, the doctrine of Holy Scripture concerning the times of the Gentiles. Secondly, The duties of Christian ministers and people, growing out thereof towards the Gentile churches. Thirdly, The doctrine concerning the present and future condition of the Jews. Fourthly, The duties growing out of the same towards the Jews. Fifthly, The system of the prophetic visions and numbers of Daniel and the Apocalypse. Sixthly, The scripture doctrine concerning the future advent of the Lord. And Lastly, the duties to the church and the world arising out of the same.[78]

A day was allotted to each subject. The morning session began at 8 a.m. with prayer by a minister, followed by one participant opening up the subject for the day. All sat round a table and took notes. This was followed by a two-hour interval for breakfast with family. The second session began at 11, before which there was time for individuals to reflect on the issues in prayer. M'Neile usually opened this session with prayer, and then asked each in turn for their views. The only appeal allowed was to the Bible, of which there were also copies in the original languages (and a Hebrew expert present in the form of Wolff). This session lasted four or five hours. After dinner, everyone reconvened informally at about 7 p.m., seated round a fire in the library; during this time participants considered questions and difficulties arising from the day's subject. About 11 p.m., proceedings concluded with a hymn and prayer.

> Such [wrote Irving] were the six days we spent under the holy and hospitable roof of Albury house, within the chime of the church bell, and surrounded by the most picturesque and beautiful forms of nature; but the sweetest spot was that council-room where I met the servants of the Lord ... , and a sweeter still was that chamber where I met in the Spirit my Lord and master whom I hope soon to meet in the flesh.[79]

---

[75] Albury, Albury Historical Society, Retta Casbard, 'Henry Drummond of Albury' (typescript, n.d.).

[76] Irving, *Preliminary Discourse*, clxxxviii–cxciv; cf. Oliphant, *Life*, 204–6. See also the simple description of a later conference which he provided for his three-year-old daughter Maggy in November 1828: Oliphant, *Life*, 251–2.

[77] M'Neile (1795–1879) had been appointed by Drummond (patron of the living) in 1822, and remained at Albury until 1834; he later became known as a champion of Protestant convictions: *BDEB*.

[78] Irving, *Preliminary Discourse*, clxxxix.

[79] Ibid. cxcii. Of course, Sunday would not have been one of the six days of study referred to.

Drummond evidently exercised a dominant role behind the scenes, even though he did not chair the sessions. We find him asking one participant, J. J. Strutt, to settle with Irving a list of subjects for consideration at the 1827 gathering; these, like the invitation list, would depend on whether the object should be to get those of differing opinions to agree, or those who agree in general to establish the extent of their agreement on details.[80] Soon after that, Irving writes to his wife that he has been invited to dine with Drummond to settle who should be invited to the next Albury conference; Drummond wants to be more cautious as some from the previous year have not been very faithful.[81] But it is Irving who dominates the discussions themselves. Given his tendency to express himself confidently and dogmatically, it is not surprising that the story should have been told that on one occasion at Albury, he burst out: 'It is a sore trial to the flesh for a man to have more light than his brethren!'[82]

The discussions of the first three conferences provided the raw materials for three volumes of *Dialogues on Prophecy* edited by Drummond, who included a disclaimer to the effect that these were not reports of actual discussions so much as speeches put into the mouths of conference participants (all identified by pseudonyms). The theology of these volumes is worth examining in its own right, but in a biography of Irving there is not space to do so. Suffice it to say that they represent Drummond's edited version of the conferences' consensus, in which Irving is sometimes criticized and Drummond himself highly praised, 'a detail which anticipates the elimination of Irving's influence from the Catholic Apostolic Church in 1833 and 1834'.[83]

* * *

Isabella was enthusiastic about her husband's letters to her describing the first conference. To her parents she wrote: 'Oh how much his spirit was refreshed & his faith strengthened by the delightful meeting at Albury at which he much wished you had been.'[84] However, John Martin was never to share his daughter's enthusiasm. In

---

[80] Strutt letters: Drummond to Strutt, 21 July 1827. The following year, Drummond invited Irving and Strutt to dine with him and settle the subjects for the next gathering so that they could be studied over the summer by participants: Strutt letters, Drummond to Strutt, 15 April 1828.

[81] Oliphant, *Life*, 243: Irving to Isabella Irving, 4 August 1828. Drummond's later recollection was that those invited were men known to believe in the restoration of the Jews to their land and the personal return of Christ to the earth: Henry Drummond, *Narrative of the Circumstances which led to the setting up of the Church of Christ at Albury* (typescript, n.d.; first publ. 1834), 7.

[82] Washington Wilks, *Edward Irving: An Ecclesiastical and Literary Biography* (London: William Freeman, 1854), 187.

[83] Oliver, *Prophets and Millennialists*, 113.

[84] Isabella Irving to her parents, 29 December 1826 (in private hands).

a letter whose date and recipient are not given, but which may have been a response to the one above from Isabella, he wrote:

> You say, 'had I been at Albury.' Perhaps it was better that I was not there. Unless I had resolved to be nothing more than a listener, I fear I might have disturbed the harmony of the meeting, by disputing many things about which its members seem too confident to allow them easily to be impugned, especially as their impressions of their importance must grow with those of their truth: and my doubts would have acted like cold water on the animating glow of expectation under which they look forward to approaching developments of prophetic Scripture. For, though I trust I am not sceptical with regard to any thing the Lord has thought it necessary to reveal, so far as I understand it; yet I cannot help being very sceptical with respect to many interpretations of his revelations, which our excellent friends seem to consider as matters now advanced into the rank of axiomatical or elementary truths, rather than as subjects of inquiry or hesitation. I do not pretend to say they are wrong. Things may be so. But I cannot see that they are so. The views given by Mr Scott in his commentary, come much nearer to those which I think most probable in regard to the Millennium, than such as are so undoubtingly set forth by Basilicus, and others who think with him. Meanwhile, I certainly think the Christian world is indebted to them for endeavouring to direct its attention to those most important topics. And, meanwhile, let us be diligent in our endeavours to convert sinners to Christ, to convince them, of sin, righteousness, and judgment; and that will be the best means of preparing them for the coming of the Lord, whether at an earlier or later date, whether in person or in spirit. ... [in this way] we shall do them more service than if we could expound to them, in all its details, the new system of prophetic interpretation ...[85]

Undaunted, Isabella asserted that her father's objections were invaluable to Irving 'as they stir him up to fortify his position the more strongly'.[86] Whilst the family never came to one mind on this issue, Martin assured his daughter that her husband's conduct was 'that of a generous lover of his fellow-creatures, and a faithful ambassador of Christ'.[87]

---

[85] Anon., *Remains of the late Reverend John Martin, D.D. Minister of Kirkaldy: Consisting of Sermons, Essays, and Letters. With a memoir* (Edinburgh: William Oliphant, 1838), 22, 24; cf. his comments in similar vein about the 1827 conference: 'They do assume that it is the Holy Ghost who has taught them these interpretations. They would really require high authority, to make one swallow them': Cambridge, URCHS, letter 18: John Martin to Miss Elizabeth A. Martin, Kirkcaldy, 20 December 1827.
  Thomas Scott (1747—1821) was a moderate evangelical Anglican who produced an influential commentary on the Bible.

[86] Isabella Irving to Mrs John Martin sr, 3 April 1828 (in private hands).

[87] Oliphant, *Life*, 252: John Martin to Isabella Irving, [December 1828].

* * *

Mrs Oliphant's astounding verdict on the first conference was that 'What their deliberations were, or the results of them, is neither important to this history, nor is the present writer qualified to enter into such a subject.'[88] With this dismissal virtually every subsequent writer has differed! Albury was important because it did much to establish the main outlines of a particular view of the Last Things which was known as historicist premillennialism[89] – 'historicist' because it interpreted the Bible in the light of the conviction that Scripture was not merely about events in what might be termed 'Bible times', but that it foretold the course of human history leading up to the Second Advent. That being so, it was an irresistible temptation in turbulent times such as the 1820s to try to correlate the Bible and the newspaper. This view was 'premillennial' because in it Christ's Second Advent was seen as preceding the millennium, a time of unparalleled earthly peace and blessing. Clearly such Evangelicals were more earthly-minded than has often been thought, and some writers have seen this as indicating a secularizing tendency at work in their thinking which would blossom in later theologians such as F. D. Maurice.[90] As summarized by Drummond, the first gathering's conclusions were:

1. That the present Christian dispensation is not to pass insensibly into the millennial state by gradual increase of the preaching of the Gospel; but that it is to be terminated by judgments, ending in the destruction of this visible Church and polity, in the same manner as the Jewish dispensation has been terminated.
2. That during the time that these judgments are falling upon Christendom, the Jews will be restored to their own land.
3. That the judgments will fall principally, if not exclusively, upon Christendom, and begin with that part of the Church of God which has been most highly favoured, and is therefore most deeply responsible.
4. That the termination of these judgments is to be succeeded by that period of universal blessedness to all mankind, and even to the beasts, which is commonly called the Millennium.
5. That the second Advent of Messiah precedes or takes place at the commencement of the Millennium.

---

[88] Ibid. 206.

[89] For the theology emanating from Albury, see Mark Rayburn Patterson, 'Designing the Last Days: Edward Irving, The Albury Circle, and the Theology of *The Morning Watch*' (Ph.D. thesis, King's College, London, 2001); idem and Andrew Walker, '"Our Unspeakable Comfort": Irving, Albury and the Origins of the Pre-Tribulation Rapture', in Stephen Hunt, ed., *Christian Millenarianism from the Early Church to Waco* (London: Hurst, 2001), 98–115.

[90] See, for example, Oliver, *Prophets and Millennialists*, who describes Irving as 'groping toward a secular Christianity' (102) and his thought as marked by a 'profound if implicit secularity' (106). However, I cannot help wondering whether Oliver was reading Irving in the light of the secularizing theologies of the 1960s and 1970s.

6. That a great period of 1260 years commenced in the reign of Justinian, and terminated at the French Revolution; and that the vials of the Apocalypse began then to be poured out; that our blessed Lord will shortly appear, and that therefore it is the duty of all, who so believe, to press these considerations on the attention of all men.[91]

Following from this was a profoundly pessimistic estimate of Christendom as a whole. Its collapse was believed to be foretold by Scripture, and whereas a previous generation of Evangelicals had engaged in mission with the hope of eventually seeing the world converted (the French Revolution having paved the way for this by striking a mortal blow at the papacy), Irving and others believed that this was a delusive hope. For them, all that could be done was to rescue a few awakened individuals from the Babylon of organized Christianity. Much of this became the basis of later premillennial thought, thus influencing English-speaking Evangelicalism, especially in North America.[92] It is therefore worth going into a little more detail concerning the Albury theology and Irving's role in formulating it, with assistance from Mark Patterson, whose thesis provides the only full-length examination of this topic.[93]

Irving considered the harmony which prevailed among the participants as evidence of the Spirit's guidance in their deliberations, and urged readers of his *Preliminary Discourse* to 'weigh well such an unanimous voice of various divines; and to consider well ere thou scornest unheard, or unexamined dost reject the sum and substance of the great doctrine of the second advent'.[94] He longed, moreover, to see the Church of Scotland awakening to the importance of this truth as believers in other denominations were doing.

What is important to note about the conferences is not merely the conclusions reached but the methodology which participants adopted in interpreting Scripture. Albury worked with a literal mode of interpreting Scripture, which Irving explained: 'When I say *literal*, I do not mean to the exclusion of the figures and metaphors with which it hath abounded; I mean *honest*, according to the natural sense of such language, plain or figurative, as the prophet useth.'[95] However, the text had a typological as well as a literal meaning: events and individuals in one period of God's dealings with humanity (types) were interpreted as foreshadowing and corresponding to similar events and individuals in later periods (antitypes). In particular, God's dealings with the Jews could be seen as prefiguring those with the church. Thus a knowledge of how God dealt with previous generations could assist

---

[91] [Drummond], ed., *Dialogues*, 1.ii–iii.

[92] Premillennialism exists in several varieties, the differences between which need not be explored here; for further information, see Bebbington, *Evangelicalism*, 85–6; Paul Boyer, *When Time Shall Be No More: Prophecy Belief in Modern American Culture* (Cambridge, MA: Belknap, 1992), esp. chs 2–3.

[93] See also Patterson and Walker, '"Our Unspeakable Comfort"'.

[94] Irving, *Preliminary Discourse*, cxciii.

[95] *MW* 1 (1829), 609, quoted by Patterson, 'Designing the Last Days', 70.

in understanding divine activity in the present and future. As Irving put it, God 'did so order the events approximate and the events ultimate as that one set of words should be applicable to both, and capable of describing and foretelling both – applicable, not by any straining of their import but by a true faithful interpretation of them',[96] The interpreter's task was to correlate type and antitype, thus upholding the Bible's divine origin by rational demonstration. The whole Bible could, in this way, be viewed as a prophetic work, and so 'The Second Coming of Christ was made the lens through which every event and doctrine was interpreted and applied.'[97]

As for the conclusions reached, Patterson claims that 'it is incontrovertible that Irving held to a pretribulation doctrine in a form that is developed and remarkably similar to contemporary dispensational views'.[98] In other words, the expectation was that Christian believers would be 'raptured' (caught up to heaven) before a final great period of tribulation preceding the visible return of Christ to earth. He finds the first explicit mention of such a view, which has become a keystone of much modern fundamentalist thinking, in the *Morning Watch* for December 1829, where it is articulated by the editor, John Tudor (1784–1861), a Welsh artist and student of biblical languages.[99] After this 'rapture', God resumes his covenant dealings with the Jews. As with many modern fundamentalists, Irving, according to Patterson, makes a sharp distinction between Jewish and Gentile history, seeing the period between the Fall of Jerusalem in AD 70 and the rapture as an interruption in God's earthly dealings with the Jewish people.[100] Just as the Jews were rejected upon their rejection of Christ, but had been given a brief space to repent before AD 70, so too Christendom had been rejected but was now being called to repent; a remnant would do so, but the rest would be judged.[101] Clearly such a view did not predispose its advocates to a positive estimate of the contemporary churches, and Irving and the Albury circle became known for their sharp denunciation of those who differed from them.

* * *

Filling the gap when no further volumes of *Dialogues on Prophecy* were published was a periodical devoted to expounding the theology of the Albury circle, the *Morning Watch*. It was not the first attempt which had been made to secure a mouthpiece for the circle's views. In July 1828 Irving wrote to his wife regarding an Evangelical periodical, *The Record*, that:

> It had come to a standstill, and was going to be given up, when Mr Drummond, and Haldane, and Lord Mandeville, and a few others, resolved to take it up and make it a

---

[96] *MW* 1 (1829), 579, quoted by Patterson, 'Designing the Last Days', 77.
[97] Patterson, 'Designing the Last Days', 99.
[98] Ibid. 77.
[99] Ibid. 75–6, citing *MW* 1 (1829), 574.
[100] Ibid. 74–5, 78.
[101] Ibid. 141.

truly Christian paper, adopting *jure divino* [divine right] doctrine with respect to Church and State at home, and Protestant principles with respect to our foreign affairs, such as Cromwell taught Papal Europe to fear. The moment it was heard by the religious world (the Evangelical) that it was coming into the hands of such men, they rallied themselves, subscribed plentifully, and are resolved to carry it on ...[102]

The Record soon became one of Irving's fiercest opponents, but the following year Drummond was able to purchase an ailing journal and turn it into the *Morning Watch*, a theological quarterly which rapidly achieved a reputation both for exhaustive exposition and also for aggressiveness towards Evangelicals who espoused different interpretations or who dared to criticize those which it adopted.[103] Such vigour sprang from a sense of urgency: 'Fundamental to the message of *The Morning Watch* was the belief that their day was one of special revelation, in which the meaning, progress, and goal of history had been uniquely unveiled. This revelation gave the circle a message they believed to be unprecedented in scope and urgency.'[104] It ran from March 1829 until June 1833 under the editorship of Tudor. Irving and his teaching are central to the *Morning Watch*, although they should not be equated with it. Mrs Oliphant describes how he pervaded early issues, 'not so much an authority, as an all-influencing, unquestionable presence, naturally and simply suggesting itself to all as somehow the centre of the entire matter'; all the contributors stood up for his views and defended him when he was challenged, an attitude which she described as 'hero-worship of the most absolute, unconscious kind'.[105] Prophecy and the text and translation of Scripture were the primary foci of the magazine at first, although gradually there came to be more articles on Christology (opposition to Irving's Christology was interpreted as one more sign that the Last Days were imminent), the gifts of the Spirit, and the relation which those who held the magazine's views should adopt towards existing churches.

We have already noted some of Irving's contributions to the journal and will have cause to note others (on Christology) in the next chapter; others during its first year or two included an article 'On the Doctrine and Manifestation and Character of the Christian Apostasy' (already noticed)[106] and a lengthy series on the 'Interpretation of

---

[102] Oliphant, *Life*, 240: Irving to Isabella Irving, 28 July 1828; Mrs Oliphant dates the letter erroneously to 25 July.

[103] Even Catholic Apostolic writers were forced to recognize the controversial nature of the *Morning Watch* as 'A periodical scarcely equalled, certainly never surpassed by any other for learning, for the healthy Catholicity of its Theology, or for the sharpness of its polemical tones': St Andrews, University Library, Special Collections, Flegg Collection (MS 38594), Anon., 'The History of the Lord's Work in these last days' (typescript, [1924]), fol. 21. This is almost an exact repetition of the verdict of a major internal historical source: London, BL, 764n13, Ernst A. Rossteuscher, 'The Rebuilding of the Church of Christ upon the Original Foundations: An Historical Narrative of its Commencement. A free Translation' [by Miss L. A. Hewett] (MS, [1871]), fol. 45.

[104] Patterson, 'Designing the Last Days', 99.

[105] Oliphant, *Life*, 258.

[106] *MW* 1 (1829), 100–114.

all the Old-Testament prophecies quoted in the New'.[107] Irving holds ministers to blame for the widespread neglect of prophetic Scripture, and asserts the right of anyone to interpret the Bible for themselves with the Holy Spirit's aid. In his opinion, the great question of the literal accomplishment of the law and the prophets resolves itself into that of whether the Bible is to be interpreted like any other book, i.e. according to 'the natural meaning of the words, similitudes, metaphors, and other figures which are employed therein'. He argues that it is, and that spiritual truth is only knowable through 'the exact, honest, and common-sense interpretation of the words in which it is made known'.[108] His aim is to deliver it from the darkness with which it has been covered, 'to follow the footsteps of the Fathers and Reformers of thy church, who did make a constant use of the prophetic Scriptures, in order that the hopes of men might rest upon the word of God, and not upon the word of men'.[109] To preachers whose prosaic style and tempering of their message to this generation's tastes he abhors, Irving calls 'come here, and learn to preach'.[110] But prophetic study has a pastoral value also: he speaks of the consolation afforded by prophetic study, seeing the Gospel declared so clearly in these writings: 'Watching over sick beds, bending over the dead, and waiting for the death of those I loved, hast thou not made peace to spring up from these songs of salvation!'[111] Two points of interpretation deserve notice in passing. The first is his belief that the forty-five years in Daniel began eight years earlier; they are the last of the Gentile times, and are 'the last days',[112] and the second is the idea that the Christian dispensation is an intercalated period in the history of God's dealings with humanity; when it ends, God's ways of governing men in flesh will resume their former course and God's sons be manifested to govern the world. 'My idea is, that not the Old-Testament but the New-Testament dispensation hath an end: and then the other resumes its course, under Christ and his bride, which is his church.'[113] This parallels strikingly the teaching which, through John Nelson Darby (1800–82), became widely disseminated in North American Evangelicalism and so helped to shape much later fundamentalism.

As well as financing the publications of the Albury circle, it seems that Drummond was also assisting Irving himself. Irving, whilst extremely well paid, was not terribly well off, thanks to a habit of prodigal generosity which had been seen in his Glasgow days.[114] His house was, according to Mrs Montagu (one of

---

[107] *MW* 1 (1829), 11–36, 149–74, 315–50, 578–618; 2 (1830), 55–99, 287–319, 529–63, 777–804; 3 (1831), 35–67, 291–315; 4 (1831), 52–84, 301–17.

[108] *MW* 1 (1829), 11.

[109] Ibid. 15.

[110] Ibid. 341.

[111] *MW* 2 (1830), 296.

[112] Ibid. 780–1. Hence he would have expected the Second Advent to occur around 1867.

[113] Ibid. 788.

[114] In 1829 we find him appealing for assistance for a poor Scot who needs a few shillings to return north, not having found work. 'I have done for them the little which I

whose wild sons spent time there), 'a sort of penitentiary for the lost sheep'.[115] In December 1828 Irving wrote to seek assistance from Drummond towards the cost of getting a book printed.[116] The following July, he requested a large sum of money to help his parents:

> I am the second son of a large and much respected family. My Father and Mother are two of the most worthy and true-hearted people you have ever known. My four sisters are patterns of Wives and Mothers in their several Neighbourhoods and the youngest of us, my only surviving brother you have seen and been kind to. The Eldest Son of my Father's family a young man the pride & honour of our town went out to India as a surgeon, and died there ... It was the maxim of my father even from our childhood to give to all his children the very best Education the Country could afford both to boys and girls, and he was wont to ... in that this was all our portion.

The problem was that when John went to India, he had incurred a debt of £500 with their uncle, against their father's wishes. There had since been trouble with this uncle about money matters and so Edward wished to borrow the money to help his parents, presumably to pay off the debt.[117] Drummond appears to have responded sympathetically, as another letter of 1829 contains an acknowledgement that Irving owed him £360 plus interest.[118]

* * *

Why did the Albury conferences cease? One Catholic Apostolic view was that they became impossible once division surfaced over prophetic interpretation, and superfluous once God opened up better ways of revealing his will and purpose.[119] Without commenting on the latter, it seems undeniable that the former was true. Also, the 1830 conference, which was shorter and held in the summer rather than at Advent, seems to have been somewhat hastily arranged, and it seems likely that disagreement over spiritual gifts (which was to divide Drummond from his minister, M'Neile) presented an insuperable obstacle to the convening of further conferences, since the gifts were seen as signs and testimonies of the prophetic interpretation which the conferences had laboured to establish. In the next chapter we shall look at the controversy surrounding Irving's views concerning the person of Christ; these views not only provided the foundation for his understanding of salvation but also prepared the way for the reappearance of the charismatic 'manifestations', which we shall discuss later on.

---

can, but I am almost always in a state of exhaustion by the demands which are made upon me. And the only resource I have that the people may not starve is to recommend them to my friends': NLS, MS 967, fol. 197: Irving to John Tate, [1829].

[115] NLS, MS 1777, fol. 212: Mrs Montagu to Jane Welsh, postmark 1826.
[116] Alnwick Castle, DFP, C9/2: Irving to Drummond, 1 December 1828.
[117] DFP, C9/3: Irving to Drummond, 7, 9 July 1829.
[118] DFP, C9/4: Irving to Drummond, 1829.
[119] Rossteuscher, 'Rebuilding', fol. 49.

1. The Fish Cross, Annan; Irving was born in one of the cottages in the background, in Butts Street

2. Part of Edinburgh University (now known as Old College);
Irving attended lectures here as an Arts student

3. Kirkcaldy parish church; Irving's father-in-law John Martin was minister here, and in 1828 thirty-five lives were lost when part of a gallery collapsed

4. The only known photograph of the Caledonian Church in Hatton Garden, long after it had been vacated by Irving's congregation

5. Admission tickets for the Caledonian Church, issued in 1824
(on loan to the London Metropolitan Archive, ref. LMA/4358/C/002/6 & 7)

6. The Irvings lived in this house in London's Claremont Square from 1825 to 1828

7. The National Scotch Church from the north-west at the end of the nineteenth century

8. Interior of the National Scotch Church as it was in Irving's time
(on loan to the London Metropolitan Archive, ref. LMA/4358/C/002)

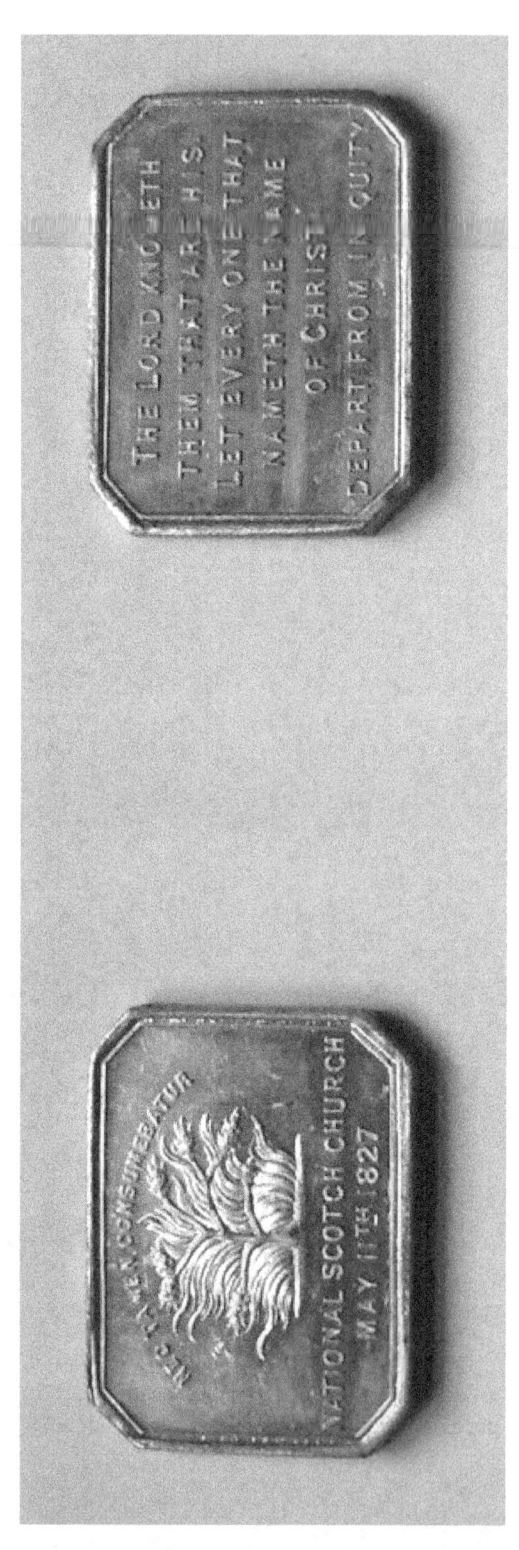

9. Communion tokens were issued to members, entitling them to take part in the Lord's Supper; these examples were issued by the National Scotch Church in 1827

10. Detail of a portrait of Irving by Faithful Christopher Pack

11. A page from the National Scotch Church burial register, showing the entry for the burial of Irving's son Gavin in 1829

12. Annan Old Parish Church, where Irving was baptized, ordained and deposed

13. This memorial tablet to Irving was erected at Regent Square about 1870; it is not known whether it survived the old building's demolition in the 1960s

14. The statue of Irving's closest friend, Thomas Carlyle, which stands near his house in Chelsea

15. This statue of Irving in the churchyard at Annan was erected in 1892

16. This blue plaque on Irving's house in Claremont Square describes Irving as
'Founder of the Catholic Apostolic Church',
an assertion which continues to engender debate

Chapter 14

Christological Heretic?

There are two issues which even today are thrown up as reasons to dismiss Irving as a crank, a fanatic or a heretic. One is his espousal of the belief that charismatic gifts such as tongues, prophecy and healing had been restored to the church, and the other is his understanding of the person of Christ, and in particular his deeply held conviction that in becoming incarnate Christ took human nature in its fallen state.[1] In this chapter we examine his views concerning the person of Christ, and the controversy which they provoked. A detailed assessment is not possible within the confines of a biography, but a little more theology than is provided by most of the biographies may be helpful to many readers. Fundamentally, Irving was concerned to respond to contemporary tendency to minimize the importance of the doctrines of the Trinity and the Incarnation. Indeed, McFarlane asserts that Irving believed traditional Christianity to be in 'deadly peril'.[2] For Irving, salvation is not to be reduced to a message about how I can escape hell; rather, he expounds it within the context of God's purpose for humanity and creation, and a developed understanding of what it is to be human, and therefore of what it meant for the Son of God to become incarnate. The Trinity is vital as a doctrine precisely because it shows us the nature of the God who saves: we could say that God does what he does because he is who he is.

---

[1] Irving's Christology has spawned a considerable amount of discussion and exposition, especially among theologians in the Reformed tradition. Much of this is more sympathetic than was the case when it was first put forth, and it is now common to claim that his views do indeed lie within the bounds of historic Christian orthodoxy. Valuable expositions include Paul Ewing Davies, 'An Examination of the Views of Edward Irving concerning the Person and Work of Jesus Christ' (Ph.D. thesis, New College, Edinburgh, 1928); Gordon Strachan, *The Pentecostal Theology of Edward Irving* (London: Darton, Longman & Todd, 1973); Graham W. P. McFarlane, *Christ and the Spirit: The Doctrine of the Incarnation according to Edward Irving* (Carlisle: Paternoster, 1996); David W. Dorries, *Edward Irving's Incarnational Christology* (Fairfax, VA: Xulon Press, 2002). Useful shorter treatments include Colin Gunton, 'Two Dogmas Revisited: Edward Irving's Christology', *Scottish Journal of Theology* 41 (1988), 359–76; Donald Macleod, 'The Doctrine of the Incarnation in Scottish Theology: Edward Irving', *Scottish Bulletin of Evangelical Theology* 9 (1990–1), 40–50; Thomas G. Weinandy, *In the Likeness of Sinful Flesh: An Essay on the Humanity of Christ* (Edinburgh: T. & T. Clark, 1993), 56–61. However, readers interested in Irving's thought would do well to read his own works first.

[2] McFarlane, *Christ and the Spirit*, 3.

Knowing God, therefore, is not a matter primarily of understanding a systematic presentation of his attributes, but of engaging with his actions in redemption.[3]

The main features of his Christology are that (i) Christ took fallen rather than unfallen human nature; (ii) nevertheless he remained sinless, through the indwelling of the Holy Spirit; (iii) it was as man anointed by the Spirit, rather than as the second person of the Trinity, that he performed his miracles; and (iv) his atoning death was as our representative rather than as our substitute. He saw these things as taught by Scripture and as upheld by the mainstream Christian theological tradition, especially as exemplified by the Scots Confession of 1560; consequently he considered himself bound as a watchman to oppose those who rejected what he taught.

Dorries attempts to show that Irving's Christology did not change in any fundamental respect throughout his London ministry.[4] This may be more than the evidence can bear, however: Irving's 1823 sermons on 'The Temptation', which formed part of his lengthy series on Luke's Gospel, emphasize the reality of Christ's humanity and his consequent liability to temptation, but unlike Dorries I do not read them as teaching that this humanity was fallen.[5] If he had taught such a view, we can be sure that it would have been picked up by the religious press. In fact, Irving's distinctive Christology first came to the notice of the wider public as a result of a sermon he preached at John Street Chapel, London, in aid of the Gospel Tract Society on 10 July 1827.[6] In the course of praising the society for its faithfulness to the doctrines of the sixteenth-century Reformers (he pointedly excludes their seventeenth-century successors, which would have made him few friends), he referred to his belief that Christ was sustained by the Spirit in his human nature, thus bearing 'all that to which sin and flesh is heir'.[7] This was exceptionable enough to some, but it was only at the end of the year that controversy really began to flare up. On 28 October, a clergyman named Henry Cole heard the last twenty minutes of Irving's evening sermon, on the strength of which he sought an interview with the preacher after the service. Cole had already gone into print with an assertion that Christ's humanity was immortal,[8] and he had been told by friends about Irving's

---

[3] Ibid. 13.

[4] Dorries, *Irving's Christology*, 73.

[5] *CW*, 2.189–243.

[6] 'Sermon to the Gospel Tract Society' [Titus 2.11], *The Pulpit*, no. 228 (2 August 1827), 417–25, 432. The chapel had been built by Drummond for a clerical seceder from the Church of England, James Harington Evans (1785–1849).

[7] Ibid. 420.

[8] Henry Cole, *The True Signification of the English Adjective Mortal, and the Awfully Erroneous Consequences of the Application of that Term to the Ever Immortal Body of Jesus Christ, Briefly Considered* (London: J. Eedes, 1827). This was published about two months before Irving's Tract Society sermon: Henry Cole, *A Letter to the Rev. Edward Irving, Minister of the Caledonian Chapel, Compton Street, in Refutation of the Awful Doctrines (held by him) of the Sinfulness, Mortality, and Corruptibility of the Body of Jesus Christ* (London: J. Eedes, 1827), v, 1. For the little that is known about Cole, see

denial of this in the Gospel Tract Society sermon,⁹ so he was hardly likely to be conciliatory in his attitude. Irving recollected that after the sermons on the Incarnation (which are discussed below) had been printed and the other two volumes were in the press,

there arose, I say not by what influence of Satan, a great outcry against the doctrine which, with all orthodox churches, I hold and maintain concerning the person of Christ: the doctrine I mean of his human nature, that it was manhood fallen, which he took up into his Divine person, in order to prove the grace and the might of Godhead in redeeming it; or, to use the words of our Scottish Confession, that his flesh was, in its proper nature, mortal and corruptible, but received immortality and incorruption from the Holy Ghost.[10]

What happened was, as Irving elsewhere recorded, that

a person of the name of Cole published a pamphlet, charging me with holding that Christ was sinful as to his flesh, and maintaining for himself that Christ's flesh was not mortal and corruptible. Of the man I knew nothing, save that a stranger once solicited conversation with me on a Lord's-day night, after public worship, of which conversation I found what purported to be the substance standing at the head of this publication.[11]

Irving invited Cole to visit him the following Thursday, but he did not,

and could reconcile his conscience to the betrayal of pastoral and ministerial confidence, and to the publication of a conversation, without ever asking me whether it was correctly reported or not. Conduct so flagrant, when coupled with doctrine so heterodox, and proceeding from a man who, I afterwards learned, had separated himself from the Church of England, I thought, would carry its own reprobation.[12]

But, to Irving's amazement, most, especially among the evangelical party, approved it. He was so troubled by accusation of heresy that he thought of sending a paper to the leading evangelical periodical, the *Christian Observer*, to contradict it, but he decided to bear the reproach instead. When, however, he saw that the church at large

---

Terry Mortensen, 'British Scriptural Geologists in the First Half of the Nineteenth Century: Part 5, Henry Cole (1792?–1858)', http://www.answersingenesis.org/tj/v13/i1/henry_cole.asp, accessed 4 July 2008.

⁹ Cole, *Letter to Irving*, 3.

[10] Edward Irving, *Sermons, Lectures, and Occasional Discourses* (3 vols, London: R. B. Seeley and W. Burnside, 1828), 1.iv.

[11] Edward Irving, *Christ's Holiness in Flesh, the Form, Fountain Head, and Assurance to us of Holiness in Flesh* (Edinburgh: John Lindsay, 1831), v. Cole's *Letter to Irving* was dated 28 December 1827: ibid. 98. Cole carelessly refers to the encounter as having taken place in the 'Caledonian Chapel, Compton Street'.

[12] Ibid. v–vi.

was in danger of believing that Christ had no temptation in his flesh to overcome, he added to his first volume of sermons (on the origin, end, act and fruit of the Incarnation) one on the method of the Incarnation (refuting the idea that Christ took unfallen flesh), and another showing the conclusions following from his doctrine; these became the third and the sixth sermons in the volume. In his opinion, Cole's doctrine was 'a pestilent heresy, which coming in will root out atonement, redemption, regeneration, the work of the Spirit, and the human nature of Christ altogether'.[13]

Cole's charges, once in print, provided grounds for many leading figures in the religious world to air their suspicions regarding Irving's orthodoxy. This was perhaps inevitable given the furore which had surrounded his *Orations* and his sermon to the London Missionary Society: Irving was never one to conform to accepted ways of doing and saying things if he was convinced that they were wrong, and his relations with Evangelicals in particular were decidedly ambivalent. On one hand, his prestige as a preacher ensured a capacity attendance if they invited him to preach in aid of some worthy cause; on the other hand, he made no secret of his contempt for the shallowness of much contemporary evangelical theology and the worldliness of the methods adopted for fund-raising by evangelical societies. They might not have been looking for a pretext to put him down, but like Cole they were hardly disposed to give him the benefit of the doubt.

* * *

The sermons on the Incarnation referred to above formed the first volume of Irving's *Sermons, Lectures and Occasional Discourses* and were subtitled *The Doctrine of the Incarnation Opened in Six Sermons*. Scholars have commented on his use of the term 'opened' as if he were giving the impression of showing his readers a mystery, but in fact these sermons are not the exposition of esoteric revelations but a solid presentation of his Christological views. Four of them were taken from a series on the doctrine of the Trinity preached in the autumn of 1825 at the Caledonian Chapel. The Trinitarian context is important for Irving's understanding of the person of Christ.[14]

---

[13] Irving, *Sermons*, 1.vi.

[14] We noted earlier that Coleridge appears to have influenced Irving's formulation of the doctrine of the Trinity, by his triad of Will, Reason or Word and Love or Life, corresponding to the Persons of Father, Son and Holy Spirit. The first of the three appears repeatedly in Irving's writing, but unlike his mentor he takes pains to ground his teaching in biblical exposition rather than philosophical abstraction: McFarlane, *Christ and the Spirit*, 59–60; see also David Yat Tang Lee, 'The Humanity of Christ and the Church in the Teaching of Edward Irving' (Ph.D. thesis, London Bible College / Brunel University, 2003). Linked with the biblical approach is his evident pastoral concern; McFarlane has commented that Irving stressed the Sonship of Christ because he was seeking to reassure his flock about the love of God: 'if the Son is not a Son from eternity,

The volume on the Incarnation was to have been published as the first of his volumes of *Sermons*, at the request of his elders, but Irving decided to delay it in order to respond to increasing criticism of his views, adding two further sermons as we noted earlier. As expanded, he wrote to Isabella that 'there is much more to God's glory in that volume than in all my other writings put together'.[15] The delay in publication had cost almost a year, the preface being dated 10 November 1828. In it, Irving explained that the Incarnation was a work of the Trinity, that Christ was subjected to every kind of temptation to which fallen flesh is heir, but that he was maintained sinless through the action of the Holy Spirit:

> The point at issue is simply this; Whether Christ's flesh had the grace of sinlessness and incorruption from its proper nature, or from the indwelling of the Holy Ghost. ... The Son said, 'I come:' the Father said, 'I prepare thee a body to come in:' and the Holy Ghost prepared that body out of the Virgin's substance. And so, by the threefold acting of the Trinity, was the Christ constituted a Divine and a human nature, joined in personal union for ever.[16]
>
> He was passive to every sinful suggestion which the world through the flesh can hand up unto the will; he was liable to every sinful suggestion Satan through the mind can hand up to the will; and with all such suggestions and temptations I believe him beyond all others to have been assailed, but further went they not. ... and so, from his conception unto his resurrection, his whole life was a series of active triumphing over sin in the flesh, Satan in the world, and spiritual wickedness in high places.[17]

In the body of his exposition, Irving explained that the end of the Incarnation was to bring glory to God by bringing into existence the complete and perfect form of being; by proclaiming the good news; and by overthrowing God's enemies. To that end, Christ assumed fallen human nature. 'That Christ took our fallen nature is most manifest, because there was no other in existence to take.'[18] Adumbrating his later thinking, Irving asserted that the baptism with the Holy Ghost not only constituted Christ as Prophet but 'was to him truly and literally that same baptism of power and holiness with which he was afterwards to baptize his church, when he should have ascended up on high'.[19] The indwelling of the Holy Spirit which he received in his conception merely enabled him to keep the Law of Moses; it was after his baptism with the Holy Ghost (which occurred at his baptism in water) that Christ began to live that life above the Law which the church should live. Then began his conflict with evil and his power to preach, heal and perform miracles.

---

then God is not Father from eternity': Graham W. P. McFarlane, *Edward Irving: The Trinitarian Face of God* (Edinburgh: St Andrew Press, 1996), 6.

[15] Oliphant, *Life*, 246: Irving to Isabella Irving, 9 September 1828.

[16] Irving, *Sermons*, 1.v–vi.

[17] Ibid. vii.

[18] Ibid. (140)ii. The curious page reference is explained by the fact that the additional sermons were inserted at pages 140 and 328 and were paginated using roman numerals.

[19] Ibid. (140)xxv.

Throughout these sermons, the stress is on Christ's active rather than passive obedience, his conquering temptation rather than his suffering. 'It is in the active obedience of Christ, in the perfect submission and obedience which he yielded, in the doing without any failure all the will of God, that he became the Author of salvation to all them that believe. The suffering which he came under was, as it were, but the putting of that will to proof'.[20] This in itself would have aroused evangelical opposition, since they made the atoning sufferings of Christ central to their understanding of his saving work. But Irving went on to oppose their views explicitly, caricaturing them somewhat in the process:

> I consider it, therefore, to be rather a low view of the Redeemer's work, to contemplate it so much in the sense of acute bodily suffering, or to enlarge upon it under the idea of a price or bargain, which is a carnal similitude, suitable and proper to the former carnal dispensation, and which should, as much as possible, be taken away for the more spiritual idea of our sanctification by the full and perfect obedience which Christ rendered unto the will of God; thereby purchasing back, and procuring for as many as believe in him, their justification and sanctification by the Holy Spirit, which is their conformity to the will of God, and reliance on his eternal purpose.[21]

Denying that God could suffer, Irving asserted that Christ suffered in his human nature only; therefore the amount of his suffering must have been finite, which went against the view (reaching back to Anselm of Canterbury in the eleventh century) that his sufferings were of infinite value. In so saying, Irving challenged much of the Western tradition of understanding regarding the atonement, which had seen sin as doing infinite dishonour to God and as such necessitating a sacrifice of infinite value to make fit reparation.

* * *

Two articles followed in the *Morning Watch*, 'On the Human Nature of Christ' in March 1829, and in June 'On the True Humanity of Christ'.[22] Asked to expand these for separate publication in Scotland, in January 1830 Irving produced *The Orthodox and Catholic Doctrine of Christ's Human Nature*, described by Mrs Oliphant as 'a controversial reassertion, strongly defensive and belligerent, of the doctrine which he had before stated with calm exposition and lofty argument'.[23] It was this work which the Presbytery of London, and later the General Assembly of the Church of Scotland, seized upon as a definitive statement of Irving's views. For that reason, we shall give it fairly detailed consideration.

In the preface, he offers a succinct statement of his position:

---

[20] Ibid. 21–2.
[21] Ibid. 22–3.
[22] *MW* 1 (1829), 75–99, cf. 240–3; ibid. 421–45.
[23] Oliphant, *Life*, 278. The many lengthy quotations in it from *The Doctrine of the Incarnation Opened* indicate that he had not changed his basic position.

whenever I attribute sinful properties and dispositions and inclinations to our Lord's human nature, I am speaking of it considered as apart from Him [sic], in itself; I am defining the qualities of that nature which he took upon him, and demonstrating it to be the very same in substance with that which we possess. To understand the work which he did, you must understand the materials with which he did it. The work which he did was to redeem, sanctify, quicken, and glorify this nature of ours, which is full of sin, and death, and rebellion, and dishonour unto God. ... his human nature was holy in the only way in which holiness under the Fall exists or can exist, is spoken of or can be spoken of in Scripture, namely, through inworking or energizing of the Holy Ghost ...[24]

He makes it as clear as he possibly can that he believes in Christ's sinlessness: 'from his conception every acting of his mind was holy, and every acting also of his flesh; but this not in its proper nature, but through the constraining and enforcing power of his Person, acting Godhead, by the Holy Ghost'.[25] The point at issue between him and his opponents is the source of such perfection: in other words,

whether during his life it [Christ's flesh] was one with us in all its infirmities and liabilities to temptation, or whether, by the miraculous, [sic] generation it underwent a change so as to make it a different body from the rest of the brethren. They argue for an identity of origin merely; we argue for an identity of life also. They argue for an inherent holiness; we argue for a holiness maintained by the Person of the Son, through the operation of the Holy Ghost. They say, that though his body was changed in the generation, he was still our fellow in all temptations and sympathies: we deny that it could be so; for change is change; and if his body was changed in the conception, it was not in its life as ours is. In one word, we present believers with a real life; a suffering, mortal flesh; a real death and a real resurrection of this flesh of ours: they present the life, death, and resurrection of a changed flesh: and so create a chasm between Him and us which no knowledge, nor even imagination, can overleap.[26]

Irving spells out what he sees as the pastoral implications of his opponents' views. If Christ's flesh were not like ours, then:

First, He is not tempted in all points as I am.
Secondly, He is not capable of being a high priest to me, which standeth in this very thing, that in all things he was likened to the brethren. Heb. v.
Thirdly, He had only two of my enemies to contend with, the devil and the world; and I have no proof that he can overcome the third, which is the flesh.
Fourthly, He never was one with me, and I know not how I can ever be one with him.

---

[24] Edward Irving, *The Orthodox and Catholic Doctrine of Our Lord's Human Nature Set Forth in Four Parts: I. Statement of the Doctrine from Scripture. II. Confirmation of it, from the Creeds of the Primitive Church and of the Church of Scotland. III. Objections to the True Doctrine Considered. IV. The Doctrines of the Faith which Stand or Fall with it* (London: Baldwin & Cradock, 1830), vii–viii.

[25] Ibid. 23.

[26] Ibid. xi.

> Fifthly, I have no evidence either of the Holy Ghost's willingness to wrestle with wicked flesh, nor yet of his ability to overcome it.
> Sixthly, As Christ's life is no prototype of the Holy Ghost's power over sinful flesh, so is Christ's resurrection no assurance of my resurrection. It is most likely a peculiarity of flesh in that new condition in which he had it.
> Seventhly, The whole Gospels are an appearance, and not a reality. They are written as if he was passive to all temptation and inclination as man is; but you say he was not: therefore you put the lie upon the whole testimony of the Scriptures.[27]

He goes on to argue that his understanding is not only consonant with the ancient creeds, but is also agreeable to the Scots Confession and the Westminster Confession.

How does Christ's death avail to save us? Irving rejects the idea that Christ died to appease God's wrath:

> This goes exactly upon the notion of the heathen, that God wanteth and will have suffering, wanteth and will have compensation, standeth to his point, and will not abate one iota of suffering to any one. And as he had a mind to save so many, Christ came and bore the sufferings which they ought to have borne: every jot of it, but not one jot more; for if he had borne one jot more, the Father would have been unjust, and if he had borne one jot less, the Father would have abated of his sternest rectitude. And therefore it is they have such an abhorrence of the idea, that Christ died for all, that he was a propitiation for all, and bore the sin of the world.[28]

As in his *Doctrine of the Incarnation Opened*, Irving holds that at-one-ment (as he likes to spell it) amounts to the fact that 'Christ took our fallen nature, with all its natural and inherent propensities; and overcame these, and brought it into union with Godhead, and hath fixed it there for ever by the resurrection'.[29] He goes on to acknowledge that it involved the death of the Lamb of God – a death which could only be possible if he had come in a nature subject to death, and assumed flesh which was mortal and corruptible. Such a death was not merely for his own humanity but for that of all, as his humanity is one with ours. The infinity and meritoriousness of Christ's work consisted not in his suffering, then, but in his freely condescending to become incarnate.

* * *

At some point during the spring of 1830, Irving received almost £100 from friends in Edinburgh. Writing to thank them, he informed them that his one remaining desire was to expound the Epistle to the Hebrews in that city, an epistle which stresses the reality of Christ's humanity and his consequent ability to sympathize with, and to aid, hard-pressed believers. His reason for so desiring was that:

---

[27] Ibid. 27–8.
[28] Ibid. 100–1.
[29] Ibid. 88.

I perceive that the controversy which is now arising in the Church is not merely for the person of Christ, but for the very name of God, whether He be Love or not. ... I am ready unto the death to serve the Church of Scotland, which I believe in her constitution to be the most apostolical of the churches existent on earth. I entreat you all to reverence her ordinances, and to stand by her in the perils which are at hand.[30]

However, this was the year when the Kirk began to proceed against John McLeod Campbell, Irving's London colleague Maclean and Irving himself. Early in 1830 Maclean had been presented to the parish of Dreghorn in Ayrshire, but a petition had been sent in which objected to his Christological views. The matter was referred to the Synod of Glasgow and Ayr and ultimately to the General Assembly. In discussing the case, the Assembly expressed abhorrence of the idea that Christ possessed peccable human nature, though it reversed the sentence passed on him as the judgement had been entered on too hastily; it called on the Presbytery of Irvine to proceed according to the church's rules. Campbell's case was remitted to the Presbytery of Dumbarton, as the doctrines which he stood accused of teaching had already been condemned by the 1720 Assembly.[31] Among them were the assertions that assurance of salvation is of the essence of Christian faith, that Christ died for all and not for the elect alone, and that fear of punishment and hope of reward were not proper motives for Christian obedience: all of these were prominent in Campbell's preaching.[32]

During the sitting of the General Assembly, Irving published a pamphlet in Edinburgh entitled *The Opinions Circulating regarding our Lord's Human Nature, Tried by the Westminster Confession of Faith*. The title is significant as an indicator of his continuing desire to remain faithful to the standards of the church which had ordained him. Although he felt that he was restoring long-neglected emphases in Christian teaching, and that the church as a whole was in deadly peril because of its neglect of these, he was not intending to break new ground so much as to expound what he believed to be the authentic Christian theological tradition.[33] The work appeared anonymously, probably so that the arguments could be considered on their

---

[30] Oliphant, *Life*, 2.112: Irving to M. N. Macdonald, [1830].

[31] Edinburgh, NAS, CH1/1/81, Register of Acts of the General Assembly, 1828–31, fols 340–5: 25–26 May 1830. In 1720, the Assembly had proceeded against the 'Marrow-Men', so called from the book which gave definitive expression to their views, Edward Fisher's *The Marrow of Modern Divinity*; this was first published in 1645 and republished in 1718: Peter K. Stevenson, *God in Our Nature: The Incarnational Theology of John McLeod Campbell* (Carlisle: Paternoster, 2004), 14. Even inside the high places of the Kirk, rebellion was abroad: in the index to the Register of Acts, the anonymous compiler added a note regarding Campbell: 'One of the celebrated cases in Church history, Mr Campbell being deposed for alleged heterodoxy, particularly in regard to the doctrine of the Atonement: He is the author of various books; and was loved by all who knew him.'

[32] Stevenson, *Campbell*, 14.

[33] Oliphant, *Life*, 292: Irving to Chalmers, 2 June 1830.

own merits rather than as coming from him. The tract has a markedly less sermonic feel than *Orthodox and Catholic Doctrine*, and is more moderately expressed, doubtless in an attempt to win over his readers. In view of the controversy which was calling the General Assembly to pronounce a verdict in the Maclean case, Irving considered it time to test the opinions being expressed by the confession which elders and ministers were required to sign. He outlines the three main views, and holds them up against the teaching of the Westminster Confession, relevant sections of which he expounds phrase by phrase. The three views are (i) that Christ took fallen human nature; (ii) that he took Adam's pre-fall human nature; and (iii) that he took Mary's flesh but that it was changed by the action of the Holy Spirit into something fit for the Son of God. As one would expect, it is the first of these which he deems to be the doctrine taught in it.[34]

At about the same time and with the same objective, he co-operated with another Thomas Carlyle (1803–55),[35] who was acting as Maclean's advocate, in a second anonymous pamphlet, *The Doctrine of the Church of Scotland concerning the Human Nature of our Lord, as Stated in her Standards*. They surveyed the authoritative doctrinal standards of the Church of Scotland, and advanced the idea that the Westminster Confession possessed authority as a common standard intended for the nations of England, Scotland and Ireland, but that it was not to be regarded as superseding the Scots Confession and other earlier documents. Rather, it was to be interpreted by them, as they remained the ultimate authority.[36]

If he was hoping to influence the minds of the assembled fathers of the Kirk by either of these productions, he was to be disappointed; and relations with the Presbytery of London also began to deteriorate. This was to leave him isolated and exposed as a Church of Scotland minister. It is clear that by early 1830, relations between Irving and the presbytery were strained. Maclean was minister at London Wall when presented to Dreghorn, and Irving informed his father-in-law that he did not wish to intervene in the resulting vacancy, as the office-bearers there had 'foolishly taken it into their heads that I have had a great hand in making Mr. Maclean a churchman and a Millenarian, instead of a liberal and a nothingarian, which is the thing that goes best down in these latitudes'.[37] When, on 25 June, the presbytery advised Maclean to resign his charge (he was on leave of absence) as

---

[34] 'A Minister of the Church of Scotland' [Irving], *The Opinions Circulating concerning Our Lord's Human Nature, Tried by the Westminster Confession of Faith* (Edinburgh: John Lindsay, 1830).

[35] This Carlyle was to become an apostle in the emergent Catholic Apostolic Church; his namesake was to be irritated by the confusion between them on more than one occasion.

[36] [Edward Irving and Thomas Carlyle], *The Doctrine of the Church of Scotland concerning the Human Nature of our Lord, as stated in her Standards* (Edinburgh: John Lindsay, [1831]).

[37] Oliphant, *Life*, 2.110–11: Irving to John Martin, [early 1830]; cf. Edinburgh, EUL, MS Dc.4.103 (Irving): John Martin to Robert Paul, 3 March 1830, which repeats the allegations.

inquiries into his views were likely to be protracted and the church needed a minister, Irving dissented.[38] On 11 May a committee was appointed to consider the question of Christ's human nature: Irving was to be a member, and it was to be chaired by another of the ministers, James Miller.[39] It appears to have set to work quickly, as Irving wrote to a friend on 21 May that he was satisfied with its conclusion regarding Christ's human nature.[40] On 20 July Miller reported that the committee had found:

> That the Son of God took human nature of ye substance of his mother, which (human nature) was wholly and perfectly sanctified, by ye power of ye Holy Ghost, in the act of conception, and was upheld in the same state by the same power of ye Holy Ghost, & underwent no process or progress of sanctification, as it needed none ...[41]

Irving assented heartily to this, and later affirmed: 'By that deliverance I am willing that every sentence which I have written should be tried.'[42] However, we shall see in a later chapter that this was not enough to prevent relations between Irving and the presbytery from breaking down completely during the autumn.

* * *

Responses to Irving's works fell thick from the presses. We shall not survey them all here,[43] but deal with a few of the most interesting critical evaluations. His most formidable critic was Marcus Dods, Presbyterian minister at Belford in Northumberland and author of an extended denial of the view that Christ took fallen human nature, *On the Incarnation of the Eternal Word*, first published in 1830. Without ever naming them or their publications, Dods charged those who held this view with Nestorianism because in applying the description 'sinful' to Christ's flesh but not to Christ himself, they were in effect making a separation between the two which entailed belief that there were two persons in Christ.[44] Irving wrote to Dods

---

[38] Cambridge, URCHS, 'Minutes of the Scots Presbytery of London. Vol. 2. Apr. 28. 1823 to Nov. 11. 1834', fols 191–2.

[39] Ibid. fol. 189.

[40] Oliphant, *Life*, 2.123: Irving to M. N. Macdonald, 21 May 1830.

[41] 'Minutes, Vol. 2', fol. 193.

[42] Irving, *Christ's Holiness in Flesh*, xvii.

[43] A comprehensive survey is provided in Dorries, *Irving's Christology*, ch. 5.

[44] I have used the second edition of the work, which included a fulsome 'Recommendatory notice' from Chalmers.

Nestorius, a fifth-century Patriarch of Constantinople, was condemned by the Council of Chalcedon in 451 for allegedly holding the views discussed above. Nestorianism was to be a charge repeatedly made against Irving: Marcus Dods, *On the Incarnation of the Eternal Word* (2nd edn, London: William Allan, 1849; first publ. 1831); B. W. Newton, *Occasional Papers on Scriptural Subjects IV* (London: Houlston & Wright, 1866), Appendix IV, 'Note on the Doctrines of Mr. Irving', 188–95; David Brown, 'Personal Reminiscences of Edward Irving', *The Expositor*, 3rd series, 6 (1887), 216–28, 257–73,

on 8 March 1830; stating that it had been reported to him that Dods was the author of two critiques of his writings in the *Edinburgh Christian Instructor*. He was not a reader of that periodical and did not want to know whether in fact Dods was the author (he was), as they were said to be severe in language; in any case, 'for many years I have walked by the rule, of not reading any thing personally addressed to me, unless the name of the person who writes it be subscribed'. However, since Dods would have thought through the issues involved, Irving asked him to send a summary of his Christological thinking, and offered his own:

> till within these two years I never knew that there were two opinions in any orthodox creed and true church. I believe, then,
>
> 1st That all things with man as their Lord were created holy and sinless
>
> 2ndly That since the fall they have all with man as their head become altogether sinful without the power of redeeming themselves
>
> 3rdly That the Eternal Son of God, very God of very God, by Incarnation unto death and resurrection out of death redeemed man their head & man's inheritance
>
> 4thly That flesh in human nature was created all good, then it became all evil, then in Christ it became all holy, and by the resurrection it became all glory
>
> 5 That by generation our nature is all sinful as Adam's was after the fall, that by regeneration it is strengthened of Christ the regenerator, the second Adam, to overcome all sin, and that by resurrection it is changed into Christ's glory.
>
> 6. That sin in the regenerate ariseth not from the weakness of the spirit of Christ in them, but from their own inward wickedness, which they give place to, and so contract guilt, which needs a continual element of forgiveness whereof we are assured in the great work of God's having united himself to our nature and sanctified it.
>
> 7 With respect to the experience of the Son of God in our nature I am content to say that he was tempted in all points like as we are, and yet never sinned: when I want to have the truth expanded I study the Psalms and the Prophets which testify of him.

If Dods, who was over three hundred miles away in Northumberland, lived nearer, Irving would readily visit him – it would not be the first or second time that he had travelled a hundred miles or more to converse with men on the deep things of God. Irving expressed the hope that they might regard each other as brethren and fellow workers, and assured him of a welcome if he should come to London.[45] A second letter followed in August. Evidently Dods had offered to correspond with Irving on the subject, but domestic distress, doubtless the illness and death of his son Samuel, had hindered Irving from doing so. Irving asserts that he had corresponded with Dods on the basis that they were 'brother ministers communicating with one another

---

at 264; cf. John Stevens, *The Sinlessness of Jesus; being the Substance of some Discourses, delivered at Salem Chapel, on the Words – 'He Knew No Sin:' To which are annexed, Animadversions on the Rev. E. Irving's Doctrine of our Lord's Humanity* (London: Nichols), 1830, 49.

[45] Edinburgh, NLS, MS 1001, fol. 121: Irving to Marcus Dods, 8 March 1830 (punctuation follows the original).

concerning the Christian faith; and not ... reviewer and reviewed'. One charge had particularly affected him:

> a paper which I had written to shew that the devil was always beaten out of ... the flesh of Christ, being overcome by him in the Spirit; is from an ambiguously but not ungrammatically placed comma made to speak the very contrary, and I am represented as holding that Christ's flesh was devil-possessed. This being easily remembered has been written of me and circulated all over the world to the entire contradiction of the truth, and to the utter destruction of my good name.[46]

Even Irving's own father-in-law John Martin disagreed with him. In an unfinished and undated essay intended for a clerical meeting, 'On the Humanity of Jesus Christ', he discussed the theory advanced by Irving that Christ's humanity was fallen but preserved from sin by the Holy Spirit. He argued that Christ's flesh partook of what was penal in our condition, but not of anything sinful or morally corrupt. Martin rejected the assertion that the second person of the Godhead had become united with fallen man's tendency to sin. The virgin birth indicated that what the Spirit created in Mary was sinless; it was generated in holiness in order to be capable of union with the Godhead, rather than kept holy in consequence of the union. In his view, Irving's approach amounted to affirming and denying the same thing: saying that Christ was holy and yet that he battled with an inbuilt tendency towards sin. Christ was subject to trial and temptation, but not as a result of sinful desires. Furthermore, he rejected the idea that Christ assumed fallen human nature in order to redeem it: he came to redeem persons, not a nature.[47]

However, Irving's views received Carlyle's warm approval. Writing to his brother John, who was staying with Irving, he asked him to thank his host for his little book, most of which Carlyle had read in an afternoon (this was *The Orthodox and Catholic Doctrine*). 'In my humble opinion, if the common interpretation of the Bible is to be followed, our friend is perfectly right, nay indubitably and palpably so: at all events, the gainsayers are utterly, hopelessly, and stone-blindly *wrong*. My Mother who is a better judge than I, declared it to be soundest doctrine, often preached in her hearing'.[48]

What of subsequent scholarly critics? One of the first was the erstwhile Brethren leader B. W. Newton (1807–98), writing in 1866. Newton, an acute theological observer writing from a precisely defined Reformed standpoint, accused Irving of rejecting the realities denoted by the terms substitution and imputation, even though he kept the terms, and of rejecting as a legal fiction the idea that the cross was a propitiatory sacrifice. According to Newton, 'his hatred of the doctrine of imputation

---

[46] URCHS, letter 3: Irving to Marcus Dods, 5 August 1830.

[47] Anon., *Remains of the late Reverend John Martin, D.D. Minister of Kirkaldy: Consisting of Sermons, Essays, and Letters. With a Memoir* (Edinburgh: William Oliphant), 1838, 330–55; this essay was not included by Dorries in his survey of Irving's opponents.

[48] *CL*, 5.98: Carlyle to John A. Carlyle, 1 May 1830.

seems to have been one of the causes that led him to the conclusion that Christ was in the actual condition of the sinner'. The righteousness of Christ in which believers share was not that of his active obedience to the Law, but that into which he entered by resurrection.[49] Newton also considered that it was Irving's teaching, rather than that of his opponents, which subverted the doctrine of the Incarnation. Irving taught that Christ's human nature was to be seen as distinct from himself personally, which amounted to Nestorianism. As well as this, 'The Incarnation is represented as the imprisonment, so to speak, of the Eternal Word in sinful flesh': in other word, Christ clothed himself with a human form rather than becoming human.[50]

In its day, an influential evaluation of Irving's Christology was that of the New College, Edinburgh, professor H. R. Mackintosh. Mackintosh was more sympathetic towards Irving, asserting that

> no reader of the history of the case will deny that more than one argument on which his ecclesiastical condemnation rested was gravely docetic in its implications. Irving clung with his whole soul to Christ's sympathy with the tempted, His veritable brotherhood with man; and to secure this he felt it his duty to affirm that the Son of God in incarnation took upon Him *fallen* human nature ...[51]

Nevertheless, he accused Irving of confusing 'corruptible' with 'corrupt', and liability to decay or death with liability to sin. Moreover, a loose concept of perfection allowed Irving to assert that in Christ there was the potential for divergence from God's righteousness.[52]

More recently the Free Church of Scotland professor Donald Macleod has pointed out, in a lucid assessment of Irving's Christological thought, that even on Irving's account of the Incarnation, there is discontinuity between Christ and ourselves in the extent of his anointing by the Holy Spirit, his sinlessness, his self-consciousness as the Son of God, and his power.[53] So in a sense it could be said that we are no further forward in the quest for a Saviour with whom we can identify. Another problem has been highlighted by the Scottish Baptist Jim Purves, that just as Irving complained that traditional accounts of the person of Christ gave little place to the ongoing activity of the Spirit within the incarnate Christ, so too Irving's account gave little place to the significance of the 'hypostatic union', the union of the human nature with the second person of the Trinity:

> Other than as providing an enabling role in establishing the hypostatic union, the person of the Son of God within the hypostatic union is not perceived by Irving as

---

[49] Here Newton is spot-on: Irving had written to Isabella on 4 August 1828 that the righteousness imputed to believers was not that of the Ten Commandments but that which Christ entered into by his resurrection: Oliphant, *Life*, 242–3.

[50] Newton, 'Note on the Doctrines of Mr. Irving'; quotations at 191, 193.

[51] H. R. Mackintosh, *The Doctrine of the Person of Jesus Christ* (2nd edn, Edinburgh: T. & T. Clark, 1913), 276–7.

[52] Ibid. 278.

[53] MacLeod, 'Edward Irving'.

relevant to the ongoing earthly ministry of Christ. ... The main focus for Irving lies ... in the ministry of the Holy Spirit upon Christ's humanity. Irving interpreted Christ's divinity as serving the role of catalyst for the Spirit's action upon humanity.[54]

Along similar lines is the assessment of Damon So. He considers that Irving's portrayal of a Christ only upheld as sinless by the Holy Spirit, with a human will in bondage to sin, gives us a weak Christ and leaves no room for the lordship evident in the gospels. Irving's attribution of everything in Christ's obedience to the Spirit virtually excludes the free operation of his will in choosing to obey the Father. So argues that Irving draws too sharp a distinction between Christ's divinity, his humanity and the agency of the Holy Spirit.[55]

An original, if not entirely convincing, interpretation of Irving is offered by the American Presbyterian Mark Patterson. He argues that the centre of Irving's theology, underlying all else, is his adventism: 'Irving was a theologian of the millennium, and it is from this perspective, alone, that the real Irving, the whole Irving, may be understood.'[56] Irving's Christology was reshaped under premillennialist influence, with its essence becoming 'the spiritual, glorified and perfect Christ of the age to come'.[57] The same emphasis is to be found in Irving's anthropology, so that 'Albury's Christology and ecclesiology combine to portray the true church and faithful believer as purely spiritual, freed from the weakness and constraints of the physical creation.'[58]

For what it is worth, my own estimate of Irving's Christological and Trinitarian teaching is that he asked many of the right questions, even if instinctively I sense problems with some of the answers. In seeking to ground his doctrine in Scripture and the Church's theological tradition rather than in philosophy, he was setting a precedent which contemporary theologians would do well to follow. Likewise, his emphases on the agency of the Holy Spirit in the incarnate Christ and on the reality of Christ's mortality and experience of temptation deserve to be taken to heart, as Macleod has acknowledged. However, I find myself unconvinced by Irving's assertion that identity of Christ's human nature with ours requires us to say that his flesh was 'sinful', and by his dismissal of evangelical teaching regarding the

---

[54] Jim Purves, *The Triune God and the Charismatic Movement: A Critical Appraisal of Trinitarian Theology and Charismatic Experience from a Scottish Perspective* (Carlisle: Paternoster, 2004), 164.

[55] Damon W. K. So, *Jesus' Revelation of his Father: A Narrative-Conceptual Study of the Trinity with Special Reference to Karl Barth* (Bletchley: Paternoster, 2006), esp. 244-51.

[56] Mark Rayburn Patterson, 'Designing the Last Days: Edward Irving, The Albury Circle, and the Theology of *The Morning Watch*' (Ph.D. thesis, King's College, London, 2001), 150.

[57] Ibid. 154.

[58] Ibid. 156. I think Patterson may have underestimated the potential within premillennialism for a strong affirmation of the created order; it did not always lead to such a world-denying attitude as he implies.

substitutionary nature of the atoning work of Christ as 'Stock-exchange divinity', a dismissal which to me appears as cavalier as the version of that doctrine against which he reacted was inadequate. Furthermore, in the way that Irving formulated his Christology, he does seem to have been laying himself open to the charge of Nestorianism.[59] Nevertheless, his pastoral motivation, along with his pointing believers to Christ not only as an example to them in the fight against sin but also as one whose own humanity qualifies him to assist them in a unique way, makes him worthy of study on the part of pastoral theologians as well as historians and systematicians.

In the next chapter, however, we take a break from theological discussion to tell the story of his two preaching trips to Scotland in 1828 and 1829; all the aspects of his thought which we have so far surveyed appear in the story, but interwoven and set in the context of the land which remained to him 'home'.

---

[59] Needham points out that Irving appears to have formulated his Christology in dialogue not only with those who in his opinion failed to give due weight to the real humanity, but also with some who taught that Christ's human soul was pre-existent and that he brought it from heaven at the Incarnation: Nicholas R. Needham, *Thomas Erskine of Linlathen: His Life and Theology, 1788–1837* (Edinburgh: Rutherford House, 1990), Appendix V; cf. Irving, *Orthodox and Catholic Doctrine*, 56; idem, *Sermons*, 1.(140)viii–x. Such thinkers were found chiefly among the high Calvinists of the day, one being a literary antagonist of Irving's, a Strict Baptist pastor named John Stevens (1776–1849): Kenneth Dix, *Strict and Particular: English Strict and Particular Baptists in the Nineteenth Century* (Didcot: Baptist Historical Society, 2001), 174.

CHAPTER 15

Witness to the Truth, 1828–31

Irving's two preaching tours to Scotland in 1828 and 1829 are worth describing in some detail, not least in order to gain some inkling of his tremendous capacity for work, a capacity which would in time hasten the onset of his illness and death. The hectic pace and the frequency of his preaching engagements are accounted for by his rule that 'in whatever place I sleep a night, I should offer to the minister to preach to his people'.[1]

Early in 1828 Irving formed the plan of lecturing in Edinburgh. According to Isabella, he proposed to lecture on the prophetic parts of Scripture in Edinburgh during the General Assembly to give the ministers and laity something better to talk about than the party squabbling then current concerning the Apocrypha question. It is clear that Isabella shared his enthusiasm for prophetic study, as she urged her father: 'Do write me on prophetic subjects. I'll willingly pay a double letter any day to get some of your views.'[2] A day or two later Irving wrote to Carlyle that if he could obtain a pulpit, he hoped to spend a fortnight in Edinburgh during the Assembly, 'opening the Scriptures upon some points concerning which the Church & the world are alike asleep or deceived'.[3] Carlyle was dubious about the plan, telling his brother: 'Edward Irving talks of coming hither, in General Assembly time, to preach every night, on the Prophecies! He is not mad; but neither surely does he speak forth the words of truth with soberness.'[4] Others predicted that the whole thing would end in disaster, Mrs Montagu writing to Jane Carlyle: 'He talks of preaching in Edinburgh, during the General Assembly – he may as well talk of putting a Barrel of Gunpowder under the chair of the Moderator or whatever your President is called "He will be assailed by the whole clerical body, but he will fight to the last, and die embracing the statue of John Knox"'.[5]

After the communion season at the beginning of May 1828, Irving left London by sea; Isabella, who was seven and a half months pregnant and in delicate health, left for Kirkcaldy at the same time. Probably they travelled together as far as Leith, from where it would be but a short journey to her family at Kirkcaldy. The journey to Scotland was not an easy one, as James Simpson recorded: 'About 10 d[ays] ago Revd E. Irving sail'd by the tourist steam p[ac]k[e]t for Leith, instead of making the

---

[1] Edinburgh, NLS, MS 1765, fol. 127: Irving to Carlyle, 30 May 1829.
[2] Isabella Irving to her parents, 21–22 January [1828] (in private hands).
[3] NLS, MS 1765, fol. 86: Irving to Carlyle, 23 January 1828.
[4] *CL*, 4.320: Carlyle to John A. Carlyle, 1 February 1828.
[5] NLS, MS 1776, fol. 43: Mrs Montagu to Jane Carlyle, 27 February 1828.

Passage in two days they were four' and were nearly shipwrecked after striking a rock off Dunbar.[6] However, on arrival he threw himself into the round of preaching and travelling. Assisting his friends Robert Gordon and Andrew Thomson at a communion Sabbath in Edinburgh on the 11th, he preached at Thomson's church (St George's) on the following day, although James Simpson claimed to have heard that 'he chose an unsuitable subject & did not give satisfaction' — not an auspicious start, given his desire to secure a hearing for his message.[7] He then journeyed to Annan, where he was reunited with his family. Although he was apparently invited to enjoy the hospitality of the local gentry on his visits home, this was where he preferred to be.[8] However, his concern was not merely the performance of filial duty: Mrs Oliphant draws attention to his desire 'to warn, first his father's house and kindred, and the countryside which had still so great a hold upon his heart, and then universal Scotland through her capital, of that advent which he looked for with undoubting and fervent expectation'.[9]

While in Annan, he preached somewhere each day, often to large crowds and on prophetic passages and themes. He gained permission from the minister to preach in the parish church on the Thursday, Friday (Daniel 7, Acts 2–3) and Saturday (2 Peter 3, Revelation 19–20), considering himself 'most favoured of the Lord to open these great truths first in Scotland to my own kindred and townsmen, and in the church where I was baptized'.[10] It was possibly with reference to this visit that one writer recalled Irving preaching for several nights in Annan Old Church at some point around 1828, the building being 'filled ... to suffocation'.[11] On the Sabbath he preached twice in the open air, at the nearby village of Kirkpatrick-Fleming (on Romans 8.1–3, a passage whose interest would have been Christological rather than eschatological) and at Annan, the latter on behalf of the local Sabbath schools (he planned to preach on baptism from Romans 6, 'embodying the doctrine of the homilies'). Neighbouring ministers shut their churches on the Sunday so that they and their congregations could hear him.[12]

---

[6] NLS, Acc. 12489/1, James Simpson, 'J. G. S. Journals 1806 to 1830', 16 May 1828.

[7] Ibid. Simpson's in-laws lived in Peebles, so he may have received information through them.

[8] J. D[odds], 'About Edward Irving', *Leisure Hour*, 28 September 1872, 618–21, at 620.

[9] Oliphant, *Life*, 225.

[10] Ibid. 226: Irving to Isabella Irving, 17 May 1828.

[11] D[odds]., 'Edward Irving', 620. The same writer recalled that on another occasion so many were left standing outside that Irving preached in the churchyard for almost two hours on baptism, in a style that was 'familiar, discursive, and at times almost conversational'. Not everyone took to his preaching, however: a farmer in his open-air congregation at Brydekirk once expressed the view that he was too deep, and thought that he would have sunk in the bog!

[12] Oliphant, *Life*, 226–7.

The following Monday Irving planned to spend a few hours with his sister Margaret Fergusson in Dumfries and then to meet some clergymen and in the evening to preach at a nearby location he called Cargen (a small river and estate in the parish of Troqueer), where the minister was his 'nearest of kin'.[13] On the Tuesday he intended to preach to an entity he referred to as 'the Society': this may have referred to his sermon at Henry Duncan's church at Ruthwell in the afternoon. Once again, the congregation overflowed the building, and for his sermon at Holywood Church in the evening a preaching 'tent' was set up.[14] Once again he read Acts 3, and preached for several hours on Christ's Second Coming and personal reign. On the Wednesday, he travelled to Edinburgh.[15]

It was in the capital that the main business of his tour lay, which was to deliver twelve lectures on the book of Revelation between 22 May and 4 June, in St Andrew's Church. One writer described him as coming to Edinburgh 'like another Jonah into Nineveh'.[16] He had a burden which he believed to be from God, and he longed to see his compatriots responding to the message. Even so, on arriving at the house of his friend Bridges in Great King Street, where he was to stay, his natural affinity for children manifested itself. Having been sent away by their mother when she heard the great man arriving, they encountered him on the stairs; he greeted them, asked their names, and gave them 'the blessing, without which he could not pass any head sufficiently low to have his hand of benediction laid upon it'.[17]

Irving had chosen this time of year because clergy from all over Scotland would be present for its General Assembly. He therefore began at least some of his lectures at 6 a.m. in order to secure their audience before the assembly sessions began. Even at that hour, the church was thronged, as Mrs Oliphant recorded:

> I have heard a clergyman of the mildest aspect and most courtly manners describe how, roused by the idea that favoured persons were being admitted by another entrance, he, despite all the properties of his clerical character and the suavities of his individual disposition, was so far roused as to threaten an official in attendance

---

[13] The minister was William Thorburn (1766–1846), minister of Troqueer since 1801 and husband of Ann M'Kenzie, but his relationship to Irving is unknown: *Fasti*, 2.606, http://www.dwalker.pwp.blueyonder.co.uk/Fasti%20V.2/p.%20212%20PRESBYTERY%20OF%20DUMFRIES%20p.%20606.htm, accessed 1 August 2008. For Troqueer and Cargen, see *The New Statistical Account of Scotland*, Vol. 4, *Dumfries–Kirkcudbright–Wigton* (Edinburgh: William Blackwood, 1845), 223–30, at http://books.google.co.uk, accessed 1 August 2008.

[14] Such 'tents' were wooden constructions giving a measure of elevation and shelter from the elements, commonly erected during communion seasons to enable ministers to address the vast crowds which frequently assembled from neighbouring parishes.

[15] 'Senex', *Edward Irving in Dumfries (1828–1829)* (n.pl.: n.p., [repr. from *Dumfries Standard*, 27 February 1889]), 1–2; cf. *Morning Chronicle*, 30 May 1828 (taken from the *Dumfries Courier*); Oliphant, *Life*, 226: Irving to Isabella Irving, 17 May 1828.

[16] George Gilfillan, ed., *The History of a Man* (London: Arthur Hall, Virtue, 1856), 187.

[17] Oliphant, *Life*, 228.

with a personal assault, and descent over the besieged railing, if admittance was not straightway afforded.[18]

They did not rest content with coming once to view the spectacle but attended repeatedly, bringing children with them for a unique opportunity of hearing him. The venue was changed to the West Church, the largest in the city, in order to accommodate the crowds of prospective hearers, and still it was crowded.[19] Horatius Bonar recalled one of the lectures, which were mainly on Old Testament types: there was a commotion as he walked in, and so some called for quiet. 'He stood upright in his place, and in his solemn way spoke, saying, "Let no one say, Hush, hush; I will preserve order." All was calmness, and he proceeded to read out the Scotch psalm in his own noble way.' At the first lecture a number of ministers were present, and Irving announced as his text Acts 17.18, 'What will this babbler say?' His series of lectures was carefully prepared, albeit 'more eloquent than logical', and Bonar considered that he and others were indebted to him for sending them back to study the Scriptures.[20]

Chalmers (who had already tried once to gain admission and failed) was less positive. In his journal he recorded hearing Irving on 26 May:

> I have no hesitation in saying that it is quite woeful. There is power and richness, and gleams of exquisite beauty, but withal a mysticism and extreme allegorization which I am sure must be pernicious to the general cause. This is the impression of every clergyman I have met, and some think of making a friendly remonstrance with him upon the subject.[21]

His coolness may have been due in part to Irving's attendance at the General Assembly as a somewhat distracting spectator, doing everything he could to express his violent opposition to Chalmers' advocacy of the abolition of the Test and Corporation Acts.

Carlyle, now married and living in Edinburgh, described his friend

> preaching like a Bo[a]nerges, with (as Henry Inglis very naively remarked) 'the town quite divided about him, one party thinking that he was quite mad, another that he was an entire humbug.' For my own share I would not be intolerant of any so worthy man; but I cannot help thinking that if Irving is on the road to truth, it is no straight one. We had a visit from him, and positively there does seem a touch of extreme exaltation in him: I do not think he will go altogether mad, yet what else he will do I cannot so well conjecture. Cant and Enthusiasm are strangely commingled in him: he preaches in steamboats and all open places, wears clothes

---

[18] Ibid. 227–8.
[19] Ibid. 229.
[20] [Horatius Bonar]?, 'Edward Irving', *QJP* 14 (1862), 224–47, at 232–3.
[21] William Hanna, *Memoirs of the Life and Writings of Thomas Chalmers D.D. LL.D.* (4 vols, Edinburgh: Sutherland and Knox / London: Hamilton, Adams, 1850), 3.225–6; cf. Oliphant, *Life*, 228, 230.

of an antique cut (his waistcoat has flaps or tails midway down the thigh), and in place of ordinary salutation bids 'the Lord bless you.'[22]

From Edinburgh, Irving headed westwards. He appears to have preached in Glasgow for three nights (successively on Matthew 13; 'the Regeneration, when the apostles are to sit on thrones'; and the Resurrection), then at Rosneath (on Psalms 2, 9 and 10), Rhu (on Matthew 24), Carnwath (on Matthew 25.1–13), Bathgate (Matthew 25.14–30) and Edinburgh (on the Last Times) during the course of a week. Unusually for Scottish preachers of the time, he preached extempore rather than using a written manuscript, and found the experience highly congenial.[23] His first publisher, William Collins, offered a surprisingly positive estimate of what he heard:

> Mr. Irving preached on Thursday last in St Johns Church which was well attended. His Discourse was on Prophecy as usual. He was perfectly <u>intelligible</u> and I think carried the sympathies and convictions of the people generally along with him. ... For myself I felt that he had more to say in favour of his theory than I imagined.[24]

As we noted in chapter 11, it was at Rhu on 9 June that Irving met A. J. Scott and engaged him as his assistant, inviting him to accompany Isabella back to London. But he was at Rhu for other reasons. He had long been friends with Robert Story, who by now was the parish minister at Rosneath, on the shore of Gare Loch to the south of Rhu, and had just preached in his church. And while in Edinburgh he had met the minister of Rhu, John McLeod Campbell (1800–72),[25] who had come to share with Irving his views on the universal extent of the atonement and its relation to the question of personal assurance of salvation. Campbell related that 'I went ... to lay before them [Irving and Chalmers] the conclusions at which I had arrived on the subject of Assurance of Faith, and the practical experience as a minister with which my arriving at these conclusions was connected.' He rejoiced that both had been willing to weigh what he had said, rather than, as most ministers had done, deciding at once that he was wrong.[26]

Campbell's thinking began with the recognition that many of his flock lacked spiritual joy, a condition which he imputed to a distorted view of God. This he put down to the doctrine of 'limited atonement', the belief that Christ died only for the

---

[22] *CL*, 4.382: Carlyle to John A. Carlyle, 10 June 1828.

[23] Oliphant, *Life*, 225–6, 233 (Irving to Isabella Irving, 10 June 1828), 234. Isabella's cousin James Walker was minister at Carnwath, and her brother Samuel at Bathgate.

[24] Edinburgh, NCL, Chalmers MSS, CHA 4.91.27: William Collins to Chalmers, 7 June 1828.

[25] On Campbell and his theology, see Donald Campbell, ed., *Memorials of John McLeod Campbell, D.D.: Being Selections from his Correspondence* (2 vols, London: Macmillan, 1877); Peter K. Stevenson, *God in Our Nature: The Incarnational Theology of John McLeod Campbell* (Carlisle: Paternoster, 2004), esp. ch. 1 and App. 2.

[26] Campbell, *Memorials*, 1.51–2.

elect (as taught in the Westminster Confession) and not for everyone. Until individuals were assured of Christ's love for them personally, they would never serve him with a pure disinterested love; their motive would always be that of self-interest, seeking to prove to themselves that they were among the elect. (He noted that their repentance savoured of self-interest, rather than arising from a sense of having grieved a God who loved them.) Such assurance, which Campbell saw as normative Christian experience, must rest not on looking inside oneself for evidence that one was elect and therefore had a right to claim that one's sins had been pardoned by Christ, but on something objective, in the Gospel: Campbell therefore concluded that Christ had died for all, and that all had been pardoned and were invited to be reconciled to a God who loved them – hence his teaching was often described as 'universal pardon'. His preaching produced a dramatic effect on large numbers of hearers who had been brought up on the traditionally introspective Scottish Calvinist piety, and something of a religious revival occurred, although by the end of 1827 opposition was being expressed in ministerial circles. According to Newell, it was through conversation with Campbell and Scott after the General Assembly that Irving came to believe in universal atonement, in consequence of which he invited Scott to become his assistant.[27] At some point Irving invited Campbell to preach for him at Regent Square, which he did on the Sundays 15, 22 and 29 June, including a Gaelic sermon on the last date.[28] Irving arrived back in London on 3 July, and Campbell recorded a conversation in the latter's house, after which Irving began to preach that Christ died for all, and to exhort his hearers to exercise faith in the love which that manifested.[29] But Irving's soteriology (his understanding of the work of Christ in salvation) is not to be identified with that of Campbell.[30] Apart from anything else, Campbell sought to ground assurance in the objective manifestation of grace in the Incarnation, whereas Irving (following the Scots Confession) tends to stress the role played by the sacraments in assuring the believer, because of the objective reality which they attest.[31]

---

[27] J. P. Newell, 'A. J. Scott and his circle' (Ph.D. thesis, New College, Edinburgh, 1981), 50–1.

[28] London, RS, National Scotch Church register of services and collections from 1827; Oliphant, *Life*, 237.

[29] Campbell, *Memorials*, 1.53–4.

[30] It has been argued that Irving has less of Campbell's polemic against propitiation, and Campbell lacks Irving's developed understanding of the Spirit's role in relation to the incarnate Christ: Jim Purves, 'The Interaction of Christology & Pneumatology in the Soteriology of Edward Irving', *Pneuma* 14.1 (Spring 1992), 81–90, at 85–6. However, Stevenson's exposition of Campbell's thought demonstrates that his doctrine of the atonement is intertwined with belief that Christ shared our fallen humanity and consideration of the activity of the Spirit in the incarnate Christ. The difference between them may be one of degree.

[31] Jim Purves, *The Triune God and the Charismatic Movement: A Critical Appraisal of Trinitarian Theology and Charismatic Experience from a Scottish Perspective* (Carlisle: Paternoster, 2004), 133–4.

On Saturday 14 June, Irving reached Kirkcaldy. The Sunday was a sacrament Sabbath, so congregations would have been larger than usual even without the knowledge that Irving would be preaching. But the crowds drawn to hear him were to experience a catastrophe. John Martin's church had been built in 1807 to seat 1,800 people; at least 2,000 had crowded in for the evening service, straining the galleries and so exposing the inadequate quality of the workmanship.[32] The beam supporting the gallery joists moved under the weight of between 250 and 300 people in the gallery, and the joists were dislodged from their sockets in the wall, with the result that the gallery collapsed. Only two or three died as a result of that, but in the ensuing panic over thirty more were killed or fatally injured in the crush of those trying to get out of the building. Irving was on his way to the church to preach when a messenger met him with the news. He rushed to the site to assist, helping many out through a window, but there were those who in bitterness blamed him for attracting such a crowd and held him responsible for what had happened; he withdrew in tears, distressed and humiliated. Later, at family prayers, he burst out, 'God hath put me to shame this day before all the people'.[33] That evening, he wrote to Dinwiddie in London: 'We have had an awful visitation of God's providence this night'.[34] His response to the disaster appears to have been rooted in a belief that such sorrows were manifestations of divine judgement.[35] It was reported that on the following night Irving wanted to preach in the graveyard, but that the town's Provost dissuaded him, as graves were being opened there for those who had died in the accident. The rest of his time in Kirkcaldy was spent visiting the injured and bereaved, but this did little to assuage the resentment, which had been exacerbated by the fact that a family wedding was not postponed.[36] On 17 June he officiated at the marriage of his sister-in-law Elizabeth to William Hamilton, a merchant originally from Sanquhar, Dumfriesshire; the Hamiltons settled in London and became firm

---

[32] John Campbell, *The Church and Parish of Kirkcaldy: From the Earliest Times till 1843* (Kirkcaldy: Alex Page, 1904), 206–9.

[33] Oliphant, *Life*, 235.

[34] RS, EIL36: Irving to Dinwiddie, Sabbath evening [15 June 1828].

[35] Arnold Dallimore, *The Life of Edward Irving: Fore-runner of the Charismatic Movement* (Edinburgh: Banner of Truth, 1983), 89. Back in London, he used the event as the basis for an evangelistic appeal; referring to what had happened, he warned his hearers that the judgements to come would be far worse and urged them to flee to Christ at once: 'The Lord Jesus Christ' [probably preached on 6 July 1828], *CW*, 4.335–49, at 348.

[36] Oliphant, *Life*, 235; cf. 'Dreadfel [sic] Accident at Kirkaldy' (taken from the *Edinburgh Observer*, 17 June 1828), *The Times*, 20 June 1828, 3; Anon., *Authentic Account of the Dreadful Accident at Kirkaldy, Written by a Newspaper Reporter, who went expressly to Kirkaldy for Information* (n.pl.: n.p., [1828; repr. from the *Edinburgh Observer*, 17 June 1828]; Robert Aikenhead, *A Serious Address to the Inhabitants of Kirkcaldy and Vicinity: To which is prefixed, a brief Notice of the Catastrophe which happened in the Parish Church there, on Lord's Day, 15th June, 1828* ... (2nd edn, Edinburgh: James Robertson, 1828). Campbell, however, thought that Mrs Oliphant had overstated this as contemporary accounts made no mention of it: *Kirkaldy*, 208.

supporters of Irving until the manifestations began, and even then they continued to care for him as his health began its long terminal decline.

It is noticeable that we have little further record of him preaching during this trip. Whilst part of the reason is undoubtedly Isabella's confinement (Samuel was born on 26 June), that in itself would probably not have been enough to distract Edward entirely from his addiction to preaching. It may be that the catastrophe at Kirkcaldy had affected him, or that it was deemed better for him to keep a low profile during the remaining part of his stay, given the bitterness expressed against him in its immediate aftermath. However, he did preach on at least two occasions. The first was at Perth's East Church, late in June, on Matthew 24, a favourite Bible chapter for exponents of prophecy. One who had been there recalled that after a flash of lightning and clap of thunder, Irving paused, and in the gloom quoted from the chapter: 'For as the lightning cometh out of the east, and shineth even unto the west, so shall the coming of the Son of Man be'.[37] The second was at Kirkcaldy, the day before his departure for London,[38] when he preached on Psalm 46 with the intention of bringing 'some consolation unto this Christian congregation and flock, on which I have been the innocent occasion of bringing trouble and sorrow'.[39] He made an evangelistic appeal, but also sought to offer comfort to the bereaved: God's sovereignty was such that he could have spoken even to those who had previously given little evidence of spiritual life, and so their relatives should not despair. Even in this sermon, his prophetic views must have made themselves known, as one critical reporter took issue with them.[40]

* * *

During the spring of 1829, Irving made another trip to Scotland, once again timed to coincide with the General Assembly and with the aim of setting forth his eschatological views. This time he found it more difficult to secure a church in which to lecture, and he even considered preaching in the open air, asking his friend Macdonald to arrange for advertisements and the printing of a quantity of handbills announcing the lectures.[41]

---

[37] Oliphant, *Life*, 236.

[38] Samuel does not appear to have been a healthy baby, and Isabella stayed on in Kirkcaldy until the end of September: ibid. 248.

[39] Anon., *A Recollection of the Rev. Edward Irving, A. M. being Notes of a Sermon preached by him at Kirkcaldy, on Tuesday evening, 1ˢᵗ July, 1828: Taken in short hand. By one of his Friends* (Edinburgh: John Boyd, 1828), 9.

[40] 'The author of *Criticisms on Mr Irving's Lectures*' ['A Student of Prophecy'], *A Review of the Last Sermon preached in Scotland by the Rev. Edward Irving, at Kirkcaldy, July 1, 1828; in which his Leading Sentiments respecting the Resurrection of the Saints, the Removing of the Earth, &c. &c. contained in his Sermon, are compared with the Views of the most judicious Commentators, brought to the test of Scripture, and proved erroneous* (Edinburgh: H. & J. Pillans, 1828).

[41] Oliphant, *Life*, 259: Irving to M. N. Macdonald, n.d.

On his way he preached at Annan on 14 and 15 May, and at New Bridge, to the east of the town (16 May); and on the Sabbath (17 May) he preached twice more at Annan in a field, because the churchyard was too small to accommodate the crowd, which he estimated at nearly ten thousand. It was recorded that he preached from noon until 5.30 p.m. with only an hour's break, evidence of his prodigious strength and his passion for preaching. That night he accompanied his sister Margaret and her baby to Dumfries, from where he caught the mail coach to Edinburgh.[42]

Irving lectured on Revelation daily in Hope Park Chapel, from where a call had been issued to him in 1825, from 19 May until 5 June, the first week at 6 p.m. and the second week from 7 to 9.30 a.m. (as before, this was to avoid clashing with the sessions of the General Assembly). A number of ministers attended, and as he wrote to Isabella: 'The one thing which I have laboured at is to resist liberalism by opening the word of God.' Nevertheless, by contrast with the previous year, the building was not completely filled on the first night.[43] Irving lectured extempore, in order that he might be more dependent on the Holy Spirit. Writing in the published version of the lectures, he described how God 'delivered me from the bonds and trammels of argument and oration'; we have come a long way from his first book.[44] What led him to adopt this method was his intent to spend a fortnight preaching in his home territory after seven years' self-imposed absence as a preacher; he felt that this might be his only opportunity to testify there to the whole of God's truth, and that it would be tragic to waste it by merely reading sermons (on particular points) prepared and used elsewhere. The Spirit urged him to 'open thy heart and not thy papers to them, and trust thou Me'.[45] The result was a sense of freedom, power and 'fulness and freshness of matter' in his preaching, and he forthwith adopted the same approach with his congregation in London.[46]

The lectures were published from January 1830 as *Exposition of the Book of Revelation*, initially in monthly numbers, each prefaced by a sonnet, and then as four volumes.[47] Bonar stated that the published volumes 'bear little resemblance to their original' as they contained much more of his 'advanced theology'; for this reason, we shall defer fuller consideration of them as published until the end of the chapter. Bonar also heard Irving preach one Sunday afternoon; the service began at 2.15 p.m. but did not finish until 5.30. He recollected that many were leaving before the sermon had ended, and Irving began to tell them off before checking himself, realizing that some might have responsibilities as servants.[48]

As well as lecturing, Irving had hoped to represent the burgh of Annan at the General Assembly. On 3 April the magistrates and the Town Council had nominated

---

[42] Ibid. 261–2: Irving to Isabella Irving, 14 and 19 May 1829.

[43] *Caledonian Mercury*, 21 May 1829.

[44] *PW*, 1.697.

[45] Ibid. 698.

[46] Ibid.

[47] Oliphant, *Life*, 259–60, 264, 272; quotation from 264: Irving to Isabella Irving, 4 June 1829.

[48] [Bonar]?, 'Irving', 233–4.

him as their Commissioner to the Assembly, the nomination paper being signed by his father and brother-in-law.[49] On 6 May the Presbytery of Annan gave its approval to the nomination.[50] The legality of the appointment was challenged in the Assembly on 21 May. (Irving seems to have anticipated problems on this score, as he stated that when approached he warned them not to risk being deprived of their right to be represented by electing him; only when they were advised that it was allowable did he agree.) By 94 votes to 67, it was agreed that a committee be appointed to report on the commission. Two days later the committee tendered its report, and a debate ensued which was closely argued on both sides. Irving urged the Assembly not to disenfranchise the burghs. In his view there was nothing to prevent them from electing a minister to represent them, and the two Books of Discipline left it open for burghs to send ministers or laymen (in any case, he rejected the distinction between pastor and elder). He also called on the Assembly not to exclude all those who lived outside Scotland from its deliberations and reminded it of the needs of the many expatriate Scots, in whose interests he had agreed to attend. Andrew Thomson, then a leader of the evangelical party in the Church of Scotland, spoke on Irving's behalf, arguing that only ministers of parishes were excluded, as they were represented through their presbytery (Irving's charge did not qualify as a parish, since it lay beyond the Scottish parochial system; in addition, the Presbytery of London was not represented at the General Assembly). His speech was unavailing: the committee had reported that as a stated minister in full exercise of his office, Irving could not sit as a ruling elder for the burgh of Annan, and by 110 votes to 61 this was accepted. Thomson dissented, as did Irving's brother-in-law Samuel Martin and others.[51]

It is important to remember that the grounds on which the issue was argued did not involve the question of Irving's doctrinal views. As one commentator explained, the case settled an important point of church law, 'whether a person ordained to the ministry, and in the habitual discharge of its functions, were competent to officiate as an elder – an office in the church, the holder of which has always, in the vague and general notions of the public at least, been esteemed a lay-man'.[52] Irving certainly does not appear to have taken the decision personally. Writing to Isabella, he stated that it gave him no pain to be rejected, except as wronging the burgh of Annan and other burghs who had the right to send a minister or elder. And he was accorded honourable recognition: the Moderator (the Church of Scotland's chief official, appointed annually) asked Irving to walk with him to inform the Commissioner, who represented the monarch, that the Assembly was waiting for him (it was the custom to choose two ministers and one elder to do this). The

---

[49] Annie Steel, *Records of Annan 1678–1833* (Annan: Dumfriesshire Newspapers, 1933), 207–8.

[50] Edinburgh, NAS, Minute book of the Presbytery, CH2/13/6, fol. 32.

[51] NAS, CH1/1/81, Register of Acts of the General Assembly, 1828–31, fols 201–3; 'General Assembly', *Caledonian Mercury*, 25 May 1829; 'General Assembly', *Aberdeen Journal*, 27 May 1829; *Aberdeen Journal*, 3 June 1829.

[52] R., 'General Assembly', *Caledonian Mercury*, 1 June 1829.

Commissioner asked Irving to dine with him, the Solicitor-General for Scotland and Sir Walter Scott also being present, and the Moderator invited him to attend the Assembly and to sit in the body of the house.[53]

From Edinburgh he travelled to Dumfries, arriving on 6 June after travelling all night. He snatched a few hours' rest, before going out to visit the sick and to expound the Scriptures in a family gathering at one Miss Goldie's, albeit in the presence of a number of clergy, gentlemen and ladies. That evening, he preached at St Michael's Church on the book of Revelation; extra supports had been installed for the gallery after the Kirkcaldy accident. The next day (Sunday), Irving preached in the grounds of the Academy to a crowd of six or seven thousand (he thought it was nearer ten) on Psalm 8 and Hebrews 2, two important passages for an understanding of the person of Christ, from 11 a.m. until shortly after 2 p.m. It was so hot that several fainted and one had an epileptic fit. At 4 p.m. he officiated at Holywood to an even larger crowd, which the Annan surveyor estimated at thirteen thousand, and was almost four hours in the pulpit: 'although his sermon was a long one, he told the people he could preach till midnight'. The sermon, on Revelation 5, was said to have been easily audible to all. Irving's parents heard him at both places. On Monday he went to Dunscore, a famous Covenanting site about nine miles northwest of Dumfries, where he met Carlyle and was kindly received by him and Jane at their new home, Craigenputtock. He spent two nights with them, and he and Carlyle dined at the manse with the minister, Robert Bryde. His sermon was on 1 Corinthians 15.20,[54] although he used it as an opportunity to expound his millennial views. Again, the service lasted four hours, and the crowd was between two and three thousand – no mean achievement, given the sparsely-populated nature of the locality. Carlyle described the sermon as being 'like true discourse direct from the inner reservoirs', and stated that it was well received.[55] One reason for Irving's enthusiastic reception in the Dumfries area was that several local ministers supported his understanding of the humanity of Christ. Another, we may conjecture, was his

---

[53] Oliphant, *Life*, 263–4: Irving to Isabella Irving, 26 May 1829. Scott left his impressions of Irving on record:

I could hardly keep my eyes off him while we were at table. He put me in mind of the Devil disguised [as] an angel of light so ill did that horrible obliquity of vision harmonize with the dark tranquil features of [a] face resembling that of our Saviour in Italian pictures with the hair carefully arranged in the same manner. There was much real or affected simplicity in the manner in which he spoke. ... He boasted much of the tens of thousands that attended his ministry at the town of Annan, his native place, till he well nigh provoked me to say he was a distinguished exception to the rule that a prophet was not esteemed in his own country: *The Journal of Sir Walter Scott*, ed. and intro. W. E. K. Anderson (Edinburgh: Canongate Books, 1998), 632: 23 May 1829.

[54] 'But now is Christ risen from the dead, and become the firstfruits of them that slept.'

[55] Thomas Carlyle, *Reminiscences,* ed. C. E. Norton (London: J. M. Dent, 1932), 287; *CL*, 5.25n; *Manchester Times and Gazette*, 13 June 1829 (taken from the *Dumfries Courier*); Oliphant, *Life*, 265: Irving to Isabella Irving, 11 June 1829; Senex, *Irving in Dumfries*, 2–4.

expressed love of the Covenanting tradition, in an area where this remained very much part of a local sense of identity.

However, he was to encounter a less encouraging reception when he returned to Glasgow to preach; he was well known here, as he had been in Annan, but his ministry under Chalmers does not seem to have been remembered positively by many. On the morning of his engagement, Irving recorded: 'Collins spoke this morning to me as a heretic, and I rose and left him with offence.'[56] That evening, he preached in a chapel of ease in Albion Street, for the benefit of the Tron Church's Sabbath Schools. According to a newspaper report, the building was only half full when the service commenced at 7 p.m. After taking an hour over the 'preliminaries', which included the exposition and singing of Psalms 8 and 110, he announced as his text Revelation 1.1.[57] Introducing the subject by stating that a friend on returning from absence would usually bring a gift with them, he explained that he brought the keys to the interpretation of the Apocalypse. Anticipating restiveness, he asserted that 'he expected good breeding, not levity, from the young men present'. About 9 p.m., many began to grow impatient, and numbers left; Irving begged them to be patient and assured them that he would not be long. They would have been sorely disappointed, for an hour later:

> after requesting them to be quiet for a few minutes, he proceeded to say he was not a novice; he was not an ignorant man – he had profited at school above his equals. The town congregation were not like the fathers of the country. He had during the last three weeks preached to a congregation of 10,000, many of which had come fifteen or twenty miles to hear him, and had as far to return; and yet they heard him patiently for three hours. O the manners of the city! In the country they looked up to him as a man of God, sent to expound to them the word of God; and it often brought tears in his eyes to see young men and maids, old men and wives, with their bibles in their hands, turning up every passage as he gave it. He hoped the day was not far distant when preaching, not newspapers, would be the chief delight of men; and he hoped to be an instrument in bringing about the revival of these days. ... He then proceeded to urge the claims of the Society for whose aid the sermon was preached; but the ringing of the bells (ten o'clock) and the noise of the people hurrying out, prevented him from being heard. The Reverend Gentleman then exclaimed with great animation, 'Hear me! O! hear me; it will be long before I ask you to do so again.' Upon this order was restored, and the congregation dismissed at twenty minutes past ten.[58]

---

[56] Oliphant, *Life*, 265: Irving to Isabella Irving, 11 June 1829. Irving may have been surprised by his reception, given that Collins had been quite positive about his lecturing the previous year.

[57] 'The Revelation of Jesus Christ, which God gave unto him, to shew unto his servants things which must shortly come to pass ...'

[58] 'The Rev. Edward Irving', *Morning Chronicle*, 16 June 1829 (from the *Glasgow Chronicle*).

His trials were not over; leaving the church, he found a crowd outside, some of whom taunted him for preaching 'a Roman Catholic baptism, and a Mohammadan [sic] heeven' (a reference to his stress on the significance of the physical earth in his millennial teaching). One reason for the hostility may have been his support for Campbell, whose distinctive teachings were being strenuously opposed by Glasgow ministers.[59] Nevertheless, the Calton weavers asked him to preach for them on the following Monday (15 June), a request which is all the more remarkable given that their political views were diametrically opposed to his.

Apart from planning to preach at Paisley, Rosneath and Row, he seems to have visited his brother-in-law at Bathgate before a hasty visit to preach at Kirkcaldy; sailing home the next day, he was in his London pulpit again on the following Sunday, 21 June. It could not be possible for any human being to sustain such a pace of activity for very long, and in the next section of the story we shall trace the slow decline of Irving's health and explore the relationship between this and the quality of his ministry.

* * *

Before that, we shall examine the *Lectures on Revelation*.[60] These have been neglected by many writers, and represent an incomplete work, the fifteen published lectures only covering the book as far as Revelation 6.17. Irving's initial thought was to offer a popular exposition of the book, but as he proceeded with his lectures he concluded that what the church needed was not another scheme of interpretation but a demonstration of the valuable things contained in the book, and their usefulness for edifying believers, to counter its widespread neglect as a mysterious piece of writing.[61] He believed that it fell out of use during the period of Roman domination of the church; by contrast, 'there was no book out of which our reformers took the substance of their preaching against the Pope more than out of

---

[59] Oliphant, *Life*, 266–7.

[60] Their publishing history is complicated. *The Times,* 11 January 1830, 4, advertised the first monthly lecture as newly published. No others appear to be extant, but the text of this first lecture appears identical to that in the four-volume *Exposition of the Book of Revelation, in a Series of Lectures* (London: Baldwin and Cradock, 1831). In the preface to this, Irving explained the decision to switch to publishing in book form: 'I feel that it would be breaking faith with the readers of these Numbers, were I to proceed further on the present plan of monthly publication, which also I found inconvenient on many accounts'. He proposed bringing out the work by volumes, beginning with a fifth volume uniform with the four which would cover Revelation 6–7, 15–16 and 19–20: ibid. 1.v. This never appeared. The lectures were republished in 1864 as *The Prophetical Works of Edward Irving* (2 vols, London: Alexander Strahan). Some material from the lectures (condensed in PW, 1.546–612) was first published as 'The Church, with her Endowment of Holiness and Power', *MW* 2 (1830), 630–68 (= *CW*, 5.449–506); 'On the Gifts of the Holy Ghost, Commonly called Supernatural', *MW* 2 (1830), 850–69; 3 (1831), 473–96; 4 (1831), 84–101 (= *CW* 5.509–61); both discussed in Strachan, *Irving*, chs 8–9.

[61] *PW*, 1.vii.

this book'.[62] It was therefore highly relevant to a liberal age which regarded Romanism and Protestantism as equals. Indeed, the expression of such opinions in Edinburgh, which he deemed 'alike subversive of Church and State', were a major reason why he decided to lecture on the book in that city.[63] It was, he claimed, a preservative against 'the grand rebellion of these times against the prophetic word of God in favour of human wisdom, policy, prudence, and expediency'.[64]

For Irving there was an urgency about the situation which called for outspokenness. The difference between Rome and Protestantism was that 'The Papal is the seducer, the Protestant is the seduced.'[65] Before the Council of Trent (1545-63), the true church had existed within the Roman Catholic Church, but after the council set its seal of approval on the corruptions and abuses which had entered the church during the medieval period, that church became an apostate body. Thereafter, the visible church was not to be sought in Rome, but apart from it. In the final lecture he traces the history of the persecution of believers at the hands of Rome, as part of his exposition of how the opening of the seals has been fulfilled in the course of ecclesiastical history. In view of all this, one might have expected Irving to give his approval to Evangelicalism, which was at that time engaged in strenuous efforts in Britain and Ireland, as well as through the Continental Society, to convert Catholics. Not so; he repeatedly condemned it in the strongest terms, equating it with the church at Laodicea (Revelation 3.14-22).

The published version gives much more space than the lectures had done to the Letters to the Seven Churches. We have already noted (in chapter 11) something of what Irving had to say on the basis of these chapters regarding the Christian ministry. But its significance, theologically speaking, derives from his conviction that an exposition of the church's true constitution is a vital antidote to the advance of papal error, and at the heart of this lies his presentation of the glorified Christ portrayed in Revelation 1-3. Here Christ is shown to be the universal Bishop, the only head and high priest of the church, an implicit rebuttal of papal claims. As head of the church, Christ has three supreme rights: to be the Word of God, through whom God is communicated; to bestow eternal life and baptize with the Holy Ghost; and to feed the flock with his flesh and blood in the communion. Hence preaching (which awakens faith), baptism (through which the elect are regenerated), and the Lord's Supper (which nourishes the spiritual life of the believer) are all the prerogatives of the church's ordained ministry.

---

[62] Ibid. 25. He contrasts the Scottish love of the book with the Church of England's neglect of it: ibid. 71.
[63] Ibid.
[64] Ibid. 26.
[65] Ibid. 533.

CHAPTER 16

The Port Glasgow Manifestations, March 1830 onwards

In this chapter we shall trace Irving's contacts with Christians in the west of Scotland. He does not play a prominent role in these events, but an account is necessary because his contacts with the chief actors were to prove seminal for the development not only of his thinking about the Holy Spirit, but also, and fatefully, for his practice.

Writing in the heyday of the twentieth-century Charismatic movement, Gordon Strachan claimed that the manifestations which occurred in Scotland and in connection with Irving's ministry were distinguished from previous similar events because they were 'occasioned not by the overflow of powerful religious feeling but by faithful response to the systematic study and preaching of the Word of God. Theological understanding was central to all that happened and preceded all forms of experience of spiritual gifts.'[1] The evidence offered in this and the following chapter leads me to think that this may be a somewhat one-sided presentation of events, influenced by a concern to demonstrate the theological respectability of charismatic phenomena. Yet Strachan is surely right to draw attention to the seminal role played by Irving's preaching in creating a climate of expectation. It would be erroneous to suppose that Irving had given no real thought to the person and work of the Holy Spirit until he began to think about the possibility that the supernatural gifts (such as healing, tongues and prophecy) might be restored to the church. In his journal for 22 November 1825, he reflected on the closeness of very holy men to God: 'to me it seemed not possible to say whether He might not still work manifest wonders by their hand. Not to convince them with visible demonstrations, for that is the Catholic solicitation for an idol; but to work spiritual wonders by their means.'[2] It was probably in the summer of 1826, after his series on the Trinity, that he preached a series of evening sermons from which were taken 'The Strivings of the Holy Spirit' and 'Marks of the Divine Life'.[3] As part of his 1829 lectures in Edinburgh on the book of Revelation, he dealt with the question of spiritual gifts in 'The Church, with her Endowment of Holiness and Power'.[4] According to Strachan, Irving's

---

[1] Gordon Strachan, *The Pentecostal Theology of Edward Irving* (London: Darton Longman & Todd, 1973), 14–15.
[2] Oliphant, *Life*, 177.
[3] *CW*, 4.469–79 and 4.480–91 respectively.
[4] Reprinted in *MW* 2 (1830), 630–68; *CW*, 5.449–506.

exposition hinged on the twin convictions that the gifts were signs of Christ's coming in human flesh and foretastes of his coming again in glory.[5]

Irving explained how his thinking about the gifts had developed in a series of articles appearing in *Fraser's Magazine* in January, March and April 1832.[6] He claimed that since the opening of his new church in 1827 he had taught that the church was still held responsible for the gift of the Holy Ghost, and he believed that the supernatural gifts and operations of the Spirit were not intended to be a temporary feature of church life; however, he considered that they had disappeared as a result of the church's unbelief and he did not expect them to reappear until the Second Advent. Bearing witness to the intended permanence of the gifts prepared his people to receive them, and prepared him to act as he had done once he was convinced the gifts had been restored. But something else had to come first:

> the way had to be prepared by the full preaching of Christ's coming in our flesh, and his coming again in glory – the two great divisions of Christian doctrine which had gone down into the earth, out of sight and out of mind, and which must be revived by preaching before the Holy Spirit could have any thing to witness unto ...[7]

News of the restoration of the gifts therefore came as something of a surprise:

> Thus we stood, when the tidings of the restoration of the gift of tongues in the west of Scotland burst upon us like the morning star heralding the approach of day, and turned our speculations upon the true doctrine into the examination of a fact. ... I did rejoice with great joy when the tidings were read to me, coming through a most authentic channel, that the bridal attire and jewels of the Church had been found again.[8]

Such claims were too important to believe except on the best evidence. If true, the consequences for the church were potentially revolutionary. As we shall see in the next chapter, Irving therefore obtained evidence from witnesses, including elders and 'many of the most spiritual members of my flock' who went to see, and from the gifted persons themselves.[9]

* * *

Irving considered that it was Campbell who through his preaching had prepared the ground for the gifts to reappear, but Scott who sowed the seed. As Irving's assistant, Scott 'used to signify to me his conviction that the spiritual gifts ought still to be

---

[5] Strachan, *Irving*, 83.

[6] Edward Irving, 'Facts connected with Recent Manifestations of Spiritual Gifts', *Fraser's Magazine* 4 (1831–2), 754–61; 5 (1832), 198–205, 316–20; also published as a booklet (London: James Fraser, 1832).

[7] Irving, *Facts*, 2.

[8] Ibid.

[9] Ibid. 3.

exercised in the Church', which should be praying for their restoration.[10] Influenced by Scott, Campbell had encouraged his congregation in a sermon at the beginning of 1828 to pray for the Holy Spirit to be poured out.[11] His stirring preaching, the resulting spiritual vitality experienced by many, the controversy created by his views which would ultimately lead to heresy proceedings being initiated against him, and Irving's repeated visits, all contributed to the growth of what many have seen as religious excitement. Religion was preoccupying everyone to an unprecedented degree. Furthermore, the saintly lives of two parishioners had made their own impact.[12] Among those who had been blessed by Campbell's ministry were Isabella Campbell and her sister Mary, who lived at Fernicarry, on the border of the parishes of Rosneath and Rhu (then spelt 'Row') in what is now the village of Garelochhead. Both had been converted around 1825 after a prolonged and intense period of spiritual struggle and conviction of sin.[13] Isabella, who had achieved a reputation for saintliness which had spread beyond the locality and attracted many visitors, had died of tuberculosis on 1 November 1827.[14] Her memoir had been compiled by her minister at Rosneath, Robert Story, and it portrayed her as something of a spiritual example. When the pilgrims continued to arrive after Isabella's death, Mary assumed her sister's mantle. A few years earlier, her fiancé, with whom she had intended to go abroad as a missionary, died; in spite of her ill-health, she maintained that ambition. With her visitors, the bedridden Mary talked of mission, healing by faith, and the restoration of spiritual gifts. Several intending missionaries settled at Fernicarry and preparations began to be made during the winter of 1829–30 for their departure.[15] In his account, Irving noted that she expected the Holy Ghost to come first on the lowest of God's children. He agreed, in the light of what he felt contemporary religious leaders were doing to those who maintained the truth: 'I believe that the day of carpenters and fishermen is come again, and the day of masters in arts and doctors in divinity is gone by.'[16]

---

[10] For fuller discussion of these events and the course of relationships between Irving, his church and the 'gifted persons' in Scotland, see my article, 'The Taming of the Prophets: Bringing Prophecy under Control in the Catholic Apostolic Church', *Journal of the European Pentecostal Theological Association* 16 (1996), 58–70.

Sources for this section include Robert Norton, *Memoirs of James and George Macdonald, of Port-Glasgow* (London: John F. Shaw, 1840); Robert Herbert Story, *Memoir of the Life of the Rev. Robert Story, late Minister of Rosneath, Dunbartonshire* (Cambridge: Macmillan, 1862), 227; [C. W. Boase], *Supplementary Narrative* to *The Elijah Ministry in the Christian Church* (Edinburgh: R. Grant, 1868).

[11] J. P. Newell, 'A. J. Scott and his circle' (Ph.D. thesis, New College, Edinburgh, 1981), 37, following Donald Campbell, ed., *Memorials of John McLeod Campbell, D.D.: Being Selections from his Correspondence* (2 vols, London: Macmillan, 1877), 1.48.

[12] Oliphant, *Life*, 276–7.

[13] [Robert Story], *Peace in Believing: A Memoir of Isabella Campbell, of Fernicarry, Rosneath, Dumbartonshire* (2nd edn, Greenock: R. B. Lusk, 1829).

[14] Ibid. 156n, 471.

[15] Ibid. 194–6.

[16] Irving, *Facts*, 5.

The Macdonald family of Port Glasgow emerged as principal actors in what followed, and Robert Norton, an Anglican clergyman who in 1832 married Margaret Macdonald,[17] wrote up the events sympathetically and in considerable detail. However, the first person to experience any miraculous gift was James Grubb, a flax dresser of Port Glasgow. Terminally ill, he became bedridden, but his reputation for spirituality attracted a succession of visitors to his house. He and others foretold what was coming, knew the needs of people at a distance, and beheld in visions the glory which was to be revealed in the church. Not infrequently, according to Norton, Grubb manifested a supernatural insight into the spiritual condition of visitors or their relatives.[18] (What Norton did not recognize is that this fits into a pattern of Scottish spirituality, with similar phenomena being reported during the Covenanting era.) Irving had conversed with Grubb when preaching in the area during 1828, and continued to receive reports from Scotland through one of his deacons, David Ker, who had family in Greenock.[19]

Norton stressed that the Macdonalds read little except the Bible, and that they were attracted to Campbell's ministry because they had already arrived at the views which, according to Norton, he was advocating in his sermons. These included belief in assurance of salvation as normal for Christians (something which contrasted with the introspection and uncertainty as to one's spiritual standing then predominant in Scottish Calvinism), universal redemption (as opposed to Calvinist belief that Christ died only for the elect), the real humanity of Christ (which they understood as his having assumed fallen human nature), his premillennial advent and earthly reign, and the intended continuance of miraculous gifts in the church. For the summer of 1828, the Macdonalds took lodgings for their sisters at Rhu and the brothers, who were in the shipbuilding trade, visited at weekends. The Macdonalds commenced a prayer meeting in their home for the state of the church and the world; they joined another such gathering but were asked to cease attending, and were also excluded from the parish's Sabbath School. Their minister began to preach against their views, so they set aside time before the services to pray for him.

On such soil fell Scott's suggestion that the restoration of spiritual gifts should be expected.[20] Late in 1829, he was on a visit to the West of Scotland. Staying with his father in Greenock, he made inquiries about the Macdonalds and Grubb (who had died in the summer); what he learned strengthened his conviction that the gifts would soon be restored. Visiting Mary Campbell, he tried to convince her that there was a distinction between regeneration (i.e. the implantation of divine life in the soul) and baptism with the Holy Ghost. His arguments proving unavailing, he left her with

---

[17] London, BL, 764n13, Ernst A. Rossteuscher, 'The Rebuilding of the Church of Christ upon the Original Foundations. An Historical Narrative of its Commencement. A free Translation' [by Miss L. A. Hewett] (MS, [1871]), fol. 221. One writer states that Norton was also the Macdonald family doctor for many years: D. P. Thomson, *Women of the Scottish Church*, ([Perth: n.p.], 1975), 173.

[18] Norton, *Memoirs*, ch. 3.

[19] Irving, *Facts*, 4.

[20] Oliphant, *Life*, 276–7.

the charge to read the Acts of the Apostles and warned her against rejecting the truth (which he had just expounded). In December Mary, who had now begun to pray for the baptism with the Holy Ghost, read John 14–16, and came to see that the incarnate Christ was holy not by virtue of his divine nature but because the Holy Spirit was active in him, an understanding which matched that of Irving: 'She came to see what for six or seven years I had been preaching in London, that all the works of Christ were done by the man anointed with the Holy Ghost, and not by the God mixing himself up with the man.' From that she drew a most important conclusion: 'if Jesus as a man in my nature thus spake and thus performed mighty works by the Holy Ghost, which he even promiseth to me, then ought I in the same nature, by the same Spirit, to do likewise "the works which he did, and greater works than these"' (cf. John 14.12). Again, this was what Irving himself had been teaching: 'the end of the whole mystery of his incarnation is to shew unto mortal men what every one of them, through faith in his name, shall be able to perform'.[21]

Late in 1829 or early in 1830 Scott preached at Rhu and Greenock from 1 Corinthians 12 on the subject of the charismatic gifts. The 'Rowites' (as McLeod Campbell's keen followers were named) established home meetings in both places to seek the outpouring of the Spirit; some extraordinary things occurred, yet they had not considered the question of the restoration of supernatural gifts; his sermon proved a catalyst for the first manifestations. Irving confessed that while he could not yet bring himself to believe Scott's arguments, he found them unanswerable.[22]

On 1 February 1830 Mary Campbell, then seriously ill, experienced something akin to a trance in which she was profoundly conscious of the presence of God, and uttered a severe warning to the pastors and people of Scotland. At about the same time, Margaret Macdonald, also seriously ill, was likewise the subject of intense visionary experiences. Thereafter each woman gave occasional utterance to sentences which from their tone and content were judged by observers to be divinely inspired, culminating in Mary Campbell's speaking in an unknown tongue on 28 March. She concluded that it was the language of a group of Pacific islands, although she was not well enough to proceed there and begin her mission. In the middle of April, Margaret received the baptism in the Holy Spirit, and experienced a sudden healing at the command of her brother James immediately after he had received the baptism of the Spirit through her prayers. James wrote to Mary Campbell telling her what had occurred and commanding her to arise; she in turn was healed and took the ferry to Port Glasgow to visit the Macdonalds. While she was with them, James and George Macdonald began to speak in tongues; their minister came to visit them all. In a time of prayer James spoke in tongues again; the minister quoted St Paul's instruction to tongue-speakers, 'pray that ye may interpret',[23] whereupon both brothers began to manifest this gift also. James explained in a letter of 20 April that

---

[21] Irving, *Facts*, 4; cf. Newell, 'Scott', 71–2; Strachan, *Irving*, 64.

[22] Newell, 'Scott', 68–70; Strachan, *Irving*, 74.

[23] 1 Cor. 14.13; the context is that utterances in unknown tongues in a gathering of the church should be accompanied by 'interpretation' into the language of the hearers, like tongues a gift of the Holy Spirit.

'the words do not commend themselves to the understanding first, but he that interprets does not know what the meaning is till he hears the voice [his own] speaking them, literally the Spirit giving utterance'.[24]

As soon as word got around, visitors from all over the British Isles flocked to see what was going on. According to Mary Macdonald, 'Some of them are people enquiring what they must do to be saved; but the greater part are Christians come to glorify God, by witnessing what great things the Lord is doing amongst us; and there are a few that have come to dispute and deny the gifts.'[25] Rhu became for the moment 'a focus of national interest'.[26] Mary Campbell moved to the nearby town of Helensburgh in order to be more accessible to visitors; meetings were arranged there at which the gifts were exercised.[27] Prayer meetings seeking the restoration of these gifts were commenced in various parts of Scotland. With the spread of the twentieth-century Pentecostal and Charismatic movements, many readers will have heard speaking in tongues. But it is worth inserting a contemporary description.

> In the midst of private conversation they are often impelled to speak out in tongues. A previous silence, and an extraordinary change of countenance, will generally intimate to others its approach; and it will then often occur that they will clench the nearest friend by the hand with an iron grasp, and speak out in the tongue; part of the time perhaps with the eyes closed, and then opened with the most intensely searching and fixed look.

The writer explained that if the speakers did not believe that they would receive the interpretation of their utterance, they would go to a private room and speak in tongues there.[28]

* * *

But what did the visitors make of all this? The most influential were the party who came from London late in August 1830 to spend three weeks or more in the locality investigating the gifts. They included a young solicitor, John Cardale, his wife and daughter, a Dr Thompson, and two others. Cardale wrote up his impressions in a letter to the *Morning Watch* dated 16 November, 'On the Extraordinary Manifestations in Port-Glasgow'.[29] Describing one of the daily prayer meetings

---

[24] [Boase], *Supplementary Narrative*, 762.

[25] Ibid. 765–6: letter of Mary Macdonald, 18 May 1830.

[26] Stewart J. Brown, *Thomas Chalmers and the Godly Commonwealth in Scotland* (Oxford: Oxford University Press, 1982), 214.

[27] Thomson, *Women*, 176.

[28] Archibald M'Kerrell, *An Apology for the Gifts of Tongues and Interpretation, at present manifested in the Church of Christ, and the Words of a Vision of Prophecy, given to the Church in A.D. 1830* (Greenock: W. Johnston, 1831), 10. St Paul forbade the exercise of tongues in the meetings of the church unless interpreted (1 Cor. 14.27–8).

[29] *MW* 2 (1830), 869–73. For another party member's account of what they had witnessed, see [J. Thompson], *A Brief Account of a Visit to some of the Brethren in the*

which they had attended, he expressed his conviction that the tongues were indeed real languages. They had examined the manifestations closely, and also employed one of the gifted persons as their servant, and Cardale was certain that these people were living close to God, that they were scrupulous in performing the duties of daily life, that they were free from any trace of fanaticism, and that their gifts were indeed from God. He was anxious to testify to all of what he had witnessed, and in the next chapter we shall notice the impact of the meetings which he convened for that purpose.

As well as Cardale, a number of notable theologians inquired into these things. According to Philip Newell, 'Almost every notable Christian man of the time took the matter into devout and anxious consideration.'[30] Space does not allow a comprehensive survey, but it is important to look at the reactions of those most closely associated with the new theological views – McLeod Campbell, Story, Erskine, Scott, Chalmers and Irving.

Campbell was initially positive. The Sunday following his visit to the Macdonalds, he preached at Rhu from Haggai 2, asserting that there was no reason to believe that the charismata were intended for the early church alone.[31] Describing the manifestations of tongues, interpretation and prophecy from Mary Campbell and the Macdonald brothers, he argued that it harmonized with the descriptions of such phenomena found in 1 Corinthians 14.

> Personally it has been my faith in this department of truth for two years & upwards that the gifts enjoyed by the first christians were not characteristic of that time but of this present dispensation and therefore possessed in right of God's gift by the church, all along & until the second coming of Christ, however through lack of faith in that right, they have in point of fact been unsought & unenjoyed.

They show 'the present agency of Christ by the Spirit', as his personal acts, and edify the body 'by causing each to see Christ in his brother – and love Christ in him'.[32] Within a few years, however, Campbell would revise this estimate in view of what he perceived as the tendency of the gifts to legitimate the ecclesiasticism of the new church which was emerging in London and elsewhere; having in the meantime been deposed from the ministry of the Church of Scotland, Campbell was hardly likely to be sympathetic to institutionalism in any form.

Story also seems at first to have sympathized with the new movement. A few days after first hearing the tongues he wrote to Chalmers expressing the opinion that the phenomenon was from God and that it did sound like real languages; he also

---

West of Scotland; with Remarks on certain Doctrines contained in 'The Truth as it is in Jesus' (London: J. Nisbet, 1831).

[30] Newell, 'Scott', 98.

[31] Peter K. Stevenson, *God in Our Nature: The Incarnational Theology of John McLeod Campbell* (Carlisle: Paternoster, 2004), 36.

[32] Edinburgh, NCL, Chalmers MSS, CHA 4.134.21: J. McLeod Campbell to Chalmers, 28 April 1830.

attested Mary Campbell's longstanding passion to spread the gospel. But he would not jump to conclusions: he recognized his duty as a minister to test these phenomena as carefully as he could.[33] It was not long, however, before cautious sympathy turned to criticism, and by July 1831 Irving was writing to urge him not to stand aloof from what the Holy Spirit was doing in his locality, and advising him to 'Keep your conscience unfettered by your understanding.'[34] The following year, he accused Story of 'standing afar off from the work of the Lord, scanning it like a sceptic instead of proving it like a spiritual man'.[35]

Story's attitude appears to have changed primarily because he became disillusioned with Mary Campbell. Being the Campbells' minister and having ample opportunity to observe the phenomena (and the persons in whom they were manifest) at first hand, he was in some respects better placed than Irving to come to a judgement upon them, not that he was able to convince Irving. When the two men met in Glasgow late in 1834, McLeod Campbell explained his reasons for doubting the work; Irving replied that 'you have seen the shortcomings of the brethren in private; but I have heard the voice of the Eternal Spirit in the midst of the great congregation'.[36] Soon after, Story confessed to Irving, in a letter which did not reach him before he died), that as a local minister he should have provided a narrative for the public (and especially for his friend) of what had gone on, since he knew worse things about the gifted persons than even the scurrilous pamphlets had alleged.[37] Other factors leading Story to distance himself from the movement included the failure of the Cairds to sacrifice the things of this world by going abroad as missionaries, as had been intended (and for which Mary had claimed the gifts were intended to fit them).[38] Claiming that she had been conditioned to expect the gifts by Irving's writings, Story concluded that Irving heard in her utterances 'the echo of his own voice'.[39] Nevertheless, Story asserted that the Irvingites long sought to convert him to their way of thinking.[40]

On the other hand, W. R. Caird, who married Mary Campbell in 1831 and who later became a Catholic Apostolic evangelist, alleged much later that Story's failure to pass on to the family as promised the proceeds of his *Memoir of Isabella Campbell* (which had been a best-seller) occasioned a rift between him and the family. Story then began to doubt the reality of the manifestations, ostensibly because of the unwise conduct of the prayer meetings in which they occurred, leading

---

[33] William Charles Maughan, *Rosneath Past and Present* (Paisley and London: Alexander Gardner, 1893), 120–3.

[34] Oliphant, *Life*, 317.

[35] Glasgow, University of Glasgow, University Library, MS DC21/1: Irvings to Robert Story, 27 January 1832; quoted in Story, *Memoir*, 227.

[36] Story, *Memoir*, 229.

[37] Ibid. 230–1; cf. 222–3.

[38] Ibid. 213, 216; Edward Miller, *The History and Doctrines of Irvingism* (2 vols, London: C. Kegan Paul, 1878), 1.59.

[39] Story, *Memoir*, 215.

[40] Ibid. 227n.

to a tetchy correspondence with the Cairds and Drummond in 1834. At some point Story also wrote to Mrs Campbell, criticizing how the family had spent what they did receive and claiming that their interest in the proceeds was confined to the first edition.[41]

Thomas Erskine had been initially convinced by the manifestations and wrote a sympathetic pamphlet *On the Gifts of the Holy Spirit*.[42] In it he contended that the gifts had lapsed through want of faith but were not intended to cease until their purpose was accomplished, expressed by St Paul in 1 Corinthians 13.10 as the coming of that which is perfect.[43] He affirmed the recent occurrences as genuinely miraculous, stating that 'this is not gibberish, it is decidedly well compacted language'.[44] The following year saw him expound his views more fully in *The Brazen Serpent*. But as the focus of events shifted to London, and a new church structure began to be erected, he became more cautious, since the manifestations now served a purpose different from what he looked for.[45] His apprehension, like McLeod Campbell's, focused on the way that something was being interposed between God and the individual soul, whether an authoritative leader or a binding interpretation of Scripture; this Erskine saw as a reversion to Old Testament religion.[46] In October 1834, he wrote to Irving: 'what I feel in your letter is the entire annihilation by it of all true personal, spiritual religion or conscious communion with God'.[47] By 1837 Erskine could state in *The Doctrine of Election* that he no longer believed these manifestations to be genuine, although he continued to hold that the disappearance of the gifts posed a far greater problem than their reappearance could ever do.[48] Continuing to uphold the belief that the gifts should still be manifest, he asserted his inability to receive the manifestations he had heard as being from God.

Surprisingly, Scott does not appear to have accepted the manifestations as divine. Mrs Oliphant claimed that given Scott's tendency to question authority in religious matters, the hope of spiritual gifts may have provided 'a gleam of possible deliverance out of the ever increasing problems and perplexities of life and

---

[41] W. R. Caird, *A Letter to the Rev. R. H. Story, Rosneath, respecting certain Misstatements contained in his Memoir of the late Rev. R. Story* (Edinburgh: Thomas Laurie, 1863), 13–14, 17–20, 34. For the correspondence referred to, see Story, *Memoir*, 213–23. The *Memoir* had asserted that it was Caird who had converted the correspondence about gifts into one about money: ibid. 223. All this sheds light on Irving's defiant postscript to the letter of 27 January 1832 quoted above: 'Mrs Caird is a Saint of God & hath the gift of prophecy'.

[42] Andrew L. Drummond and James Bulloch, *The Scottish Church 1688–1843: The Age of the Moderates* (Edinburgh: Saint Andrew Press, 1973), 199.

[43] T[homas]. E[rskine]., *On the Gifts of the Spirit* (Greenock: R. B. Lusk), 1830, 5, 10.

[44] Ibid. 15, 16n.

[45] William Hanna, ed., *Letters of Thomas Erskine* (2nd edn, Edinburgh: David Douglas, 1878), 142.

[46] Ibid. 150–1: Erskine to Rachel Erskine, 21 May 1833.

[47] Ibid. 163–4: Erskine to Irving, 16 October 1834.

[48] Ibid. 166.

thought'.[49] He also seems to have been attracted to the idea that the gifts might be restored, as a sign of the divine indwelling which he believed was vital for animating the church and commending God's truth to human consciences.[50] And it is clear that his thinking stimulated expectation in others. Thus, according to her, Scott

> ... bent all his powers to laying this train of splendid mischief, I trust no one will consider that I speak with levity, or in the slightest degree prejudge what was to follow, by using this word. But the position is so remarkable, and the results were yet so much more so, that it seems to me a justifiable expression; all the more as the singular man who dropped this seed, obeying his fastidious instincts, as might have been predicted of him, afterwards rejected the phenomena which his own exertions had shaped into being.[51]

But it may be that, as she alleged, he was dismayed by what his own expectations had created: 'That which to the higher intelligence was a matter of theoretical belief, became in other hands an active principle, wildly productive, and big with results unpremeditated and unforeseen.'[52] Scott's convictions were expounded in a short work published in 1830, *Neglected Truths. No. I: Hints on I Corinthians XIV*. Its preface was dated 14 June, so he must have known about what had happened, yet although he argued for the continuance of the miraculous gifts, he made no comment on contemporary claims.[53] Ultimately, Scott, 'though still entertaining the full conviction that miraculous gifts were part of the inheritance of Christians, ... totally refused his sanction to the present utterances'.[54]

Shortly after Scott and Irving parted company, Mrs Scott was summoned to receive a message which Irving wanted conveyed to her husband. She described how the two men parted over Irving's growing preoccupation with church structures:

> I said, 'You believe that organisation produces life; Mr. Scott believes that life alone can organise: does this express your great difference?' He assented. After an hour's audience in which with awful but affectionate seriousness he stated to me what were my husband's heresies, I said, 'It is very clear to me that the antagonism of the two views is as the north to the south pole, – that they are totally and purely opposite.' He said, 'It is so. Mr. Scott or I am in dangerous error. The end will show.'[55]

---

[49] Oliphant, *Life*, 2.104.

[50] Newell, 'Scott', 67, 73, 75.

[51] Oliphant, *Life*, 2.107.

[52] Ibid. 277.

[53] [A. J. Scott], *Neglected Truths. No. I: Hints on I Corinthians XIV* (London: L. B. Seeley, 1830), 5.

[54] Oliphant, *Life*, 386. Newell suggests that this may have been because of the anti-intellectualism displayed by the 'gifted persons': 'Scott', 92.

[55] Quoted in Hanna, ed., *Letters of Erskine*, 151; Hanna believed that it was this divergence of opinion which resulted in Scott's health giving way during his trials for ordination.

Chalmers, on hearing what had taken place, affirmed his willingness to believe in the gifts if unassailable evidence could be presented in support. He got Campbell to send him samples of Mary Campbell's automatic writing, and in May 1830 took a specimen to London for scrutiny by oriental scholars; their verdict was that it was no language at all. While sympathetic to the theology which had helped to precipitate the outbreak of charismatic phenomena, Chalmers was concerned at the excesses of McLeod Campbell's followers and their failure to recognize the church's discipline.[56]

It seemed that Irving alone continued to believe in the gifts, according to Newell because he refused to exercise his understanding at the expense of his conscience.[57] As he wrote to Chalmers on 2 June 1830, 'The substance of Mary Campbell's and Margaret Macdonald's visions or revelations, given in their papers, carry to me a spiritual conviction and a spiritual reproof which I cannot express.'[58] In this, we may see the lingering influence of Coleridge's stress on the conscience as a faculty through which divine truth was apprehended. (Coleridge, who might be thought to have had little time for the manifestations, is quoted by one scholar as saying: 'I make no question but that it is the work of the Holy Spirit, and a foretaste of that spiritual power which is to be poured forth on the reviving Church of Scotland'.[59]) Newell also argues that Irving's mind was essentially made up at the start, claiming that Irving came to accept the gifts even before Scott had visited Scotland to investigate them, and certainly before he had witnessed them for himself; 'Theological compatibility, rather than evidence based upon an observation of the facts, seems to have been the determining factor in Irving's commitment'.[60] I think this over-estimates the extent to which Irving's mind was made up, but it rightly draws attention to the fact that he conducted his investigations within a developed framework of theological understanding, as the next chapter will demonstrate.

Twentieth-century assessments have often been offered in the light of the rise of the Pentecostal and Charismatic movements. A Charismatic theologian who has exercised much of his ministry in the Church of Scotland is Tom Smail. He has contended that Mary Campbell 'had found in Irving's charismatic Christology a *relevant* Christ, who operated in a humanity that was the same as hers by the power

---

[56] NCL, Chalmers MSS, CHA 4.136.50: Edward Craig to Chalmers, 29 April 1830; William Hanna, ed., *Memoirs of the Life and Writings of Thomas Chalmers D.D. LL.D.* (4 vols, Edinburgh: Sutherland and Knox, 1850), 3.258–9, 261; Brown, *Chalmers*, 216–17. His interest appears to have continued until at least 1832, when he was inquiring about the claim that Robert Baxter had spoken 'in the power' in known foreign languages: Edinburgh, Banner of Truth: Anna G. Perceval to Robert Baxter, 28 April 1832. He expressed his concerns more fully in connection with a difficult pastoral situation on which he and Irving took opposing views: see the next chapter.

[57] Newell, 'Scott', 169.

[58] Oliphant, *Life*, 292.

[59] F. Krämer, *Thomas Carlyle of the Scottish Bar (1803–1855)* (Freiburg: Universitätsverlag Freiburg Schweiz, 1966), 20, citing William A. McVickar, *The Life of the Reverend John McVickar, S.T.D.*, 131–2.

[60] Newell, 'Scott', 98.

of the Spirit that he was ready to confer upon her.'[61] Smail goes on to offer an understanding of charismatic experience with close parallels to that of Irving. By the action of the Holy Spirit, the Son of God entered our humanity, and the same Spirit works in us as worked in Christ; of Irving's Christology he writes: 'Whatever criticism and detailed correction it may require, it offers a basically dynamic, charismatic and practical representation of the Person of Christ that can provide the modern charismatic movement with a far sounder basis than the second blessing Pentecostalism on which it has hitherto relied.'[62] The comparison has been made negatively as well as positively: two other Church of Scotland ministers, Andrew Landale Drummond (Irving's psychologizing biographer) and James Bulloch, described her as 'Irving's evil genius ... responsible for the modern Pentecostal movements'.[63] Negative assessments have ensured that until recent years Pentecostals and Charismatics have been reluctant to look to Irving for precedents, and indeed they have often been unaware of what transpired in Scotland in 1830. In the next chapter, we shall begin a more detailed examination of what went on in Irving's London congregation.

---

[61] Thomas A. Smail, *Reflected Glory: The Spirit in Christ and Christians* (London: Hodder and Stoughton, 1977), 73.
[62] Ibid. 76.
[63] Drummond and Bulloch, *Scottish Church 1688–1843*, 206.

CHAPTER 17

The 'Manifestations' in London, July 1830–November 1831

In August 1830, Carlyle wrote of Irving to his brother John:

> O were I but joined to such a man! Would the Scotch Kirk but expel him, and his own better genius lead him far away from all Apocalypses and prophetic and theologic chimera, utterly unworthy of such a head, to see the world as it here lies visible and is, that we might fight together, for God's *true* cause, even to the death! With one such man I feel as if I could defy the Earth.[1]

The appearance of charismatic manifestations in London would both confirm Carlyle's high estimate of Irving's character and convince him that Irving was all but irrecoverably enthralled by them and hence blinded to 'the world as it here lies visible'.

* * *

The last day of each Albury meeting was always given to considering the practical bearing of the subjects discussed. At the final gathering (2–6 July 1830), M'Neile as chairman summed up the position which the participants had reached:

> 1. That Mr. Irving has come forward as a mark for the Infidel to shoot at, and as a standard for the believer to rally by.
> 2. That it is our duty to inquire further into the mind of God, as revealed in His word, in consequence of our success hitherto.
> 3. To humble ourselves for the state in which the Church is.
> 4. To protest against the abuses in the Church in these lands, publicly and plainly, after private prayer for the ministers, and humiliation on account of the sins of our brethren. That the matters of abuse are:– 1st, False doctrine preached; and when complained of to the Bishops, no notice taken of it: 2d, Transgression of rule, in ministers administering Baptism in private: 3d, Amalgamation with Socinians and Heretics for carrying on avowedly Christian works.
> 5. We ought to act offensively, as the Reformers did, and protest against the abuses; using, however, discriminating language, kindliness of manner; and being ourselves very reverent of ordinances.

---

[1] *CL*, 5.145–6: Carlyle to John A. Carlyle, 21 August 1830.

6. It is our duty to pray for the revival of the gifts manifested in the primitive Church; which are, wisdom, knowledge, faith, healing, miracles, prophecy, discerning of spirits, kinds of tongues, and interpretation of tongues.
7. That a responsibility lies on us to inquire into the state of those gifts said to be now present in the West of Scotland.
8. It is our duty to support the Ministers who have been ejected for their testimony.[2]

To some extent, Irving seems to have been detached from the discussions. His son Samuel was gravely ill, but he was confident that the prayers of his friends and supporters would avail to ensure the child's survival. Moreover, Isabella appears to have encouraged him to attend: on arrival the evening before the conference commenced, he wrote to her: 'Had you not been what God's grace has made you, I should not have been here. Had you signified your wish that I should remain, or even faltered in your consent, I should not have been here.' He made clear how much he valued her support, and what the church owed to it. He sent a message to Maggie, now nearly five years old, 'to stir up the gift of the Holy Ghost that is in her', and even asked to be remembered to the servants.[3] The following day he expressed his wish that his brother George and the other doctor treating Samuel should join faith to their use of medical means, and prayed that he and Isabella would be given faith to believe that their son would be restored.[4]

Ministerial duty, rather than family concerns, called him back to London on Saturday (3 July) to preach three times at Regent Square on the sabbath. Confident again that Samuel would be spared, he set out again for Albury on the Monday at 7 a.m. Soon afterwards, Samuel's condition worsened; his breathing became increasingly laboured, until he opened his blue eyes on his mother and died, just three hours after his father had left. Once again, Maggie was left as the only child – and her eyesight was giving cause for concern. Small wonder that Isabella's sister Elizabeth asked her father to say nothing to anyone of Edward's 'unaccountable' conduct in leaving home at such a time.[5]

Irving was stunned by this latest blow, lamenting to Drummond that 'my children [are] taken from me one by one'. Worst was the possibility that he had been mistaken: 'The thing which hung over my mind with dark perplexity was this, that God's word seemed to have failed; for that many of God's people had been agreed to ask this matter of him I had no doubt'. If there had been one gifted with the power to work miracles, he wrote, his son need not have died.[6] There was thus a poignancy about his appeal to the Albury conference to study 1 Corinthians 12–14 before

---

[2] Henry Drummond, *Narrative of the Circumstances which led to the setting up of the Church of Christ at Albury* (typescript, n.d.; first publ. 1834), 4.

[3] Oliphant, *Life*, 297: Irving to Isabella Irving, 1 July 1830.

[4] Ibid.: Irving to Isabella Irving, 2 July 1830.

[5] Isabella Irving to John Martin, 5 July 1830; Elizabeth Hamilton to John Martin, 5 July [1830] (both in private hands).

[6] Alnwick Castle, DFP, C/9/5: Irving to Drummond, 7 July 1830.

parting, chapters in which the apostle Paul reflected on the nature and significance of the charismatic gifts and gave instructions regarding their use.

Edward buried his son in the family vault on 10 July; it must have been painful for him to have commenced a Sabbath School (which apparently he did about this time), and to conduct a special service commemorating the death of George IV on 15 July 1830.[7] But he continued to fulfil his pastoral responsibilities. In time, too, he and Isabella would rejoice at the birth of another son: on 21 February 1831 Martin Howy Irving came into the world. Martin would not only survive to maturity but also achieve eminence as Professor of Classics and Chancellor of Melbourne University, with a spell in between as a successful headmaster.[8]

* * *

According to Carlyle's brother John, who was lodging with the Irvings during the summer of 1830, Irving talked of going to open a church in Paris for both Scots and French.[9] But it was to Ireland, not to France, that he went next. One Monday, probably the 30th,[10] he left for Ireland with Isabella and Maggie. They were to be guests of Lady Powerscourt, an earnest Evangelical who would later host conferences of the early Brethren on her beautiful estate some miles south of Dublin in County Wicklow. This area was the centre of gravity of Anglo-Irish Evangelicalism: the Rector of Powerscourt was Robert Daly, a leading Evangelical, and Dublin was the setting for several noteworthy evangelical ministries, Anglican and Dissenting.[11] Although this was supposed to be a holiday, as usual Irving packed it with engagements. Preaching at Bath and Bristol on the way, we find him in the pulpit on 3 September at Powerscourt. On both the following days he preached twice in Dublin; on the 6th at Bray, south of Dublin; and on the 7th at Delgany, near Powerscourt. Isabella, in a letter to her sister, stated that his sermon there 'made a deep impression upon many, and was understood by the poorest of the people'. When he preached at the Scots chapel in Kingstown (now Dun Laoghaire) on Sunday

---

[7] St Andrews, University Library, Special Collections, Flegg Collection (MS 38594): John Caw to William Bonar, 13 October 1830 (typescript copy).

[8] On Martin Irving, see John Martin, *Martin Howy Irving: Professor, Headmaster, Public Servant* (Melbourne: University of Melbourne History of the University Unit, 2006).

[9] *CL* 5.146n: John A. Carlyle to Thomas Carlyle, 12 August [1830]. The prime mover in this abortive project was probably Pierre Méjanel, a Reformed pastor and Continental Society agent who welcomed the gifts when they appeared in Scotland and later became an 'Irvingite' minister: Timothy C. F. Stunt, *From Awakening to Secession: Radical Evangelicals in Switzerland and Britain 1815–35* (Edinburgh: T. & T. Clark, 2000), 385.

[10] Oliphant, *Life*, 299. According to the Regent Square collection record book Irving preached there each Sunday in July and August apart from 8 August; he was then absent from the pulpit the whole of September.

[11] Stunt, *Awakening*, passim; Tim Grass, *Gathering to His Name: The Story of Open Brethren in Britain and Ireland* (Milton Keynes: Paternoster, 2006), 14–22.

17th, to an audience which included a number of prominent Roman Catholics, a window had to be removed so that he could be heard by the hundreds sat on benches outside.[12] According to Isabella, Edward preached thirteen times in eight days, but she did not worry about his health as she was certain that he was doing God's work.[13] He concluded his 'holiday' by preaching five times at a Presbyterian church in Belfast (apparently to open it), admission being by ticket only [14]

The warm reception which he had received in Ireland contrasted with the stiffness of his fellow Scots. Back in London, Irving was all too aware of gathering opposition, and in preaching on the Church he stressed that Christ's followers would be hated in this world just as their Saviour had been.[15] It was in such a setting that John Cardale and his party testified that autumn to invited groups concerning what they had witnessed in Scotland. For example, at a meeting in the house of the artist John Owen Tudor (later to become an apostle), they spoke to an audience which included Drummond, Spencer Perceval (son of the assassinated Prime Minister and himself also to become an apostle), M'Neile, Irving and others.[16] About this time, too, Cardale began regular prayer meetings in his house for the gifts to be poured out in London. A few days after the first one, an event occurred which was to electrify the London evangelical world and contribute to the increasing polarization of opinion concerning Irving. A Miss Fancourt, daughter of an Anglican clergyman, had been an invalid for some years, but claimed to have been healed after being prayed for by a friend of the family. Although no tongues or prophecy were involved, her claim provoked a furore and was inevitably associated with the manifestations.

* * *

Miss Fancourt's healing came just as Irving's relations with the Presbytery of London were worsening irretrievably. The members present on 11 May had constituted themselves a committee to consider the question of Christ's human nature, with Irving's teaching in mind.[17] Millar as their chairman reported their conclusion on 20 July:

> That the Son of God took human nature of ye substance of his mother, which (human nature) was wholly and perfectly sanctified, by ye power of ye Holy Ghost, in the act

---

[12] *Times*, 18 September 1830, 2; Oliphant, *Life*, 300.

[13] Oliphant, *Life*, 300.

[14] *Belfast News-Letter*, 7, 17 September 1830, 21 June 1831. For a critique of Irving's doctrine from an orthodox Presbyterian standpoint, see 'The Rev. Edward Irving', *Belfast News-Letter*, 24, 28 September 1830.

[15] Caw to William Bonar, 13 October 1830.

[16] [H. B. Copinger], 'Annals: The Lord's Work in the Nineteenth and Twentieth Centuries' (typescript, n.d.), 19.

[17] Cambridge, URCHS, 'Minutes of the Scots Presbytery of London. Vol. 2. Apr. 28. 1823 to Nov. 11. 1834', fol. 189.

of conception, and was upheld in the same state by the same power of ye Holy Ghost, & underwent no process or progress of sanctification, as it needed none ...'[18]

Irving was entirely happy with this statement, as he later recorded: 'By that deliverance I am willing that every sentence which I have written should be tried.'[19] But Millar was not minded to let the matter rest; on 21 September he gave notice that he intended to bring to the Presbytery's attention Irving's *Orthodox and Catholic Doctrine of Christ's Human Nature*.[20]

At the next meeting, on 12 October, A. J. Scott returned the call extended to him by the church at Woolwich, announcing that he could not subscribe to the Westminster Confession. Irving was one of a small committee appointed to try to persuade Scott to change his mind.[21] The same day, it was Irving's turn to preach before the presbytery. He spoke for two hours, 'opening the subject of the Church as a co-essential part of the purpose of God, with the Incarnation of the Son, unto which this was the preparation and likewise the way, and all the means and all the life of it'.[22] Not surprisingly, his sermon did nothing to persuade them to suspend their action against him: on the 19th they agreed to seek satisfaction concerning certain statements in his book. As the only dissentient, he withdrew from their jurisdiction, appealing over their heads to the Church of Scotland.[23] James Simpson watched him take his cloak, hat and staff, and move out of the court to sit in the aisle of the church.[24] Even Mrs Oliphant, for all her hero-worship, was constrained to admit that his action was 'somewhat wilful and lofty'.[25]

Irving's withdrawal did not stop a committee from being appointed to examine the book in the light of the teaching of the Bible and the doctrinal standards of the Church of Scotland. A committee was also appointed to receive Irving's protest at the presbytery's proceedings and to consider what steps should be taken.[26] Reporting back on 9 November, it rejected his claim that they had failed to act according to the guidelines laid down in Matthew 18.15–20 for dealing with an offending brother, arguing that he had precipitated things by preaching before them

---

[18] Ibid. fol. 193.

[19] Irving, *Christ's Holiness in Flesh, the Form, Fountain Head, and Assurance to us of Holiness in Flesh* (Edinburgh: John Lindsay, 1831), xvii. The lengthy preface gives his version of the somewhat complicated course of events.

[20] 'Minutes, Vol. 2', fols 191–2.

[21] Ibid. fol. 205; 'Scotch Presbytery in London', *The Times*, 13 October 1830, 3.

[22] Oliphant, *Life*, 301: Irving to Elizabeth Hamilton, 13 October 1830.

[23] Irving, *Christ's Holiness in Flesh*, xix. His view was that as a body lacking legal standing in the Church of Scotland, the presbytery had no right to try his standing as a minister: ibid. xxxix.

[24] Edinburgh, NLS, Acc. 12489/1, James Simpson, 'J. G. S. Journals 1806 to 1830', 21 October 1830.

[25] Oliphant, *Life*, 306.

[26] 'Minutes, Vol. 2', fols 206–7.

with great fulness & particularity, & with much heat & zeal, y⁵ very doctrine which, in the Pamphlet, he knew had given offence to his Brethren; & seeing, that, in this Court, [the] Protester did himself declare, that knowing y⁵ doctrine contained in y⁵ said pamphlet had become a matter of controversy, he had on purpose laid it on y⁵ Presb. table for their consideration ...'[27]

Furthermore, he had no right to withdraw from its jurisdiction: as a voluntary body, its authority was the stronger because its members had chosen to submit to it rather than being obliged to do so. At his ordination, he had promised to submit to whatever presbytery he might be connected with, and had effectively renewed that commitment at his induction.[28]

The report on his book was received on 14 December, and Irving was declared no longer to be a member of the presbytery; he might be readmitted only if he submitted to its authority and renounced the errors detailed in the report.[29] To a friend soon afterwards, Irving expressed his conviction that 'The Lord has given me the honour of being the first to suffer'.[30] Once again, it seems, he saw himself as following in the steps of the Covenanter martyrs. The following day Irving's officers issued a declaration asserting the orthodoxy of his teaching.[31] It was sent to the newspapers and on the succeeding Sunday it was read from the pulpit.[32] This served only to raise the temperature of the controversy further.

In January 1831, therefore, the presbytery resolved to publish their own account of what had gone on, in order to show that their proceedings had been grounded on a sound grasp of Irving's teaching and that they had not proceeded against him unjustly.[33] They had thought that the statement agreed the previous summer struck at the root of Irving's views and that as a result he would see his error, but instead it was being claimed that they had adopted his opinions. At the December meeting they had agreed not to make the matter public, except to have their decision read out in churches whose sessions deemed it necessary, but Irving's actions had forced their hand. As for the declaration from Regent Square, they were forced to conclude that

---

[27] Ibid. fol. 209.

[28] Ibid. fols 209–10.

[29] Ibid. fols 215–26.

[30] Oliphant, *Life*, 2.157.

[31] It appears in full in Oliphant, *Life*, 307. The declaration had been thought to have been drafted by Irving, but the editor of the *Edinburgh Christian Instructor* inserted a note he had received from a member of the Session at Regent Square, explaining that Irving had known nothing of the declaration, which was drawn up by several members of session, until it was brought to him for signature: *ECI* 30 (1831), 298; cf. Edward Irving, 'Declaration from the National Scotch Church, London', *MW* 3 (1831), 247–8.

[32] James Simpson, 'J. G. S. Journals 1806 to 1830', 21 December 1830.

[33] 'Minutes, Vol. 2', fol. 228; Anon., *A Brief Statement of the Proceedings of the London Presbytery, in Communion with the Established Church of Scotland, in the Case of the Rev. Edward Irving, and of a Book, written by him, and entitled 'The Orthodox and Catholic Doctrine of our Lord's Human Nature'* (London: Basil Steuart, 1831). Irving was responding to the latter in his preface to *Christ's Holiness in Flesh*.

'either the spirit, as well as the words of this Confession, are in direct opposition to the doctrine taught by Mr. Irving; or that it is couched in language, which, though it be not meant, is most assuredly calculated to deceive'.[34] The controversy marks a significant step in Irving's thought away from loyalty to the polity of the Church of Scotland. As a later writer not unfairly observed, Irving 'was the foremost to contend for Calvinistic orthodoxy till his own was impugned, the most uncompromising upholder of the Church's honest discipline by Sessions, Presbyteries, and Assemblies, *till that discipline fell upon himself*'.[35]

At the same time as all this was going on, Irving and his officers were drawing up a petition for a national fast. With an eye to the revolutionary ferment which had resurfaced that year in parts of Europe, they expressed their apprehension of imminent divine judgement on account of the spread of democracy and infidelity. In Britain, there had been failure to acknowledge the hand of God in national affairs; failure of the churches in doctrine and discipline; dissolution of hierarchical social bonds as a consequence of shortcomings of the nobility; and the desire of merchants to grow rich had led to the oppression of the workers, who had thus become morally degraded and ready to overthrow the institutions of government. The insurrections which had broken out in various parts of the country were 'grievous evidence of the miserable condition to which the poor have come through ignorance, neglect, and destitution'. Reform, Irving asserted, must begin at the top.[36] The petition, which had been agreed on 6 December, was presented to the King through the Home Secretary, Lord Melbourne, on the 21st by Irving and three of his elders. Horatius Bonar described what happened:

> A curious scene took place when he & his elders went to Lord Melb[o]urn[e]s to present it. They went in a body. Melbourne was long of coming in, & they engaged in prayer till he came. When he came in Mr. Irving stept forward & told him, here was a petition which he must be very careful to deliver to his Majesty & then concluded by a very solemn admonition to Melburne of his duty, till Melburne was much affected. before they left the house they again engaged in prayer. three days after this the recommendation of the Council to pray for the disturbances was issued.[37]

---

[34] Anon., *Brief Statement*, 19.

[35] [Horatius Bonar]?, 'Edward Irving', *QJP* 14 (1862), 224–47, at 246.

[36] London, LMA, LMA/4358/C/002/25, *To the King's most Excellent Majesty: The Petition of the Minister, Elders, and Deacons of the National Scotch Church, Regent Square, London, in Session assembled.*

[37] NLS, MS 15996, fol. 14: Horatius Bonar to John Bonar, 13 January 1831.

* * *

But what of the manifestations? Later Catholic Apostolic writers tended to minimize Irving's role in the appearance of the gifts in London.[38] Rossteuscher, for example, states that his *Morning Watch* article in Autumn 1830 showed a certain caution concerning them, and that he was absent for a lengthy spell because of his health. It was only when attending Cardale's meeting in October that he was convinced, and even then he was preoccupied with developments in his own church until the following May. He preached during the winter on baptism with the Holy Ghost, but was not yet ready for practical action. Indeed, some of his congregation had advanced further than he had:

> Members of his own flock, who were longing for the revival of spiritual gifts in their midst, and who were not fully satisfied with his own prayers bearing upon the subject, as he offered them in the church, frequently urged him to consent to special prayer meetings. But he was not to be moved. It went against his high church tendencies to allow of social or family gatherings for prayer for such purposes outside of the church.[39]

However, once some of his flock began to prophesy in the context of their own family worship, he felt himself duty-bound to investigate.[40] Such an interpretation may be overstated but it is closer to the truth than that which sees Irving as the prime mover in what happened: he himself admitted that he had not encouraged his flock to seek the restoration of the gifts, and it can be argued that for much of the time he was (in modern parlance) reactive rather than proactive.

Irving developed a biblical basis for his approach to the gifts in a series of *Morning Watch* articles, 'On the Gifts of the Holy Ghost, Commonly called Supernatural', which appeared between December 1830 and September 1831 and hence predate the appearance of the gifts in Sunday services, and for the most part also the prayer meetings.[41] In these articles he argued for the permanence of the gifts (especially tongues), intended by the ascended Christ for building the church as God's dwelling-place, 'to prepare for God such a living temple, such a speaking, acting body, as shall declare his presence to every beholder'.[42] The absence of the gifts he put down to the lack of an adequate testimony to the work of Christ for them to

---

[38] Cf. William W. Andrews, *Edward Irving: A Review* (2nd edn, Glasgow: David Hobbs, 1900), 98–108.

[39] London, BL, 764n13, Ernst A. Rossteuscher, 'The Rebuilding of the Church of Christ upon the Original Foundations. An Historical Narrative of its Commencement. A free Translation' [by Miss L. A. Hewett] (MS, [1871]), fols 226–33; quotation at fol. 232.

[40] Ibid. fol. 239.

[41] 'On the Gifts of the Holy Ghost, Commonly called Supernatural', *MW* 2 (1830), 850–69; 3 (1831), 473–96; 4 (1831), 84–101; repr. in *CW* 5.509–61. He followed these up with 'The Mystery of Speaking with Tongues', *MW* 5 (1832), 78–84.

[42] Irving, 'Gifts', 856.

attest, and to the exaltation of human reason and effort in place of dependence on divine life and power. Tongues, he asserted, were 'the sign of the baptism with the Holy Ghost',[43] a gift for all to seek. Given his relative lack of personal experience of these gifts at this stage, he offered a surprisingly full account of how the gift of tongues should be exercised. But he stressed that he was writing as judge rather than jury, laying down the relevant principles on which a right estimate of contemporary manifestations could be attained. Nevertheless, he was predisposed to accept the gifts by his belief that when they prayed, God would not have given them other than what they requested (cf. Luke 11. 11–13).[44] As Stunt puts it: 'Irving and his followers had, for years, been praying for an outpouring of the Holy Spirit: they were hardly likely to question closely the authenticity of the healings and glossolalia of the early 1830s.'[45]

It was Mrs Cardale who was the first to speak in the Spirit in London, at home on 30 April 1831, uttering the words, 'The Lord will speak to His people! The Lord hastens His coming! He comes, He comes.'[46] The Cardales belonged to an evangelical Anglican congregation (St John's, Bedford Row), but their minister, Baptist Noel, refused to come and hear her; accordingly they sought advice from Irving and began attending Regent Square. Soon after, Cardale's sister Emily also received the gifts of tongues and prophecy, and came to exercise considerable influence among the 'gifted persons'. Several of Irving's flock also experienced the gift of prophecy in their family worship, and informed him. The gifts also appeared in the regular Saturday meetings at Irving's house for prayer and Bible study. At these meetings, participants gathered in Irving's study at 5 p.m., moving to the living room an hour later and finishing towards 10.[47] Jane Simpson recorded that on one occasion, when a number of the nobility were present, 'the Tea was scarcely removed when Mrs Caird was filled with the Spirit, and spoke first in a tongue then in English at great length'.[48] All this took place in private homes; the first prayer meetings which Irving organized in the church were the daily meetings at 6.30 a.m. during May to pray for the forthcoming General Assembly.

---

[43] Ibid. 91.

[44] Oliphant, *Life*, 317. This was a standard argument in early apologetic for the gifts.

[45] Timothy C. F. Stunt, '"Trying the Spirits": The Case of the Gloucestershire Clergyman (1831)', *JEH* 32 (1988), 95–105, at 95.

[46] Rossteuscher, 'Rebuilding', fol. 238. Rossteuscher dates this to 5 April, but 30 April is more commonly given: [Copinger], 'Annals', 20; Gordon Strachan, *The Pentecostal Theology of Edward Irving* (London: Darton Longman & Todd, 1973), 99, following John Hair, *Regent Square: Eighty Years of a London Congregation*, (London: James Nisbet, 1899), 104. [C. W. Boase], *Supplementary Narrative* to *The Elijah Ministry in the Christian Church* (Edinburgh: R. Grant, [1868]), dates it to 7 May.

[47] Michael Hohl, *Bruchstücke aus dem Leben und den Schriften Edward Irving's, gewesenen Predigers an der schottischen Nationalkirche in London*, (St Gallen: C. von Scheitlin, 1839), 132–8.

[48] NLS, Acc. 12489/10, Jane Simpson, Diary, 1831, fol. 92. The date of this meeting is unclear, but her husband recorded Mrs Caird speaking at such a meeting in mid-June: 'J. G. S. Journal 1806–1830', 20 June 1831.

* * *

It was with good reason that Irving felt the need to engage in prayer for the General Assembly, as he knew that his doctrines would probably be condemned there. For some months he had been thinking about undertaking another fortnight's lectures in Edinburgh, this time on the Incarnation. In December, he told his friend, the Edinburgh advocate M. N. Macdonald, that he would do so over Christmas. His plan had been to lecture on the Epistle to the Hebrews, but Isabella suggested adding a series of prophetic expositions in the mornings. However, the presbytery proceedings against him meant that on 16 December he had to inform Macdonald that the session had advised him not to go.[49]

But Irving was using other means to reach his fellow ministers. In the spring of 1831 he published a short work entitled *Christ's Holiness in Flesh, the Form, Fountain-Head, and Assurance to us of Holiness in Flesh*. This, as well as his *Orthodox and Catholic Doctrine*, were written as replies to J. A. Haldane, the ablest of Irving's critics in the area of Christology. He was fighting two forms of error, one being that Christ's human nature was that of Adam unfallen, and not derived from Mary; (making it immortal, incorruptible, and not subject to our infirmities), and the other being that Christ's nature was Mary's, but that in the moment of generation it was purged from all sin.[50] Irving sought to measure these against the Westminster Confession (unlike others around him, he had not yet abandoned it).[51] He arranged for the work to be sent to the ministers of the Church of Scotland,[52] but this was doubtless regarded as an inflammatory gesture.

Although he had longed to preach and lecture for a week in Edinburgh during the Assembly,[53] his lectures were never to be delivered. Neither did he attend it, although it was to prove fateful for his future course. His friend McLeod Campbell, on trial for heresy, initially maintained the compatibility of his teaching with the Westminster Confession, but during his trial he changed his ground to appeal, as Scott was doing, from the Confession to Scripture.[54] On 25 May, therefore, Campbell was deposed from the ministry. The withdrawal of Hugh Maclean's licentiate was affirmed on the following day, as was that of Sandy Scott's on the 27th.[55] Irving was aware that his turn could not be long delayed. James Simpson

---

[49] Oliphant, *Life*, 2.157.

[50] Irving, *Christ's Holiness in Flesh*, xv–xvi.

[51] Andrew Landale Drummond, *Edward Irving and his Circle: Including some Consideration of the 'Tongues' Movement in the Light of Modern Psychology* (London: James Clarke, [1937]), 113.

[52] Edinburgh, NAS, CH1/1/81, Register of Acts of the General Assembly, 1828–31, fol. 566; cf. Oliphant, *Life*, 311.

[53] Oliphant, *Life*, 311.

[54] Oliphant, *Life*, 2.178; A. C. Cheyne, *The Transforming of the Kirk: Victorian Scotlands [sic] Religious Revolution* (Edinburgh: Saint Andrew Press), 1983, 62.

[55] Register of Acts, 1828–31, fols 509, 527–8; Andrew L. Drummond and James Bulloch, *The Scottish Church 1688–1843: The Age of the Moderates* (Edinburgh: Saint Andrew Press, 1973), 203–4.

recorded in his diary that on 24 May, Irving heard that the Assembly had appointed a committee to examine his works.[56] Two days later he wrote to Macdonald asking how to proceed if the Assembly were to be asked for judgement against him or his book. He made it clear that he did not intend to suffer the loss of his ministerial standing without a fight: 'I am deeply impressed with the duty of contesting every inch of ground with these perverters of the Gospel and destroyers of the vineyard'.[57] The committee reported back on 30 May, citing passages in *The Orthodox and Catholic Doctrine* and *Christ's Holiness in Flesh* which it regarded as teaching the corruption of Christ's human nature and hence as falling within the condemnation of Bourignonianism which every minister and licentiate of the Church of Scotland was required to subscribe.[58] Accordingly, the Assembly laid down that if Irving should claim the privileges of a licentiate or minister, the local presbytery would be bound to inquire whether he was the author of certain works and then to proceed as it thought fit.

Irving's father-in-law was deeply grieved at the Assembly's handling of the issues, especially the harsh and uncharitable things said by some in debate. But he considered that to some extent Irving had brought it upon himself: 'I think, and I have told him over and over, that his language, if not his meaning[,] is heterodox, and gives abundant occasion for all that has been said and done against him. I am not the only one of his Friends who has said and written this to him'.[59] The language of Irving's reaction to the Assembly's decisions bore out Martin's opinion:

> the people should no longer hear those ministers who cast them out and the truth of God with them, until these ministers have returned to the preaching of the truth. For they have declared themselves Antichrist in denying that Christ came in the flesh; and they have denied both the Father and the Son. ... I say, therefore, it is the duty of the people to come out and be separate.[60]

Writers have sometimes been puzzled at Chalmers' silence in the Assembly debate. In his journal, he merely recorded: 'General Assembly. Mr Irving's case.'[61] He himself claimed that it would have taken too long for him to master the literature

---

[56] James Simpson, 'J. G. S. Journals 1806 to 1830', 13 and 24 May 1830.

[57] Oliphant, *Life*, 315: Irving to Macdonald, 26 May 1831.

[58] Bourignonianism was so named from the seventeenth century Flemish mystic Antoinette Bourignon. According to the General Assembly, she taught that Christ had a twofold human nature derived from Adam and from the Virgin Mary, the former being corrupt and sinful.

[59] Cambridge, URCHS, letter 22: John Martin to William Hamilton, June 1831 [copy].

[60] Oliphant, *Life*, 317: Irving to Story, July 1831.

[61] Edinburgh, NCL, Chalmers MSS, CHA 6.1.11: 'Journal No. 7' (1827–34), 28 May 1831.

and to prepare himself for participation in the debate.[62] It may also be, as Stewart Brown has suggested, that public defence of Irving's views would have cost him his professorial chair.[63] The story was told that when Chalmers saw a newspaper report of Irving's condemnation, he exclaimed with relief that 'one vote would not have made any difference'.[64] In any case, Chalmers 'was to have a long history of abstention from Assembly divisions'.[65] Probably, however, his silence was in part the result of a developing estrangement between him and Irving resulting from a complex pastoral situation in which Chalmers felt that Irving had acted discreditably. It concerned a converted Jew, Ridley Herschell, and Helen Mowbray, the daughter of a Leith merchant. Irving often attended Bible studies led by Herschell in London, to which one of Herschell's baptismal sponsors brought Helen. She was a friend of the Irvings, a keen prophetic student and a member of the flock at Regent Square.[66] When, early in 1830, Herschell and Miss Mowbray intimated their intention of marrying, her parents asked Chalmers to intervene and use his influence to stop things going any further. It seems that the girl was claiming that Irving had advised her to act as she had, and so the following March Chalmers asked Drummond to get Irving to intervene, but Irving claimed that the dictates of the Holy Spirit took precedence over parental authority. Moreover, Campbell also refused to get involved, claiming to know nothing of Herschell or Helen Mowbray; Chalmers thought he was lying, and the affair ended his friendship with Irving: their correspondence appears to have ceased, and in October 1831 he complained that Irving's recent letters on the topic had 'completely broken up all my confidence ... in thinking of him'.[67]

---

[62] William Hanna, *Memoirs of the Life and Writings of Thomas Chalmers D.D. LL.D.* (4 vols, Edinburgh: Sutherland and Knox, 1850) 2.227–8, quoted in David W. Dorries, *Edward Irving's Incarnational Christology* (Fairfax, VA: Xulon Press, 2002), 48.

[63] Stewart J. Brown, *Thomas Chalmers and the Godly Commonwealth in Scotland* (Oxford: Oxford University Press, 1982), 218.

[64] [John Tulloch], Review of Oliphant's *Life* and Story's *Memoir*, *Edinburgh Review* 116 (1862), 426–60, at 455.

[65] D. Chambers, 'Doctrinal Attitudes in the Church of Scotland in the Pre-Disruption Era: The Age of John McLeod Campbell and Edward Irving', *Journal of Religious History* 8 (1974–5), 159–82, at 168.

[66] Ridley H. Herschell, ed., *'Far above Rubies': Memoir of Helen S. Herschell by her Daughter* (London: Walton and Maberly, 1854), 113–14; [G. B. Sanderson], *Memoir of Ridley Haim Herschell, late Minister of Trinity Chapel, Edgware Road* ([Edinburgh]: printed for private circulation, 1869), 76; A. Temple Patterson, *Radical Leicester: A History of Leicester 1780–1830* (Leicester: University College, 1954), 208.

[67] NCL, Chalmers MSS, CHA 3.14.12: Chalmers to Fergus Jardine, 11 October 1831. See also 4.144.40: M. M. Mowbray to Chalmers, 11 March 1830; 4.154.46: Campbell to Chalmers, 18 March 1831; DFP, C/1/87: Chalmers to Drummond, 15 March 1831; Hanna, *Chalmers*, 3.287; Brown, *Chalmers*, 217; J. C. G. Binfield, 'Jews in Evangelical Dissent: the British Society, the Herschell Connection and the Pre-Millenarian Thread', in M. Wilks, ed., *Prophecy and Eschatology*, Studies in Church History Subsidia 10 (Oxford: Basil Blackwell, 1994), 225–70.

A published letter sheds considerable light on the affair, and on Chalmers' developing attitudes towards the manifestations and thus towards Irving. Written to Irving's friend McDonald, it protested against

> the mischievous delusion, by which, under the guise of religious principle, they have not only done what in them lay to contravene the will and rightful privileges of a father; but by the extravagance and folly of their most unscriptural imaginations, may, if suffered to pass without notice or correction, inflict the utmost damage and discredit on the cause of serious Christianity ...[68]

Those involved claimed to have been assured in prayer that the marriage was divinely approved, but none had been able to give any reason for their certainty. Chalmers, with his stress on the importance of reason in Christian living and thinking, saw this as potentially dangerous: arguing that God speaks to us through Scripture, he claimed to have found a principle at work among the Rowites which would lay the church open to all sorts of errors under the guise of special revelations; from accepting revelations which added to Scripture, they would come to countenance things opposed to Scripture, as this marriage did in contravening the Fifth Commandment. He therefore abjured 'the false lights and revelations by which you and your party have been of late so bewildered'.[69]

* * *

The General Assembly's condemnation of Irving's teaching made little difference to life at Regent Square, as he continued with his preaching and pastoral work. On 19 June he preached in aid of a fund opened for the relief of starving Irish peasants. Mrs Montagu told Jane Carlyle that he had 'preached very nobly for the poor famishing Irish, and the congregation have nobly seconded him, having raised at one sermon 350£ the largest collection ever made in London at any place of worship'.[70] *The Times* commented: 'Such a liberal contribution deserves notice, and challenges imitation.'[71] Irving's regular sabbath routine was described by a Swiss student in London, Michael Hohl. He would be invited by Irving to his house for a meal between services; besides the family, there were generally six to eight present, including Irving's brother George. Irving would return to church at 3 p.m., to listen to his missionary conduct the afternoon service; Hohl not seldom accompanied him, returning to his house afterwards for a cup of tea or something to eat.[72] The evening service followed, at which Irving usually preached. The picture is of a minister whose door was open to strangers of various nationalities, who lived simply enough,

---

[68] 'Dr. Chalmers and the Tenets of the late Rev. E. Irving', *The Pulpit*, no. 652 (9 April 1835), 444–8, at 445.
[69] Ibid. 448.
[70] NLS, MS 1776, fol. 63: Mrs Montagu to Jane Carlyle, 23 June 1831.
[71] *The Times*, 20 June 1831, 2.
[72] Hohl, *Bruchstücke*, 122–4.

and whose Sundays appear to have been rather hectic, especially when one takes into consideration the vestry interviews, urgent sick calls, and other demands upon a minister's time.

However, Irving remained concerned to respond to the Assembly's decisions. During the summer he issued a compendium of the Kirk's main doctrinal standards, *The Confessions of Faith and the Books of Discipline of the Church of Scotland, of date Anterior to the Westminster Confession*.[73] To this he provided a lengthy historical preface discussing the relative status and merits of the different documents,[74] and a summary of Scottish church history which held up the Celtic monks as models of spirituality and ministry over against Rome, whose influence had caused the Scottish church to decay. Although the immediate stimulus to publication was his conviction that the courts of the Church of Scotland were failing to act according to these foundation documents,[75] he appears to have had such a work in mind as early as January 1827, when Isabella informed her parents that he was writing a short account of Protestantism for a new edition of the Kirk's confessions.[76] Seeking to vindicate his position as a Presbyterian minister, and to justify his lack of love for the Westminster Confession, he expressed his decided preference for the Scots Confession, which he had been accustomed to read to his church twice a year during communion seasons; its article on sacraments had 'delivered me from the infidelity of evangelicalism'.[77] By contrast, the Westminster Confession, was 'a great snare to tender consciences, a great trial to honest men', including his friends;[78] it was too abstract and detailed, and the Assembly which had produced it had been convened during a time when revolutionary principles held sway and the nation's constitution was effectively in abeyance. 'I never liked that Assembly, and would much rather our Church had never adopted its books. As it is, however, we must bow to the awards of Providence, and make the best use of them.'[79] Indeed, he omitted most of the Westminster family of documents from his compilation on the basis that they had not been produced by the Church of Scotland. This was historically true, but his action would have won him no friends in a church which made the Westminster Confession its primary doctrinal standard. As if that were not enough, his independence manifested itself in his assertion that local congregations were to be self-sufficient, a presbytery being a body of elders within a congregation rather than one drawn from several congregations. Synods and other

---

[73] *The Confessions of Faith and the Books of Discipline of the Church of Scotland, of Date anterior to the Westminster Confession: To which are prefixed a Historical View of the Church of Scotland from the Earliest Period to the Time of the Reformation, and a Historical Preface, with Remarks* (London: Baldwin and Cradock, 1831). The *Historical View* was reprinted in *CW*, 1.543–96.

[74] Reprinted as 'Notes on the Standards of the Church of Scotland', *CW*, 1.599–645.

[75] Irving, *Confessions*, clix.

[76] Isabella Irving to her parents, 5 January 1827 (in private hands).

[77] Irving, *Confessions*, xcix.

[78] Ibid. clii.

[79] Ibid. cl.

such gatherings were for emergencies only, and not part of the regular mechanism of church government. Thus he, as a minister, had an authority and freedom of action which paralleled those of a bishop of the Church of England, or the leading minister of a presbytery of the Church of Scotland.[80] Furthermore, he asserted that God could yet restore apostles and prophets to the church, and that the latter had indeed reappeared, the prophetic office being exercised by those who spoke in tongues.[81]

A markedly more negative response came the following March, in his article 'A Judgment – as to what Course the Ministers and the People of the Church of Scotland should take in consequence of the Decisions of the last General Assembly'.[82] He held the Assembly guilty of denying the reality of Christ's humanity, and hence his work on earth, as well as that of the Spirit in preserving him sinless. To disallow the appeal to Scripture against the Confession was no better than the papacy, and the Assembly had acted against God and his truth. Those who had been ejected by it for the truth's sake should be welcomed as ministers of Christ. Whilst he had formerly opposed separating from the Kirk, his studies in Revelation 2–3 had led him to conclude that separation was justified in these circumstances. The faithful should cease attending services conducted by those who taught error and meet under a faithful minister; if none were available, 'let them meet together, and worship amongst themselves, crying to the Lord to raise them up Apostles, Evangelists, Prophets, Pastors and Teachers, and Elders and Deacons, and the other office-bearers in his house'.[83]

This was followed in June by 'The Responsibility of a Baptized Man, of a Preacher of the Gospel, and of a Pastor in Christ's Flock, to Christ and the Church', which elaborates and applies ideas already given expression in his *Lectures on Revelation*.[84] Irving has in view the instruction given to the Presbytery of Annan to investigate his teaching, and argues in this paper that as baptized he is responsible only to the church where he is at present; as a pastor, he is directly responsible to Christ.[85] In all cases, his responsibility to God is paramount. As for his ministerial status, that did not come ultimately from the presbytery: 'They did not give it; they did but discern that God had given it; and that which God hath given He only can revoke'.[86] He can thus reject the General Assembly's claim to jurisdiction over him as usurpation and refuse to submit to it. The determinations of presbyteries and synods are binding only as far as pastors see them to be conformable to the mind of Christ. Since, in his opinion, God had given up on the presbyteries, faithful ministers should quietly withdraw, pastor their people, mourn in prayer over the

---

[80] Ibid. cxxii–cxxiii.

[81] Ibid. cxviii.

[82] *MW* 5 (1832), 84–115; also published separately (Greenock: R. B. Lusk, 1832); references are to the latter.

[83] Ibid. 23.

[84] *MW* 6 (1832), 430-50.

[85] Recognition of this had helped him and his flock to remain steadfast when he was put out of the Presbytery of London: *PW*, 2.86.

[86] Ibid. 437; cf. *PW*, 1.240.

state of the church, and lead their flocks into the truth. Significantly, he signs the article as 'Pastor of Christ's Flock in London', indicative of the way his remnant ecclesiology was developing.

* * *

After the Assembly concluded, the focus of the early morning meetings at Regent Square shifted to prayer for the outpouring of the Holy Spirit and spiritual gifts.[87] At these meetings Irving would call on anyone known to him to read the Scriptures and pray, whether they were a member of his church or not, minister or layman.[88] A regular attender that summer describes the proceedings:

> the morning prayers were composed of three services (each about half an hour's duration), the first of which was conducted by a person called on by the pastor or president; the second by any person present who desired to undertake the office; and the third by the pastor, which he concluded with the usual blessing. Each of these leaders was, for the service, considered the *mouth* of the congregation; and, having selected a psalm, which the whole assembly (generally about seventy or eighty in number) joined in singing, he read a chapter of the Bible, and offered an extempore prayer.[89]

Irving tested the gifts and the gifted persons, seeking to establish that the gifts were being exercised in conformity with Scripture, that the persons were living godly lives, and that everything upheld sound doctrine. Only when he was satisfied would he allow the gifts to be exercised in public – but by now he was not so much cautious as convinced of the reality of what was taking place, and thus his approach shifted from evaluation to preparing his flock for the eventual public exercise of gifts which to all but the gifted would be totally unlike anything they had ever witnessed. Indeed, by the summer, inspired utterances complained that he was hindering the exercise of the gifts. The first utterance at the early morning prayer meeting occurred late in the summer of 1831; soon after, Irving decided to go against the advice of the Trustees by allowing the gifts to be exercised at the prayer meetings, so that the

---

[87] Oliphant, *Life*, 316; Rossteuscher, 'Rebuilding', fols 241–2.

[88] Robert Baxter, *Narrative of Facts, Characterizing the Supernatural Manifestations, in Members of Mr. Irving's Congregation, and Other Individuals, in England and Scotland, and Formerly in the Writer Himself* (London: James Nisbet, 1833), 12.

[89] George Pilkington, *The Unknown Tongues Discovered to be English, Spanish, and Latin; and the Rev. Edw. Irving proved to be Erroneous in attributing their Utterance to the Influence of the Holy Spirit: Also a Private Arrangement in his Closet, Previous to a Prayer Meeting and Consultation in the Vestry, to which the Writer was invited by Mr. Irving, because he believed him to be in 'the Spirit,' and prayed that he might receive the Gift of Interpretation; Various interesting Colloquies between the Writer and Mr. Irving and his Followers; and Observations, which manifestly show that they are all under a Delusion* (2nd edn, London: Field & Bull, 1831), 7n.

congregation could have opportunity to observe them before they occurred in the regular services.[90]

Not all were sympathetic. James Simpson recorded that at the house meeting on 25 June Irving read 1 Corinthians 14; many critical remarks were made by those present, but a manifestation from Mrs Caird exhorted them to put away criticism. More formal criticism was also being voiced. On 27 July Simpson attended a meeting of the Guardians of the Caledonian Asylum, which had been called to obtain a vote by subscribers to sanction removal of its boys from attending Irving's services. Although it failed, the criticism would develop into something more serious.[91] It was not long before James Nisbet, one of Irving's elders, was contemplating resignation, not only on account of the manifestations but also because of Irving's theological views. Nisbet's theological unease was triggered by the criticisms of the Church of Scotland's doctrinal standards expressed in Irving's *Confessions of Faith*, and Irving defended his action in a letter of 27 September by arguing that every church allowed men a measure of latitude to comment on the deficiencies of its standards. As for the manifestations:

> I have great tenderness for the scruples of a Brother on the subject of the manifestations, and while I as a responsible man and a Minister of the Lord Jesus Christ do plainly and honestly express & maintain my own opinion, I will never thereby involve any Elder or member of my flock in the consequences of my opinion and faith though I may long & labour to bring them to the same because I believe it both to be true and important.

Irving exhorted him not to act hastily but to be open, and especially to wait until he had finished the exposition of the gifts which he had begun on Wednesday evenings.[92] However, events would confirm Nisbet in his opposition.

* * *

There were many accounts of what happened when the manifestations first appeared in public worship at Regent Square; most were unsympathetic and consequently skewed in their presentation. It may therefore be worth offering an alternative and less readily accessible but just as significant eyewitness account, a letter from John Tudor to Robert Baxter penned a few days after the first manifestation during Sunday

---

[90] Some sources date this to 25 August: Robert Baxter, *Irvingism, in its Rise, Progress, and Present State* (London: James Nisbet, 1836), 16; [Edward Trimen], 'Rise and Progress of the Work of the Lord' (typescript, n.d.), 53. Another source, however, gives this as the date of the schoolmaster Taplin's first utterance, locating it at Irving's house: [Boase], *Supplementary Narrative*, 785. Others place it in September: Gordon Strachan, 'Carlyle, Irving, and the "Hysterical Women"', *Carlyle Annual* 12 (1991), 17–32, at 20; cf. Copinger, 'Annals', 22; Rossteuscher, 'Rebuilding', fols 243–4. Most give Taplin as the speaker, though Strachan states that it was a Miss Dixon.

[91] James Simpson, 'J. G. S. Journals 1806 to 1830', 27 June 1831, 29 July 1831.

[92] Edinburgh, EUL, MS Dc.4.103, Irving to James Nisbett [sic], 27 September 1831.

worship on 16 October. (Tudor would become an apostle in the new church, and Baxter was about to achieve great influence as a prophet.)

> You know how diligently Mr Irving & his church have been waiting for the gifts of the Spirit, you know also that Mr Irving thought it disorderly that they should be manifested on the Lord's day when the church was assembled for the service of God, but that he considered our morning prayer meetings an occasion when they might properly be exercised, though he did not see it right to advise the women to speak even there, & Miss Emily Cardale rushed out into the vestry that she might disburden herself of a message from the Lord, without doing offence to Mr Irving whom she considered as set over the house of the Lord. I was in still more difficulty than Mr Irving, seeing the necessity of keeping order, & not seeing any difference between the congregation on the Lord's day & that for morning worship, as both assembled under the Pastor & elders of the church; & not myself perceiving how the Pastor's praying & teaching singly in the former case, & calling upon others to join with him in leading the worship in the latter, changed the principle so far as to allow interruption in the latter but not in the former. Things went on as when you were in London till the Sunday before last Octr 16. 1831 a day which I think will be memorable in the history of the Church. Mr Taplin & Miss Hall had both felt pressed in Spirit to speak on the preceding Sunday, but not having received permission from Mr Irving held their peace. On the 16th however, Miss Hall again feeling the power upon her, went out of the church into the vestry,[93] after Mr Irving had finished reading the chapter in the morning service, & there she broke forth very loud, & before the door could be shut, I heard the words 'How dare ye' & I understand she went on to condemn the daring to suppress the voice of the Spirit in the congregation but the sound of the voice alone was heard in the church & not the words uttered[.] There was some agitation in the congregation, but Mr Irving calmed it by saying that she was one of those persons upon whom the Lord had bestowed a gift, but that he had not seen it his duty to allow the ordinary service of the Lord's day to be broken in upon but had desired them to restrain the utterance: but that he did now feel it to be a most unseemly thing, that any one should be constrained to flee from a Christian congregation thus; because the Lord would not suffer her to be silent, & they would not hear the Lord's message. He then gave out a suitable Psalm, & instead of continuing his discourse as usual on Ephesians, he opened the first half of the XIIth of 1 Cor, & nothing more took place in the morning.[94]
> In the evening, before beginning the service, Mr Irving stated from the pulpit, that he felt as if he had done wrong in suppressing what he believed to be the voice of God any where; but that he had been greatly perplexed & had chosen to cast himself upon the mercy of God rather than of men, in rather risquing [sic] offending him by being too slow in obeying, than offending cruel & bigotted man in being

---

[93] Apparently this complied with an order made by the session: James Simpson, 'J. G. S. Journals 1806 to 1830', 17 October 1831.

[94] According to another member of the congregation, Irving explained that 'he had been for some time considering the propriety of introducing it; but, though satisfied of the correctness of such a measure, he was afraid of dispersing the flock: nevertheless, as it was now brought forward by God's will, he felt it his duty to submit': Pilkington, *Unknown Tongues*, 10.

too hasty, & if he had offended he prayed the Good God to pardon.[95] He said he thought himself bold, but he was not bold enough to resist God, & therefore he called upon those to whom God had given his gift to search themselves thoroughly, to assure themselves that the power & the impulse was of God & not of themselves, & if they could not restrain it, then they ought not to rush out from the house of God where his voice might be heard nor might the congregation to be surprised at hearing the voice of that God whom they continually professed to come up to meet & hold communion with in his own house. The service then went on as usual & Mr Irving discoursed from the latter half of 1 Cor XII, at the end of which while he was alluding to the occurrence of the morning, Mr Taplin broke out in a tongue & concluded in these words in English 'Do you fly from the voice of God, when he is in the midst of you! Where then will you fly in the day of judgement?' At the first sounds of his voice there was much confusion from great numbers rising to ascertain the cause or see the person; & the loudness & unknown sounds occasioned such agitation & rustling, that the English was heard imperfectly, but after Mr Irving had tranquilized the people, he repeated the words, & made some suitable remarks. A few went out of the church during the first alarm, & some more during the singing of the Psalm but nine tenths or perhaps more of the congregation not only remained but seemed greatly impressed, & in anything rather than a scoffing mood. Since that time there has been speaking continually at the morning prayers & multitudes regularly attend. There was no speaking last Sunday [23 October] but very crowded congregations to hear discourses from Mr Irving of more than his usual power & demonstration, as you would expect. His session of Elders & Deacons met twice last week, to deliberate on the course to be now pursued; & they have resolved not to put down the voice of the Spirit either on the Lord's day or at any other time, only recommending the greatest care & vigilance to the gifted persons; to be stewards & ministers of the gift & not to let it have Lordship over them; lest the gift itself should be a bondage & a snare, instead of a privilege; lest the gift should be made an idol, & put in the place of the Lord & giver; lest they should become passive irresponsible tools, instead of active & accountable servants to do the will of the Lord.[96]

A less sympathetic observer claimed that in the confusion of that first Sunday evening service, some thought a murder had been committed and one man called to the pew openers and the beadle to stop the perpetrator from escaping;

it would be impossible to describe the confusion produced by this display of fanaticism. There was, indeed, in the strange unearthly sound and extraordinary power of voice enough to appal the heart of the most stout-hearted! A great part of the congregation standing upon the seats, to ascertain the cause of alarm, and the Rev. Gentleman, standing with arms extended, and occasionally beckoning them to silence, formed a scene which, perhaps, partook as much of the ridiculous as of the sublime! No attempt was made to stop the individual, and after two or three minutes

---

[95] That afternoon, Miss Cardale had declared 'in the power' that the church had been resisting the Holy Spirit: James Simpson, 'J. G. S. Journals 1806 to 1830', 17 October 1831.

[96] Edinburgh, Banner of Truth: J. O. Tudor to Robert Baxter, 26 October 1831.

he became exhausted, and sat down, and then the Rev. Gentleman concluded the service. Many were so alarmed, and others so disgusted, that they did not return again into the church; others formed themselves into groups at the entry of the church, and discussed the propriety of the Rev. Gentleman suffering the exhibition; and altogether a sensation was produced which will not be soon forgotten by those present.[97]

It is a measure of the strength of the friendship between Irving and Carlyle that even their inability to understand each other's view of the tongues did not end it. Yet it is noteworthy that this episode put more strain on the relationship than had Carlyle's declaration that he had abandoned orthodox Christian faith. Whilst the latter remained respectful towards those who were serious and balanced in their religious practice (few though they were in his view), he felt unable to regard the tongues-speakers in this light. This disagreement brought out the difference in their world-views, with Irving espousing an interventionist understanding of God's activity in human history which Carlyle could not accept.

The evening after Miss Hall broke the silence, the Carlyles paid a call on Irving, unaware of what had happened. The Irvings were hosting a meeting of gifted persons, and

As we talked a moment with Irving who had come down to us, there rose a shriek in the upper story of the house, and presently he exclaimed, '*There* is one prophecying [sic]; come and hear her!' we hesitated to go, but he forced us up into a back-room, and there we could hear the wretched creature raving like one possessed; *hoo*ing and *ha*-ing, and talking *as* sensibly as one would do with a pint of brandy in his stomach; till after some ten minutes she seemed to grow tired, and became silent. Nothing so shocking and altogether unspeakably deplorable was it ever my lot to hear. Poor Jane was on the verge of fainting; and did not recover the whole night.[98]

A few days later, Carlyle wrote to his brother: 'Poor George ... spoke to us of it almost with tears in his eyes; and earnestly entreated me to *deal* with his Brother; which, when he comes hither (by appointment on Tuesday) I partly mean to attempt, tho' now I fear it will be useless.'[99] Indeed it was, as he informed his mother:

Irving comes but little in our way; and one does not like to go and seek him in his own house, in a whole posse of enthusiasts, ranters and silly women. He was here once, taking tea, since that work of the 'Tongues' began: I told him with great earnestness my deepseated unhesitating conviction that it was *no* special work of the Holy Spirit, or of any Spirit save of that black frightful unclean one that dwells

---

[97] An Earnest Contender for 'The Faith which was Once Delivered to the Saints', *The Unknown Tongues!! &c. or, the Rev. Edward Irving and the Rev. Nicholas Armstrong arraigned at the Bar of the Scriptures of Truth, and found 'Guilty.' To which are added, Two Letters by the Rev. H. B. Bulteel, M.A. late Curate of St. Ebbe's, Oxford* (6th edn, London: William Kidd, 1832), 6.

[98] *CL*, 6.25: Carlyle to Margaret A. Carlyle, 20 October 1831.

[99] Ibid. 33: Carlyle to John A. Carlyle, 21 October 1831.

in Bedlam. He persists mi[l]dly-obstinate in his Course; greatly strengthened therein by his wife, who is reckoned the beginner of it all.[100]

Carlyle later recalled that when he went to remonstrate with Irving, he challenged his friend's biblicism, arguing that Irving was building far too much on a small part of Scripture, and that in any case God did not speak only in an ancient book. Irving, he argued, should be looking forwards and reckoning with the realities and challenges of contemporary society, not back to the New Testament era.[101] Irving's closest friend feared not merely that he would lose his congregation, but that he might lose his mental balance. Jane, for her part, considered it

> truly distressing to see a man of such talents and such really good and pious dispositions as Mr Irving given up to an infatuation so absurd – ready to sacrifice to it his dearest friends, his reputation, all his worldly prospects. Most people think it all a humbug – which is quite reasonable in those who do not *know* him. but [sic] a man more sincere in his professions does not exist.[102]

Therein lies a crucial point: if Irving had not been so 'good' and had possessed less integrity, he would not have persisted in acknowledging the gifts at such cost to himself – it was his consistency of character which made him so faithful to what he believed was God's voice.

How did Irving handle the appearance of the gifts in Sunday worship? Irving broke from his regular course of exposition to preach on the issues raised. We have already seen that on the first Sunday he changed his sermon topic in order to expound the teaching of 1 Corinthians 12 regarding the gifts. Several of his sermons appeared in print, assured of wide circulation. On 23 October, he preached in the morning on 'The duty of importuning the Father for the Gifts of the Holy Ghost'.[103] Before the service began, he explained what the tongues were and how they had come to be manifested among his congregation. The gifted persons were bearing witness to what he was already preaching – the nearness of the Second Coming – and were sent to bid everyone to prepare for that day. During the course of the service, he stated that 'no person with whose spiritual qualifications he was not well acquainted, would be allowed to display the gift of tongues before the congregation'.[104] The following morning's prayer meeting saw the body of the church filled with 'respectable people' hoping to hear the tongues. A reporter, after giving examples of the utterances, was

---

[100] Ibid. 41: Carlyle to Margaret A. Carlyle, 10 November 1831.

[101] Thomas Carlyle, *Reminiscences,* ed. C. E. Norton (London: J. M. Dent, 1932), 299.

[102] *CL,* 6.35: Jane Welsh Carlyle to Helen Welsh, 26 October [1831].

[103] *The Pulpit,* no. 466 (27 October 1831), 117–26. However, a newspaper report stated that he preached from Joel 2.28: 'The Rev. Edward Irving and the Unknown Tongue', *Caledonian Mercury,* 29 October 1831 (taken from the *Morning Herald).* Possibly one formed the sermon and the other the exposition.

[104] 'The Rev. Edward Irving and the Unknown Tongue', *Caledonian Mercury,* 29 October 1831.

constrained to confess: 'These unknown tongues are fearful matters for a reporter.'[105] Within a few weeks, almost a thousand people were attending the prayer meetings.[106] It should not be forgotten that around this time a cholera outbreak was causing great apprehension.[107] Irving's reaction was that 'Civil war and pestilence are abroad; but have faith, my brethren. The cholera shall rage throughout the country, and it will approach to the very gates of our city, but will not enter.'[108]

On 26 October, Irving preached at the midweek service on 'The Gift of Tongues Enjoyed in the Church'. Tongues were not intended for preaching to the nations, but as a refutation of infidelity – not by means of rational arguments but by a church doing works of power. In an utterance, the unknown tongue was the sign of inspiration; and the known tongue provided the content. They were loud because they were intended to awaken those asleep – presumably spiritually.[109] However, James Simpson recorded the divisions occasioned in the session by the tongues: Irving, along with Duncan Mackenzie and David Ker, thought that the gifts should not be restrained at any time. By contrast, Nisbet was 'in a very irritated state of Mind towards Mr Irving and all who profess to have received the Gifts of the Spirit'.[110]

The Sunday services attracted much greater congregations than the prayer meetings, Rossteuscher stating that those unable to gain entrance 'continued to throng the neighbouring streets till long after the commencement of the service'.[111] The packed congregations presented a serious hazard, and concern lest the catastrophe at Kirkcaldy be repeated may have been a factor in Irving's decision to restrict the exercise of the gifts to the prayer meetings.[112] *The Times* urged the curious to stay away, not only to avoid countenancing what it considered a disgraceful exhibition but also lest they become infected by the contagion.[113] On the other hand, a believer would undoubtedly have felt themselves back in the days of the Acts of the Apostles. From whatever viewpoint, it was a dramatic time for the church.

On 30 October he explained why he dared not continue to forbid the exercise of the gifts during Sabbath worship. When someone interrupted his sermon, Irving asked that he be stopped, asserting: 'All persons who speak in the Tongues are

---

[105] 'Specimens of the Unknown Tongues', *Caledonian Mercury*, 29 October 1831.

[106] Oliphant, *Life*, 326: Irving to M. N. McDonald, 7 November 1831; cf. David Brown, 'Personal Reminiscences of Edward Irving', *The Expositor*, 3rd series, 6 (1887), 216–28, 257–73, at 268.

[107] On 18 October the Privy Council issued instructions regarding the action to be taken by communities to inhibit its spread: Norman Longmate, *King Cholera: The Biography of a Disease* (London: Hamish Hamilton, 1966), 9.

[108] *Belfast News-Letter*, 18 November 1831.

[109] 'The Gift of Tongues Enjoyed in the Church', *The* Pulpit, nos 468 (3 November 1831), 154–9; 469 (10 November 1831), 165–9.

[110] James Simpson, 'J. G. S. Journals 1806 to 1830', 28 October 1831.

[111] Rossteuscher, 'Rebuilding', fol. 249.

[112] Cf. ibid. fol. 250.

[113] 'The Rev. Mr. Irving', *The Times*, 29 October 1831, 5; cf. *Caledonian Mercury*, 14 November 1831.

known to *me;* all others are but brawlers.'[114] Unfortunately for Irving, his opponents had a rather different definition of who constituted a brawler, as his trial before the London Presbytery would demonstrate.

A report in *The Pulpit* stated that congregations were rapidly increasing, and that Irving was available in the vestry at Regent Square from 10 until 12 each morning to speak to doubters. It went on to quote an advertisement for the first number of a new work by Irving, *The Day of Pentecost,* which was expected to run to three or four more numbers, published at intervals. The first was being published now in order to 'prevent, as far as he is able, the hideous ruin upon which the church and nation are precipitating themselves by blaspheming the work of the Holy Ghost'.[115] In the event, no more were published, but in this one Irving explained the importance which the baptism of the Holy Ghost had assumed in his thinking about the work of Christ, the privileges of the church, and the nature of Christian experience. The great office of Christ which God had commissioned John the Baptist to herald was that of baptizing with the Holy Ghost. Christ's life, death and resurrection were the means to this end, and it was by the baptism with the Holy Ghost that Christ's resurrection life was communicated to the church.[116] The 'standing sign' of this baptism was speaking with tongues; those who believed would do the same works as Christ did on earth, and greater ones too.[117] Irving explained speaking with tongues as being a mode of prophecy, and as subsidiary to the latter gift:

> accordingly we find, in all the instances which in divers places have now occurred of this gift, that the person doth only, as it were, introduce his discourse with some words, or at most sentences, of the unknown tongue, and straightway flows on in a strain of English words, most easy to be understood, uttered with great power, and commonly enforced with frequent repetitions. It is nothing more than prophecy, for which the people are prepared by a few words of an unknown tongue, that they may assuredly know that the power which is upon the speaker is not power of his own, but power of God.[118]

A time of crisis was approaching. Once the full manifestation of the Spirit was in evidence, the church would have to decide whether to accept or reject it; the latter course would lead to everlasting perdition.[119]

In the midst of this ferment came the half-yearly Communion season. Irving reported that there had been almost a hundred new communicants during the previous

---

[114] Earnest Contender, *Unknown Tongues!!*, 16–18; this was apparently lifted without acknowledgement from a report in *The Pulpit.*

[115] 'Further Particulars of the Rev. E. Irving and the Unknown Tongues', *The Pulpit*, no. 468 (3 November 1831, 159–60.

[116] Edward Irving, *The Day of Pentecost, or the Baptism with the Holy Ghost* (n.pl.: n.p., 1831), 2, 4–5.

[117] Ibid. 28, 35–7.

[118] Ibid. 65.

[119] Ibid. 109.

six months, although some of his congregation had drawn back because of the gifts. Noting that the Holy Spirit had always allowed the service to be completed before any manifestations occurred, he recorded that the previous evening Brown had preached from Psalm 91 about the cholera to a congregation which probably numbered three thousand; two manifestations afterwards had described it as a judgement, especially on those who scoffed at God's truth.[120] That scoffing was no figment of Irving's imagination. The following Sunday evening, an utterance followed Irving's sermon;

> A person in the gallery called out 'Blasphemy!' many hissed, and a strange disturbance took place, which cannot be described. A variety of persons barricaded the doors on both sides of the gallery: about fifty persons then commenced a general harangue, and called upon Mr. Irving to discuss the subject with them, which he declined. During all this disorder, the Rev. Gentleman commenced his prayer that the tumult of the people might be stayed.[121]

According to James Simpson, a large number of supporters of the atheist lecturers Richard Carlile and Robert Taylor had come to disturb the service. Apparently about fifty supporters of these two men heckled Irving for forty-five minutes, and when calm had been restored Irving advised the congregation that the tongues would henceforth be exercised only in the early prayer meetings.[122] Isabella Irving told a friend that in fact this had been the only occasion when a disturbance occurred in the church.[123]

The following Sunday, 20 November, Irving preached three times; each of his chosen passages related to the question of the gifts. His morning passage was John 16, in which Jesus spoke of the ministry of the Holy Spirit in and through his disciples. In the afternoon he expounded Malachi 3 (a prophecy of the one who should prepare the way of the Lord) and preached from John 7.37–9 (Jesus' promise that whoever believed in him would receive 'rivers of living water' within themselves, an image of the Holy Spirit). At the evening service he expounded Jesus' teaching in Mark 13 about the events associated with his Second Coming, and preached on Isaiah 28.9–14, in which hearing people speak in an unknown tongue was said to be a sign of God's judgement upon his disobedient people.[124] The gifts themselves were heard again that day. In the morning, Irving read 1 Corinthians 14 and paused; a manifestation from Miss Cardale followed, urging the congregation not

---

[120] Oliphant, *Life*, 326: Irving to M. N. McDonald, 7 November 1831.

[121] Earnest Contender, *Unknown Tongues!!*, 14–15; quotation at 15. Another report had a man interrupting Miss Hall and being invited by Irving to meet him in the vestry after the service: 'Disturbance at Mr. Irving's Church', *The Record*, no. 405 (14 November 1831).

[122] James Simpson, 'J. G. S. Journals 1806 to 1830', 16 November 1831; cf. *Newcastle Courant*, 26 November 1831.

[123] Terling, Terling Place, Strutt letters: Isabella Irving to Mrs Probyn, 20 January 1832.

[124] Oliphant, *Life*, 333: Irving to William Hamilton, 21 November 1831.

to despise the word of God. During the singing of a psalm, Archibald Horn, one of the session, came to the pulpit and asked Irving's permission to read from the Bible his reasons for leaving the church; on being refused, 'he went into vestry, took his hat, and went right down the church'. That evening, Irving judged it wiser to keep the doors locked, even though people outside were beating on them. According to an account in *The Pulpit*, Irving stated after preaching that to keep the promise he made the previous week, there had been no manifestations that night, but they would be allowed once again, as tongues were intended for scoffers (such as those who had created the previous week's disturbance) as well as believers.[125] As he explained the week after,

> the ordinance that I have set forth is, that after the reading of this chapter, and after the sermon, there shall be a pause; during which the church and congregation shall sink into silence and wait on the Lord, considering the things that they have heard; and, if it please the Lord to speak to us, listening reverently to what is said. I have required the *five persons*, whom I have proved in this church, and who have my authority, who are covered with my authority (which is no less than the authority of Him who gave me authority in the church) – I have placed them on my right hand and on my left, in the front of the gallery, to speak from thence, if it please the Spirit to speak by them.[126]

Apparently, it was when Irving was unable to secure police assistance to maintain order (because they insisted on being allowed to arrest any other speaker) that he decided to allow the gifts, trusting God to protect the congregation.[127]

Mrs Oliphant pointed out that most of the gifted persons at Regent Square were newcomers.[128] By contrast, many of Irving's established flock were disturbed by these events. James Simpson, whose wife was one of the 'gifted persons', had spoken with many members who thought that the gifts were not of God. He had been unable to convince his pastor to restrain them on Sundays, and now feared the break-up of the congregation.[129] By the end of November, it was being reported that most of Irving's elders and deacons had left in protest against the tongues.[130]

On 19 November the Trustees met in response to the previous Sunday's tumult. Irving was present at his own request (normally he did not attend such meetings) and stated his views on tongues and prophecy in church life.[131] In a letter to his brother-in-law, who was away from London, he explained that he had outlined to them his

---

[125] Ibid; cf. 'Scotch Church, Regent Square', *The Pulpit*, no. 472 (1 December 1831), 228.

[126] *Morning Service at the National Scotch Church, Regent Square, Sunday, Nov. 27, 1831* (n.pl.: n.p., [1832]), 30.

[127] Cf. Rossteuscher, 'Rebuilding', fol. 250.

[128] Oliphant, *Life*, 295, 323.

[129] James Simpson, 'J. G. S. Journals 1806 to 1830', 12 November 1831.

[130] *John Bull*, 28 November 1831, 379.

[131] LMA/4358/A/006, 'Trustees Minute Book' (1825–48), fols 24–5; Hair, *Regent Square*, 112–13.

understanding of the Trust Deed as giving him sole responsibility for all aspects of worship. After discussion, they adjourned the meeting until the following Tuesday.[132] As Irving did not plan to attend, he wrote to them outlining his order for the public exercise of the gift of prophecy and reiterating his belief that it was the minister's prerogative to order all aspects of public worship. If they could not support what he was doing, he urged them not to oppose it lest they be found fighting against God. If they were still minded to take steps to prohibit the exercise of the gifts, he requested a 'friendly conference' with them first. With the letter, he sent each of them a copy of *The Day of Pentecost*.[133] The Trustees welcomed his intent to seek a legal ruling and called a friendly meeting with him.[134] What happened next will be revealed in the following chapter.

It was rapidly becoming evident that although there were claims to manifest gifts of tongues and prophecy, the concomitant gift of discernment of spirits had not been given, and therefore Irving and the gifted persons were struggling when it came to testing claimants to the gifts. This is especially clear in what Timothy Stunt has called 'The Case of the Gloucestershire Clergyman'.[135] The clergyman in question was the Reverend E. C. Probyn, the evangelical Vicar of Longhope and Rector of Abinghall. He, with his wife and seven-year-old son Julian, visited Irving's church at the point in October 1831 when the gifts were first manifested in the Sunday services. Julian's twin sister, Juliana, had been left at home in the care of the family governess, Miss Banks, who was given to religious enthusiasm. While the rest of the family were in London, Juliana spoke 'in the Spirit', and the parents when they returned encouraged her. Julian also began to prophesy, which Stunt suggests may have been a case of twins communicating through a secret language. Irving explained what happened:

> One child who received the Spirit there, and after her, her twin brother, son and daughter (about eight years old, twins) of a clergyman, a particular friend of mine, both spake with tongues and prophesied. The Spirit betrayed himself, would not

---

[132] Oliphant, *Life*, 333: Irving to William Hamilton, 21 November 1831. The Hamiltons would spend some months in Scotland, where William consulted with Isabella's father. When he reappeared at Regent Square, he was said to have looked ten years older: ibid. 332, 334.

[133] Irving to the Trustees of the National Scotch Church, received 22 November 1831 (in private hands); reproduced in Oliphant, *Life*, 335–6.

[134] 'Trustees Minute Book' (1825–48), fols 28–9.

[135] This paragraph draws on Henry Drummond to J. J. Strutt, 10 November 1831; Isabella Irving to Rev. Probyn, 25 November 1831 (both among the Strutt letters); 'Spirit of Prophecy and Gift of Tongues', *Monmouthshire Merlin*, 12 November 1831; 'A Lying Devil', *Monmouthshire Merlin*, 19 November 1831; Stunt, '"Trying the Spirits"' (*JEH*). Cf. idem, 'Trying the Spirits: Irvingite Signs and the Test of Doctrine', in Kate Cooper and Jeremy Gregory, eds, *Signs, Wonders, Miracles: Representations of Divine Power in the Life of the Church*, Studies in Church History 41 (Woodbridge: Boydell, 2005), 400–9; Anon., 'Spiritual Gifts and Demoniacal Possession', *MW* 5 (1832), 145–60, at 152–4.

take the test (1 John iv. 1–3), forbad to marry, and played many more antics, and was at last expelled. It was a true possession of Satan, preached a wondrously sweet Gospel, had a desire to be consulted about everything, disliked prayer, praise, and reading the Scriptures, and otherwise wrought wondrously.[136]

Lest we exaggerate the influence exercised by the children, we should note that it was Wolfe, Probyn's curate, who informed the congregation on 30 October that Christ would return that week; millennarian friends in Gloucester urged the family to give up all and emigrate to Jerusalem. They proceeded to distribute their possessions, guided by prophecy from the children. On the night of 7 November, Probyn's father employed constables to stop the party (about fifteen in number) if they attempted to leave. In sorting out the mess, Irving decided that the children's spirit must be tested, after he had met Miss Banks and learning that many of her prophecies had failed. On the evening of 7 November Julian had threatened the adults if they did so, and his father failed to stand up to him. The following morning, Wolfe adjured the spirit in Julian to confess Christ as having come in human flesh (cf. 1 John 4.1–6), which it refused to do; Wolfe then exorcized the children. Probyn, speaking in church the next Sunday, blamed it all on the Devil. In London, Irving called together a number of the gifted persons and other leaders and read them two letters from Probyn; Miss Cardale prophesied of their need for the gift of discernment, and others urged them to seek it. Irving also sought prophetic guidance from the Port Glasgow brethren. Stunt's conclusion is that in his letters during this period and after, Irving comes across as 'a realistic and consistent person, a man of principle struggling to find a place for the manifestations within the life of the Church and, at the same time, acutely aware of the need for pastoral discernment and restraint'.[137] The problem for Irving and his colleagues was that it was one thing to be aware of the need, and another to be equipped to meet it.

The need to be able to discern the spirits was also highlighted by those who claimed to have received a miraculous gift but then repudiated it, an early and celebrated instance being George Pilkington. A recent convert from Deism, he had attended Irving's early prayer meeting for almost three months before 16 October. In the weekday meetings he began to speak in interpretation of the utterances in tongues, but his gift was not recognized, and he was accused of attempting to interpret by his own understanding because he thought the tongues often sounded like snatches of foreign languages, which he then translated. Rejecting the gifts as being of human origin, he published an account of his experiences, *The Unknown Tongues Discovered to be English, Spanish, and Latin*. Appearing in mid-November 1831, it had gone into a sixth edition by the end of December.[138] In response, Irving explained that he had sought to help Pilkington ascertain whether or not his gift was genuine:

---

[136] Oliphant, *Life*, 2.212: Irving to M. N. Macdonald, 19 November 1831.
[137] Stunt, '"Trying the Spirits"' (*JEH*), 104.
[138] *The Times*, 19 November 1831, 3; 28 December 1831, 4.

After a few days' intercourse, I clearly made out, to the man's own satisfaction, that it was not a spiritual gift, but a delusion, arising partly from an unclean heart, partly from a confused head, and chiefly from an erroneous idea as to what the gift of interpretation consists in: and so I dismissed him with all loving-kindness and some exhortation, believing him to be a pious and well-principled man; nor had I any reason to suspect the contrary until I heard of his publication. The man can do us no harm, if he tell the truth. That he should do himself the harm of betraying private ministerial confidence, and speaking evil of those who sought his good, I sincerely regret; but do in some measure forgive it, as I have heard that he is in very needy circumstances, and published his book for bread.[139]

To Andrew Drummond, Pilkington's experience indicated the existence of 'an organised group, united on a given basis, and hostile to the intrusion of individuals and ideas out of harmony with its principles'.[140] We shall see later on that this may have been a factor in Irving's rejection of Jane Simpson's gift.

Other problems soon surfaced. Women had initially been allowed to prophesy regarding matters of church government, but once a man had been raised up to prophesy, they were only permitted to give 'refreshing streams'.[141] A Mr W. faked the gift of prophecy in order to obtain business.[142] Ultimately, the need for discernment of spirits was met by the assertion of the superiority of apostles, something to which that Irving found difficult to submit, although in theory he accepted it.

---

[139] One of the Congregation of the National Scotch Church, *A Word for Inquiry previous to Decision in the Matter of the present Manifestations of, or Pretensions to, the Gifts of Speaking with Unknown Tongues and Prophesying, with an Appendix containing Extracts from the Writings of the Rev. Edward Irving, and his rejected Letter to the Editor of the Times &c. &c.* (2nd edn, London: W. Harding, 1832), 52.

[140] Drummond, *Irving*, 173. Drummond's solid account of Irving's life offers a valuable corrective to Mrs Oliphant's lack of theological grasp, but includes extensive discussion of the psychology of tongues-speaking and other charismatic phenomena which now comes across as hopelessly dated. Moreover, he has been accused of having 'virtually psychologised the man out of existence', and his biography condemned as 'a direct, and intelligent, rational attack upon Pentecostalism *per se*': Andrew Walker, 'Will no one stand up for Edward Irving?', *The Listener*, 6 December 1984.

[141] Henry J. Marks, *Narrative of Henry John Marks, a Jew; now a Follower of the Lord Jesus Christ* (3rd edn, (London: the author, 1842), 122–3.

[142] B. Shillingford, *Errors of Irvingism Exposed; or, Modern Popery Unmasked* (2nd edn, London: Ebenezer Palmer, 1836; first publ. 1831), 9n.

CHAPTER 18

The Presbytery moves against Irving, December 1831–May 1832

The winter of 1831–2 saw the manifestations continue at Regent Square, and gradually assume greater significance in terms of the way the congregation was run. Inevitably, therefore, the conflict between Irving and the Trustees would come to a head.

For the moment, however, things appeared to settle down; on 22 December *The Times* reported that the tongues had been heard again the previous Sunday after a gap of two or three weeks. Prayer meeting attendance also appears to have declined; on Thursday 15th, there had been a hundred and fifty to two hundred present, it being a day of humiliation on account of the differences between Irving and the Trustees.[1] *The Times* had taken a consistently critical line regarding the manifestations, and Irving offered it two or three letters setting out the facts connected with the work, probably in an attempt to set the record straight; the editor promised to try to make room for them, but they did not appear.[2] However, we have already noticed the three articles on this theme which appeared in *Fraser's Magazine* during 1832; the first was Irving's initial rejected letter of 27 December 1831. Irving had planned to send the newspaper a second letter on the nature of the gift of tongues, and a third on its proper use in the church; these formed the second and third of the articles as published.[3]

During this period several of the prophets caused Irving considerable heartache, most notably Miss Hall (who had precipitated so much of the opposition by speaking on 16 October), Jane Simpson (whose gift was to be a factor in the deterioration of relationships between the gifted persons in Scotland and those in London), and Robert Baxter. We shall look at each case in turn.

---

[1] 'The Scotch Church', *The Times*, 22 December 1831, 3 (from *The Globe*).

[2] *The Times*, 5 December 1831, 3.

[3] Edward Irving, 'Facts connected with Recent Manifestations of Spiritual Gifts', *Fraser's Magazine* 4 (1831–2), 754–61; 5 (1832), 198–205, 316–20; cf. 'One of the Congregation of the National Scotch Church', *A Word for Inquiry previous to Decision in the Matter of the present Manifestations of, or Pretensions to, the Gifts of Speaking with Unknown Tongues and Prophesying, with an Appendix containing Extracts from the Writings of the Rev. Edward Irving, and his rejected Letter to the Editor of the Times &c. &c.* (2nd edn, London: W. Harding, 1832), 50–2.

Mary Hall was a governess in the household of Spencer Perceval, who had been to the fore in the public exercise of the gifts. In March 1832, she confessed that she had been faking them. John Tizard, who is otherwise unknown to us but in whose home she was staying at the time, wrote to Baxter:

> It has pleased the Lord in His great faithfulness completely to discover the heart of poor Mary Hall (who was during your last visit & still is remaining in my house) through a very powerful testimony from Mrs Caird & Miss Emily Cardale that the whole work of utterance in her has been entirely of the flesh. By degrees her own conscience has been fully convicted of it, & she is suffering in the flesh much bitterness & grief from the consequences. I fear that all her knowledge of the Lord has gone no deeper than the intellect, for her heart appears now to be quite shut up from the Lord. The whole work in her she sees plainly to have been nothing else than strong excitements in the flesh. ... It is remarkable that the first utterance in public at the Morning Prayer Meeting in Mr Irving's Church was by a Miss Dixon who it has since appeared has spoken only in the flesh, & the first utterance in the public Sunday Service was by poor Mary Hall, who now tells me that her own conscience shewed her at that very time that it was but the flesh. Even when Mr Irving had all the gifted persons together, & by the command of the Spirit from Miss E. Cardale tried them all, the flesh was sufficient to enable Mary Hall to confess equally with them as she herself now acknowledges.[4]

Once again, the lack of ability to 'discern the spirits' had been demonstrated, as had the inadequacy of the tests devised by Irving. A Catholic Apostolic writer recorded how Irving dealt with her:

> Miss Hall's case had nothing supernatural in it_ It was a mixture of fleshly excitement & sinful imposture & imitation, which she confessed _ & was very penitent _ It was while Mr Irving was still in the Scotch Church, & tho' he was very kind & pastoral in his treatment of her, yet he followed the custom of Presbyterians _ & would not admit her again to the Holy Communion, till she had, (as I heard him express it), 'borne the rebuke of the Church'.
>
> And on the day he had fixed for this, she was called out by name, & stood in the middle of the Church, while he spoke to her of her grievous & blasphemous sin_ She was afterwards received again to Communion_ & remained a penitent & faithful member of his flock.[5]

More difficult to deal with was Jane Simpson: her case shows the difficulty in which Irving found himself trying to weigh up competing claims to represent the voice of God. Jane recorded that Mrs Caird came to London in April 1831, and that she [Jane] was filled with the Holy Spirit one Sabbath following a conversation in which she exhorted Jane to plead with God for this. Thereafter the Spirit's

---

[4] Edinburgh, Banner of Truth: John Tizard to Robert Baxter, 26 March 1832.

[5] Alnwick Castle, DFP, C/13/2, undated ms note. However, another note claimed that 'Miss Hall – declared she too had been deluded, left the Body, & adopted a different course of life': DFP, C/13/4, undated ms note.

inspiration was manifested in singing God's praise but Jane received no gift of supernatural utterance until she met Mrs Caird again in November at the Irvings'. At a later meeting, Mrs Caird said to Jane, 'ye are the Temple of the holy Ghost now', and Jane appears to have begun to speak two or three weeks later. Shortly after, Mrs Caird and Irving 'pressed the exercise of this gift in Church' and Jane was assigned a seat at the front of the church with those recognized as prophets. Being of a timid disposition, she found this a trial. On the first morning she spoke in church, Miss Cardale had breakfast with her, warning her 'in the power' against trusting in the gift and advising her to be 'passive in the hands of Jesus'. The Cairds spent a day with Jane talking about Miss Hall, and Mary Caird was made to say to her, 'Jesus has had his arms around you[;] he would not suffer you to stumble'. A few days later, Miss Cardale advised Irving that Jane should only exercise her gift in his presence; he sent a note of this to her, calling her to be in church with the gifted persons as much as possible. Jane sought to comply.[6] Clearly some of the other gifted persons were less than encouraging towards Jane and her gift; things became more tense once she began to speak in public more frequently.

At the end of May, entertaining the Taplins and Irving one evening, James Simpson recorded:

> We had some conversation regarding the free use one of the Prophets in the Church has made of her Gift in reproving her fellow Prophets. I maintained that this [was] an abuse of the Gift, and Mr Irving held that it was a use sanction'd of God, 'Letting two or three speak and let the Rest discern' [1 Corinthians 14.29]. I believe this is, Discern the spiritual meaning and profit of the Utterances, and not as Mr Irving believes, a Discerning whether the Individual is speaking by the Power of God, the Devil, or the Flesh.[7]

The point at issue was whether the gift of discernment was inherent to that of prophecy, as the Simpsons believed, or a distinct gift which only some possessed, as Irving was arguing. If the latter was the case, then the prophets were more accountable, since their gift had to be approved by those able to discern its genuineness. The other gifted persons claimed to discern that Jane's gift was not genuine, a claim which she and her husband rejected, feeling themselves perfectly competent to ascertain that point and convinced that Jane's sense of the divine presence overrode whatever objections Irving and others might advance.

The best known of the three individuals was Robert Baxter (1802–89). An earnest and well-connected Evangelical with a growing law practice in Doncaster, he had been known to Irving since 1823. Before the gifts appeared in London, he had been permitted on occasion to conduct part of the early morning prayer meetings. In August 1831, he was arguing with Irving, speaking against the tongues, when an

---

[6] Edinburgh, NLS, Acc. 12489/10, [J. G. Simpson Journal] 27 March – 11 November [30 December] 1831, 30 December 1831.

[7] NLS, Acc. 12489/1, James Simpson, 'J. G. S. Journals 1806 to 1830', 31 May 1832.

utterance made him fall prostrate.[8] It was probably soon after this that Isabella Irving wrote to urge him to seek utterance from the Lord.[9] Although he appears to have begun to speak 'in the power' privately around that time, it was once he began to do so in public that he exercised enormous influence at Regent Square, though he was only in London occasionally. On 24 January Irving wrote: 'The Lord hath anointed Baxter of Doncaster after another kind, I think the apostolical; the prophetical being the ministration of the word, the apostolical being the ministration of the Spirit.'[10] Baxter, he informed Story, was one 'on whom the Lord has poured down his Spirit after a different kind from what we have hitherto seen amongst us'. After six months of private utterance, his mouth had been opened at the early service, apparently on 13 January. According to Irving, Baxter was saying that 'the two orders of witnesses were now present in the Church, the 1260 days of witnessing are begun, and that within three and a half years, the saints will be taken up, according to the 12th chapter of the Apocalypse'. Ordination by the visible church was 'cut short in judgment', and God was about to set forth 'a spiritual ministry' to replace it. Church and state were both accursed and would be destroyed; pestilence and sword were to come upon the nation but the saints (including the King) would be preserved; those looking for the second coming were to set their house in order. God, Irving announced, was preparing to do a great work in his congregation.[11]

Influenced by Baxter's prophecies, Irving began to preach 'the interpretation of the trumpets [Revelation 8–9], and the doctrine of the baptism by fire, and forthcoming apostolic mission'.[12] One Sunday, after an utterance from Baxter, Irving extolled him as a spiritual minister, he himself being only a fleshly one. As Baxter recalled, the utterances at Regent Square always distinguished the spiritual church and ministry from the visible, with the consequence that subsequent utterances disparaged the physical sacramental elements;[13] what mattered was the inner baptism of fire which would purge out all sin, not the outward baptism with water. Many of these themes would exercise a decisive influence on the thinking of the movement which later became the Catholic Apostolic Church, although it did not reject outward sacraments. Such was Irving's esteem for Baxter that he was ready to invite him to officiate in the pulpit and to be the congregation's pastor, but the Holy Ghost

---

[8] Edinburgh, NCL, Chalmers MSS, 4.179.8: Lord Elgin to Chalmers, 11 April [1832].

[9] Banner of Truth: Isabella Irving to Robert Baxter, 26 August 1831.

[10] Oliphant, *Life*, 2.234: Irving to M. N. Macdonald, 24 January 1832.

[11] Glasgow, University of Glasgow, University Library, MS DC21/1, Irvings to Robert Story, 27 January 1832; cf. Oliphant, *Life*, 343–4. Baxter offered a similar summary of the content of the utterances, which he noted as being taken up in Irving's preaching: *Irvingism, in its Rise, Progress, and Present State* (London: James Nisbet, 1836), 19–20.

[12] Robert Baxter, *Narrative of Facts, Characterizing the Supernatural Manifestations, in Members of Mr. Irving's Congregation, and Other Individuals, in England and Scotland, and Formerly in the Writer Himself* (London: James Nisbet, 1833), 71.

[13] Ibid. 77–8.

forbade it.[14] All the same, as Irving wrote, we 'much desire your reappearing in the midst of us with the full power of an apostle to minister the Spirit unto us by the laying on of hands'.[15]

Things did not proceed as expected, however: prophecy had indicated that after forty days Baxter would be filled with power to undertake his apostolic commission; when the fortieth day passed and nothing happened, daily prayer was made in Irving's church that Baxter 'might speedily receive the full endowment of an apostle'.[16] An utterance was given at home that 'the power was not given on the fortieth day because the church in London had failed in love towards the visible church, which God had cast off'.[17] Baxter, however, recanted, issuing two sensational works, a *Narrative of Facts* (1833) and *Irvingism* (1836). A cache of letters held by the Banner of Truth Trust in Edinburgh offers further evidence concerning his change of views. He came to believe that his first utterance had been by satanic power, and that the rest were human productions.

Baxter was led to investigate Irving's views more thoroughly by a Lichfield clergyman, Peter Blackburn, who argued that if Irving had been teaching error, as prophetic utterance had stated, it could not be the Holy Spirit speaking or he would have been rebuked. Baxter wrote to Irving with his conclusions, confident they would be accepted because Irving thought him destined to be an apostle.[18] Irving promptly laid Baxter's missive before Mrs Caird and Miss Cardale, 'two prophetesses of the Lord who have been his mouth of wisdom & of warning to me & my church in all perplexities'. In his reply to Baxter, Irving stated that he read this and another letter from Baxter to Mrs Caird, Miss Cardale and Isabella; utterance came through Miss Cardale that

> you [Baxter] had been snared, by departing from the word & the testimony; that I had maintained the truth, and that the Lord was well pleased with me for it; that I must not flinch now but be more bold for it than heretofore; that he had honoured me for it, and that I must not draw back; that in some words I had erred, and that the word of the Spirit by you was therefore true, and that if I waited upon the Lord he would shew me them by his Spirit, but that he had forgiven it because he knew my heart was right towards him; that I had maintained the truth; and must not draw back from maintaining it ...

---

[14] Anon., 'Mr. Irving's Church THE Sign of the Times', *MW* 6 (1832), 224–8, at 227.

[15] Banner of Truth: Irving to Baxter, postmarked and endorsed 2 March 1832; quoted in Baxter, *Irvingism*, 22.

[16] Baxter, *Narrative*, 82.

[17] Ibid. 89–90.

[18] Ibid. 101–2; Peter Blackburn, *Reasons for thinking Mr Irving deceived; or a Discussion of some Questions relating to the Gift of Tongues, in which the Statements of St Paul in 1 Cor. XIV. are carefully considered, and Mr Irving's Interpretation of them as set forth in the third Volume of the Morning Watch is examined and found erroneous* (2nd edn, Cambridge: J. G. & F. Rivington, 1834), i.

The general import of the utterances at this conference was that Baxter had sought to apply his own prophetic words using his understanding, and so had taken the reference to Irving's error as applying to whole of his book (presumably *The Day of Pentecost*) rather than to two particular sentences.[19]

Irving's reply to Baxter proved to be the key factor in opening his eyes: since it stated that the gifted persons had reacted against what Baxter had written, it was clear that the gifts were supporting Irving's views.[20] He travelled to London to inform Irving of his change of opinions, reaching him on 26 April, the day the latter's trial began.[21] He told Irving and Cardale, who was to be Irving's counsel during the trial, that 'we had all been speaking by a lying spirit, and not by the Spirit of the Lord'.[22] Irving's assistant David Brown was at Irving's house for breakfast after the usual prayer meeting, when a visitor was announced and Irving left the room for a few minutes to speak with him. On his return, he called the company to prayer, the burden of his heart being:

> Have mercy, Lord, on thy dear servant, who has come up to tell us that he has been deceived, that his word has never been from above but from beneath, and that it is all a lie. Have mercy on him, Lord: the enemy has prevailed against him, and hither he has come in this time of trouble and rebuke and blasphemy, to break the power of the testimony we have to bear this day to this work of thine.[23]

Baxter saw Irving again that evening and the following morning, but could make no headway in convincing him.[24]

Apart from the doubts induced by non-fulfilment of prophecies (cf. Deuteronomy 18.15–22), Baxter rejected the manifestations because he had come to reject Irving's view of Christ as heretical and as pastorally dangerous:

> If ever any doctrine was made plain to me, it is plain that Mr Irving, in holding the law of sin to have been in the flesh of Jesus, is in a fearful heresy. His doctrine concerning the believer's holiness is yet more fearful, and the two clergymen who with me were made partakers of the power whereby I spoke, are both horror-struck at the doctrine. I wrote Mr I. in the full persuasion that he would see the error; but, to my dismay, he not only upheld it, but sent me two utterances in favour per Miss Cardale and Mrs Caird, declaring I was in the wrong, and he in the right. ... I had endured the apparent failure of the word for six weeks, and was not shaken; but when

---

[19] Banner of Truth: Irving to Baxter, 21 April 1832, cf. Baxter, *Narrative*, 103–8.

[20] Baxter, *Narrative*, 103–4, 109.

[21] One newspaper reported that Baxter had been summoned as a witness, but had informed Irving that if called he would have to denounce that which his evidence would have been expected to uphold: 'Expulsion of the Rev. Edward Irving from the Scotch Church', *Examiner*, 6 May 1832.

[22] Baxter, *Narrative*, 118.

[23] David Brown, 'Personal Reminiscences of Edward Irving', *The Expositor*, 3rd series, 6 (1887), 216–28, 257–73, at 272.

[24] Baxter, *Narrative*, 118–19.

I found the same power had again and again spoken words *which were not fulfilled*, exercised in London in sustaining false doctrine, I could no longer restrain the conclusion, that 'surely this is not of God.' ... On my seeing Mr Irving, I found him so entirely under the influence of this power as not even to weigh my representations, and I am indeed so overwhelmed to see one whom I so much love so utterly deluded.[25]

Irving's explanation of Baxter's defection was that he had tried to interpret prophetic words by his own understanding. In addition, he should have stayed where his mouth had been opened (probably a reference to Irving's church?) until the promised power was given.[26] To this Irving later added the assertion that as a church they had caused Baxter's stumbling through their unbelief.[27] But it was the earlier assertion which remained at the heart of all later interpretations of Baxter, whose case history remains worthy of serious study.

David Brown, who had first preached at Regent Square on 3 January 1830, was another who left Irving at this time.[28] He offered two rather different explanations of his actions. According to the first, he had been to see Isabella the day before Irving's trial commenced, to explain why, after increasing unease at the course of Baxter's prophetic career, he had come to reject the divine origin of the utterances; he stated that things had been brought to a head by his discovering things about one of the gifted women (perhaps Miss Hall) that were 'fatal to any Divine source in *her* utterances'. When Baxter came to tell Irving that he had recanted, Brown was stunned at the unexpected confirmation of what he had said the day before, and forthwith arranged to terminate his engagement. After some days, Irving came to see him, and Brown explained that he had only left once he had no grounds left for thinking that what was going on could possibly be from God. Irving, 'with a good deal of suppressed feeling' asserted 'Your intellect, sir, has destroyed you.' So they parted.[29] The second version was that he had left Irving after an unsatisfactory conversation attempting to clarify the latter's Christological views. Whilst Irving's understanding was in Brown's view less unsound than often thought, on other subjects his outlook

---

[25] [Horatius Bonar]?, 'Edward Irving', *QJP* 14 (1862), 224–47, at 236: Baxter to Mrs P., 30 April [1832]. Mrs P. may have been Spencer Perceval's wife.

[26] Edward Irving, 'What caused Mr. Baxter's Fall?', *MW* 7 (1833), 129-40, at 131.

[27] Edward Irving, 'Exposition and Sermon delivered at the Horse Bazaar, Gray's Inn Road, on Friday Evening, September 28, 1832', in *The Discipline of the Church, by the Rev. E. Irving; with two Addresses in the Open Air, by Missionaries* (London: W. Harding, [1832]), 2–4. Cf. Anon., 'The Voice of God', *MW* 5 (1832), 297–306, at 305–6, which also accused Baxter of excessive self-confidence as evidenced by his making himself the centre of his own predictions and the interpreter of his own words.

[28] Brown, 'Personal Reminiscences'; William Garden Blaikie, *David Brown D.D., Ll.D.: Professor and Principal of the Free Church College, Aberdeen. A Memoir* (London: Hodder and Stoughton, 1898), 32–6.

[29] Brown, 'Personal Reminiscences', 271–3. Close friends believed that it was through Brown's influence that Baxter recanted his belief in the gifts, although the latter gives no hint of this: Blaikie, *Brown*, 40n.

was 'so evidently calculated to open the floodgates of error, and to confound the truth of God with the vagaries of enthusiasm' that Brown left him, convinced that the Church of Scotland must soon exclude him; Irving 'laid his understanding as it were a sacrifice on the altar of mistaken devotion'.[30]

* * *

It is now time to trace the course of events leading to Irving's eviction from Regent Square. On 2 December 1831 Presbytery conferred with Irving, Cardale (his legal advisor), and Mackenzie, who by now was his only sympathetic elder. It was resolved that they would await the result of a forthcoming session meeting.[31] It is clear that all parties were finding great difficulty in reaching a decision on what to do. The session minutes for 20 December record that they had met twice since the conference of the 2nd; every effort had been made to convince Irving that his strategy for dealing with the gifts in worship outlined in his letter of 22 November was not consistent with the discipline of the Church of Scotland, but to no avail. They therefore resolved to take action against him, feeling themselves bound to uphold the standards of the Kirk. Irving remained steadfast, writing to the session on 24 December to warn them against hindering the work and standing by his November letter to the Trustees.[32]

Family ties led William Hamilton to ask to be exonerated from any measures taken.[33] This was not, however, because he sympathized with what his brother-in-law was doing; as he had written to John Martin on 8 December,

> I feel it to be difficult to attend the church and to maintain that composure of mind with which I desire to worship; for Edward is so very pointed in his prayers in returning thanks to God for that which I consider to be a delusion, that my mind involuntarily recoils from it, and feelings are engendered which are anything but pleasant or becoming the solemnity of the service.[34]

Even so, in another letter he paid tribute to Edward's character as a Christian (as did many who disagreed with him):

> I believe that a large proportion of the present congregation agree with Edward in the belief of the reality of those manifestations, and that they will follow him wherever he may remove to; and I must say that they are in general very pious people, zealous for God, and most exemplary in the discharge of their religious

---

[30] David Brown, 'Reminiscences of Edward Irving', *Free Church Magazine* 8 (1851), 14–17.

[31] London, LMA, LMA/4358/A/006, 'Trustees Minute Book' (1825–48), fol. 29.

[32] Oliphant, *Life*, 340.

[33] 'Trustees Minute Book' (1825–48), fols 30–2.

[34] John Hair, *Regent Square: Eighty Years of a London Congregation* (London: James Nisbet, 1899), 114–15.

duties. ... I never knew a man so devoted to the service of his Master, or more zealous in the performance of what he conceives to be his duty.[35]

Following the session's decision, the Trustees resolved on 31 December to submit a copy of Irving's letter of 22 November to the Solicitor-General, Sir Edward Sugden, for a legal opinion, seeking his advice as to how to stop the churchmatic proceedings and as to the extent of their powers.[36] At their meeting on 20 February 1832, they received his opinion. Sugden was clear that Irving's conduct was not warranted by the Trust Deed, nor was it covered by his discretionary powers as minister. 'The Trustees ought to proceed immediately to remove Mr. Irving from his pastoral charge by making complaint to the London Presbytery in the manner pointed out by the deed.' Since this process could take some time, they could eject Irving and shut the chapel until the case was decided. In the meantime, they had the power to prevent anyone not a seatholder from disturbing the congregation, and to remove miscreant seatholders under the power vested in them by the Trust Deed. At all events, it was their duty to act promptly. Three Trustees, Horn, Goldie and Mann (who took a leading role in proceedings) were appointed to wait on Irving with this opinion and to ascertain whether he would relieve them from having to act on it. When they did so, Irving promised his response in a few days.[37]

It came first in the form of a public statement. On the following Sunday, 26 February, he made a statement after each service. William Hamilton reported it to Kirkcaldy:

> I do not know whether I may ever look this congregation again in the face in this place, and whether the doors of my church will not be shut against me during this week. If it be so, it will be simply because I have refused to allow the voice of the Spirit to be silenced in this church. No man has anything to say against me. I have offended no ordinance of God or man, and I have broken no statute of man. No one has found any fault with me at all except in the matter of my God – nay, on the contrary, every one has pronounced me even more abundant in my labours and more diligent in my duties of late; and also that my preaching has been more simple and edifying than formerly. The church has been enlarged; many souls have been converted by the voice of the Spirit; the church has fallen off in nothing; and altogether the work of the Lord has been proceeding. ... What are you to do? You must not come here. Here the Spirit of God has been cast out, and none can prosper who come here to worship. Go not to any church where they look shyly on the work of the Spirit. We must 'not forsake the assembling of ourselves together as the manner of some is.' This, then, I advise for the present, that each householder who is a member of this flock do gather round him those in his neighbourhood who are not householders, and joining to them the poor, do [sic] exhort them and expound

---

[35] Oliphant, *Life*, 352.
[36] 'Trustees Minute Book' (1825–48), fol. 37.
[37] Ibid. fols 39–41; quotation at fol. 40.

to them the words of the Lord ... All the other meetings of the church will be held in my house.[38]

It was, however, some weeks before Irving was finally locked out, and when he was, his house would have been far too small to accommodate those who left with him. Irving had to make another statement the following Sunday, explaining that his previous one had been misrepresented by the newspapers, but the speculation continued: 'It is rumoured that several distinguished personages are taking a very warm interest in the decision of the question, and that, should Mr Irving be finally ejected, a chapel at the west end of the town is in readiness for his reception.'[39]

Two days after the first statement, Irving gave a written response to the Trustees, which although friendly remained unyielding: 'The principle on which I have acted is to preserve the integrity of my ministerial character unimpaired, and to fulfil my office according to the word of God.' If they must 'act to prevent me and my flock from assembling to worship God, according to the word of God' then he and his flock would trust him to look after them.[40]

Hamilton's letter indicates the growing isolation which Irving felt, as even his family deserted him. As Edward wrote to his father-in-law,

> Your letters concerning the work of the Holy Ghost in my church, and my conduct in respect thereto, do trouble and grieve me very much, because of your rashness in coming to a conclusion on so awful a question without the materials for a judgment; and because of the unqualified manner in which both you and Samuel and all condemn me, without any adequate information, and, as seems to me, without due tenderness and love.[41]

If this were God's work, how could he hinder it? (This was his basic conviction throughout, and serves to explain his conduct far better than any explanation couched in terms of mental instability or quest for popularity.) 'I never made any agreement, at any time, to suppress the voice of the Spirit in the public assemblies of the church, and never will do.' Moreover, his ministry was prospering more than ever in conversions and attracting new hearers. But one wonders what Martin made of his son-in-law's advice to 'look to your own dead, and heretical, and all but apostate church at home, and see what repentance and humiliation can be offered for it. Rejoice that there is one church in this land where the voice of the Holy Ghost, speaking in the members, is heard.'[42] This was somewhat harsh since Martin was alone in recognizing that, believing as he did, Irving had no other course open to him; the Trustees only sought the suppression of the manifestations in public

---

[38] Oliphant, *Life*, 348.
[39] *Caledonian Mercury*, 5 March 1832.
[40] Oliphant, *Life*, 349: Irving to the Trustees, 28 February 1832.
[41] Oliphant, *Life*, 2.252: Irving to John Martin, 7 March, 1832.
[42] Ibid. 2.253.

worship, not in the early morning services, but even such a compromise would have been unacceptable to Irving.[43]

The Trustees now referred the matter to the presbytery. At its meeting on 13 March, the Moderator laid before it a memorial and complaint, and a 'Case & Opinion' from the Trustees, accusing Irving of 'certain abuses in worship & discipline' and asking it to advise whether Irving should be deposed.[44] However, the complaint stated that Irving had always conformed to the doctrine and practice of the Church of Scotland, a statement which the presbytery found unacceptable because it had previously charged him with teaching erroneous doctrine.[45] The hitch was resolved when, on 5 April, the presbytery agreed to proceed without prejudice to their previous decisions regarding Irving, and his trial was fixed for three weeks later.[46]

On 17 March, Irving set out his defence in a letter to the Trustees and the Building Committee. He began by asserting that he had been enabled to be indifferent to the result of their deliberations, 'though it should deprive me of all income and cast me after ten years of hard service upon the wide world with my wife and my children, forth from a house which we built almost entirely upon the credit of my name, and primarily for my life enjoyment, where also the ashes of my children repose'. Still more was he indifferent because he had stood alone for so long as a minister of Christ, 'who hath been honoured of Him to bring forth from obscurity a whole system of precious truth', especially regarding the Second Coming. He warned them that 'whosoever lifteth a finger against the work which is proceeding in the Church of Christ under my Pastoral care, is rising up against the Holy Ghost', and listed the factors which had convinced him of the work.

> Many months of most painstaking and searching observation, the most varied proofs of every kind taken with all the skill and circumspection which the Lord hath bestowed upon me; the substance of the doctrine, the character of the speech and the form and circumstances of the utterances tried by the Holy Scriptures, and whatever remains most venerable in the traditions of the Church, the present power and penetration of the word spoken over the souls of the most holy persons, with the abiding effects of edification upon hundreds who have come under my own personal knowledge; the nature of the opposition which from a hundred quarters, most of them unholy, indifferent, infidel and atheistical hath arisen against it, together with the effects which the opposition hath had upon the minds of honest and good persons who have stumbled at it, their haste and headiness, their unrest and trouble of mind; the attempts of Satan by mimicry of the work and thrusting in upon it of seductive and devil-possessed persons to mar it, and the jealous holiness with which God hath detected all these attempts and watched over his own work to keep it from intermixture and pollution; and above all the testimony of the Holy Ghost in

---

[43] Oliphant, *Life*, 336.
[44] Cambridge, URCHS, 'Minutes of the Scots Presbytery of London. Vol. 2. Apr. 28. 1823 to Nov. 11. 1834', fols 258–9.
[45] 'Trustees Minute Book' (1825–48), fols 45–6: 17 March 1832.
[46] Ibid. fol. 54.

my own conscience as a man serving God with all my house, the discernment of the same Holy Ghost in me as a minister over his truth and watchman over his people...

The complaint against him was not a matter of immorality, error, neglect of duty, breach of good faith, change of ordinance, or departure from the constitutions of the Kirk. In his view, the Trust Deed had never been intended to prevent these gifts, nor had the constitutions. He urged them to consider the fleshly motives which had actuated them, such as dislike of the work, fear of popular odium, and complacency. If they cast out the Holy Spirit, the church would be dead, and so he appealed to them to repent. His parting shot was that he had read his letter an hour before in the presence of a gifted person, who foretold terrible things if they persisted in their course.[47]

In the meantime, Irving occupied himself with his punishing round of preaching (up to seven times a week) and pastoral work. Most of his appearances in print from 1831 were published reports of sermons. Irving's preaching in his latter years probably fell short of its powerful best (thanks in part to his practice of extempore delivery), and the onset of illness must have affected his ability to preach by sapping his physical strength, but there is no doubt that he continued to view the specific topics with which he dealt (often related to the manifestations) as part of a comprehensive system of Christian teaching. The problem was that the negative strain which had always been present in his thought became much more pronounced as he reacted to the condemnation of his teaching and practice; in addition, when preaching about the tongues, he was on ground which was totally unfamiliar to the majority of his hearers. Small wonder that given this and the general opposition to the manifestations, 'It was no longer to a national influence, but to a remnant saved from all nations, a peculiar people, that his earnest eyes were turned.'[48] As Irving himself explained, 'The work which God is setting his hand to, is not of reconstituting the primitive church, but redeeming his church out of the captivity of Babylon'.[49] To some extent this resembled the conventicle preaching condemned in his *Farewell Discourse* of 1822. Yet on occasion there could still be a big vision in his preaching, as is evident in his utterances on the national fast day appointed for 21 March on account of the cholera epidemic. Services were held at many churches, including Regent Square. In the morning,

> it was expected that the Rev. Mr. Irving would deliver a discourse on national transgressions and the judgments which would follow – but the Rev. Mr. Brown officiated, Mr. Irving having in the first instance expounded a portion of the 24th chapter of Isaiah: and in concluding his remarks, he said (in allusion to the passage he had been reading) – cry aloud for the King – for the Princes – the Senators – the

---

[47] Irving to the Trustees and Building Committee of the National Scotch Church, 17 March 1832 (in private hands).

[48] Oliphant, *Life*, 339.

[49] Edward Irving, 'Interpretation of the Fourteenth Chapter of the Apocalypse', *MW* 5 (1832), 306–24; 6 (1832), 18–44, 262–85, at 284.

Nobles – the merchants and traders – yea, for the people of the land, and especially that poor; a class who should never be forgotten. It is probable that this will be the last national fast which will be known in England; hence, my brethren, admit of its importance, and spend it as you ought – namely, in prayer and supplication.[50]

That evening Irving preached on 'England's Rejection of Christ', taking as his text Zechariah 12.10, in which God promised to pour out on his people a spirit of repentance and supplication so that they would mourn as they beheld the one whom they had pierced (traditionally taken as a reference to Christ).[51] He expected the fulfilment of this prophecy within a few months or years as Christ returned. England had rejected Christ as head of the church, as King of kings and Lord of lords (by its espousal of democracy), as owner of all, and as the poor man's friend. He called on his hearers to repent, stating his conviction that 'we shall never see another fast in the realm of Britain until it is too late!' He applied his call to repentance to a range of groups: the poor, employers, those in power, and ministers. Clearly, with the emphasis on prophecy, there continued to be a strong vein of social critique in his preaching: we must not imagine that he abandoned the one for the other.

As well as preaching at Regent Square, in March Irving began preaching in Islington on Sunday afternoons, in a workshop in South (later Basire) Street, New North Road, which had been fitted up as Zion Chapel the previous year.[52] It was not long before this became too small (if indeed he ever used it) and he announced a move to the open air. That brought its own problems: two men were brought to court accused of picking the pockets of members of Irving's audience.[53] A newspaper report indicates that he did not pull his punches when preaching to the unchurched:

The Rev. Edward Irving had another field-day at Islington yesterday. The numbers present were variously estimated at from 2,000 to 4,000. After reading part of the 24th chapter of Isaiah, the rev. gentleman poured forth his denunciations against sin for at least an hour and three quarters, without experiencing the least interruption from the motley crowd by which he was surrounded. Mr. Irving frequently announced the approaching destruction of the world, as the consequence of mankind's perversity in rejecting the new born doctrine of the tongues. London, because of its superlative wickedness, would be the first example of the judgments of God; and, as this metropolis had been favoured above all other places, the judgments upon it would be in the same proportion fearfully terrible. After the

---

[50] *Morning Chronicle*, 24 March 1832.

[51] 'England's Rejection of Christ', *The Pulpit*, no. 489 (29 March 1832), 136–44.

[52] 'Islington: Protestant Nonconformity', *A History of the County of Middlesex: Volume 8: Islington and Stoke Newington Parishes* (1985), 101–115; http://www.british-history.ac.uk/report.aspx?compid=9522, accessed 7 October 2008.

[53] *The Times*, 3 April 1832, 4. A correspondent had earlier stated that Irving was to have opened a chapel in Popham Terrace, Islington, but adjourned to Britannia Fields because of the size of the crowd. In addition, members of Irving's flock had engaged over twenty chapels and rooms for preaching purposes: 'Rev. E. Irving', *The Times*, 27 March 1832, 3.

service, Mr. Irving, accompanied by Mr. Armstrong and several other friends, proceeded through Islington and Pentonville, followed by a crowd of 200 or 300 persons. Britannia field, which has been chosen by Mr. Irving for these displays, is now called 'The Field of the Tongues.'[54]

* * *

The day of the trial arrived at last; it seems to have been something of a public spectacle, *The Times* reporting that on one morning large numbers were waiting for the doors to be opened.[55] Underlying the different interpretations of events put forward by Irving and his opponents was a fundamental question: was this a matter of procedure or of doctrine? The Trustees and the presbytery treated it as the former, and in so doing they were acting in line with the General Assembly, where matters of morals and doctrine had often been raised under the guise of procedural issues;[56] Irving saw it as the latter, and sought to argue the biblical basis for his actions. Related to this was another issue – the legitimacy of appealing in a court of the Church of Scotland to the Scriptures over against the Kirk's doctrinal standards.

The moderator (the Rev. J. R. Brown) constituted the meeting by prayer, interrupted by Taplin in tongues and English, 'telling the members of the Presbytery that they were there assembled in their own name and strength, and condemning them for their past proceedings'.[57] The complainants for the Trustees (Mann, Nisbet and others) laid the charges that: (i) Irving allowed public worship to be interrupted by those who were neither ministers nor licentiates of the Church of Scotland; (ii) he allowed public worship to be interrupted by those who were neither members nor seatholders of the National Scotch Church; (iii) he allowed and encouraged public worship to be interrupted by women; (iv) he allowed and encouraged public worship to be interrupted by lay members; (v) he had appointed suspensions in the course of worship for the gifts to be exercised by these people. The Trustees then outlined the course of events which had brought them before the presbytery.[58]

Of the ten Trustees, two did not share in the complaint – Horn (for reasons unknown) and Hamilton. (When the Trustees met on 2 March, Hamilton had taken the minutes, and had explained that his family relationship to Irving precluded him from taking any part in the matter although he could not fairly oppose the

---

[54] NLS, MS 967, fol. 204: cutting from *The Newcastle Courant*, 7 April 1832.

[55] *The Times*, 3 May 1832, 3.

[56] D. Chambers, 'Doctrinal Attitudes in the Church of Scotland in the Pre-Disruption Era: The Age of John McLeod Campbell and Edward Irving', *Journal of Religious History* 8 (1974–5), 159–82, at 161.

[57] W. Harding, *The Trial of the Rev. Edward Irving, M.A. before the London Presbytery; containing the whole of the Evidence; exact Copies of the Documents; verbatim Report of the Speeches and Opinions of the Presbyters, &c.; being the only authentic and complete Record of the Proceedings, taken in Shorthand by W. Harding* (London: W. Harding, 1832), 1.

[58] Ibid. 3.

complaint.) After hearing the complaint read, Irving was asked whether he had a written defence. He said that he had not, as Christ had commanded his followers not to premeditate their defence in such situations.[59]

Mann proceeded to call witnesses for the prosecution. Mackenzie was cross-examined by Irving, but the moderator disallowed the latter's question whether the manifestations were scriptural because the issue before the court was whether they were in accordance with the Church of Scotland's polity. ('Hisses and great disorder' ensued.) There was a procedure for the reception of new doctrinal understanding, which had not been followed in this case: if a minister thought he had received new light on Scripture, he could put it before the presbytery, and they could send it up to the Assembly for transmission to all presbyteries for their considered opinion. Irving, however, protested at not being allowed to appeal to the Bible, condemned the gathering as 'a court of Antichrist', and intimated that he would put no more questions.[60]

That evening, apart from meeting Baxter, Irving preached at Regent Square from Acts 2.37 on 'The Baptism of the Holy Ghost', the doctrine for which he saw himself as on trial. It was 'the proper distinction of the Christian dispensation ... the great and particular subject out of which every thing that is distinctive of the Christian dispensation flows'; 'this gift of the Holy Ghost is that without which religion will go back to Moses'.[61]

The following day saw Irving giving his defence from 11.45 a.m. until 3.50 p.m., with interruptions when the court deemed him out of order or abusive.[62] He argued first that Christ's office was to be that of baptizer with the Holy Ghost. 'It is for the name of Christ, as "baptizer with the Holy Ghost," that I am this day called in question before this court'.[63] In his speech, he aimed: (i) to justify the phenomena from Scripture; (ii) to show that this was what had been received at Regent Square, and that it was for all; (iii) to show how he had ordered the manifestations, and that his procedure was according to Scripture and the standards of the Church of Scotland; and (iv) to explain how the parties in the case stood, and how in his opinion the case stood before the court.

At the early morning prayer meetings, 'We cried unto the Lord for apostles, prophets, evangelists, pastors and teachers, anointed with the Holy Ghost the gift of Jesus, because we saw it written in God's word that these are the appointed

---

[59] Ibid, 6–10; [William Harding], *A Word of Testimony: or, a Corrected Account of the Evidence adduced by the Trustees of the National Scotch Church, in support of their Charges against the Rev. Edward Irving, and his Defence* (London: Adam Douglas, 1832), 5. Irving had in mind the situation of believers on trial for their faith (cf. Luke 21.12–15).

[60] Harding, *London Trial*, 10–12.

[61] 'The Baptism of the Holy Ghost', *The Pulpit*, no. 493 (26 April 1832), 201–6; quotations at 201, 206.

[62] Harding, *London Trial*, 19–50.

[63] Ibid. 19.

ordinances for the edifying of the body of Jesus.'[64] And when the gifts appeared, Irving tested them

> first, by the walk and conversation of the persons; secondly, by trying it according to the form of Scripture, seeing whether it had the sign of the tongue, and whether the prophesying was for edification, and exhortation, and comfort; thirdly, by the consciousness of the Spirit within myself, bringing conviction to my own heart; fourthly, by submitting it to all the people ...[65]

The presbytery was not competent to decide whether the gifted persons spoke by the Holy Ghost, as it had never heard them – but this, he asserted, was the real issue. As for allowing women to speak, it was not women speaking but the Holy Ghost speaking in them: 'it is not persons but the Holy Ghost that speaketh in the church'.[66] The tendency of the complaint was to deny Christ's office as baptizer with the Holy Ghost, to take away the gifts of tongues and prophecy from the church, to take away the Spirit's liberty to speak in the church, and to take away the minister's standing as responsible directly to Christ rather than to any human entity. It was small thing for him to lose the building, as his flock could meet outdoors and God could provide another meeting place, but a big thing for the presbytery to gainsay the Spirit's work: 'it will be a burdensome thing, not to this Presbytery alone, but to this city, if you shall shut the only church within it in which the voice of the Holy Ghost is heard – if you shall shut the only church in Britain in which the voice of the Holy Ghost is heard'.[67] His conclusion was that Protestant churches were in a Babylonish state as much as the Roman Catholics; accordingly he separated himself and his flock from them, 'constituting no schism, but a minister believing that his Lord is soon to appear, and desiring that his church, by the baptism of the Holy Ghost, should be made meet for his appearing'.[68]

The trial was adjourned until 2 May, but in the intervening period a memorial was drawn up for presentation to the presbytery. One writer recollected that at an early prayer meeting, a paper was laid on the table for attenders to sign.[69] It stated that many of the signatories had subscribed to the building; that Irving's ministry had been blessed; and that the Church of Scotland's forms had been adhered to. While some were not in sympathy with the manifestations, they were prepared to leave God to sort things out. The right of the Trustees to call Irving to account in this way was rejected; indeed, it was claimed, not one-twentieth of the members would approve of their proceedings. The memorialists urged the presbytery to proceed with caution,

---

[64] Ibid. 23–4.
[65] Ibid. 34.
[66] Ibid. 41.
[67] Ibid. 49.
[68] Ibid. 50.
[69] [Louisa Perina Courtauld Clemens], *Narrative of a Pilgrim and Sojourner on Earth, from 1791 to the present Year, 1870* (Edinburgh: H. Armour, 1870), 113.

lest their decision lead to litigation and a congregation of thousands be separated from the Kirk.[70]

When the trial was reconvened Irving was allowed to answer Mann's case as a favour, the London Presbytery being unable to appeal to any higher church court. Mackenzie asked leave to present the memorial, but this was disallowed.[71] Irving reiterated his belief that this was not merely a question of discipline but one of doctrine. He reminded his hearers that he had zealously set about restoring the church's standards: in doctrine, in the observance of communion, in the public practice of baptism, and in regular lecturing and preaching. Those who spoke in the services were not unauthorized: he had authorized them, after testing their gifts. He had been willing to leave Regent Square, but felt the Lord telling him not to as he was not a private individual but a pastor. Irving set his defence in the context of the congregation's flourishing: in the six months since the last communion service his preaching had added two hundred members, twenty at least 'converted from the depths of infidelity and immorality'. All told, he knew of over a thousand converted through his ministry.[72] The court arranged to adjourn at 3.45 p.m., forcing Irving to give his apologies for the evening session as he was due to preach. Mann then asked whether Irving thought he had been honest in not acknowledging that Miss Hall had been deluded. Irving's heartfelt response was that: 'She is one of the lambs of my flock – she is carried in my bosom!'[73]

That evening, it emerged that the presbytery had been reluctant to have anything to do with the case; indeed, it narrowly escaped being refused a hearing, but the duty had been forced on them by the Trust Deed. In his summing up, the moderator opined that in view of all that Irving had been teaching on the subject, and the excitement which had marked the prayer meetings, 'The wonder ... is, not that the manifestations did occur, but that they did not occur sooner.'[74] The presbytery found all five charges fully proven, and 'while deeply deploring the painful necessity thus imposed on them, they did, and hereby do decern [a Scottish legal term meaning 'judge' or 'decree'] that the said Rev. Edward Irving has rendered himself unfit to remain the minister of the National Scotch Church aforesaid, and ought to be removed therefrom, in pursuance of the conditions of the trust-deed of the said church'.[75]

The following day (Thursday), the Trustees resolved unanimously that Irving could no longer be allowed to continue as minister. They arranged to send him a copy of their resolution, and to have a certified copy of the presbytery's decision formally served upon him; two of them would accompany their agent to take back the church keys.[76] They determined to close the church at once, although Hamilton

---

[70] Harding, *London Trial*, 89.
[71] Ibid. 61.
[72] Ibid. 64–9.
[73] Ibid. 71.
[74] Ibid. 84.
[75] Ibid. 88.
[76] 'Trustees Minute Book' (1825–48), fols 61–2.

had urged them to allow it to remain open till after the sacrament; they refused his request as they considered that their absence from communion would, according to the Trust Deed, deprive them of a voice in the choice of a future minister, and because two hundred new members (who would be supportive of Irving) were due to be admitted.[77]

That night Irving preached his last sermon at Regent Square. It was an utterance of defiant confidence that the Lord would guide him and his flock. The previous Sunday evening, he came into the vestry and found a letter on the mantelpiece, presenting him with a portable pulpit. God would provide them with a house, as he had provided a pulpit. As for the approaching communion, tokens would be given out as usual;[78] if need be, the deacons would seek another venue and people would be posted at the door of the church to tell the congregation where and when it would be celebrated.[79] If it were not, then they were 'to be kept (if not delivered up on Sunday), as a bond of union till such time as the Lord shall guide the flock to some other place of refuge', according to one member.[80]

On Friday morning the congregation worshipped in front of the church doors; Irving then read the Trustees' resolution and their high opinion of his character. But he also did something which if understandable was less than commendable. It was probably Horatius Bonar who, reviewing Mrs Oliphant's biography, noted the intolerance which marred Irving's final years; others were ejected from their ministries for less cogent reasons but they did not behave as he had done. On this occasion Irving cursed all connected with Regent Square, 'praying that there might never be another pastor there; that a blight would rest upon it' and so on, inveighing 'both against its walls and its worshippers'.[81]

That day Irving went to the nearby Horse Bazaar and explained the facts; the proprietor immediately assured him that 'You shall have with all my heart whatever accommodation I can give.'[82] The hall in question, at 277 Gray's Inn Road, had been built during the late 1820s as stabling and auction facilities for horses. In 1831 the social reformer and atheist Robert Owen helped establish an Institution of the Society to Remove the Cause of Poverty and Ignorance, the following year opening an Equitable Labour Exchange, where artisans could barter skills for goods.[83] On

---

[77] Oliphant, *Life*, 368–9.

[78] It was customary in Presbyterian churches to issue members with tokens, admitting them to communion as participants.

[79] *The Last Sermon preached at the National Scotch Church, Regent Square, on Thursday Evening, the 3d of May, 1832* (London: W. Harding, [1832]), 6–7.

[80] Oliphant, *Life*, 368.

[81] [Bonar]?, 'Edward Irving', 243–4. What would Irving have said when the building was bombed in 1945?

[82] Irving, *Last Sermon*, 8.

[83] David A. Hayes, *East of Bloomsbury* (London: Camden History Society, 1998), 68–9; Walter H. Godfrey and W. McB. Marcham, eds, *Survey of London, Volume 24*, British History Online, http://www.british-history.ac.uk/report.aspx?compid=65568, accessed 28 January 2009. Owen soon moved elsewhere, as did Irving, and the building

Friday evening the intending communicants met there, probably for a preparatory service.

One supporter gave eloquent expression to the confidence of those who went out:

> The towers and pinnacles of the building from whence they have been ejected may aptly symbolize the antiquated church, garnished with men's devices, which has cast Mr. Irving out; but the plain and hasty building which will now be erected will better suit with our condition of 'strangers and pilgrims' here below, and more fitly symbolize that 'house not made with hands,' whither we hope speedily to arrive, the 'city which hath foundations, whose maker and builder is God.'[84]

In the event, no building was erected, but a converted picture-gallery served as the congregation's home for twenty years; by the 1850s, the church's outlook had developed to the point where it would erect one of the most imposing ecclesiastical buildings in London, in Gordon Square.

* * *

Events, and the advance of illness, were beginning to take their toll on Irving. Carlyle informed his father in December 1831 that they had seen Irving only once since the tongues began. 'He looked hollow and haggard; thin, greywhiskered, almost an old man: yet he was composed and affectionate and patient. I could almost have wept over him, and did tell him my mind with all plainness.'[85] Irving's mental powers were, he felt, beginning to atrophy: 'I am glad to think that he will not go utterly *mad* (not madder than a Don Quixote was); but his intellect seems quietly settling into a superstitious *caput mortuum;* he has no longer an opinion to deliver worth listening to on any secular matter'.[86] When Carlyle's father died in January 1832, Irving's attempts to minister proved sadly inadequate. As Thomas explained to his mother, they had kept all visitors away until the time of the funeral, when Irving was admitted, and prayed with them. He meant well, but Carlyle found his prayer and conversation disturbing: 'his whole mind is getting miserably crippled and weakened; his inane babble about his tongues and the like were for me like froth to the hungry and thirsty'.[87]

Before illness took hold, however, Irving was buoyed up by an experience of healing from cholera, after he had been preaching on the gift of healing. On 29 March, after leaving the prayer meeting, he had been taken ill and could eat no breakfast. His condition worsening, he went to bed, praying and confessing his sin.

---

became the Royal London Bazaar. After Irving departed, the building was occupied briefly by Madame Tussaud's waxworks.

[84] Anon., 'The Ark of God in the Temple of Dagon', *MW* 5 (1832), 441–56, at 456.
[85] *CL*, 6.65: Carlyle to James Carlyle sr, 13 December 1831.
[86] Ibid. 127: Carlyle to John A. Carlyle, 16 February 1832.
[87] Ibid. 110–11: Carlyle to Margaret A. Carlyle, 30 January 1832.

He was due to preach at Regent Square at 11.30 a.m. (by this time there was a regular Thursday morning service). David Brown took his place, but Irving got up.

> As soon as the prayer was finished he walked up the Pulpit Stairs with a face, pale as a sheet & <u>many</u> years <u>older</u> to look at – Mr Brown begged him to desist, but he was not to be daunted – He read a chapter, but as he proceeded his eye became dim, his voice thick & his head so swam that he could not make a word of comment – He gave out a Psalm & sat down with all eyes turned on him – His heart was fixed on Jesus, and he felt it to be a struggle whether Jesus was stronger in his soul than Satan in his body – just at this time a cold sweat came out over all his body & the pang was gone past – He was still weak but preached one of the sweetest sermons, the people present ever had heard – In the evening he again preached to 200 poor folk in one of the School rooms ...

He did not tell anyone that he had had cholera until a Dr Marshall from the cholera ship (presumably a kind of isolation hospital set up on the Thames during the emergency) visited him a few evenings later and told of his healing from it. Irving then stated what had happened, convincing Marshall (who had been to the West of Scotland to observe the manifestations there) that he had truly been stricken with the disease and been healed.[88]

---

[88] St Andrews, University Library, Special Collections, Flegg Collection (MS 38594): John Caw to William Bonar, 3 April 1832. For Irving's account, see 'Visions – Miraculous Cures – Cholera', *MW* 5 (1832), 416–29, at 425–9.

CHAPTER 19

Deposed as Pastor, May 1832–March 1833

The sharing of the Horse Bazaar by Edward Irving and Robert Owen during the summer of 1832 was, as one paper put it, 'perhaps, the strangest conjunction that ever design or accident produced'.[1] Carlyle informed his brother that Irving 'has rented Owen's huge ugly Bazaar (they say) in Grey's Inn Road, at 7 guineas a week, and lectures there every morning: Owen the Atheist, and Irving the Gift-of-Tongueist time about [by turns]: it is a mad world'.[2] In the words of the *Morning Watch*, 'Mr. Irving and his Church have been ejected from Babylon, and have found a refuge in the jaws of Antichrist.'[3] But the congregation still had to endure a rather peripatetic existence: a note appended to the published version of Irving's last sermon at Regent Square intimated that each Sunday and once in the week, there would be a meeting for them at which he would preside. Twice each Sunday the word would be preached in the highways, and he would also preach once each Sunday in any place provided for him. The early morning services were to continue, as would those on Wednesday evenings. The editor had heard that Irving's friends had engaged Mr Cubitt to build a chapel near Sidmouth Street, to be completed in two months.[4] At the end of May, one member reported:

---

[1] 'The Rev. Mr. Irving', *Times*, 5 May 1832, 2.

[2] *CL*, 6.185: Carlyle to John A. Carlyle, 2 July 1832. Timothy Stunt points out that the hall in question was Owen's Socialist Lecture Hall, not, as often stated, the Socialist Rotunda in Blackfriars: *From Awakening to Secession: Radical Evangelicals in Switzerland and Britain 1815–35* (Edinburgh: T. & T. Clark, 2000), 265 n.96.

Conveniently, Britannia Fields, where Irving preached on Sunday afternoons, was across Constitution Row from Owen's hall: Lillian W. Kelley, 'Edward Irving Preaching in Britannia Fields Summer 1832: A Portrait by Faithful Christopher Pack, R.R.P.', *JPHSE* 5.1 (1932), 21–30, at 22.

[3] Anon., 'The Ark of God in the Temple of Dagon - Mr. Irving's Church and the London Presbytery', *MW* 5 (1832), 441-56, at 441.

[4] *The Last Sermon preached at the National Scotch Church, Regent Square, on Thursday Evening, the 3d of May, 1832* (London: W. Harding, [1832]), 8. Of the three Cubitt brothers, Thomas, William and Lewis, it was probably William who was approached, as his building firm was located in Gray's Inn Lane: 'William Cubitt (MP)', http://en.wikipedia.org/wiki/William_Cubitt_(MP), accessed 26 January 2009.

We have resolved to build a Church capable of seating 1500 in the neighbourhood of Regent Square – it is to cost about £4,000 – & plain & seat free – This week each of the <u>members</u> of the Church (there are nearly 700) is to receive a ticket on which he will mark his own subscription & whatever his friends will add to the same – Will you<u> do something for us and give me your returns within</u> three or four weeks, about which time we are to give in our tickets – already 400 or £500 has been collected at the doors of the house ...

Mr Irving preaches twice on the Sunday in the open air in Cold bath Fields & Islington Green – On Wednesday evg at the former place & on Saturday at the <u>Jew's</u> district East London – The Lord is graciously helping him, thousands come round him & hear the word of God with gladness – all our own folk assemble round the pulpit, as many as are weak bringing camp stools & many sweet women are not ashamed or wearied to stand for hours ...[5]

There was no let-up in the amount of work which Irving undertook; it seems that he was too busy even to attend his father's funeral in July, although George did so. Edward, according to Carlyle, was 'preaching in the fields about London; at Hampstead Heath, his precentor in a tree'.[6]

It was during this period that things came to a head with the Simpsons: the problems Irving experienced in dealing with Jane's prophetic gift, which was not accepted as genuine by other gifted persons, indicate that he was ultimately unable to integrate his belief in the restored charismata with his practice of ministry: in practice, things just did not work out as tidily as they did in his theoretical pronouncements on the subject. It was one thing to insist that the Spirit's voice must be heard in the church as the complement and answer to the voice of Christ through the minister, but quite another to discern when the utterances proceeded from the Spirit and when they were counterfeit. As noted earlier, deadlock resulted because she refused to recognize any authority which denied her gift, whilst Irving insisted on the acceptance of his authority.[7]

The Cardales in particular became increasingly hostile to Jane. Indeed, Miss Cardale's lack of love had become so evident in the congregation that some had spoken to the Simpsons about it. When Irving tested Jane's gift in mid-May, she passed the doctrinal and personal tests which he applied; he also read her an article on Revelation 14 which he was writing for the *Morning Watch*, for the Spirit to

---

[5] St Andrews, University Library, Special Collections, Flegg Collection (MS 38594): John Caw to William Bonar, 29 May 1832.

[6] *CL*, 6.196: Carlyle to John A. Carlyle, 31 July 1832.

[7] Edinburgh, NLS, Acc. 12489/14, John Home Simpson, Typescript work on the Simpsons and their relationship to Irving, c. 1985, fol. 97.

For the following paragraphs, see the Simpson papers for the period, especially Acc. 12489/11, 'A Brief Account of Mr & Mrs Simpson's Visit to Portglasgow in 1832'; Gordon Strachan, 'Carlyle, Irving, and the "Hysterical Women"', *Carlyle Annual* 12 (1991), 17–32.

respond through her.⁸ He accepted all those utterances, but a succession of meetings took place during May and June, which saw Irving take the side of the Cardales and Mary Caird, all of whom by now rejected Jane's prophetic gift.

Jane and her husband became convinced that the disagreement was due to the lack of the gift of discernment of spirits. She was convinced that her experience had been from God, and that she had received repeated confirmation of this in her spirit. Irving felt obliged to obey the voice of those who were recognized as prophets in his church, and appeared to have no solution to the dilemma except an appeal to his authority. She thanked him warmly for all she had received under his ministry, but insisted she could not resist the power and must accordingly separate from him: 'if my Husband will permit I will go to the Land of my Fathers, I will go to the Brethren in the West and have communion with them, and from thence to my Kindred', to which Irving objected as it would throw suspicion on the prophets in his church.⁹ A succession of meetings and letters served only to polarize things, the Simpsons warning Irving that his ministry would be blighted if he persisted in rejecting Jane's gift, an argument which paralleled those he had used against the Trustees. On 22 July, therefore, the couple left for Scotland.

They went first to Greenock and Port Glasgow, where they spent time with the Macdonalds. Without being told what had happened in London, Margaret prophesied that there were divisions and confederacies there. James Simpson read an account of the matter which he had compiled to the Macdonalds and their group; James Macdonald then prayed that Irving might be humbled and yet saved, and all present spoke in the power, the import of their utterances being 'bring him down, down, down, to the dust, to the dust'.¹⁰ The Simpsons were accepted into full communion and Jane's gift acknowledged. A few days later, three members of Irving's congregation arrived, doubtless attempting to limit the damage.

James returned to London early in August and on 8 August Irving denounced Jane to the church; James wrote to inform him that they were no longer members of his flock, but he refused to accept this, visiting them on 26 November with Cardale and others to get them to submit to his authority. On 6 December Irving wrote to Jane, effectively excommunicating them for insubordination (ironically, given his own rejection of the authority of the London Presbytery). The body of Irving's letter bears quoting in full because it shows how high a view he continued to have of his office.

> You have grievously offended against the Lord Jesus Christ the Chief Shepherd, who hath called me in his grace to watch over your soul, in that you have set at nought all my counsels and would [have] none of my reproof; and arise in direct rebellion against my authority and the Church of which I am the Angel under the Lord Jesus Christ. I require and command you, as you value your precious soul for

---

⁸ It was published as 'Interpretation of the Fourteenth Chapter of the Apocalypse', *MW* 5 (1832), 306–24; 6 (1832), 18–44, 262–85.

⁹ Acc. 12489/4, Diary, 15 July 1832 – September 1838, fol. 38.

¹⁰ Acc. 12489/11, 'A Brief Account of Mr & Mrs Simpson's Visit to Portglasgow in 1832', unpaginated.

which He died, and which is His[,] that you would lay down the weapons of your rebellion and humiliate yourself in the sight of the Lord and confess your sin before His Church, and be absolved from it, and delivered out of the hands of the Enemy, who hath you now and if you repent not will have you for ever.

You have not resisted man but you have resisted the Holy Ghost, and do resist Him; and He declareth of you that if you repent not, Jesus will come and cut you altogether out of his vine, wherein you have been grafted, and should bear fruit unto the Father's glory.

Oh let me have joy of thee who hast caused me so much sorrow. Thou hast troubled Christ's Church, beware lest He trouble thee. I beseech thee by the mercies of God, that thou obey the word which he speaketh unto thee through his Minister & through his Prophets.

Meanwhile I have seen it to be my duty to set your Husband and you on the outside of the fold by resuming [taking back] your Tokens, and I do call upon you to return again into the bosom of it by humbling yourself in the dust, and repenting, and confessing your sins. Then shall my heart rejoice which now grieveth over you.[11]

Strachan, who interprets the disagreement as a power struggle, describes Cardale as 'kingmaker' because 'he had behind him the two most "inspired," powerful, and manipulative women in the whole movement, his wife and sister'; he was their mouthpiece and through him they controlled all the power broking of the new ecclesiastical hierarchy as it emerged.'[12] Without going so far and implying that there was any deliberate attempt at manipulation, we may nevertheless acknowledge the possibility that in any such group of people, there is the possibility of factors other than spiritual ones being operative, often at the subconscious level, and affecting the judgement.

* * *

Meanwhile, Irving and his congregation continued to preach wherever they could. On occasion this brought them into conflict with the authorities, whether for blocking the thoroughfare (and attracting pickpockets) or for creating a disturbance.[13] Whilst the young men asserted before the magistrates their divine commission to preach, Irving advised them to be more circumspect; urging them on one occasion to 'beseech his mercy on the city which is thus setting itself in opposition to the preaching of the word', he warned them not to throw their liberty away but to choose

---

[11] NLS, MS 1676, fols 232–3: Irving to Jane Simpson, 6 December 1832. The tokens were those issued to communicants; taking them back was tantamount to excommunication.

[12] Strachan, 'Carlyle, Irving, and the "Hysterical Women"', 32.

[13] For example, 'Police', *The Times*, 13 April 1832, 3; 'Police', *The Times*, 8 May 1832, 4.

a spot to preach where they were not blocking the thoroughfare.[14] Irving also preached regularly to Jewish audiences, which provoked some trouble. According to one report, 'every Saturday morning he expounds the Scripture prophecies to the Jewry, and declares their restoration to Palestine to be at hand'.[15] Application was made by a Jew to magistrates to prevent Irving from preaching in Goodman's Fields; he had made statements which Jewish hearers considered offensive and so they 'had determined to pelt him with rotten eggs on his next appearance'. The magistrates thought that Irving would have to take some of the consequences, but directed an officer to keep the peace.[16]

Cholera, which was widespread in London that summer, gave Irving's open air sermons an added impact. Preaching on it, he claimed that God's anger was seen in its impact on Paris and in the civil unrest there, but God's mercy in its lesser impact on London and in the nation's preservation from revolution.[17] Nevertheless, it represented a divine chastisement, and 'I tell you of a verity, there is no protection from this disease save in the name of our God.' The only defence against the disease was outlined in Psalm 91, which he proceeded to expound evangelistically.[18]

One reason why he preached outdoors was the crowds who came to hear him, often in the hope of witnessing the manifestations. Irving's humility when the manifestations confirmed his preaching was, according to Mrs Oliphant, 'a sight, if that voice were true, to thrill the universe; a sight, if that voice were false, to make angels weep with utter love and pity'. Perhaps even more moving for many was the occasion when a poorly clothed small child had become separated from its parents while Irving was preaching on the regeneration of infants in baptism. Brought to the front, it was given to Irving, who held it against his shoulder and continued his sermon, using the child as an illustration. It was content in his arms, and was restored to its parents (who had been able to see where their child was) at the end of the service.[19] Edward's love of children meant that he and Isabella rejoiced when their new baby was born late in September. Isabella informed her family that God had kept her from having any need for medicine, and the new baby was doing very well. He had a fine head of black hair, and 'I believe Edward means to name dear Baby Bryce Johnstone [sic]'.[20] In the end, however, he was named Ebenezer.

---

[14] *The Discipline of the Church, by the Rev. E. Irving; with two Addresses in the Open Air, by Missionaries* (London: W. Harding, [1832]), 7.

[15] *Caledonian Mercury*, 28 May 1832.

[16] *Morning Chronicle*, 31 May 1832.

[17] *Exposition and Sermon by the Rev. Edward Irving, M.A. at Cold-Bath Fields, Sunday Morning, June 10th, 1832; together with a Manifestation by Miss Cardale* (London: W. Harding, [1832]), 11.

[18] 'The Cholera – a Call for National Repentance: Open Air Service, at the Back of Coldbath-Fields Prison, Clerkenwell, on Wednesday Evening, July 18, 1832', *The Pulpit*, no. 507 (26 July 1832), 58–64; quotation at 60.

[19] Oliphant, *Life*, 370–1.

[20] Isabella Irving to Mrs Martin, 29 September 1832 (in private hands).

* * *

In the course of his business as a solicitor, Cardale had had premises offered to him at 14 Newman Street, to the north of Oxford Street, during September. He took a builder to view them and a lease was taken out in Irving's name for thirty-three years.[21] Isabella looked forward to its opening, assuring her mother that 'It will not only be most convenient & set forth the ancient form of the Church but elegant & commodious.'[22] It was opened on Friday, 19 October, the service including manifestations from Miss Cardale, Mrs Caird, Taplin and Henry Drummond, and the baptism of Ebenezer Irving by Nicholas Armstrong.[23] (The name appears to have been chosen with the church's situation in mind, Irving referring to him as 'our stone of help', a witness to God's faithfulness.[24]) According to *The Times*, about 1,600 people were present at the opening, attendance at which was restricted to members and friends of Irving's congregation.[25]

The following Sunday Irving preached from John 3.14–17, 'On the Universality of the Gospel Invitations'. It was an evangelistic sermon, as were many of his recorded sermons from this period; it seems that he believed himself to be preaching the full gospel, which he considered others were not doing because they did not preach the Second Coming of Christ or the baptism with the Holy Ghost.[26] God, he announced, had provided them with this house, having stayed them by prophecy from building one. It would be open for public worship ten times a week: each morning at 6.30, Sundays at 3 p.m., Wednesdays at 6 p.m., and Fridays at 11.30 a.m.; there would also be three services restricted to the church on Fridays at 6 p.m. and Sundays at 10 a.m. and 6 p.m. Unusually for a church at that time, and in contrast to the practice at Regent Square, there were to be no seat rents to raise funds: 'I am resolved that there never shall where I minister – for I believe it to be among one of the prejudices to the preaching of the gospel'. However, collections would be taken at the door until the expense of taking the building had been

---

[21] [H. B. Copinger], 'Annals: The Lord's Work in the Nineteenth and Twentieth Centuries' (typescript, n.d.), 28.

[22] Isabella Irving to Mrs Martin, 11, 13 October [1832] (in private hands).

[23] *Exposition and Sermon delivered at the Opening of the New Chapel, Newman Street, Oxford Street, Sunday Afternoon, October 21, 1832* (London: W. Harding, [1832]), 8. Armstrong was a Church of Ireland clergyman who had accepted the gifts and resigned from his post as a preacher with the Reformation Society; he would become an apostle in the new church.

[24] Henry Drummond, *Narrative of the Circumstances which led to the setting up of the Church of Christ at Albury* (typescript, n.d.; first publ. 1834), 21: Irving to David Dow, 25 April 1833.

[25] *The Times*, 22 October 1832, 4.

[26] *Exposition and Sermon at the Opening*, 4; cf. Edward Irving, 'Exposition delivered at Salem Chapel, Deverill Street, Dover Road, ... together with a Manifestation by Mr. Taplin, October 8, 1832', *Expositions and Sermons by the Rev. E. Irving and the Rev. N. Armstrong* (London: W. Harding, [1832]), 1–7.

cleared.²⁷ The attempt to restrict entry to some services may not have lasted long, as an editorial note to a sermon preached a few days later says that the plan to admit members only to some services was given up.²⁸

Finance was openly discussed: at the end of one service in November, Irving made a statement about the needs of the cause. When the agreement was made with the proprietor, he had decided to be responsible himself 'in order that I might not again, by the hands of trustees, be, myself and my flock, cast out to the streets'. The two elders who had supported him became sureties, but he considered that the flock and congregation should bear the financial responsibility. Anticipating modern practice, he called for pledges of annual or six-monthly giving, which the officers would record in a book.²⁹ At Regent Square Irving's stipend had never been less than £500 (the highest figure for any minister of the Presbytery of London),³⁰ and it is likely that his income had suffered quite a drop; letters to Drummond indicate that by the spring of 1833 he was finding it hard to make ends meet. Not surprisingly, one old friend expressed concern at Irving's state of health and the responsibilities which he had taken on:

> I went a few days since to see Edward Irving in his new House, in Newman Street, He was very glad to see me he looked dreadfully pale, and was much emaciated, but he seemed more tranquil than usual. He took me over his Chapel, which is beautifully fitted up ... he has built, a place beyond, for visitors, pious Clergymen, Travellers &c containing six Bed rooms and a sitting room and the Front House is a very handsome one, much better than the one you saw – He has *taken upon himself* a rent of 400£ a year & Taxes in proportion, – while he is popular this may do – but with this rent they must collect 1000£ at the Chapel to enable him to live at all ...³¹

---

²⁷ *Exposition and Sermon at the Opening*, 7; cf. Anon., 'Mr. Irving's Church THE Sign of the Times', *MW* 6 (1832), 224–8, at 225, which stated that the congregation had in fact collected sufficient money to erect a building, no others being available, and that Newman Street seated more people than Regent Square.

²⁸ *Exposition and Sermon, delivered at the Church in Newman-Street, on Wednesday Evening, October 24, 1832* (London: W. Harding, [1832]), 7–8. The restriction of some services to members arose because Irving had observed that the gifts of tongues and prophecy were rarely manifested when unbelievers were present, and this had led him to judge that it would be more consonant with the mind of the Spirit, seeing that unbelievers quenched the Spirit, to separate the unbelievers and have meetings where believers alone were admitted': Robert Baxter, *Narrative of Facts, characterizing the Supernatural Manifestations, in Members of Mr. Irving's Congregation, and other Individuals, in England and Scotland, and formerly in the Writer himself* (London: James Nisbet, 1833), 47.

²⁹ 'The Exposition and Sermon, at the Church in Newman Street, Sunday Evening, November 11, 1832, by the Rev. E. Irving, A.M.', *Two Services at the Rev. E. Irving's Chapel, Newman Street, November 4th and 11th* (London: W. Harding, [1832]), 16.

³⁰ George G. Cameron, *The Scots Kirk in London* (Oxford: Becket, 1979), endpapers.

³¹ *CL*, 6.313n: Mrs Montagu to Jane Carlyle, 2 January 1833.

Yet he continued open-handed in his hospitality. In August Isabella wrote to her parents, begging them to pay a visit and evidently hoping that they would then be convinced of the work. Edward added his voice, telling them not to worry about expense, 'for we were never so rich since we began house-keeping'. Thirty or forty men from the church preached in the streets, and every two months nearly fifty members were added to the church. 'I believe the Lord is doing a work in my church, wherein the whole world shall have reason to rejoice.'[32] Crucial to the success of that work was Irving's continued commitment to the hard graft of pastoral care. At the turn of the year, for example, he addressed sixty-four new members (it appears that such were received every two months), and it is noteworthy that the large numbers already in his care did not stop him from knowing them well enough to address a personal exhortation to each one.[33]

* * *

The Presbytery of London, as a voluntary association possessing doubtful legal status, had no right of appeal to the General Assembly of the Church of Scotland.[34] However, that did not preclude those who believed Irving to be teaching Christological error from seeking his deposition from the ministry by other means. On 7 March 1832 Dr Dickson moved (successfully) to a commission of the Assembly that a committee be appointed to inquire into Irving's 'reported doctrines and proceedings' since the Assembly of the previous year.[35] The committee reported back on 26 May, and Principal Macfarlan of Glasgow recommended accepting its recommendations and instructing the Presbytery of Annan to initiate proceedings against Irving, a recommendation which was agreed to without a vote.[36] The presbytery was to write an official letter to him and deliver it personally, requiring him to avow or disavow authorship of three works, *The Orthodox and Catholic Doctrine*, *The Day of Pentecost*, and *A Judgment*; if necessary, they were to draw up a libel and require him to appear before them.[37]

Irving replied to their letter on 1 September, indicating that he intended to take the full two months allowed to answer the questions put by them so as to avoid rashly involving them or himself in the consequences which flowed from his

---

[32] Oliphant, *Life*, 2.317–18.

[33] *Exposition and Sermon, by the Rev. E. Irving, A.M., at his Chapel, Newman Street, on Sunday Afternoon, December 23, 1832: To which is added an Address delivered at the Church in Newman Street, Friday Evening, Jan. 4th, 1833, previous to the Distribution of Sacramental Tokens to Sixty-Four New Communicants* (London: W. Harding, [1832]), 9–16.

[34] The Irving case led the Presbytery of London to seek recognition in 1833 as an official court of the Church of Scotland: Cameron, *Scots Kirk*, 247–8.

[35] *The Pulpit*, no. 488 (22 March 1832), 128.

[36] *Presbyterian Review and Religious Journal* 2 (1832), 452–3.

[37] Edinburgh, NAS, CH2/13/6, Presbytery of Annan minutes, fol. 97: 4 July 1832.

answer.[38] Six weeks later he avowed his authorship of the works in question and upheld the doctrine contained in them. The friendly and respectful tone of the earlier letter, to men who had known his family, was replaced by a more belligerent one; he stated that the third work had been written

> to denounce the General Assembly of the Church of Scotland as one of the most wicked of all God's enemies upon the face of the earth for having denied and fought against all the foundations of the truth as it is in Jesus, and cast out his servants for preaching the same. With that wicked assembly now three times tried of God, and three times found wanting, and with all who adhere to, or in any way aid and abet, its evil deeds, I can maintain no relationship but that of avowed and open enmity.

Grieved that they should obey it and so share in its evil deeds, he called on them to separate from it lest they share in its judgement.[39]

The day of the trial had been fixed for 13 March 1833.[40] On the way to Annan Irving had stopped to visit his sister Elizabeth Kennedy and her family in Manchester; he arrived at his brother-in-law Dickson's house in Annan by the mail coach early that morning, to be met by his deacon, David Ker. By the time the trial commenced at noon, about two thousand people had packed into the parish church. Several reporters were present, including one of Irving's friends (probably William Harding, who was publishing his sermons at this time). At one point in the proceedings, some gallery seats cracked as if giving way, though nothing further happened.

Irving objected to the libel which had been prepared, since it asserted Christ's sinfulness in his human nature but did not mention that he was kept holy by the Holy Spirit. He was removed from the court while the presbytery deliberated and agreed to add the word 'peccability' to it, which would make it correspond to that against Maclean and also would remove Irving's objection to it as unfounded.[41] Called back in, he refused to state whether it was now relevant to his case. He and

---

[38] Edinburgh, NCL, Box 9.3.15: Irving to James Monilaws, 1 September 1832.

[39] NCL, Box 9.3.19: Irving to the Ministers and Elders of the Presbytery of Annan, 13 October 1832.

[40] For the following paragraphs, see Anon., *Trial of Mr Edward Irving, late Minister of the National Scotch Church, Regent Square, London, before the Presbytery of Annan, on 13th March, 1833; with an Appendix, containing Copies of some of his Letters, and other Documents, a Refutation of his Errors, and an Account of the supposed Supernatural Manifestations exhibited by the 'Gifted' of his Congregation; also some Notices of similar Manifestations in the French Prophets, and others* (Dumfries: Journal Office, 1833); [William Harding]?, *The Trial of the Rev. Edward Irving, A.M. before the Presbytery of Annan, on Wednesday, March 13, 1833: Also Mr. Irving's Letter to his Congregation. Taken in Short Hand* (London: W. Harding, 1833); Oliphant, *Life*, 391–5.

[41] 'Peccable' meant that Christ was capable of sinning, rather than that he was actually a sinner, which was implied by a bald statement that Christ assumed sinful human nature, especially since, as Irving protested, it made no mention of Christ's being preserved sinless by the indwelling of the Holy Spirit.

the presbytery therefore retired for a half-hour conference, 'when God gave me grace to refuse to every one of them the right hand of fellowship' and not to eat with them; he said that he 'would hold no conference of friendship with them but be at open and avowed enmity until they had ceased from persecuting his faithful members'.[42] Agreement was not forthcoming, but the presbytery concluded that the libel was relevant and that they would proceed on the basis of it. At some points, Irving not only refused to answer questions, like Christ before Pilate, but sat with his face in his hands.

Finally, Irving stood to begin his defence. Undoing his long blue cloak, he raised his hand briefly to his brow, produced a Bible from his pocket, and began to speak. After insisting that he upheld the holiness of the incarnate Christ and rejecting the General Assembly as heretical, he told the presbytery that it was for them to do what they thought right.

> But I stand here as a witness for the Lord Jesus – to tell men what he did for them; And what he did was this: – He took your flesh and made it holy, thereby to make you holy; and therefore he will make every one holy who believes in Him. ... I dare ye to say that the Lord your Saviour had an easier passage through life than you had...[43]

He backed up his claims by expounding Psalm 40, which he interpreted as speaking of the experience of the incarnate Christ, a procedure which he justified by asserting that 'The apostles taught out of the Psalms, and not from confessions of faith, and traditionary documents.'[44] When his old acquaintance Henry Duncan charged him with preaching his doctrines to the people rather than defending himself to the presbytery, and the moderator suggested that he imagined he was preaching to his congregation in London, Irving replied that he had not forgotten where he was, for this was the church where he had been baptized and ordained; in any case, he made no distinction between the ministers present and their flocks. He had an intensely practical object, not a speculative one: 'Ye ministers, elders, and presbytery! This is no question of scholastic theology. I speak for the sanctification of men. I wish my flock to be holy – and unless the Lord Jesus has contended with sin, as they are commanded to do, how can they be holy when they follow him?'[45]

A robust defence followed of his *Doctrine of the Incarnation Opened*. Irving explained that when the building of his new church was under way, he wished to contribute a volume of sermons, the proceeds of which could be put towards the cost. His elders discussed this and asked him to publish the sermons on the Incarnation as the first of the three proposed volumes. When Andrew Thomson took it up (in the *Edinburgh Christian Instructor*), Irving was minded to retaliate but remembered the Lord's injunction to raise such issues with a brother privately first;

---

[42] Oliphant, *Life*, 2.351.
[43] [Harding]?, *Annan Trial*, 13.
[44] Ibid. 14.
[45] Ibid. 15.

he wrote him a letter but never sent it and still had it. Then a friend told him that a controversial review of the work would be appearing in print, so he 'wrote this tract which my Church have found so edifying, in order to neutralize the efforts of my opponents'.[46] When he heard that the Assembly had condemned it, he retired to his session house to spend some days reading it before the Lord, but he found nothing to alter; it was, he asserted, 'strong medicines for a dying church'.[47] If he were a heretic, would God not have given him up to sin? But they all knew what kind of an example he had shown them (and he had preached in all their pulpits).

He then challenged their loyalty to the General Assembly. They were Christ's servants, not those of an Assembly which had cast out one greater even than John Knox – McLeod Campbell, whose holiness required that Irving take his part. He had made the three-hundred mile journey to Annan not because he was obliged to (indeed, the presbytery had no authority to act as it had done, calling him to account when he was not within its bounds), but freely. And it was at considerable inconvenience to himself: they had taken him from his flock of nine hundred (besides children) and 'from ruling among my apostles and elders'.[48] In closing, he called his hearers to repent and purify themselves, for the Lord was coming soon. Irving had spoken for nearly two hours.

The moderator then called each of the ministers to give their opinion on the case. Duncan's judgement was that Irving could no longer remain a minister of a church which he had sworn to maintain but whose faith he had renounced. He found it hard to offer such a verdict, as he esteemed Irving, but he had seen his mind gradually led astray from the truth. The other ministers followed, each in turn judging Irving guilty of heresy and deserving of deposition from the ministry of the Church of Scotland. The moderator was about to pray before pronouncing sentence, when a loud voice broke the tense silence: 'Arise, depart! Flee ye out, flee ye out of her! ... How can ye pray to Christ whom ye deny? ...' Only when a clergyman held aloft a candle in the evening gloom was it seen who the speaker was – David Dow, who had been deposed the previous August as minister of Irongray, west of Dumfries.[49] He then rose to leave, Irving following him, calling 'As many as will obey the voice of the Holy Ghost, let them depart.' The deposition was thus pronounced in his absence.

Irving sent Ker and another supporter, Robert Smith, to stand at his sister's house adjoining the church and announce that he would preach in a field almost opposite the church the next morning. About 1,700 people gathered to hear him and afterwards, according to an eye witness, he was surrounded by hundreds wanting to

---

[46] It is not clear whether he had in mind *The Day of Pentecost*, which was named in the libel, or *The Orthodox and Catholic Doctrine*, which was about the person of Christ.

[47] Anon., *Annan Trial*, 32.

[48] [Harding]?, *Annan Trial*, 19.

[49] An eyewitness at McLeod Campbell's trial recalled one of the Macdonalds rushing out of the church, red in the face and crying 'Come out of her, my people' (cf. Rev. 18.4): Gregory Bateson, ed., *Perceval's Narrative: A Patient's Account of his Psychosis 1830–1832* (London: Hogarth Press, 1962), 21.

shake his hand or touch his clothes.[50] The same day he sent a letter to his flock recounting what had happened at the trial and rejoiced that he had been delivered after testifying faithfully to the truth: to him Dow's prophecy had come as an intimation of release: 'He sent me that wonderful word and set me free'. In view of the unenlightened state of the local ministers and people, he judged it his duty to remain for some days and preach wherever opportunity was given, which he did to large crowds.[51] Carlyle's judgement was that in effect Irving was appealing to the people by preaching to them.[52] He was popular with the country folk but 'his very name is an offence to decent society'.[53] According to a local newspaper, Irving denounced the ministers who had condemned him as 'incompetent, negligent, and ignorant'. But the reporter offered a shrewd assessment of the justice of the sentence: 'whether the amount of difference between him and the Church justified deposition, may be questioned by third parties. But, certainly, according to Mr Irving's estimate, it does; for it is quite plain, that if the Church had not rejected him, he must, in common consistency, have rejected the Church.'[54]

The treatment Irving received from the Church of Scotland undoubtedly reinforced the remnant strand in his ecclesiology which treated the church as a company of faithful believers gathered in Christ's name out of an apostate religious body; there was also an increasing emphasis on the true ministry as one which was anointed by the Holy Spirit. Where these ideas were to lead we shall discover in the following chapter.

---

[50] Frank Miller, 'Edward Irving and Annan', *RSCHS* 4, repr. in idem, *Poems from the Carlyle Country: Together with Papers on Two of Carlyle's early Friends and some Fragments in Prose* (Glasgow: Jackson Son & Co., 1937), 39–47, at 46.

[51] Oliphant, *Life*, 2.350–3; quotation at 352; cf. *The Record*, no. 507 (25 March 1833), following the *Dumfries Courant*.

[52] Thomas Carlyle, *Reminiscences*, ed. C. E. Norton (London: J. M. Dent, 1932), 301.

[53] *CL*, 6.364: Carlyle to John A. Carlyle, 29 March 1833.

[54] Anon., 'Deposition of Mr. Irving', *Dumfries Times*, 20 March 1833, 43–44, at 43.

CHAPTER 20

Ordained as Angel, March 1833–August 1834

Ever since Carlyle and Mrs Oliphant blamed the new church for silencing Irving after his deposition, controversy has surrounded this action. Carlyle followed Mrs Oliphant in alleging that on returning from Scotland Irving was prohibited from ministering in Newman Street for a week because he had gone beyond his instructions, perhaps by his open-air preaching.[1] Mrs Oliphant's account, in which the prohibition was portrayed as an inappropriate way to treat one who had just suffered for the truth and as not expected by Irving, was taken as a criticism of the church and its new leaders. She felt it necessary to add a footnote to the one-volume edition of her biography accepting the assurance offered by J. B. Cardale (the 'Pillar' or *primus inter pares* of the apostles in the Catholic Apostolic Church) that this action was not intended to humiliate her hero but pointing out that he wrote as an insider, she as an outsider.[2]

The facts were these: on 31 March, Irving was about to receive into the church an infant which had been baptized at home, when Cardale in his capacity as apostle caught his hand and stopped him (at this stage apostles were expected to act as such only when inwardly impelled by the Holy Spirit). Irving obeyed, asking the parent to postpone the rite.

> Then the Lord further signified that it was His will we should know, and the whole church feel, that we were without ordinances, to the end we might altogether feel our destitute condition, and cry to Him for the ordinances from heaven. Then I discerned, that He had indeed acknowledged the act of the fleshly church, taking away the fleshly thing; and that He was minded, in His grace, to take us under His own heavenly care, and constitute us into a church directly in the hands of the Great Shepherd and Bishop of our souls ...[3]

The previous Sunday, prophecy had stated that 'what the Church of Scotland had given the Church of Scotland could withdraw, and therefore he should not administer

---

[1] Thomas Carlyle, *Reminiscences,* ed. C. E. Norton (London: J. M. Dent, 1932), 301.
[2] Oliphant, *Life,* 396–7.
[3] Henry Drummond, *Narrative of the Circumstances which led to the setting up of the Church of Christ at Albury* (typescript, n.d.; first publ. 1834), 11: Irving to David Dow, April 1833.

the Sacraments until he had again received ordination'.[4] Irving does not appear to have seen this as a humiliation at all; given the expectation that he would soon be ordained to what Baxter had called the 'spiritual ministry', there is no reason why he should have done. One writer records that when hindered from baptizing, he threw off his gown, exclaiming: 'Thank God, I am free from the trammels of men.' In any case, his inhibition followed from his own teaching about the true spiritual ministry.[5]

His ordination as angel followed on Good Friday, 5 April, in response to prophetic direction.[6] The act of ordination was conducted by Cardale as apostle, who laid hands on Irving and prayed for him. Communion followed, during the preparation for which Cardale read the letters to the Seven Churches in Revelation 2–3 'in the power' (i.e. as inspired by the Spirit). These chapters, on which Irving had lectured and written at such length, were to play an important part in Catholic Apostolic liturgical rites, and the root of this lay in Irving's belief that 'what is spoken to the angel is spoken to the churches in the angel, and what is spoken to the churches is spoken to the angels over the churches; for these times are they written, for churches having angels are they written'.[7] Reflecting on the service, Irving concluded that it represented:

> 1st, A casting off, so far as London is concerned ... of the old ordinances, which they have polluted, and a giving of them anew from His own hand from heaven. 2dly, A purging out of the old leaven of the flesh, and the requirement of a purely spiritual service, which we must grow up from childhood into manhood, beginning from that day, by the forgetting of the former things, and the never bringing them into mind. 3dly, A constituting of the church in the angel, by the taking of him bound in all the words spoken by the Lord to the churches, that we might henceforth cease altogether from the canons and laws of men.[8]

The new order meant radical changes for the open air preaching ministry. At the session meeting the morning after Irving's ordination, word came by the apostle shutting the mouths of those who had been preaching in the streets. As Irving explained that Easter Sunday, 'The Lord hath shown yesterday that the witness in the streets shall be no longer but by those whom He shall send forth.' He thanked them for their efforts and sufferings, but enjoined them to silence, calling the congregation

---

[4] Oliphant, *Life*, 397; [H. B. Copinger], 'Annals: The Lord's Work in the Nineteenth and Twentieth Centuries' (typescript, n.d.), 31.

[5] C. Kegan Paul, *Biographical Sketches* (London: Kegan, Paul, Trench, 1883), 31, 33. The Catholic Apostolic explanation of events was given by W. W. Andrews: 'The authority of the Church of Scotland was vindicated by his submission to his sentence, and the wrong that she had done him was redressed by a higher ordination': *Edward Irving: A Review* (2nd edn, Glasgow: David Hobbs, 1900), 147.

[6] For a detailed account of the ordination service, see his first letter to Dow: Drummond, *Narrative*, 11–14.

[7] Ibid. 13.

[8] Ibid. 14.

to 'Pray that God would speedily name the evangelists & send them forth.'[9] The following Saturday evening (13 April), the new church's first evangelists were ordained, having been called to their office by prophecy. Irving was directed to lay hands on them as angel and send them out. He was ready for this, as

> the Lord had shewn me in the light of His truth, that while it was the prophet's part to call by name, and the apostle's to endow with the gift, it was mine, as the constituted angel of the church, and head of authority in this city, to give them of my authority to go forth within that bound, and fulfil the ministry which they had received of the Lord ...[10]

But their mission was now somewhat different: 'From all that has been spoken to the evangelists, it seems that it is not preaching the Gospel to the heathen, but preaching deliverance and life to the captives of Babylon.'[11] In other words, it was directed to those caught up in the existing religious systems, rather than those who made no claim to Christian allegiance.

The Sunday morning after he had laid hands on the evangelists, Irving did so on the newly called elders and their assistants ('helps'), 'giving them power and authority to minister the word and sacraments within the bounds of this city, and sharing with them of the gift which the Lord had given to me'. It is clear that Irving saw his role as angel as crucial to the good order of the new church: 'Surely this is the mystery of the angel to be the rule and discerner of whatever is said and done in the flock by pastor, evangelist, prophet, or apostle.'[12] His approach would result in some tension between him and other ministers as they worked out their respective roles; we shall return to this below.

The size of the flock and the lack of ministers coming with them from Regent Square made it imperative that deacons as well as elders be appointed. Irving's second letter to Dow regarding events during April 1833 explained that at first, the two deacons and two elders which he had would meet regularly with him, the gifted persons also being present. Each week they would pray that their numbers would be made up. The first additional deacons were chosen later in April, but were not ordained by the laying on of hands because, according to the apostle (Cardale), 'there was not yet a church filled with the Spirit to choose deacons'.[13] There was thus a degree of provisionality about the arrangements.[14]

While all this was going on, the Irving's infant son Ebenezer lay dangerously ill.

---

[9] St Andrews, University Library, Special Collections, Flegg Collection (MS 38594): Andrew Bonar, Notes dated 25 April 1833 concerning arrangements at Newman Street.

[10] Drummond, *Narrative*, 15.

[11] Ibid. 14. Developed Catholic Apostolic understanding was similar to this.

[12] Ibid. 16.

[13] Ibid. 17: Irving to David Dow, 25 April 1833.

[14] I shall offer a fuller account of the development of the church's polity in my forthcoming work on the Catholic Apostolic Church, *The Lord's Work*; the focus here is on Irving and on developments as they related to the course of his life and ministry.

> The Lord hath laid much affliction upon me and my children of whom the youngest dear Ebenezer is dangerously ill, we have cast them entirely upon the Lord, believing that he knows best what is good for them and for us; not despising medicines but content to be afflicted which we are afflicted [sic]; and seeking to return unto the Lord from all our backslidings.[15]

William Hamilton's wife Elizabeth claimed that Isabella had said that Ebenezer's illness was God's punishment for Edward's having remained in Scotland longer than he should have done; apparently he had been rebuked in the church for doing so.[16] This may have been overstating things a little, but Isabella informed her father that it had been a trial to her that he was grieving the Lord by neglecting his charge in London.[17] That Irving could give such attention to church affairs during this family crisis is thought-provoking, although we have no record of Isabella's reaction to her husband's tendency to immerse himself in his work, a work with which she heartily sympathized.

Remarkably, Irving's second letter to David Dow was written just four days after Ebenezer's death, as he lay in the next room 'laid out for his burial ... Oh, he is such a monument of our unbelief!' On the day he died, Sunday 21 April, the elders came to pray for him,

> nor departed until the Lord had taken him, and refused to give him back to our prayers. He was a child filled with the beauty of God from his mother's womb: peace, patience, and joy, and boundless love, were in all his ways, until about the time I was cast out by the church; when he was smitten with a gradual fading away, and never smiled again. After I returned he never smiled; and before he never but smiled: and now he lieth in peace ...[18]

Announcing the loss to the family at Kirkcaldy, Irving interpreted it as chastisement for the sins of himself, his family and the flock. Touchingly he recorded that like Edward he appeared to have possessed divine life from his birth onwards: 'when, in faith, I addressed words of godliness to nourish the seed of faith which was in him, his patient heed was wonderful'.[19] Once again, the family vault at Regent Square was opened for Irving to conduct the burial. One wonders what went through his mind as he stood in the building which he had so lately cursed. In a touch of courtesy, the burial register refers to him as 'Rev.', notwithstanding his deposition from the ministry.

Only a few weeks later, on the morning of 8 May, Irving's brother George also died. According to Carlyle, he had been 'dangerously ill, of inflammation of the lungs'.[20] Isabella informed her father the same day, assuring him that he had died

---

[15] Alnwick Castle, DFP, C/9/15: Irving to Drummond, 27 March 1833.
[16] Oliphant, *Life*, 398.
[17] Ibid.: Isabella Irving to John Martin, n.d.
[18] Drummond, *Narrative*, 21.
[19] Oliphant, *Life*, 399: Irving to John Martin, 23 April 1833.
[20] *CL*, 6.386–7: Carlyle to John A. Carlyle, 17 May 1833.

trusting the Lord. This death, like the previous one, she saw as evidence of God's refining and chastising work. George, whose surgical practice had done quite well, left most of his property to his mother, apart from his gold watch (which went to Edward) and some small bequests to his partner and an apprentice.[21] Edward buried him at Regent Square on 13 May.

In June the *Morning Watch* ceased publication. Irving's account of the decision to take this step shows that it was not only in response to the pressure of church work but also a realistic decision given its precarious finances, even though circulation was continuing to increase.

> This morning the Lord spake at my breakfast-table to dear Tudor, to the effect that he was a vessel now chosen of the Lord for his own work, and that he must cease from the work whereto the Lord had not called him, and entirely devote himself to the Lord's work; and other words clearly shewing to us all that the Lord's mind was the Morning Watch should no longer be continued. He told me afterwards that there was nearly a debt of £200 upon it, we must raise it for him amongst us. For dear man, through the badness of the times leaving two of his homes upon his hands, he told me what I may tell you but not another, that his whole income to live upon was but £35 a year.[22]

* * *

Before following Irving through the events of 1834, we must examine briefly the development of the relationship between him and the apostles. The restoration of the apostleship had not been anticipated by Irving or by the gifted persons in Scotland. Miss Cardale, two or three years after visiting Port Glasgow, recalled being struck to hear:

> these people, (when in mighty power), praying to God to have pity upon His weary heritage (His poor Church scattered and divided), utter this petition – 'O Lord send Apostles in Thy compassion, none else can heal the schisms of Thy Church' and like expressions, and, Miss Cardale adds, 'we used to say "Apostles! What can it mean?"'[23]

In his *Confessions of Faith*, Irving had claimed the support of the Second Book of Discipline for his exhortation to prayer for the restoration of the offices of apostle, evangelist and prophet mentioned alongside those of pastor and teacher in Ephesians

---

[21] Isabella Irving to her parents, 8 May 1833 (in private hands).

[22] DFP, C/9/18: Irving to Drummond, 4 May 1833. Tudor's statement in the final issue makes no mention of his financial problems: 'Conclusion of the *Morning Watch*', *MW* 7 (1833), 399–403.

[23] [Edward Trimen], 'Rise and Progress of the Work of the Lord (typescript, n.d.), 46.

4.11–12.[24] However, he did not consider what the practical implications of such a restoration might be, and it appears that he was caught off balance by the way things developed. The new church order, the 'spiritual ministry' of Baxter's prophecies, was to have at its pinnacle the apostles, called by prophecy and charged with ruling the movement. While Irving's ministry had done much to bring it into existence, so much so that it was often known by outsiders as 'Irvingism', he was neither an apostle nor a prophet. Instead, he served as an angel.[25] However, his high view of the angel's office was to cause problems, especially as Cardale's background was not Presbyterian but Anglican, and he was therefore familiar with a different understanding of ministerial orders. Until Drummond's ordination as apostle on 25 September 1833, Cardale was the only one, but thereafter others were called; by the time Irving died there were six.

One reason for the tension was that Irving had been used to his independence, even to the extent of withdrawing from the presbytery, but he was now placed under a higher ministry. For another, it was in his church in Newman Street that this ministry was developing.[26] He appears to have seen his office as enabling him to exercise a measure of authority over the prophets; one writer records that a servant girl speaking in the power was told by Irving to speak more to the point as Scripture taught that the spirits of the prophets were subject to the prophets.[27] Irving continued to weigh and act on words of prophecy himself, rather than leaving that to the apostles.[28] In his view, 'The angel of the Church is over the apostle, and the apostle is over the angel of the Church.' He clarified this by explaining that the Letters to the Seven Churches had been addressed to their angels, but written by an apostle. 'So receive I, through an apostle, my instructions; and having received them, the apostle himself is the first man that must bow to them, and I will take good care that he doth so, lest he should exalt himself to the seat of our common Master, who alone is complete within Himself'.[29]

Irving's letters to Drummond show that he supported the changes in worship and church polity which were taking place. We see them discussing how particular changes should be implemented, and how various prophecies should be understood. But the relationship does not appear always to have proceeded smoothly. On one occasion we find Irving confessing, with a sensitivity of spirit which does him credit:

---

[24] Edward Irving, *The Confessions of Faith and the Books of Discipline of the Church of Scotland, of Date anterior to the Westminster Confession: To which are prefixed a Historical View of the Church of Scotland from the Earliest Period to the Time of the Reformation, and a Historical Preface, with Remarks* (London: Baldwin and Cradock, 1831), cxvi.

[25] Oliphant, *Life*, 396n.

[26] Andrews, *Irving*, 148–9.

[27] Anon., *A Letter to a Friend in the Country on reading Robert Baxter's* Narrative of Facts (London: James Nisbet, 1833), 14.

[28] Oliphant, *Life*, 402.

[29] Oliphant, *Life*, 2.334: Irving to Alan Ker, 30 April 1833.

I do thank you much for your many acts of loving kindness and for the continual ministry of your prayers on behalf of me and of my flock: and I am conscious to myself of having come far short of a loving and bountiful requital of your goodness, and of having judged by the appearance and so of having judged unrighteous judgment. For though I bear to you and to all saints a true and loving heart and am willing to give up all for Christ's sake, I have seen that the enemy hath much in me which I suspected not, but which my God daily revealeth, and putteth away through the sprinkling of the blood of Jesus upon my conscience. Therefore I desire to be reconciled unto you my brother for all evil thoughts words and deeds which I have been guilty of towards you, although unknown to yourself or to me, and to be forgiven of you and of Christ whose little one you are, so shall I come and lay my gift upon the altar, that it may be accepted of God and made profitable to you, for he alone it is who maketh to profit.[30]

He was aware of his tendency to be a fault-finding Scotsman,[31] but nevertheless considered that he had a responsibility to indicate to Drummond how the latter should obey the prophecies received. So, contemplating Drummond's spending a while in London away from his congregation in Albury, Irving can write: 'As a man you are under me, as a spiritual minister bringing the word of God I am under you.'[32]

Slowly Irving came to terms with the relationship developing between apostles, prophets and angels; but to the end of his life the issue was not completely resolved. In two final letters to his congregation, Irving confessed to having been impatient with apostolic government and to having put the angel in place of Christ as head of the church,[33] and we shall see that shortly before his death he sent for one of the apostles (Woodhouse) in order to confess his sin in having resisted the bringing out of the apostleship and his jealousy for his flock.[34]

Problems also arose in dealing with Edward Taplin, by now the chief among the prophets at Newman Street. Relations between Irving and Taplin had been strained for some months; in September 1833 Irving had confided to Drummond that

While the Church is truly exercised in such a way as, I believe, to retain the ordinance of a Prophet, poor Mr. Taplin seems doing every thing to provoke God to supersede him, and to cast him off. He baffles all dealings, and makes void all

---

[30] DFP, C/9/25: Irving to Drummond, after 13 October 1833.
[31] Cf. DFP, C/9/36: Irving to Drummond, 2 April 1834.
[32] DFP, C/9/37: Irving to Drummond, 7 April 1834.
[33] Washington Wilks, *Edward Irving: An Ecclesiastical and Literary Biography* (London: William Freeman, 1854), 281.
[34] Cf. [Copinger], 'Annals', 50; cf. London, BL, 764n13, Ernst A. Rossteuscher, 'The Rebuilding of the Church of Christ upon the Original Foundations. An Historical Narrative of its Commencement. A free Translation' [by Miss L. A. Hewett] (MS, [1871]), fol. 527.

prayers. I am almost in despair of him. No one knows how my heart has been broken with that man.[35]

In March 1834, while the apostles were away in Edinburgh ordaining ministers to serve the new church, Taplin and Irving called sixty men of the congregation to serve as evangelists; for this independent action they were rebuked by Cardale from Edinburgh and forced to reverse the appointments. Irving called them together and told them that he had acted in error, but Taplin left the church and did not return until Irving had died: before setting out on his last journey Irving declared publicly that Taplin was in open rebellion against him.[36]

* * *

Irving entered the final year of his life busy and yet in declining health. One of the last of his sermons to be published was delivered on 12 January 1834 at Newman Street and based on Isaiah 5.8–12, it sounds the same note of passionate social critique which had been evident throughout his ministry, as he included the desire for riches among the sins calling forth God's judgement. His belief that true believers were but a remnant of the visible church found expression two weeks later: preaching from Isaiah 10, he denounced the churches as worshipping an idol rather than the true God. Nevertheless, God would send forth and empower his messengers: 'he shall catch them up unto the throne of God and of the Lamb; he shall put upon them his mighty power; he shall send them forth, first in sackcloth, his witnesses, to publish the gospel in shame and contempt, as I now publish, and as the Evangelists, whom he hath called in this city, do publish it'.[37] Parliaments and bishops could not reform the church, but God was preparing a sheepfold by the ministry of apostles, prophets, evangelists and pastors (what was to become the 'fourfold ministry' of the Catholic Apostolic Church). Accordingly he urged his hearers to withdraw from the existing churches: 'Leave those houses of iniquity, the churches; come out, for they will cast out every thing that hath a hold of truth.'[38] In a sermon from the gospels which followed (it appears that the practice at Newman Street was to have one sermon from the Old Testament and another from the gospels), his high view of the civil power appears in his instructing his hearers when persecuted not to resist God's ordinance as the Covenanters had done but to endure passively, awaiting God's deliverance.

Irving's negative attitude towards the churches affected his relationships with Isabella's family. He accused her brother Samuel of not following on to know the Lord, of allowing the truth he had been given as a minister to be hidden under a

---

[35] DFP, C/9/22: Irving to Drummond, 16 September 1833.

[36] Robert Baxter, *Irvingism, in its Rise, Progress, and Present State* (London: James Nisbet, 1836), 29–30; [Copinger], 'Annals', 40–1. In one of Irving's last letters to his congregation, he called them to pray for Taplin as a 'chosen vessel': Wilks, *Irving*, 283.

[37] *Scripture Reading and Exposition by the Late Rev. Edward Irving, A.M. at the Church in Newman Street, on Sunday Afternoon, 12th January 1834* (n.pl.: n.p., n.d.), 17.

[38] Ibid. 29.

bushel, and of failing to stand up for those who proclaimed the truth. His people were dying of religious formalism. True Christianity was 'the coming of the Lord in his judgments and his glory, ... the victory of the Lord in our flesh, ... the presence of his fulness in his Spirit in the Church, ... the abiding and abounding love of God the Father over the prodigal children of men, in Christ Jesus their elder brother'.[39] Isabella's denunciations of Scotland's religious state were almost as vigorous as her husband's, and one wonders what it takes to write a letter to a close family member wholly composed of such rebukes.

The churches being written off in this way, Irving and his followers sought to establish places of refuge for those who heeded their message.[40] These came in two forms, expected to develop simultaneously: Albury, it was said, was planted as a new church fitted for mission as the seat of the apostles, while the other emerging congregations were transplants, intended to witness within the existing divisions of Christendom.[41] Before Irving died, groups or congregations appear to have been formed at five locations in London and thirty-two elsewhere.[42] It was once apostles began to be called to office and to travel around the country preaching, setting up congregations and appointing ministers, that things really got off the ground. Irving played some part, but not as a systematic church-planter; where he was involved, it appears usually to have been as a catalyst through his preaching and private conferences with local clergy. So, for example, we find him lecturing at Southampton on Monday evenings from November 1832 to January 1833,[43] with a church being formed there soon after. Where he was involved in a more formal way, it was often under apostolic and prophetic direction, as when he was directed by prophecy on 25 January 1834 to go to Scotland with Taplin and William Tait (the former minister of the Collegiate Church in Edinburgh, who had been deposed on account of his support for the manifestations), to deal with problems which had arisen in the infant congregation in Edinburgh; these centred on the exercise of the gift of prophecy, which needed to be brought into line with practice elsewhere in the churches being gathered under apostles.[44] Arriving on 29 January, Irving spent a

---

[39] Cambridge, URCHS, letter 16: Irvings to Samuel Martin, 22 January 1834.

[40] For a fuller account of the formation of congregations during this period, see *The Lord's Work*, as well as [Copinger], 'Annals'; Rossteuscher, 'Rebuilding', Book II, ch. 3.

[41] DFP, C/9/12, Irving to Drummond, 5 February 1833; cf. Rossteuscher, 'Rebuilding', fol. 303, for this as a standard Catholic Apostolic interpretation of events.

[42] They were: Aberystwyth, Albury, Barmoor / Lowick, Bath, Belfast, Birmingham, Bridgnorth, Brighton, Bristol, Cambridge, Chatham, Chelmsford, Chepstow, Chester, Dudley, Edinburgh, Eynsham, Frome, Greenock, Kirkcudbright, Lymington, Melksham, Norwich, Paisley, Portsmouth, Rickmansworth, Salcombe, Southampton, Uxbridge, Ware, Wells and Wolverhampton; and in London: Bishopsgate, Newman Street, Chelsea, Islington and Southwark.

[43] [Copinger], 'Annals', 29.

[44] Ibid. 38–9. Cf. Tim Grass, '"The Taming of the Prophets": Bringing Prophecy under Control in the Catholic Apostolic Church', *Journal of the European Pentecostal Theological Association* 16 (1996), 58–70.

week teaching the flock and drawing on his experience of handling the gifts, with the church being duly set up on 6 February.[45]

From the start of his ministry Irving had tried to show that he could do without a full text in the pulpit (as on the occasion when he dropped his manuscript), and he had been moving away from writing out full sermon notes for some years in the interests of greater dependence on the Spirit's inspiration; but the benefit of this was not evident to some of his hearers. In a letter Irving described how he decided what to preach about on his Sunday in Edinburgh:

> while I was in doubt what to teach, the Lord, before the service began, opened the mouth of the prophet to encourage the flock to bow their understandings, and guide me to teach the manner of God's worship, of the holy race, and the altar, which I did forenoon and afternoon, with greater presence and power of teaching than I ever felt ... In the evening the power came upon the prophet to direct me to Ezekiel xxxvii., which I chose of myself, and had power to minister it, marvellous to myself.[46]

However, Horatius Bonar's estimate of Irving's preaching that week was very different.

> The place looked dingy, being but poorly lighted; and the audience was small. How strange the contrast between this and the 'West Kirk' in 1828! An 'apostle' or 'angel' was in the pulpit, and Mr Irving occupied the desk under him. To us all was melancholy. Irving looked twenty years older; his black hair had become gray; his cheeks thin and sunk. Only the old eye and forehead remained to tell of other days. Even his voice was not what it had once been. He expounded a passage in Jeremiah, if we remember aright; but the exposition was bare and feeble. He prayed; and the tones of his voice still sound to us afar; low, wailing tones of profound melancholy; while the burden of his hopeless cry was, 'Have pity, Lord, upon Thy desolate heritage!' He looked dispirited and wan and feeble; a man whose heart had already begun to break.[47]

Irving returned to London in mid-February. He was unwell and was losing his strength; friends took him away on Monday mornings so that on that day at least he would not have to receive visitors, as was his usual practice, but he still used the time to work, dictating letters.[48] Isabella filled out the picture in a letter to her mother. Apologizing that he had not been to Kirkcaldy during his visit to Scotland ('Edward was much grieved that it was not in his power to come to see you ... but his time is truly not his own neither is he his own master.'), she assured them that although very ill on his return he was now much better although still with a cough. The doctor had found 'a little chronic inflammation on the upper part of the Chest &

---

[45] London, British Library, 764m13 (uncatalogued), 'Rev. William Cannon's Account of Tongues and Prophecy', undated ms note shelved with *MW* 6; Oliphant, *Life*, 405–6.

[46] Oliphant, *Life*, 406: letter of 2 February 1834.

[47] [Horatius Bonar]?, 'Edward Irving', *QJP* 14 (1862), 224–47, at 238.

[48] Oliphant, *Life*, 407–8.

the external muscles of the Lungs too much strained', but Edward was now almost entirely healed by the Lord.[49] A few days later she informed them that Edward was almost completely better, though he had not quite regained his usual vigour, and had been able to take all his services except one. Reading between the lines, we may guess that family relationships were still somewhat delicate. Samuel, it appears, had walked from Bathgate to Edinburgh but missed seeing Edward (had he intended to discuss the letter he had just received, which we noted above?), while Isabella lamented that her father 'seems to feel he cannot come to us'.[50]

On 23 March the Irvings' last child, Isabella, was born. Her mother was grateful that the delivery had been easy, and informed the family that the baby had a Martin face. Edward, however, was not looking at all well. He still had the fatigue and cold which he had picked up in Scotland, and was working incessantly, constantly speaking (sometimes in hot overcrowded places), listening to the problems of his flock, and overseeing the church. By now he suffered from constant lassitude, but refused to believe himself ill.[51] Close friends were becoming really concerned about his health; this is illustrated by Carlyle's account of a meeting in Kensington Gardens in May 1834, after a gap of over two years.

> In look he was almost friendlier than ever; but he had suddenly become an old man. His head, which I had left raven-black, was grown grey, on the temples almost snow-white; the face was hollow, wrinkly, collapsed; the figure, still perfectly erect, seemed to have lost all its elasticity and strength. ... He admitted his weak health, but treated it as temporary, it seemed of small account to him. Friends and doctors had advised him to Bayswater for better air; had got him a lodging there, a stout horse to ride; summer, they expected, would soon set him up again. His tone was not despondent; but it was low, pensive, full of silent sorrow.[52]

He tried on several occasions to visit Irving and finally, as he explained to his mother,

> on Saturday last, [I] spent two hours with him. He seemed to have wonderfully recovered his health, and I trust will *not* perish in these delusions of his. He is still

---

[49] Isabella Irving to Mrs Martin, 5 March 1834 (in private hands). After giving details of the children's progress, she commented that although two of her servants gave her great satisfaction, a third, Lilly, 'breaks out occasionally in sad fits of passion & that is very disturbing & greatly grieving & dishonouring to the Lord.'

[50] Isabella Irving and Elizabeth Hamilton to Mrs Martin, 10 March 1834 (in private hands).

[51] Elizabeth Hamilton to Mrs Martin, 24 March 1834 (in private hands).

[52] Carlyle, *Reminiscences*, 302–3; cf. *CL*, 7.150–1: Carlyle to Jane Welsh Carlyle, 17 May 1834. Irving was staying at 14 Westbourne Terrace, which appears to have been the house of his brother-in-law William Hamilton: Barbara Waddington, *The Rev. Edward Irving & the Catholic Apostolic Church in Camden and beyond* (London: Camden History Society, 2007), 30.

a good man; yet woefully given over to his idols; and enveloped, for the present, and high choked, in the despicablest coil of cobwebs ever man sat in the midst of.[53]

For the moment, however, it was Isabella's health rather than Edward's which was giving cause for concern. On 10 July she suffered a miscarriage, 'brought on three weeks ago by a sad fright we were put into of having lost our precious Margaret in the ocean of London'.[54] As if that were not enough, on 26 July Edward wrote that it had looked as if he would lose her to the cholera; thankfully, he was able to testify that 'the Lord hath this morning heard the Confession & supplication of the Elders and we are much lightened. It hath been a wonderful dealing both with her and me for the subjugation of my intractable spirit to the Lord's own way.'[55] He recounted to his father-in-law that they called for the elders (as prescribed in James 5) and confessed their sin to them; the Elders then went up to her room and each prayed for her. Five minutes after their departure, she asked for food. Irving recognized the doctor as an instrument of healing in her case and could see God's hand at work in her healing as much as in his own, in which no doctor, medicine, or 'ordinance' (i.e. a rite performed by a minister of the church) had been involved. He was looking forward to the visit of his parents-in-law to London, and it seems that a few months had done much to restore their frank and friendly relationship.[56]

Margaret, by now eight years old, had evidently been sent to Macclesfield to stay with one of Irving's supporters, a Mrs Wales. From there she wrote to her aunt that she was learning botany, going for drives in the country, memorizing Scripture, poems and hymns, and sewing. But what is revealing is her total acceptance of her father's message: 'dear papa says Christ is near to come and he says.[sic] be thou holy or thou wilt never see him or be with him and he says the Holy Ghost only can make thee holy therefore pray mightily for the Holy Ghost'. She continues: 'poor Miss Clay is sick in her mind but what are we[;] we are not in our right mind unless we are sitting at the feet of Jesus[.] Miss Clay is frightened at the cows'.[57]

* * *

Shortly after Isabella's restoration, Carlyle again tried repeatedly to visit Edward. He was convinced (and William Hamilton agreed) that she had withheld his calling cards from her husband: 'I never in my time was concerned in another such despicability as I was forced to suspect her of'. (This goes a long way to explain her unsympathetic portrayal in his *Reminiscences*.) When he finally obtained admission, Edward did not rise from the sofa, nor did Isabella, who was sitting at his feet. 'He complains of biliousness, of a pain at his right short-rib; has a short thick cough which comes on at the smallest irritation.' He 'looked weak, dispirited, partly embarrassed', and

---

[53] *CL*, 7.196: Carlyle to Margaret A. Carlyle, 30 May 1834.
[54] DFP, C/9/41, Irving to Drummond, 10 July 1834.
[55] DFP, C/9/42, Irving to Drummond, 26 July 1834.
[56] Oliphant, *Life*, 2.373–4: Irving to John Martin, July 1834.
[57] Margaret Irving to Aunt [Anne Martin?], n.d. (in private hands).

continued to work even though the doctor ordered him to rest.[58] By September Carlyle described him to a friend as

> evidently very far from well; broken-looking, ten years older than when you saw him last; all *hoary* round the cheeks and under the chin; has a short ugly cough and hardness of breathing that comes upon him at the smallest effort is so weak that he cannot lift his little child to his head.' The Doctor's account is that his lungs *are* affected, tho' as yet only superficially; but that if he persist in the same course of excitement and agitation the affection *will* get deep enough.[59]

But by now, Irving had already left London for the last time; to Carlyle's lasting resentment, he would 'persist in the same course'. Carlyle's frustration showed itself in hostility towards the ministers of Irving's church: 'I often think I might do something for him, were we in free intercourse; but the "four-and-twenty elders" will it not, and must have their way.'[60] This was a misunderstanding of the situation, but one which persists today. In the next chapter, we shall examine the various explanations given of Irving's decision to go to Scotland, a decision which undoubtedly hastened his death.

---

[58] *CL*, 7.272: Carlyle to John A. Carlyle, 15 August 1834.
[59] Ibid. 298: Carlyle to William Graham, 14 September 1834.
[60] Ibid. 255: Carlyle to William Graham, 5 August 1834.

CHAPTER 21

'If I die, I die unto the Lord', September–December 1834

The great question thrown up by the final months of Irving's life is a simple one, although it has never received a completely satisfactory answer: why did he decide to go to Scotland? Various explanations exist, which we shall attempt to survey, but first we should note his expressed desire to return to Scotland to preach; he had been unable to do so in 1831 as planned, but took advantage of the opportunity given by his trial in 1833. At the afternoon service on Sunday 14 April, which had usually been devoted to evangelistic preaching, he informed the congregation that since his calling as angel, 'I have felt my gift of preacher or evangelist failing, as it were, not for want of will, but for want of warrant'. He asked them to pray that when the church could cope with his absence, God 'would spare me to come to Scotland, in the full commission of an evangelist; for his word hath passed upon me to that effect, and I long much to serve Him there'.[1]

Irving's father-in-law claimed that some of the prophets in London had asserted that God wished him to go to Scotland and undertake a great work there.[2] Baxter had prophesied that Irving 'would not be given the apostolic office, but would be sent as a prophet to Scotland, to bear the Lord's warning before the carnage which would ensue from the cholera there'.[3] According to the Catholic Apostolic minister C. W. Boase,

> A word of prophecy some years before having spoken emphatically of Mr Irving being a witness to his own land, he, when he felt his health rapidly declining, was seized with an intense desire to fulfil this duty in a more direct manner than hitherto, by going to Scotland and counselling such of his brethren of the clergy of the Church of Scotland who should seek to him; and many did come to him to confer

---

[1] Henry Drummond, *Narrative of the Circumstances which led to the setting up of the Church of Christ at Albury* (typescript, n.d.; first publ. 1834), 17.

[2] William Hanna, ed., *Memoirs of the Life and Writings of Thomas Chalmers D.D. LL.D.* (4 vols, Edinburgh: Sutherland and Knox, 1850), 3.287n.

[3] Robert Baxter, *Narrative of Facts, characterizing the Supernatural Manifestations, in Members of Mr. Irving's Congregation, and other Individuals, in England and Scotland, and formerly in the Writer himself* (London: James Nisbet, 1833), 67, cf. 69.

on the state of things generally in the Church, and upon those matters of which he had such intimate knowledge. In the fulfilment of this supposed duty he died ...[4]

As a result, it was believed by some that his departure was in obedience to instructions received. Carlyle, who despaired of being able to do anything to help his friend, told his brother that Irving was 'off to Glasgow for some tongue-work, being ordered to it'. The doctor had insisted that he should go to Madeira, but to no avail.[5] Mrs Oliphant thought this explanation plausible when she produced the first edition of her biography:

> Either the time had now arrived for that great work, and he was authoritatively commanded to go forth and do it, which is the explanation given by his alarmed and disapproving relatives of his journey; or else the Church at Newman Street, anxious for the restoration of his health, gladly pronounced an authoritative sanction to his wish to wander ...[6]

Cardale and others in the Catholic Apostolic Church evidently objected to this, as the one-volume edition reads:

> The explanation given by his alarmed and disapproving relatives of his journey is that the time had now arrived for that great work, and that he was authoritatively commanded to go forth and do it. The representatives of the Church in Newman Street, however, do not admit this. 'It was not without remonstrance on the part of many,' but 'we were met by the suggestion that it was his native air,' writes an influential member of the community. They yielded, however, to his wish, which was to wander ...[7]

She suggested that the leaders may have seen that he would never seek health for its own sake, and that his presence was 'already an unacknowledged embarrassment, preventing or at least hindering the development of all its [the church's] new institutions'.[8] That being so, both they and he may have felt an unacknowledged sense of relief when he left. Whatever Cardale and the others felt, David Ker in his response to Mrs Oliphant asserted that 'the friends who entreated him to go to a

---

[4] [C. W. Boase], *Supplementary Narrative to The Elijah Ministry in the Christian Church* (Edinburgh: R. Grant, [1868]), 812. The wording is virtually identical to that in [F. V. Woodhouse], *A Narrative of Events affecting the Position and Prospects of the whole Christian Church: Part I. Second Edition, with a Second Part, containing a Continuation to the Present Time* (London: Bedford Bookshop, 1938; first publ. 1885), 38, the first part of which had appeared in 1847.

[5] *CL*, 7.329: Carlyle to John A Carlyle, 28 October 1834.

[6] Oliphant, *Life*, 2.374.

[7] Oliphant, *Life*, 408. In a footnote on the next page she expressed sorrow that such a statement should have pained his friends, but refused to retract it.

[8] Ibid. 409.

southern latitude, offered to defray the expense of the journey'.[9] There can be little doubt that Drummond would have been willing to contribute generously to this, and it was therefore unjust of Carlyle to hold him and others responsible for not doing more to help Irving.

To sum up, we may say that Irving longed to return to Scotland to preach; that prophecy had previously indicated that he would be a prophet to his native land; that he was advised against making the journey by people who would willingly have paid for him to go abroad to spend the winter resting in a milder climate; and that the leaders at Newman Street went along with his wishes. In the end, he went to Scotland because he was committed to what he saw as his vocation. Nobody else should be charged with the responsibility for his decision.

* * *

Irving left London at the beginning of September. Travelling via Birmingham, he spent 10 days in Shropshire before making his way via Herefordshire to Aberystwyth. From here he worked his way northwards during the first week or so of October, and then returned along the coast to Liverpool, which he reached on the 13th. Sailing from here to Greenock, he arrived in Glasgow on the 29th,[10] where he stayed with the Taylor family. Such, in brief, was the itinerary, and it may well have owed something to a desire to meet people with whom he had already been in contact, or to explore promising openings; but he packed the journey with sightseeing as well as speaking, sending home regular reports on his progress, health and doings. These are as revealing as the journal which he kept for Isabella in 1825, and like the earlier document are fully reported by Mrs Oliphant.[11]

Irving kept his children supplied with letters describing the sights he had seen, and offering lively retellings of historical events, such as this one from Ironbridge on 16 September. Its account of his visit to the oak tree in Shropshire where the future Charles II hid is tinctured with Irving's own 'divine right' views:

> The people rose up against [Charles I], and warred against him till they took him, and then cut off his head at Whitehall, in London; and his poor son [to become Charles II] they pursued, to take him and kill him also, and he was forced to flee away and hide himself, as King David did hide himself. ... we went upstairs into an ancient bedroom, whose floor was sore worn with age, and by the side of this bedroom was a door leading into a little, little, room, and the floor of that room lifted up in the middle, and underneath was a narrow dark dungeon or hiding-place,

---

[9] David Ker, *Observations on Mrs Oliphant's 'Life of Edward Irving:' and Correction of certain Misstatements therein: With a Reprint of Mr Irving's Speeches before the Presbytery of London, in March 1832* (Edinburgh: Thomas Laurie, 1863), xvi–xvii.

[10] Some sources give the date as 25 October, but cp. Isabella Irving to Miss Martin, 29 October 1839 (in private hands), in which she recalled arriving in Glasgow five years ago to the day.

[11] Carlyle thought this the most lifelike part of her book: *Reminiscences*, ed. C. E. Norton (London: J. M. Dent, 1932), 305.

in which the King of all this island was glad to hide himself, in order to escape from his persecutors; this narrow place opened below by narrow stairs into the garden, where is a door in the wall hidden behind ivy. Then we went up another stair to the garret, and at the top of it there was another board in the floor, that lifted up, and went down by a small ladder into another hiding-place. But all these hiding-places were not enough to hide the King from his persecutors, armed soldiers on horseback, who entered the house to search it. Then the King fled out by the door behind the ivy in the garden, and leapt over the garden wall into a field, and climbed up an oak-tree, and hid himself among its thick branches. Papa saw this tree. It is done round with a rail, to distinguish it from the rest and to keep it sacred ... Then the soldiers, not finding him in the house, galloped about into the wood, and passed under the very tree; but God saved the King, and they found him not. ... There are many lessons to be learned from this, which your mother will teach you, for I am tired, and my horse is getting ready.[12]

He continued to preach or teach wherever openings presented themselves. At Chepstow, where an evangelist from Newman Street named Sturgeon had sown the seed, 'I am watering it with words of counsel and instruction, teaching them the way of worshipping God, and encouraging them to gather together and call upon His name. I think there is the foundation of a Church laid in this place.' At the Sturgeons' home he had had great numbers attend family worship, and he had also been in conference with all the young clergy locally.[13] He was confident regarding his own state of health and encouraged by that of his son, who had been ill:

... I am indeed very much better, and hardly conscious of an invalid's feelings ... I continue to use Dr. Darling's prescriptions, and find the good of them. Now, as concerneth speaking, I am fully persuaded, by experience, that it is the proper exercise of the lungs, and, being taken in measure, it is always good for me. But nothing has done me so much good as to hear of dear Martin's recovery. That was indeed healing both to body and soul.[14]

Two days later he informed Isabella that he was riding thirty miles a day, and walking downhill. 'I have you and the children in continual remembrance before God, and them also that are departed, expressing my continual contentedness that they are with Him.'[15]

But as he worked his way back eastwards along the North Wales coast, he began to long for Isabella's company, and asked her to be ready to join him. After getting wet viewing the Menai Bridge, he spent a feverish night, which the next day's ride did not completely cure. Further on, his headache returned, this time with sickness.[16]

---

[12] Oliphant, *Life*, 412–3: Irving to Isabella Irving, 23 September 1834.

[13] Ibid. 414–15: Irving to Isabella Irving, 27 September 1834. A newspaper report claimed that he had been lecturing at a lady's residence near Chepstow: *Bristol Mercury*, 4 October 1834.

[14] Oliphant, *Life*, 415: Irving to Isabella Irving, 27 September 1834.

[15] Ibid. 416: Irving to Isabella Irving, 29 September 1834.

[16] Ibid. 419–20: Irving to Isabella Irving, 11 October 1834.

The next letter describes how he had fought his fever for three days, but was now, apparently, coming to terms with the reality that his illness was worsening: he therefore felt it best to sail direct from Liverpool (where he was staying) to Greenock. Perhaps the clearest indication of his state of mind and body was the confession that 'Now I feel unable to take care of myself, and my calm judgment is that you should be my nurse and companion.'[17] Isabella herself wrote to Drummond that 'He is ill[,] very ill[,] and faith alone can support me.' She thought that Satan was seeking to shake Edward's faith and to hinder him from trusting God for healing, since 'the promise of the Lord is distinctly I will put none of these diseases upon you', and sickness in his people dishonoured the Lord. It was, she felt, evidence that sin continued to cling even to believers.[18]

Once Isabella had joined Edward in Liverpool and he had recovered a little, they sailed by the packet boat to Greenock, and made their way to Glasgow. Even here, he would not cease working. The hope was that he would plant a church there, and services were being held in the Lyceum room each Sabbath, though he did little himself except speak a few words to the congregation before the service ended.[19] McLeod Campbell had been preaching there each Sunday since the beginning of January 1833, and the two men often rode out together while Irving was in Glasgow.[20] Campbell may have been hoping to reclaim Irving from his errors: to his father he wrote, 'I do not feel that I have made any impression on him as yet. But it may yet be. I do not find him at all like the rest [i.e. the emissaries from London].'[21] However, Irving felt that he had come in a suspicious and accusatory spirit, trying to put him right. In the same letter Irving described his daily routine:

> ... I feel it my duty to take all ease of this mortal body which the Lord hath redeemed by His blood. I wish to strengthen my digestion by eating only the most nourishing meats with bread & drinking one or two glasses of very fine East India Madeira & sometimes instead of it a tumbler of excellent ale. Also I make a ride two hours or two hours & a half every day about midday & after dining at 2 o'clock I rest till 5 without seeing any one. I am sponged with vinegar and rubbed with a coarse towel every morning before getting out of bed & I have never yet gone out after dinner save to take a short walk with my wife when the weather is fine_[22]

Isabella remained confident that Edward would be healed, as prophecy had assured him of success in Scotland.[23] To her father, Edward dictated a letter on 21 November in which he described himself as being 'in pretty good health'. The cold mountain air

---

[17] Ibid. 420-1: Irving to Isabella Irving, 12-13 October 1834.
[18] Alnwick Castle, DFP, C/9/43: Isabella Irving to Drummond, 19 October 1834.
[19] William Arnot, *Life of James Hamilton, D.D., F.L.S.* (London: J. Nisbet, 1870), 65-6: Hamilton to Jane Hamilton, 28 November 1834.
[20] Donald Campbell, ed., *Memorials of John McLeod Campbell, D.D.: Being Selections from his Correspondence* (2 vols, London: Macmillan, 1877), 1.102, 104.
[21] Ibid. 125: Campbell to his father, 30 October 1834.
[22] DFP, C/9/44, Irving to Drummond (in Isabella's hand), 11 November 1834.
[23] Oliphant, *Life*, 422-3.

gave him great pleasure and he was not affected by the rain; 'My frame cries out for cold air & not for Madeira or Malta or any such places'. As for his reasons for being in Glasgow,

> with respect to some work that you have followed the newspapers in believing I am sent to do here that work is just to rest [illegible] and abide patiently and to give counsel to those whom the Lord shall bring to me for counsel and that I may not even be burdened with this the Lord hath sent Francis Woodhouse Esq one of the Elders of my Church, and named to be an Apostle, to be joined with me ...

In this letter he says that he was available for consultation from noon till 6 p.m., and far from feeling burdened by his schedule, he asked: 'can there be a man out of health surrounded with more blessed conditions than I am? I wish you would praise God with me instead of murmuring & complaining about me.' John Martin had evidently written a letter which had upset them, and Irving asked him not on any account in his letters to speak with contempt of what they believed to be a work of the Holy Spirit. God, he asserted, had allowed him to be seen to be weak and helpless before sending him fully armed against 'that Babylon of which you are still a watchman'. He and Isabella hoped to be in Edinburgh soon and planned to visit Samuel on the way.[24]

Others were less sanguine about his condition. Soon after their arrival in Glasgow, the Irvings spent a day with David Ker's sister-in-law (and her husband), who recorded her impressions:

> I never saw anything more affecting than the change in his appearance. To human appearance, he is sinking under a deep consumption. His gigantic form bears all the marks of age and weakness; his tremendous voice is now often faltering; and when occasionally he breaks forth, with all his former feeling, into such flowing, eloquent commendations, of the excellent glory of the Man Christ Jesus, and tells the dishonour done to His name, one sees that his bodily powers are exhausted by his still vigorous mental occupations. ... His heart seemed to flow out in love to all mankind, and to bear down all the barriers which names and sects have raised to obstruct its exercise.[25]

Another who was concerned was Francis Woodhouse. The youngest of the apostles, he had come from London to assist the Irvings and to teach the flocks in Glasgow and Edinburgh about the nature of the apostolic office (and doubtless by so doing to counter the influence of the Macdonalds). He was convinced of the seriousness of Irving's condition, and told Drummond that, in line with a prophecy recently given that Satan gained power over an angel through the sin of his church, 'his restoration must come from the cry of the people of whose common sin he is

---

[24] Cambridge, URCHS, letter 9: Irving to John Martin, 21 November 1834 (in Isabella's hand, but signed by Edward and endorsed 'Edward's last').

[25] Mary Pryor Hack, *Christian Womanhood* (London: Hodder and Stoughton, 1883), 200–1.

the sign & manifestation'. The state to which Irving had been brought gave Woodhouse cause for sober reflection; 'there', he wrote, 'is the Pride of Scotland[,] moral[,] intellectual and personal[,] brought to nought by the hand of the Lord'.[26] As late as 29 November Irving expressed his confidence that 'when He sees fit, He will renew my strength'.[27] But Woodhouse perhaps gave a truer picture when he told Drummond: 'He is wounded with a very heavy dealing; his faith has almost left him'. Although Irving evidently still hoped to go to Edinburgh and testify to the work, Woodhouse refused to contemplate it 'while every step of our way would put him to torture'. Two days earlier, he had shown Irving a letter from Drummond, in response to which Irving acknowledged that he had been jealous of the apostles and was still afraid that they were taking too much on themselves, but confessed his sin and expressed his longing to be delivered from jealousy and suspicion.[28]

During the autumn Irving addressed two final letters to his flock.[29] It is clear that he viewed himself as 'the chief instrument of bringing in that sin for which the hand of the Lord hath long lain heavy upon us' and his illness as a chastisement for this. In his first letter, therefore, he sought to explain what he believed that sin had been, as the first step to dealing with it. Describing it as 'the making of a calf' (cf. Exodus 32), he explains that God had planned to set in London 'a complete and perfect pattern of what His Church should be', but that the church had exalted him as its angel to the place of headship over it which belonged to Christ alone (and which was exercised through apostles). His action with Taplin in naming the sixty evangelists was a manifestation of this error, as was sending them forth without ordination. The church had, he asserted, been 'impatient of the government of Apostles, of the Lord in them'. Urging them to repent, he also calls them to 'Cry for the prophet, for he was a chosen vessel. Hold ye him against his own rebellious heart. Let him not go; and if he will not return, oh! be ye guiltless of his fall.'[30] The second letter, dated 25 October, returns to the idea that he and they were being chastised on account of their sin, but added to this the conviction that 'the Lord will utterly separate my name from the work which He worketh for the blessing of the whole world. Oh! what a grief it hath been to me that my name should be familiarly joined with the work of the Lord.'[31] A concluding excerpt from his letter to Cardale of 5 November reiterated

---

[26] DFP, C/9/46, Woodhouse to Drummond, 20 November 1834; Oliphant, *Life*, 425; [H. B. Copinger], 'Annals: The Lord's Work in the Nineteenth and Twentieth Centuries' (typescript, n.d.), 43.

[27] Oliphant, *Life*, 2.400: Irving to William Hamilton, 29 November 1834.

[28] DFP, C/9/47, Woodhouse to Drummond, 29 November 1834.

[29] *To the Church of God in London, with the Elders and the Deacons* [Two pastoral letters 'to the Flock of God, which the Lord Jesus Christ hath given into my hand'], ed. J. B. Cardale (London: Mills, Jowett & Mills, [1835]); reproduced in Washington Wilks, *Edward Irving: An Ecclesiastical and Literary Biography* (London: William Freeman, 1854), 280–7.

[30] Wilks, *Irving*, 283.

[31] Ibid. 285. This is one reason why Catholic Apostolics have refused to accept the designation 'Irvingites'.

the conviction that God was separating him from the flock in order to guard against any tendency to idolatry on their part.

Carlyle claimed that Irving's letter from Glasgow (presumably he meant both) was 'full of questionings, dubieties upon the *Tongues* and such points; full of wanderings in deep waters, with one light fixed on high, "Humble ourselves before God, and He will show us!"[32] Irving was clearly perplexed by the turn which events had taken, but it is going too far to say that this had led him to doubt the reality of the gifts. Some words from a prayer he had uttered in January well sum up the conviction which sustained him: 'They say we are fools for waiting for thee; but we wait for thee ... we hold fast our confidence, and we will not let it go.'[33]

On 28 November, Isabella wrote her parents a letter which they must have expected but dreaded receiving; Edward had said that they would write if his condition worsened, and now it had. He was very ill but she still believed that God would intervene in his own time.[34] The Martins hastened to Glasgow, as did Edward's mother and sister. In London, the church held a day of prayer and fasting. The Irvings' governess wrote that they had broken him down but the Lord could raise him up.[35] Clearly their belief, in line with the prophecy referred to above, was that he was suffering on account of their sin.

On Sunday 7 December, Edward twice expressed a desire to depart and be with Christ; at various points he asked his wife to read him Psalm 18, Ephesians 4 and 1 Thessalonians 4–5. To his father-in-law he testified to the depths of peace and joy which he experienced in Christ. When his mother asked if he had anything to say concerning Isabella and the children, he expressed the confidence that the elders in London would look after them. Then he lapsed into unconsciousness for the last six hours, moaning a great deal.[36] The fullest account of his death was given by John Martin in a letter to William Hamilton. Although unconscious, Edward had continued to speak but very indistinctly; the most Martin could catch was 'and if I die _ I die to the Lord. Amen!'[37] His mind had been wandering since the previous

---

[32] Carlyle, *Reminiscences*, 306; cf. A. L. Drummond's comment that in it 'we can feel an undercurrent of deep disappointment with the hierarchy and its subjective basis': *Edward Irving and his Circle: Including some Consideration of the 'Tongues' Movement in the Light of Modern Psychology* (London: James Clarke, [1937]), 226. Carlyle alleged that Henry Drummond and others had suppressed and destroyed the letters after having them printed for private circulation. If so, and there is no other evidence to confirm his claim, it was futile, since the letters had already been reprinted in the *Gospel Magazine* for May 1835.

[33] *Expositions and Sermons by the Rev. E. Irving, Jan. 29th, and Feb. 1st; and Rev. N. Armstrong, January 27th, 1833* (London: W. Harding, [1833]), 2.

[34] Isabella Irving to her parents, 28 November 1834 (in private hands).

[35] Caroline Rooke to Isabella Irving, postmarked December 1834 (in private hands).

[36] Campbell, ed., *Memorials*, 1.127: Campbell to his sister, 16 December 1834; Ker, *Observations*, xvii.

[37] It was probably Woodhouse who wrote to Cardale after Irving died that he had said '*If* I die', implying he might not; whether or not this was so, it seems that Irving was

night, always in the direction of spiritual things. 'He was often praying for the Church – confessing sin – giving praise for mercies. Sometimes he was exhorting the Church, sometimes giving counsel to individuals, and so forth.' Around 5 p.m. he began repeating 'Lord pardon all'; unable to finish the sentence, he kept repeating the word 'all'. Another fragment of speech ended 'keep unto that day'.[38] Once Martin observed that Edward mixed some foreign words in his speech, some Hebrew; he repeated the first verse of Psalm 23 in Hebrew, and Edward immediately replied with what appeared to be the second and third. Isabella had had almost no sleep for over a week watching over him, nor had her mother. Martin took up his pen again at 12.40 a.m. on 8 December, to announce that Edward had died half an hour earlier. Isabella was now 'bereaved of her almost idolized husband'. In spite of his rejection of the gifts, he acknowledged that 'Good Mr. Woodhouse has acquitted himself, with the most devoted attention, of the trust committed to him; doing every thing in his power to assist or serve either Edwd or his wife. I shall ever esteem and love him for what I have seen of the unassuming goodness of heart, which he has displayed.'[39] The immediate cause of death remains unclear; according to Campbell, the doctors attending Irving 'said that his death was not connected with any affection [sic] of the lungs, though to ordinary eyes it appeared consumption'.[40]

* * *

The funeral was held on Friday 12 December in Glasgow Cathedral, where Irving lies buried in the crypt, in a grave offered by a Mr Laurie, a business partner of William Hamilton.[41] Among the large congregation were, it was claimed, most of the Glasgow ministers and most of the elders and deacons from St John's:[42] they may have disagreed with his theology, but were constrained to acknowledge him as a saintly man. *The Times* quoted a Scottish newspaper report to the effect that 'every other consideration was forgotten in the universal and profound sympathy with which the information was received'.[43] One writer states that the funeral sermon was preached by Chalmers, but I have found no confirmation of this.[44] The story got

---

struggling to understand why he was to die, but that the struggle ended in an expression of trust: Ker, *Observations*, xvii.

[38] From 2 Timothy 1.12, a confession of St Paul near the end of his life: 'I know whom I have believed, and am persuaded that he is able to keep that which I have committed unto him against that day'.

[39] John Martin to William Hamilton, 7–8 December 1834 (in private hands).

[40] Campbell, ed., *Memorials*, 1.128: Campbell to his father, 18 December 1834.

[41] Isabella Irving to Mr and Mrs Laurie, [December 1834] (in private hands).

[42] *The Times*, 20 December 1834, 3; Oliphant, *Life*, 427; Drummond, *Irving*, 227.

[43] 'Death of the Rev. Edward Irving', *The Times*, 12 December 1834, 2 (from the *Scottish Guardian*, 9 December 1834).

[44] William Landels, 'Edward Irving: A Lecture', in *Lectures delivered before the Young Men's Christian Association* ... (London: James Nisbet, 1863), 39–89, at 44. Gordon Strachan asserts that the text of the sermon was 2 Sam. 3.38, 'Know ye not that there is a

about that a band of white-robed women kept watch over the grave expecting Irving's resurrection, although Story's son denied it, his father having been one of the last to leave the scene.[45]

Another funeral sermon was preached in London on 14 December by John Cumming at Crown Court Church of Scotland.[46] In his opinion, Irving had 'made a deeper sensation among the religious public, than any other minister since the days of Luther and of Knox, and who being dead speaks volumes'. But mixed with admiration for Irving was the intent to portray his latter course as a cautionary tale.

> 'When I came first to this great metropolis, I found in Mr. Irving a friend when I had none besides, and in his session much spiritual and religious comfort. I was in the habit of spending many Saturday evenings along with a few ministers of England and Scotland, in meditations on the Greek Testament; and when I remember the child-like simplicity, the striking humbleness of mind, and the kind hospitality of that great and good man, I cannot but grieve at the awful eclipse under which he came, and the early tomb he has found. He is gone to the grave, I have reason to believe, with a broken heart. However much he continued to adhere to the unscriptural and enthusiastic notions he broached, he could not yet shut his eyes to the awful discoveries made concerning the conduct of some of his professedly inspired followers.[47]

Lessons to learn from Irving included the dangers of a lofty intellect (like the eagle, he soared too close to the sun and was blinded, 'misled by sparks of his kindling'); the dangers of ministerial popularity; the danger of self-confidence; and the danger of leaving truth for novelty.[48]

Tributes were paid by many who had differed from Irving during his ministry. Baxter described him as 'A man of noble powers, warm affections, and of unconquerable energy; used as an instrument for much good until overtaken by this

---

prince and a great man fallen this day in Israel?' but gives no source for this: *The Pentecostal Theology of Edward Irving* (London: Darton Longman & Todd, 1973), 201.

[45] Robert Herbert Story, *Memoir of the Life of the Rev. Robert Story, late Minister of Rosneath, Dunbartonshire* (Cambridge: Macmillan, 1862), 233. The myth proved persistent: among those to repeat it was A. L. Drummond, on the evidence of a minister who had been present at the funeral: *Irving*, 227–8; cf. Arnold Dallimore, *The Life of Edward Irving: Fore-runner of the Charismatic Movement* (Edinburgh: Banner of Truth, 1983), 169. H. C. Whitley's version was that on the night after the funeral, 'superstitious crowds stood around the Cathedral half expecting some last, great miracle out of the grave': *Blinded Eagle: An Introduction to the Life and Teaching of Edward Irving* (London: SCM, 1955), 34.

[46] J. Cumming, 'The Moral Influence we exert after Death', *British Pulpit* 2 (1834), 541–8. Cumming was the Church of Scotland minister at Crown Court, where his predictions (including setting dates for the Second Coming) brought him considerable notoriety.

[47] Ibid. 545.

[48] Ibid. 546.

delusion, under which he withered.'[49] Writing to Armstrong in 1835, Baxter claimed to 'know the doubts of the work with which he was torn, when I was with him, and I believe the contradictions and hindrances, confusion and increasing doubts in the work, hastened his dissolution'.[50] Erskine called him 'a man of much child-like feeling to God, and personal dependence on Him, amidst things which may well appear unintelligible and strange in his history',[51] Robert Murray M'Cheyne, then an Edinburgh divinity student but later to become a saintly and effective minister in Dundee, wrote on hearing of Irving's death, 'I look back upon him with awe, as on the saints and martyrs of old. A holy man in spite of all his delusions and errors. He is now with his God and Saviour, whom he wronged so much, yet, I am persuaded, loved so sincerely.'[52]

Perhaps the final tribute should come from an article in *Fraser's Magazine* published soon after Irving's death. The magazine emanated from the literary circles which he had sought to influence at the start of his London ministry, and the author was probably Carlyle. At any rate, the article asserted that those who only saw the London Irving could have no inkling of what the 'Scottish uncelebrated Irving' was like. Abandoned by the fashion-seekers, he still had his Bible. And he posed a question which summed up not only Irving's ministry but his life: 'If it is the written word of God, shall it not be the acted Word too?'[53]

---

[49] Robert Baxter, *Irvingism, in its Rise, Progress, and Present State* (London: James Nisbet, 1836), 30.

[50] Ibid. 46: Baxter to Nicholas Armstrong, 9 August 1835.

[51] William Hanna, ed., *Letters of Thomas Erskine* (2nd edn, Edinburgh: David Douglas, 1878), 165: Erskine to Miss Stuart, 13 December 1834.

[52] Andrew A. Bonar, *The Life of Robert Murray M'Cheyne* (London: Banner of Truth, 1960; first publ. 1844), 35; cf. [Horatius Bonar]?, 'Edward Irving', *QJP* 14 (1862), 224–47, at 242.

[53] Anon., 'Edward Irving', *Fraser's Magazine* 11 (1835), 99–103, at 102. For the authorship, see Anon., 'Edward Irving', *Fraser's Magazine* 67 (1863), 62–73, at 62.

Chapter 22

Epilogue

Ever since Thomas Carlyle's *Reminiscences*, it has been common to view Irving as a good man who not only strayed into what was then deemed theological error but who also suffered at the hands of the leaders in the church which his ministry had done so much to create. Irving is portrayed as the man with a big vision; they as the petty-minded and bureaucratic functionaries whose system had no place for its creator. Whilst it is true, as we have seen, that Irving was caught on the back foot by some of the developments which occurred in the new church, Carlyle's judgement is fair neither to Irving nor to the apostles. The fact is, as we have shown, that Irving believed these developments to come from the hand of God (and his Romanticism would have predisposed him to long for supernatural divine intervention in the life of what he saw as the moribund church of his day), and his consistency of character meant that inevitably he would accept them and do his part to implement them. He certainly had questions which went unanswered, and he admitted to difficulties in working out his obedience to the divine purpose (especially when it came to relating to the apostles and prophets), but still he obeyed, although he proved unable to integrate the manifestations into his high doctrine of the ministerial office: had he held a lower view of the latter, this would have been easier.

A review of the *Collected Writings* expressed the conviction that Irving had gone astray 'because he was too logical, too consistent, and too honest to hold certain principles for truth and yet deny their legitimate and inevitable consequences'.[1] I believe this is true, and that it can be demonstrated by reference to his views on subjects as diverse as missionaries and the manifestations. Irving was accused of many things, but his accusers were to the fore in giving him full credit for his sincerity. The picture which has emerged in this biography is of a man passionately convinced of the truth of his message, prepared to proclaim it without fear or favour, and by his very simplicity of character perhaps blinded to the considerations of prudence which tended to moderate the conduct and speech of many of his clerical contemporaries. Irving was a man – and a minister – of high ideals, and of high reverence for the ideal and for its perceived exemplars, an attitude which the Romantic climate of the day would have reinforced.

To accompany each of his *Lectures on Revelation*, Irving penned a sonnet expressing its leading truths. In one dedicated to the memory of a clerical friend, he summed up the minister's task:

---

[1] *Scotsman*, 25 October 1865, 6.

Thou wast a churchman of the ancient seed;
A shepherd, who thy care did ne'er abate;
A watchman, who the nation's weal did heed;
Which drew upon thee sons of Belial's hate.[2]

Each of those three epithets is capable of application to Irving himself. He was, firstly, a *churchman*. His high view of the church and his conviction of the perpetual necessity of the ministry (which arose from the unchanging needs of its members) meant that he was bound to place stress on this aspect of ministerial duty. And this did not involve myopic dedication to the affairs of the congregation to which a minister was called: Irving always kept an eye on religious developments beyond his own congregation and approved of other ministers who did likewise. A high view of the church's calling and glory meant, too, that he could never be satisfied with a 'maintenance' model of ministry. This, and his own early experience of rejection, helped to strengthen his sense of frustration with existing views.

Irving was a *shepherd*. In spite of his tendency to authoritarianism (a trait evident in his schoolmastering days and reinforced by his high view of the ministry), he never lost the ability to relate to ordinary people or to voice their concerns in critiques of contemporary business practice or government policy. We have seen that he laid himself out in ministering to those in need, that his home was always open to them, and that he possessed the rare pastoral gift of being able to retain in his mind and heart an intimate understanding of the circumstances and spiritual condition of a large number of people.

Irving was a *watchman*. For much of his career he attempted to relate to the world outside as well as to the church. In the Preface, I explained what lay behind the chosen title for this book – *The Lord's Watchman*. His sense of duty to God and his consistency of character ensured that he continued to speak what he saw as the truth, in and out of season. However, this ministry came at a considerable personal cost, as he explained:

> If I had not comfort and strength in my God, and assurance of His salvation, the thickening shapes of evil ... would drive me to despair. For my heart was never cruel, and much labour in the pastor's office hath made it more tender, than well befits the messenger of such heavy news as God hath called me to bear to this nation and the nations of Christendom.[3]

To my mind, the last line of the quotation from Irving's sonnet is most significant. In any examination of his life and work, one note continually makes itself heard: that of the ministry as warfare. Irving's references to the subject, as well as his practice, repeatedly affirmed the necessity of contending for the truth, of fighting the forces of evil, of equipping the saints for battle. While much of this derives from the particular cast of his theology as an expression of early nineteenth-

---

[2] *PW*, 1.786.
[3] Ibid. 2.56.

century radical Evangelicalism, it could be argued that Irving thrived on disagreement; condemnation from others reinforced his sense of being persecuted for righteousness' sake, and blanket condemnation of the shortcomings of the religious and political world formed a major part of his preaching and writing. According to the *Ordination Charge*, his ideal minister was also to be ready for combat. Here is a reflection of his Christology, with its consistent stress upon the Incarnate Christ as one who shared our nature (just as Irving could stand in the shoes of his parishioners) and thus contended with, and overcame, sin in the flesh by the power of the Spirit.

Irving's legacy remains the subject of debate. For many, its most obvious aspect is the Catholic Apostolic Church. He is often, and incorrectly, described as its 'founder', although a more appropriate word would be 'catalyst'. My examination of its debt to him must await the forthcoming volume on the church, *The Lord's Work*. But his ministry provided the soil in which there could take root an unusual plant: thoroughly and uncompromisingly biblicist, yet unlike other contemporary biblicists intensely sacramental and with a rich appreciation of the material dimension to worship. Furthermore, it succeeded in combining a firm adherence to the Scriptures as the revealed word of God with an expectation that the God who spoke in 'Bible times' could still speak in the nineteenth century. Yet after its last apostle died in 1901 the church began quietly to fade away, convinced that its particular part in God's purpose was to outward appearances accomplished.

For some, it is Irving's version of Evangelicalism, with its emphasis on the study of biblical prophecy, which was a major part of his legacy. But the scheme of interpretation propounded by the Albury circle and perpetuated in essentials by the Catholic Apostolic Church did not ultimately prove very influential; its historicist premillennialism, although popular during the mid-nineteenth century, would lose out to a futurist version as propagated by J. N. Darby and the Brethren and later adopted by much of the Pentecostal movement.

Perhaps the most significant part of his theological legacy may have been his emphasis on the Incarnation rather than the Atonement. This was taken up enthusiastically and developed by the Anglican theologian F. D. Maurice, perhaps the foremost theologian of the Broad Church wing of Anglicanism. Something similar appears to have happened in the Church of Scotland under the leadership of men like Norman Macleod. Even so, Irving should not be seen as the sole source of this new emphasis; more significant was his friend John McLeod Campbell. Irving's distinctive Christology, however, was to a considerable extent his own, and its emphasis on Christ's human nature as fallen has secured the approval of some influential theologians within the Reformed tradition who have sought to rehabilitate Irving as orthodox.

Coupled with this distinctive Christology was Irving's emphasis on Christ as the prototype Christian anointed with the Holy Spirit. Mary Campbell drew from this the conclusion that we may do the works which Christ did, a conclusion similar to that which has helped to motivate Pentecostal and Charismatic Christians. Yet few of them have been aware of Irving until recent decades; if they were, it was only so that they could distance their teaching from his, especially where his Christology was concerned.

So, if no area of Irving's theology can be said to have commanded widespread interest and approval, or to have influenced large numbers, are we to say that his ministry was wasted? By no means. For those who will read his works and penetrate beyond his tendency to dogmatism and excessive condemnation of opponents, there is a rich vein of biblical and theological exposition to be mined. Lesser theologians than he have had their works reprinted in our day; perhaps it is time that consideration was given to the production of a scholarly edition of Irving's most significant works. The appearance of an edition of his letters from the same publisher as this work, edited by the archivist of what was his church, Barbara Waddington, is a welcome first step towards this.

In the end, however, I suspect that what will continue to attract the most attention is his life and in particular his approach to preaching and pastoral ministry. A biography of him seems to have appeared in almost every generation since his death. I hope that this one, which among other things has sought to draw attention to his neglected pastoral sermons and writings, will prove a worthy member of that succession.

Appendix I
Irving's Family

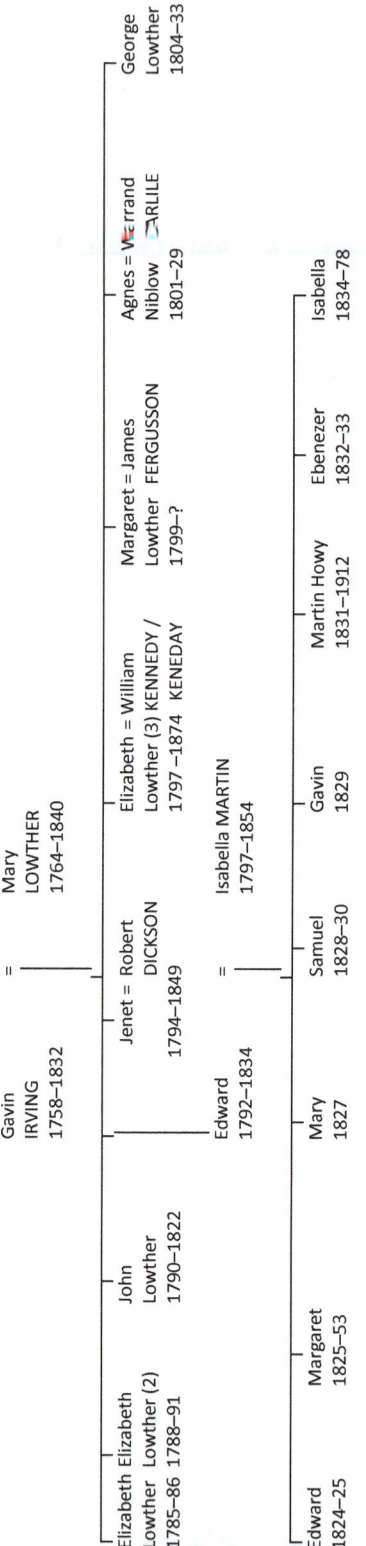

APPENDIX 2

A Chronology of Irving's Life

1792	August 4: Born at Annan
1805	November: Enters Edinburgh University
1809	April: Graduates Master of Arts; commences Divinity course; becomes schoolmaster at Haddington
1810	Becomes tutor to Jane Welsh
1812	September 29: Resigns post at Haddington; becomes master of new school at Kirkcaldy
1815	June: Completes Divinity course, licensed to preach by Presbytery of Kirkcaldy
1818	Summer: Resigns his post; moves to Edinburgh
1819	September: Becomes assistant to Chalmers at St John's, Glasgow
1822	June: *Farewell Discourse to the Congregation and Parish of St. John's, Glasgow*. His first published work
	June 19: Ordained by Presbytery of Annan
	July 14: Begins ministry at Caledonian Chapel
	August 4: Brother John dies in India
	October 16: Inducted by presbytery
1823	May 19: Congregation resolve to build a new church
	July: *For the Oracles of God, four Orations: For Judgment to Come, an Argument, in nine Parts*
	August 16: by now living at 7 (later 4) Myddelton Terrace
	October 14: Marriage to Isabella at Kirkcaldy
1824	'Introductory Essay' to the *Life of Bernard Gilpin*
	May 13 (publ. 1825): Sermon to the London Missionary Society, Tottenham Court Chapel; first part publ. as *For Missionaries after the Apostolical School*
	July 1: Laying of the foundation-stone of the National Scotch Church
	July 22: Edward born
1825	*Introductory Essay to Bishop Horne's Commentary on the Psalms*
	Spring (publ. 1826): Sermon to the Continental Society, *Babylon and Infidelity Foredoomed of God: A Discourse on the Prophecies of Daniel and the Apocalypse which relate to these Latter Times, and until the Second Advent*
	early Summer (publ. 1827): *Homilies on Baptism*

	July: Refuses call to Hope Park Chapel, Edinburgh
	Autumn: by now living in Claremont Square
	October 2: Margaret born
	October 11: Son Edward dies
1826	November 30 – December 8: First Albury Conference
1827	'Homilies on the Lord's Supper', *CW*, 2.433–642
	February 23: Mary born
	March 15: Preaches at Maclean's ordination
	April 19: Publication of *Ben Ezra* and *Preliminary Discourse*
	May 11: National Scotch Church opened
	Sermons, Lectures and Occasional Discourses: Vol. II. On the Parable of the Sower. Preface dated 28 September 1827
	October 28: Cole hears Irving preach on Christ's humanity
	November/December: Albury Conference
	December 14: Mary dies
1828	January 1: *A Pastoral Letter ... from the Scotch Presbytery in London to the Baptized of the Scotch Church residing in London and its Vicinity and in the Southern Parts of the Island*. Preaches Fast Day sermon, publ. as *An Apology for the ancient Fulness and Purity of the Doctrine of the Kirk of Scotland*
	Sermons, Lectures and Occasional Discourses: Vol.III. On Subjects National and Prophetical. Preface dated 10 January 1828
	January – May: Sermons on 'The Last Days'; publ. as *The Last Days: A Discourse on the evil Character of these our Times*
	before 11 May: *A Letter to the King on the Repeal of the Test and Corporation Laws, as it affects our Christian Monarchy*
	May 22 – June 4: Twelve lectures in St Andrew's, Edinburgh, on Revelation
	June 15: Gallery collapses at Kirkcaldy
	June 26: Samuel born
	Sermons, Lectures and Occasional Discourses: Vol. I. The Doctrine of the Incarnation Opened; preached 1825; delayed in response to criticisms; preface dated 10 November 1828
	December 1: by now living at 13 Judd Place East
1829	*The Church and State Responsible to Christ, and to One Another: A Series of Discourses on Daniel's Vision of the Four Beasts*
	The Signs of the Times
	January 15: Publication of three volumes of *Sermons, Lectures and Occasional Discourses*
	May 19 – June 5: Lectures on Revelation in Edinburgh; publ. 1831 as *Lectures on [Exposition of] the Book of Revelation*; also as *Prophetical Works*
	July 28: Gavin born and dies
1830	Publ. January 26: *The Orthodox and Catholic Doctrine of our*

Appendix 2

	Lord's Human Nature
	Publ. ?May: [with Thomas Carlyle], *The Doctrine of the Church of Scotland concerning the Human Nature of our Lord, as stated in her Standards*
	May–June: *The Opinions circulating regarding our Lord's Human Nature, tried by the Westminster Confession of Faith* publ. during General Assembly
	June 30 – July 6: Final Albury Conference
	July 5: Samuel dies
	September: Cardale and party go to Scotland to investigate manifestations
	October 19: Withdraws from Presbytery in protest at its treatment of his *Orthodox and Catholic Doctrine*
	December 14: Declared to be no longer a member of Presbytery
	December 15: Declaration of church officers and congregation affirms his orthodoxy
1831	*Christ's Holiness in Flesh, the Form, Fountain-Head, and Assurance to us of Holiness in Flesh*
	The Confessions of Faith and the Books of Discipline of the Church of Scotland, of Date anterior to the Westminster Confession: To which are prefixed a Historical View of the Church of Scotland from the Earliest Period to the Time of the Reformation, and a Historical Preface
	The Day of Pentecost or The Baptism with the Holy Ghost
	February 21: Martin born
	April 30: Miss Cardale speaks in tongues, the first in London
	May 25–26: General Assembly finds Campbell, Maclean and Scott guilty of heresy
	October 16: Miss Hall speaks in tongues in vestry
	December 20: Trustees agree that the manifestations must be stopped
1832	publ. March: *A Judgment, as to what Course the Ministers and the People of the Church of Scotland should take in consequence of the Decisions of the Last General Assembly*
	publ. January–April: *Narrative of Facts connected with recent Manifestations of Spiritual Gifts*
	March: Miss Hall confesses she had been faking gifts
	April 26: Baxter recants
	April 26–27, May 2: Trial before Presbytery of London; deposed in his absence
	May 3: *The Last Sermon preached at the National Scotch Church*
	July 17: Edward's father dies
	Late September: Ebenezer born
	October 19: Newman Street opened

1833	January 22: by now living at 14 Newman Street
	March 13: Trial and deposition by Presbytery of Annan
	March 24: Inhibited by prophecy from administering sacraments until apostolically ordained
	April 5: Reordained as Angel
	April 21: Ebenezer dies
	May 8: Brother George dies
1834	March 23: Isabella born
	early September: Leaves London
	late October / early November: *To the Church of God, which the Lord Jesus Christ hath given into my hand* [two pastoral letters, ed. J. B. Cardale]
	December 8: Dies in Glasgow, 12.10 a.m.
	December 12: Funeral, Glasgow Cathedral

APPENDIX 3

Contents of Irving's *Collected Writings*

NB: The dates given are those of publication, unless indicated by an asterisk, in which case they are the dates of composition. Details of other works by Irving can be found in the Bibliography.

Vol. 1

ON THE WORD OF GOD (first published as *For the Oracles of God, Four Orations* (1823))
I. The Preparation for Consulting the Word of God	p.1
II. The Manner of Consulting the Word of God	p.18
III. The Obeying of the Word of God	p.34
IV. The Obeying of the Word of God – *continued*	p.50

THE PARABLE OF THE SOWER (1828)
Introductory. How it is possible to teach Spiritual Things by Natural Emblems	p.69
Lecture I. The Seed that fell by the Wayside, which the Birds of the Air snatched away	p.98
Lecture II. The Seed on the Rock, which was burnt up of the Sun	p.150
Lecture III. The Seed which fell among Thorns, and was choked before it could bring forth Fruit	p.194
Lecture IV. The Seed which fell on the Soil of a good and honest Heart, and brought forth abundantly	p.259
Lecture Supplementary. The improvement of the Doctrine taught in this and the preceding Lectures, concerning a Soil in Man prepared for the Word	p.319
THE BOOK OF PSALMS (1825)	p.383

MISSIONARIES AFTER THE APOSTOLICAL SCHOOL (*1824, first published 1825)
Dedication	p.427
Preface	p.429
The Missionary Charter	p.437
The Occasion and Method of the Addresses	p.439
I. Messiah's Constitution for the Missionary Estate	p.447
II. The Perpetuity of this Missionary Constitution proved	p.467
III. The Perpetuity of this Missionary Constitution proved – *continued*	p.490

Conclusion p.512
ORDINATION CHARGE (*1827)
Ordination Charge to the Minister of the Scots Church, London Wall p.527
HISTORICAL VIEW OF THE CHURCH OF SCOTLAND BEFORE
THE REFORMATION (from *The Confessions of Faith and the Books of
Discipline of the Church of Scotland*, 1831)
Part I. The early Plantation, Progress, and Prosperity of the Church in
the Realm of Scotland p.543
Part II. The Church of Scotland wrestling against Antichrist p.572
NOTES ON THE STANDARDS OF THE CHURCH OF
SCOTLAND (1831) p.599

Vol. 2

JOHN THE BAPTIST (*1823)
Lecture I. Luke III. 1, 2 p.3
Lecture II. Luke III. 3 p.16
Lecture III. Luke III. 7, 10 p.29
Lecture IV. Luke III. 10 p.40
Lecture V. Luke III p.56
Lecture VI. Luke III. 15–18 p.69
Lecture VII. Luke III. 16–18 p.81
Lecture VIII. Matt. III. 13; Luke III p.95
Lecture IX. John I. 19–28 p.105
Lecture X. John III. 23 p.113
Lecture XI. John III p.127
Lecture XII. Luke III p.136
Lecture XIII. Luke III; Matt. XIV p.148
Lecture XIV. Luke III; Matt. XIV; Mark VI p.161
Lecture XV. Luke III; Matt. XIV; Mark VI p.174
THE TEMPTATION (*1823?; five lectures on Luke IV) p.191
HOMILIES ON BAPTISM (*1825, published 1827)
Dedication p.247
Homily I. The Signification of this Ordinance p.249
Homily II. The Sealing Virtue of Baptism p.270
Homily III. The Doctrine Taught in Baptism p.289
Homily IV. The New Standing into which Baptism Bringeth the Church,
and the Engaging Parent or Sponsor, towards the Child p.306
Homily V. The Duties of the Church and the Engaging Parent or Sponsor p.321
Homily VI. The Standing of the Baptized in the Church p.343
Homily VII. The Standing of the Baptized with respect to the Lord's Supper p.358
Homily VIII. Conclusions of Doctrine flowing from Baptism p.375
Homily IX. Practical Conclusions flowing from Baptism p.395

Appendix 3

Homily X. Justification and Recapitulation of the Whole Doctrine contained in the above Homilies	p.414
HOMILIES ON THE LORD'S SUPPER (*1827?)	
Homily I. On Self-Examination	p.435
Homily II. The thing which is signified in the Lord's Supper	p.482
Homily III. The Invitation, Admonition, and Argument for all Baptized Persons to come unto the Table of the Lord	p.502
Homily IV. The invisible Grace signified and conveyed to the Faithful in the receiving of the Bread	p.526
Homily V. The receiving of the Cup	p.552
Homily VI. The invisible Grace signified and conveyed to the Faithful in the receiving of the Cup	p.578
Homily VII. The Lord's Supper as a Commemorative Act	p.589
Homily VIII. The Substance of the Doctrine contained in the Lord's Supper	p.605

Vol. 3

ON PRAYER (*1823–4)	
I. The Reasonableness and Rule of Prayer	p.3
II. The inestimable Advantage of Prayer	p.15
III. Its appropriate Place and Occasion	p.26
IV. The Spirit of Approach to God	p.38
V. The Character of Him to whom we pray	p.51
VI & VII. The misapprehension of God's Grace	p.62
VIII. Prayer and Action	p.87
IX–XIV. The Lord's Prayer (six lectures)	p.96
ON PRAISE (*1823–4?; four lectures)	p.165
ON FAMILY AND SOCIAL RELIGION (*1823–4?)	
I & II. Serving God in the Household	p.217
III. Duty to Parents	p.244
IV. Matrimony	p.258
V. Duties of Parents to Children	p.268
VI. For the estate of Orphanage	p.276
VII. On Friendship	p.297
VIII. Social Religion the natural outflow of Private Religion	p.309
IX. The good of Social Religion to the Religious	p.324
DISCOURSES DELIVERED ON PUBLIC OCCASIONS	
I. Farewell Discourse at St John's, Glasgow (1822)	p.343
II. Preparatory to the Laying of the Foundation-Stone of the National Scotch Church, Regent Square (1824)	p.363
III. Thanksgiving after Laying the Foundation of the National Scotch Church, Regent Square (1824)	p.370
IV. On Education (*1825, published 1828)	p.382

V. The Cause and the Remedy of Ireland's Evil Condition (*1825,
published 1828)   p.430
VI. The Spiritual Economy of Scotland (*1826)   p.470
VII. Last Sermon in the Caledonian Church (*1827)   p.500
VIII. First Sermon in the National Scotch Church (*1827)   p.520

Vol. 4

MISCELLANEOUS DISCOURSES
I. Idolatry (*1825)   p.3
II. Idolatry of the Imagination (*1825)   p.17
III. Idolatry of the Sense (*1825)   p.32
IV. Idolatry of Forms (*1825)   p.48
V. Idolatry of Symbols and Forms (*1825)   p.61
VI. Idolatry of the Book – the Bible (*1825)   p.75
VII. Idolatry of the Sacraments (*1825)   p.86
VIII & IX. On Intellectual Life (*1822–3?)   p.100
X–XIII. On Moral Life (*1822–3?; four discourses)   p.123
XIV. The Bondage in Egypt (*1822–32)   p.178
XV. The Kingdom of David and Solomon (*1822–32)   p.202
XVI–XXI. God our Father (*1827; six discourses)   p.222
XXII. The Lord Jesus Christ (*1827)   p.335
XXIII. God's Glory in the Church (*1826–32?)   p.350
XXIV & XXV. On the Death of Children (1827)   p.367
XXVI. The Deceitfulness Of Riches (*1826)   p.391
XXVII–XXX. The Love of Money (*1826; four discourses)   p.402
XXXI. Covetousness produced by natural Affection (*1822–32)   p.444
XXXII. The Peacefulness of those who cast their care upon God (*1822–32)   p.458
XXXIII. The Strivings of the Holy Spirit (*1825–6?)   p.469
XXXIV. Marks of the Divine Life (*1825–6?)   p.480
XXXV. Christian Discipline (*1822–32)   p.492
XXXVI. The Theology of the Natural Man (*1823?)   p.504
XXXVII. The Rest of the Sabbath (*1822–32)   p.515
XXXVIII. Jesus our Example, that we should follow his Steps (1832)   p.526

Vol. 5

THE DOCTRINE OF THE INCARNATION OPENED (*1825,
published 1828)
Preface   p.3
Epistle Dedicatory   p.7
I. That the beginning or origin of the Mystery, that the Eternal Word
should take unto Himself a body, is the holy will and good pleasure of God   p.9
II. The End of the Mystery of the Incarnation is the Glory of God   p.59

Part I. By Manifestation
Part II. By Action
III. The Method is by taking up the fallen Humanity   p.114
Part I. The Composition of Christ's Person
Part II. The Universal Reconciliation wrought by His Death, and
the Particular Election ministered by His Life in Glory
Part III. The Removal of the Law, and the bringing in of Grace
Part IV. Conclusions
IV. The Preparation for, and the very Act of, the Incarnation of Christ   p.258
Part I. The Humiliation in Flesh unto Death
Part II. The Descent into Hell
V. The Fruits of the Incarnation   p.312
Part I. Grace and Peace
Part II. The Promulgation or Preaching of the same
Part III. The Personal Application of the same
VI. Conclusions Concerning the Subsistence of God, and the Subsistence
of the Creature, derived from reflecting upon the Incarnation   p.398
THE CHURCH
The Church, with her Endowment of Holiness and Power (from *Lectures
on the Book of Revelation*, *1829, published 1831)   p.449
ON THE GIFTS OF THE HOLY GHOST
On the Gifts of the Holy Ghost commonly called Supernatural (1830–1)   p.509
APPENDIX
Appendix to the Treatise on the Incarnation (1828)   p.563

Bibliography

Manuscript and Unpublished Material

Albury, Albury Historical Society

Casbard, Retta, 'Henry Drummond of Albury', typescript, n.d.

Alnwick, Alnwick Castle / Oxford, Bodleian Library

The Archives of the Duke of Northumberland at Alnwick Castle, Drummond Family Papers, letters from or relating to Irving (microfilms of sections of these papers are held at the Bodleian Library, MSS Film 1606–9, accessible by permission from the Archivist at Alnwick Castle)

Annan, Public Library

Gilchrist, George, 'Memorials in Annan Old Burial Ground', typescript, 1963

Cambridge, Westminster College, United Reformed Church Historical Society

Letters and papers relating to Irving and the National Scotch Church
Minute books of the Presbytery of London

Dublin, Representative Church Body Library

MS/61/2/11, J. B. Leslie, 'Biographical Succession List of Kilmore'
MS/61/4/1, J. B. Leslie, 'Biographical Index of the Clergy of the Church of Ireland'

Dumfries, Dumfries and Galloway National Health Service Archives

Case notes re. David Ferguson

Edinburgh, Banner of Truth Trust

Letters to, by and relating to Robert Baxter

Edinburgh, National Archive of Scotland

B30/13/21, Haddington Burgh Registers: Council Book 1806–1812
B30/19/4, Haddington Burgh Registers: Treasurer's Accounts 1803–35
CH1/1/81, 82, Register of Acts of the General Assembly, 1828–31, 1832–4
CH1/2/149–156, Assembly Papers, main series, 1828–33
CH2/13, Minute book of the Presbytery of Annan
CH2/224, Minute book of the Presbytery of Kirkcaldy

Edinburgh, National Library of Scotland

Acc. 8813(1), W. R. Caird and G. Ryerson, 'Journal of a Voyage to New York; and several places in Canada made by W. R. C. and G. R. of London commencing 1st Feby 1834'

Acc. 12489, Journals and papers of James G. and Jane Simpson; /1, 'J. G. S. Journals 1806 to 1830' [actually 9 March 1806 – 2 July 1832); /4, Diary, 1832–8; /5, 'J. G. S. Journals 1838 to 1845'; /9, Jane Simpson, Diary, 1826–8; /10, idem, Diary, 1831; /11, 'A Brief Account of Mr & Mrs Simpson's Visit to Portglasgow in 1832'; /14, John Home Simpson, Typescript work on the Simpsons and their relationship to Irving, c. 1985; /15, miscellaneous letters

MS 1799, Thomas Carlyle, Marginal annotations on Friedrich Althaus, 'Thomas Carlyle', *Unsere Zeit* 2 (1866), 1–41

MS 10997, Prayer in Irving's hand

MSS 15996–8, Letters to or from members of the Bonar family

MS 16481, 'Account of Books borrowed from the public Library of the Town of Haddington from 1st April 1792 and forward'

Letters from or relating to Irving (MSS 665, 740, 967, 1001, 1030, 1676, 1764, 1765, 1771, 1774, 1776, 1777, 1810, 3112, 3823, 5139, 9848, 14836, 23204)

Letters to and from Mrs M. O. W. Oliphant (MSS 4133, 4172, 23210)

Edinburgh, New College Library

Irving, Edward [?], manuscript volume of 'Heads and skeletons of sermons'

Letters from the Chalmers collection

Edinburgh, University Library, Special Collections

MS Dc.4.103 (Irving), Letters by or relating to Irving

'Matriculation Roll of the University of Edinburgh. Vol. II. 1775–1810', 'Vol. III. 1811–1829'

'The Roll-Book of Students of Divinity in the University of Edinburgh, From November 17th 1801 to April 9th 1831'

Glasgow, University of Glasgow, University Library

MS DC21/1, Irvings to Robert Story, 27 January 1832

Kirkcaldy, Museum and Art Galleries

Letter of Irving to the members and office-bearers of the Caledonian Church, 16 July 1825.

London, British Library

764h10, Bound volume of Irving's sermons, from *The Pulpit* and *The Preacher*, 1823–33

764h11, Extracts from various periodicals relating to the Catholic Apostolic Church, 1830–77

764h18, Extracts from various periodicals, relating to Edward Irving, 1831–65

764m13, (uncatalogued), 'Rev. William Cannon's Account of Tongues and Prophecy', undated ms note shelved with *MW* 6

764n13, Ernst A. Rossteuscher, 'The Rebuilding of the Church of Christ upon the Original Foundations: An Historical Narrative of its Commencement. A free Translation' [by Miss L. A. Hewett], MS, [1871]

764n19, Newspaper cuttings relating to Edward Irving and the Catholic Apostolic Church, 1835–1905

Add. MSS 49191–2, Perceval Papers

London, Lambeth Palace Library

MS 1812, fol. 70, Irving to C. E. H. Orpen, 21 July 1831

MS 2689, R. Somerset Ward, 'The Death of a Church and the Problems arising therefrom: An Account of that Body which called itself "the Catholic Apostolic Church," and was sometimes called by its Opponents "the Irvingites"', typescript, 1935

London, London Metropolitan Archive

LMA/4358, Regent Square Presbyterian Church, Trustees' Minute Book 1825–48, Annual Reports, Baptismal Registers, and Scrapbooks

London, Lumen (formerly Regent Square) United Reformed Church

Letters to and from Irving

'National Scotch Church Burial Register'

National Scotch Church, Register of services and collections from 1827

'National Scotch Church Committee Minute Book No.3'

St Andrews, University Library, Special Collections, Flegg Collection (MS 38594)

Anon., 'The History of the Lord's Work in these Last Days', typescript, [1924]

Bonar, Andrew, Notes dated 25 April 1833 concerning arrangements at Newman Street

Bonar family, Typescript copies of letters 1830–33 concerning Irving

Terling Place, Terling, Essex, Strutt Family Archives

Letters to the Hon. J. J. Strutt by Henry Drummond, the Irvings and others, in the possession of the fifth Baron Rayleigh

Privately Held

Belcher, A. H., Typescript family history
Irving, Edward, 'Diary. Haddington 18th July 1810'
Letters and papers relating to the Irving, Gardiner, and Martin families

Theses, Dissertations and other Unpublished Works

[Copinger, H. B.], 'Annals: The Lord's Work in the Nineteenth and Twentieth Centuries', typescript, n.d.

Dingley, Robert James, 'Some Studies in Apocalyptic Themes and Images in English Literature and Art 1790–1850', D.Phil. thesis, University of Oxford, 1980

Elliott, Peter, 'Edward Irving: Romantic Theology in Crisis', draft thesis, in private hands

Elliott, Peter, 'Edward Irving's Hybrid: Towards a Nineteenth-Century Apostolic and Presbyterian Pentecostalism', paper delivered at a conference of the Commission Internationale d'Histoire et d'Études du Christianisme, Canterbury, April 2008

Enright, William Gerald, 'Preaching and Theology in Scotland in the Nineteenth Century: A Study of the Context and Content of the Evangelical Sermon', Ph.D. thesis, University of Edinburgh, 1968

Lee, David Yat Tang, 'The Humanity of Christ and the Church in the Teaching of Edward Irving', Ph.D. thesis, London Bible College / Brunel University, 2003

Newell, J. P., 'A. J. Scott and his Circle', Ph.D. thesis, New College, Edinburgh, 1981

Patterson, Mark Rayburn, 'Designing the Last Days: Edward Irving, the Albury Circle, and the Theology of *The Morning Watch*', Ph.D. thesis, King's College, London, 2001

Rennie, Ian S., 'Evangelicalism and English Public Life 1823–1850', Ph.D. thesis, University of Toronto, 1962

Sitwell, Francis, 'Copy of a Letter from Mr. Francis Sitwell to his Sister, Mary (Probable date 1834)', typescript, n.d.

Stewart, Kenneth J., 'Restoring the Reformation: British Evangelicalism and the "Réveil" at Geneva 1816–1849', Ph.D. thesis, New College, Edinburgh, 1992 (publ. as *Restoring the Reformation: British Evangelicalism and the Francophone 'Réveil' 1816–1849*, Bletchley: Paternoster, 2006)

Strachan, Gordon, 'Lacking Discernment: The Lack of the Gift of Discernment of Spirits in the Charismatic Group surrounding Edward Irving, 1831–32 as Recorded in the hitherto unpublished Diaries of James and Jane Simpson, Members of Regent Square Church: Edited with Commentary by John Simpson, Gifford, East

Lothian 1988', paper given at a conference at Regent Square United Reformed Church, London, 27 September 1992

[Trimen, Edward], 'The Rise and Progress of the Work of the Lord', typescript, n.d.

Whitley, H. C., 'Edward Irving: An Interpretation of his Life and Theological Teaching', Ph.D. thesis, New College, Edinburgh, 1953

Young, Stephen Edward, 'William Dodsworth 1798–1861: The Origins of Tractarian Thought and Practice in London', Ph.D. thesis, Open University, 2003

Upton, Liam, chapters of an uncompleted, untitled thesis, in private hands

Works by Irving

An Apology for the Ancient Fulness and Purity of the Doctrine of the Kirk of Scotland: A Sermon preached on the Occasion of a Fast appointed by the Presbytery of London, to be held in all their Churches on the First Day of the present Year, because of the low Ebb of Religion among the Children of the Scottish Church residing in these Parts, London: James Nisbet, 1828

Babylon and Infidelity Foredoomed of God: A Discourse on the Prophecies of Daniel and the Apocalypse, which relate to these Latter Times, and until the Second Advent, Glasgow: William Collins, 1828

The Christian's Cure for the Cholera: Open Air Service, at the Back of Coldbath-Fields Prison, Clerkenwell, on Wednesday Evening, July 18, 1832, London: W. Harding, [1832]

The Church and State Responsible to Christ, and to One Another: A Series of Discourses on Daniel's Vision of the Four Beasts, London: J. Nisbet, 1829

'The Church, with her Endowment of Holiness and Power', *MW* 2 (1830), 630–68

Collected Writings, ed. Gavin Carlyle, 5 vols, London: Alexander Strahan, 1864–6

The Confessions of Faith and the Books of Discipline of the Church of Scotland, of Date anterior to the Westminster Confession: To which are prefixed a Historical View of the Church of Scotland from the Earliest Period to the Time of the Reformation, and a Historical Preface, with Remarks, London: Baldwin and Cradock, 1831

The Day of Pentecost, or the Baptism with the Holy Ghost: A Treatise in Three Parts: I.– The Promise contained in all the Scriptures. II.– The Fulfilment on the Day of Pentecost. III.– The Effect in the Edification of the Church. No. I. London: Baldwin and Cradock, 1831

The Discipline of the Church, by the Rev. E. Irving; with two Addresses in the Open Air, by Missionaries, London: W. Harding, [1832]

'On the Doctrine and Manifestation and Character of the Apostasy in the Christian Church', *MW* 1 (1829), 100–15

Exposition of the Book of Revelation, in a Series of Lectures, 4 vols, London: Baldwin and Cradock, 1831

Exposition and Sermon, delivered in the Open Air, Cold-Bath-Fields, on Wednesday Evening, August 8, 1832, n.pl.: n.p., [1832]

The Exposition, Sermon, and Services, at the National Scotch Church, Regent Square, with the Exhortation by the Gifted Sister, Miss Hall, &c. Sunday, Dec. 18, 1831, n.pl.: n.p., [1832]

Exposition and Sermon, by the Rev. E. Irving, A.M., at his Chapel, Newman Street, on Sunday Afternoon, December 23, 1832: To which is added an Address delivered at the Church in Newman Street, Friday Evening, Jan. 4th, 1833, previous to the Distribution of Sacramental Tokens to Sixty-Four New Communicants, London: W. Harding, [1832]

Exposition and Sermon by the Rev. Edward Irving, M.A. at Cold-Bath Fields, Sunday Morning, June 10th, 1832; together with a Manifestation by Miss Cardale, London: W. Harding, [1832]

Exposition and Sermon by the Rev. E. Irving, M.A. delivered in the Fields at Clerkenwell, on Sunday Morning, May 6th. 1832, London: W. Harding, [1832]

Exposition and Sermon, by the Rev. E. Irving, May 17, 1833: Also an Address to the Elders, April 12, 1833, n.pl.: n.p., [1833]

Exposition and Sermon, delivered at the Church in Newman Street, Oxford Street, January 9, 1833, by the Rev. E. Irving, A.M., London: W. Harding, [1833]

Exposition and Sermon, delivered at the Church in Newman-Street, on Wednesday Evening, October 24, 1832, London: W. Harding, [1832]

Exposition and Sermon delivered at the Opening of the New Chapel, Newman Street, Oxford Street, Sunday Afternoon, October 21, 1832, London: W. Harding, [1832]

Exposition and Sermon, delivered in the Open Air, Cold-Bath-Fields, on Wednesday Evening, August 8, 1832, London: W. Harding, [1832]

'Facts connected with Recent Manifestations of Spiritual Gifts', *Fraser's Magazine* 4 (1831–2), 754–61; 5 (1832), 198–205, 316–20; also publ. London: James Fraser, 1832

Farewell Discourse to the Congregation and Parish of St. John's, Glasgow, Glasgow: Chalmers and Collins, 1822

Gathered Gems from the Orations of Edward Irving: Systematically arranged, London: James Nisbet, 1857

'On the Gifts of the Holy Ghost, commonly called Supernatural', *MW* 2 (1830), 850–69; 3 (1831), 473–96; 4 (1831), 84–101 (= *CW*, 5.509–61)

Homilies on the Sacraments, Vol. I: *On Baptism*, London: Andrew Panton, 1828

'On the Human Nature of Christ', *MW* 1 (1829), 75–99, 240–3

'Interpretation of the Fourteenth Chapter of the Apocalypse', *MW* 5 (1832), 306–24; 6 (1832), 18–44, 262–85

'Introductory Essay' to William Gilpin, *The Life of Bernard Gilpin*, Glasgow: Chalmers and Collins, 1824

'Introductory Essay' to George Horne, *A Commentary on the Book of Psalms*, New York: Robert Carter, 1845

'Jesus our Ensample, that we should follow his Steps', *MW* 6 (1832), 103–17 (= *CW*, 4.526–59)

A Judgment, as to what Course the Ministers and the People of the Church of Scotland should take in Consequence of the Decisions of the Last General Assembly, Greenock: R. B. Lusk, 1832 (extracted from *MW* 5 (1832), 84–115)
The Last Days: A Discourse on the Evil Character of these our Times, proving them to be the 'Perilous Times' of the 'Last Days', London: J. Nisbet, 1850
The Last Sermon preached at the National Scotch Church, Regent Square, on Thursday Evening, the 3d of May, 1832, London: W. Harding, [1832]
Lectures on the Book of Revelation, as (in substance) preached in Edinburgh during the Sitting of the General Assembly, in May 1829, Lecture I: On the Name, Authority, Subject Matter and Sanctions of the Book, London: Baldwin and Cradock, 1829
A Letter to the King on the Repeal of the Test and Corporation Laws, as it affects our Christian Monarchy, London: James Nisbet, 1828
Miscellanies from the Collected Writings of Edward Irving, London: Alexander Strahan, 1866
For Missionaries after the Apostolical School, a Series of Orations: In four Parts. I. The Doctrine. II. The Experiment. III. The Argument. IV. The Duty. Part First. The Doctrine, in three Orations, London: Hamilton, Adams, 1825 (BL copy, shelfmark C61c8, with annotations by Coleridge)
Morning Service at the National Scotch Church, Regent Square, Sunday, Nov. 27, 1831, n.pl.: n.p., [1832]
'The Mystery of Speaking with Tongues', *MW* 5 (1832), 78–84
'Minister of the Church of Scotland, A' [Irving], *The Opinions circulating concerning Our Lord's Human Nature, tried by the Westminster Confession of Faith*, Edinburgh: John Lindsay, 1830
For the Oracles of God, four Orations: For Judgment to Come, an Argument, in nine Parts, London: T. Hamilton, 1823; 3rd edn, London: T. Hamilton, 1824
The Orthodox and Catholic Doctrine of Our Lord's Human Nature set forth in four Parts: I. Statement of the Doctrine from Scripture. II. Confirmation of it, from the Creeds of the Primitive Church and of the Church of Scotland. III. Objections to the true Doctrine considered. IV. The Doctrines of the Faith which stand or fall with it, London: Baldwin & Cradock, 1830
The Nature and Use of the Gift of Tongues, as stated in the Scriptures, Greenock: R. B. Lusk, [1830?]
A Pastoral Letter from the Scotch Presbytery in London, addressed to the Baptized of the Scottish Church residing in London and its Vicinity, and in the Southern Parts of the Island, London: James Nisbet, 1828
'On the Prophetical Aspect of all God's Works and Ways', *MW* 7 (1833), 52–73
Prophetical Works, ed. Gavin Carlyle, 2 vols, London: Alexander Strahan, 1867/70
'The Responsibility of a Baptized Man, of a Preacher of the Gospel, and of a Pastor in Christ's Flock, to Christ and the Church', *MW* 6 (1832), 430–50
The Rev. Edward Irving's Preliminary Discourse to the Work of Ben Ezra: entitled The Coming of Messiah in Glory and Majesty: To which is added, an Ordination

Charge, delivered by Mr. Irving in 1827; And also his Introductory Essay to Bishop Horne's Commentary on the Psalms, London: Bosworth & Harrison, 1859

Scripture Reading and Exposition by the Late Rev. Edward Irving, A.M. at the Church in Newman Street, on Sunday Afternoon, 12th *January 1834*, n.pl.: n.p., n.d.

Selections from the Collected Writings of Edward Irving, ed. Gavin Carlyle, Paisley. Alexander Gardner, 1915

Sermons and Lectures, ed. Gavin Carlyle, London: Alexander Strahan, 1864 (= Vol. 2 of *CW*)

Sermons, Lectures, and Occasional Discourses, 3 vols, London: R. B. Seeley & W. Burnside, 1828

The Signs of the Times, London: Andrew Panton, 1829

'Signs of the Times, and Characteristics of the Church', *MW* 1 (1829), 641–66; 2 (1830), 141–62

A Tale of the Times of the Martyrs [extracted from *The Anniversary* for 1829], n.pl.: n.p., [1850?]

Thirty Sermons ... Preached during the First Three Years of his Residence in London: From the Accurate Notes of Mr. T. Oxford, Short-hand Writer, London: John Bennett, 1835

'Thoughts, Moral and Divine, touching God's Method and Order of Revealing Himself', *MW* 5 (1832), 383–94

To the Church of God in London, with the Elders and the Deacons, ed. J. B. Cardale, London: Mills, Jowett & Mills, [1834]

To the King's most Excellent Majesty: The Petition of the Minister, Elders, and Deacons of the National Scotch Church, Regent Square, London, in Session assembled, London: Ellerton & Henderson, [1830]

'On the True Humanity of Christ', *MW* 1 (1829), 421–45

Two Services at the Rev. E. Irving's Chapel, Newman Street, November 4th *and 11*th, London: W. Harding, [1832]

'What caused Mr. Baxter's Fall?', *MW* 7 (1833), 129–40

'The Widow's Son raised', *The British Pulpit* 2 (1834), 534–40

[with Thomas Carlyle], *The Doctrine of the Church of Scotland concerning the Human Nature of our Lord, as stated in her Standards*, Edinburgh: John Lindsay, [1831]

(trans. and intro.) Juan Josafat Ben-Ezra [Manuel Lacunza], *The Coming of Messiah in Glory and Majesty, Translated from the Spanish, with a Preliminary Discourse, by the Rev. Edward Irving, A.M.*, 2 vols, London: L. B. Seeley, 1827

(annotated) Orlando W. Roberts, *Narrative of Voyages and Excursions on the East Coast and in the Interior of Central America ... with Notes and Observations by Edward Irving*, Edinburgh: Constable, 1827

(with Nicholas Armstrong), *Expositions and Sermons by the Rev. E. Irving, Jan. 29*th*, and Feb. 1*st*; and Rev. N. Armstrong, January 27*th*, 1833*, London: W. Harding, [1833]

(with Nicholas Armstrong), *Expositions and Sermons by the Rev. E. Irving and the Rev. N. Armstrong*, London: W. Harding, [1832] (with Nicholas Armstrong), *Sermons and Expositions by the Rev. E. Irving, A.M., and the Rev. N. Armstrong, A.B.*, London and Edinburgh: [various publishers], 1831–3

Editor's Preface to [John Lacy], *The General Delusion of Christians, touching the Ways of God's revealing himself to and by the Prophets, evinced from Scripture and Primitive Antiquity; and many Principles of Scoffers, Atheists, Sadducees, and Wild Enthusiasts, refuted*, London: R. B. Seeley and W. Burnside, 1832

Other Published Items (reviews have not been included)

'Actor, An', *Shakespeare, and Honest King George, versus Parson Irving and the Puritans; or, Taste and Common Sense, refuting Cant and Hypocrisy*, London: C. Harris, 1824

Aikenhead, Robert, *A Serious Address to the Inhabitants of Kirkcaldy and Vicinity: To which is prefixed, a brief Notice of the Catastrophe which happened in the Parish Church there, on Lord's Day, 15th June, 1828 ...*, 2nd edn, Edinburgh: James Robertson, 1828

Aliquis, 'Spiritual Gifts, their Nature, Uses, Period of Continuance, and Incompatibility with present Circumstances', *ECI* n.s. 1 (1832), 579–89

Allen, David, 'A Belated Bouquet: A Tribute to Edward Irving (1792–1834)', *Expository Times* 103 (1991–2), 328–31

Allen, David, 'Edward Irving (1792–1834), an all-round Charismatic Ministry', *Renewal*, no. 198 (November 1992), 34–6

Allen, David, 'Regent Square Revisited: Edward Irving, Precursor of the Pentecostal Movement', *Evangel* 22 (2004), 75–80

Andrews, William W., *Edward Irving: A Review*, 2nd edn, Glasgow: David Hobbs, 1900

Andrews, W. W., *Martin Luther and Edward Irving: Their Work and Testimony compared*, London: Thos Bosworth, 1884

Anon., 'The Ark of God in the Temple of Dagon', *MW* 5 (1832), 441–56

Anon., 'Augustus Welby Pugin', *Blackwood's Edinburgh Magazine* 90 (1861), 670–89

Anon., *Authentic Account of the Dreadful Accident at Kirkaldy, Written by a Newspaper Reporter, who went expressly to Kirkaldy for Information*, n.pl.: n.p., [1828; repr. from the *Edinburgh Observer*, 17 June 1828]

Anon., *An Account of the whole Proceedings in the Case of the Rev. H. B. Maclean, before the Presbytery of Irvine and the Synod of Glasgow and Ayr*, Irvine: E. Macquistan, 1830

Anon., *A Brief Statement of the Proceedings of the London Presbytery, in Communion with the Established Church of Scotland, in the Case of the Rev. Edward Irving, and of a Book, written by him, and entitled 'The Orthodox and Catholic Doctrine of our Lord's Human Nature'*, London: Basil Steuart, 1831

Anon., *A Catalogue of the Graduates in the Faculties of Arts, Divinity, and Law, of the University of Edinburgh, since its Foundation*, Edinburgh: Neill, 1858

Anon., 'Dr. Chalmers and the Tenets of the late Rev. E. Irving', *The Pulpit*, no. 652 (9 April 1835), 444–8

Anon., 'Edward Irving', *Fraser's Magazine* 11 (1835), 99–103

Anon., 'Edward Irving', *Fraser's Magazine* 67 (1863), 62–73

Anon., 'Edward Irving', *North British Review*, no. 73 (August–November 1862), 94–131

Anon., 'Edward Irving', *United Presbyterian Magazine* 8 (1862), 350–4, 395–403

Anon., 'Edward Irving's Works', *QJP* 17 (1865), 331–57

Anon., *An Eloquent, Evangelical, and Orthodox Ministry exemplified in a Letter to a Christian Friend, in answer to repeated Interrogatories as to the Qualifications and Evangelical Orthodoxy of the Rev. Edward Irving, Minister of the Caledonian Church, Hatton-Garden, London*, London: William Booth, 1824

Anon., *Extracts of Correspondence of the Continental Society for the Diffusion of Religious Knowledge over the Continent of Europe*, no. 46, London: Macintosh, [1832]

Anon., *Fifteenth Annual Report of the Session to the Congregation of the Presbyterian Church, Regent Square, at a Meeting of the Members held in the Church, on Wednesday, 23rd January, 1861*, London: Hayman Brothers, 1861

Anon., *A Full Report of the Proceedings in the General Assembly of the Church of Scotland, in the Case of the Rev. John M'Leod Campbell, late Minister of Row, on the 24th and 25th of May, 1831*, 2nd edn, Greenock: R. B. Lusk, 1831

Anon., *Haddington: Royal Burgh, A History and a Guide*, East Linton: Tuckwell, 1997

Anon., *The History of the Times: 'The Thunderer' in the Making 1785–1841*, London: The Times, 1935

Anon., ed., *Horatius Bonar: A Memorial*, London: James Nisbet, 1889

Anon., 'Mr. Irving's Church THE Sign of the Times', *MW* 6 (1832), 224–8

Anon., 'Irving's Four Orations, and Argument in Nine Parts', *Edinburgh Magazine* 13 (1823), 214–18

Anon., *Isabella Campbell, of Rosneath, Scotland*, Philadelphia, PA: Tract Association of Friends, n.d.

Anon., *A Letter to a Friend in the Country on reading Mr. Baxter's* Narrative of Facts, London: James Nisbet, 1833

Anon., 'The Life of Edward Irving', *Blackwood's Edinburgh Magazine* 91 (1862), 737–57

Anon., *List of the Graduates in Medicine in the University of Edinburgh, from MDCCV to MDCCCLXVI*, Edinburgh: Neill, 1887

Anon., *The London Scotch Presbytery and the Rev. Edward Irving, A.M.*, [London: W. Harding, 1832]

Anon., *Lowndes' British Librarian, or Book-Collector's Guide to the Formation of a Library in all Branches of Literature, Science, and Art, arranged in Classes, with Prices, Critical Notes, References, and an Index of Authors and Subjects, Class I. – Religion and its History*, 11 parts in 2 vols, London: Whitaker, 1839

Anon., 'On "The Manifestations," &c. with a Letter from some Members of Mr. Irving's congregation and the Editor's Reply', *Christian Herald*, no. 35 (September 1833), 208–16

Anon., 'Memoir of the Rev. Edward Irving, A.M.', *European Magazine* 84 (1823), 291–3

Anon., *The Metropolitan Pulpit; or Sketches of the most Popular Preachers in London*, London: George Virtue, 1839

Anon., 'Miraculous Gifts: old and new Claimants', *QJP* 7 (1855), 99–121

Anon., *Modern Miracles compared with Scripture*, Norwich: Jarrold, 1831

Anon., 'No. XII. The Rev. Edward Irving, M.A. Late Minister of the National Scotch Church', *Annual Biography and Obituary* 20 (1836), 138–56

Anon., Obituary of Irving, *Gentleman's Magazine* n.s. 3 (1835), 664.

Anon., 'Pretended Miracles – Irving, Scott, and Erskine', *Edinburgh Review* 53 (1831), 261–305

Anon., *Proceedings of the Continental Society, for the Diffusion of Religious Knowledge over the Continent of Europe: Seventh Year, 1824–1825*, London: A. Macintosh, 1825

Anon., 'Proceedings of the General Assembly', *ECI* n.s. 2 (1832), 541–60

Anon., *A Recollection of the Rev. Edward Irving, A.M. being Notes of a Sermon preached by him at Kirkcaldy, on Tuesday Evening, 1st July, 1828: Taken in short hand. By one of his Friends*, Edinburgh: John Boyd, 1828

Anon., 'Records of a Stage Veteran – IV', *New Monthly Magazine*, no. 43 (March 1835), 356–60

Anon., *Remains of the late Reverend John Martin, D.D. Minister of Kirkaldy: Consisting of Sermons, Essays, and Letters. With a Memoir*, Edinburgh: William Oliphant, 1838

Anon. [Editors], 'Remarks on Mr. Irving', *Gospel Magazine*, 4th series, 10 (1835), 226–33

Anon., 'The Rev. Edward Irving', *The Hive* 2.51 (1823?), 369–72

Anon., 'The Rev. Edw. Irving, A.M.', *The Examiner*, no. 807 (14 July 1823), 453

Anon., 'The Rev. Edward Irving and his Adversaries', *Fraser's Magazine* 3 (1831), 423–8

Anon., *Reasons for concluding that the Gifted People may be in the Right*, 2nd edn, London: William Harding, n.d.

Anon., 'Spiritual Gifts and Demoniacal Possession', *MW* 5 (1832), 145–60

Anon., *The Storehouses of Babylon*, London: A. Douglas, [1833]

Anon., *Substance of the Trust Deed of the New National Scotch Church*, [London: n.p., 1827]

Anon., *Through the Lens 24: Glimpses of old Annan Burgh*, Dumfries: Dumfries and Galloway Libraries, Information and Archives with the Friends of Annandale and Eskdale Museums, 2003

Anon., *The Trial of the Rev. Edward Irving, A.M. before the Presbytery of Annan, on Wednesday, March 13, 1833: Also Mr. Irving's Letter to his Congregation. Taken in Short Hand*, London: W. Harding, 1833

Anon., *Trial of Mr Edward Irving, late Minister of the National Scotch Church, Regent Square, London; before the Presbytery of Annan, on 13th March, 1833; with an Appendix, containing Copies of some of his Letters, and other Documents, a Refutation of his Errors, and an Account of the supposed Supernatural Manifestations exhibited by the 'Gifted' of his Congregation; also some Notices of similar Manifestations in the French Prophets, and others*, Dumfries: Journal Office, 1833

Anon., *Trial of the Rev. Edward Irving, M.A.: A Cento of Criticism*, London: E. Brain, 1823; 10th edn, London: Knight and Lacey, 1825

Anon., *'Try the Spirits.' 1 John iv. 1*, London: James Nisbet, 1831

Anon., 'The Voice of God', *MW* 5 (1832), 297–306

Anon., *The Whole Proceedings in the Case of the Rev. John M'Leod Campbell, late Minister of Row, before the Presbytery of Dumbarton, the Synod of Glasgow and Ayr, and the General Assembly of the Church of Scotland; including, besides all the Documents, the Speeches in the different Church Courts*, Greenock: R. B. Lusk, 1831

Anti-Cabala, *A Morning Visit to the Rev. E. Irving's, and an Inquiry into the alleged Return to the Church of the Gift of Tongues; with Remarks, Inferences, and Suggestions, also, an Appendix, containing Facts and Notices illustrative of the whole Subject*, London: J. Kelly, 1831

Archibald, Raymond Clare, *Carlyle's First Love, Margaret Gordon, Lady Bannerman: An Account of her Life, Ancestry and Homes, her Family and Friends*, London: John Lane the Bodley Head, 1910

Armour, R. W. and R. F. Howes, *Coleridge the Talker*, Ithaca, NH: Cornell University Press, 1940

Arnot, William, *Life of James Hamilton, D.D., F.L.S.*, London: J. Nisbet, 1870

[Ashley, John], *The Doctrine of the Gift of Tongues and Prophesying, impartially Considered, and Scripturally Vindicated, as being the Privilege of the Gospel Dispensation under which we live, and as said to be possessed by some of the Members of the Rev. Mr. Irving's Church*, London: J. Jaques, 1832

Ashton, Rosemary, *The Life of Samuel Taylor Coleridge: A Critical Biography*, Oxford: Blackwell, 1996

Ashton, Rosemary, *Thomas and Jane Carlyle: Portrait of a Marriage*, London: Chatto & Windus, 2001

Basilicus [Lewis Way], *Thoughts on the Scriptural Expectations of the Christian Church*, London: A. Panton, 1826

Bateson, Gregory, ed., *Perceval's Narrative: A Patient's Account of his Psychosis 1830–1832*, London: Hogarth Press, 1962

Baxter, Robert, *Irvingism, in its Rise, Progress, and Present State*, London: James Nisbet, 1836

Baxter, Robert, *Narrative of Facts, characterizing the Supernatural Manifestations, in Members of Mr. Irving's Congregation, and other Individuals, in England and Scotland, and formerly in the Writer himself*, London: James Nisbet, 1833

Bebbington, D. W., 'Religion and National Feeling in Nineteenth-Century Wales and Scotland', in S. J. Mews, ed., *Religion and National Identity*, Studies in Church History 18, Oxford: Blackwell, 1982, 489–503.

Bebbington, D. W., *Evangelicalism in Modern Britain: A History from the 1730s to the 1980s*, London: Unwin Hyman, 1989

Beverley, R. M., *A Sermon preached at Hull, on the XIII. of November, MDCCCXXXI. on the Unknown Tongues*, London, London: Frederic Westley and A. H. Davis, 1831

Binfield, J. C. G., 'Jews in Evangelical Dissent: the British Society, the Herschell Connection and the Pre-Millenarian Thread', in M. Wilks, ed., *Prophecy and Eschatology*, Studies in Church History Subsidia 10, Oxford: Basil Blackwell, 1994, 225–70

Black, Kenneth Macleod, *The Scots Churches in England*, Edinburgh: William Blackwood, 1906

Blackburn, Peter, *Reasons for thinking Mr Irving deceived; or a Discussion of some Questions relating to the Gift of Tongues, in which the Statements of St Paul in 1 Cor. XIV. are carefully considered, and Mr Irving's Interpretation of them as set forth in the third Volume of the Morning Watch is examined and found erroneous*, 2nd edn, Cambridge: J. G. & F. Rivington, 1834

Blaikie, William Garden, *David Brown D.D., Ll.D.: Professor and Principal of the Free Church College, Aberdeen. A Memoir*, London: Hodder and Stoughton, 1898

[Boase, C. W.], *Supplementary Narrative* to *The Elijah Ministry in the Christian Church*, Edinburgh: R. Grant, [1868]

Bolitho, Hector and Derek Peel, *The Drummonds of Charing Cross*, London: George Allen and Unwin, 1967

[Bonar, Horatius]?, 'Edward Irving', *QJP* 14 (1862), 224–47

[Bonar, Horatius]?, 'Irvingism.' *QJP* 18 (1866), 209–25, 313–33

[Bonar, Horatius], 'Irvingism in 1831', *QJP* 23 (1871), 300–4

[Bonar, Horatius], 'Irvingism in 1832', *QJP* 23 (1871), 382–6

Bonar, Marjory, ed., *Reminiscences of Andrew A. Bonar, D.D.*, London: Hodder and Stoughton, 1895

Boyer, Paul, *When Time Shall Be No More: Prophecy Belief in Modern American Culture*, Cambridge, MA: Belknap, 1992

Boys, Thomas, *The Christian Dispensation miraculous: Republished from the Jewish Expositor for February, 1831*, London: L. B. Seeley, 1831

Boys, Thomas, *The suppressed Evidence: or, Proofs of the miraculous Faith and Experience of the Church of Christ in all Ages, from authentic Records of the Fathers, Waldenses, Hussites, Reformers, United Brethren, &c.: An Historical Sketch, suggested by the Hon. and Rev. B. W. Noel's 'Remarks on the Revival of Miraculous Powers in the Church'*, London: Hamilton, Adams, 1832

Brash, Thomas, *Thomas Carlyle's Double-Goer and his Connection with the Parish of Row: A Lecture delivered to the Guild of Park United Free Church, Helensburgh, on 15th February 1904*, Helensburgh: Macneur & Bryden, [1904]

Brooke, Richard Sinclair, *Recollections of the Irish Church*, London: Macmillan, 1877

Brown, Callum G., 'Rotavating the Kailyard: Re-imagining the Scottish "Meenister" in Discourse and the Parish State since 1707', in Nigel Aston and Matthew Cragoe, eds, *Anticlericalism in Britain c. 1500–1914*, Stroud: Sutton, 2001, 138–58

Brown, David, 'Letter to a Friend entangled in Error', *ECI* n.s. 2 (1833), 73–86, 145–53

Brown, David, 'Personal Reminiscences of Edward Irving', *The Expositor*, 3rd series, 6 (1887), 216–28, 257–73

Brown, David, 'Reminiscences of Edward Irving', *Free Church Magazine* 8 (1851), 14–17

Brown, Stewart J., *Thomas Chalmers and the Godly Commonwealth in Scotland*, Oxford: Oxford University Press, 1982

[Bull, John], *Puritanical Treason!! The King and Honest John Bull versus Parson Irving, Doctor Collyer, and their Proselytes; or Truth unmasking Hypocrisy, Deceit, and Bigotry! A Satirical Epistle*, London: W. Chubb, n.d.

Burleigh, J. H. S., *A Church History of Scotland*, London: Oxford University Press, 1960

Burns, Robert, *The Church revived without the Aid of unknown Tongues: A Sermon preached in the Scots Church, Swallow Street, on Sabbath, the 6th of November, 1831, to which are now added, a few prefatory Remarks*, London: A. Douglas, 1831

Burns, William, *The Law of Christ Vindicated from Certain False Glosses of the Rev. Edward Irving, contained in his Argument on a Judgment to Come*, London: R. Hunter, 1824

Caird, W. R., *A Letter to the Rev. R. H. Story, Rosneath, respecting certain Misstatements contained in his Memoir of the late Rev. R. Story*, Edinburgh: Thomas Laurie, 1863

Cameron, George G., *The Scots Kirk in London*, Oxford: Becket, 1979

Campbell, Donald, ed., *Memorials of John McLeod Campbell, D.D.: Being Selections from his Correspondence*, 2 vols, London: Macmillan, 1877

Campbell, Ian, 'Carlyle and the Secession', *RSCHS* 18 (1972), 48-64

Campbell, Ian, 'Edward Irving, Carlyle and the Stage', *Studies in Scottish Literature* 8 (1971), 166–73

Campbell, Ian, *Thomas Carlyle*, Edinburgh: Saltire Society, 1993 (first publ. 1974)

Campbell, John, *The Church and Parish of Kirkcaldy: From the Earliest Times till 1843*, Kirkcaldy: Alex Page, 1904

[Campbell, John McLeod], *On Keeping a Conscience void of Offence towards God and towards Man, while considering what claims to be of God*, Greenock: Greenock Intelligencer Office, 1834

Campbell, John McLeod, *Reminiscences and Reflections, referring to his early Ministry in the Parish of Row, 1825–31*, ed. and intro. Donald Campbell, London: Macmillan, 1875

Cardale, John B., 'On the extraordinary Manifestations in Port-Glasgow', *MW* 2 (1830), 869–73
Carlyle, A. J., 'The Centenary of Edward Irving', *Modern Churchman* 24 (1934–5), 588–97
Carlyle, Alexander, ed., *The Love Letters of Thomas Carlyle and Jane Welsh*, 2 vols, London: John Lane, The Bodley Head, 1909
Carlyle, Thomas, *Reminiscences*, ed. K. J. Fielding and Ian Campbell, Oxford: Oxford University Press, 1997
Carlyle, Thomas, *Reminiscences*, ed. James Anthony Froude, London: Longmans, Green, 1881
Carlyle, Thomas, *Reminiscences,* ed. C. E. Norton, London: J. M. Dent, 1932
Carruthers, William, 'Edward Irving and Marcus Dods', *JPHSE* 1 (1914–19), 55–6
Carter, Grayson, *Anglican Evangelicals: Protestant Secessions from the* Via Media, *c. 1800–1850*, Oxford: Oxford University Press, 2001
Chalmers, Thomas, 'On the Respect due to Antiquity: A Sermon, preached on Friday, May 11, 1827, at the Opening of the Scotch National Church in London', in idem, *Works*, vol. 11, Glasgow: William Collins, n.d., 123–59
Chambers, D., 'Doctrinal Attitudes in the Church of Scotland in the Pre-Disruption Era: The Age of John McLeod Campbell and Edward Irving', *Journal of Religious History* 8 (1974–5) 159–82
Charteris, A. H., 'Edward Irving', in *Teachers and Preachers of Recent Times*, Edinburgh: William P. Nimmo, 1881, 176–89
Cheyne, A. C., *The Transforming of the Kirk: Victorian Scotlands [sic] Religious Revolution*, Edinburgh: Saint Andrew Press, 1983
Cleland, James, *The Rise and Progress of the City of Glasgow, Comprising an Account of its Public Buildings, Charities, and other Concerns*, Glasgow: James Brash, 1820
[Clemens, Louisa Perina Courtauld], *Narrative of a Pilgrim and Sojourner on Earth, from 1791 to the present Year, 1870*, Edinburgh: H. Armour, 1870
Clubbe, John, ed., *Carlyle and his Contemporaries: Essays in honor of Charles Richard Sanders*, Durham, NC: Duke University Press, 1976
Coghill, Mrs Harry, ed., *Autobiography and Letters of Mrs Margaret Oliphant*, intro. Q. D. Leavis, Leicester: Leicester University Press, 1974
Cole, Henry, *A Letter to the Rev. Edward Irving, Minister of the Caledonian Chapel, Compton Street, in Refutation of the awful Doctrines (held by him) of the Sinfulness, Mortality, and Corruptibility of the Body of Jesus Christ*, London: J. Eedes, 1827
Conolly, Matthew Forster, *Biographical Dictionary of Eminent Men of Fife*, Cupar: John C. Orr / Edinburgh: Inglis & Jack, 1866
Contemporary, A, *Traits of Character; being twenty-five Years' literary and personal Recollections*, 2 vols, London: Hurst and Blackett, 1860
Craig, Edward, *A Letter to Thomas Erskine, Esq. in Reply to his recent Pamphlet in Vindication of the West Country Miracles*, Edinburgh: William Oliphant, 1830
Criticus, 'The Rev. Edward Irving', *European Magazine* 84 (1823), 47–8, 245–8

'Crito', *The Superiority of Practice to Speculation*, Edinburgh: for the author, 1831

Cumming, J., 'The Moral Influence we exert after Death', *The British Pulpit* 2 (1834), 541–8

Dale, Thomas Pelham, *A Life's Motto, illustrated by Biographical Examples*, London: Virtue, n.d.

Dallimore, Arnold, *The Life of Edward Irving: Fore-runner of the Charismatic Movement*, Edinburgh: Banner of Truth, 1983

D'Arblay, A. C. L., *The Apostolic Gift of Tongues, contrasted with some modern Claims to Inspiration: A Sermon, preached in Camden Chapel, St. Pancras, on January VIII, MDCCCXXXII, being the Sunday following the Epiphany: preceded by an Introductory Discourse on the prevailing Spirit of the Times, and its Effects on National Religion. To which is added, an Appendix, containing an Answer to Hume on Miracles, and to Laplace on Atheistical Necessity*, London: J. G. & F. Rivington, 1832

D[arby]., J. N., *Letters of J. N. D.*, 3 vols, Kingston-on-Thames: Stow Hill Bible and Tract Depot, n.d.

Davenport, J. S., *Edward Irving and the Catholic Apostolic Church*, New York: John Moffet, 1863

Davenport, Rowland A., *Albury Apostles: The Story of the Body known as the Catholic Apostolic Church (sometimes called 'the Irvingites')*, London: Free Society, 1973 (first publ. 1970)

Davie, George Elder, *The Democratic Intellect: Scotland and her Universities in the Nineteenth Century*, Edinburgh: University Press, 1961

Dix, Kenneth, *Strict and Particular: English Strict and Particular Baptists in the Nineteenth Century*, Didcot: Baptist Historical Society, 2001

Dodds, James, *Personal Reminiscences and Biographical Sketches*, Edinburgh: Macniven & Wallace, 1887

D[odds]., J[ames]., 'About Edward Irving', *Leisure Hour*, 28 September 1872, 618–21

Dods, Marcus, *On the Incarnation of the Eternal Word*, 2nd edn, London: William Allan, 1849 (first publ. 1831)

Dorries, David W., *Edward Irving's Incarnational Christology*, Fairfax, VA: Xulon Press, 2002

[Dowglass, Thomas], *A Chronicle of certain Events which have taken place in the Church of Christ, principally in England, between the Years 1826 and 1852*, London: Charles Goodall, 1852

Drummond, Andrew Landale, *Edward Irving and his Circle: Including some Consideration of the 'Tongues' Movement in the Light of Modern Psychology*, London: James Clarke, [1937]

Drummond, Andrew L., and James Bulloch, *The Scottish Church 1688–1843: The Age of the Moderates*, Edinburgh: Saint Andrew Press, 1973

Drummond, Henry, *Abstract Principles of Revealed Religion*, 2nd edn, London: Thomas Bosworth, 1876 (first publ. 1845)

[Drummond, Henry], *No. I. The Church of Christ. A.D. 1834*, Greenock: W. Johnston, [1834]

[Drummond, Henry], *No. IV. The Church of Christ. A.D. 1834*, London: Robson, [1834]

[Drummond, Henry], ed., *Dialogues on Prophecy*, 3 vols, London: James Nisbet, 1828–9

Drummond, Henry, *Narrative of the Circumstances which led to the setting up of the Church of Christ at Albury*, typescript, n.d. (first publ. 1834)

Duns, John, *Memoir of the late Rev. Samuel Martin, Minister of the Free Church, Bathgate*, Edinburgh: W. P. Kennedy, 1854

Duncan, George John C., *Memoir of the Rev. Henry Duncan, D.D., Minister of Ruthwell*, Edinburgh: William Oliphant, 1848

Durie, Bruce, *Kirkcaldy & East Fife in old Photographs*, Stroud: Sutton Publishing, 2002

Earnest Contender for 'The Faith which was Once Delivered to the Saints, An, *The Unknown Tongues!! &c. or, the Rev. Edward Irving and the Rev. Nicholas Armstrong arraigned at the Bar of the Scriptures of Truth, and found 'Guilty.' To which are added, Two Letters by the Rev. H. B. Bulteel, M. A. late Curate of St. Ebbe's, Oxford*, 6th edn, London: William Kidd, 1832

E[rskine]., T[homas]., *On the Gifts of the Spirit*, Greenock: R. B. Lusk, 1830

Espin, T. E., *Critical Essays*, London: Rivingtons, 1864

[Ferguson, David], 'Reminiscences of Edward Irving', *The New Moon, or Crichton Royal Institution Literary Register* 20 (1864)

Festing, Gabrielle, *John Hookham Frere and his friends*, London: James Nisbet, 1899

Fielding, Kenneth J. and David R. Sorensen, eds, *Jane Carlyle: Newly selected Letters*, Aldershot: Ashgate, 2004

Findlater, J., 'The Propaganda of Futurism', *Evangelical Quarterly* 9 (1937), 169-79

Flegg, Columba Graham, *'Gathered under Apostles': A Study of the Catholic Apostolic Church*, Oxford: Clarendon, 1992

Fleming, James, *The Life and Writings of the Rev. Edward Irving, M.A.*, London: Knight and Lacey, 1823

Fletcher, Joseph, *On the miraculous Gifts of the Primitive Churches, and modern Pretensions to their Exercise: a Discourse, delivered at Stepney Meeting, on Lord's Day Evening, Nov. 27, 1831*, London: Frederick Westley and A. H. Davis, 1832

Fox, Caroline, *Memories of Old Friends*, ed. Horace N. Pym, 2 vols, 3rd edn, London: Smith, Elder, 1882

Frere, B. S., *A Record of the Frere Family of Suffolk & Norfolk*, [Stamford: the author], 1982

Frere, J. H., *The Great Continental Revolution marking the Expiration of the Times of the Gentiles, A. D. 1847–8*, London: J. Hatchard, 1848

Froom, LeRoy E., *The Prophetic Faith of our Fathers*, vol. 3, Washington, DC: Review & Herald, 1946

Froude, James Anthony, *Thomas Carlyle: A History of the First Forty Years of his Life 1795–1835*, 2 vols, London: Longmans, Green, 1882

Garrett, Clarke, *Respectable Folly: Millenarians and the French Revolution in France and England*, Baltimore, MD: Johns Hopkins University Press, 1975

George, David, *The Scriptural Doctrine of the Second Advent. An Essay: read before one of the Associations of the Edinburgh Young Men's Society. By a Member of the Society*, Edinburgh: J. T. Smith, 1833

George, M. Dorothy, *Catalogue of political and personal Satires preserved in the Department of Prints and Drawings in the British Museum*. Vol. X, *1820–1827*; Vol. XI, *1828–1832*, London: British Museum Trustees, 1952, 1954

Gibb, Andrew, *Glasgow: The Making of a City*, London: Croom Helm, 1983

Gilbert, Josiah, ed., *Autobiography and other Memorials of Mrs Gilbert (formerly Ann Taylor)*, 2 vols, London: Henry S. King, 1874

Gilchrist, George, *Annan Parish Censuses 1801–1821*, Scottish Record Society n.s. 4, Edinburgh: Econoprint for the Scottish Record Society, 1975

Gilfillan, George, ed., *The History of a Man*, London: Arthur Hall, Virtue, 1856

Gilley, Sheridan. 'Edward Irving, The National Scotch Church and the Catholic Apostolic Church', in *Caledonia Gothica: Pugin and the Gothic Revival in Scotland*, Architectural Heritage 8 (1997), 37–46

Gilley, Sheridan, 'Edward Irving, Prophet of the Millennium', in Jane Garnett and Colin Matthew, eds, *Revival and Religion since 1700: Essays for John Walsh*, London: Hambledon, 1993, 95–110

Goode, William, *The Modern Claims to the Possession of the Extraordinary Gifts of the Spirit, stated and examined; and compared with the most remarkable Cases of similar kind that have occurred in the Christian Church: with some General Observations on the Subject*, London: J. Hatchard, 1833

Gordon, T. Crouther, 'Edward Irving', in Ronald Selby Wright, ed., *Fathers of the Kirk*, London: Oxford University Press, 1960

Gould, Brian, 'Irving, Carlyle, & the Apostolic Church in Birmingham', *JPHSE* 14 (1968–72), 201–5

Graduate, A, *A Word Decisive of the Present Pretensions to the Gifts of speaking with Tongues and Prophesying*, Oxford: W. Baxter, 1834

Grass, Tim, *Gathering to His Name: The Story of Open Brethren in Britain and Ireland*, Milton Keynes: Paternoster, 2006

Grass, Tim, 'The Taming of the Prophets: Bringing Prophecy under control in the Catholic Apostolic Church', *Journal of the European Pentecostal Theological Association* 16 (1996), 58–70

Gray, W. Forbes and J. H. Jamieson, *East Lothian Biographies*, Transactions of the East Lothian Antiquarian & Field Naturalists' Society, Haddington: D. & J. Croal, 1941

Gray, W. Forbes and J. H. Jamieson, *A Short History of Haddington*, Stevenage: SPA Books, 1995; first publ. Edinburgh: East Lothian Antiquarian & Field Naturalists' Society, 1944

Greenwood, Thomas, *The Latest Heresy, or modern Pretensions to the miraculous Gifts of Healing and of Tongues, condemned by Reason and Scripture*, London: William Harding, 1832

[Greville, Charles Cavendish Fulke], *The Greville Memoirs*, ed. Lytton Strachey and Roger Fulford, 8 vols, London: Macmillan, 1938

Gribben, Crawford and Timothy C. F. Stunt, eds, *Prisoners of Hope? Aspects of Evangelical Millennialism in Britain and Ireland, 1800–1880*, Carlisle: Paternoster, 2005

Griggs, E. L., ed., *Collected Letters of Samuel Taylor Coleridge*, Vols 5 and 6, Oxford: Clarendon, 1971

Gunton, Colin, 'Two Dogmas Revisited: Edward Irving's Christology', *Scottish Journal of Theology* 41 (1988), 359–76

Grub, George, *An Ecclesiastical History of Scotland from the introduction of Christianity to the Present Time*, 4 vols, Edinburgh: Edmonston and Douglas, 1861

Gunton, Colin E., *The Promise of Trinitarian Theology*, 2nd edn, Edinburgh: T. & T. Clark, 1997

Hack, Mary Pryor, *Christian Womanhood*, London: Hodder and Stoughton, 1883

Hair, John, *Regent Square: Eighty Years of a London Congregation*, London: James Nisbet, 1899

Haldane, Alexander, *The Lives of Robert Haldane of Airthrey, and of his Brother, James Alexander Haldane*, 2nd edn, London: Hamilton, Adams, 1852

Haldane, J. Aylmer L., *The Haldanes of Gleneagles*, Edinburgh: William Blackwood, 1929

Hall, Sophy, *Dr Duncan of Ruthwell: Founder of Savings Banks*, Edinburgh and London: Oliphant, Anderson & Ferrier, 1910

[Hamilton, James?], 'Edward Irving', *Evangelical Christendom* n.s. 7 (March 1866), 111–14

Hanna, William, ed., *Letters of Thomas Erskine*, 2nd edn, Edinburgh: David Douglas, 1878

Hanna, William, *Memoirs of the Life and Writings of Thomas Chalmers D.D. LL.D.*, 4 vols, Edinburgh: Sutherland and Knox, 1850

Hanson, Laurence and Elisabeth, *Necessary Evil: The Life of Jane Welsh Carlyle*, London: Constable, 1952

[Harding, William]?, *The Trial of the Rev. Edward Irving, A.M. before the Presbytery of Annan, on Wednesday March 13, 1833: Also, Mr. Irving's letter to his congregation. Taken in Short Hand*, London: W. Harding, 1833.

Harding, William, *The Trial of the Rev. Edward Irving, M.A. before the London Presbytery; containing the whole of the Evidence; exact Copies of the Documents; verbatim Report of the Speeches and Opinions of the Presbyters, &c.; being the only authentic and complete Record of the Proceedings, taken in Shorthand by W. Harding*, London: W. Harding, 1832

[Harding, William]?, *A Word of Testimony: or, a corrected Account of the Evidence adduced by the Trustees of the National Scotch Church, in support of their Charges against the Rev. Edward Irving, and his Defence*, London: Adam Douglas, 1832

Hardinge, Henry, *Remarks on the Twelfth and Fourteenth Chapters of St Paul's First Epistle to the Corinthians, with other Observations, on the Use and Abuse of the Gift of Tongues, &c.*, London: G. Groombridge, 1836

[Hardman, John], *An Exposition of Chapters XII. XIII. and XIV. of 1. Corinthians, with Observations on the Present State of the Church*, Dublin: William Curry, Jun., 1834

Harrison, J. F. C., *The Second Coming: Popular Millenarianism 1780–1850*, London and Henley: Routledge & Kegan Paul, 1979

Hayes, David A., *East of Bloomsbury*, London: Camden History Society, 1998

Hazlitt, William, *The Spirit of the Age or Contemporary Portraits*, ed. E. D. Mackarness, 2nd edn, Plymouth: Northcote House, 1991

Heffer, Simon, *Moral Desperado: A Life of Thomas Carlyle*, London: Phoenix, 1996

Hempton, D. N., 'Evangelicalism and Eschatology', *JEH* 31 (1980), 179–94

[Henderson, Miss E.], *Modern Fanaticism unveiled*, London: Holdsworth and Ball, 1831

Herschell, Ridley, ed., *'Far above Rubies': Memoir of Helen S. Herschell by her Daughter*, London: Walton and Maberly, 1854

Hilton, Boyd, *The Age of Atonement: The Influence of Evangelicalism on Social and Economic Thought 1785–1865*, Oxford: Oxford University Press, 1988

Hohl, Michael, *Bruchstücke aus dem Leben und den Schriften Edward Irving's, gewesenen Predigers an der schottischen Nationalkirche in London*, St Gallen: C. von Scheitlin, 1839

Holmes, Richard, *Coleridge: Darker Reflections*, London: HarperCollins, 1998

Hooper, John, *The Present Crisis, considered in relation to the Blessed Hope of the Glorious Appearing of the Great God, even our Saviour Jesus Christ*, 2nd edn, London: James Nisbet, 1831

Horrocks, Don, *Laws of the Spiritual Order: Innovation and Reconstruction in the Soteriology of Thomas Erskine of Linlathen*, Carlisle: Paternoster, 2004

Howse, Ernest Marshall, *Saints in Politics: The 'Clapham Sect' and the Growth of Freedom*, London: George Allen & Unwin, 1971

[Hulbert, C.], *Some Account of the Irvingites, their Opinions and Predictions: Also those of the French Prophets of the Last Century; the Followers of Anne Lee & Jemima Wilkinson. With short Notices of each; and a brief Memoir of the Rev. E. Irving*, Hulbert: Providence Grove, Shrewsbury, 1837

Ireland, Mrs Alexander, *Life of Jane Welsh Carlyle*, 2nd edn, London: Chatto & Windus, 1891

Irving, John Beaufin, *The Irvings, Irwins, Irvines, or Erinveines: or any other Spelling of the Name: An Old Scots Border Clan*, 2nd fascsimile edn, Dumfries: Dumfries and Galloway Libraries, 1996 (first publ. 1907)

Jay, Elizabeth, ed. and intro., *The Autobiography of Margaret Oliphant: The complete Text*, Oxford: Oxford University Press, 1990

Jay, Elisabeth, *Mrs Oliphant: 'A Fiction to Herself': a literary Life*, Oxford: Clarendon, 1995

Johnson, Harry, *The Humanity of the Saviour: A Biblical and Historical Study of the Human Nature of Christ in relation to Original Sin, with special reference to its soteriological Significance*, London: Epworth, 1962

Johnston, Bryce, *A Commentary on the Revelation of St. John*, 2 vols, Edinburgh: William Creech, 1794

Johnston, James, *Annan's Most illustrious Son (and other Great Men)*, Annan: privately published, 1987

Jones, William, *Biographical Sketch of the Rev. Edward Irving, A.M. late Minister of the National Scotch Church, London: With Extracts from, and Remarks on his Principal Publications*, London: John Bennett, 1841

Keir, David, *The House of Collins: The Story of a Scottish Family of Publishers from 1789 to the Present Day*, London: Collins, 1952

Kelley, Lillian W., 'Edward Irving Preaching in Britannia Fields Summer 1832: A Portrait by Faithful Christopher Pack, R.R.P.', *JPHSE* 5.1 (1932), 21–30

Kennedy, James, W. A. Smith, and A. F. Johnson, eds., *Dictionary of Anonymous and Pseudonymous English Literature (Samuel Halkett and John Laing)*, new and enlarged ed., Edinburgh: Oliver and Boyd, 1926

Kent, Muriel, 'Edward Irving, 1792–1834', *Hibbert Journal* 23 (1934–5), 277–89

Ker, David, *Observations on Mrs Oliphant's 'Life of Edward Irving:' and Correction of certain Misstatements therein: With a Reprint of Mr Irving's Speeches before the Presbytery of London, in March 1832*, Edinburgh: Thomas Laurie, 1863

Kirby, Thomas A., 'Carlyle and Irving', *ELH: A Journal of English Literary History* 13 (1946), 59–63

Krämer, F., *Thomas Carlyle of the Scottish Bar (1803–1855)*, Freiburg: Universitätsverlag Freiburg Schweiz, 1966

Landels, William, 'Edward Irving: A Lecture', in *Lectures delivered before the Young Men's Christian Association* ..., London: James Nisbet, 1863, 39–89.

'Layman, A', *An Examination and Defence of the Writings and Preaching of the Rev. Edward Irving, M.A. Minister of the Caledonian Church, Cross Street, Hatton Garden: Including copious Extracts from his 'Four Orations for the Oracles of God,' and his 'Argument for Judgment to Come'*, London: John Fairburn, [1823]

Leishman, James Fleming, *Matthew Leishman of Govan and the Middle Party of 1843: A Page from Scottish Church Life and History in the Nineteenth Century*, Paisley: Alexander Gardner, 1921

The Author of 'The Circular on the Revolutions' [James Leslie], *Letter to the Rev. Edward Irving, Minister of the National Scots Church, London, on the Gift of Tongues*, Edinburgh: J. Lindsay, 1832

Lewis, Donald M., ed., *The Blackwell Dictionary of Evangelical Biography 1730-1860*, 2 vols, Oxford: Blackwell, 1995

Lines, William J., *An all-consuming Passion: Origins, Modernity, and the Australian Life of Georgiana Molloy*, Berkeley, CA: University of California Press, 1996

[Lockhart, J. G.], 'The Rev. Mr Irving's Orations', *Blackwood's Magazine* 14 (1823), 145–62

Longmate, Norman, *King Cholera: The Biography of a Disease*, London: Hamish Hamilton, 1966

L[usk]., R. B., *The Testimony of Facts concerning the Continuation of Miracles in the Church*, Greenock: R. B. Lusk, 1832

Lynch, T. T., *The Mornington Lecture*, London: James Clarke, 1885

M., J. J., *An Address to all Christians*, London: W. Harding, [1832]

Marrat, Jabez, *Northern Lights; or, Pen and Pencil Sketches of Twenty-one modern Scottish Worthies*, 3rd edn, London: T. Woolmer, 1885

M'Clellan, John, *Speech delivered at the Bar of the General Assembly, in the Case of the Rev. William Dow: With considerable Additions, and an Appendix containing the Minutes of the Proceedings of the Presbytery of Kirkcudbright, and the Judgment of the Assembly, in that Case*, Edinburgh: William Whyte, 1832

M'Farlan, Helen, *Selections from Letters and Journals of Ruthwell Manse Life 1871–1889*, Edinburgh: privately printed, 1914

McFarlane, Graham W. P., *Christ and the Spirit: The Doctrine of the Incarnation according to Edward Irving*, Carlisle: Paternoster, 1996

McFarlane, Graham W. P., *Edward Irving: The Trinitarian Face of God*, Edinburgh: St Andrew Press, 1996

McFarlane, Graham W. P., 'Edward Irving and the Uniqueness of Christ', in Antony Billington, Tony Lane and Max Turner, eds, *Mission and Meaning: Essays presented to Peter Cotterell*, Carlisle: Paternoster, 1995, 217–29

McFarlane, Graham, 'Strange News From Another Star: An Anthropological Insight from Edward Irving', in Christoph Schwöbel and Colin E. Gunton, eds, *Persons, Divine and Human: King's College Essays in Theological Anthropology*, Edinburgh: T. & T. Clark, 1991, 98–119

McGee, Gary B., 'Taking the Logic "a little further": late nineteenth-century References to the Gift of Tongues in Mission-related Literature and their Influence on early Pentecostalism', *Asian Journal of Pentecostal Studies* 9 (2006), 99–125

M'Kerrell, Archibald, *An Apology for the Gifts of Tongues and Interpretation, at present manifested in the Church of Christ, and the Words of a Vision of Prophecy, given to the Church in A. D. 1830*, Greenock: W. Johnston, 1831

Mackintosh, H. R., *The Doctrine of the Person of Jesus Christ*, 2nd edn, Edinburgh: T. & T. Clark, 1913

Mackintosh, Robert James, ed., *Memoirs of the Life of the Right Honourable Sir James Mackintosh*, 2 vols, London: Edward Moxon, 1835

MacLeod, Donald, 'The Doctrine of the Incarnation in Scottish Theology: Edward Irving', *Scottish Bulletin of Evangelical Theology* 9 (1990–1), 40–50

Macmillan, Donald, *Representative Men of the Scottish Church*, Edinburgh: T. & T. Clark, 1928

M'Neile, Hugh, 'On Discrimination in Doctrine', *British Pulpit* 1 (1833–4), 213–226

M'Neile, Hugh, *Letters to a Friend, who has felt it his Duty to secede from the Church of England, and who imagines that the Miraculous Gifts of the Holy Ghost are revived among the Seceders*, London: J. Hatchard, 1834

M'Neile, Hugh, *Miracles and Spiritual Gifts*, London: James Nisbet, 1832

Marks, H. J., *Narrative of Henry John Marks, a Jew; now a Follower of the Lord Jesus Christ*, 3rd edn, London: the author, 1842

Martin, John, *Martin Howy Irving: Professor, Headmaster, Public Servant*, Melbourne: University of Melbourne History of the University Unit, 2006

Martine, John, *Reminiscences and Notices of the Parishes of the County of Haddington*, repr. Haddington: East Lothian Council, 1999

Martine, John, *Reminiscences of the Royal Burgh of Haddington*, Edinburgh: John Menzies, 1883

Maughan, William Charles, *Rosneath Past and Present*, Paisley and London: Alexander Gardner, 1893

Maxwell, Sir Herbert, ed., *The Creevey Papers: A Selection from the Correspondence & Diaries of the late Thomas Creevey, M.P. born 1768 – died 1838*, 2 vols, London: John Murray, 1903

Mechie, Stewart, 'Education for the Ministry in Scotland since the Reformation', *RSCHS* 14 (1983), 115-33, 161-78

Merricks, William S., *Edward Irving: The Forgotten Giant*, East Peoria, IL: Scribe's Chamber Publications, 1983

Miller, Edward, *The History and Doctrines of Irvingism*, 2 vols, London: C. Kegan Paul, 1878

Miller, Frank, *A Bibliography of the Parish of Annan: With Biographical Memoranda respecting the Authors catalogued*, Dumfries: reprinted from the *Transactions of the Dumfriesshire and Galloway Natural History and Antiquarian Society*, 1925

Miller, Frank, 'Edward Irving and Annan', *Records of the Scottish Church History Society* 4, repr. in idem, *Poems from the Carlyle Country: Together with Papers on Two of Carlyle's early Friends and some Fragments in Prose*, Glasgow: Jackson Son & Co., 1937, 39–47

Miller, James, *The Lamp of Lothian or the History of Haddington*, Haddington: Sinclair, 1900

Morris, A. J., *Glimpses of Great Men: or, Biographic Thoughts of Moral Manhood*, London: Ward, 1853

Munn, James, *Commentary on the Publication, entitled 'An Account of the whole Proceedings in the Case of the Rev. H. B. Maclean, before the Presbytery of Irvine and Synod of Glasgow and Ayr'*, Kilmarnock: Chronicle Office, 1831

Myers, Thomas, *The Norrisian Prize Essay for the Year 1832: To which the Gold Medal was awarded by the University of Cambridge*, London: W. H. Dalton, 1833

'Nealum, W.', *Rev. Edw. Irving's Defence of himself against the Critics: Being a Full Report of all the Documents and Speeches read and delivered on Feb. 3, 1824, at a meeting of the Scottish Convocation, called* in hunc effectum *by Mr. I.*, London: John Walker, 1824

Needham, Nicholas R. *Thomas Erskine of Linlathen: His Life and Theology, 1788–1837*, Edinburgh: Rutherford House, 1990

Nelson, Thomas, *A Biographical Memoir of the late Dr Walter Oudney and Captain Hugh Clapperton, both of the Royal Navy, and Major Alex. Gordon Laing ...*, Edinburgh: Waugh and Innes, 1830

Newell, J. Philip, 'Scottish Intimations of modern Pentecostalism: A. J. Scott and the Clydeside Charismatics', *Pneuma* 4.2 (Fall 1982), 1–18

Newton, B. W., '*Occasional Papers on Scriptural Subjects IV*, London: Houlston & Wright, 1866

Noel, Baptist W., *Remarks on the Revival of Miraculous Powers in the Church*, London: James Nisbet, 1831

Norfolk Curate, A [John Browne], *A Sermon on our Lord's Human Nature, in which it is shown from Scripture that Jesus Christ took our Nature entirely free from all Taint of Sin*, London: Simpkin & Marshall, 1832

Norton, Robert, *Memoirs of James and George Macdonald, of Port-Glasgow*, London: John F. Shaw, 1840

O[liphant]., [Mrs] M. O. W., 'Thomas Carlyle', *Macmillan's Magazine* 43 (1881), 482–96

Oliphant, Mrs [M. O. W.], *The Life of Edward Irving, Minister of the National Scotch Church, London*, 2 vols, London: Hurst and Blackett, 1862

Oliphant, Mrs [M. O. W.], *The Life of Edward Irving, Minister of the National Scotch Church, London*, 5th edn, London: Hurst and Blackett, n.d.

[Oliphant, Mrs M. O. W.], 'Edward Irving', *Blackwood's Edinburgh Magazine* 84 (1858), 567–86

Oliver, W. H., *Prophets and Millennialists: The Uses of Biblical Prophecy in England from the 1790s to the 1840s*, [Auckland]: Auckland University Press and Oxford University Press, 1978

One of the Congregation of the National Scotch Church, *A Word for Inquiry previous to Decision in the Matter of the present Manifestations of, or Pretensions to, the Gifts of Speaking with Unknown Tongues and Prophesying, with an Appendix containing Extracts from the Writings of the Rev. Edward Irving, and his rejected Letter to the Editor of the Times &c. &c.*, 2nd edn, London: W. Harding, 1832

Orme, William, *An Expostulatory Letter to the Rev. Edward Irving, A.M. Occasioned by his Orations for Missionaries after the Apostolical School*, London: B. J. Holdsworth, 1825

Owen, Robert Dale, 'Interesting People whom I met in London. A Chapter of Autobiography', *Atlantic Monthly* 32 (1873), 560–72

P., 'Remarks on the Life, Character, and Death of the Rev. Edward Irving, A.M.', *The Watchman; or, Prophetical Journal*, 341–51

Palmer, H. P., *Joseph Wolff: His romantic Life and Travels*, London: Heath Cranton, 1935

Palmer, Samuel, *St. Pancras; being Antiquarian, Topographical, and Biographical Memoranda, relating to the extensive Metropolitan Parish of St. Pancras, Middlesex: With some Account of the Parish from its Foundation*, London: Samuel Palmer, 1870

Parkin, T., *An Answer to Mr. Irving's Letter to the King, imploring his Majesty to withhold the Royal Assent from the Bill to repeal the Test and Corporation Acts*, London: Wightman and Cramp, 1828

Pastor [Andrew Thomson], *The Rev. Edward Irving's Newspaper Declaration considered; or Mr. Irving convicted of ascribing Original Sin to our Lord Jesus Christ: In a Letter to the Editor of the Edinburgh Christian Instructor*, Edinburgh: William Whyte, 1831

Patterson, A. Temple, *Radical Leicester: A History of Leicester 1780–1830*, Leicester: University College, 1954

Patterson, Mark and Andrew Walker, '"Our Unspeakable Comfort": Irving, Albury and the Origins of the pre-tribulation Rapture', in Stephen Hunt, ed., *Christian Millenarianism from the Early Church to Waco*, London: Hurst, 2001, 98–115

Paul, C. Kegan, *Biographical Sketches*, London: Kegan Paul, Trench, 1883

Paul, C. Kegan, *Memories*, London: Kegan Paul, Trench, Trübner, 1899

Paull, H. A., *The Trial: or, Unknown Tongue and False Prophecy arraigned, judged, and condemned, for presumptuously counterfeiting the Gifts of the Holy Ghost, in the Arminian, Son-of-God Denying Kirk, (alias Mr. Irving's)*, London: for the author, 1831

Pennington, Arthur Robert, *Recollections of Persons and Events*, London: Wells, Gardner, Darton, 1895

Pilkington, George, *The Doctrine of Particular Providence, or the Divine Guardianship over the most minute Concerns of Man: Illustrated and defended in Biographical Reminiscences*, London: Edmund Fry, 1838

Pilkington, George, *The Unknown Tongues discovered to be English, Spanish, and Latin; and the Rev. Edw. Irving proved to be erroneous in attributing their Utterance to the Influence of the Holy Spirit: Also a Private Arrangement in his Closet, previous to a Prayer Meeting and Consultation in the Vestry, to which the Writer was invited by Mr. Irving, because he believed him to be in 'the Spirit,' and prayed that he might receive the Gift of Interpretation; Various interesting Colloquies between the Writer and Mr. Irving and his Followers; and Observations, which manifestly show that they are all under a Delusion*, 2nd edn, London: Field & Bull, 1831

A Presbyter of the Church of England [A. P. Perceval], *An Enquiry into the late supposed Manifestations of the Holy Spirit*, London: J. G. & F. Rivington, 1832

Purves, Jim, 'The Interaction of Christology & Pneumatology in the Soteriology of Edward Irving', *Pneuma* 14.1 (Spring 1992), 81–90

Purves, Jim, *The Triune God and the Charismatic Movement: A Critical Appraisal of Trinitarian Theology and Charismatic Experience from a Scottish Perspective*, Carlisle: Paternoster, 2004

[de Quincey, T.], 'Sketches of Life and Manners; from the Autobiography of an English Opium-Eater', *Tait's Edinburgh Magazine* 7 (1840), 629–37

Railton, Nicholas M., *No North Sea: The Anglo-German Evangelical Network in the middle of the Nineteenth Century*, Studies in Christian Mission 24, Leiden: Brill, 2000

Redivivus, John Bunyan, *The Holy War. A Vision. A Poem in five Books. To which is added, The Holy War, in Prose; In illustration of the Times, Characters, and Associations, which marked the first Quarter of the 19th Century. Also, Men's Duties in the Present Times, argued from St. John's Address to the various Classes who attended his Preaching*, London: William Cole, 1825

Roberts, H. V. Molesworth, '"Regent Square" The Cathedral of English Presbyterianism', *JPHSE* 10 (1952–5), 54–8

Robertson, A., *A Vindication of 'The Religion of the Land' from Misrepresentation; and an Exposure of the absurd Pretensions of the Gairloch Enthusiasts: In a Letter to Thomas Erskine, Esq., Advocate*, Edinburgh: William Whyte, 1830

Ross, H. S., 'Birmingham Presbyteriana: Some Notes', *JPHSE* 11 (1956–9), 211–12

Sandeen, E. R., *The Roots of Fundamentalism: British and American Millenarianism 1800–1930*, Chicago, IL: University of Chicago Press, 1970

Sanders, Charles Richard, et al., eds, *The Collected Letters of Thomas and Jane Welsh Carlyle*, 35 vols so far, Durham, NC: Duke University Press, 1970 onwards

Saunders, Laurance James, *Scottish Democracy 1815–1840: The Social and Intellectual Background*, Edinburgh: Oliver and Boyd, 1950

Schaff, Philip, ed., *The Creeds of Christendom*, 3 vols, 6th edn (1931), repr. Grand Rapids, MI: Baker, 1998

Schlossberg, Herbert, *The Silent Revolution & the making of Victorian England*, Columbus, OH: Ohio State University Press, 2000

Schmidt, Leigh Eric, *Holy Fairs: Scotland and the making of American Revivalism*, 2nd edn, Grand Rapids, MI: Eerdmans, 2001

[Scott, A. J.], *Neglected Truths. No. I: Hints on I Corinthians XIV*, London: L. B. Seeley, 1830

Scott, Hew, ed., *Fasti Ecclesiae Scoticanae*, rev. ed. William S. Crockett and Francis Grant, 7 vols, Edinburgh: Oliver & Boyd, 1915-28 (first publ. 1866-71)

Scott, Walter, *The Journal of Sir Walter Scott*, ed. and intro. W. E. K. Anderson, Edinburgh: Canongate Books, 1998

De Selincourt, Ernest, *Dorothy Wordsworth: A Biography*, Oxford: Clarendon Press, 1933

'Senex', *Edward Irving in Dumfries (1828–1829)*, [Dumfries]: n.p., [1889]

Shaw, P. E., *The Catholic Apostolic Church, sometimes called Irvingite*, Morningside Heights, NY: King's Crown Press, 1946

S[haw]., W. B., 'An Irvingite Token', *JPHSE* 2 (1920–3), 165

Shillingford, B., *Errors of Irvingism Exposed; or, Modern Popery Unmasked*, 2nd edn, London: Ebenezer Palmer, 1836 (first published 1831)

Shillingford, B., *An Appendix to the Errors of Irvingism Exposed ...*, London: Ebenezer Palmer, 1837

Simpson, Patrick Carnegie, *The Life of Principal Rainy*, London: Hodder and Stoughton, 1909

Skabarnicki, Anne M., 'Annandale Evangelist and Scotch Voltaire: Carlyle's *Reminiscences* of Edward Irving and Francis Jeffrey', *Scotia* 4 (1980), 16–30

Sloan, J. M., *The Carlyle Country; with a Study of Carlyle's life*, London: Chapman & Hall, 1904

Smail, Thomas A., *Reflected Glory: The Spirit in Christ and Christians*, London: Hodder and Stoughton, 1977

Smith, James, E., *'Shepherd' Smith the Universalist: The Story of a Mind*, London: Sampson, Low, Marston, 1892

Smith, Walter C[halmers?]., 'Edward Irving', *Good Words* 25 (1884), 44–7, 103–7, 179–82

Smout, T. C., *A History of the Scottish People 1560–1830*, London: Fontana, 1985

So, Damon W. K., *Jesus' Revelation of his Father: A Narrative-Conceptual Study of the Trinity with Special Reference to Karl Barth*, Bletchley: Paternoster, 2006

Southey, Robert, *A Vision of Judgment by Robert Southey, Esq. L.L.D.*[sic] *Author of Wat Tyler, to which is added, A Vision of Judgment by Lord Byron*, London: William Dugdale, 1824

Stanley, Arthur Penrhyn, *The Life and Correspondence of Thomas Arnold, D.D.*, 2 vols, London: B. Fellowes, 1845

Steel, Annie, *The Church of Annan, 1171–1934*, Annan: Dumfriesshire Newspapers, 1934

Steel, Annie, *Records of Annan 1678–1833*, Annan: Dumfriesshire Newspapers, 1933

Stevens, John, *The Sinlessness of Jesus; being the Substance of some Discourses, delivered at Salem Chapel, on the Words – 'He Knew No Sin:' To which are annexed, Animadversions on the Rev. E. Irving's Doctrine of our Lord's Humanity*, London: Nichols, 1830

Stevenson, Peter K., *God in our Nature: The Incarnational Theology of John McLeod Campbell*, Carlisle: Paternoster, 2004

Stewart, David Dale, *Memoir of the Life of the Rev. James Haldane Stewart, M.A.*, London: Thomas Hatchard, 1856

[Story, Robert], *Peace in Believing: A Memoir of Isabella Campbell, of Fernicarry, Rosneath, Dumbartonshire*, 2nd edn, Greenock: R. B. Lusk, 1829

Story, R. Herbert, 'Edward Irving', in Anon., ed., *Scottish Divines 1505–1872*, Edinburgh: Macniven and Wallace, 1883, 225–72

Story, Robert Herbert, *Memoir of the Life of the Rev. Robert Story, late Minister of Rosneath, Dunbartonshire*, Cambridge: Macmillan, 1862

Stout, Harry S., *The Divine Dramatist: George Whitefield and the Rise of modern Evangelicalism*, Grand Rapids, MI: Eerdmans, 1991

Strachan, Gordon, 'Carlyle, Irving, and the "Hysterical Women"', *Carlyle Annual* 12 (1991), 17–32

Strachan, Gordon, 'Edward Irving and Regent Square: A Presbyterian Pentecost', *JPHSE* 14 (1972), 186–95

Strachan, Gordon, *The Pentecostal Theology of Edward Irving*, London: Darton Longman & Todd, 1973

Strachan, Gordon, 'Theological and cultural Origins of the nineteenth century Pentecostal Movement', in Paul Elbert, ed., *Essays on Apostolic Themes*, Peabody, MA: Hendrickson, 1995, 144–157

Strutt, Hon. C. R., 'The Strutt Family of Terling, 1650–1873', London: privately printed, 1939

'Student of Prophecy, A', *Criticisms on the Leading Sentiments in the Lectures of the Rev. Edward Irving, delivered at Edinburgh from 22d May to 4th June 1828: A bird's eye View of the whole Subject in the Book of the Revelations: Also an Address to Mr Irving, and to the Public*, Edinburgh: for the booksellers [H. & J. Pillans], 1828

'Student of Prophecy, A', *A Review of the Last Sermon preached in Scotland by the Rev. Edward Irving, at Kirkcaldy, July 1, 1828; in which his Leading Sentiments respecting the Resurrection of the Saints, the Removing of the Earth, &c. &c. contained in his Sermon, are compared with the Views of the most judicious Commentators, brought to the Test of Scripture, and proved erroneous*, Edinburgh: for the booksellers [H. & J. Pillans], 1828

Stunt, Timothy C. F., *From Awakening to Secession: Radical Evangelicals in Switzerland and Britain 1815–35*, Edinburgh: T. & T. Clark, 2000

Stunt, Timothy C. F., 'Trying the Spirits: Irvingite Signs and the Test of Doctrine', in Kate Cooper and Jeremy Gregory, eds, *Signs, Wonders, Miracles: Representations of Divine Power in the Life of the Church*, Studies in Church History 41, Woodbridge: Boydell, 2005, 400–9

Stunt, Timothy C. F., '"Trying the Spirits": The Case of the Gloucestershire Clergyman (1831)', *JEH* 32 (1988), 95–105

Surtees, Virginia, *Jane Welsh Carlyle*, Wilton, Salisbury: Michael Russell, 1986

[Tarbet, William], *Edward Irving and the Catholic Apostolic Church: By one of its Members*, London: Bosworth & Harrison, 1856

[Tarbet, William], *Remarks on Mr. Baxter's Narrative of Facts, characterising the supernatural Manifestations in Members of Mr. Irving's Congregation, and other Individuals in England & Scotland, and formerly in the Writer himself: In a Letter to a Friend. With an Appendix containing Extracts of Letters from Individuals who are Subjects of the Manifestations*, 2nd edn, London: A. Douglas, 1833

[Taylor, Isaac], *Natural History of Enthusiasm*, 6th edn, London: Holdsworth and Ball, 1832

Thom, David, *The Miracles of the Irving School shewn to be unworthy of serious Examination*, London: Longman, 1832

Thom, David, 'On the Scotch Kirks and Congregations in Liverpool: being a brief Sketch of their Rise and Progress', *Historic Society of Lancashire and Cheshire Proceedings and Papers* 2 (1849–50), 69–84, 229–31

Thomson, Andrew, *Principal Harper, D.D.*, Edinburgh: Andrew Elliot, 1881

Thomson, D. P., *Women of the Scottish Church*, [Perth: n.p.], 1975

Thomson, J. H., *The Martyr Graves of Scotland*, ed. Matthew Hutchinson, intro. D. Hay Fleming, Edinburgh: Oliphant, Anderson & Ferrier, [1903]

Thomson, John A., *History of Annan and District: Vol. 2, from 1603–1837*, Annan: the author, 1999

[Thompson, J.], *Brief Account of a Visit to some of the Brethren in the West of Scotland; with Remarks on certain Doctrines contained in 'The Truth as it is in Jesus'*, London: J. Nisbet, 1831

Trustees of the National Scotch Church, Printed letter to subscribers, 20 August 1832

[Tudor, J. O.], 'Conclusion of the *Morning Watch*', *MW* 7 (1833), 399–403

Tulloch, John, *Movements of Religious Thought in Britain during the Nineteenth Century*, intro. A. C. Cheyne, Leicester: Leicester University Press, 1971 (first publ. 1885)

Upton, Liam, '"Our Mother and our Country": The Integration of Religious and National Identity in the Thought of Edward Irving (1792–1834)', in Robert Pope, ed., *Religion and National Identity: Wales and Scotland c. 1700–2000*, Cardiff: University of Wales Press, 2001, 242–67

Vaughan, Edward Tho[ma]s, *A Letter to the Rev. Edward Bickersteth, Principal Secretary of the Church Missionary Society, on the Lawfulness, Expediency, Conduct and Expectation of Missions*, Leicester: T. Combe, 1825

Waddington, Barbara, *The Rev. Edward Irving and the Catholic Apostolic Church in Camden and beyond*, London: Camden History Society, 2007

Walker, Andrew, 'Will no one stand up for Edward Irving?', *The Listener*, 6 December 1984

W[alker]., N. L., 'Trials of Irving and Campbell of Row', *British and Foreign Evangelical Review*, no. 50 (April 1867), 331–54

Walker, Richard, *Regency Portraits*, 2 vols, London: National Portrait Gallery, 1985

Ward, James, *New Trial of the Spirits: in reply to Two Sermons, preached in the Parish Church of Upper Chelsea, and published by the Rev. Henry Blunt, M.A., written in a Letter to a Friend*, London: Sherwood, Gilbert, and Piper, 1835

Watt, D., *Guide to Annan and Neighbourhood, historical, traditional, descriptive, with Business Directory*, 4th ed., Annan: D. Watt, [1902]

Watt, Hugh, *Thomas Chalmers and the Disruption*, Edinburgh: Thomas Nelson, 1943

Weinandy, Thomas G., *In the Likeness of Sinful Flesh: An Essay on the Humanity of Christ*, Edinburgh: T. & T. Clark, 1993

Whitley, H. C., *Blinded Eagle: An Introduction to the Life and Teaching of Edward Irving*, London: SCM, 1955

[Wilks, S. C.], *Case of Miss Fancourt. The Documents and Correspondence in the Christian Observer on the alleged miraculous Cure of Miss Fancourt*, London: J. Hatchard, 1831
Wilks, Washington, *Edward Irving: An Ecclesiastical and Literary Biography*, London: William Freeman, 1854
Williams, Meade C., 'Edward Irving', *Princeton Theological Review* 1 (1903), 1–22
Williams, Merryn, *Margaret Oliphant: A Critical Biography*, Basingstoke: Macmillan, 1986
Wiseman, Nathaniel, *Michael Paget Baxter: Clergyman – Evangelist, Editor and Philanthropist*, London: Chas. J. Thynne & Jarvis, 1923
Wolff, Joseph, *Journal of the Rev. Joseph Wolff for the Year 1831*, London: James Fraser, 1832
Wolff, Joseph, *Travels and Adventures of the Rev. Joseph Wolff, D.D., Ll.D.*, London: Saunders, Otley, 1860
[Woodhouse, F. V.], *A Narrative of Events affecting the Position and Prospects of the whole Christian Church: Part I. Second Edition, with a Second Part, containing a Continuation to the Present Time*, London: Bedford Bookshop, 1938 (first publ. 1885)
Wordsworth, Dorothy, *Recollections of a Tour made in Scotland A.D. 1803*, ed. J. C. Shairp, Edinburgh: Edmonston and Douglas, 1874
Wylie, James A., *Disruption Worthies: A Memorial of 1843: With an Historical Sketch of the Free Church of Scotland from 1843 down to the Present Time*, Edinburgh: Thomas C. Jack, [1881]
Y[orke]., O[liver]., 'The Fraserians; or, the commencement of the year Thirty-Five. A Fragment', *Fraser's Magazine* 11 (1835), 1–27

Newspapers and Periodicals

Annandale Observer
Baptist Magazine
Blackwood's Edinburgh Magazine
British Press
Christian Herald
Christian Observer
Country Literary Chronicle and Weekly Review
Dumfries Times
Eclectic Magazine of Foreign Literature
Eclectic Review
Edinburgh Christian Instructor
Edinburgh Magazine
Edinburgh Review
English Review
Evangelical Magazine
Evangelical Times

Fraser's Magazine
Gentleman's Magazine
Gospel Magazine
Haddingtonshire Courier
John Bull
London Christian Instructor / Congregational Magazine
London Quarterly Review
Monmouthshire Merlin
Morning Chronicle
New Evangelical Magazine
Presbyterian Review and Religious Journal
Pulpit
Quarterly Christian Magazine
Record
Scotsman
Theological Critic
United Presbyterian Magazine
Westminster Review

Electronic Resources

Oxford Dictionary of National Biography
Gale Digital Collection
Scotsman
Times Digital Archive
General Register Office, Scottish parish registers [online], www.ScotlandsPeople.gov.uk, accessed May 2009
Letters from 'North American Women's Letters and Diaries', http://www.alexanderstreet4.com, ccessed 13 November 2006
Anon., *Letter from Kirkaldy*, http://www.nls.uk/resources/pdf/74414732.pdf, accessed 1 March 2007
Anon., 'Colonial CD Books: Carlile', http://www.colonialcdbooks.com/carlile.htm, accessed 15 May 2009
Anon., 'The Coming of Messiah with Glory and Majesty: Introduction', http://www.lacunza.fsnet.co.uk/intro.htm, accessed 25 December 2001
Anon., 'Islington: Protestant nonconformity', *A History of the County of Middlesex: Volume 8: Islington and Stoke Newington parishes* (1985), 101–15, http://www.british-history.ac.uk/report.aspx?compid=9522, accessed 7 October 2008
Anon., *Letter from Kirkaldy*, http://www.nls.uk/resources/pdf/74414732.pdf, accessed 1 March 2007
Anon., *The New Statistical Account of Scotland*, Vol. 4, *Dumfries-Kirkcudbright-Wigton*, Edinburgh: William Blackwood, 1845, 223–30, http://books.google.co.uk, accessed 1 August 2008

Anon., 'Ossian: Fact or Fiction', http://www.bbc.co.uk/legacies/myths_legends/scotland/highland/, accessed 13 March 2009

Anon., 'The Revelation of the Coming: Margaret Macdonald's Revelation', http://www.banner.org.uk/misc/rapture.html, accessed 26 April 1999

Anon., 'Rushings; or, British Popular Vagaries', *Fraser's Magazine* 26 (1842), 213–23, http://books.google.co.uk/books?id=bMURAAAATAAJ&pg=PA213&d q=%22fraser%27s+magazine%22+1842+%22edward+irving%22&lr=, accessed 30 April 2009

Anon., *Second Statistical Account of Scotland*, vol. 2, *Haddington, County of Haddington (1834–45)*, 1–17, http://stat-acc-scot.edina.ac.uk/link/1834-45/Haddington/Haddington/, accessed 15 November 2005

Anon., *Second Statistical Account of Scotland*, vol. 9, *Kirkcaldy, County of Fife*, 740–70, http://stat-acc-scot.edina.ac.uk/link/1834-45/Fife/Kirkcaldy/, accessed 15 November 2005

Anon., *Statistical Account of Scotland: Account of 1791–99*, vol. 19: *Annan, County of Dumfries*, http://stat-acc-scot.edina.ac.uk//link/1791-99/Dumfries/Annan/, accessed 22 October 2005

Anon., 'William Cubitt (MP)', http://en.wikipedia.org/wiki/William_Cubitt_(MP), accessed 26 January 2009

Anon., 'Mr Wroe's Virgins', http://gayandmike.co.uk/johnwroe.htm, accessed 1 December 2008

Barclay, George, *Statistical Account of Scotland 1791–99*, 21 vols, Edinburgh: William Creech, 1791–9, vol. 6, http://stat-acc-scot.edina.ac.uk/link/1791-99/Haddington/Haddington/, accessed 15 November 2005

Blair, George, *Biographic and Descriptive Sketches of Glasgow Necropolis*, Glasgow: Maurice Ogle, 1857, http://books.google.co.uk/books?id=rcUH AAAAQAAJ&printsec=frontcover&dq=blair+%22glasgow+necropolis, 30 April 2009

Coates, Chris, 'A Man of Peculiar Appearance', http://www.utopia-britannica.org.uk/pages/John%20Wroe.htm, accessed 1 December 2008

Cunningham, Allan, *The Life of Sir David Wilkie: With his Journals, Tours, and Critical Remarks ...*, 3 vols, London: John Murray, 1843, vol. 3, http://books.google.co.uk/books?id=k_YDAAAAQAAJ&printsec=frontcover&dq= cunningham+wilkie, accessed 30 April 2009

Darwin, Emma, *A Century of Family Letters, 1792-1896*, ed. Henrietta Litchfield, 2 vols, New York: D. Appleton, 1915, http://books.google.co.uk/books?id= vMgEAAAAIAAJ&q=%22emma+darwin%22+%22family+letters%22&dq=%22e mma+darwin%22+%22family+letters%22&pgis=1, accessed 30 April 2009; ibid. London: John Murray, 1915, http://darwin-online.org.uk/content/ frameset?viewtype=text&itemID=F1553.1&keywords=edward+irving&pageseq=26 4, accessed 30 April 2009

Dobson, Peter, 'A Journey Through East Lothian Places and Personalities', http://www.grantsbraes.org.uk/pdf/a-journey-through-east-lothian.pdf, accessed 13 March 2009

Eyre-Todd, George, ed., *The Book of Glasgow Cathedral*, Glasgow: Morrison, 1898, 405, http://www.archive.org/stream/bookofglasgowcat00eyreuoft/bookofglasgow cat00eyreuoft_djvu.txt, accessed 6 May 2009

Godfrey, Walter H., and W. McB. Marcham, eds, *Survey of London, Volume 24*, British History Online, http://www.british-history.ac.uk/report.aspx?compid= 65568, accessed 28 January 2009

King, William Davies, 'Performing the Holy Ghost: Revelations of the Reverend Edward Irving in 1830-31' *Journal of Religion and Theatre* 1.1 (Fall 2002) [online journal], http://www.fa.mtu.edu/~dlbruch/rtjournal/vol_1/no_1/king.html, downloaded 13 November 2008

Latham, J. E. M., *The Search for a New Eden. James Pierrepont Greaves (1777-1842): The Sacred Socialist and his Followers*, London: Associated University Presses, 1999, http://books.google.co.uk/books?id=i6BzfM3zRSMC&pg= PP1&dq=%22search+for+a+new+eden%22&lr=, accessed 30 April 2009

Mortensen, Terry, 'British Scriptural Geologists in the First Half of the Nineteenth Century: Part 5, Henry Cole (1792?–1858)', http://www.answersingenesis. org/tj/v13/i1/henry_cole.asp, accessed 4 July 2008

Roberts, Andrew, 'Biographies of Honorary (Unpaid) Lunacy Commissioners 1828–1912: Spencer Perceval MP', http://www.mdx.ac.uk/testarea/www/ users/study/6bioH.htm#H21, accessed 16 September 2008

Scott, Hew, ed., *Fasti Ecclesiae Scoticanae*, rev. ed. William S. Crockett and Francis Grant, 7 vols, Edinburgh: Oliver & Boyd, 1915–28 (first publ. 1866-71), http://www.dwalker.pwp.blueyonder.co.uk/Ministers%20Index.htm, accessed on various dates

Sizer, Stephen, 'Edward Irving (1792–1834), The Rapture and Rupture between Israel and the Church', http://www.virginiawater.co.uk/christchurch/irving1.html, accessed 26 April 1999

Williams Wynn, Frances, 'Diaries of a Lady of Quality: The Rev. Edward Irving', http://diariesofaladyofqualityblogspot.com/2005/12/rev-edward-irving.html, accessed 11 January 2006

Index

Albigenses 2
Albury circle 5, 144, 171
Albury Conferences 149, 163-70, 216-18, 306-7
Andrews, W. W. 79-80, 93, 223, 277
Angel, office of 118, 266, 277, 278, 281-2
Annan 1, 23, 120, 191, 198
Annan Academy 3-4, 9, 19
Annan Old Parish Church 4
Antichrist 101, 144, 148, 150, 162, 226, 258
Apostles 230, 243, 247, 276, 278, 280-3, 294, 295, 300
Armstrong, Nicholas 257, 269

Babylon 152-3, 162, 163, 169, 255, 259, 264, 278, 294
Baptism with the Holy Spirit 208
Baxter, Robert 214, 233, 246-50, 281, 289, 298-9, 307
Belfast 29, 219, 284
Ben Ezra *see* Lacunza, Manuel
Blackburn, Peter 248
Blyth, David 114, 115
Bolton (East Lothian) 12, 14, 22, 96
Books of Discipline 56, 112, 199, 280
Bonar, Horatius 161, 193, 222, 261, 285
Bonshaw 2, 5
Bourignonianism 226
Brougham, Henry 54, 57, 75, 141
Brown, David 56, 161, 239, 249, 250-1, 263
Byron, Lord 71

Caird, Mary 206, 207-8, 209, 210, 211, 214-15, 232, 245-6, 248, 266, 269, 302
Caird, W. R. 211-12, 224
Caledonian Asylum 40
Caledonian Chapel 40-1, 54, 108

Campbell, Isabella 206, 211
Campbell, John McLeod 182, 194-5, 202, 205-6, 207, 210, 211, 212, 225, 227, 274, 293, 297, 302, 307
Campbell, Mary *see* Caird, Mary
Canning, George 53-4, 57
Cardale, Emily 209, 224, 234, 239-40, 242, 245-6, 248, 265, 267, 269, 280, 307
Cardale, J. B. 209-10, 219, 223, 224, 233, 249, 251, 267, 269, 276, 277, 278, 281, 290, 307
Cardale, Mrs 209, 224, 267
Carlyle, Alexander J. 36-7
Carlyle, Gavin 33-4
Carlyle, Jane 14, 36-9, 42, 61, 81-3, 147, 235, 236
Carlyle, Thomas xiii, 1, 4, 6, 17, 18-21, 23, 27, 34-6, 38, 42, 57-8, 60, 69, 77-8, 81, 82-4, 86-8, 92, 101, 107, 146, 147, 157-8, 186, 190, 193-4, 216, 235-6, 262, 264, 275, 276, 286-7, 290-1, 296, 299, 300
Carlyle, Thomas (advocate) 183
Carter, Grayson 149
Catholic Apostolic Church xiii, xiv, 5, 64, 85, 104, 105, 118, 173, 223, 247, 276, 277, 278, 283, 284, 290, 295, 302
Chalmers, Grace 32, 47
Chalmers, Thomas 12-13, 25, 29-32, 47, 51, 52, 53, 75, 82, 90, 107-8, 109-10, 142, 154, 155, 156, 193, 214, 226-8, 297
Chepstow 292
Cholera 237, 239, 255, 262-3, 268, 287, 289
Church of Scotland 24-5, 43, 122, 302
Clapperton, Hugh 4
Cobbett, William 76
Cole, Henry 175-7, 306

Coleridge, S. T. 67, 78, 92-3, 96, 99, 101, 102, 110, 154, 177, 214
Collins, William 49, 194, 201
Communion 58, 113, 238-9, 261
Continental Society 94, 103, 145, 151, 163, 203
Covenanters 4-5, 74, 112, 132-3, 140, 145, 201, 207, 221
Cumming, John 298

Dallimore, Arnold 76, 107, 117, 120
Darby, J .N. 172, 302
Dialogues on Prophecy 166, 168-9
Dickson, Robert 4
Dingley, R. J. 148, 152-3
Dinwiddie, William 43-4, 55, 114-15, 159
Discernment of Spirits, gift of 241-3, 245-6, 265-6
Disruption, The 13, 25
Dixon, Miss 232, 245
Dods, Marcus 184-6
Dorries, David 106-7, 175, 184, 186
Dow, David 274-5
Drummond, A. L. 16-17, 61, 79, 215, 243, 296, 298
Drummond, Henry 102-5, 121, 141, 145, 149, 163, 164-6, 170-1, 172-3, 175, 212, 219, 269, 281, 282, 291, 296
Dublin 218
Duncan, Henry 192, 273, 274
Dunscore 200

Ecclefechan 5-6, 19, 50
Edinburgh Christian Instructor 20, 185, 221, 274
Edinburgh Review 20, 136
Elliott, Peter 19, 92, 154
Erskine, Thomas 153, 212, 299
Evangelicalism 51, 140, 148, 149, 168, 169, 172, 302; in Church of Scotland 25
Evangelists 277-8, 283, 292, 295

Faber, G. S. 148
Fancourt, Miss 219
Fernicarry 206

French Revolution 101, 140, 148, 153, 169
Frere, J. H. 100-2, 104, 151, 154, 164
Froude, J. A. 36-7

Gardiner, S. R. 61-2
General Assembly 24, 28-9, 116, 179, 182-3, 198-200, 225-6, 257, 271, 274, 307
'Gifted persons' 224, 231, 235, 236, 240, 249, 255, 259
Gilley, Sheridan 149
Glasgow 31, 293; St John's Church 29-31, 297; St Mungo's Cathedral 64, 297-8
Glen, William 5
Gordon, Margaret 35, 37
Gordon, Robert 59, 108, 154-5, 191
Gordon Square (London) 262
Greenock 29, 115, 207, 208, 293
Grubb, James 207
Gunton, Colin xv

Haddington 12, 36, 39, 45, 69, 82
Haldane, J. A. 13, 225
Haldane, Robert 13, 103
Hall, Miss 233, 239, 244-5, 250, 260, 307
Hamilton, Elizabeth 88, 196-7, 217, 279
Hamilton, William 55, 110, 114, 115, 159, 196-7, 241, 251-2, 257-8, 260-1, 286, 287
Hazlitt, William 67-8, 73-4
Healing 208, 219, 262-3, 286, 293
Helensburgh 209
Herschell, Ridley 227
Highland Society 40, 55
Historicism 101, 168, 302
Hohl, Michael 228
Holywood 7, 192, 200
Hooker, Richard 9-10, 78, 128
Hope, Adam 3, 4, 5
Horn, Archibald 114, 115, 240, 252, 257
Horse Bazaar 261-2, 264
Horsley, Samuel 163

Index 351

Howie, John (of Lochgoin) 2, 111
Howy, Thomas 2
Huguenots 2

Irving, Agnes, later Carlile (1801-29) 33, 130-1
Irving, Edward (1792-1834). birth and early life 1-7, 134, 305; his appearance 9, 16, 32, 68, 193-4, 285, 286, 288, 294; caricatures of 74, 76; portraits of 42, 82, 158; his squint 2-3, 9, 66; his health 2, 60, 91, 125, 130, 156, 190, 202, 262-3, 270, 283, 285-6, 287-8, 290-3; Arts student 8-11, 305; early reading 9-10, 19; schoolmaster at Haddington 10, 12-15, 305; Divinity student 10-11, 21, 305; involvement in Bible societies 14, 26, 32, 96, 145-6, 150; schoolmaster at Kirkcaldy 15, 16-26, 305; engagement 20-1, 36-8, 81; actor at Kirkcaldy? 21; licensed to preach 21-2, 305; attitude to Westminster Confession 22, 27, 56, 129, 182-3, 225, 229; attitude to Scots Confession 56, 113, 128, 129, 175, 183, 195, 229; first sermon at Annan 23; leaves Kirkcaldy for Edinburgh 26, 27; visits Ulster 29-30; assistant to Chalmers 29-34, 46, 305; offered a call to Jamaica 39, 41; offered a call to New York 39; called to Caledonian Chapel 41-5; trials and ordination 43, 45, 305; induction at Caledonian Chapel 52, 305; popularity 53-5, 57-8, 60, 66-7, 77, 112; nicknamed 'Doctor Squintum' 68; responds to critics 78-9, 176-7, 185-6, 226, 243; London homes: Myddelton Terr 85, 305; Claremont Sq 85, 306; Judd Pl East 130, 306; Newman St 270-1, 308; marriage 81-3, 124, 305; sermon to London Missionary Society 94-5, 305; foundation-stone laid for National Scotch Church 56, 305; sermon to Continental Society 94, 305; refuses call to Hope Park Chapel, Edinburgh 59-60, 306; opens National Scotch Church 107-11, 306; appoints Scott as missionary 115-16, charged with Nestorianism 184-5, 187, 189; preaching tours of Scotland 190-202, 306; gallery collapses at Kirkcaldy 196, 306; parts company with Scott 213; preaching tour of Ireland 218-19; withdraws from Presbytery of London 220-2, 307; declaration by officers affirming his orthodoxy 221-2, 307; early morning prayer meetings 224, 231-2, 236-7, 239, 244, 258-9, 264; views condemned by General Assembly 226; trial by Presbytery of London 225, 238, 249, 257-60, 307; removed from Regent Sq 251-61; opens new church in Newman St 269-70, 307; trial by Presbytery of Annan 61, 271-4, 308; inhibited from administering sacraments 276-7, 308; ordained as Angel 277, 308; visits Edinburgh (1834) 284-5; last journey 291-4, 308; illness and death in Glasgow 293-7, 308; funeral 297-8, 308
character 4, 12-13, 14-15, 16-17, 18, 20, 34, 38, 69, 133, 236, 251-2, 253, 261, 299, 300, 301
children: Ebenezer 268, 269, 278-9, 307, 308; Edward 86, 89-91, 127, 128, 279, 305, 306; Gavin 130, 306; Isabella 61, 286, 308; Margaret (Maggie) 89, 165, 217, 218, 287, 306; Martin 37-8, 61, 218, 292, 307; Mary 125, 127, 128, 306; Samuel 125, 197, 217-18, 306, 307
evangelistic concern 59, 64, 70-1, 73, 76-7, 119-20, 191, 196, 268, 269, 289
hospitality 44, 88, 119, 172-3, 271, 298, 301

preaching 6, 9, 23-4, 25, 28, 30, 31, 32, 42-3, 49-50, 51, 52, 53, 61-80, 94-5, 102, 112-13, 116, 124, 159, 190, 191-4, 197, 198, 200-2, 218-19, 247, 255-7, 265, 267-8, 274-5, 283, 285
as a Reformed theologian 106, 110, 111, 122, 128, 130, 140, 144
as a Romantic 28, 36, 38, 79, 137, 300
as a Scot 132-7, 229-30, 291
views on: Apocrypha 145-6, 152, 153; assurance 195; atonement 161, 175, 179, 181, 186-7; baptism 91, 114, 126-9, 191, 202; baptism with the Holy Ghost 224, 238, 258; Bible 27, 69-71, 73, 100, 169-70, 172; Calvinism 57, 100, 136; charismatic gifts 33, 128, 205, 208, 214, 217-18, 223-4, 230, 231-2, 236, 239-40, 253, 254-5, 265, 296; Christology 159, 174-89, 208, 219-20, 225, 272, 273, 302; Church 111, 118, 124, 129, 170, 203, 230-1, 255, 258-9, 275, 277, 283-4, 301; Church of England 118, 141; Church of Scotland 28-9, 118, 136-7, 143, 169, 182, 222, 226, 229-31, 272, 275; Church and State xiv, 5, 78, 137, 140-5, 283, 291-2; communion 129-30; deaths of his children 90, 125-7, 217-18, 279; Dissenters 56, 136, 141; education; election 25, 57, 129; Evangelicalism 2, 25, 58-9, 70, 72-3, 77, 123, 160-1, 177, 179, 203; healing 33, 217, 279, 287; Holy Spirit 119, 128, 130, 204; infidelity 19, 136, 146, 152, 155, 162; Jews 151, 157, 160, 162, 170, 268; marriage and family life 14, 33, 35, 86, 107, 127, 134-5; Millennium 157, 160, 188; ministerial office xiv, 6, 18, 44-5, 46-9, 64, 66, 88, 117-20, 230-1, 266-7, 275, 277, 278, 281, 301; missions and missionaries 28, 41-2, 46, 93-7, 169; patronage 26, 27, 138; politics 112, 140-1, 144-5; preaching 13, 14, 19, 24, 28, 47-8, 51-2, 63-5, 70-1, 111, 112-13, 117, 120-4, 133; prophecy, gift of 230, 238, 241, 259; prophecy in Scripture 5, 78, 99-100, 101-2, 103-4, 124, 131, 136, 141, 143-5, 146, 148-73, 202-3, 247; publishing 42, 49, 95-6, 121-2; Roman Catholicism 104, 108, 110, 141-5, 150, 151, 155, 156, 157, 162, 203; sacraments 128, 195; slavery 66, 95; social injustice 49, 64, 65-6, 89, 137-9, 158-60, 255-6, 283; theatre 76; tongues 224, 230, 236-8, 239-40, 296
as a watchman xiv, 137, 175, 301
writings:
Apology for the ancient Fulness and Purity of the Doctrine of the Kirk 136-7, 306
Argument for Judgment to Come see *Orations*
Babylon and Infidelity Foredoomed 94, 101-2, 103-4, 151-4, 305
'Cause and Remedy of Ireland's Evil Condition' 59, 94, 143
Christian's Cure for the Cholera
Christ's Holiness in Flesh 221, 225, 226, 307
'Christ the Propitiation' 58
Church and State 144-5, 306
Church of God in London, To the 295
'Church, with her Endowment of Holiness and Power, The' 202, 204-5, 313
Collected Writings 61, 309-13
Confessions of Faith and Books of Discipline of the Church of Scotland 229-30, 280, 307, 310
'Curse as it hath degraded Man,

Index

The' 65-6
Day of Pentecost 238, 241, 249, 271, 307
'Death of Children, On the' 125-7, 312
'Deceitfulness Of Riches' 139, 312
Doctrine of the Church of Scotland 183, 307
'Doctrine and Manifestation and Character of the Apostasy' 144
'Education' 94, 311
'Facts connected with Recent Manifestations' 205, 244, 307
'Family and Social Religion' 63, 85-6, 311
Farewell Discourse to St. John's, Glasgow 46-9, 305, 311
'First Sermon in the National Scotch Church' 111-12, 312
Flock of God, To the 308
'Gifts of the Holy Ghost' 202, 223-4, 313
'God our Father' 312
Homilies on Baptism 63, 91, 128-9, 306, 310-1
'Homilies on the Lord's Supper' 129-30, 306, 311
'Idolatry' 63, 312
'Intellectual Life' 62, 64-5, 312
'Interpretation of the Fourteenth Chapter of the Apocalypse' 265-6
'Interpretation of Old Testament Prophecies' 171-2
Introductory Essay to Bishop Horne's Commentary on the Psalms 305, 309
'Introductory Essay' to *Life of Bernard Gilpin* 117, 305
'Jesus our Ensample, that we should follow his Steps' 312
'John the Baptist' 62, 64
'Judgment, in consequence of the Last General Assembly' 230, 271, 307
Last Days 22, 121, 158-61, 306
'Last Sermon in the Caledonian Church' 108-9, 312
Last Sermon at the National Scotch Church 261, 307
Lectures on Revelation 198, 202-3, 300, 306
Letter to the King 142, 306
'Lord Jesus Christ, The' 196
'Love of Money, The' 139, 312
Missionaries after the Apostolical School 93-9, 305, 309-10
'Moral Life' 62, 64-5, 312
'Notes on the Standards of the Church of Scotland' 310
Opinions circulating regarding our Lord's Human Nature 182-3, 307
Orations [For the Oracles of God] 62, 69-79, 305, 309
Ordination Charge 117, 302, 310
Orthodox and Catholic Doctrine 179-81, 186, 220, 225, 226, 271, 306-7
Pastoral Letter from the Scotch Presbytery 135-6, 306
'Plan of the Apocalypse' 150
'Praise' 63, 311
'Prayer' 63, 99-100, 311
Preliminary Discourse to Ben Ezra 157, 165, 169, 306
Prophetical Works see *Lectures on Revelation*
'Responsibility of a Baptized Man' 230-1
Sermons I. Doctrine of the Incarnation Opened 63, 69, 100, 121-2, 176-9, 273-4, 306, 312-13
Sermons II. Parable of the Sower 121-4, 306, 309
Sermons III. On Subjects National and Prophetical 121-2, 306
Signs of the Times 161-3, 306
'Signs of the Times, and Characteristics of the Church' 160
'Spiritual Economy of Scotland'

133-5
'Spiritual and national Benefits from Erection of a New Church' 56
'Tale of the Times of the Martyrs' 132-3
'Temptation, The' 63, 175, 310
'Theology of the Natural Man' 78, 312
Thirty Sermons 62
'Three Spirits' 155
Irving, Elizabeth, later Kennedy (1797-1874) 33, 272
Irving, Gavin (1758-1832) 1-2, 6, 135, 265, 307
Irving, George (1804-33) 3, 17, 85, 125, 217, 228, 235, 265, 279-80, 308
Irving, Jenet (Janet), later Dickson (1794-1849) 14
Irving, John (1790-1822) 3, 6, 81, 90, 173, 226, 305
Irving, Isabella (1797-1854) 20-1, 36-8, 81-3, 84, 87, 88, 89, 90, 91, 101-2, 104, 121-2, 125, 128, 130, 136, 147, 156, 158, 166-7, 190, 197, 217, 219, 225, 236, 239, 247, 248, 268, 271, 279, 284, 287, 291, 293, 297
Irving, Margaret, later Fergusson (b.1799) 192, 198
Irving, Mary (1764-1840) 2, 120, 134, 296
Irvingism / Irvingites 16, 281, 295

Jewsbury, Geraldine 36
Johnston, Bryce 7

Ker, David 207, 237, 272, 274, 290-1, 297
Kirkcaldy 16, 196
Knox, John 12, 106, 274, 298

Lacunza, Manuel 155-7
Liverpool 110, 293
London Society for the Propagation of Christianity among the Jews 163

Lorimer, Robert 13, 15
Luther, Martin 47, 106, 298

Macaulay, Z. 146
M'Cheyne, R. M. 299
Macdonald, George and James 207, 208-9, 210, 266, 294
Macdonald, Margaret 207, 208, 266
Macdonald, Mary 209
Macdonald, M. N. 197, 225-6
McFarlane, Graham 174, 177-8
Mackenzie, Duncan 114, 115, 237, 251, 258, 260
Mackintosh, H. R. 187
Maclean, H. B. 182-4, 225, 307
Macleod, Donald 187

M'Neile, Hugh 165, 173, 216, 219
'Manifestations' in London 223-43, 244-50, 268
'Manifestations' in Scotland 204-15, 228
Mann, J. H. 252, 257, 260
Martin, Elizabeth *see* Hamilton, Elizabeth
Martin, Isabella *see* Irving, Isabella
Martin, John 16, 18, 20, 86, 89, 90, 166-7, 186, 253, 286, 289, 294, 296-7
Martin, Mrs John 21, 297
Martin, Samuel 20, 81, 86, 120, 194, 199, 253, 283-4, 286
Maurice, F. D. 168, 302
Méjanel, Pierre 218
Melbourne, Lord 222
Merricks, W. S. 106
Milton, John 16, 71, 72, 78, 140-1
Moderates 25, 65
Moncrieff, William 4, 33, 45
Montagu, Anna and Basil 83, 89, 90, 92, 122, 125, 130, 136, 154, 173, 190, 228, 270
Morning Watch 144, 152, 170-1, 264, 280
Mowbray, Helen 227

National Scotch Church 55, 107, 110, 298, 305

Trustees of 127, 231, 240-1, 244, 252-4, 257-8, 259, 260-1, 307
Needham, Nicholas R. 189
Newell, J. Philip 195, 210, 213, 214
Newton, B. W. 186-7
Nisbet, James 110, 114, 115, 232, 237, 257
Norton, Robert 207

Oliphant, Mrs M. O. W. xiii, xiv, 1, 10, 37, 43, 52, 84, 93, 125, 129, 131, 168, 171, 191, 196, 212-13, 220, 240, 243, 276, 290, 291
Oliver, W. H. 106, 159, 168
Ossian 10
Overall, Bishop 140
Owen, Robert 261, 264

Paine, Peggy 3
Panton, Andrew 114
Parnell, J. V. 99
Patronage 25
Patterson, Mark 106, 169-71, 188
Perceval, Spencer 219, 245
Perth 197
Pilkington, George 242-3
Port Glasgow 207, 208, 242, 266
Powerscourt, Lady 218
Premillennialism 169, 188, 302
Presbyterianism 13, 24-5, 261
Presbytery of Annan 45, 199, 271
Presbytery of Haddington 11, 22
Presbytery of Kirkcaldy 21-2
Presbytery of London 43, 52, 108, 116, 137, 142, 179, 183-4, 199, 219-22, 252, 254, 270, 271
Presbytery of Paisley 115, 116
Probyn, E. C. 241-2
Prophecy, gift of 224, 233-4, 241-3, 274-5, 276-7, 278, 284
Prophets 246, 248, 266, 267, 281-2, 283, 300
Pulpit 62, 75-6
Purves, Jim 187-8, 195

de Quincey, Thomas 67

Rapture, The 170

Record 170-1
Regent Square *see* National Scotch Church
Robertson, Andrew 40, 43, 53, 55
Rossteuscher, Ernst A. 171, 223
Row (Rhu) 115, 194, 206, 207, 208, 209

Scott, A. J. 112, 115-16, 194-5, 205-6, 207-8, 212-13, 220, 225, 307
Scott, Walter 200
Seceders, Burgher 5-6, 19
Simpson, James and Jane 51, 110, 114, 115, 116, 124, 156, 191, 240, 243, 244, 245-6, 265-7
So, Damon 188
Smail, Tom 214-15
Smith, John 95
Southey, Robert 71
Stevens, John 189
Stewart, J. H. 164
Story, Robert 12, 50, 158, 206, 210-12, 298
Strachan, Gordon 106, 204-5, 267, 297-8
Strachey, Mrs 42, 88
Strutt, J. J. 156, 166
Stunt, Timothy C. F. 224, 241-2, 264

Tait, William 284
Taplin, Edward 232, 233-4, 246, 257, 269, 282-3, 284, 295
Thomson, Andrew 20, 25, 29, 111, 191, 199, 274
Times 228, 237, 297
Tongues 208-9, 210-11, 212, 224, 233-4, 235-6
Trial of Edward Irving: A Cento of Criticism 74
Tudor, J. O. 170, 219, 233, 280

University College, London 146
Upton, Liam 54, 132-3

Waddington, Barbara 82, 303
Walker, Andrew 243

Way, Lewis 102, 156, 163
Wedgwood, Charlotte 109
Welsh, Jane *see* Carlyle, Jane
Welsh, Mrs 69
Westminster Confession 115, 116, 195, 220

Whitley, H. C. xiv, 129, 298
Wolff, Joseph 163-4
Woodhouse, F. V. 282, 294-5, 296-7
Wordsworth, Dorothy 68-9

York, Duke of 41

www.ingramcontent.com/pod-product-compliance
Lightning Source LLC
Chambersburg PA
CBHW071756300426
44116CB00009B/1104